Fourth edition

revised & expanded edition

BISEXUAL RESOURCE GUIDE

Robyn Ochs,
editor

Bisexual Resource Center

Bisexual Resource Center
PO Box 1026
Boston MA 02117-1026

United States of America

© 2001

ISBN 0-9653881-3-1

Printed in the United States of America

Contents

Introduction

In the mid 1980s I was at a conference on bisexuality sponsored by what is now known as the Bisexual Resource Center and someone said, "Wouldn't it be great if someone made a list of all of the bi groups out there? That way we could all keep in touch with each other." I remember thinking, "What a good idea! SOMEBODY should do that." Well, that somebody turned out to be me. I pulled together the first edition of the *International Directory of Bisexual Groups* later that year. It was six pages long and listed about 40 groups in a handful of countries.

Things change. Movements grow. Listing 352 bi groups and 2129 bi-inclusive groups in 66 countries, as well as bibliographies, film guides and some awesome quotes and photos, the *Bisexual Resource Guide, 4th Edition* is evidence that the bi movement has indeed come a long way. The growth in the number of bi groups over the years is evidence of a burgeoning movement, but perhaps even more powerful a statement is the number of groups which formerly ignored (or even denied access to) bisexual people which now include us. This expansion of "community" is a continuing international trend, and it will help to make it easier for bisexual people to identify as such, and easier for all of us – lesbian, gay, bisexual, heterosexual, transgendered, intersexed, queer, and questioning – to find comfort with ourselves and a sense of community with others, even if and when our identities change over our lifetimes.

A Chinese woman recently wrote to me, wondering why we would be interested in including Asian resources in a Guide produced in the United States. It is my belief that we are all empowered by the knowledge that there is widespread organizing by bisexuals and other sexual minorities in so many countries throughout the world. We can gain nourishment and strength by looking across oceans, and sometimes even by looking across town in our own communities. This book is evidence that we are not alone, and we are in good company.

This guide includes several other important sections: an extensive bibliographic section, an annotated list of recommended films, advertising, information on safer sex, photos, great quotes, cartoons by Alison Bechdel and Roberta Gregory, an electronic resources section, and of course listings of resources in 66 countries.

The *Bisexual Resource Guide, 4th edition* is truly a community undertaking. Approximately 200 people from around the world contributed their time and talents to make it happen. A list of some of these people follows. This project couldn't have happened without you! And we need even more people to help with the next *Guide*. Besides giving of your money (hint, hint!), you can also help by writing to me and giving me feedback. I especially need the input of folks outside the U.S. What other information would *you* like to see in the next edition of this guide? What books and films have you read that you think should appear on the lists (but don't yet)? Are there groups that you know about that I don't? Are there listings that are incorrect? I won't know unless you tell me. You can write to me c/o BRC or send me e-mail at: ochs@bi.org.

Bi for now,

Robyn

Roberta Gregory

Bi Stuff
from the
Bisexual Resource Center

P.O. Box 1026
Boston, MA 02117
617-424-9595
brc@biresource.org

The BRC can help you show your Bisexual Pride in all sorts of ways! We have stylish tanks and t-shirts, buttons, and bumperstickers. Check out our selection at **www.biresource.org/biproducts**.

The BRC website is the one place that stocks virtually every bi book, video, and music CD available. **And** we have many of these products at *below list price*. In addition, the BRC receives a commission on every sale, which goes to support our award-winning work.

Visit the BRC merchandise sites:
www.biresource.org/bookstore
www.biresource.org/videostore
www.biresource.org/musicstore

Angelica R (Mexico), Alejandra A (Argentina), Anne B (France), Arlene K (USA), Amjad (Pakistan), Amatul H (USA), Adia (Peru), Agnes (Singapore), Ales (Slovenia), Audrey S (USA), Arthur C (USA), Axel G (Germany), Ananda L (USA), Alan H (USA), Armin D (Germany), Annalee N (USA), Autumn C (USA), Alex K (UK), Astrid N (USA), Adrian M (Australia), Ailsa W (Australia), Alison Wheeler (UK), Andrew M (Australia), Amy H (USA), Angel (Australia), Amy C (USA), Ann K-N (UK), Alexei G (USA), Ann Marie S (UK), Alan T (USA), Andreas (Germany), Andrea C (USA), Anna H (Australia), Ali B (UK), Abi D (USA), Alison W (UK), Abby (USA), Angela G (USA), Anna H (Australia), Amanda U-K (USA), Alison R (UK), Ann S (USA), Andy C (UK), Annie S (USA), Annie H (USA), Annie G (USA), Albert B (UK), Alan S (USA), Beth (Australia), Bruce S (Canada), Bill B (USA), Bill B (USA), Beth W (USA), Brett B (USA), Bill B (USA), Barry S (USA), Beth F (USA), Beth R (USA), Beth C (USA), Benno S (Germany), Bearpaw M (USA), Bobbi K (USA), Betty B (USA), Betty A (USA), Beth F (USA), Bruce G (USA), Barb N (USA), Beila K (USA), Bill W (USA), Ben P-D (UK), Ben S (USA), Basem S (USA), Buz de V (UK), Bill I (USA), Bethany R (USA), Brad R (USA), Brad D (USA), Buzz H (USA), Brenda B (USA), Catherine D (France), Cianna S (USA), Cath L (Australia), Carol Q (USA), Clare H (UK), Carmen O (USA), Carinna G (Germany), Cecilia T (USA), Cianna S (USA), Craig W (Australia), Charles K (USA), **"Never doubt** (USA), Carolyn R (Canada), Carl S (USA), Corinna G (Germany), Camille C (USA), Claire P (UK), Cidneye G (USA), Carmen C (Paraguay), Cathy J (USA), Cornelius Y (USA), Cathy C (USA), Clare T (UK), Claire M (USA), Caramel Q (UK), Cliff A (USA), Chandini (US **that a small group of** A (USA), Carla I (USA), Chris S (UK), Cecilia T (USA), Chris O (USA), Cl. V (France), Darragh D (Ireland), Desmond K (UK), David L (USA), Daniel O (Philippines), David R (USA), David B (UK), Dorian S (USA), Davey N (UK), Drew L (**thoughtful, committed citizens** USA), David J (Australia), Dean D (Australia), David R (USA), Dana D (USA), David D (UK), Debbie B-S (USA), Daniel W-L (France), Dania P (USA), Dan A (Canada), Dave M (USA), Dawn A (USA), Dennis M (USA), David S (USA), D **can change the world;** USA), Denise P (USA), Deborah D (USA), Elias F-J (USA), Fabio D (Italy), Erich S (USA), Elaine B (USA), Elaine K (Australia), Erin R (USA), Edwin H (Germany), Ellen H (USA), Ellyn R (USA), Erwin H (Netherlands), Emily D (USA), Emil **indeed, it's the only thing** lyn M (USA), Evey (Australia), Ellen S (USA), Ehse M (USA), Ellyn R (USA), Elisabeth M (USA), Elizabeth G (USA), Efrain G (USA), Fritz K (USA), Franco R (Italy), Frank S (Netherlands), Francisco (Costa Rica), Francis S (Ge **that ever does."** H (Germany), Fred V-G (Netherlands), Gert D (Denmark), Graham M (Australia), Gabrielle F (Austria), Gillian E (Australia), Gigi W (USA), Gail C (USA), Geoffrey V (New Zealand), Gail Z (USA), Gerard P (USA), Gwenyth J (USA), Gerhard H (Germany), Gary L (USA), Gary N (USA), Geert W (Belgium), Gabriel C (USA), Grant D (UK), Ginny L (USA), Greta C (USA), Ganapati D (USA), Glenn V (Australia), Gilly R (USA), **Margaret Mead** (Australia), Haruka K (Japan), Hok G (Australia), Hanna B (Sweden), Heidi V (USA), Hannie H (Netherlands), Hilde V (Netherlands), Heidi J (USA), Heleina C (UK), Hinde S (USA), Heleen R (Netherlands), Hoppe (USA), Howard H (UK), Helga (Germany), Hap S (USA), Hannie H (Netherlands), Hester T (UK), Holly N-F N(USA), Heather F(USA), Ian W (UK), Iain (UK), Indigo S (USA), Jason S (Australia), Julia B (Australia), Jill N (USA), Julie B (France), Julie W (USA), Jürgen H (Germany), Julia P (USA), Julie K (USA), Jolie B (Netherlands), Julius C (USA), Julie R (USA), Julie L (USA), Jan H (USA), John H (UK), Jackie H (UK), Joan W (USA), Jace K (USA), Jean K (Australia), Jon S (USA), John F (UK), Jennifer Y (USA), Jack R (USA), Jay S (USA), Jim U (UK), Jennifer H (USA), Jeroen T (Netherlands), Jace M (USA), Jo D (UK), Jay P (USA), Joanne M (USA), Jill N (USA), Jim F (USA), Jo E (UK), Jolanda A (Netherlands), John V (USA), Jen Y (UK), John R (USA), John S (USA), Jean B (UK), Joy O (USA), Julie B (UK), Jonathan W (USA), Jennifer M (UK), John C (USA), Judyboy (Ireland), June J (USA), Jean F (USA), Judith G (UK), Jennifer F (USA), Jonathan U (USA), Kuwaza I (USA), Kevin L (UK), Katie-Lee W (Netherlands), Kris R (USA), Karin G (Germany), Keith B (USA), *Kathe M (USA), Kas H (Netherlands), Karin B (USA), Kate W (UK), Kevin S (USA), Kata O (USA), Krayg (UK), KJ (USA), Klaus (Austria), Kory D-M (USA), Koen B (Germany), Karla R (USA), Kate Y (UK), Kenneth C (USA), Kate Y (UK), Linda E (Finland), Lani K (USA), Loraine H (USA),

(USA), Laura S (USA), Lisa O (USA), Lucinda O (USA), Leah S (USA), Luisa S (USA), Kyle S (USA), Kevin S (UK), Kurt C (Canada), Kripton (Italy), Kuwaza I (USA), Luka (Italy), Lawrence B (UK), Kevin M (USA), Kate H (Australia), Kurt Z (Canada), Kirsty C (Australia), Kai M (USA), Koen B (Germany), Kathy L (USA), Kevin S (UK), Katie M (USA), Kevin L (UK), Karen Y (USA), Kath A (UK), Lou H (USA), Luigi F (USA), Kerry E (UK), Karen O (USA), Karla R (USA), Kate F (Scotland), Kathrine D (USA), Katrina R (New Zealand), Lillian (Estonia), Lawrence B (UK), Lawrence (France), Liz H (USA), Laura S (USA), Liz K (Australia), Laura Ann S (Australia), Lis G (Denmark), Lisa S (USA), Lisa L (UK), Linda P (USA), Leon P (Australia), Luigi F (USA), Linda Sue D (USA), Lisa E (USA), Liz H (USA), Lani K (USA), Laura P (USA), Lilliane (Canada), Louis A (USA), Lynn D (USA), Lou H (USA), Lillian (Canada), Megan P (New Zealand), Megan M (USA), Megan (USA), Milla R (USA), Meeghan F (USA), Marcia D (USA), Maria B (Netherlands), Michael B (USA), Michael S (Australia),

This book is dedicated to the many individuals who have been working over the past thirty years to create space for bisexual people and identities.

We are pioneers, and we have changed the world in ways previously unimaginable. Yes, we have a long way to go, but we must also remember, with great pride, the distance we have come.

Never underestimate your ability to bring about change.

Robyn Ochs

WHAT ARE BI WOMEN DOING IN THE WORLD?

Power and Joy: Celebrating Women, by Robin Colodzin. Copyright 2000.

A LOT!!!!!

Find out all about it by subscribing to *BiWomen*, a bimonthly newsletter of the Boston Bisexual Women s Network. Each issue has a theme and includes news, reviews, interviews, personal essays, poetry, and artwork by women from around Boston and around the country.

For a year's subscription, send $20 to:
BBWN, P.O. Box 400639, Cambridge, MA 02140.
For a sample issue, send $3 to the above address.

Words of Thanks

The most amazing thing about this project is the extent to which it is a community effort. More than 200 people around the world have given generously of their time and energies to make it happen. The following people all deserve thanks:

THE CORE GROUP:

Editor: Robyn Ochs
Editor for Listings: Lynda Dyndiuk
Business Manager: Arthur Cohen
Database Designer/Wizard of Technology: David Rothcheck

REGIONAL EDITORS

ARGENTINA: Marcelo Ferreyra, Biblioteca GLTTB
AUSTRALIA: **ACT**: Angel; **NSW**: Sean + Will Letts (wletts@csu.edu.au); **QL**: Wayne Roberts (Australian Bisexual Network); **TAS**: Teddie (teddieboo@primus.com.au); **VIC**: Evey; **WA**: A. Hepworth hepworth@essun1.murdoch.edu.au)
AUSTRIA: Klaus
BELGIUM: Sofie Verhalle (sofie_v@hotmail.com) + Paul Bavo
BRAZIL: Carmen Oquendo
CANADA: **ALBERTA**: Danielle Ladoucer (sandouce@home.com); **BC, SASK, MB**: Carolyn Reitzel (carer@direct.ca); **MANITOBA**: Trevor/Bi Pride (trevorlee2000@hotmail.com); **MARITIMES**: Angela; **ONTARIO**: Stephen Harvey (steve@bi.org); **QUEBEC**: Liliane from bisexuelle.qc.ca;
COSTA RICA: Francisco at CIPAC/DDHH (cipacdh@racsa.co.cr)
DENMARK: Trine Brekke
ESTONIA: Lillian Kotter (eluell@saturn.zzz.ee
FINLAND: Linda Eklöf

Left to right: Linda (layout), Eddie (intern), Wayne (Reel Bisexuals), Virginia (layout)

Editors, eft to right: Morgan (USA: Oregon), Axel (Germany), Bill (USA: Central & Western Massachusetts), Carmen (Brazil & Puerto Rico), Kripton (Italy)

FRANCE: Anne Bensoussan (annebens@club-internet.fr)
GERMANY: Axel Griessman (axl@axl.org
INDIA: Sherry Joseph (sherry@vbharat.ernet.in)
IRELAND: Judyboy Kisses (judyboy@excite.com)
ISRAEL: Jared Goldfarb (jared@pobox.com)
ITALY: Kripton
MEXICO: Mariaurora Mota
NETHERLANDS: Maurice Snellen (maurice@lnbi.demon.nl)
NEW ZEALAND: Robyn Hopkins (oceannz@hotmail.com)
NORWAY: Trine Brekke (trineb82@hotmail.com)
PAKISTAN: Amjad
PARAGUAY: Carmen Colazo
PERU: Adia
PHILIPPINES: Daniel Ocampo
RUSSIA/CIS: Rosa Carson
SINGAPORE: Agnes
SLOVENIA: Ales
SPAIN: Eduardo Zamanillo (alega@nodo50.org)
SWEDEN: Hanna Bertilsdotter (hanna.bertilsdotter@spray.se)
SWITZERLAND: Antenne Bisexuelle Romande InfoBi (infobi@gmx.ch)
UNITED KINGDOM: Andy Cork + Laurence Brewer
(Raseyfantasey@netscapeonline.co.uk) + Jules (jules@kingginer.com) + Lisa Geary

Left to right: Jolie (Netherlands), Teddie (Australia), Stephen (Canada), Gary (USA)

UNITED STATES :

AL/MS: Christine ""Stine"" Fletcher; AR/OK: Deborah Dixon; AZ: Melody Rector; CA: Denise (central), Mik Scheper (mikz@poboxes.com) (northern except San Francisco) + Dani Bautier (northern), Gary North, Bi Consultation Services (bisexuals@aol.com) (southern); CO: Lisa Diguardi diguardi@mscd.edu + Lin E., BiNet Colorado; CT: Silvia Glick; DC/DE: Susan B. Lander, Esq.; FL- Kathryn Schnaible; GA: Chris Duro; IA: Mark Pearson (dharmayoop@hotmail.com); ID: Sandy James & Sparrow; IL: Mary Lamb Sheldon; IN: Tania Gadbout; KS: Emily Hadley; MA: Bill Rogers (Central & Western), Debbie Block-Schwenk (Eastern), Lauree (eastern); ME: Virginia Slawson (vslawson@midcoast.com); MI: Holly Nannette + Andrea; MN: Heather Franek (hfranek@coolmail.net) + Victor Raymond; MO: Jonathan Zucker (zucker@alliesproject.org); NB: Terri Ann Johnson; NC/ND: Laura Y.; NH: Chris; NJ: Tom Limoncelli (tom@limoncelli.org) + Robin Renée (www.robinrenee.com, menage98@aol.com); NM: David Walker; NV: Pete Glass; NY-Upstate: Brian Utter; OH: Sarah Young (sarah_whitman_young@hotmail.com); OR: Morgan Madrid (morgan@biportland.org) + Allyn Bowers (allyn@biportland.org); PA: Karen Stern (biunity@netaxs.com) (Philadelphia) + Jamie Phillips (jphillips@hotmail.com) + Milla Rosenberg (millarose00@hotmail.com) (Pittsburgh); PR: Carmen Oquendo; RI: Susan Rooney (sarooney@kpmg.com); TN: Melinda Brown (tn_grrl@yahoo.com); TX: Gigi Raven Wilbur; VA: Steve Kadar (stevekadar@yahoo.com); VT: Kim Ward; WA/WV: Alexei Guren; WA: Julie Levitt; WI: William Atewell; WY: Pete Chvany (khvastun@world.std.com); ZIMBABWE: Dumisane

STUDENT INTERNS:

Liz Janiak

Laure de Vulpillieres (aka Voop)

Amy Albert

Eddie Bruce

Left to right: Marcelo (Argentina), MikZ (Northern California), Pete (USA, Wyoming), Allyn (USA, Oregon)

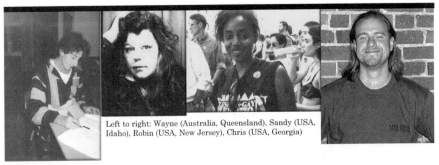
Left to right: Wayne (Australia, Queensland), Sandy (USA, Idaho), Robin (USA, New Jersey), Chris (USA, Georgia)

ADVERTISING: Arthur Cohen

PUBLICITY/PRESS RELEASES: Arthur Cohen, Elizabeth Washer

PRODUCTION: We extend our gratitude to Tiffany Voorhees at McNaughton & Gunn, Inc., for going "the extra step" (actually, *several* extra steps) for us. Thank you for your good humor and patience.

WRITERS:
Films with Bisexual Characters: Wayne Bryant
Bi The Book: Robyn Ochs, Ron Fox, Sherry and Deep
Safer & Sexier: Cianna Stewart

Getting Bi on the Internet: Voop, building on work formerly done by Audrey Beth Stein, Gilly Rosenthal, John Valentine, and Kathryn Foote

Why Bi: Compiled by Liz Janiak. Contributors: Antonio Ferrera, Russ Stein, Jude, Donna Huen, Koen Brand, Alex Lee, Carrie Peterson, Barry Saiff, Ronan Watters, Sheeri Kritzer, Mariaurora Mota, Sparrow, Axel Griessmann, Ellyn Ruthstrom, Marcella Bucknam, Daniel M. Ocampo, Mark Pearson, Ramki Ramakrishnan, Sophie Verhalle, Adia, Marcia Deihl. (Layout: Ellyn Ruthstrom)

DESIGN:

Hilde Vossen (left), Maurice Snellan (right)

Cover Design: Melissa Kulig (Maksimum Design - maksimum@mindspring.org) Interior Design: Robyn Ochs & Kathleen Hepburn

Layout/Desktop Publishing: Robyn Ochs & Kathleen Hepburn, with lifesaving help from Virginia Slawson, Linda Blair, Kathleen Hepburn, Ellyn Ruthstrom.

VARIOUS TYPES OF SUPPORT: Vivienne Esrig, Rosa Carson, Brockton Bi Couple, Heidi Vanderheiden, Alan Hamilton, Tanya Godbout, Amy Conger, Elena O'Malley, Nick Smith, Dana Shaw, Sarah McKibben, Ian Watters, Amatul Hannan

PROOFREADING: Linda Dyndiuk, Bhavana Chawla, Sarah McKibbon, Elena O'Malley, Audrey Beth Stein, Marjorie Charney, Anke, Debbie Block-Schwenk

TECHNICAL SUPPORT: Anke, Carla Imperial, Kathleen Hepburn

Jamie (Pittsburgh PA, USA)

PHOTOGRAPHY: Hilde Vossen; Ellyn Ruthstrom; Robyn Ochs, Efrain J. Gonzalez, Holly Danyliu, A. Dubois, Matt LeGrant, Marcia Deihl, Peg Preble, Rachel Lanzerotti, Wayne Bryant, Wayne Roberts, & others.

Thanks to the following for their various roles in helping move this project along: Brett Beemyn (for his repeated offers to help out!), Wayne Bryant, Gabriela Carrión, Julianne Chatelaine, Children From The Shadows/True Colors, Alvin Fritz, Stephen Harvey, The International Gay and Lesbian Human Rights Commission, Sheeri Kritzer (BRC Treasurer), Beth Firestein (for her editorial talents), Ron Fox, Mary Ann Greanier, Bobbi Keppel, Stephanie Moore-Fuller, Barb Nicely, David Reiffel, Alejandra Sarda, Ellen Keyne Seebacher, D. Shaw, P.K. Simons, Nick Smith, Russ Stein, Aletha Taber, Elizabeth Reba Weise, Jessica Wilder, Jen Yockney, and to those who wished to remain anonymous and to those whose names I simply forgot to include (sorry).

To all of the board members and volunteers, past and present, of the Bisexual Resource Center.

For financial support, special thanks to Dr. Fritz Klein and the American Institute of Bisexuality, as well as to the people who responded to our call for donations to hire interns.

Editors, left to right: Andy (UK), Tom (USA, New Jersey), Carmen (Paraguay), Maurice (Netherlands), Mary (USA, Illinois)

Thank you to Alison Bechdel and to Roberta Gregory for giving permission to use your cartoons and sketches. And Alison, thanks for Sparrow!.

I am eternally indebted to the Fabulous Kathleen Hepburn, (The Extremely Great) who laid out the earlier editions of the Guide and who contributed her technical wizardry, her amazing knowledge of PageMaker, and many hours of her time to this project.

And finally, to my partner Peg Preble, who put up with me while I was working on this project, and to fur-faces Pixel, Kiddle and Emma, for serving as paperweights and lap (and sometimes, unfortunately, keyboard) warmers during many long hours. And to my mom, who gets it.

Arthur Cohen

Melissa Kulig

Voop

Ellyn Ruthstrom being appreciated by Natalie (l) and Robyn (r)

David Rothcheck

Linda Dyndiuk

Kathleen Hepburn

Robyn Ochs

What is Bisexuality?

bi Robyn Ochs

Some people are attracted to men. Some people are attracted to women. And some people are attracted to men and to women. And some of us go through periods in our lives when we may not be particularly attracted to anyone.

Simple.

Sexologist Alfred Kinsey and his colleagues tried to chart this diversity by developing what ended up being called "The Kinsey Scale," a seven point scale in which people who were exclusively heterosexual in their attractions and behaviors were assigned a zero, people who were exclusively homosexual a six, with lots of combinations of heterosexuality and homosexuality in the one to five range. One of the most surprising findings of the *Kinsey Report* was that almost half of his male respondents, and about one-fourth of his female respondents reported adult sexual experience with both men and women. And this was in the late 1940s! Kinsey addressed the fluidity of sexuality in the following statement:

> *Males do not represent two discrete populations, heterosexual and homosexual. The world is not divided into sheep and goats. Not all things are black, nor all things white. It is a fundamental of taxonomy that nature rarely deals with discrete categories. Only the human mind invents categories and tries to force facts into separated pigeon-holes. The living world is a continuum in each and every one of its aspects. The sooner we learn this concerning human sexual behavior the sooner we shall reach a sound understanding of the realities of sex.*

Similarly, anthropologist Margaret Mead stated in a 1975 article in *Redbook*,

> *Even a superficial look at other societies and some groups in our own society should be enough to convince us that a very large number of human beings – probably a majority – are bisexual in their potential capacity for love. Whether they will become exclusively heterosexual or exclusively homosexual for all their lives and in all circumstances or whether they will be able to enter into sexual and love relationships with members of both sexes is, in fact, a consequence of the way they have been brought up, of the particular beliefs and prejudices of the society they live in and, to some extent, of their own life history.*

Given statements like this, it is surprising that Western culture has held on to its dichotomous concept of sexual orientation, which posits that everyone is *really* either gay or straight. In this mode of thinking, bisexuality exists only as an oddity, a transitional phase, a blip in the natural order of things.

But those who attempt to dichotomize sexuality are closing their eyes to the very real experiences of some very real people. Anthropologist Esther Newton wrote that "desire, we begin to think, is less like a heart, throbbing the same everywhere, and more like music, and every culture has its own—not only songs, but tonality, instruments and occasions." Not only does every culture and every subculture have its own understanding of sexuality and its meaning, but every individual is different, with our own unique sexuality. We each have the right to use the labels we choose, and to live as we choose, providing that all parties involved are fully consenting adults.

My advice to you is this:

Be good to yourself.

Be good to your loved ones.

Be honest.

Be thoughtful.

Play safe.

Communicate.

Get the support and information you need.

And celebrate the gift of your sexuality!

And that's the purpose of this book.

 **Bisexual**

is a name for a richly varied reality that any one narrow definition cannot full describe. We asked hundreds of people to comment on their bisexuality — what bisexuality means to them personally, how they discovered their own bisexuality, and why they do or do not use the word "bisexual" to describe themselves. Following is a selection of their responses, the full range of which reflects what "bisexuality" means to people who define it by living it. *Why Bi? was compiled by Elizabeth Janiak, who is a student in Cambridge, Massachusetts.*

I've always had a problem with dichotomies.

My mother used to tell me that when I was about five I would point at the cherry tree in our garden and say, "when I was a boy, I used to climb that tree." I was 21 before I realized that my attraction to women was about more than platonic bonding and I wondered for about a year whether I was gay; I certainly enjoyed hanging out with like-minded gay men and women, but would catch myself looking at men and thinking rather lustful thoughts about them. My best female

friend came out as bisexual around this time and all of a sudden I had a whole new set of referents in which I could frame my identity. I came to realize that the label 'bisexual' is the only one that fits me — for now. The important thing about my identity (for how can I speak about the identity of any other bisexual?) is not who I have a relationship with or how I choose to have that relationship, but rather an attempt to understand love better, and an attempt to unlearn many linguistic/conceptual categories which are taken to be universal Truths. I try to remind myself that most binary categories we use are relatively modern, Western, dominant-male ones,

Jude & her friend Justin

Why Bi?

can be related to power differences, and that I am free to use the same categories in different ways if I choose, or make my own categories if I need to.

Jude is 26, lives in Dublin, Ireland and hopes to embark on a Ph.D. soon.

I consider myself bisexual because it is the only appropriate term I can see to describe my emotional, physical, and sexual attraction to both women and men. Not limited by so-called societal norms of heterosexuality, I have learned to get involved in different levels with women and men of different backgrounds. I think that is what being bisexual means to me: you do not really look at another person as woman or man but see them for the real person they are and, if it's possible, to explore if you can reach different levels of relating to each other. Having more freedom in terms of not having to choose who you could have a relationship with (which is often limited by gender) is one of the better points of being bisexual. I am bisexual because **I do not choose to have attractions to only women or men but because I have more options of finding people to explore life with.**

Daniel M. Ocampo is from The Philippines.

A lesbian friend once told me that, when coming out to her brother, he asked her: "How do you know that you don't like men since you haven't been with any?" "How do you know you are not gay since you haven't been with men?" was her reply, to which he answered "because I don't feel the need to be with men." "Me neither," she said... I call myself bisexual **because I feel the need to be with both men and women.**

Antonio Ferrera, from Spain, is 36 years old with a Ph.D. in physics. He is fond of good meals, good wines, flamenco dancing late into the night, and anything related with having a good time in general, i.e., bon vivant wannabe.

To me, the word bisexual has evolved in meaning over the years. I originally used it to describe my state of being attracted to some men and some women, regardless of whether I chose to act on that attraction. But nowadays it has come to mean my being attracted to very specific kinds of people — those who challenge, and occasionally demolish, the limits of gender in their lives. Specifically, I find myself attracted to feminine males, butch females, and other transgendered people.

Ramki Ramakrishnan

My awareness of androgyny in myself has led to my reclaiming the older meaning of bisexual ('two sexes in the same body') and a political position from which to tackle the institutions of gender and heterosexism, and the way we marginalize some people and privilege others based on their gender-role conformity.

Ramki Ramakrishnan is a biologist, musician, and queer community organizer, last sighted in Austin, Texas. He is founder-member of Trikone-Tejas, a pan-Asian student alliance dedicated to ending racism, sexism, and homophobia at UT Austin.

I have been calling myself bisexual since the age of 14 (when I came across it in a dictionary). For me, **one's sexual identity**, however contradictory that may seem, **is more than a sexual thing**: it also has to do with feelings, social contacts, friendship, etc. At first, I assumed I was 50-50 (50% for guys, 50% for the girls), but now I realize it is more complex than

Why Bi?

Why Bi?

that: I easily have a crush on girls, I am more easily attracted to girls than boys. I don't often fall in love with guys but when I do, it's 'serious.' I am now in a (monogamous) relationship with a girl and I find it very fulfilling. I certainly have no need for a man. I would say that I am more attracted to girls on the whole but identify as bisexual since I have had some meaningful relationships with boys in the past, because that might happen in the future (if my girlfriend and I would break up — God forbid!), and because guys still seem to interest me.

Sofie Verhalle is the Resource Guide editor from Belgium.

I've identified as bi for fifteen years. To me **bisexuals are people who dread the idea of only being erotically involved with one of the two sexes for the rest of their lives**; but, despite all this, in truth they are as likely to be seduced into monogamy as anyone else.

Mark Pearson is 43 and lives a simple life in Iowa, USA.

I am bisexual by default, in that it is the only word in common usage that approximates my sexual orientation. To me the word implies the existence of only two genders or sexes, when I believe there are many more. **I am attracted to a wide range of gender expressions**, and many times the only way I can describe myself to people who still believe in the binary gender system (the idea that there are only male and female genders) is to say that I am bisexual. I use this identity with reservations, as the word itself is inadequate and fails to challenge the traditional oppressive model of sex and gender.

Alex Lee, 23, is an Asian American transgender community organizer in San Francisco.

Why do I label myself Bisexual? It is because I have discovered within myself a yearning not only for my wife but also for members of my own sex. I have denied these feelings until I was 46 years old. Then I came out to my wife and myself. **We accepted these feelings as something that would change but not end our marriage.** I started to look for information about bisexuality, reading about it in books and on the Internet, meeting people that were more experienced at a bisexual support group and at a mailing list. And from that information and after a lot of communication with my wife I started accepting my own feelings.

Because I wanted the label to confirm my inner feelings I now call myself Bisexual. At the bisexual support group I met another man in a similar situation, and with the consent of our wives we developed a relationship. Accepting my feelings for both genders makes me feel more complete and balanced than before.

Koen Brand is 47 years old and happily married for 26 years. Since his coming out in February 1999, he has become an active member of the Dutch Bisexual Network. He is a member of the committee that is busy organizing the first European Bisexual Conference (EBC1) to be held in Rotterdam in June 2001.

Koen Brand

I call myself bisexual because I feel comfortable saying it. While it doesn't define all of who I am, it may help people understand me better, just as saying, "I like to do beadwork" may help people understand me. It's nice to be able to have a safe place to say it, either out loud, or implicitly (ie, by wearing a bi pride shirt or button). As an individual, my bisexuality is about whom I care about, whom I'm attracted to, and whom I love. As part of a community, **calling myself bisexual helps attract visibility.**

Sheeri Kritzer lives and works as a freelance web programmer in Somerville, MA, USA.

Why Bi?

I began by thinking I was a lesbian. That identification fell apart when I admitted to myself that I found men attractive as well. Then I identified as bisexual. That identification fell apart when I fell in love with a gender-bending transsexual who had decided, halfway through the switch, to stay "in the middle." With an attraction to three sexes, how could I be bisexual? Trisexual? No, that's the punchline of a bad joke. For a while, I adopted the seventy-something-year-old term "pansexual" but I got tired of defining the word for people. There are already too many aspects of my life that appear cryptic to most people; why intentionally add another? I want a self-label that brings people closer to me, not one that sends them running for their dictionaries.

I've found freedom in the term bisexual even though it hints at a simple dichotomy that I've long since discarded. Like most symbols, the word bisexual is an icon that depicts a transcendent reality, a meaning too large for that symbol to effectively capture and box away. When I label myself bisexual, I am calling myself open. **Open to possibilities, open to the ebb and flow of people past the shores of my life.** Though the word 'sex' is contained within the word 'bisexual,' to me it's about so much more than sex (a vast realm itself!). It's about opening my heart and my life to the winds of time and learning to love as much as I can, as long as I can, as full and deep and wide as an ocean.

Sparrow is a 33-year-old bisexual person who used to be a lesbian before she came out of more closets than you can shake a stick at. She lives in Southeastern Idaho, USA with a lover and some pets. A retired sex worker, Sparrow now writes erotica and non-fiction under the pseudonym Magdalene Meretrix.

Sparrow

I am a 27-year-old, Irish, Queer Activist, Socialist, bi guy who is sometimes into kinky sex. I can be all or a mix of these at any one time. These identities link me to other people in the form of communities and friendships — they are part of who I am. An important thing for me is that none of them are fixed and what those words mean to me now is different from what they meant a year ago and in another year's time they may have a different meaning again. I don't know the reason but **I have always felt more at home with things that aren't fixed and static.** I have always liked having a range of very different projects and plans on the go at any one time. Firstly, it keeps me interested in what I am doing, and secondly, it gives me more room to move about. When I was younger I did this because I didn't know what I wanted to be or do when I grew up

Ronan Watters

and settled down (as I was told I would have to). Now, while I still don't know what I want to do in a few years time, I do know I still want to have as many options open to me as possible then as now.

Ronan Watters lives in Ireland and is involved with Bi Irish.

I am bisexual because I do not judge according to outside features, but on what's behind that. **I am attracted to mind before anatomy.**

Carrie Peterson

Why Bi?

I call myself Bisexual because, since puberty, I have
been attracted to,
fantasized about sex with,
wanted to be with, stared at longingly,
And, at various points in my life,
been sexual with,
been loving with,
been involved intimately with both men and
women.
Because I have enjoyed being sexual with both
men and women.

Because the word Bisexual has tremendous power.

To name, to identify, to distinguish yourself
As what you are,
And what you are not
Enables you to live your life
As yourself.

Barry Saiff (at left) and Luigi Ferrer at a
BiNet meeting.

Because as a teenager and a twenty-something I was very confused.
Not because I am Bisexual
But because I did not understand then that I am Bisexual.
And because as a teenager I never heard the word spoken.
Because I don't want anyone else to lose the time that I have lost
Time that slowed me down
In building the kind of life I want,
In being a happy Bisexual.
Because too many times I have been told that there are no real Bisexuals.
And because, too many of those times, I was still not sure myself.
Yes, we all want a world where we don't need labels.
But we still need the word Bisexual,
And those of us who use it,
Those of us who wield the word Bisexual proudly in the world,
Even those of us who are not Bisexual who are not afraid to say, "Bisexual!"
Are performing an essential service to everyone.

*Barry Saiff currently serves as one of five Interim Steering Committee members and
Fundraising Coordinator for BiNet USA. He has been a Bisexual activist for 9
years, and at various times has also been a war tax resister, peace activist, ending
hunger activist, and fundraiser. He lives and works in San Francisco.*

I spent my life coming out...and every coming out was a lie. I had lived for years alternating between calling myself a lesbian and then slipping back into the het world, depending on whom I was dating. But I knew that every identity I assumed was a lie and I always felt guilty whether I was expounding the wonder of sex with women or talking about how much I liked men. It was my guilty secret that I didn't really fit either category and my dreams were of lovers of any gender. Also, as so many bisexuals do, I feared I was the only one in the world who felt that way. I finally reached a point where I could no longer live with the lies and I told a friend about my secret attraction to both genders. I was terrified I would lose her friendship, but the pain of the lie was more terrible than the possible loss. She looked at me and said "Oh, you're bisexual! OK." The look on my face must have told a very strange story. Inside I was faced with a sudden realization. I had never told anyone about my feelings, and yet there was a whole word that described how I felt! There must be other people who felt as I did — other bisexuals! The simple fact that a word existed not only gave me an identity, but it also opened a whole world of new possibilities! And even though it was several years before I met another person who identified as bi, it changed everything at that moment. Now I hear people say they don't like the word bisexual. They feel it has negative and limiting connotations. But for me it will always be a cherished doorway to a new world. It represents freedom, honesty, and self-realization as no other word ever has.

Marcella Bucknam is a former national coordinator for BiNet USA currently living in Omaha, Nebraska, USA.

I identify myself as bisexual because it reflects my openness to the opportunity to love or relate to everybody. I wonder if the people that are incapable of loving one or the other gender have a defective chromosome.

Mariaurora lives and works in Monterrey, Mexico. She was one of the founding members of the Metropolitan Community Church in Monterrey and now is the director of OASIS, a sexual diversity community center.

Why Bi? For me becoming bi was a non-miraculous epiphany late in life. As a young adult, I had recovered from stunning depression — we are a small and so far secret band — and that was a miracle!

My high school and college years were straight, shy, dry and non-sexual. Moving to New York, I met the love of my life, a woman painter who took my twenty-eight-year virginity and introduced me to the Art Students League and Will Barnet, her and my beloved mentor. Art and this love affair and a spiritual grounding later in the Human Potential movement opened me up again.

Back in Boston in my thirties, I began volunteering intensively in state mental hospitals, four of them, and eventually was hired as a rehabilitation counselor, starting a new career. At night, I lurked in gay bars, another new career of sorts. I came out in 1982 at age 56. I have few lovely memories of my 17 years as a gay man, part of which was tangled up in booze! Less and less do I buy into the clichés of gay and straight thinkers. **I started calling myself bisexual in my seventies** — that's now — and after a particularly moving exchange of confidences with a stranger who may or may not be gay, I realized hey! I'm bi.

Russ Stein is a retired psychotherapist living in Franklin, Massachusetts, USA. He has been a gay/bi activist for many years and is a member of the board of SpeakOut Boston.

Why not? It is my firm belief that **all humans are born bisexual**. It is just a natural thing to be bi.

Axel Griessmann lives in Hamburg, Germany. He is working in the computer and communications business. In his little spare time he likes listening to music of all kinds and building, restoring, and riding his motorcycles.

Axel Griessmann

Three words: **Truth in advertising.**

Marcia Deihl has been a musician, writer, and activist in the Cambridge area (USA) for 25 years. She co-wrote a chapter (with Robyn Ochs) in Homophobia: How We All Pay the Price *(Beacon, 1992) and also has a chapter in* Blessed Bi Spirit

(Continuum International Press, 2000), as well as music, theater, and feature articles for Sojourner: A Women's Forum. *Along with Robyn Ochs, she was a co-founder of the Boston Bisexual Women's Network (1983). Currently, she's a member of the Cambridge Lavender Alliance and a book reviewer for the* Harvard Review.

Marcia Diehl (far right) and Amanda Udis-Kessler and Gilly Rosenthal.

In questions of sexuality, I prefer not to use labels to define myself. But considering that we live in a society that needs these "damned" labels, I prefer to use the term "bisexual." Considering my personal preferences, **calling myself "bisexual" covers a wider territory regarding my capacity to fall in love** and to share the life of a couple with another person without taking into consideration these questions of gender. Like all labels, identifying oneself as bisexual has certain disadvantages, because there exists a prejudice (very widespread) that bisexuality implies promiscuity. This idea exists in hetero as well as homosexual groups, and one suffers certain discrimination, as a result of the view that bisexuality represents an easy out, when in reality, for me it has to do with an open perspective.

Adia is 24, lives in Lima, Peru, and has a B.A. in literature.

Why Bi?

I have loved and been loved by men and by women and I hope that pattern will continue in my life. I am a very woman-focused person because even before I defined my sexuality I defined myself as a feminist. Some people may misinterpret my sexuality because of that focus, but I know who gets me hot, and I know who has found their way into my heart. Bi community is a wonderful place to come out in. I have found the bi community to be **one of the most accepting spaces for anyone to spend time in.** And something that I don't think we are given credit for is that we provide an incredibly safe space for

Ellyn Ruthstrom

lesbians and gays to come out within. We don't really care if you define yourself as other than bisexual; if you're happy, so are we. I love that.

Ellyn Ruthstrom is 41 years old and lives in Somerville, Massachusetts, USA. She is the editor of the BiWomen *newsletter and is on the board of the Bisexual Resource Center in Boston.*

Calling myself bisexual was a long and often troubling journey. In a world that persists in seeing sexuality as dichotomous, I came to see bisexual **as the most honest representation of who I am sexually.** I now am active in anti-homophobia work in my community, and find that maintaining this label, while confusing and even abhorrent for some, is necessary for me. I also believe that in some small way I am a role model for young people who might otherwise be too scared to call themselves bisexual.

Donna Huen lives in Winnipeg, Canada.

How to Start a Bisexual Support Group

bi Robyn Ochs

Bisexual support groups are springing up all over the world. Is there one in your town? If not, you may want to start one. Here are some pointers to help you create the safe space essential for creating a positive bisexual identity.

What is a Support Group?

It's up to you to decide what type of group you want. It can be a social group, a facilitated or unfacilitated discussion group, it can be closed or open to newcomers. Each type of group will require different skills to run.

Rule Number One: There Are No Rules.

There is no simple formula for the successful creation of a bisexual support group. Even within a given country, every community has its own character. Organizing in Minneapolis is not the same as organizing in a small town in New Hampshire. And a small town in Manitoba may be different from a small town in Quebec. Therefore, what follows are guidelines and suggestions, not hard and fast rules. You will need to adapt this information to your own community's resources and needs, and to your own personal desires.

A Group will be More Successful if its Members Feel a Sense of Ownership.

If you are beginning a group, do everything possible to make sure that the group, and not one person, shares responsibility and decision making. Therefore, while it is important to go into your first meeting with some ideas about what you would like a group to be, be open to other people's ideas. Failure to do so will result in a situation where all members will not get what they need from the group, and you will get stuck doing all of the work, because other people will not feel invested in the group. And if you burn out or lose interest, the group may cease to exist.

Logistics

The first step in forming a new group is to organize a meeting. This process of organization has several components: finding a space, letting people know that the meeting is going to happen, and deciding upon the actual agenda for the meeting.

Finding a space: In many communities it is possible to obtain meeting space at little or no charge. Public libraries, schools, city or town halls, someone's home, women's or progressive bookstores, food cooperatives, religious meeting houses (Quakers and Unitarian Universalists are usually particularly receptive) may have meeting space available. Keep in mind issues such as safety, accessibility to public transportation and wheelchair accessibility, and try to select a place which is fairly neutral, to allow closeted people, or people new to bisexual identity the maximum possible safety. When you have found a meeting space, make sure to leave time to advertise. Usually 6-8 weeks is sufficient.

Contact information: It can be very helpful to list contact info so that people can contact your groupfor more information: address, phone number, e-mail, websites. Should you list your own address or phone number? Some people feel comfortable doing this, others do not. One woman lists her telephone number with a pseudonym. That way she knows immediately whether someone is calling as a result of her ads or posters, and she feels safer because she is not giving out her real name. If you list your own number and have restrictions on when you are willing to be called, state that clearly in the flier or ad, such as "for info. call Maria at 222-2222 between 6 pm and 9 pm." Another option is to rent a voice mailbox (approximately $10/month), or to ask a local (or not too far away) lesbian/gay hotline, or lesbian/gay center, or women's center to serve as your contact phone number, at least for a limited time. Whatever method you choose, be sure to return all calls promptly, and to be discreet. Remember: homophobia exists, and not everyone is out to his/her roommate, parents, spouse, etc.

Covering Expenses: Keep expenses as low as possible, then "pass the hat" at the meeting. State what your expenses were, and propose a suggested amount, asking people to pay what they can.

Getting the Word Out: Advertising

Once you have located a site for your first meeting, you must let as many people as possible know that it is happening. There are a number of ways to do this, mostly through newspapers, fliers, and word of mouth.

Newspaper calendars and classified ads: Many newspapers will list events open to the public in a "calendar" section. Check your local newspaper to see whether they do this. Calendar listings are usually free. If a calendar listing is not possible, you my want to consider placing a brief classified ad. Keep it as short and inexpensive as possible. For example:

> *BISEXUAL support/discussion group forming. First meeting November 22, 7:30 p.m. at Local High School Cafeteria. Call (789)456-1234 for info.*

Try to get this listing into as many publications as possible: the newspapers of nearby colleges, the nearest gay paper (even if it is based in another city or town), regional e-mail lists or bulletin boards, any local or regional newsletters (does a nearby Unitarian Universalist Church have a newsletter? Is there a women's center newsletter published nearby?)

Fliers: Make up a clear, concise 8 1/2 x 11 inch or other standard size poster about the meeting. State the time and place of the meeting, whether it is wheelchair accessible, what its purpose is (i.e. "to discuss the possible formation of an ongoing bisexual support group"). Statements about confidentiality may be helpful, especially in a more conservative environment. Get these posters up in as many locations as possible: on bulletin boards in local progressive stores, on local campuses, in bookstores, at the nearest food coop, gay bars, etc. Use your imagination. One place you may want to consider postering is the inside of bathroom stalls. They sometimes stay up longer before getting pulled down, you will have a captive audience, and interested people can read them and copy down the information in total privacy.

Remember: when choosing where to place calendar listings and to hang posters, keep in mind that bisexual people are a very diverse group, and to reach the maximum number of people you will want to get the word out in many different locations. This means reaching people from all economic, racial, and ethnic backgrounds who are bi, gay, and straight identified.

Your First Meeting

Come to your first meeting prepared. Arrange chairs in a circle so that everyone can see each other and everyone is included. Here is one possible format for a first meeting: ▼ **Welcome everyone**. Discuss ground rules (respect for one another, confidentiality, sharing air time, no one has to speak who does not wish to.) Review the evening's agenda. Many people feel more comfortable when they know what to expect. Make sure that everyone is comfortable physically: let them know where the bathroom is, where they may and may not smoke, that they may get up and leave the room if they wish to, etc. ▼ **Do some sort of "go-around"** in which each person gets a chance to speak. Have each person say their name and answer a question or two (why they came, what they would like to get out of the meeting, an interesting fact about themselves.) One exercise which can be a good icebreaker is to have people divide into pairs. Within each pair, have each person interview the other for 3 minutes, then switch roles. When each has interviewed a partner, come back to the main group and go around the room,

having each person introduce her/his partner: "This is Teresa. She is the mother of two children. She hates lima beans and likes to play rugby and the violin." ▼ **Have a moderated discussion**. Most people in a new group have had little or no opportunity to talk about issues related to bisexuality and are starving for a chance to talk. ▼ **Set aside time to decide on the next step**. Do people want to have another meeting, to start a group, etc.? Make sure that you do not leave the meeting without scheduling your next meeting. Pass around a phone list so that you (or someone else who is designated) have a way to reach people interested in meeting again.

Make sure that this meeting does not last more than 2 hours, or people will start to drift out and will miss the planning segment of the meeting. Keep an eye on the time, and try to leave 40 minutes or so for the planning segment. You may have to cut off an interesting conversation, but explain that you are asking people to cut the current conversation short to work out a way to continue the discussion later.

Subsequent Meetings

Depending upon the needs and desires of its members, support groups usually take one of four formats: ▼ **Focus on personal support or empowerment.** A personal support group would meet regularly and might focus on "go-arounds," with each member giving an update on current issues in her or his life. Other group members would listen and, sometimes, if asked, offer comments or advice. Occasionally, issues raised in the go-arounds might lead to impassioned political discussions over sexual politics and other issues. ▼ **Focus on discussion of topics.** A discussion-focused group would pick a topic in advance of each meeting. Topics might include: a book or article that everyone agreed to read and discuss, or a subject (the politics of marriage, bisexuality and feminism, coming out to one's children, parents, friends, partners, etc., dating, gender differences in relationships, monogamy and open relationships, safer sex, being bi in the gay community, etc.) ▼ **Focus on activities.** An activity-focused group might meet regularly for social activities: going out dancing, bowling, to the movies, to the beach, or renting and watching videos. ▼ **A combination of the above.** Brief go-arounds followed by a topic discussion, or go-arounds some weeks and topic discussions on others, with periodic social activities.

The group must decide where and how often to meet, and you must decide what type of commitment is expected from members. One suggestion is to meet weekly for a fixed period of time to form a sense of community and group cohesion and then to adjust your meeting to a less-intensive schedule. Another suggestion is to begin a personal support and empowerment group with several weeks of topic discussions to allow members time to build trust. You also need to decide whether to be an open or closed group. You might begin as an open group and then decide to close the group to new members at a later date, as the group coalesces. If you decide to close your group, you may wish to set up a mechanism for helping others form their own support groups. You may choose to rotate facilitators, or to have a regular volunteer or professional facilitator.

It is important to remember that, no matter what you do, not all groups will last. The group chemistry may not be right. If this happens, you may want to try again from the beginning.

Words Of Advice

Whenever possible, **talk to other people** who have experience in what you are trying to do. Talk to people who have started bisexual support groups in areas similar to yours, or who have started other types of support groups in your own community. We can learn from others' successes and mistakes.

Embrace diversity. While it may sometimes be more comfortable to have a group filled with people who are like you in terms of class, race, politics, etc., sometimes we learn more in a group where a variety of diverse voices are present.

Try, to the greatest extent possible, to **accommodate people's needs**. Is your meeting place wheelchair accessible? Are there pets, cigarette smoke, or other environmental substances present that members may be allergic to? Is your meeting place on public transportation for members without cars?

An occasional individual may contact you or show up at your meetings whose needs cannot be met by a support group. You may wish to have the names and phone numbers of the nearest hotline and of a couple of supportive therapists so that you can provide appropriate referrals.

Be clear in your advertising, and to new members that your group is not a dating service. Some support groups have policies stating that group members should not get romantically involved with one another.

Be aware that your group will provide support for many more people than actually attend meetings. The simple knowledge that there is a bisexual group meeting out there may be affirming to more people than you will ever know. And that is another good reason to get the word out.

If your group is an open group, try to make meeting time, place and contact information consistent. Some people may be terrified at the idea of attending a bisexual support group, and it may take them months to get up the courage to come to their first meeting. Make sure these people can find you.

Once your group is established, don't forget to get listed in the *Bisexual Resource Guide*.

[*Note: This information originally appeared in the form of a pamphlet published by the Bisexual Resource Center. I am aware that this information is directed primarily at readers in the United States and Canada, and that some of the information contained herein may not fully apply to those organizing in other countries. Readers in other countries: please take what is useful, and forgive the rest. —Robyn Ochs*]

Members of Bi Irish

Safer & Sexier

bi Cianna P. Stewart

So I've been asked to talk to you about safer sex. But really I'd rather just talk about sex because it's more fun to talk about enjoying having good sex and how to keep having it. Really, safer sex is about sex. I know sometimes we forget that. Even more importantly, staying safe doesn't start when you're already having sex. But we'll get to that.

So about sex...

Do you like having sex?

What kind of sex do you like?

What do you mean by "sex"?

Do you know what will make you feel good during sex?

Do you like to talk during sex?

Do you like to talk before having sex?

Do you hate to talk about sex?

Do you only talk about sex when you're not having it?

Do you know how to ask for what you want?

Can you say something would feel better if...

Can you tell a sex partner that something they're doing does not feel good?

What words do you use to describe your body?

What words do you use for different sexual/sensual acts?

What kind of sex makes you feel unsafe?

What are your boundaries?

What are your partner's boundaries?

Are you more willing to stop having sex or to try doing it with latex?

HIV

So there's this thing out there called HIV (the virus that's been linked to AIDS), and while it seems like it's everywhere, you can actually track its path, and stop it before it gets to you. Really.

Who, me?

HIV has no biases for or against a group of people. It does, however, have a particular fondness for bodily fluids that have a high level of white blood cells, and for activities which transmit those fluids from one person to another. It therefore affects all people doing certain "unsafe activities," regardless of sexual identity, gender, age, race, class or regional location.

Yes, you.

What else is out there?

There are many other diseases and infections you could potentially contract or transmit through sex. These diseases and infections can almost all be treated, but they can cause problems ranging from sores to very painful infections. Syphilis, hepatitis A, B, and C, gonorrhea, and chlamydia can all be transmitted through sex. Genital herpes and genital warts are transmitted through contact with the herpes or warts. Safer sex will help protect you from all of these. Pubic lice can also be transmitted through sex or any close physical contact, or through sharing clothing.

Syphilis is caused by bacteria. In addition to causing sores on the genitals, anus, or mouth, it produces fever and can damage internal organs if left untreated. Antibiotics are very successful in treating syphilis if it's detected early. Hepatitis is a virus that causes inflammation of the liver. Vaccines are available for Hepatitis A and B. Gonorrhea and chlamydia are bacterial infections treatable with antibiotics. Herpes and warts are both viruses and thus cannot be permanently cured, but symptoms can be eased through the treatment of outbreaks. Pubic lice, while easy to catch, are also easily treated with medicated lotions.

There are many bacteria and viruses out there that would love to make their home in your body. But this doesn't mean you should panic. It means that if you have strange symptoms, including sores on the genitals or mouth, strangely colored urine, or burning/unusual discharge from the genitals, then you should contact a doctor to see if you've contracted a disease or infection through sexual contact. And remember, playing safe can help to protect you from these problems.

What about pregnancy?

For men and women having sex, pregnancy prevention can be very important. Remember that pregnancy prevention is not the same as safer sex. Though the Pill or a diaphragm can usually prevent pregnancy, they can't protect you from sexually transmitted diseases or infections.

If you or your partner do get pregnant without wanting to, you have several options. While many people chose parenting or giving their child up for adoption, some choose to abort the pregnancy. Abortions are usually performed during the first two trimesters of a pregnancy. Legal restrictions on abortion vary from country to country and within the United States from state to state. Many states in the U.S. restrict a young woman's access to abortion, often requiring a woman under the age of 18 to obtain her parents' permission before obtaining an abortion. In some areas, certain abortion methods, like partial extraction, are restricted. Those who can contact a local or national reproductive health provider and/or advocacy group, such as Planned Parenthood in the United States, can find out more specific information about abortion access in their area. Be warned, though, that many places called "pregnancy crisis centers" are not reproductive health clinics. They encourage adoption and parenting only and are anti-abortion.

"Bodily fluids"?

HIV lives in white blood cells. The fluids in your body with a high concentration of white blood cells are blood, semen, and vaginal fluids (i.e. cum, discharge, ejaculate, etc.). HIV may also be transmitted through breast milk. Menstrual blood contains regular blood, and could easily transmit HIV. Saliva, tears, and sweat have such low traces of white blood cells that you'd have to drink gallons to put yourself seriously at risk. Urine is sterile and does not transmit HIV. Feces, however, often have blood in them and are therefore considered unsafe.

"Unsafe activities"?

A short (and incomplete) list of activities that are potentially unsafe when engaged in without the use of a barrier:

- Sexual intercourse involving penetration by a penis
- Anal finger play or fisting
- Vaginal finger play or fisting
- Oral sex on a penis or vagina
- Sharing any part of a rig used for injecting drugs or hormones
- Cuttings, piercings, or whipping until blood is drawn
- Kissing while there are open sores on the mouth

Safer injecting

Injection drug and hormone use is responsible for an increasingly high percentage of new HIV infections. This is especially true in urban areas, and for women. While many people think of addicts when hearing about injection drugs, the number of people who use drugs recreationally at dance clubs and parties is growing, and many of them are sharing their works. Hormones and steroids are also injected, and therefore share the same risks as injection drugs.

The important thing to remember is that it's not important what is injected, simply that you are injecting something. Blood can stay in the needle, syringe, or any other part of the rig. Because of this, using someone else's rig (also called "sharing works") makes it possible to inject their blood along with everything else.

Bleach will kill HIV, but only if it stays in the rig for at least 30 seconds. Drawing up water and bleach alternatively at least 5 times will usually fill the time minimum. Most people don't take this much time when they're using bleach. Also, there's always a possibility that some bleach will stay in the rig and this hurts when it's injected.

The most effective way to stay safe if you inject drugs, hormones, steroids, or anything else, is to own your own rig, and not to share needles, syringes, cottons, cookers, or water with anyone else. Having your own works means that you care about staying alive.

Safer Sex: what it means and doesn't mean

"Safer sex" means using barriers during sex to keep yourself and your partner(s) from exchanging bodily fluids which carry HIV. Using safer sex also protects you from other sexually transmitted diseases.

Safer sex does not mean asking your partners about who they've slept with and then deciding, based on that information alone, that it's okay to have unsafe sex. This ignores the fact that there are a number of ways to contract HIV, including sharing rigs while using injection drugs. This also does not ask what kinds of sex they had, whether safe or not, and does not at all address what partners their partners have had. This is not a safe method for many bisexual people, since both homophobia and biphobia on the part of our partners can affect how we answer and/or how they answer us. Beyond that, people may change their answer based on whether they think you'll still sleep with them if they answer honestly.

Safer sex does not mean simply being in a monogamous relationship. You may have been monogamous for all of two weeks. Or perhaps either you or your partner is a serial monogamist, who still has had many partners in one year.

Safer sex does mean educating yourself, planning enough to get the supplies, and keeping them close at hand. If you have to get out of bed, go into another room, or if you simply left the stuff at home, you're giving yourself one more excuse not to play safely. Keep some next to your bed, in the kitchen, out by the pool, in your jacket, in your car, at the office, wherever you have sex. (Lucky you – at the office?)

Safer Sex

Condoms

So available, so colorful, so user friendly. Condoms are usually unrolled over a hard penis before penetration. They can also be used to cover dildoes, vibrators, and other sex toys so that they're easier to clean and safer to share. You can also cut a condom into a flat sheet and use it to protect yourself when doing oral sex on a vagina.

Condoms have gotten a bad rap in some circles about breaking, but when a condom breaks it's usually because it was used incorrectly. Check the expiration date on the package. Keep condoms (and all latex stuff) away from heat (unless it's your body heat!). Always be sure to use a lubricated condom, or use some lube with unlubed condoms. NEVER use a petroleum-based lube with latex (like Vaseline, baby oil, Penzoil, whatever your fetish) – it breaks down the latex and will cause it to tear.

Tips:

- Put a little lube in the end of the condom before unrolling it onto the penis. It makes the tip much more sensitive.

- Try different kinds of condoms. Some feel better than others and the shape is very personal.

- Put on two condoms, then part-way through, remove one. The increased sensation is fabulous.

- If you're sharing a toy (like a dildo or vibrator) put a couple of condoms over it first. Then before you trade it, take one off. It's much faster than putting on a fresh condom in the middle of playing.

Gloves

For all "digital play" (i.e. using your fingers in someone's vagina or anus) wear a latex glove, and use lots of lubricant. Gloves can be cut open by removing the fingers and thumb and cutting open one side to give you nice, large, stretchy piece of latex for oral sex on women or for rimming. I love gloves because they make everything smoother, silkier. They are a fashion statement, especially when you coordinate the colored ones with your outfit. You can get boxes of gloves at beauty supply houses and medical supply stores.

Tips:

- If you're sensitive to the powder on gloves (or on latex), pre-rinse them in water, then let them dry. They'll be all ready to use when the occasion arises.

- If you'll be changing orifices mid-play (e.g. anus to vagina, one butt to another, etc.), put two gloves on at the beginning. Then when you want to switch, just take one off, and you're ready.

- Try lube on the inside of the glove. You'll feel more and the glove seems thinner.

Lubricant

For a lot of sex play, especially with latex, using a lubricant of some kind is highly recommended. Use a water-based one, because petroleum products break down latex. Lube makes everything wet and slippery. I can feel more. So can my partner(s). I can play longer. A lot longer. I have become a major lube fetishist. So can you.

Tips:

- Many lubes contain Nonoxynol-9, which does help fight HIV, but may also cause an allergic reaction. Women are especially sensitive to it. Check the ingredient list.

- Keep some water in a spray bottle or a squirt gun near wherever you have sex. If your lube begins to dry out, add water.

- For your travel pack, pick up lube samples from anywhere you buy lube. You can also often get some for free from health offices, AIDS outreach services, and from HIV testing sites.

Plastic Wrap

Plastic wrap is an excellent barrier for oral sex. Thin, clear, and tasteless, it allows you to feel and smell everything you want in sex. Also, it can be torn off in large sheets so you can cover everything that you need to.

Be sure to use a name brand plastic wrap – they're usually stronger and more rigidly tested. And in case you've heard some warnings: It's o.k. to use microwavable wrap (unless your body heats up to over 150°F).

Tips:

- Take the roll out of the box before you start to play. The cutter on the side of the box is too easy to cut yourself on (especially when distracted).

- Wrap the sheet around each leg (not too tightly) to create a barrier that you don't have to hold in place.

- Drip some lube on your partner's skin before setting down the sheet. This will help hold the plastic in place and increase the sensation.

What if your protection fails?

If you are engaged in an activity with a particularly high risk for HIV infection and your protection fails. For example, if a condom breaks during anal or vaginal intercourse, or you use someone else's rig while injecting, then you can take high doses of anti-HIV medications for four to six weeks. This procedure is called Post Exposure Prophylaxis and must be started within 72 hours of the incident. PEP is not guaranteed, and it is no substitute for safer injecting or safer sex. Being safer is also simpler and potentially more fun.

Coming out to your doctor

There are many other health concerns for all people, bi, gay, lesbian, straight, trans, or pansexual. But to get the care we all need to stay healthy, we need to be honest with our doctors. Many people are tempted to lie to their doctors about things like smoking or drug use, because they are embarrassed or worried about confidentiality, even though doctors are normally required to keep what we tell them confidential. For queer people of all kinds there is the added concern of homophobia and biphobia. Coming out to your doctor can greatly improve the quality of your care, not only because it helps you be honest with him or her about your sexual activity in the past and the present, but also because honesty and comfort with your healthcare provider(s) is important for the kind of positive relationship that leads to your improved health.

Coming out to healthcare providers is not for everyone. If you cannot come out, don't feel guilty. But do know that you have a right to quality care from a doctor who isn't prejudiced against you. There are services available to help you find a doctor who is queer-friendly. The best references for a healthcare provider are your queer or queer-supportive friends.

If you do want to come out to your doctor, here are some tips: Assure confidentiality if you need to. If you aren't out to your community, it might make you feel better just to hear your doctor promise you that s/he will respect your right to confidentiality. Also, wait until you feel comfortable. Maybe you don't want to come out to your doctor on the first visit. Get to know her first if it will make you feel safer. You might never feel 100% comfortable coming out to your doctor, but that's okay, too. It's your doctor's job to look after your health, and by coming out you are helping him or her to do that job well.

That's all for now. Now go get turned on and have some excellent sex.

Cianna P. Stewart lives in San Francisco, and she's hoping to keep having sex for as long as possible. Liz Janiak contributed to the updating of this article.

Unlimited Desires: An International Anthology of Bisexual Erotica

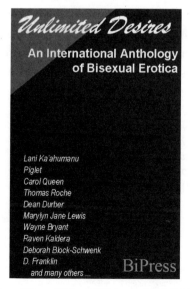

Features stories from Piglet, Carol Queen, Marylyn Jaye Lewis, Lani Ka'ahumanu, Jamie Joy Gatto, Rachel Martin, Deborah Block-Schwenk, Raven Kaldera, Isabelle Lazar, Thomas S. Roche, Paul Cowdell, Gabriella West, Wayne Bryant, Dean Durber, D. Franklin and many others.

Edited by the BiPress collective (Laurence Brewer, Trish Oak, Kevin Lano).

Quotes

``An impressive collection of positive and unashamed bisexual writing -- it's about time." Kathleen Kiirik Bryson, author of Mush and editor of erotic fiction, Virgin Publishing

``Really first rate writing, the collection goes right to the heart of the matter. It carries a social punch even more valuable than its (considerable) erotic charge." Tom Robinson

Web: http://bipress.bi.org/
Email: diversity33@hotmail.com

Address: BiPress, PO Box 10048, London SE15 4ZD, UK
Price: 6.50 pounds / 12 US dollars inc. P&P. Payments by cheque to "BiPress"

ELEANOR ROOSEVELT VOTING FOR THE FIRST TIME

♥ Think bisexual.

SUBSCRIBE TO

ANYTHING THAT MOVES

Since 1991, *Anything That Moves* magazine has been a vital forum for bisexual and transgendered people. An outspoken link in the growing network of out and active bisexuals, we also bring together isolated and closeted people in gay and straight communities. They come to us for the outstanding news, features, art, photography, fiction, reviews and poetry that we print in every issue. Won't you join them?

Subscribe online at **www.anythingthatmoves.com**
or write to
2261 Market St. #496
San Francisco, CA 94114-1600
or to **info@anythingthatmoves.com**

ATM is a non-profit, volunteer-run organization that appreciates your support. The efforts of volunteers and the generosity of donors are what keep us going. Thanks!

Trying to reach the bi and trans communities? *Anything That Moves* has an intensely loyal following. With an international distribution of approximately 15,000, we have the largest readership of any bisexual magazine. Contact business@anythingthatmoves.com for advertisement dimensions and rates, or call 415.626.5069.

Biphobia

bi Robyn Ochs

Bisexuality makes people uncomfortable. Many people wish that we would just go away, or at least keep quiet about it, because our very existence is perceived as a threat to the social order. A declaration of bisexual identity often results in experiences of discrimination, hostility, and invalidation. We are frequently viewed by gay- and lesbian-identified individuals as either confused or interlopers possessing a

"Your fence is sitting on me" at MOW, 1993

degree of privilege not available to gay men and lesbians and are viewed by many heterosexuals as amoral, hedonistic spreaders of disease and disrupters of families. Why all the fuss?

To understand the dynamic of biphobia, it helps to understand the dynamics of oppression in general, in order to separate out what is actually about bisexuality itself, and how much of it is just about silly humans, and how we tend to behave as social creatures.

Sociology 101

First off, Western society likes to construct things in binaries. Male/Female. Good/ Evil, and of course, Gay/Straight. In each of these binaries, one is given high status, the other lower.

Prejudicial behavior, or discrimination, is widespread. People in many categories and in many cultures have long been denied access to opportunities in areas such as employment, housing, and civil liberties. We are also denied the luxury of being able to see people who look and live like ourselves fairly represented on television, in the movies, in newspapers and in magazines.

Another example of prejudicial behavior and discrimination is stereotyping. For example, bisexuals have been stereotyped as indecisive and promiscuous. Sexual orientation is what Gordon Allport called "a label of primary potency," one that is seen as so significant that "it magnifies one attribute out of all proportion to its true significance, and masks other important attributes of the individual." (p. 179) The spotlight of attention is focused on this one aspect of ourselves, and all of our other qualities and characteristics get thrown into shadow. Bisexuality, once known, thus becomes foregrounded.

It is important to remember that despite this, each person has numerous simultaneous identities. I, for example, identify as bisexual, able-bodied, athletic, a dancer, left-handed, an activist, an academic, a student, a public speaker, a daughter, aunt, and sister, and as someone in a "lesbian" relationship. Many of us are members of more than one identity group within a given category: I, for example, identify as mixed-class, and my religious/ethnic heritage is mixed. I am Jewish but not religious, one of my three parents was Christian. I have lived in Boston for 20 years but identify strongly as a New Yorker. Some of our identifications may be as members of the majority or in-group; others may be as members of the minority, or out-group. Thus, few of us are in all respects privileged or in all respects oppressed.

Another factor directly affecting bisexuals' experience of oppression is the invisibility of our particular minority population. Individuals in an identity category that is visually identifiable (by the fact of sitting in a wheelchair, or because their skin is of a particular hue) have to deal with the difficulties that accompany their constant visibility. They do not have the option of "passing" as a member of the dominant group in order to avoid discrimination in a given context. Groups with identities that are not readily apparent, such as bisexuals, gays, and lesbians, have a different experience. While we are not constantly identifiable, which may in certain contexts protect us from discrimination, we have the disadvantage of not being able to identify others like ourselves, resulting in feelings of isolation and an underestimation by both bisexuals and non-bisexuals of our large numbers. In addition, the "privilege" of passing also carries as its counterweight the onus of having to repeatedly announce ourselves in order to avoid being assumed to be in the dominant group, as well as feelings of guilt or discomfort when we are silent. We carry the weight of constantly having to make the decision of how and when to come out and at what cost.

Homophobia

Biphobia cannot be understood in isolation. It shares many characteristics with other forms of oppression, especially with homophobia. Audre Lorde (1984) defines homophobia as the belief in the inherent superiority of one pattern of loving, and thereby the right to dominance and the fear of feelings of love for a member of one's own sex, and therefore the hatred of those feelings in others.

The Campaign to End Homophobia, an organization dedicated to raising awareness among heterosexuals, divides homophobia into four distinct but interrelated types: personal, interpersonal, institutional, and cultural. Personal homophobia is an individual's own fears or feelings of discomfort toward homosexual people or homosexuality. Interpersonal homophobia is defined as that same fear manifest in hurtful behaviors, such as name-calling, negative jokes, or the physical violence

directed at bisexuals, gay men, and lesbians, known as "gay bashing." Institutional homophobia consists of a broad range of discriminatory practices toward lesbian, gay, or bisexual people, such as prohibiting same-sex couples from obtaining social benefits under their partners' policies or denial of legal protection against discrimination in employment, housing, or public accommodations. Cultural homophobia is defined as cultural standards and norms that pervade society, such as the assumption that all people are heterosexual or silence around issues of homosexuality (Thompson & Zoloth, 1990).

There is no doubt that homophobia and heterosexism exist. One need only look at the prevalence of bomb threats, murder, physical assaults, arson, vandalism, telephone harassment, and police abuse against GLBT people.

How does homophobia affect bisexuals, gays, and lesbians? Gordon Allport (1954) laid out multiple ways in which individuals respond negatively to stigmatization, including two of importance to the discussion of biphobia: aggression and blame directed at one's own group, and prejudice and discrimination directed against other minorities. Theoretically, this may assist us in understanding two phenomena frequently observed in sexual minority populations: (a) internalized homophobia and (b) the hostility directed at bisexuals and transgendered persons by some gay men and lesbians. Feelings of victimization may get acted out through anger and rejection of those who are perceived as even less acceptable than oneself. There is a fear that these "marginal people" will give all gays and lesbians an even worse image than that which they already hold in the eyes the dominant culture, further impeding gays' and lesbians' struggle for acceptance.

Where Does Biphobia Overlap With Homophobia?

There is a considerable overlap between homophobia and biphobia, as well as specific ways in which each is unique. Furthermore, homophobia and biphobia affect men and women differently.

Visible bisexuals, like visible lesbians and gay men, may be targeted for discrimination. If theories of the "lesser oppression" of bisexuals were to hold true, the bisexual teacher whose sexual orientation has been disclosed would merely be reduced to half-time employment, and the bisexual individual being targeted by homophobic teens would get only half-gay bashed (punched and kicked half as many times, or perhaps half as hard?). Homophobia and biphobia inevitably intersect through the common experience of discrimination. To the bigot, we are all alike.

AND YOU KNOW WHAT ELSE? IT BUGS ME THAT SHE CAN COME IN HERE AND SOAK UP LESBIAN CULTURE, THEN GO HOME. TO HER SAFE, SOCIETALLY APPROVED **BOYFRIEND.**

AAH, WHAT ARE YOU AFRAID OF, MO? THERE'S ROOM FOR EVERYBODY! I SAY THE MORE PEOPLE SOAK-ING UP LESBIAN CULTURE, THE BETTER!

Another area of congruence between the experience of biphobia and the experience of homophobia may be with respect to "coming out" issues. A bisexual coming to terms with a same-sex attraction is likely to experience shame, ambivalence, and discomfort similar to that experienced by lesbians and gay men. Most world cultures deny both homosexuality and bisexuality, present distorted images of both homosexuals and bisexuals, and prevent the dissemination of accurate information about both groups to people in the general population.

In summary, we are all oppressed, and we can all be targeted. Whether the cause of this oppression is called "homophobia" or "biphobia," it hurts everyone.

Biphobia

Most bi people I have met come laden with painful stories of rejection and hurt, by both heterosexuals and lesbians and gay men.

A primary manifestation of biphobia is the denial of the very existence of bisexual people, attributable to the fact that many cultures think in binary categories, with each category having its mutually exclusive opposite. This is powerfully evident in the areas of sex and gender. Male and female, and heterosexuality and homosexuality are seen as "opposite categories." Those whose sexual orientation defies simple labeling or those whose sex or gender is ambiguous may make us profoundly uncomfortable.

Thus, bisexuals create discomfort and anxiety in others simply by the fact of our existence. We are pressured to remain silent, as our silence allows the dominant culture to exaggerate the differences between heterosexual and homosexual and to ignore the fact that human sexuality exists on a continuum. It is much less threatening to the dominant heterosexual culture to perpetuate the illusion that homosexuals are "that category, way over there," very different from heterosexuals. If "they" are extremely different, heterosexuals do not have to confront the possibility of acknowledging same-sex attractions within themselves and possibly becoming "like them." There is considerable anxiety in being forced to acknowledge that the "other" is not as different from you as you would like to pretend.

Because of our cultural erasure, bisexuality tends to be invisible except as a point of conflict. Given that studies reveal that only a small percentage of bisexuals are simultaneously involved with persons of both genders (Rust, 1991) and that we tend to assume that a person's sexual orientation corresponds to the sex of his or her current partner, it is difficult to make one's bisexuality visible in one's day-to-day living. As a result, we usually "see" bisexuality only in the context of uncomfortable situations: a closeted married man contracts HIV from sex with another man and his wife contracts

cartoon bi Alison Bechdel

the virus; a woman leaves her lesbian relationship for a male lover. Often, when bisexuality is given attention, it is portrayed as a transitional category, an interim stage in an original or subsequent coming-out process, usually from heterosexual to homosexual. This has the effect of associating bisexuality in many people's minds with conflict and impermanence.

The word *bisexual* itself may be seen as a product of binary thinking and, therefore, problematic. Many people struggling to understand bisexuality can only imagine the concept as a 50-50 identity. In their minds, if there is to be a third category, then it must fall midway between the other two categories and have clearly defined, unchanging parameters. Using this measurement, they will find very few "true" bisexuals. Many people also assume that a bisexual *must* need a lover of each sex to be satisfied, raising the specter of non-monogamy, another hot button for many.

This association of bisexuality with non-monogamy is a source of biphobia within heterosexual communities, especially since the arrival of HIV and AIDS. In the minds of many, bisexuality has come to be strongly identified with images of married, closeted men bringing HIV to their wives and children through unsafe sex with other men, and these stereotypes are amply reinforced in the media.

Biphobia directed at bisexuals by gay men and lesbians is complex and has its roots in the dynamics of oppression and the particular historical contexts affecting the growth and development of individual gay, lesbian, and bisexual communities. Coming out and living as gay can be very difficult. Most gay men and lesbians have experienced a great deal of hurt and rejection, and shared pain is one of the foundations on which many "lesbian and gay" communities have historically been based. External oppression may create a sense of not being safe and a strong need to maintain a clear boundary between "us" and "them." Bisexuals are by definition problematic in this regard, blurring the boundaries between insider and outsider. And further, bisexual visibility within the lesbian and gay community calls into question the inaccurate assumption that there is a monolithic lesbian and gay community with a single set of standards and values, composed of individuals who all behave similarly and predictably.

Lesbians and gay men may also fear that they are unable to compete with the benefits accorded by our culture to those in heterosexual relationships, believing that those who have a choice will ultimately choose heterosexuality. Many lesbians and gay men believe that bisexuals have less commitment to "the community," and that whatever a lesbian or gay man might have to offer to their bisexual partner will not be enough to

cartoon bi Alison Bechdel

outweigh the external benefits offered to those who are in heterosexual relationships. There is some realistic basis for this fear: Heterosexual relationships *are* privileged, and many bisexuals, as well as many lesbians and gay men, adopt at least a public front of heterosexuality to avoid family censure, develop careers, and raise children with societal approval. However, I also believe that there is some internalized homophobia in this line of reasoning. Many bisexuals, although having this perceived choice, still choose same-sex relationships. What gets lost in the fear is the fact that same-sex relationships also offer benefits not available in heterosexual relationships: the absence of scripted gender roles, freedom from unwanted pregnancy, the ease of being with someone with more similar social conditioning, and so on. Most important, the psychic cost of denying one's love for a particular person can be astronomical.

Internalized Biphobia

Biphobia does not come only from the outside. Internalized biphobia can be powerful, sometimes overpowering, and the experience of isolation, illegitimacy, shame, and confusion felt by many bisexuals can be disempowering, even disabling.

Even today, with modest improvements in this area, there are few role models available to us. Due to bisexual invisibility and the paucity of bisexual role models or bisexual community, most bisexuals develop and maintain our bisexual identities in isolation.

Most bisexuals spend a majority of our time in the community that corresponds with the sex and sexual orientation of our romantic partner. This can result in a sense of discontinuity if we change partners and our partner is of a different sex or if we shift back and forth between two differing communities over time. Other bisexuals have a strong social affiliation with either a heterosexual, lesbian, or gay community. This can result in another set of conflicts: if our partner is not of the "correct" sex, then we may feel guilt or shame for having "betrayed" our friends and community. Because of these potential difficulties, many people privately identify as bisexual but, to avoid conflict and preserve their ties to a treasured community, choose to identify publicly as lesbian, gay, or straight or to stay silent, allowing others to presume that they do, further contributing to bisexual invisibility.

Therefore, it is not surprising that some bisexuals feel that their bisexual desire is more a burden than a gift. They may feel a pressure or a wish to make a choice between heterosexuality and homosexuality to make their lives easier and avoid internal and external conflict. Many desire the ease they imagine would come with having one clear, fixed, socially acceptable identity.

The behavior of individual bi people, as members of a stigmatized group, is frequently seen as representative of *all* bisexuals. Thus, a bi-identified person may feel a sense of shame when any bisexual person behaves in such a way as to reinforce negative stereotypes of bisexual people. And we can feel an even more profound sense of shame when our own behavior happens to mirror one of the existing stereotypes of bisexuals (such as practicing polyamory, or leaving one relationship for another). Although some bisexual people do behave in ways that conform to negative stereotypes about bisexuals, it is actually the dynamics of prejudice that cause others to use such actions to generalize their stereotyping and prejudicial behavior to an entire group.

Ironically, bisexual individuals in monogamous relationships may also experience difficulties, feeling that their maintenance of a bisexual identity constitutes a double betrayal of both their community of primary identification (straight or gay) and of their partner. Alternatively, the bi person's partner may feel that a bi person's decision to continue to identify as bisexual, despite the fact of being in a monogamous relationship, is somehow a withholding of full commitment to the relationship and a holding on to the possibility of other relationships. This overlooks the fact that one's identity is, in actuality, separate from particular choices made about relationship involvement or monogamy.

So, how do we make things better?

Given so many obstacles, both internal and external, discussed above, how can a bisexual person come to a positive bisexual identity?

Understand the social dynamics of oppression and stereotyping. Get support and validation from others. Join a support group, subscribe to an email list, attend a conference, read books about bisexuality. Get a good bi-positive therapist, and find a friend (or two or twenty) to talk to.

Silence kills. I encourage bisexual people to come out as bisexual to the maximum extent that you can do so safely. Life in the closet takes an enormous toll on our emotional well-being. Bisexuals must remember that neither bisexuals nor gays and lesbians created heterosexism and that as bisexuals, we are its victims as well as potential beneficiaries. Although we must be aware that we, as bisexuals, sometimes have privileges that have been denied to gays, lesbians, and transgendered persons of any orientation, this simply calls for us to make thoughtful decisions about how to live our lives. We did not create the inequities, and we must not feel guilty for who we *are*; we need only be responsible for what we *do*.

Bisexuals, along with lesbians, gay men, and supportive heterosexuals must open our hearts and minds to celebrate the true diversity among us. Our success lies in creating a space where the full spectrum of our relationships is respected and valued, including those that are unlike our own. We must remember that each person is unique and also that we have much in common. Labels can unite us, but they can also stifle us and constrict our thinking when we forget that they are merely tools. Human beings are complex, and labels will never be adequate to the task of representing us. It is impossible to reduce a lifetime of experience to a single word.

If biphobia and homophobia are not allowed to control us, we can move beyond our fears and learn to value our differences as well as our similarities.

Bibliography

Allport, Gordon, *The Nature of Prejudice.* Reading MA, etc.: Addison Wesley Publishing Co., 1954.

Lorde, Audre, *Sister Outsider.* Freedom, CA: The Crossing Press, 1984.

Rust, Paula, "The Politics of Sexual Identity: Sexual Attraction and Behavior Among Lesbian and Bisexual Women," in *Social Problems*, Vol. 39, No. 4. (Nov. 1992).

Thompson, Cooper and Zoloth, Barbara, "Homophobia," a pamphlet produced by the Campaign to End Homophobia (Cambridge MA, 1990).

BI THE BOOK

This section is organized into four parts.

Finding Bisexuality in Literature

bi Robyn Ochs
... asks the questions "What is a "bisexual book"? What makes a fictional character "bisexual"?

Bisexual Stories

by Robyn Ochs
... is an annotated listing of fiction, poetry, and short stories.

A Reader's Guide to Non-Fiction Books, Chapters, and Journal Articles on Bisexuality

bi Ron Fox
... is a comprehensive annotated bibliography of non-fiction resources, arranged by subject.

Special Section on GLBT Literature and Film in India

bi Sherry and Deep
... was sent to us from India. It's an excellent bibliography on GLBT literature and films in India.

Together, they constitute the first and only published comprehensive bibliography on bisexuality.

Finding Bisexuality in Literature

bi Robyn Ochs

This section of the Bisexual Resource Guide contains an annotated bibliography (or Bi- bliography) of books with bisexual content: books about the subject of bisexuality as well as books with bi characters. Now it's very easy to tell if a non-fiction book is about bisexuality: it's usually called *Bisexual Lives*, or *Bisexual Politics*, or something like that. But it's a lot harder to tell if a work of fiction is a "bisexual book."

After all, how do you determine who is "really" bisexual? Is a female character who is heterosexual at the beginning of the book and then falls in love with another woman and at the end of the book is still deeply in love with that woman "really" a bisexual, or is she "really" a lesbian? If she never labels herself as lesbian or bisexual, the reader will obviously be making a subjective interpretation. It is important to keep in mind that the author's intent and a reader's interpretations are not always the same.

This was demonstrated to me very clearly in the winter of 1996 as I was organizing a panel at the Out/Write conference here in Boston. I provided conference organizer Michael Bronski with a list of approximately one dozen fiction writers whom I thought would be appropriate for a panel on bi characters in fiction. Michael called those on my list whom he thought most likely to attend the conference, and he reported back to me that one woman whom he had called, *several* of whose novels appear on my list of books with bi characters, had wondered aloud to him why she was being asked to be on this particular panel. "I don't write about bisexuals," she said, "I write about straight women who become lesbians." Well, she certainly could have fooled me, and, to be quite honest, I felt a sense of personal hurt and rejection when Michael reported what the novelist had said, though of course I recognize the right of the author to understand her own creations as she chooses.

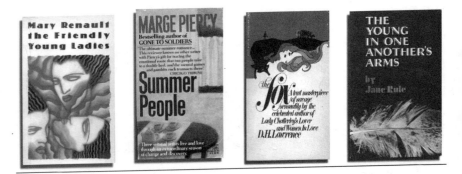

It would not be an understatement to say that we are starved for reflections of our varied bisexual lives, and as a result we grab at whatever scraps we can find.

So, how *can* you recognize a bisexual? There is a presumption in Western cultures that all people are heterosexual, expanded somewhat in this century to the presumption that all people are either heterosexual *or* become homosexual. Bisexuality, for the most part, remains invisible—invisible, that is, except as a point of conflict or transition. In other words, an action or event must occur in order to make bisexuality visible to the viewer. Thus, with rare exceptions, the only bisexuals who are seen as bisexual are those who are known to be in relationships with more than one partner (of more than one sex), and bisexuals who are leaving a partner of one sex for a partner of a different sex. Bisexuals whose lives are celibate, monogamous, and/or non-conflictual are not read as bisexual by the outside viewer, but rather as either straight or gay. Hence, there is an inevitable association of bisexuality with non-monogamy, conflict and transition.

In our review of bisexuality in literature, certain general themes can be found.

One major theme is **triangulation**, usually accompanied by jealousy and the fracturing of one relationship for another. The bisexual person is usually located at the triangle's apex. Two examples of this are Anaïs Nin's *Henry and June*, which is about a triangulated relationship with between Henry, June and Anaïs, with June at the apex; and Earnest Hemingway's *Garden of Eden*, with Catherine at the apex between Marita and David.

Then there's the "**discovery novel**," popular in lesbian literature of the 1970s, in which a previously heterosexual woman *discovers* her lesbianism by falling in love with a woman. Because at the end of the book she is blissfully paired with another woman, she is commonly read as someone who has discovered her "true" nature and is now a lesbian. But does this invalidate her previous relationships? Does she self-identify as lesbian? If so, will her new identity remain stable over time? What might this woman's future hold should her current relationship end? Despite statistical probability, because we live in a "happily ever after" culture, we are not supposed to ask this latter question. Another common character found in discovery novels is the woman (sometimes the (ex)partner of the woman described above) who can't handle the societal stigma attached to a same-sex relationship and "goes back" to men (is she *really* a lesbian unwilling to admit it, or is she really bi, or really straight?)

Another place we can sometimes find bisexuality is in **fantasy/science fiction/ Utopian** novels. Here, bisexuality is *normal*, a given, not stigmatized. By setting a story outside of the current reality, a great deal more leeway is allowed. A few examples are Starhawk's *The 5th Sacred Thing*, Samuel Delaney's *Dhalgren*, Marge Piercy's *Woman on the Edge of Time*, James Varley's *Titan, Wizard, and Demon* Series, and Melissa Scott's *Burning Bright* and *Shadow Man*.

Historical novels are another place to locate the elusive bisexual. Here, safely far away from the present time, men (and almost all of the historical bisexuals I've been able to located are male) are bisexual — no big deal — though they're not called bisexual or gay. Examples: most of the historical novels by Mary Renault (about ancient Greece), and Lucia St. Clair Robson's *Tokaido Road* (which is set in 17th century Japan).

And then there's what I call "**1970s bisexuality**" where bisexuality equals free love. These novels are usually written by men and, in contrast to historical novels, the bisexual characters are almost always women who share their voluptuous bodies with both women and (primarily) with men. Authors Robert Heinlein, Tom Robbins, and John Irving would all be included under this heading.

Then there's **adolescent bisexuality**, sometimes written off as youthful teenage experimentation: Hanif Kureishi's *The Buddha of Suburbia*, and Felice Picano's *Ambidextrous*.

Finally, there's the **hedonistic bisexual** who is often self-destructive and may leave a trail of broken lives (including his or her own), for example, Leonard Cohen's *Beautiful Losers*, Rupert Everett's *Hello Darling, Are You Working?*, and Carole Maso's *The American Woman in the Chinese Hat*.

But few authors actually use the "B-word." Among the few who do are Emma Donohue, Larry Duplechan, E. Lynn Harris, Dan Kavanagh, M.E. Kerr, and poets Michael Montgomery & Michelle Clinton.

In *Vice Versa: Bisexuality and the Eroticism of Everyday Life,* author Marjorie Garber says that we write our life histories backward, from the present, eliminating facts that do not fit our current stories. Someone who currently identifies as a gay man, therefore, might discount all past heterosexual experience, even if it felt meaningful and "real" at the time. And authors may do the same for their characters. Unlike those of us in the real world, the authors, of course, have this right: they *can* see into their characters minds. The characters are, after all, their creations.

Perhaps one thing I learned from my experience of trying to organize the writers' panel is that, in my hunger to find myself in fiction, perhaps I was focusing too hard. Perhaps I can find aspects of myself not only in fictional characters that self-identify as bisexual, but also in the experiences of characters of various sexual orientations.

Labels are tools, which help us to describe ourselves to ourselves as well as to others. They are not fixed and unchanging *essences*. The reality is that each of us is unique. Labels, however useful, will never be fully adequate to the task of describing real people, and should not be confused with reality. In that sense, we may be able to find our own bisexual experiences in fiction, regardless of the self-identification of the character or the intent of the author.

That said, I present you with a list of books that contain within their pages some degree of bisexual content. Enjoy!

BISEXUAL STORIES
An annotated bi-bliography

bi Robyn Ochs

All of the books listed below deal in some way with bisexual identity and/or behavior, though few of the narrators or characters in the books listed below use the word "bisexual." Rather, each book has at least one character whose life history can be interpreted to be bisexual. This list is by no means exhaustive; rather it is a place to begin. Your suggestions for books to be listed in future editions of this Guide are welcome. All books listed below are in English, except as noted. Many of these books can be ordered through the "Bisexual Bookstore" on the World Wide Web: http://www.biresource.org/bookstore/index.html.

BIOGRAPHIES/AUTOBIOGRAPHIES

Elizabeth Andrew, **Swinging on the Golden Gate**. Skinner House Books, 2000. (Can be purchased from www.uua.org/bookstore) Memoir of a woman reconciling the experience of being bisexual with the Christian faith. Highly recommended.

James Broughton, **Coming Unbuttoned**. San Francisco: City Lights Books, 1993. Born in 1913, poet and independent filmmaker Broughton takes us through his life in the San Francisco Bay Area, London and Paris. Though he does not delve into the meaning of his bisexual identity, he (and many others in his story) clearly identifies as such and had a number of relationships with men and women over the course of his life.

John Cheever, **The Journals of John Cheever**. NY: Knopf, 1990. Includes discussion of writer's bisexuality and extramarital relationships. (In case you were wondering, none of Cheever's fictional writings discuss bisexuality.)

Cyril Collard, **Savage Nights**. Woodstock, NY: The Overlook Press, 1993 (originally published in French as **Les Nuits Fauves**). French writer, film director and actor writes of his HIV diagnosis and subsequent relationships with a 17 year old woman and two young men. Set in present-day Paris, this disturbing and powerful story includes discussions of unprotected sex, anonymous s/m sex, and the difference for the author between sex with male and female partners. The author self-identifies as bisexual.

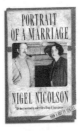

Samuel R. Delaney, **The Motion of Light in Water.** NY: Arbor House, 1988. Fascinating autobiography of science fiction writer's teens and twenties in New York City, 1957-1965. While Samuel Delaney currently identifies as gay, his history and his former identification are bisexual.

Barbara Guest, **Herself Defined: The Poet H.D. and Her World.** NY: Doubleday, 1984. Biography of American expatriate writer H.D. (1886-1961). Thorough and respectful representation of her significant romantic relationships, which included both women and men.

Jean Larkin, ed., **A Woman Like That: Lesbian and Bisexual Writers Tell Their Stories.** NY: Perennial (Harper Collins), 2000. EXCELLENT anthology of coming out stories by 31 US writers, 4 bisexually-identified: Wendy W. Fairey, Tristan Taormino, Cecilia Tan and Pat Califia.

Anchee Min, **Red Azalea.** NY: Berkeley Books, 1994. Fascinating autobiography of a woman growing up in Maoist China. The woman Min loves in her youth, and perhaps Min herself, are bisexual.

Anaïs Nin, **Henry and June.** NY: Harcourt, Brace, Jovanovich, 1986. Nin's diary from 1931-1932, recounting her relationships with her husband, Hugo, and with Henry and June Miller. Beautiful writing, much about her relationships and their meaning to her.

Kate Millett, **Flying.** NY: Simon & Schuster, 1974. and **Sita.** NY: Simon & Schuster, 1976. Two autobiographical novels by a self-identified bi who has been a leader of the modern women's movement.

Nigel Nicolson, **Portrait of a Marriage.** London: Weidenfeld & Nicolson, 1973. Biography of Vita Sackville-West & Harold Nicolson by their son. Born late 19th-century, Vita was a self-identified bi woman of the British upper class in love with Violet Trefusis.

Queen, Carol, **Real Live Nude Girl: Chronicles of sex-positive culture**. Pittsburgh, PA: Cleis Press, 1997. Autobiographical essays by a leading bi-identified exponent and proponent of sexual diversity and sex-positivity.

Rusterholtz, Wallace P., **My not-so-gay life.** Chicago: First Unitarian Society of Chicago, 1996. Rusterholtz, born in 1909, discusses his experiences as a bisexual man, his World War II service in Iran, memories of the Chicago Unitarian church, and opinions on current political and religious issues.

Blanche Weisen, **Eleanor Roosevelt.** 2 vols. NY: Penguin, 1992. Includes substantial discussion of her intimate relationships.

In German

Irmela v.d. Lühe, **Erika Mann: Eine Biografie** (luhe irmela von der 1947/ 1993). "Life story of a woman with contradictions and ruptures in life who did not keep her same and other sex relationships secret yet when editing her father's letters she erased homoerotic hints. Reads like a novel.

POETRY

Michelle Clinton, **Good Sense & The Faithless**. Albuquerque, NM: West End Press, 1994. About life, complexity, racism, being bisexual, politics, and more.

M.S. Montgomery, **Telling the Beads**. Baltimore: Chestnut Hills Press, 1994. (available for $11.50 from New Poets Series, 541 Picadilly Rd., Baltimore MD 21204) An explicit and emotionally gripping book of sonnets, a journey across the life of one bisexual man.

COMICS

Leanne Franson, **Assume Nothing: Adventures of a Bi-Dyke Starring Liliane**. Slab-o-Concrete Publications, 2000. **Teaching Through Trauma**. Hove, UK: Slab-o-Concrete Publications, 1999.

Alison Bechdel, **Post-Dykes to Watch Out For**. Ithaca: Firebrand Books, 2000. Bisexual pride buttons can be found pinned on 2 of the 8 striped shirts on the cover of this book! Alison grapples with lesbians loving men, girls becoming boys, etc.

FANTASY & SCIENCE FICTION

Gael Baudino, **Gossamer Axe**. NY: Penguin Books. 1990. Ancient Irish Pagan religion meets heavy metal. The story of a harper born in the 6th century who has found her way to present-day Denver, where she uses the forces of heavy metal to try to rescue her true love from centuries of imprisonment. Both Christa and Siudb, her love, are bisexual. **Maze of Moonlight**. NY: Penguin Books, 1993. Set in Europe during the time of the Crusades and the last days of the Elves. A couple of the male characters are behaviorally bisexual.

Greg Bear, **Anvil of Stars**. NY: Warner Books, 1992. A ship of children are set on a mission to locate and punish those who have destroyed Earth. These childrens are not bound by the old rules, and neither monogamy nor heterosexuality is enforced, although both seem to be presented as somewhat more satisfying and, perhaps, a sign of a more mature, adult relationship.

Samuel Delaney, **Dhalgren**. NY: Bantam Books, 1975. Disturbing story of a young drifter who enters the remains of a destroyed city. Set on earth in the more or less present time. The protagonist is bi, and a couple of the other characters have bisexual histories or experiences.

Diane Duane, **Door Into Fire**. NY: Tom Doherty Associates, Inc., 1979. **Door Into Shadow**. NY: Tom Doherty Associates, Inc., 1984. **Door into Sunset**. NY: Tom Doherty Associates, Inc., 1992. Well-written fantasy series in which most people are bisexual, and homophobia is nonexistent.

Robert A. Heinlein, **Friday**. NY: Ballantine Books, 1982. Set in a future society where casual sex, polyamory and sex between women are all considered acceptable. Interestingly (and a statement about the author and the time in which the book was written), heterosexual relationships are still privileged, and almost all of the women, but *none* of the men in the book are actively bisexual. **I Will Fear No Evil**. NY: Ace, 1970. This one is all free love, sex, and almost *everyone* is bisexual. It's also so full of gender stereotypes I almost vomited reading it. It's the story of an old man who gets his brain

transplanted into the body of a young woman, after which he suddenly acquires a strong desire to have sex with men, to wear spiked heels and makeup, and to be passive and manipulative. Go figure...

Ellen Kushner, **Swordspoint**. NY: Tor Books, 1987. In a society where conflicts are settled by duels, a professional swordsman whose current relationship is with a man, and whose past love was a woman, is involved in the intrigues of the nobles, one of whom is a bisexual man.

Mercedes Lackey and Ellen Guon, **Knight of Ghosts and Shadows.** NY: Baen Publishing Enterprise, 1990. Set in Los Angeles, on the grounds of a Renaissance Fair, elves and musicians fight magic-destroying evil. The protagonist finds himself falling in love with both a female human and a male elf. **Summoned to Tourney.** NY: Baen Publishing Enterprise, 1992. Set in San Francisco and more or less in the present, a male elf is involved in a three way relationship with two humans (one male, one female). They are street musicians who ride magic steeds that look like motorcycles, and struggle to save San Francisco from destruction.

Ursula LeGuin, **The Dispossessed.** NY: Granada Publishing, 1975. Set far in the future on a moon far from earth, this social utopian novel about anarchy involves a society in which there is no stigma attached to sexual orientation or sexual behavior. The protagonist, though primarily heterosexually oriented, has homosexual experiences as well.

Vonda N. McIntyre, **Starfarers.** NY: Ace Books, 1989. Set on a research spaceship, a woman and two men are in a romantic partnership, and are considered by some old-fashioned because theirs is a closed relationship.

R.M. Meluch, **Chicago Red.** NY: Roc-Penguin ,1990. Set in post-democracy North America, where a king rules over impoverished peasants. Tow, the "king's assassin" and all around not at all likeable man, is bisexual.

Pat Murphy, **Nadya.** NY: Tom Doherty, 1996. Set in the 1800s, a chronicle of the adventures of a young woman who becomes a wolf once a month. She travels from Missouri to the west coast, and in the course of her travels falls for a man, and then a woman, and then a different man.

Marge Piercy, **Woman on the Edge of Time.** NY: Fawcett Cress, 1976. Sci-fi/fantasy novel about a Latina woman in a NYC mental hospital who time travels to a future utopian society in which bisexuality & homosexuality are completely accepted.

J.F. Rivkin, **Silverglass.** NY: Ace Fantasy, 1986; **Web of Wind.** 1987; **Witch of Rhostshyl.** 1989. Sci-fi/fantasy trilogy about two women, a mercenary and a noblewoman, both happen to be bisexual.

Mary Rosenblum, **Chimera.** NY: Del Ray/Ballantine Books, 1993. It's the future, when for many people life takes place as much in virtual reality as in the flesh world. At least one character in this book, David Chen, a virtual reality artist is clearly bisexual, though the "b-word" is not used. A good read.

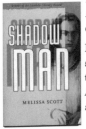

Melissa Scott, **Burning Bright.** NY: Tor/Tom Doherty Associates, 1993. Hi-tech sci-fi based on concept of virtual reality games. One male character and (likely) the female protagonist are bi. **Shadow Man.** NY: Tor/Tom Doherty Associates, 1995. It's the future, and it has finally been determined that there are 5 sexes, not two. But the people on this one colony, unlike those on all of the other planets, haven't accepted that yet, with a resultant culture clash between indigenes and off-worlders. With 5 sexes, there are 9 different sexual orientations, including bi, omni, demi and hemi.

Starhawk, **The Fifth Sacred Thing**. NY: Bantam Books, 1993. Futuristic utopian novel with two competing cultures: one egalitarian in which bisexuality is taken for granted, and the other oppressive and authoritarian.

John Varley, **Steel Beach**. NY: Putnam, 1992. After the invasion of the earth, humans have moved to the moon (and elsewhere). In this society, people, who can now live a very long time, can be hetero-, homo-, or bisexually oriented, and also can (and sometimes do) change sexes surgically. The main character is (almost entirely) heterosexual, and is attracted to woman when his is a man, and to men when she is a woman. Other characters are differently oriented.

Margaret Weis and Tracy Hickman, **Rose of the Prophet**, Volumes I (1988), II (1988) and III (1989). NY: Bantam Books. Twenty Gods rule the world, each with different abilities and his or her own followers, but now they are at war. This trilogy is the story of this war and the people involved. Mathew, an androgynous man, is in love with the other two central characters, a woman and her husband, though he never has a sexual relationship with either.

Walter Jon Williams, **Aristoi**. NY: Tom Doherty Associates, 1992. Set in the far future, all sexual orientations are accepted. Gabriel, the protagonist, the creator and leader of a number of worlds, has a number of concurrent relationships with men (including one whom he impregnates) and women.

SELECTED OTHER FICTION

(This list is far from exhaustive.)

Alice Adams, **Almost Perfect**. NY: Fawcett, 1993. Lifestyles of the (almost) rich and famous. Daugher of Mexican mother and famous Anglo father meets Anglo commercial artist who is unpredictable, drinks too much and is somewhat of a misogynist. Oh, and he is bisexual too.

Lisa Alther, **Five Minutes in Heaven**. NY: Dutton, 1995. Three of the four main characters could all be classified more or less Kinsey-5s, and the fourth is -- who knows, but much as she'd like to be, she's not a Kinsey 0. **Bedrock**. NY: Ivy Books, 1990. 2 married women, best friends, & their love for each other. **Other Women**. NY: Knopf (Random House), 1984. A woman with a bi history comes to terms, through therapy, with herself & her love for women. **Original Sins**. NY: Signet, 1982. Story of 5 people growing up in Tennessee, including 2 with bisexual experiences. **Kinflicks**. NY: Knopf, 1976. Woman with bi history struggles to understand herself & her relationship with her mother.

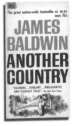

Carol Anshaw, **Aquamarine**. NY: Washington Square Press, 1992. Interesting and thought-provoking novel which takes the life of a competitor in the 1968 Olympics and projects twenty years into her future. Three different possible futures are presented, each based on the reverberations of choices made shortly after the Olympics. In each of her equally possible futures, she has married or remained single, loved women or men, become a parent or not, stayed in her Missouri hometown or moved to New York City. **Seven Moves**. NY: Mariner Books (Houghton Mifflin), 1996. A lesbian therapist's lover disappears. One of her best friends (a minor character) is a woman married to a man who is also seeing another woman.

James Baldwin, **Another Country**. NY: Dell, 1985 [1960]About race, sexuality & friendship between men. **Giovanni's Room**. NY: Dell, 1988[1956] Two male expatriates in France, one from the US, one Italian, fall in love. One is engaged to be married to a woman. Beautifully written, lots of internal struggle and self-hatred. **Tell Me How Long The Train's Been Gone**. NY: Dell, 1968. About an-African American man who becomes an actor. Probably the most clearly bisexual of all of Baldwin's characters.

Ann Bannon, **Odd Girl Out** (Tallahassee: Naiad, 1983 [1957] and **Beebo Brinker** (Tallahassee: Naiad, 1986 [1962]. Two in a series of five novels published in the late 50s and early 60s, these are fascinating representations of gay and bisexual life in that time period. **Odd Girl Out** is the story of two young college women who have a relationship until one leaves the other for a man. **Beebo Brinker** is the story of a lesbian in NY's Village scene. Several of the characters in the book could be characterized as bisexual. But beware: none of these characters are overly loveable.

Pat Barker, **The Eye in the Door**. NY: Plume/Penguin, 1993. Set in England during World War I, psychological novel about Billy Prior, an intelligence agent who is bisexual, as is one other male character. **The Ghost Road**. NY: Plume, 1996. More about Billy Prior. Both of these books are excellent reads.

Christopher Bram, **Almost History**. NY: Plume/Penguin, 1993. Fascinating historical novel about a gay American diplomat who spends much of his career in the Marcos-controlled Phillipines. Beginning in the 1950s and moving forward in time to just beyond the fall of the Marcos regime, many of the secondary male characters are bisexual in identity and/or behavior.

Rita Mae Brown, **Rubyfruit Jungle**. Plainfield, VT: Daughters, Inc., 1973. Most of the characters behave bisexually. About sexuality & growing up poor. **Six of One**. US & Canada: Bantam Books, 1978. Set in a small southern town & spanning 1909-1980, the book has 2 bi women: the narrator and Ramelle. **Southern Discomfort**. NY: Bantam Books, 1982. Set in Alabama,in the early 20th century, two secondary characters, Grace and Payson, are bisexual. **Venus Envy.** NY: Bantam Books, 1993. Set in present-day Virginia, about a woman's relationships with family and friends.

Jackie Calhoun, **Lifestyles**. Tallahassee, FL: The Naiad Press, 1990. Can be read as a bisexual or lesbian coming out story. A woman who has been left by her husband of many years meets and falls in love with another woman.

Susan Taylor Chehak, **Dancing on Glass**. NY: Fawcett Crest, 1993. Man goes back to the town of his childhood to resurrect his family name. Falls in love with a woman whose family is historically interwoven with his, marries her, but then becomes obsessed with a teenaged boy. Kind of soap-operatic.

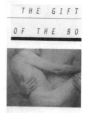

Leonard Cohen, **Beautiful Losers**. NY: Vintage, 1966. Yes, *that* Leonard Cohen. The songwriter. Poetic, erotic and disturbing novel set in Montreal. Both of the male characters are bisexual.

Nicole Conn, **Claire of the Moon**. Tallahassee: The Naiad Press, Inc., 1993. A (formerly) straight woman discovers love with a lesbian therapist (no, not hers) at a writers' retreat. Just like the movie of the same name.

Fiona Cooper, **Rotary Spokes**. UK: Brilliance Books, 1989. Rather odd novel about a female mechanic from the wrong side of the tracks of a tiny town somewhere in the western United States who discovers her sexuality by falling into bed with a woman. This first woman (someone says about her:"She still messing you around with all that peace, love and bisexuality shit?") and a teenager of the "anything that moves" variety are among the characters in this book who could be considered bisexual.

Stephanie Cowell, **Nicholas Cooke: Actor, Soldier, Physician, Priest**. NY: W.W. Norton & Co., 1993. Historical fiction about the contemporaries of Shakespeare in Elizabethan England. A young boy comes to London where he becomes an actor who, in his teens, is infatuated with playwright Christopher Marlowe, and later with a fellow soldier and various women. This book is quite clear about Nicholas' bisexual desires, it also makes clear that the protagonist understands his heterosexual desires to be the more mature ones, supplanting his adolescelent homosexuality.

Emma Donohue, **Stir Fry**. NY: HarperCollins, 1994. In Dublin, a 17-year old woman begins university, discovers her two new women roommates are a couple. One of these self-identifies as bi. **Hood**. NY: Harper Collins, 1996. A lesbian in Ireland's life partner is a woman who has has a history with both men and women. Note: Emma Donohoe is a contributor to the **Bisexual Horizons** anthology (above).

Larry Duplechan, **Eight Days A Week**. Boston: Alyson, 1985. Takes place in Los Angeles, in the pre-AIDS era. Johnny Ray Rousseau, a 22-year-old African-American nightclub singer by night, legal secretary by day, meets and falls for a blond bisexual banker who is portrayed as somewhat of a jerk-- not, however, because he is bisexual, but because he is possessive and wants Johnny Ray to give up his nightclub career to be home with him at night. Explicit sexuality and lots of musical references.

Andrea Dworkin, **Mercy**. NY: Four Walls, Eight Windows, 1990. Unsettling story written in the first person of a girl who grows up and is abused by one man after another. Some of her sexual relationships are with women. Well-written, very graphic.

Brett Easton Ellis, **The Rules of Attraction**. NY: Penguin, 1987. Pretty depressing book about students at a private college with no direction who take lots of drugs, sleep with each other (while drunk or high), and never go to class. Most of the men sleep with lots of men and women; the women sleep with the men.

Rupert Everett, **Hello Darling, Are You Working?** NY: Avon Books, 1992. The British narrator, Rhys, is a bisexual actor, drug addict, and sometimes prostitute.

Harvey Fierstein, **Torch Song Trilogy.** NY: Villard Books, 1983. In this play, the protagonist's lover/ex-lover Ed is a self-identified bisexual. He is also closeted and would prefer to be straight, but he makes makes progress through the play. Some focus on Arnold's unwillingness to accept that Ed might actually be bisexual.

E.M. Forster, **Maurice.** NY: W.W. Norton & Co., 1971. About a homosexual man in love with another homosexual man who "goes straight." Is he bisexual? Historically. Is he in denial of his homosexual feelings? Probably. Are his heterosexual feelings "real"? Probably. Listed here mainly because it was written in 1913-1914, is beautifully written, and is one of the only early gay-themed novels that ends happily.

Paul Goodman, **Making Do.** NY: Macmillan, 1963. Set in the very early 60s, several of the male characters are bisexual, none of the women. This book is definitely disturbing, replete with racism, misogyny, violence, though interesting as a look at a specific time and place in history. Certainly helps you to understand the subsequent rise of feminism & lesbian separatism.

Stephanie Grant, **The Passion of Alice.** NY: Houghton Mifflin, 1995. Set in Massachusetts in the mid 1980s, the story of a hospitalized anorexic woman. Maeve, a bulimic woman on the same ward, and a major character in this book, is behaviorally bisexual, though there is no discussion of identity.

Brad Gooch, **Scary Kisses.** NY: Pocket Books: Simon & Schuster, 1988. Sex, drugs and emptiness in the modeling world of 1980 NY, Milan and Paris.

Carol Guess, **Seeing Dell.** Pittsburgh: Cleis Press, 1995. Dell, a taxi driver, has died suddenly, leaving behind two lovers, one male, one female. Set in a small town in the midwestern United States, it's refreshing to see a novel about working-class people.

Diana Hammond, **The Impersonator.** NY: Doubleday, 1992. Story of a sexually compelling man who lacks inner direction and gets through life by dissembling and by attaching himself to various lovers, one of whom is a man. There are 2 male characters who could be called bisexual.

Joseph Hansen, **Job's Year.** NY: Plume Fiction, 1983. About a primarily gay actor with other bi characters as well; **A Smile in His Lifetime.** NY: Plume Fiction, 1981. A married man dealing with his homosexuality. **Backtrack.** NY: The Countryman Press, 1987. A primarily gay young man trying to find out who murdered his primarily gay father. **Steps Going Down.** NY: Penguin Books, 1982. There are two bisexual men in this crime book, both utterly unlikeable-- but then this book contains unlikeable characters of several sexual orientations.

E. Lynn Harris, **Invisible Life.** NY: Doubleday,1991 and **Just As I Am.** NY: Doubleday,1994. Upper middle class African American man struggles to deal with his bisexuality and with issues of coming out. Issues such as: relationships, being in the closet, dis/honesty, HIV, etc. **And This Too Shall Pass.** NY: Doubleday, 1996. A pro football player comes to identify as gay. A few of the other male characters in the book could be identified as bisexual, especially Basil the closeted and dishonest man who appears in Harris' earlier books. **Abide With Me.** NY: Doubleday, 1999. Continues the sagas of the same characters, adding, this time, a bi woman who has a close and caring relationship with Nicole, the book's primary female character, who is heterosexual. **Not a Day Goes By**. NY: Doubleday, 2000. Two of this series' most unpleasant characters, Basil and Yancey, find each other and, perhaps, get what they deserve.

Ernest Hemingway, **The Garden of Eden**. NY: Collier Books, 1986 (written 1961). is last work, about a male/female couple & a woman who enters their relationship. Transgender issues, jealousy, bisexuality. Also, among his collections of short stories is one called "The Sea Change" in which a woman tells her male beloved that she has fallen in love with a woman.

Sparkle Heyter, **The Chelsea Girl Murders**. UK: No Exit Press , 1999. (www.noexit.co.uk) Set in NYC's Chelsea Hotel, a TV newscaster finds herself entangled in intrigue, murder, and guerilla art. A couple of minor male characters are described in passing, and in a matter of fact way, as bisexual. The author is Canadian, the story is set in the US, and the book is published in the UK. Go figure.

Greg Johnson, **Pagan Babies**. NY: Plume (Penguin), 1993. Since their days together in Catholic school, Janice and Clifford's lives are intertwined. Janice is straight, and Clifford gay—well, except that he and Janice are boyfriend/girlfriend for years, with an active sexual relationship during some of that time. This novel is about growing up Catholic in the US, about AIDS, friendship, expectations and disappointments.

Dick Kavanagh (pseudonym of Julian Barnes), **Duffy**. NY: Pantheon Books, 1980; **Fiddle City**, **Putting the Boot In**. NY: Penguin, 1987; and **Going to the Dogs**. NY: Penguin, 1987. Standard English detective fare, except that the protagonist, Duffy, is a bisexual ex-cop.

M.E. Kerr, **Hello, I Lied**. NY: Harper Collins, 1997. A teenaged boy summering in East Hampton in a cottage on an estate where his mother is employed as cook for a retired rock star, has a boyfriend back in New York, is dealing with what it means to have a gay identity, and then falls in love with a French girl who is a guest of the rock star. Oops. Is he really gay? What are his friends going to think now?

James Kirkwood, **P.S. Your Cat is Dead**. NY: Warner Books, 1972. An underemployed NYC actor/writer catches the (bi) burglar who is in the process of robbing him (not for the first time), and ties him up in his kitchen. The actor's recently deceased best friend and one other caracter, are also bisexual. Entertaining.

Edith Konecky, **A Place at the Table**. NY: Ballantine Books, 1989. Middle aged Rachel is "a perfectly ordinary woman who sometimes falls in love with other women."

Hanif Kureishi, **The Buddha of Suburbia**. NY, London, etc.: Penguin Books, 1990. In suburban London, the story of the bi son of an Indian father & English mother.

D.H. Lawrence, **The Fox**. NY: Bantam Books, 1923, 1951. In rural England, two women living together as a couple. Tensions arise with the arrival of a man who courts one of the women. No explicit bisexuality, but the two women are obviously, sexual or not, a couple.

Jane Lazarre, **The Powers of Charlotte**. Freedom, CA: The Crossing Press, 1987. A psychological novel about a woman from a Jewish Communist family. Bisexuality is not a central theme, but 4 characters have varying degrees of bisexual history.

Rosamond Lehman, **Dusty Answer**. London/NY: Harcourt Brace Janovich, Inc., 1927. A young wealthy English woman's search for love. Both the man and the woman with whom she falls in love are, ultimately, unattainable. Quite an amazing book, considering it was published in 1927. I'm surprised it isn't better known.

Bill Lee, **Different Slopes: A Bisexual Men's Novel**. San Francisco: GLB Publishers, 1996. Set in World War II, this semi-pornographic novel is the story of a man's sexual and romantic adventures as he follows his libido. This is most certainly a biSEXUAL novel.

Jennifer Levin, **Water Dancer**. NY: Penguin Books, 1994. A marathon swimmer, training for a race, stays with her trainer and his wife. This book is about motivation, relationships, and swimming, and has a bisexual character.

Erika Lopez, **Flaming Iguanas: An Illustrated All Girl Road Novel Thing**. NY: Simon & Schuster, 1997. Two twenty-something Puerto Rican women from New Jersey take off across the US on newly acquired motorcycles. Tomato Rodriguez, the narrator, is trying to figure out whether she's bisexual. This book is unique and highly entertaining.

Daniel Magida, **The Rules of Seduction**. Boston: Houghton Mifflin, 1992. Jack Newland is a wealthy New York socialite who has had relationships with both men and with women, as have some of his male friends.

Dacia Maraini, **Women at War**. NY: Italica Press, 1988. (originally published in Italian as **Donna in guerra**.) A working class schoolteacher and her mechanic husband vacation in the Bay of Naples. Previously passive and unpolitical, Vannina meets various people and begins to develop a feminist and political consciousness. This book has female and male bisexual characters. **Letters to Marina** (originally published in Italian in 1981 as **Lettere a Marina**) (Freedom, California: The Crossing Press, 1988). A feminist woman talks about her past and current experiences in the form of a series of letters to Marina, a woman who is her ex-lover. She and some of her past and present lovers, love both men and women. When I told her of this project, the author herself referred me to this book.

Carole Maso, **The American Woman in the Chinese Hat**. NY: Penguin Books, 1994. Shortly after her brother's death from AIDS, a New York writer named Catherine leaves her woman lover of 12 years and comes to the French Riviera, where she comes apart, having a number of affairs, with men and women, in the process.

Valerie Miner, **Movement**. Trumansburg, NY: The Crossing Press, 1982. A decade in the life of a journalist who is married to a draft resister in the 60s & 70s. She, and one of her woman friends have bisexual experience/attractions.

Elias Miguel Munoz, **Crazy Love**. Houston, TX: Arte Publico Press (Univ. of Houston, Houston TX 77004), 1988. About growing up in one Cuban American family. Focus on family dynamics and expectations, and on his sexual experiences, both consensual (with women and men) and nonconsensual (with men), while growing up and as an adult.

Gloria Naylor, **Bailey's Cafe**. NY: Vintage Contemporaries (Random House), 1993. A book about suffering & survival, with a bi character, Jesse Bell.

O'Brien, Edna, **The High Road.** NY: Plume, 1988. An Irish woman goes to an island in Spain to recover from a broken heart caused by a relationship with a man, becomes attracted to a Spanish woman. **Also Casualties of Peace,** 1966 in **An Edna O'Brien Reader.** NY: Warner Books, 1994. O'Brien is an Irish author whose books were banned in Ireland in the 1960s. From an Irish woman's perspective, she deals quite explicitly with life, sexuality, and emotion.

Felice Picano, **Late in the Season.** NY: Gay Presses of New York, 1984. Gay-identified man in a long term relationship with a man meets and gets involved with a college aged woman. **Ambidextrous.** NY: Gay Presses, 1985. A currently-gay identified man looks back on his bisexual childhood and adolescence in NYC.

Marge Piercy, **Summer People.** NY: Fawcett Crest, 1989. The story of two women & a man in a triad relationship.

Manuel Puig, **Kiss of the Spider Woman.** NY: Vintage Books, 1980. Story of two men, a homosexual window dresser & a heterosexual revolutionary who are imprisoned in the same cell in a Latin American prison. Involves situational bisexuality.

Jane Ransom, **Bye Bye.** NY: New York University Press, 1997. A psychological satire of NYC and its art scene. The story of a New York woman thrown out by her "too-perfect" husband because of her nonconsensual infidelities, who decides to change her identity. She disappears, and then reappears as "Rosie" and has three lovers, two women and a man.

Mary Renault, **The Persian Boy.** NY: Vintage Books, 1972. A fictionalized version of the story of the Persian king Darius and Alexander the Great, told from the eyes of the eunoch slave boy Bagoas. Darius and Alexander are both portrayed as bisexual, with Alexander way up there on the Kinsey Scale, and Darius somewhere in the middle. **The Last of the Wine.** NY: Vintage Books, 1975 [1956]. Set in ancient Athens, some men are heterosexual, some homosexual, and some bisexual. Lysis, the male lover of the male protagonist, is bisexual.

Tom Robbins, **Even Cowgirls Get the Blues.** NY, etc.: Bantam Books, 1976. A straight man's perspective of female bisexuality.

Lucia St. Clair Robson, **The Tokaido Road.** NY: Ballantine Books, 1991. Set in 17th-century Japan, many of the male characters are behaviorally bisexual.

Jane Rule, **The Young in One Another's Arms.** Tallahassee: Naiad Press, 1984. About a multigenerational boarding-house-becomes-communal-group in Vancouver. There are two women who have relationships with women (each other) and with men. This book deals with triangulation, with redefinition of "family." **This is Not for You.** Tallahassee: Naiad, 1982. Set in the US and London, the story of a group of friends beginning in their college years. The narrator is a lesbian?/bisexual? women who is in love with another woman from college but refuses to allow a romantic or sexual relationship to develop, despite the reciprocity of feeling. The narrator later has a relationship with a woman married to a man.

May Sarton, **Mrs. Stevens Hears the Mermaids Singing.** New York: W.W. Norton and Company, 1965. A poet looks back over her long life and recalls her past loves, male and female, trying to understand their relationship to the development of her poetry and her self. Sarton herself self-identified, at various times, as lesbian and bisexual.

Cathleen Schine, **Rameau's Niece.** NY: A Plume Book (Penguin), 1994. A present day 28 year old New Yorker, who has published a bestselling book on 18th-century French fiction, is married to a 39 year old English professor. Her life begins to get caught up in and confused with the story in a manuscript she is reading, and her life spins away from normalcy. Her sexual fantasies run rampant, their subjects are both male and female.

Sarah Schulman, **People in Trouble.** NY: E.P. Dutton, 1990. One of the 3 main characters is Kate, an artist and married woman who loves her husband and also falls in love with a lesbian AIDS activist named Molly. As is the case with all of Schulman's books, this is a fascinating if sometimes depressing look at NYC life.

Elizabeth Searle, **A Four-Sided Bed.** Saint Paul, MN: Graywolf Press, 1998. Someone told me this was the "most bisexual book" she'd ever read. A beautifully-written novel about relationships, honesty & dishonesty, the relationship between the past and the present time, mental illnesses, AIDS. There is some discussion of identity, and even a mention or two of the "b-word."

Dani Shapiro, **Playing With Fire.** NY: Doubleday, 1989. Two young women meet at Smith College, one from a religious Jewish family, the other a Christian socialite. They begin to fall in love with each other, and then are pulled apart by a third party. A novel about family and boundaries, set in high society.

April Sinclair, **Coffee Will Make You Black.** NY: Hyperion, 1994, and **Ain't Gonna Be The Same Fool Twice**. NY: Avon Books,1996. Growing up and coming of age novels about Jean "Stevie" Stevenson. Set in the 1970s, Stevie experiences desire for both men and women, as well as disco dancing, yoga, hot tubs, and free love.

Tom Spanbauer. **The Man Who Fell in Love With the Moon.** NY: Atlantic Monthly Press, 1991. Several bi characters in this novel set in 19th-century Idaho.

Carole Spearin McCauley, **The Honesty Tree.** Palo Alto, CA: Frog in the Well Books, 1985. Novel about twowomen in a relationship.

Darcy Steinke, **Suicide Blonde.** NY: Washington Square Press, 1992. Set in San Francisco, a (possibly, kinda) bisexual woman is obsessed with her lover, a bisexual man. Full of compulsion, alcohol and drugs, and destruction. Disturbing.

Junichiro Tanizaki, **Quicksand.** NY: Alfred A. Knopf, 1993 [1947]. Set in Japan in the 1920s, a female married art student falls in love with a woman. A story of obsession and betrayal. Both women are bisexual.

Carla Tomaso, **Matricide.** NY: Plume, 1994. One of the narrator's sidekicks is a woman just out of high school who self-identifies as bisexual.

Alice Walker, **The Color Purple.** New York: Harcourt Brace Janovich, 1982. Shug, a major character, is bisexual. **Possessing the Secret of Joy.** NY: Pocket Books, 1992. Pierre, a self-declared bisexual, is a minor character who discusses, briefly, not only his own bisexuality, but his pan-sexual identity. **By The Light of My Father's Smile.** NY: Ballantine, 1998. In this complex story of love, sexuality, motivations, interrelatedness, Suzanne, over the course of the book (and of her life) has three lovers: a man, then a woman, then another man. The "b-word" is not used, but there is no doubt in my mind that this is one of the most bisexual books I have read.

Edmund White, **The Beautiful Room is Empty.** NY: Ballantine Books, 1988. The narrator's best female friend, Maria, self-identifies as bisexual. Also minor male bisexual character. Autobiographical novel about growing up gay in New York in the 50s and 60s.

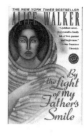

Stevie White, **Boy Cuddle.** London: Penguin, 1992. British novel about a bisexual boxer in love with a prostitute who has sex with men for money and an ongoing relationship with the protagonist, who also becomes seriously involved with a female prostitute. About life on the streets of South London. The front cover says "Amoral. Bisexual. In love ...?"

Mary Wings, **She Came By The Book.** NY: Berkeley Prime Crime Book, 1996. Set in San Francisco's gay community, this murder mystery includes a *very, very* minor bisexual plot twist. It's interesting nonetheless, if you're interested in a story that's not too far off from real-life community politics.

Jeanette Winterson, **The Passion.** NY: Vintage International (Random House), 1987. Set in France and Italy during Napoleon's reign, one of the protagonists is a bisexual woman. **Written on the Body.** NY: Vintage International (Random House), 1992. Set in the present, a tale of love between the narrator and a married woman. The name and gender of the narrator (who talks of past relationships with men and with women) is never stated. Reading this book is an interesting and somewhat unsettling experience. **Gut Symmetries.** NY: Knopf, 1997. Two physicists, one male, one female, have an affair. He is married, she is single. She meets and falls in love with his wife. Beautifully written story of a romantic triangle.

Lois Ann Yamanaka, **Name Me Nobody.** New York: Hyperion, 1999. Teen novel. Emi Lou and Von have always been best friends, but Emi Lou can't understand Von's feelings for another girl; although she is involved with a boy from school she still feels jealous of Von and her new girlfriend.

Shay Youngblood, **Soul Kiss.** NY: Riverhead Books, 1997. Young African-American girl is left at age seven by her addict mother with two "aunts" (actually a couple). This book is about her growing up, her search for love, and the development of her sexuality. I'm not sure whether she would call herself bisexual, but her experience is bisexual. This book is beautifully written. **Black Girl in Paris.** NY: Riverhead Books, 2000 has four characters – all women – including the protagonist – whom I would consider bisexual. This is the story of an African-American aspiring writer in her 20's who goes to Paris in search (literally and metaphorically) of James Baldwin. I strongly recommend this one.

Eda Zahl, **Fluffy Butch.** London: Mandarin Fiction, 1994. Quirky novel about a young woman living in Los Angeles who dates men and women. The back cover says: "How do you learn to love men? Mary learns by shaving her head, moving to Los Angeles and dating women. To her amazement bald Mary begins to view the world from a man's point of view. She even begins to sympathise with them. Worse, she starts to date them again. Mary finds herself having affairs with men and women, sometimes women and men— who knows who she'll end up with?"

SHORT STORIES:

Ruthann Robson, **Eye of a Hurricane.** Ithaca, New York: Firebrand Books, 1989. Some of these short stories have bisexual characters.

Jane Rule, **Inland Passage.** Tallahassee, FL: Naiad Press, 1985. "His Nor Hers," "Puzzle," and possibly also "Inland Passage" have bisexual characters.

IN THE FAMILY

The Magazine for
Queer People and
Their Loved Ones

$22 per year—4 issues
P.O. Box 5387
Takoma Park, MD 20913
302-270-4771

BLACK BOOKS

books and magazines
for the bi zeitgeist

• *Best Bisexual Erotica*
series ($19 each for BBE
vol. 1 and BBE vol. 2)

• *Black Sheets* magazine
($6 for sample issue)

**SPECIAL: order BBE or
Blask Sheets from this ad
and take 20% off!**

More titles, including many
books on bisexuality, all in
our free catalog, from:

Black Books, PO Box
31155-BG, San Francisco
CA 94131-0155

email: BG@blackbooks.com

credit card orders:
800.818.8823

ARTISTIC LICENTIOUSNESS

The Adult comic book that shows
you should NEVER make assumptions
about anybody's sexuality.....
including your OWN!
Issue #1 - $3.00 ppd. #2 - $3.50 ppd.
BOTH for only $6 ppd.
(can. add 20% - foreign add 30%.) ALSO,
you MUST say you're over 18 yrs old!
OR. Just send S.A.S.E. for catalogue...
ROBERTA GREGORY. Box 27438.
SEATTLE. WA. 98125

www.robertagregory.com

MediaFocus: Bisexual Visibility

MediaFocus: Bisexual Visibility is an initiative of the Cultural Interest Media Project which focuses on the diversity of the lesbian, gay, bisexual and transgender community. The Bisexual Visibility initiative helps GLAAD achieve its mission by focusing on and advocating for fair, accurate and inclusive representations of bisexual people in the media.

Through the course of history, bisexuality in the media has remained relatively invisible. When it was dealt with, representations were often unfair or inaccurate. In 1996, GLAAD formed the organization's first Bi Visibility Team (BVPT), a group of local New York bi activists, GLAAD members and staff, to discuss and implement programs to increase the media's understanding of bisexuality, and to respond to biphobia.

In 1997, the BVPT launched the Bi Visibility Web Page, which can be accessed through GLAAD Online at www.glaad.org.

We encourage you to take an active role telling the media how you feel about the portrayals (positive, negative and invisible) of bisexual people by volunteering! If you are interested or have more questions, please feel free to contact Loren Javier, GLAAD's Cultural Interest Media Manager, at 415.861.2244 (San Francisco/Bay Area) or by e-mail at javier@glaad.org.

Cultural Interest Media Project

San Francisco
1360 Mission Street
Suite 200
San Francisco, CA 94103

Los Angeles
8455 Beverly Boulevard
Suite 305
Los Angeles, CA 90048

Kansas City
1509 Westport Road
Kansas City, MO 64111

Atlanta
159 Ralph McGill Blvd
Suite 506
Atlanta, GA 30308

New York
248 West 35th Street
Suite 200
New York, NY 10001

Washington, DC
1825 Connecticut
5th Floor
Washington, DC 20009

A Reader's Guide to Non-Fiction Books, Chapters, and Journal Articles on Bisexuality

bi Ronald C. Fox

The following books, book chapters, and journal articles are a diverse collection of recommended non-fiction readings that focus on bisexual identity and/or behavior and take an affirmative approach to bisexuality and bisexual issues. A few items in each section have been highlighted with a * symbol and are good places to begin or continue your reading in the non-fiction literature. All materials listed below are in English, except as noted. This list is by no means exhaustive; rather it is a work in progress. Your suggestions for books, chapters, and journal articles to be listed in future editions of the **Guide** are welcome, including those in languages other than English. Many thanks to Robyn Ochs for her encouragement, suggestions, and collaboration in making a place in the *BRG* for this guide to the non-fiction literature on bisexuality. Many of the books listed below can be ordered through the "Bisexual Bookstore" on the World Wide Web, located at: www.biresource.org/bookstore/.

Codes: ♀: Primarily about Women; ♂: Primarily about Men; ♀♂: About both Women and Men

NON-FICTION BOOKS SPECIFICALLY ON BISEXUALITY

Aggleton, Peter. (Ed.). (1996). **Bisexualities & AIDS: International perspectives.** London: Taylor & Francis. ♂ Collection of essays and reviews of the research literature on bisexual behavior among men in a number of modern cultures, including Australia, Brazil, Canada, China, Costa Rica, the Dominican Republic, France, India, Mexico, Papua New Guinea, Peru, the Philippines, and the U. K.

Bi Academic Intervention (Phoebe Davidson, Jo Eadie, Clare Hemmings, Ann Kaloski, & Merle Storr). (Eds.). (1997). **The Bisexual Imaginary: Representation, identity, and desire.** London: Cassell. ♀♂ Collection of essays on bisexuality in history, literature, film, and cultural studies.

*Bisexual Anthology Collective (Leela Acharya, Nancy Chater, Dionne Falconer, Sharon Lewis, Leanna McLannan, & Susan Nosov) (Eds.). (1995). **Plural desires: Writing bisexual women's realities.** Toronto: Sister Vision Press. ♀ An anthology of writings by a diverse group of Canadian & US women.

Bode, Janet (1976). **View from another closet: Exploring bisexuality in women.** New York: Hawthorne. ♀ One of the first books on bisexuality, based on the author's intervi ws with bisexual women.

Bryant, Wayne. (1997). **Bisexual characters in film: From Anaïs to Zee.** New York: Harrington Park Press. ♀♂ What it says. More descriptive than analytical.

Cantarella, Eva. (1992). **Bisexuality in the ancient world.** New Haven, CT: Yale University Press. ♀♂ Translated from the Italian. A scholarly examination of bisexuality in ancient classical Greece & Rome.

*Firestein, Beth A. (Ed.). (1996). **Bisexuality: The psychology and politics of an invisible minority.** Thousand Oaks, CA: Sage. ♀♂ A collection of essays that provides the most comprehensive overview and review of bisexuality and psychology to date, with chapters by Ron Fox, Loraine Hutchins, Carol Queen, Maggie Rubenstein, Paula Rust, Robyn Ochs, and others.

Fraser, Mariam. (1999). **Identity without selfhood: Simone de Beauvoir and bisexuality.** New York: Cambridge University Press. ♀ The author examines how feminism, queer theory, and post-modern analysis have viewed Simone de Beauvoir and how the emphasis on deconstruction of Western approaches to sexuality present obstacles to acknowledging and validating bisexuality as a sexual orientation and identity.

Garber, Marjorie. (1995). **Vice versa: Bisexuality & the eroticism of everyday life.** New York: Simon & Schuster. ♀♂ If you are interested in an in-depth look at bisexuality in literature, popular culture, or psychoanalysis, this book is for you.

Geller, Thomas. (Ed.). (1990). **Bisexuality: A reader & sourcebook.** Ojai, CA: Times Change Press. ♀♂ Collection of interviews & articles.

George, Sue. (1993). **Women & bisexuality.** London: Scarlet Press. ♀ An examination of bisexual identity and relationships, based on the author's survey study of 150 self-identified bisexual women in the United Kingdom.

Haeberle, Edwin J., & Rudolph Gindorf. (1998). **Bisexualities: The ideology and practice of sexual contact with both men and women.** New York: Continuum. ♀♂ Translated from the German. Collection of essays by participants in the 1990 International Berlin Conference for Sexology. Most chapters reflect the beginnings of the shift in scholarly thinking about bisexuality that has come about as a result of subsequent and more current research on bisexuality and bisexual identity.

Hall, Donald. E., & Maria Pramaggiore. (Eds.). (1996). **RePresenting bisexualities: Subjects & cultures of fluid desire.** New York: NYU Press. ♀♂ Collection of essays on bisexuality in queer theory, literature, film, and cultural studies.

*Hutchins, Lorraine, & Lani Kaahumanu. (Eds.). (1991). **Bi any other name: Bisexual people speak out.** ♀♂ Boston: Alyson. Diverse collection of 75 essays and autobiographical narratives by bi-identified people from the United States.

Klein, Fritz. (1993). **The bisexual option** (2nd ed.). New York: Harrington Park Press. (see display ad elsewhere in this *Guide*.) ♀♂ Second edition of one of the first published books on bisexuality (1978) written from an affirmative perspective (Charlotte Wolff's 1979 book, **Bisexuality: A Study,** listed below, is the other). The author is also the creator of the well-known Klein Sexual Orientation Grid (KSOG), a multi-dimensional scale of sexual orientation & sexual identity (See Klein, Sepekoff, & Wolf, 1986 below under "Sexual orientation: Non-dichotomous approaches" for their original article).

Klein, Fritz, & Timothy J. Wolf. (Eds.). (1985). **Two lives to lead: Bisexuality in men and women.** New York: Harrington Park Press. ♀♂ The first published scholarly collection of reports on 1980s research on bisexuality. Originally a special issue of the prestigious *Journal of Homosexuality* (1985, Vol. 11, Issue 1/2).

*Kohn, Barry, & Alice Matusow. (1980). **Barry & Alice: Portrait of a bisexual marriage.** Englewood Cliffs, NJ: Prentice-Hall. ♀♂ An autobiographical account of the authors' marriage and the impact on their relationship of their coming to terms with their bisexuality.

Kolodny, Debra R. (Ed.). (2000). **Blessed bi spirit: Bisexual people of faith.** New York: Continuum. ♀♂ A wide-ranging anthology, with contributions by 31 bisexual people of faith speaking in a most affirmative way about the intersection of spirituality and sexuality in their lives.

*Ochs, Robyn. (2001). **Bisexual Resource Guide** (4th ed.). Cambridge, MA: Bisexual Resource Center. ♀♂ Contains an extensive bibliography of books, chapters, and journal articles with bi content, list of recommended films, merchandise guide, announcements and relevant notices, articles, and listings of more than 2500 bisexual & bi-inclusive groups & e-mail lists. Available for $13.95 from the Bisexual Resource Center, or through the BRC website online at: www.biresource.org/biproducts/guide.html

Off Pink Collective. (1988). **Bisexual lives.** London: Off Pink Publishing. ♀♂ Collection of personal narratives by bisexual women and bisexual men in the U. K.

*Orndorff, Kata. (Ed.). (1999). **Bi Lives: Bisexual Women Tell Their Stories.** Tucson, AZ: See Sharp Press. ♀ A collection of very thoughtfully done interviews with a diverse group of 18 women, with a focus on how they became aware of and came to terms with their bisexuality.

*Rose, Sharon, Cris Stevens, & The Off-Pink Collective. (Eds.). (1996). **Bisexual horizons: Politics, histories, lives.** London: Lawrence & Wishart. ♀♂ Diverse collection of 54 essays and autobiographical narratives by bi-identified people, mostly from the UK.

Rust, Paula C. (1995). **Bisexuality & the challenge to lesbian politics: Sex, loyalty & revolution.** New York: NYU Press. ♀ The author traces the origins of the controversy about bisexuality among lesbians to the 1970s lesbian feminist debates, out of which, she argues, developed an environment in which bisexuality inevitably became a challenge to lesbian politics. She also discusses likely developments in the sexual politics of the future.

*Rust, Paula C. Rodríguez (Ed.). (2000). **Bisexuality in the United States: A Social Science Reader.** New York: Columbia University Press. ♀♂ Comprehensive collection of classic journal articles and book chapters on bisexuality, including many references in this reading list. In-depth reviews by the editor precede each of the book's sections. Highly recommended.

Sigma Research. (1993). **Behaviourally bisexual men in the UK: Identifying need for HIV prevention.** London: UK Health Education Authority. ♂ Results of a government sponsored survey study of sexual behavior and HIV/AIDS awareness.

Storr, Merl. (Ed.). (1999). **Bisexuality: A critical reader.** London: Routledge. ♀♂ Psychological, sociological, activist, and post-modern/cultural criticism perspectives are all included in this edited volume of previously published articles, book chapters and book excerpts. Features material by Freud, Ellis, and Kinsey, as well as bi authors Fritz Klein, Amanda Udis-Kessler, Sue George, Jo Eadie, Amber Ault, Clare Hemmings, and Ann Kaloski.

Tielman, Rob A. P., Manuel Carballo, & Aart C. Hendriks. (Eds.). (1991). **Bisexuality & HIV/ AIDS: A global perspective.** Buffalo, NY: Prometheus. ♂ Collection of essays and reviews of research on bisexual identity and behavior among men in a number of modern cultures, including Australia, India, Indonesia, Latin America, Mexico, the Netherlands, New Zealand, Sub-Saharan Africa, Thailand, the United Kingdom, and the United States.

*Tucker, Naomi, with Liz Highleyman & Rebecca Kaplan. (Eds.). (1995). **Bisexual politics: Theories, queeries, & visions.** New York: Harrington Park Press. ♀♂ (Order info: 1-800-342-9678). Diverse collection of essays exploring the history, philosophies, visioning, and strategies of bisexual politics in the United States.

Weinberg, Martin S., Colin J. Williams, & Douglas W. Pryor. (1994). **Dual attraction: Understanding bisexuality.** New York: Oxford University Press. ♀♂ Results of the authors' interview and survey research on bisexual identity and relationships in 1980s San Francisco. Includes personal narratives, the authors' views on how bisexual identity develops, comparison of bisexual, heterosexual, and lesbian/gay patterns of sexual attractions and relationships, and a portrait of the impact of HIV/AIDS on the lives of individuals from their original interviews.

Weise, Elizabeth R. (Ed.). (1992). **Closer to home: Bisexuality & feminism.** Seattle: Seal Press. ♀ Collection of 23 essays by bisexual feminist women on bisexuality, feminism, and their intersection.

Williams, Mark J. K. (1999). **Sexual pathways: Adapting to dual attraction.** Westport, CT: Praeger. ♀♂ A study of bisexual identity and relationships, based on the author's interviews with 30 American bisexual women and men.

*Wolff, Charlotte. (1979). **Bisexuality: A study.** London: Quarter Books. ♀♂ One of the first books on bisexuality written from an affirmative perspective (Fritz Klein's **Bisexual Option**, listed above, is the other), based on the author's survey research on bisexual women and men in the U. K.

In French:

*Mendès-Leité, Rommel, Catherine Deschamps, & Bruno-Marcel Proth. (1996). **Bisexualité: Le dernier tabou.** [Bisexuality: The last taboo]. Paris: Calmann Levy. ♀♂ Portrait of bisexual identity and behavior among bisexual men in France today, based on the authors' interviews.

In Dutch:

*Hansson, Hannie, (Ed.). (1990). **Bisexuele levens in Nederland.** [Bisexual lives in the Netherlands]. Amsterdam: Orlando. ♀♂ Portrait of bisexual identity and relationships, based on the author's interviews with bisexual women and men.

Kuppens, A. (1995). **Biseksuele identiteiten: Tussen verlangen en praktijk.** [Bisexual identities: Between desire and behavior]. Nijmegen: Wetenschapswinkel. ♀♂ Theoretical overview and discussion of bisexual identities, based on interviews with bisexual women and bisexual men.

van Kerkhof, Marty P. N. (1997). **Beter Biseks. Mythen over biseksualiteit ontrafeld.** [Better bisexuality: Myths about bisexuality revealed]. Amsterdam: Schorer Boeken. ♀♂ Examination of bisexual identity and relationships, based on interviews with bisexual women and bisexual men.

In German:

*Feldhorst, Anja. (1996). (Ed.). **Bisexualitäten.** [Bisexualities]. Berlin: Deutsche AIDS-Hilfe. ♀♂ Collection of essays on bisexual identity, relationships, and communities in Germany.

Geissler, Sina-Aline. (1993). **Doppelte Lust: Bisexualität heute— Erfahrungen und Bekenntnisse.** [Dual desire: Bisexuality today— Experiences and confessions]. Munich: Wilhelm Heyne. ♀♂ An exploration of bisexuality in Germany today, based on the author's interviews with bisexual women and bisexual men.

*Gooß, Ulrich. (1995). **Sexualwissenschaftliche Konzepte der Bisexualität von Männern.** [The concept of bisexuality in scientific discourse about human sexuality]. Stuttgart: Ferdinand Enke. ♀♂ Scholarly examination by a German psychiatrist of the origins and development of the concept of bisexuality in the fields of psychology and sexology, including an overview of current theory and research.

Haeberle, Erwin J., & Rolf Gindorf. (Eds.). (1994). **Bisexualitäten: Ideologie und Praxis des Sexualkontes mit beiden Geschlectern.** [Bisexualities: Theory and practice of sexual relations with both sexes]. Stuttgart: Gustav Fischer Verlag. ♀♂ A collection of scholarly essays on bisexuality by participants in the 1990 International Berlin Conference for Sexology. English translation is listed above.

Honnens, Brigette. (1996). **Wenn die andere ein Mann ist: Frauen als Partnerinnen bisexueller Männer.** [When the other person is a man: Women partners of bisexual men]. Frankfurt: Campus. ♀♂ Explores the experiences of women in marriages with bisexual men in Germany, based on the author's interviews.

*Hüsers, Francis & Almut König. (1995). **Bisexualität.** [Bisexuality]. Stuttgart: Georg Thieme. ♀♂ A sociologist and a psychiatrist provide a comprehensive and affirmative picture of and guide to bisexuality in Germany today.

In Spanish:

Archivo Lesbico y de Mujeres Diferentes. (1998). Escrita en el cuerpo. [Written in the body]. Retrieved from the World-Wide Web: www.bi.org/~ba.biwomen/ ♀ Collection of original and translated articles, in Spanish, on bisexuality and bisexual issues.

BI-INCLUSIVE NON-FICTION BOOKS

Sexual Orientation

*Bohan, Janis S. (1996). **Psychology & sexual orientation: Coming to terms.** New York: Routledge. ♀♂ Excellent bi-inclusive historical and contemporary overview of the field of sexual orientation and sexual identity.

*Bohan, Janis S., Glenda M. Russell & Vivienne Cass. (1999). **Conversations about psychology and sexual orientation.** New York: New York University Press. ♀♂ Excellent and informative book on psychology and sexual orientation. Includes a chapter by Fritz Klein on the importance of a multidimensional approach to sexual orientation and a chapter by Vivienne Cass, in which she updates her widely known and often cited stage theory of gay and lesbian identity formation with a much more open and inclusive theoretical framework for sexual identity development that acknowledges the multiple pathways that many people take in coming to terms with and potentially changing their sexual identities over time.

Rust, Paula C. (Ed.). (1997). **Sociology of sexuality & sexual orientation: Syllabi & teaching materials.** Washington, DC: American Sociological Association. ♀♂ Collection of college course syllabi, including the syllabus for Robyn Ochs' course "Contexts and constructs of identity: Bisexuality."

Health Care, Counseling, and Psychotherapy

Appleby, George Alan, & Jeane W Anastas. (1998). **Not just a passing phase: Social work with gay, lesbian, and bisexual people.** New York: Columbia University Press. ♀♂ A bi-affirmative handbook of social work practice with LGB people, including sections on identity development, community, relationships, LGB families, aging, HIV, and mental health issues.

SINA-ALINE GEISSLER

Doppelte Lust

Bisexualität heute –
Erfahrungen und Bekenntnisse

Cabaj, Robert P., & Terry S. Stein, (Eds.). (1996). **Textbook of homosexuality and mental health.** Washington, DC: American Psychiatric Press. ♀♂ A ground-breaking LGB-affirmative book, with chapters by Ron Fox (on bisexual identity) and Dave Matteson (on bisexual counseling issues) and other bi-inclusive chapters on a diverse range of LGB psychiatry and psychology issues.

*Eliason, Michele J. (1996). **Who cares?: Institutional barriers to health care for lesbian, gay, and bisexual persons.** New York: NLN Press. ♀♂ A bi-inclusive thorough examination of obstacles to quality health care for lesbians, gay men, bisexual women, and bisexual men.

Gruskin, Elisabeth Paige. (1999). **Treating lesbians and bisexual women: Challenges and strategies for health professionals.** Thousand Oaks, CA: Sage. ♀ This book provides an overview of the important issues facing health care professionals in providing affirmative treatment for lesbians and bisexual women.

Hunter, Ski, Coleen Shannon, Jo Knox, & James I. Martin. (1998). **Lesbian, gay, and bisexual youths and adults: Knowledge for human services practice.** Thousand Oaks, CA: Sage. ♀♂ This bi-affirmative volume provides an overview of knowledge important to providing services to LGB youth and adults.

Kominars, Sheppard B., & Kathryn D. Kominars. (1996). **Accepting ourselves and others: A journey into recovery from addictive and compulsive behaviors for gays, lesbians and bisexuals.** Center City, MN: Hazelden. ♀♂ A bi-inclusive LGB-centered guide to the process of recovery.

Longres, John F. (Ed.). (1996). **Men of color: A context for service to homosexually active men.** New York: Harrington Park Press. ♂ Contributions to this volume focus on how identity, behavior, and community figure into providing affirmative social services for gay and bisexual men of color.

Neal, Charles, & Dominic Davies. (Eds.). (2000). **Issues in therapy with lesbian, gay, bisexual and transgender clients.** Buckingham, England, UK: Open University Press. ♀♂ A collection of essays on psychotherapy with LGBT clients, including a contribution by therapists Liz Oxley and Claire Lucius on bisexual issues with clients in therapy.

*Niesen, Joseph H. (1994). **Counseling lesbian, gay, and bisexual persons with alcohol and drug abuse problems.** Arlington, VA: National Association of Alcohol and Drug Abuse Counselors. ♀♂ A bi-inclusive handbook on alcohol and drug abuse treatment with LGB persons by the director of New Leaf, a San Francisco agency serving the LGBT community.

*Perez, Ruperto M., Kurt A. DeBord, & Kathleen J. Bieschke. (Eds.). (2000). **Handbook of counseling and psychotherapy with lesbian, gay, and bisexual clients.** Washington, DC: American Psychological Association. ♀♂ A well done bi-inclusive volume, with contributions on: LGB identity development; issues of diversity in counseling LGB clients; adapting and applying psychological theories to clinical practice; research and training issues; and affirmative approaches to individual, couples, and group counseling with LGB clients.

Identity

Atkins, Dawn. (1996). (Ed.). **Looking Queer: Body Image and Identity in Lesbian, Bisexual, Gay and Transgender Communities.** New York: NYU Press. ♀♂ An excellent collection that includes a number of bi voices and essays dealing with bisexuality: Greta Christina, Kate Woolfe, Catherine Lundoff, Nina Silver, Susanna Trnka, Julie Waters, Morgan Holmes, Raven Kaldera, Laura Cole, Layli Phillips, Ganapati Durgadas and Jill Nagle. Over 400 pages of excellent reading.

Burch, Beverly. (1994). **On Intimate Terms: The Psychology of Difference in Lesbian Relationships.** Urbana & Chicago: University of Illinois Press. ♀ Burch, a psychotherapist, draws a distinction between "primary" and "bisexual" lesbians, and posits that there may be a complementarity, or attraction, between the two. She sees "bisexual lesbians" as women who identify as lesbian later than "primary lesbians" and may have had significant heterosexual relationships and/or continue to recognize heterosexual relationships as a possibility. Primarily about women who identify as lesbian rather than bisexual, but extensive discussion of bisexuality.

Burch, Beverly. (1997). **Other women: Lesbian/bisexual experience and psychoanalytic views of women.** New York, NY: Columbia University Press. ♀ The author's second book focusing on lesbian and bisexual women, their identities and relationships, in the context of classical and contemporary psychoanalytic theory and practice.

D'Augelli, Anthony R., & Charlotte J. Patterson. (Eds.). (1995). **Lesbian, gay, and bisexual identities over the lifespan: Psychological approaches.** New York: Oxford University Press. ♀♂ Groundbreaking LGB psychology book that includes a chapter by Ron Fox on bisexual identities.

*Esterberg, Kristin G. (1997). **Lesbian & bisexual identities: Constructing communities, constructing selves.** Philadelphia: Temple University Press. ♀ An in-depth study of lesbian and bisexual identity development, based on the author's interviews with a diverse group of women in a Northeastern community in the U.S.

*Johnson, Brett K. (1997). **Coming out every day: A gay, bisexual, or questioning man's guide.** Oakland, CA: New Harbinger. ♂ The queer man's comprehensive & bi-inclusive guide to coming out and maintaining a positive self-accepting identity.

Norris, Stephanie, & Emma Read. (1985). **Out in the open: People talking about being gay or bisexual.** London: Pan. ♀♂ A diverse collection of profiles of gay men, lesbians, bisexual men and bisexual women in the United Kingdom.

Savin-Williams, Ritch C., & Kenneth M. Cohen. (Eds.). (1996). **The lives of lesbians, gays, and bisexuals: Children to adults.** Fort Worth, TX: Harcourt Brace. ♀♂ A bi-inclusive collection addressing developmental issues of lesbians, gay men, bisexual women, and bisexual men over the lifespan.

Van Gelder, Lindsay, & Pamela Robin Brandt. (1996). **The Girls Next Door: Into the Heart of Lesbian America.** New York: Simon & Schuster. ♀ This entertaining book about lesbians in America includes substantial discussions about lesbians who sleep with men but self-identify as lesbians, attitudes of lesbians about bisexuals, and, in general, for many of us, the fluidity of our sexual desire. It's a fun read, with discussions of the Michigan Womyn's Music Festival, the Dinah Shore Party Circuit and the Lesbian Avengers, among other things.

Wishik, Heather, & Carol Pierce. (1991). **Sexual orientation & identity: Heterosexual, lesbian, gay, & bisexual journeys.** Laconia, NH: New Dynamics. ♀♂ An in-depth and affirmative exploration of sexual orientation and the development of sexual identity with interwoven theory and personal narratives.

Sexuality

Bright, Susie. (1992). **Susie Bright's sexual reality: A virtual sex world reader.** Pittsburgh, PA: Cleis Press. ♀ Collection of bi-affirmative autobiographical essays on sexuality and sexual diversity.

Laumann, Edward O., John H. Gagnon, Robert T. Michael, & Stuart Michaels. (Eds.). (1994). **The social organization of sexuality: Sexual practices in the United States.** Chicago: University of Chicago Press. ♀♂ This interesting and controversial book contains results of the most recent large-scale study of sexuality in the USThe study was carried out with private funding after the United States Congress refused to provide public funding. Chapter 9 titled "Homosexuality" includes the most recent statistics from research of this type on same-sex behavior and relationships, bisexual attractions and behavior, and LGB self-identification.

*Marrow, Joanne. (1997). **Changing positions: Women speak out on sex & desire.** Holbrook, MA: Adams Media. ♀ Comprehensive and enlightening contemporary portrait of women's sexuality, based on the author's interviews with bisexual, lesbian, and heterosexual women.

Pasle-Green, Jeanne, & Jim Haynes. (1977). **Hello, I love you: Voices from within the sexual revolution.** New York: Times Change Press. ♀♂ Diverse collection of 1970s personal narratives on sexual behavior, relationships, and bisexuality.

*Queen, Carol., & Lawrence Schimel. (Eds.). (1997). **Pomosexuals: Challenging assumptions about gender and sexuality.** San Francisco: Cleis Press. ♀♂ A bi-affirmative, bi-inclusive collection of essays celebrating gender and sexual diversity.

Relationships and Families

Abbott, Deborah, & Ellen Farmer. (Eds.). (1995). **From wedded wife to lesbian life: Stories of transformation.** Freedom, CA: Crossing Press. ♀ Collection of personal narratives of 43 women about their coming out experiences.

*Buxton, Amity P. (1994). **The other side of the closet: The coming out crisis for straight spouses & families.** New York: John Wiley & Sons. ♀♂ An exploration of the issues involved in heterosexual marriages in which of one of the partners comes out as gay or bisexual, with a focus on the experiences of the female spouses of gay & bisexual men.

Cassingham, Barbee J., & Sally M. O'Neil. (Eds.). (1993). **And Then I Met This Woman.** Racine, WI: Mother Courage Press. ♀ About previously married women's journeys into same-sex relationships. Most of the women in the book identify as lesbian, a few identify also as bisexual. First person accounts, may be helpful for women coming out from heterosexual identities.

Dickens, Joy, & Ian McKellen. (1996). **Family outing: Guide for parents of gay, lesbian, and bisexual people.** London: Dufour Editions. ♀♂ This book from the UKfocuses on the issues faced by parents and families of LGB people.

Faderman, Lillian. (1991). **Odd girls & twilight lovers.** New York: Penguin. ♀ Fascinating history of lesbian life in 20th-century USIncludes numerous references to bisexuality, especially in the 1920s and 1980s.

Gochros, Jean Schaar. (1989). **When husbands come out of the closet.** New York: Harrington Park Press. ♀♂ Study of the impact of the coming out process on the spouses of gay and bisexual men and their marital relationships.

Kaeser, Gigi, Peggy Gillespie, & Kath Weston. (1999). **Love makes a family: Portraits of lesbian, gay, bisexual, and transgender parents and their families.** Boston: University of Massachusetts Press. ♀♂ A collection of photographs and statements from a diverse group of LGBT persons and their families.

Patterson, Charlotte J., & Anthony R. D'Augelli. (Eds.). (1998). **Lesbian, gay, and bisexual identities in families: Psychological perspectives.** New York: Oxford University Press. ♀♂ A collection of essays on LGB identities in families.

Scott, Jane. (1978). **Wives who love women.** New York: Walker. ♀ Based on the author's interviews with married lesbian and bisexual women.

Strock, Carrie. (1998). **Married women who love women.** New York: Doubleday. ♀ Portrait of currently lesbian-identified married women, their attractions and relationships with other women, and the impact of these experiences on their heterosexual marriages. Based on interviews and the author's personal experiences. May be helpful for women with current or past similar experiences.

Whitney, Catherine. (1990). **Uncommon lives: Gay men and straight women.** Penguin: New York. ♀♂ Based on the author's interviews with gay and bisexual men and heterosexual women.

Polyamory

Anapol, D. M. (1997). **The new love without limits: Secrets of sustainable intimate relationships.** San Rafael, CA: IntiNet Resource Center. ♀♂ A bi-inclusive classic on polyamory.

*Easton, Dossie & Catherine A. Liszt. (1997). **The ethical slut: A guide to infinite possibilities.** San Francisco: Greenery Press. ♀♂ A comprehensive bi-inclusive guide to polyamorous relationships.

Foster, Barbara M., Michael Foster, & Letha Hadady. (1997). **Three in love: Menages à trois from ancient to modern times.** New York: Harper Collins. ♀♂ Overview of threesomes throughout history.

*Lano, Kevin, & Claire Parry. (Eds.). (1995). **Breaking the barriers to desire: Polyamory, polyfidelity & non-monogamy— New approaches to multiple relationships.** Nottingham, England, UK: Five Leaves Publications. ♀♂ Collection of essays on diverse forms of multiple relationships.

Munson, Marcia, & Judith P. Stelboum. (Eds.). (1999). **The lesbian polyamory reader: Open relationships, non-monogamy, and casual sex.** New York: Haworth Press. ♀ A collection of essays on polyamory and lesbian and bisexual women.

Nearing, Ryam. (1992). **Loving more: The polyfidelity primer.** Boulder, CO: Loving More. ♀♂ Another classic guide to committed polyamorous relationships.

West, Celeste. (1995). **Lesbian polyfidelity.** San Francisco: Booklegger Press. ♀ Comprehensive guide to committed polyamorous relationships among women.

Youth

*Bass, Ellen & Kate Kaufman. (1996). **Free your mind: The book for gay, lesbian, and bisexual youth—and their allies.** New York: Harper Perennial. ♀♂ A broad-ranging bi-inclusive contemporary guide for LGB youth, allies, and families.

*Bernstein, Robin, & Seth Clark Silberman. (Eds.). (1996). **Generation Q: Gays, lesbians, and bisexuals born around 1969's Stonewall riots tell their stories of growing up in the age of information.** Boston: Alyson. ♀♂ Diverse collection of personal narratives by gay, lesbian, and bisexual youth.

Findlen, Barbara. (Ed.). (1995). **Listen Up: Voices From the Next Feminist Generation.** Seattle: Seal Press. ♀ An anthology of autobiographical writings by feminists in their 20s. Several contributors self-identify as bisexual, including Anastassia Higgenbotham, Laurel Gilbert, Jee Yeun Lee, and Christine Doza.

*Gray, Mary L. (Ed.). (1999). **In your face: Stories from the lives of queer youth.** New York: Harrington Park Press. ♀♂ An impressive collection of personal perspectives by a diverse group of LGB youth.

Mastoon, Adam. (1997). **The shared heart: Portraits and stories celebrating lesbian, gay, and bisexual young people.** New York: William Morrow. ♀♂ A collection of photographs and personal narratives from a diverse group of LGB youth.

Owens, Robert E. (1998). **Queer kids: The challenges and promise for lesbian, gay, and bisexual youth.** New York: Haworth Press. ♀♂ Provides an overview of typical issues facing LGB youth, including sexual identity development, coming out, difficult school conditions and situations, parental reactions, LGB youth programs, and counseling issues.

Pollack, Rachel, & Cheryl Schwartz. (1995). **The journey out: A guide for and about lesbian, gay and bisexual teens.** New York, NY: Viking. ♀♂ A bi-inclusive guide to coming out and LGB identity for teenagers, their families, and their friends.

Sanlo, Ronni L. (1998). **Working with lesbian, gay, bisexual, and transgender college students: A handbook for faculty and administrators.** Westport, CT: Greenwood Press. ♀♂ The Coordinator of the LGBT Student Resources Center at the University of California Los Angeles provides a comprehensive source of information on working with LGBT college students.

The Bisexual Resource Guide 4th Edition

Sherrill, Jan-Mitchell, & Craig A. Hardesty. (1994). **The gay, lesbian & bisexual students' guide to colleges, universities, & graduate schools**. New York: NYU Press. ♀♂ Comprehensive guide to LGB affirmative institutions of higher learning.

Transgender Persons and Identities

Denny, Dallas. (Ed.). (1998). **Current concepts in transgender identity**. New York: Garland. ♀♂ An up-to-date collection of essays representing emerging affirmative approaches to transgender identities and issues, including chapters on gender identity and sexual orientation by Ira Pauly and Jamison Green.

Wilchins, Riki Ann. (1997). **Read my lips: Sexual subversion and the end of gender**. Ithaca, NY: Freehand Books. ♀♂ Collection of autobiographical essays by a bi-identified transgender activist celebrating sexual and gender diversity.

Ethnic, Racial, & Cultural Diversity

*Asian & Pacific Islander Wellness Center. (1997). **Understanding Asian & Pacific Islander sexual diversity: A handbook for individuals**. San Francisco: Asian & Pacific Islander Wellness Center. ♀♂ An excellent overview of historical and contemporary sexual diversity in the Asian and Pacific Islander communities, including a list of community organizations and a reading list.

Lim-Hing, Sharon. (Ed.). (1994). **The very inside: An anthology of writing by Asian & Pacific Islander lesbian & bisexual women**. Toronto: Sister Vision Press. ♀ A collection of essays and poetry that includes several pieces by bi-identified women.

Ratti, Rakesh, (Ed.). (1993). **Lotus of another color: An unfolding of the South Asian Lesbian & Gay Experience**. Boston: Alyson. ♀♂ An anthology that includes three essays by bi-identified people.

Summerhawk, Barbara, Cheiron McMahill, & Darren McDonald. (Eds.). (1998). **Queer Japan: Personal stories of Japanese lesbians, gays, transsexuals, and bisexuals**. Norwich, VT: New Victoria. ♀♂ A groundbreaking collection of personal narratives from Japanese LGBT persons.

Note: The following books describe same-sex and/or transgender behavior and relationships in diverse cultures around the world. There is ample material in these volumes demonstrating that bisexuality and persons with both same-sex and other-sex behavior and relationships have been an accepted and integral part of many cultures both currently and historically.

*Blackwood, Evelyn, & Saskia E. Wieringa. (Eds.). (1999). **Female desires: Same-sex relations and transgender practices across cultures**. New York: Columbia University Press.

Brown, Lester B. (Ed.). (1997). **Two Spirit people: American Indian lesbian women and gay men**. New York: Harrington Park Press.

*Carrier, Joseph. (1995). **De los otros: Intimacy and homosexuality among Mexican men**. New York: Columbia University Press.

*Herdt, Gilbert H. (1984). **Ritualized homosexuality in Melanesia**. Berkeley, CA: University of California Press.

Hinsch, Bret. (1990). **Passions of the cut sleeve: The male homosexual tradition in China**. Berkeley, CA: University of California Press.

Leong, Russell. (Ed.). (1996). **Asian American sexualities: Dimensions of the gay and lesbian experience**. New York: Routledge.

Leupp, Gary P. (1995). **Male colors: The construction of homosexuality in Tokugawa Japan**. Berkeley, CA: University of California Press.

Murray, Stephen O. (1984). **Social theory, homosexual realities**. New York: Gay Academic Union.

Murray, Stephen O. (Ed.). (1987). **Male homosexuality in Central and South America**. New York: Gay Academic Union.

*Murray, Stephen O. (1992). **Oceanic homosexualities**. New York: Garland Publishing.

*Murray, Stephen O. (2000). **Homosexualities**. Chicago: University of Chicago Press.

Murray, Stephen O., & Will Roscoe. (Eds.). (1997). **Islamic homosexualities: Culture, history, and literature**. New York: New York University Press.

*Murray, Stephen O., & Will Roscoe. (Ed.). (1998). **Boy-wives and female-husbands: Studies of African homosexualities**. New York: St. Martins Press.

*Ruan, Fang Fu. (1991). **Sex in China: Studies in sexology in Chinese culture**. New York: Plenum Press.

*Schmitt, Arno, & Jehoeda Sofer. (Eds.). (1992). **Sexuality and eroticism among males in Moslem societies**. New York: Harrington Park Press.

Saikaku, Ihara. (1990). **The great mirror of male love**. (P. G. Schalow, Trans.). Stanford, CA: Stanford University Press.

Schneebaum, Tobias. (1988). **Where the spirits dwell: An odyssey in the jungle of New Guinea**. New York: Grove.

Schifter, Jacobo. (2000). **Public sex in a Latin society**. New York: Haworth.

*Schifter, Jacobo, & Johnny Madrigal Pana. (2000). **The sexual construction of Latino youth: Implications for the spread of HIV/AIDS**. New York: Haworth.

Seabrook, Jeremy. (1999). **Love in a different culture: The meaning of men who have sex with men in India**. London: Verso.

Watanabe, Tsuneo, & Iwata, Jun'ichi. (1987). **The love of the Samurai: A thousand years of Japanese homosexuality**. (D. R. Roberts, Trans.). London: GMP Publications.

Queer Theory/Cultural Studies/Literary Criticism

*Beemyn, Brett, & Mickey Eliason. (Eds.). (1996). **Queer studies: A lesbian, gay, bisexual, & transgender anthology**. New York: NYU Press. ♀♂ Includes essays by Paula Rust, Amanda Udis-Kessler, Ruth Goldman, Amber Ault, Christopher James, Warren J. Blumenfeld and others. An impressive bi-inclusive mixed orientation collection, with several chapters on bisexuality in the context of queer studies.

Spirituality

*Conner, Randy P., David Hatfield Sparks, & Mariya Sparks. (1997). **Cassell's encyclopedia of Queer myth, symbol and spirit**. London: Cassell. ♀♂ A wide-ranging bi-affirmative encyclopedia of LGBT spirituality.

Kimball, Richard S. (Ed.). (2000). **Our whole lives: Sexuality education for adults**. Boston, MA: Unitarian Universalist Association and United Church Board of Homeland Ministries. Stuart, Elizabeth et al. (1998). **Religion is a queer thing: A guide to the Christian faith for lesbian, gay, bisexual and transgendered people**. New York: Cassell. ♀♂ A sexuality curriculum featuring a section on sexual orientation by bi activists and educators Bobbi Keppel and Alan Hamilton.

Sweasey, Peter. (1997). **From queer to eternity: Spirituality in the lives of lesbian, gay and bisexual people**. New York: Cassell. ♀♂ Exploration of spirituality and LGB people.

Tigert, Leanne McCall. (1996). **Coming out while staying in: Struggles and celebrations of lesbians, gays, and bisexuals in the church**. Cleveland, OH: United Church Press. ♀♂ Another volume exploring spirituality in the lives of LGB people.

Lesbian, Gay, Bisexual, & Transgender Communities

Colker, Ruth. (1996). **Hybrid: Bisexuals, multiracials, & other misfits under American law**. New York: NYU Press. ♀♂ An examination of how the legal system treats and mistreats those who don't fit standard categories, including bisexual and multiracial people.

Gamson, Joshua. (1998). **Freaks Talk Back: Tabloid Talk Shows and Sexual Nonconformity.** Chicago: University of Chicago Press. ♀♂ Well-written and chock full of stories about US talk shows and their treatment of lesbian, gay, bi and transgendered people. Explores the issues from many angles, including how, while being used by talk shows, LGBT activists in return use talk shows to educate the public about LGBT issues. Includes substantial discussion of how bi's in particular are treated, including a number of entertaining behind the scenes stories.

Harris, Paul. (1999). **The queer press guide 2000**. New York: Painted Leaf Press. ♀♂ Comprehensive listing of LGBT newspapers and magazines.

Hertzog, Mark. (1996). **The lavender vote: Lesbians, gay men, and bisexuals in American electoral politics**. New York: New York University Press. ♀♂ Focus on the impact of LGB people on the electoral process.

Shepard, Curtis F., Felice Yeskel, & Charles Outcalt. (1996). **Lesbian, Gay, Bisexual, and Transgender Campus Organizing: A Comprehensive Manual**. Washington, DC: National Gay and Lesbian Task Force. Also available online at: http://www.ngltf.org/ ♀♂ A guide to LGBT campus organizing.

Swan, Wallace. (1997). **Gay/lesbian/bisexual/transgender public policy issues: A citizen's and administrator's guide to the new cultural struggle**. New York: Harrington Park Press. ♀♂ Focus on GLBT public policy issues.

Working Group on Funding Lesbian & Gay Issues. (1999). **Funders of lesbian, gay & bisexual programs: A directory for grantseekers** (3rd ed.). New York: Working Group on Funding Lesbian & Gay Issues. ♀ ♂ Available for $15 from the Working Group on Funding Lesbian & Gay Issues, 116 E. 16th St., 7th Fl., New York, NY 10003. Phone: (212) 475-2930. (Also accessible online at: http://www.workinggroup.org/resource.htm#Directory).

BOOK CHAPTERS AND JOURNAL ARTICLES ON BISEXUALITY

Complete information is provided for all listed chapters and articles, with the exception of chapters from the following anthologies:

Beemyn & Eliason, **Queer studies**; Bernstein & Silberman, **Generation Q**; Bisexual Anthology Collective, **Plural desires**; Findlen, **Listen up**; Hall & Pramaggiore, **RePresenting bisexualities**; Hutchins & Kaahumanu, **Bi any other name**; Rose, Stephens, & the Offpink Collective, **Bisexual horizons**; Rust, **Bisexuality in the United States: A social science reader**; Tucker, **Bisexual politics**; Weise, **Closer to home.** For chapters from these anthologies, the authors' names, chapter titles, book titles, and page numbers are given, and the reader is referred to the relevant book sections above for complete references. For books that were already described above in the book sections, a list of authors and titles are given at the beginning of each section, and the reader is referred to the book sections for complete references.

Special Issues of Journals and Magazines

Asian Pacific Journal. (1993, Spring/Summer, Vol. 2, No. 1). Special issue titled "Witness aloud: Lesbian, gay & bisexual Asian/Pacific American writing." A collection primarily by lesbian and gay identified authors. Includes writing by bi authors Indigo Chih-Lien Som and Jee Yeun Lee.

Dulwich Centre Journal. (1999, No. 1). Special issue of new Australian journal titled: "Bisexuality: Identity, politics and partnerships." Guest edited by Ruth Gibian, with articles from Australia and the U. S., as well as interviews with bisexual youth, Australian Bi Network activist Mark Trudinger, and author Dennis Altman.

Journal of Bisexuality. The first issue of this new quarterly journal was published in the Fall of 2000. Edited by well-known bi author Fritz Klein, the **Journal** will include essays, research, book and film reviews, and personal narratives on bisexuality.

Journal of Gay, Lesbian, and Bisexual Identity. (1997, Vol. 2, Issue 1). Special issue on bisexual theory: Collection of essays, articles, poetry, and book reviews on bisexuality in literature, film, autobiography, community, and cultural studies. Please note that this journal has been renamed **International Journal of Sexual and Gender Studies**.

Journal of Homosexuality. (1985, Vol. 11, Issue 1/2). Special issue on bisexuality: Collection of scholarly reports on 1980s research on bisexuality.

Lavender Network: Oregon's Lesbian and Gay Newsmagazine. (1993, January) Special issue on bisexuality. Includes articles by Sharon Sumpter, Elias Farajajé-Jones, and others.

Loving More: New Models for Relationships. (1997, Fall). Special issue, titled "Bi love." Includes articles by Loraine Hutchins, Mark Silver and others.

Open Hands: Reconciling Ministries with Lesbians and Gay Men. (1991, Fall). Special issue on bisexuality. Includes articles by Beth Weise and others.

Open Hands: Reconciling Ministries with Lesbians and Gay Men. (1998, Summer). Special issue titled "Bisexuality: Both/and rather than either/or." Includes articles by Amanda Udis-Kessler, Ben Roe, and others.

Sexual Orientation: Multidimensional Approaches

For *Books* on sexual orientation, see the *Bi-Inclusive Books* section above: Under *Psychology, Sexual Orientation*: Bohan, 1996; Bohan, Russell, & Cass, 1999; Rust, 1997.

Psychological and Sociological Perspectives

Berkey, Braden R., Terri Perelman-Hall, & Lawrence A. Kurdek. (1990). The multidimensional scale of sexuality. **Journal of Homosexuality,** 19(4), 67-87.

*Cass, Vivienne. (1999). Bringing psychology in from the cold: Framing psychological theory and research within a social constructionist psychology approach. In J. S. Bohan, G. M. Russell, & V. Cass (Eds.), **Conversations about psychology and sexual orientation** (pp. 106-128). New York: New York University Press.

Coleman, Eli. (1987). Assessment of sexual orientation. **Journal of Homosexuality,** 14(1/2), 9-24.

Keppel, Bobbi, & Alan Hamilton. (2000). Your sexual orientation: Using the Sexual and Affectional Orientation and Identity Scale to teach about sexual orientation. In R. S. Kimball (Ed.), **Our whole lives: Sexuality education for adults** (pp. 157-161). Boston, MA: Unitarian Universalist Association and United Church Board of Homeland Ministries.

Klein, Fritz. (1999). Psychology of sexual orientation. In J. S. Bohan, G. M. Russell, & V. Cass (Eds.), **Conversations about psychology and sexual orientation** (pp. 129-138). New York: New York University Press.

*Klein, Fritz, Barry Sepekoff, & Timothy J. Wolf. (1985). Sexual orientation: A multi-variable dynamic process. **Journal of Homosexuality,** 11(1/2), 35-50.

Peplau, Letitia Anne, & Linda D. Garnets. (2000). A new paradigm for understanding women's sexuality and sexual orientation. **Journal of Social Issues,** 56(2), 329-350.

Rothblum, Esther D. (2000). Sexual orientation and sex in women's lives: Conceptual and methodological issues. **Journal of Social Issues,** 56(2), 193-204.

Rust, Paula C. (1996). Finding a sexual identity & community: Therapeutic implications & cultural assumptions in scientific models of coming out. In E. D. Rothblum, & L. A. Bond (Eds.), **Preventing heterosexism and homophobia** (pp. 87-123). Thousand Oaks, CA: Sage.

Rust, Paula C. Rodríguez. (2000). Alternatives to binary sexuality: Modeling sexuality. In P. C. R. Rust (Ed.), **Bisexuality in the United States: A Social Science Reader** (pp. 33-54). New York: Columbia University Press.

Sell, Randall L. (1996). The Sell Assessment of Sexual Orientation: Background and scoring. **Journal of Gay, Lesbian, & Bisexual Identity,** 1(4), 295-310.

Shively, Michael, & John DeCecco. (1977). Components of sexual identity. **Journal of Homosexuality,** 3(1), 41-48.

Personal and Political Perspectives

*Gibian, Ruth. (1992). Refusing certainty: Toward a bisexuality of wholeness. In **Closer to home** (pp. 3-16).

Kaplan, Rebecca. (1995). Your fence is sitting on me: The hazards of binary thinking. In **Bisexual politics** (pp. 267-280).

Bisexual Identity

Psychological and Sociological Perspectives

For *Books* on bisexual identity, see also the following sections above: *Books Specifically on Bisexuality*: Bode, 1976; George, 1993; Klein, 1993; Klein & Wolf, 1985; Rust, 1995, 2000; Weinberg, Williams & Pryor, 1994; M. Williams, 1999. In *Dutch*: Hanson, 1990; Kuppens, 1995; van Kerkhof, 1997; Wolff, 1979. In *French*: Mendès-Leité, Deschamps, & Proth, 1996. In *German*: Feldhorst, 1996; Geissler, 1993; Gooß, 1995; Hüsers & König, 1995. *Bi-Inclusive Books*: Under *Identity*: Atkins, 1996; Burch, 1994; Esterberg, 1997; Johnson, 1997; Wishik & Pierce, 1991. Under *Relationships & Families*: Patterson & D'Augelli, 1998. Under *Ethnic, Racial, & Cultural Diversity*: Asian & Pacific Islander Wellness Center, 1997.

Blumstein, Philip W., & Pepper Schwartz. (1977). Bisexuality: Some social psychological issues. **Journal of Social Issues,** 33(2), 30-45. Reprint appears in P. C. R. Rust, **Bisexuality in the United States: A Social Science Reader** (pp. 339-352).

Coleman, Eli. (1998). Paradigmatic changes in the understanding of bisexuality. In E. J. Haeberle, & R. Gindorf (Eds.), **Bisexualities: The ideology and practice of sexual contact with both men and women** (pp. 107-112). New York: Continuum.

*Firestein, Beth A. (1996). Bisexuality as paradigm shift: Transforming our disciplines. In B. A. Firestein (Ed.), **Bisexuality: The psychology & politics of an invisible minority** (pp. 261-291). Thousand Oaks, CA: Sage.

*Fox, Ronald C. (1995). Bisexual identities. In A. R. D'Augelli, & C. J. Patterson (Eds.), **Lesbian, gay, and bisexual identities over the lifespan: Psychological perspectives** (pp. 48-86). New York: Oxford University Press.

*Golden, Carla. (1996). What's in a name? Sexual self-identification among women. In R. C. Savin-Williams, & K. M. Cohen (Eds.), **The lives of lesbians, gays, & bisexuals: Children to adults** (pp. 229-249). Ft. Worth, TX: Harcourt Brace.

MacDonald, A. P., Jr. (1983). A little bit of lavender goes a long way: A critique of research on sexual orientation. **Journal of Sex Research,** 19(1), 94-100. Reprint appears in P. C. R. Rust, **Bisexuality in the United States: A Social Science Reader** (pp. 24-30).

Ochs, Robyn. (1997). Contexts & constructs of identity: Bisexuality. In P. Rust (Ed.), **Sociology of sexuality & sexual orientation: Syllabi & teaching materials** (pp. 100-107). Washington, DC: American Sociological Association.

*Paul, Jay P. (1996). Bisexuality: Exploring/exploding the boundaries. In R. C. Savin-Williams, & K. M. Cohen (Eds.), **The lives of lesbians, gays, & bisexuals: Children to adults** (pp. 436-461). Ft. Worth, TX: Harcourt Brace. Reprint appears in P. C. R. Rust, **Bisexuality in the United States: A Social Science Reader** (pp. 11-23).

Queen, Carol. (1995). Sexual diversity and bisexual identity. In **Bisexual politics** (pp. 151-160).

Reynolds, Amy L., & William F. Hanjorgiris. (2000). Coming out: Lesbian, gay, and bisexual identity development. In R. M. Perez, K. A. DeBord, & K. J. Bieschke (Eds.), **Handbook of counseling and psychotherapy with lesbian, gay, and bisexual clients** (pp. 35-55). Washington, DC: American Psychological Association.

Rust, Paula C. (1992). Who are we & where do we go from here? Conceptualizing bisexuality. In **Closer to home** (pp. 281-310).

*Rust, Paula C. (1996). Sexual identity & bisexual identities: The struggle for self-description in a changing sexual landscape. In B. Beemyn, & M. Eliason (Eds.), **Queer studies: A lesbian, gay, bisexual, & transgender anthology** (pp. 64-86). New York: NYU Press.

Rust, Paula C. Rodríguez. (2000). Bisexuality: A contemporary paradox for women. **Journal of Social Issues,** 56(2), 205-221.

Rust, Paula C. (2001). Two many and not enough: The meanings of bisexual identities. **Journal of Bisexuality,** 1(1), 31-68.

Schwartz, Pepper, & Philip Blumstein. (1998). The acquisition of sexual identity: Bisexuality. In E. J. Haeberle, & R. Gindorf (Eds.), **Bisexualities: The ideology and practice of sexual contact with both men and women** (pp. 182-212). New York: Continuum.

Seif, Hinda. (1999). To love women, or to not love men: Chronicles of lesbian identification. In D. Atkins (Ed.), **Lesbian sex scandals: Sexual practices, identities, and politics** (pp. 33-44). New York: Haworth.

Shuster, Rebecca. (1987). Sexuality as a continuum: The bisexual identity. In The Boston Lesbian Psychologies Collective (Eds.), **Lesbian psychologies: Explorations & challenges** (pp. 56-71). Urbana & Chicago, IL: University of Illinois Press.

Wishik, Heather R. (1996). Life maps: Tracking individual gender and sexual identity construction in the contexts of cultures, relationships, and desires. **Journal of Gay, Lesbian, & Bisexual Identity,** 1(2), 129-152.

Zinik, Gary. (1985). Identity conflict or adaptive flexibility? Bisexuality reconsidered. **Journal of Homosexuality,** 11(1/2), 7-19. Reprint appears in P. C. R. Rust, **Bisexuality in the United States: A Social Science Reader,** pp. 55-60.

Personal and Political Perspectives

For *Books* with personal and political perspectives on bisexual identity, see also the following sections above:

Books Specifically on Bisexuality: Bisexual Anthology Collective, 1995; Hutchins & Kaahumanu, 1991; Kolodny, 2000; Off Pink Collective, 1988; Orndorff, 1999; Rose, Stevens & the Off-Pink Collective, 1996; Tucker, 1995; Weise, 1992. In *Spanish*: Archivo Lesbico y de Mujeres Diferentes, 1998.

Bi-Inclusive Books: Under *Identity*: Norris & Read, 1985; Van Gelder & Brandt, 1996. Under *Youth*: Findlen, 1995. Under *Ethnic, Racial & Cultural Diversity*: Lim-Hing, 1994; Ratti, 1993.

Chater, Nancy, & Lilith Finkler. (1995). "Traversing wide territories": A journey from lesbianism to bisexuality. In **Plural desires** (pp. 14-36).

Cooper, Laurie A., Michelle E. Hynes, & Edith R. Westfall. (1995). The Kinsey three. In **Plural desires** (pp. 261-275).

*Eadie, Jo. (1996). Being who we are (and anyone else we want to be). In **Bisexual horizons** (pp. 16-20).

*Fox, Ann. (1991). Development of a bisexual identity. In **Bi any other name** (pp. 29-36).

Hamilton, Louis. (1996). Deaf bisexuality. In **Bisexual horizons** (pp. 144-148).

McKeon, Elizabeth. (1992). To be bisexual and underclass. In **Closer to home** (pp. 27-34).

Lipstadt, Helena. (1997). From lesbian to has-bian: Taking the long view of friendship and bisexuality. **In the Family: A Magazine for Gays, Lesbians, Bisexuals and Their Relations,** 2(3), 10-12, 22.

Montgomery, Michael S. (1996). An old bottle for old wine: Selecting the right label. In **Bisexual horizons** (pp. 21-24).

Queen, Carol A. (1991). The queer in me. In **Bi any other name** (pp. 17-21).

Reinhardt, Regina U. (2001). From Europe with love: A bisexual biography. **Journal of Bisexuality,** 1(1), 163-172.

*Shuster, Rebecca. (1992). Bisexuality and the quest for principled loving. In **Closer to home** (pp. 147-154).

Starr, Christina. (1995). **Making a sexual choice.** In **Plural desires** (pp. 185-190).

*Sumpter, Sharon F. (1991). Myths/realities of bisexuality. In **Bi any other name** (pp. 12-13).

*Udis-Kessler, Amanda. (1996). Challenging the stereotypes. In **Bisexual horizons** (pp. 45-57).

Zipkin, Dvora. (1992). Why bi? In **Closer to home** (pp. 55-73).

Bisexual Attractions and Behavior

Psychological and Sociological Perspectives

Findings of research on bisexual attractions & behavior. For a review of the social science literature on bisexual identity, see Fox, "Bisexuality in perspective" (cited in this section).

For *Books* on bisexual attractions and behavior, see also the following sections above:

Books Specifically on Bisexuality: Aggleton, 1996; Bode, 1976; George, 1993; Haeberle & Gindorf, 1998; Klein, 1993; Klein & Wolf, 1985; Rust, 1995, 2000; Sigma Research, 1993; Tielman, Carballo & Hendriks, 1991; Weinberg, Williams & Pryor, 1994; Wolff, 1979. In *French*: Mendès-Leité, Deschamps, & Proth, 1996.

Bi-Inclusive Books: Under *Sexuality*: Laumann, Gagnon, Michael & Michaels, 1994; Marrow, 1997.

Bagley, Christopher, & Pierre Tremblay. (1998). On the prevalence of homosexuality and bisexuality, in a random community survey of 750 men aged 18 to 27. **Journal of Homosexuality**, 36(2), 1-18. (Canada)

Bhugra, Dinesh, & Padmal De Silva. (1998). Dimensions of bisexuality: An exploratory study using focus groups of male and female bisexuals. **Sexual and Marital Therapy**, *13*(2), 145-157. (UK)

Binson, Diane, Stuart Michaels, Ron Stall, Thomas J. Coates, John H. Gagnon, & Joseph A. Catania. (1995). Prevalence & social distribution of men who have sex with men: United States & its urban centers. **Journal of Sex Research**, 32(3), 245-254.

Blumstein, Philip, & Pepper Schwartz. (1976). Bisexuality in women. **Archives of Sexual Behavior**, 5(2), 171-181.

Blumstein, Philip, & Pepper Schwartz. (1976). Bisexuality in men. **Urban Life, 5**(3), 339-358.

Diamond, Lisa M., & Ritch C. Savin-Williams. (2000). Explaining diversity in the development of same-sex sexuality among young women. **Journal of Social Issues**, *56*(2), 297-313.

*Doll, Lynda S., Lyle R. Petersen, Carol R. White, Eric S. Johnson, John W. Ward, & The Blood Donor Study Group. (1992). Homosexually & nonhomosexually identified men who have sex with men: A behavioral comparison. **Journal of Sex Research**, 29(1), 1-14.

*Fox, Ronald C. (1996). Bisexuality in perspective: A review of theory & research. In B. A. Firestein (Ed.), **Bisexuality: The psychology & politics of an invisible minority** (pp. 3-50). Thousand Oaks, CA: Sage. Reprint appears in B. Greene & G. L. Croom (Eds.). (2000). **Education, research, and practice in lesbian, gay, bisexual, and transgendered psychology: A resource manual** (pp. 161-206). Thousand Oaks, CA: Sage.

Gagnon, John H., Cathy S. Greenblat, & Michael Kimmel. (1998). Bisexuality: A sociological perspective. In E. J. Haeberle, & R. Gindorf (Eds.), **Bisexualities: The ideology and practice of sexual contact with both men and women** (pp. 81-106). New York: Continuum.

Gindorf, Rolf, & Alan Warran. (1998). Bisexualities: Heterosexual contacts of "gay" men, homosexual contacts of "heterosexual" men. In E. J. Haeberle, & R. Gindorf (Eds.), **Bisexualities: The ideology and practice of sexual contact with both men and women** (pp. 213-220). New York: Continuum.

Lever, Janet, William H. Rogers, Sally Carson, David E. Kanouse, & R. Hertz. (1992). Behavior patterns and sexual identity of bisexual males. **Journal of Sex Research, 29**(2), 141-167. Reprint appears in P. C. R. Rust, **Bisexuality in the United States: A Social Science Reader**, pp. 185-202.

Loewenstein, Sophie F. (1984). On the diversity of love object orientations among women. **Journal of Social Work & Human Sexuality,** 3(2-3). Reprint appears in P. C. R. Rust, **Bisexuality in the United States: A Social Science Reader,** pp. 203-216.

McKirnan, David J., Joseph P. Stokes, Lynda Doll, & Rebecca G. Burzette. (1995). Bisexually active men: Social characteristics & sexual behavior. **Journal of Sex Research,** 32(1), 65-76.

Messiah, Antoine, & Emmanuelle Mouret-Fourme. (1993). Homosexualité, bisexualité: Éléments de socio-biographie sexuelle [Homosexuality, bisexuality: Elements of a sexual social biography]. **Population,** 48(5), 1353-1380.

*Queen, Carol. (1996). Bisexuality, sexual diversity, & the sex-positive perspective. In B. A. Firestein (Ed.), **Bisexuality: The psychology & politics of an invisible minority** (pp. 103-124). Thousand Oaks, CA: Sage.

Rogers, Susan M., & Charles F. Turner. (1991). Male-male sexual contact in the U.S.A.: Findings from five sample surveys, 1970-1990. **Journal of Sex Research,** 28(4), 491-519.

Ross, Michael W., & Jay P. Paul. (1992). Beyond gender: The basis of sexual attraction in bisexual men & women. **Psychological Reports,** 71, 1283-1290. Reprint appears in P. C. R. Rust, **Bisexuality in the United States: A Social Science Reader** (pp. 92-98).

Rudy, Kathy. (1999). Sex radical communities and the future of sexual ethics. In D. Atkins (Ed.), **Lesbian sex scandals: Sexual practices, identities, and politics** (pp. 133-142). New York: Haworth.

*Rust, Paula C. (1992). The politics of sexual identity: Sexual attraction & behavior among lesbian & bisexual women. **Social Problems,** 39(4), 366-386.

Rust, Paula C. Rodríguez. (2000). Review of statistical findings about bisexual behavior, feelings, and identities. In P. C. R. Rust (Ed.), **Bisexuality in the United States: A Social Science Reader** (pp. 129-184). New York: Columbia University Press.

Sell, Randall L., James A. Wells, & David Wypij. (1995). The prevalence of homosexual behavior & attraction in the United States, the United Kingdom & France: Results of national population-based samples. **Archives of Sexual Behavior,** 24(3), 235-248.

Stokes, Joseph P., Robin L. Miller, & Rhonda Mundhenk. (1998). Toward an understanding of behaviourally bisexual men: The influence of context and culture. **Canadian Journal of Human Sexuality,** 7(2), 101-113.

Weinrich, James D. (1988). The periodic table model of the gender transpositions: II. Limerent and lusty sexual attractions and the nature of bisexuality. **Journal of Sex Research,** 24, 113-129. Reprint appears in P. C. R. Rust, **Bisexuality in the United States: A Social Science Reader,** pp. 78-91.

Wellings, Kaye, Julia Wadsworth, & Anne M. Johnson. (1994). Sexual diversity & homosexual behaviour. In A. M. Johnson, J. Wadsworth, K. Wellings, & J. Field, **Sexual attitudes & lifestyles** (pp. 183-224). Oxford: Blackwell Scientific Publications.

Personal and Political Perspectives

For *Books* with personal and political perspectives on bisexual attractions and behavior, see also the following sections above:

Books Specifically on Bisexuality: Bisexual Anthology Collective, 1995; Hutchins & Kaahumanu, 1991; Off Pink Collective, 1988; Rose, Stevens & the Off-Pink Collective, 1996; Tucker, 1995; Weise, 1992.
Bi-Inclusive Books: Under *Sexuality*: Bright, 1992; Marrow, 1997; Pasle-Green & Haynes, 1977; Queen & Schimel, 1997.

*Christina, Greta. (1995). Bi sexuality. In **Bisexual politics** (pp. 161-166).

*Klassen, Karen. (1991). Talking about sex, gender, and desire. In **Bi any other name** (pp. 329-334).

Barragan C. J. III, (1991). More than a footnote. In **Bi any other name** (pp. 17-21).

Farajajé-Jones, Elias. (2000). Loving "queer": We're all a big mix of possibilities of desire just waiting to happen. **In the Family: A Magazine for Gays, Lesbians, Bisexuals and Their Relations**, 6 (1), 6-13.

Field, Nicola. (1996). Trade secrets. In **Bisexual horizons** (pp. 133-141).

*Goswami, Changini. (1991). My underself. In **Bi any other name** (pp. 60-63).

Hutchins, Loraine. (1991). Love that kink. In **Bi any other name** (pp. 335-343).

Johnson, Laura. (1991). Making my own way. In **Bi any other name** (pp. 40-42).

*Ripley, Rebecca. (1992). The language of desire: Sexuality, identity and language. In **Closer to home** (pp. 91-102).

Stone, Dave. (1996). Living with the Janus people. In **Bisexual horizons** (pp. 127-132).

Tan, Cecilia. (1995). Bisexuality and S/M: The bi switch revolution. In **Bisexual politics** (pp. 167-170).

Yost, Lisa. (1991). Bisexual tendencies. In **Bi any other name** (pp. 74-76).

Bisexual Relationships and Families

Psychological and Sociological Perspectives

For *Books* on bisexual relationships and families, see also the following sections above:
Books Specifically on Bisexuality: Bode, 1976; George, 1993; Klein, 1993; Klein & Wolf, 1985; Rust, 1995, 2000; Weinberg, Williams & Pryor, 1994; M. Williams, 1999. In *Dutch*: Hanson, 1990; Kuppens, 1995; van Kerkhof, 1997; Wolff, 1979. In *French*: Mendès-Leité, Deschamps, & Proth, 1996. In *German*: Feldhorst, 1996; Geissler, 1993; Honnens, 1996.
Bi-Inclusive Books: Under *Relationships & Families*: Burch, 1994, 1997; Buxton, 1994; Dickens & McKellen, 1996; Faderman, 1991; Gochros, 1989; Patterson & D'Augelli, 1990; Whitney, 1990. Under *Polyamory*: Easton & Liszt, 1997; Munson & Stelboum, 1999.

Coleman, Eli. (1985). Bisexual women in marriages. **Journal of Homosexuality**, 11(1/2), 87-99.

Coleman, Eli. (1985). Integration of male bisexuality & marriage. **Journal of Homosexuality**, 11(1/2), 189-208.

Halpern, Ellen L. (1999). If love is so wonderful, what's so scary about MORE? In M. Munson, & J. P. Stelboum (Eds.), **The lesbian polyamory reader: Open relationships, non-monogamy, and casual sex** (pp. 157-164). New York: Haworth.

*Labriola, Kathy. (1999). Models of open relationships. In M. Munson, & J. P. Stelboum (Eds.), **The lesbian polyamory reader: Open relationships, non-monogamy, and casual sex** (pp. 217-226). New York: Haworth.

*Rust, Paula C. (1996). Monogamy & polyamory: Relationship issues for bisexuals. In B. A. Firestein (Ed.), **Bisexuality: The psychology & politics of an invisible minority** (pp. 127-148). Thousand Oaks, CA: Sage.

Rust, Paula C. Rodríguez. (2000). Heterosexual gays, heterosexual lesbians, homosexual straights. In P. C. R. Rust (Ed.), **Bisexuality in the United States: A Social Science Reader** (pp. 279-306). New York: Columbia University Press.

Tuerk, Catherine. (2000). Uncommon wisdom: Help for parents of a bisexual daughter. **In the Family: A Magazine for Gays, Lesbians, Bisexuals and Their Relations**, 5(3), 5, 25.

*Wolf, Timothy J. (1985). Marriages of bisexual men. **Journal of Homosexuality,** 11(1/2), 135-148.

Personal and Political Perspectives

For *Books* on bisexual relationships and families, see also the following sections above:
Books Specifically on Bisexuality: Bisexual Anthology Collective, 1995; Bode, 1976; Hutchins & Kaahumanu, 1991; Kohn & Matusow, 1980; Off Pink Collective, 1988; Rose, Stevens & the Off-Pink Collective, 1996; Tucker, 1995; Weise, 1992.
Bi-Inclusive Books: Under *Relationships & Families*: Abbott & Farmer, 1995; Cassingham & O'Neil, 1993; Kaeser, Gillespie & Weston, 1999; Scott, 1978; Strock, 1998; Whitney, 1990. Under *Sexuality*: Pasle-Green & Haynes, 1977; Under *Polyamory*: Anapol, 1997; Foster, Foster & Hadady, 1997; Lano & Parry, 1995; Nearing, 1992; West, 1995.

*Arden, Karen. (1996). Dwelling in the house of tomorrow: Children, young people and their bisexual parents. In **Bisexual horizons** (pp. 247-257).

Bassein, Richard S. (1991). A day in the life. In **Bi any other name** (pp. 171-173).

Brewer, Michael. (1991). Two-way closet. In **Bi any other name** (pp. 140-143).

*Bryant, Wayne. (1991). Love, friendship, and sex. In **Bi any other name** (pp. 69-73).

Cade, Felicity. (1996). Marriage and bisexuality. In **Bisexual horizons** (pp. 114-118).

Fenario, Jane. (1996). Dating and the bisexual, single mom. **In the Family: A Magazine for Gays, Lesbians, Bisexuals and Their Relations**, 1(3), 14-15.

Girard, Chris. (1991). A few brave and gifted people. In **Bi any other name** (pp. 167-170).

Glenn, Roland. (1991). Proud father of a bisexual son. In **Bi any other name** (pp. 254-257).

*Gonsalves, Sharon. (1992). Where healing becomes possible. In **Closer to home** (pp. 115-125).

Harris, Jane. (1997). Straight but not narrow: The story of a straight spouse. **In the Family: A Magazine for Gays, Lesbians, Bisexuals and Their Relations**, 2(4), 19-20.

*Jones, Billy, & Peaches Jones. (1991). Growing up with a bisexual dad. In **Bi any other name** (pp. 159-166).

Kalamka, Juba. (1999, Summer). We are family? **Anything That Moves**, (20), 32-35.

Keppel, Bobbi. (1999, Summer). Swimming upstream: Queer families and change. **Anything That Moves**, (20), 12-14.

Key, Mattie. (1991). Never, never boring. In **Bi any other name** (pp. 174-176).

Miller, Marshall, & Dorian Solot. (1999). The fine art of white picket fence-sitting: Bisexuality, marriage, and family diversity. **Anything That Moves**, (20), 20-22.

Montgomery, Michael S. (1997). The marrying kind: Bisexual life, partnered identity. **Journal of Gay, Lesbian, & Bisexual Identity**, 2(1), 77-82.

*Nachama. (1991). Double quest. In **Bi any other name** (pp. 79-82).

Norrgard, Lenore. (1991). Can bisexuals be monogamous? In **Bi any other name** (pp. 281-284).

Peter, Leonie, & Ron Owens. (2001). Forget 2001, It's 20/10 for us. **Journal of Bisexuality**, 1(1), 71-86.

Rose, Sharon. (1996). Against marriage. In **Bisexual horizons** (pp. 119-121).

*Silver, Nina. (1992). Coming out as a heterosexual. In **Closer to home** (pp. 35-46).

Trnka, Susanna. (1992). "A pretty good bisexual kiss there...". In **Closer to home** (pp. 103-113).

*Weise, Elizabeth R. (1991). Bisexuality, *The Rocky Horror Picture Show*, and me. In **Bi any other name** (pp. 134-139).

Yoshizaki, Amanda. (1991). I am who I am— A married bisexual teacher. In **Bi any other name** (pp. 25-26).

Bisexual Youth

Bi-inclusive resources on and for bisexual youth.

For *Books* on bisexual youth, see also the following book section above: *Bi-Inclusive Books*: Under *Identity*: Johnson, 1997. Under *Youth*: Bass & Kaufman, 1996; Owens, 1998; Pollack & Schwartz, 1995; Sanlo, 1998; Sherril & Hardesty, 1994.

Psychological and Sociological Perspectives

*D'Augelli, Anthony R. (1996). Enhancing the development of lesbian, gay, & bisexual youths. In E. D. Rothblum, & L. A. Bond (Eds.), **Preventing heterosexism & homophobia** (pp. 124-150). Thousand Oaks, CA: Sage.

Diamond, Lisa M., Ritch C, Savin-Williams, & Eric M. Dube. (1999). Sex, dating, passionate friendships, and romance: intimate peer relations among lesbian, gay, and bisexual adolescents (pp. 175-210). In E. W. Furman & E. B. B. Brown (Eds.), **The Development of Romantic Relationships in Adolescence.** New York: Cambridge University Press.

Evans, Nancy J., & Anthony R. D'Augelli. (1996). Lesbians, gay men, & bisexual people in college. In R. C. Savin-Williams, & K. M. Cohen (Eds.), **The lives of lesbians, gays, & bisexuals: Children to adults** (pp. 201-226). Fort Worth, TX: Harcourt Brace.

Floyd, Frank J., Terry S. Stein, Kristina S. M. Harter, April Allison, & Cynthia L. Nye. (1999). Gay, lesbian, and bisexual youths: Separation-individuation, parental attitudes, identity consolidation, and well-being. **Journal of Youth & Adolescence**, 28(6).

Harbeck, Karen M. (1993). Invisible no more: Addressing needs of gay, lesbian & bisexual youth & their advocates. **High School Journal,** 77(1-2), 169-176.

Hershberger, Scott L, & Anthony R. D'Augelli. (1995). The impact of victimization on the mental health and suicidality of lesbian, gay, and bisexual youths. **Developmental Psychology**, 31(1), 65-74.

Lock, James, & Hans Steiner. (1999). Gay, lesbian, and bisexual youth risks for emotional, physical, and social problems: Results from a community-based survey. **Journal of the American Academy of Child & Adolescent Psychiatry**, 38(3).

McFarland, William P. (1998). Gay, lesbian, and bisexual student suicide. **Professional School Counseling**, 1(3), 26-29.

Nesmith, Andrea A., David L. Burton, & T. J. Cosgrove. (1999). Gay, lesbian and bisexual youth and young adults: Social support in their own words. **Journal of Homosexuality**, 37(1).

Nichols, Sharon L. (1999). Gay, lesbian, and bisexual youth: Understanding diversity and promoting tolerance in schools. **Elementary School Journal**, 99(5).

Pope, Raechele L., & Amy L. Reynolds. (1991). Including bisexuality: It's more than just a label. In N. J. Evans, & V. A. Wall (Eds.), **Beyond tolerance: Gays, lesbians, and bisexuals on campus** (pp. pp. 205-212). Alexandria, VA: American College Personnel Association.

Savin-Williams, Ritch C. (1995). Lesbian, gay male, & bisexual adolescents. In A. R. D'Augelli, & C. J. Patterson (Eds.), **Lesbian, gay, & bisexual identities over the lifespan: Psychological perspectives** (pp. 165-189). New York: Oxford University Press.

*Savin-Williams, Ritch C. (1996). Self-labeling & disclosure among gay, lesbian, & bisexual youths. In Laird, J. & R-J. Green (Eds.) **Lesbians & gays in couples & families: A handbook for therapists** (pp. 153-182). San Francisco: Jossey-Bass.

Savin Williams, Ritch C. (1998). The disclosure to families of same sex attractions by lesbian, gay, and bisexual youths. **Journal of Research on Adolescence**, 8(1), 49-68.

Personal and Political Perspectives

For *Books* with personal and political perspectives on bisexual youth, see also the following sections above:
Books Specifically on Bisexuality: Bisexual Anthology Collective, 1995; Hutchins & Kaahumanu, 1991; Rose, Stevens & the Off-Pink Collective, 1996; Tucker, 1995; Weise, 1992.
Bi-Inclusive Books: Under *Youth*: Bernstein & Silberman, 1996; Findlen, 1995; Gray, 1999; Mastoon, 1997.

*Arnaoot, Nadya. (1996). Me and my gender(s). In **Generation Q** (pp. 221-223).

Arnaoot, Nadya. (1996). Stone. In **Generation Q** (pp. 146-148).

*Cooper, Charlotte. (1996). Fitting. In **Generation Q** (p. 59-64).

Doza, Christine. (1995). Bloodlove. In **Listen up** (pp. 249-257).

*Gilbert, Laurel. (1995). You're not the type. In **Listen up** (pp. 102-112).

*McDade, Pete. (1996). A difficult floating garden. In **Generation Q** (pp. 102-105).

*Medina, Dalissa. (1996). Tune in, get off, come out: California dreamin' and my age of Aqueerius. In **Generation Q** (pp. 59-64).

Pemberton, Sarah. (1996). *Rocky Horror* schoolgirl. In **Generation Q** (pp. 69-72).

Older Bisexual Women and Bisexual Men

Psychological and Sociological Perspectives

> For *Books* on older bisexual women and bisexual men, see also the following section above:
> *Bi-Inclusive Books*: Under *Relationships & Families*: Buxton, 1994; Gochros, 1989; Marrow, 1997.

Boxer, Andrew M. (1997). Gay, lesbian, and bisexual aging into the twenty-first century: An overview and introduction. **Journal of Gay, Lesbian, & Bisexual Identity**, 3 (3/4), 187-197.

Linsk, Nathan L. (1997). Experience of older gay and bisexual men living with HIV/AIDS. **Journal of Gay, Lesbian, & Bisexual Identity**, 3 (3/4), 265-285.

Personal and Political Perspectives

> For *Books* with personal and political perspectives on older bisexual women and bisexual men, see also the following sections above:
> *Books Specifically on Bisexuality*: Bisexual Anthology Collective, 1995; Hutchins & Kaahumanu, 1991; Kohn & Matusow, 1980; Off Pink Collective, 1988; Rose, Stevens & the Off-Pink Collective, 1996; Tucker, 1995; Weise, 1992.
> *Bi-Inclusive Books*: Under *Relationships & Families*: Abbott & Farmer, 1995; Cassingham & O'Neil, 1993; Faderman, 1991; Scott, 1978; Strock, 1998.

*Keppel, Bobbi. (1991). Gray-haired and above suspicion. In L. Hutchins & L. Kaahumanu. (Eds.), **Bi any other name** (pp. 154-158).

*Utz, Cornelius. (1991). Ninety-three people = 110% acceptance. In **Bi any other name** (pp. 22-24).

Bisexuality & Transgender Persons and Identities

Psychological Perspectives

> For *Books* addressing transgender persons and identities, see also the following section above:

Bi-Inclusive Books: Under **Transgender Persons & Identities**: Denny, 1998.

Bentler, Peter M. (1976). A typology of transsexualism: Gender identity theory and data. **Archives of Sexual Behavior,** 5, 567-584.

Coleman, Eli, Walter O. Bockting, & Louis Gooren. (1993). Homosexual & bisexual identity in sex-reassigned female-to-male transsexuals. **Archives of Sexual Behavior,** 22(1), 37-50.

*Denny, Dallas, & James Green. (1996). Gender identity & bisexuality. In B. A. Firestein (Ed.), **Bisexuality: The psychology & politics of an invisible minority** (pp. 84-102). Thousand Oaks, CA: Sage.

*Devor, Holly. (1993). Sexual orientation identities, attractions, & practices of female-to-male transsexuals. **Journal of Sex Research,** 30(4), 303-315.

Gainor, Kathy A. (2000). Including transgender issues in lesbian, gay, and bisexual psychology: Implications for clinical practice and training. B. Greene, & G. L. Croom (Eds.), **Education, research, and practice in lesbian, gay, bisexual, and transgendered psychology: A resource manual** (pp. 131-160). Thousand Oaks, CA: Sage.

*Green, Jamison. (1998). FTM: An emerging voice. In D. Denny (Ed.), **Current concepts in transgender identity** (pp. 145-162). New York: Garland.

Miller, Marshall. (1998, Spring). Transman Matt Rice on the new queer identity. **Anything That Moves,** (16)42-45.

Pauly, Ira B. (1990). Gender identity and sexual preference. In D. Denny (Ed.), **Current concepts in transgender identity** (pp. 237-248). New York: Garland.

Personal and Political Perspectives

For *Books* with personal and political perspectives on transgender persons and identities, see also the following section above:
Bi-Inclusive Books: Under *Transgender Persons & Identities*: Wilchins, 1997.

*Antoniou, Laura. (1997). Antivenom for the soul. In C. Queen, & L. Schimel (Eds.), **Pomosexuals: Challenging assumptions about gender and sexuality** (pp. 114-121). San Francisco: Cleis Press.

Franek, Heather. (1998, Summer). Talking about the issues no one's expressing: Telling it like it is in the world of bi-trans romance. **Anything That Moves,** 17, 28-31.

Harrison, David. (1997). The personals. In C. Queen, & L. Schimel (Eds.), **Pomosexuals: Challenging assumptions about gender and sexuality** (pp. 129-137). San Francisco: Cleis Press.

*Hemmings, Clare. (1996). From lesbian nation to transgender liberation: A bisexual feminist perspective. **Journal of Gay, Lesbian, & Bisexual Identity,** 1(1), 37-60.

Martin-Damon, Kory. (1995). Essay for the inclusion of transsexuals. In **Bisexual politics** (pp. 241-250).

Michaela-Gonzalez, Andrea. (1998, Summer). It's what you think you see that counts: True tales from the edges of the bi-trans continuum. **Anything That Moves,** 17, 22-25.

*O'Connor, Rachel. (1996). The transgender identity as a political challenge. In **Bisexual horizons** (pp. 243-246).

Valerio, Max Wolf. (1998, Summer). The joker is wild: Changing sex and other crimes of passion. **Anything That Moves**, 17, 32-36.

*Wilchins, Riki Anne. (1997). Lines in the sand, cries of desire. In C. Queen, & L. Schimel (Eds.), **Pomosexuals: Challenging assumptions about gender and sexuality** (pp. 138-149). San Francisco: Cleis Press.

Bisexuality and Ethnic, Racial, & Cultural Diversity

> For *Books* on bisexuality and ethnic, racial, & cultural diversity, see also the following sections above:
> *Books Specifically on Bisexuality*: Aggleton, 1996; Cantarella, 1992; Tielman, Carballo & Hendriks, 1991.
> *Bi-Inclusive Books*: Under *Ethnic, Racial, & Cultural Diversity*: Asian & Pacific Islander Wellness Center, 1997.

Overview

*Rust, Paula C. (1996). Managing multiple identities: Diversity among bisexual women & men. In B. A. Firestein (Ed.), **Bisexuality: The psychology & politics of an invisible minority** (pp. 53-83). Thousand Oaks, CA: Sage.

Smith, Althea. (1997). Cultural diversity and the coming-out process: Implications for clinical practice. In B. Greene (Ed.), **Ethnic and cultural diversity among lesbians and gay men** (pp. 279-300). Thousand Oaks, CA: Sage.

Psychological and Sociological Perspectives

*Carballo-Diéguez, Alex. (1995). The sexual identity & behavior of Puerto Rican men who have sex with men. In G. M. Herek, & B. Greene (Eds.), **AIDS, identity, & community: The HIV epidemic & lesbians & gay men** (pp. 105-114). Thousand Oaks, CA: Sage.

Collins, J. Fuji. (2000). Biracial-bisexual individuals: Identity coming of age. **International Journal of Sexuality & Gender Studies**, 5(3), 221-253.

Fukuyama, Mary A., & Ferguson, Angela D. (2000). Lesbian, gay, and bisexual people of color: Understanding cultural complexity and managing multiple oppressions. In R. M. Perez, K. A. DeBord, & K. J. Bieschke (Eds.), **Handbook of counseling and psychotherapy with lesbian, gay, and bisexual clients** (pp. 81-105). Washington, DC: American Psychological Association.

Greene, Beverly. (2000). African American lesbian and bisexual women. **Journal of Social Issues**, 56(2), 239-250.

*Kochems, Lee M., & Sue-Ellen Jacobs. (1997). Gender statuses, gender features, & gender/sex categories: New perspectives on an old paradigm. In S. E. Jacobs, W. Thomas, & S. Lang (Eds.), **Two-spirit people: Native American gender identity, sexuality, & spirituality** (pp. 255-264). Urbana, IL: University of Illinois Press.

*Lang, Sabine. (1997). Various kinds of Two-spirit people: Gender variance & homosexuality in Native American Communities. In S. E. Jacobs, W. Thomas, & S. Lang (Eds.), **Two-spirit people: Native American gender identity, sexuality, & spirituality** (pp. 100-118). Urbana, IL: University of Illinois Press.

Liu, Peter. & Connie S. Chan. (1996). Lesbian, gay, & bisexual Asian Americans & their families. In Laird, J. & R-J. Green (Eds.) **Lesbians & gays in couples & families: A handbook for therapists** (pp. 137-152). San Francisco: Jossey-Bass.

Manalansan , Martin F IV. (1996). Double minorities: Latino, Black, & Asian who have sex with men. R. C. Savin-Williams, & K. M. Cohen (Eds.), **The lives of lesbians, gays, & bisexuals: Children to adults** (pp. 393-415). Fort Worth, TX: Harcourt Brace.

*Morales, Eduardo S. (1996). Gender roles among Latino gay & bisexual men: Implications for family & couple relationships. In Laird, J. & R-J. Green (Eds.), **Lesbians & gays in couples & families: A handbook for therapists** (pp. 272-297). San Francisco: Jossey-Bass.

Williams, Walter L. (1996). Two-spirit persons: Gender nonconformity among Native American & Native Hawaiian youths. In R. C. Savin-Williams, & K. M. Cohen (Eds.), **The lives of lesbians, gays, & bisexuals: Children to adults** (pp. 416-435). Ft. Worth, TX: Harcourt Brace.

Zamora-Hernandez, Carlos E., & Davis G. Patterson. (1996). Homosexually active Latino men: Issues for social work practice. In John F. Longres (Ed.), **Men of color: A context for service to homosexually active men** (pp. 69-91). New York: Harrington Park Press.

Anthropological and Cross-Cultural Perspectives

For *Books* on anthropological and cross-cultural perspectives on bisexuality, see also the following sections above:
Books Specifically on Bisexuality: Aggleton (1996) contains chapters on bisexuality in Australia, Brazil, Canada, China, Costa Rica, the Dominican Republic, France, India, Mexico, Papua New Guinea, Peru, the Philippines, and the UKTielman (1991) contains chapters on bisexuality in Australia, India, Indonesia, Latin America, Mexico, the Netherlands, New Zealand, Sub-Saharan Africa, Thailand, the U. K., and the United States.
Bi-Inclusive Books: Under *Ethnic, Racial, & Cultural Diversity*: Blackwood & Wieringa, 1999; Brown, 1997; Carrier, 1995; Herdt, 1984; Hinsch, 1984; Hinsch, 1990; Leong, 1996; Leupp, 1995; Murray, 1984, 1987, 1992, 2000; Murray & Roscoe, 1998; Ruan, 1991; Schmitt & Sofer; Saikaku, 1990; Schifter, 2000; Schifter & Pana, 2000; Seabrook, 1999; Watanabe & Jun'ichi, 1987.

Adam, Barry D. (1985). Age, structure, & sexuality: Reflections of the anthropological evidence on homosexual relations. **Journal of Homosexuality**, 11(3/4), 19-34.

Blackwood, Evelyn. (1985). Breaking the mirror: The construction of lesbianism & the anthropological discourse on homosexuality. **Journal of Homosexuality**, 11(3/4), 1-18.

*Callender, Charles, & Lee M. Kochems. (1985). Men & not-men: Male gender-mixing statuses & homosexuality. **Journal of Homosexuality**, 11(3-4), 165-178.

*Carrier, Joseph M. (1985). Mexican male bisexuality. **Journal of Homosexuality,** 11(1/2), 75-86.

De Cecco, John P. (1998). Bisexuality and discretion: The case of Pakistan. In E. J. Haeberle, & R. Gindorf (Eds.), **Bisexualities: The ideology and practice of sexual contact with both men and women** (pp. 152-156). New York: Continuum.

Herdt, Gilbert H. (1984). A comment on cultural attributes & fluidity of bisexuality. **Journal of Homosexuality,** 10(3/4), 53-62.

Wong, Joseph. (1998). Bisexuality in early Imperial China: An introductory overview. In E. J. Haeberle, & R. Gindorf (Eds.), **Bisexualities: The ideology and practice of sexual contact with both men and women** (pp. 140-151). New York: Continuum.

Personal and Political Perspectives

For *Books* with personal and political perspectives on bisexuality and ethnic, racial, & cultural diversity, see also the following sections above: *Books Specifically on Bisexuality*: Bisexual Anthology Collective, 1995; Hutchins & Kaahumanu, 1991; Rose, Stevens & the Off-Pink Collective, 1996; Tucker, 1995; Weise, 1992.
Bi-Inclusive Books: Under *Ethnic, Racial, & Cultural Diversity*: Lim-Hing, 1994; Ratti, 1993.

*Acharya, Leela, Amina, Amita, Farzana Doctor, & Gogia. (1995). "Purifying" the (identi)ghee: South Asian feminists **Gup-shup**. In **Plural desires** (pp. 101-118).

Alexander, Christopher. (1991). Affirmation: Bisexual Mormon. In **Bi any other name** (pp. 193-197).

Barlow, Valerie. (1996). Bisexuality and feminism: One Black women's perspective. In **Bisexual horizons** (pp. 38-40).

Blasingame, Brenda. (1991). The palmist knew. In **Bi any other name** (pp. 144-146).

Chaudhary, Kamini. (1993). The scent of roses. In R. Ratti (Ed.), **A lotus of another color: An unfolding of the South Asian gay and lesbian experience** (pp. 145-150).

Chaudhary, Kamini. (1993). Some thoughts on bisexuality. In R. Ratti (Ed.), **A lotus of another color: An unfolding of the South Asian gay and lesbian experience** (pp. 54-58).

Chen, Shu Wei— Andy. (1991). A man, a woman, attention. In **Bi any other name** (pp. 179-180).

*Choe, Margaret Mihee. (1992). Our selves, growing whole. In **Closer to home** (pp. 17-26).

*Dajenya. (1991). Sisterhood crosses gender preference lines. In **Bi any other name** (pp. 247-251).

Fehr, Tracy Charette. (1995). Accepting my inherent duality. In **Plural desires** (pp. 128-129).

*Gollain, Françoise. (1996). Bisexuality in the Arab world: An interview with Muhammed. In **Bisexual horizons** (pp. 58-61).

Gorlin, Rebecca. (1991). The voice of a wandering Jewish bisexual. In **Bi any other name** (pp. 252-253).

*Jadallah, Huda, & Pearl Saad. (1995). A conversation about the Arab Lesbian and Bisexual Women's Network. In **Plural desires** (pp. 252-259).

*Kaahumanu, Lani. (1991). Hapa haole wahine. In **Bi any other name** (pp. 306-325).

*Lakshmi & Arka. (1993). Extended family. In R. Ratti (Ed.), **A lotus of another color: An unfolding of the South Asian gay and lesbian experience** (pp. 265-278).

Lee, Jee Yeun. (1995). Beyond bean counting. In B. Findlen (Ed.), **Listen up: Voices from the next feminist generation** (pp. 205-211). Seattle: Seal Press.

*Leyva, Obie. (1991). ¿Que es un bisexual? In **Bi any other name** (pp. 201-202).

Paul. (1996). On being bisexual and black in Britain. In **Bisexual horizons** (pp. 95-99).

*Pollon, Zélie. (1995). Naming her destiny: June Jordan speaks on bisexuality. In **Plural desires** (pp. 77-82).

*Prabhudas, Yasmin. (1996). Bisexuals and people of mixed-race: Arbiters of change. In **Bisexual horizons** (pp. 30-31).

Reichler, Rifka. (1991). A question of invisibility. In **Bi any other name** (pp. 77-78).

*Rios, Joe. (1991). What do Indians think about? In **Bi any other name** (pp. 37-39).

*Silver, Alan. (1991). Worth the balancing. In **Bi any other name** (pp. 27-28).

Som, Indigo Chih-Lien. (1995). The queer kitchen. Bisexual Anthology Collective (Eds.), **Plural desires** (pp. 84-88).

*Tucker, Naomi. (1996). Passing: Pain or privilege? What the bisexual community can learn from the Jewish experience. In **Bisexual horizons** (pp. 32-37).

Uwano, Kei. (1991). Bi-loveable Japanese feminist. In **Bi any other name** (pp. 185-187).

*Whang, Selena J. (1991). [untitled]. In **Bi any other name** (pp. 177-178).

Bisexuality & HIV/AIDS

For *Books* on bisexuality & HIV/AIDS, see also the following sections above:
Books Specifically on Bisexuality: Aggleton, 1996; Sigma Research,1996; Tielman, Carballo & Hendriks, 1991.

Overview

Bajos, N., J. Wadsworth, B. Ducot, A. Johnson, F. Le Pont, K. Wellings, A. Spira, & J. Field. (1995). Sexual behaviour & HIV epidemiology: Comparative analysis in France & Britain. The ACSF Group. **AIDS**, 9(7), 735-43.

*Doll, Lynda S., Ted Myers, Meaghan Kennedy, & Dan Allman. (1997). Bisexuality & HIV risk: Experiences in Canada & the United States. **Annual Review of Sex Research**, VIII, 102-147.

Rust, Paula C. Rodríguez. (2000). Bisexuality in HIV research. In P. C. R. Rust (Ed.), **Bisexuality in the United States: A Social Science Reader** (pp. 355-400). New York: Columbia University Press.

Bisexuality, Women, & HIV/AIDS

*Gómez, Cynthia A., Delia Garcia, Valerie J. Kegebein, Starley B. Shade, & Sandra R. Hernandez. (1996). Sexual identity versus sexual behavior: Implications for HIV prevention strategies for women who have sex with women. **Women's Health: Research on Gender, Behavior, & Policy**, 2(1/2), 91-110.

Moore, Jan, Dora Warren, Sally Zierler, Paula Schuman, Liza Solomon, Ellie E. Schoenbaum, & Meaghan Kennedy. (1996). Characteristics of HIV-infected lesbians & bisexual women in four urban centers. **Women's Health: Research on Gender, Behavior, & Policy**, 2(1/2), 49-60.

Rila, Margo. (1996). Bisexual women & the AIDS crisis. In B. A. Firestein (Ed.), **Bisexuality: The psychology & politics of an invisible minority** (pp. 169-184). Thousand Oaks, CA: Sage.

Ziemba-Davis, Mary, Stephanie A. Sanders, & June Machover Reinisch. (1996). Lesbians' sexual interactions with men: Behavioral bisexuality & risk for sexually transmitted disease (STD) & Human Immunodeficiency Virus (HIV). **Women's Health: Research on Gender, Behavior, & Policy**, 2(1/2), 61-74.

Bisexuality, Men, & HIV/AIDS

*Aoki, Bart, Chiang Peng Ngin, Bertha Mo, & Davis Y. Ja. (1989). AIDS prevention models in Asian-American communities. In V. M. Mays, G. W. Albee, & S. F. Schneider (Eds.), Primary Prevention of AIDS: Psychological Approaches (pp. 290-308). Newbury Park, CA: Sage.

*Boulton, Mary, Graham Hart, & Ray Fitzpatrick. (1992). The sexual behaviour of bisexual men in relation to HIV transmission. **AIDS Care**, 4(2), 165-175.

Chu, Susan Y., Thomas A. Peterman, Lynda S. Doll, James W. Buehler, & James W. Curran. (1992). AIDS in bisexual men in the United States: Epidemiology & transmission to women. **American Journal of Public Health**, 82(2), 220-224.

Davis, Mark, Gary Dowsett, & Ullo Klemmer. (1996). On the beat: A report on the Bisexually Active Men's Outreach project. In **Bisexual horizons** (pp. 188-199).

Diaz, Rafael M., Eduardo S. Morales, Edward Bein, Eugene Dilan, & Richard A. Rodriguez. (1999). Predictors of sexual risk in Latino gay/bisexual men: The role of demographic, developmental, social cognitive, and behavioral variables. **Hispanic Journal of Behavioral Sciences**, 21(4).

*Diaz, Theresa, Susan Y. Chu, Margaret Frederick, Pat Hermann, Anna Levy, Eve Mokotoff, Bruce Whyte, Lisa Conti, Mary Herr, Patricia J., Cornelis A. Rietmeijer, Frank Sorvillo, & Quaiser Mukhtar. (1993). Sociodemographics & HIV risk behaviors of bisexual men with AIDS: Results from a multistate interview project. **AIDS**, 7(9), 1227-1232.

Kegeles, Susan M., & , Joseph A. Catania. (1991). Understanding bisexual men's AIDS risk behavior: The risk-reduction model. In R. A. P. Tielman, M. Carballo, & A. C. Hendriks (Eds.), **Bisexuality & HIV/AIDS: A global perspective** (pp. 139-147). Buffalo, NY: Prometheus.

*Magaña, J. Raul, & Joseph M. Carrier. (1991). Mexican & Mexican American male sexual behavior & spread of AIDS in California. **Journal of Sex Research**, 28(3), 425-441.

Matteson, David R. (1997). Bisexual and homosexual behavior and HIV risk among Chinese-, Filipino- and Korean-American men. **Journal of Sex Research**, 34(1), 93-104.

Morales, Eduardo S. (1990). HIV infection & Hispanic gay & bisexual men. **Hispanic Journal of Behavioral Sciences**, 12(2), 212-222.

Nemoto, Tooru, Frank Y. Wong, Alison Ching, Chwee Hye Chng, Paul Bouey, Mark Henrickson, & Robert E. Sember. (1998). HIV seroprevalence, risk behaviors, and cognitive factors among Asian and Pacific Islander American men who have sex with men: A summary and critique of empirical studies and methodological issues. **AIDS Education and Prevention**, 10(Supplement A), 31-47.

Peterson, John L. (1995). AIDS-related risks & same-sex behaviors among African American men. In G. M. Herek, & B. Greene (Eds.), **AIDS, identity, & community: The HIV epidemic & lesbians & gay men** (pp. 85-104). Thousand Oaks, CA: Sage.

Roffman, R. A., J. Picciano, L. Wickizer, M. Bolan, & R. Ryan. (1998). Anonymous enrollment in AIDS prevention telephone group counseling: Facilitating the participation of gay and bisexual men in intervention and research. **Journal of Social Service Research**, 23, 5-22.

Roffman, R.A., R.S. Stephens, L. Curtin, J.R. Gordon, J.N. Craver, M. Stern, B. Beadnell, & L. Downey. (1998). Relapse prevention as an interventive model for HIV risk reduction in gay and bisexual men. **Aids Education and Prevention**, 10(1), 1-18.

Stokes, Joseph P., Kittiwut Taywaditep, Peter Vanable, & David J. McKirnan. (1996). Bisexual men, sexual behavior, & HIV/AIDS. In B. A. Firestein (Ed.), **Bisexuality: The psychology & politics of an invisible minority** (pp. 149-168). Thousand Oaks, CA: Sage.

Tafoya, Terry. (1989). Pulling coyote's tale: Native American sexuality & AIDS. In V. M. Mays, G. W. Albee, & S. F. E. Schneider (Eds.), **Primary prevention of AIDS: Psychological approaches** (pp. 280-28). Newbury Park, CA: Sage.

Wong, Frank Y., Chwee Lye Chng, & Wilson Lo. (1998). A profile of six community based HIV prevention programs targeting Asian and Pacific Islander Americans. **AIDS Education and Prevention**, 10((Suppl 3)), 61-76.

*Wood, Robert W., Leigh E. Krueger, Tsilke C. Pearlman, & Gary Goldbaum. (1993). HIV transmission: Women's risk from bisexual men. **American Journal of Public Health**, 83(12), 1757-9.

*Wright, Jerome W. (1993). African-American male sexual behavior & the risk for HIV infection. **Human Organization**, 52(4), 431-431.

Bisexual Youth & HIV/AIDS

Bettencourt, Troix, Antigone Hodgins, G. J. Huba, & Gilbert Pickett. (1998). Bay area young positives: A model of a youth based approach to HIV/AIDS services. **Journal of Adolescent Health**, 23(2), 28-36.

*Cochran, Susan D., & Vicki M. Mays. (1996). Prevalence of HIV-related sexual risk behaviors among young 18 to 24 year-old lesbian & bisexual women. **Women's Health: Research on Gender, Behavior, & Policy**, 2(1/2), 75-90.

Cranston, Kevin. (1991). HIV education for gay, lesbian, & bisexual youth: Personal risk, personal power, & the community of conscience. **Journal of Homosexuality**, 22(3/4), 247-259.

*Hayes, Robert B., & Susan M. Kegeles. (1991). HIV/AIDS risks for bisexual adolescents. In R. A. P. Tielman, M. Carballo, & A. C. Hendriks (Eds.), **Bisexuality & HIV/AIDS: A global perspective** (pp. 165-174). Buffalo, NY: Prometheus.

Rosario, Margaret, Heino F. L. Meyer-Bahlburg, Joyce Hunter, & Marya Gwadz. (1999). Sexual risk behaviors of gay, lesbian, and bisexual youths in New York City: Prevalence and correlates. **Aids Education & Prevention**, 11(6).

*Rotheram-Borus, Mary Jane, & Cheryl Koopman. (1991). Sexual risk behavior, AIDS knowledge, & beliefs about AIDS among predominantly minority gay & bisexual male adolescents. **AIDS Education & Prevention**, 3(4), 305-312.

Transgendered Persons and HIV/AIDS

Bockting, Walter O., B. E. Robinson, & B. R. Simon Rosser. (1998). Transgender HIV prevention: A qualitative needs assessment. **AIDS Care**, 10, 505-526.

Nemoto, Tooru, D. Luke, L. Mamo, A. Ching, & J. Patria. (1999). HIV risk behaviours among male-to-female transgenders in comparison with homosexual or bisexual males and heterosexual females. **Aids Care**, 11(3).

Personal and Political Perspectives

Bishop, Dolores. (1991). Another senseless loss. In **Bi any other name** (pp. 258-260).

Danzig, Alexis. (1990). Bisexual women & AIDS. In **The ACT UP/New York Women and AIDS Book Group** (pp. 193-198). Boston: South End Press.

Dutton, Jackie. (1996). It's about numbers. In **Bisexual horizons** (pp. 169-175).

George, Sue. (1996). HIV, AIDS and safer sex: Introduction. In **Bisexual horizons** (pp. 159-165).

Highleyman, Liz. (1996). Bisexuals and AIDS. In **Bisexual horizons** (pp. 166-168).

Lawrence, Robert Morgan, & Queen, Carol. (2001). Bisexuals help create the standards for safer sex: San Francisco, 1981-1987. **Journal of Bisexuality**, 1(1), 145-162.

Lourea, David. (1991). Just another lingering flu. In **Bi any other name** (pp. 99-102).

Sands, David. (1996). Tony. In **Bisexual horizons** (pp. 211-213).

Stewart, Hap. (1991). A healing journey. In **Bi any other name** (pp. 147-150).

Stewart, Hap. (1994, Spring). Surviving HIV: Some thoughts for my brothers and sisters. **Anything That Moves**, (7), 41, 42, 51.

Wright, Joe. (1998, Spring). Surviving the storm: Bisexual men and HIV. **Anything That Moves**, 16, 34-37.

Health Care, Counseling, and Psychotherapy

For *Books* on bisexuality and psychology, and on affirmative approaches to health care, counseling and psychotherapy with bisexual persons, see also the following sections above:

Books Specifically on Bisexuality: Firestein, 1996; Klein, 1993; Wolff, 1979. In German: Gooß, 1995; Hüsers & König, 1995.*Bi-Inclusive Books*: Under *Identity*: D'Augelli & Patterson, 1995; Savin-Williams & Cohen, 1996. Under *Health Care, Counseling, & Psychotherapy*: Appleby & Anastas, 1998; Cabaj & Stein, 1996; Eliason , 1996; Gruskin, 1999; Hunter, 1998; Kominars & Kominars 1996; Longres, 1996; Neal, 2000; Niesen, 1994; Perez, DeBord, & Bieschke, 2000.

American Psychological Association. (2000). **Guidelines for Psychotherapy with Lesbian, Gay, and Bisexual Clients.** Washington, DC: American Psychological Association. Available online at: http://www.apa.org/pi/lgbc/publications/guidelines.html

Dworkin, Sari H. (2000). Individual therapy with lesbian, gay, and bisexual clients. In R. M. Perez, K. A. DeBord, & K. J. Bieschke (Eds.), **Handbook of counseling and psychotherapy with lesbian, gay, and bisexual clients** (pp. 157-181). Washington, DC: American Psychological Association.

Falco, Kristine L. (1996). Psychotherapy with women who love women. In R. P. Cabaj & T. S. Stein, **Textbook of homosexuality & mental health** (pp. 397-412). Washington, DC: American Psychiatric Press.

Fassinger, Ruth E. (2000). Applying counseling theories to lesbian, gay, and bisexual clients: Pitfalls and possibilities. In R. M. Perez, K. A. DeBord, & K. J. Bieschke (Eds.), **Handbook of counseling and psychotherapy with lesbian, gay, and bisexual clients** (pp. 107-131). Washington, DC: American Psychological Association.

*Lourea, David. (1985). Psycho-social issues related to counseling bisexuals. **Journal of Homosexuality**, 11(1/2), 51-62.

*Markowitz, Laura M. (1995). Bisexuality: Challenging our either/or thinking. **In the Family: A Magazine for Lesbians, Gays, Bisexuals & their Relations**, 1(1), 6-11, 23.

*Matteson, David R. (1996). Counseling & psychotherapy with bisexual & exploring clients. In B. A. Firestein (Ed.), **Bisexuality: The psychology & politics of an invisible minority** (pp. 185-213). Thousand Oaks, CA: Sage.

Morrow, Susan L. (2000). First do no harm: Therapist issues in psychotherapy with lesbian, gay, and bisexual clients. In R. M. Perez, K. A. DeBord, & K. J. Bieschke (Eds.), **Handbook of counseling and psychotherapy with lesbian, gay, and bisexual clients** (pp. 137-155). Washington, DC: American Psychological Association.

Nichols, Margaret. (1989). Sex therapy with lesbians, gay men, & bisexuals. In S. R. Leiblum, & R. C. Rosen (Eds.), **Principles & practice of sex therapy: Update for the 1990s** (2nd ed.). (pp. 269-297). New York: Guilford.

Poelzl, Linda. (2001). Bisexual issues in sex therapy: A bisexual surrogate partner relates her experiences from the field. **Journal of Bisexuality**, 1(1), 121-142.

Weasel, Lisa H. (1996). Seeing between the lines: Bisexual women & therapy. **Women & Therapy,** 19(2), 5-16.

Wolf, T. J. (1987). Group counseling for bisexual men. **Journal of Homosexuality**, 14(1/2), 162-165.

Wolf, T. J. (1987). Group psychotherapy for bisexual men & their wives. **Journal of Homosexuality**, 14(1/2), 191-199.

Attitudes toward Bisexuality: Biphobia, Heterosexism, Discrimination

For *Books* on attitudes toward bisexuality, see also the following sections above: *Books Specifically on Bisexuality*: For psychological and sociological perspectives: Colker (1996), Eliason (1996), and Rust (1995).Firestein, 1996; Klein, 1993; Wolff, 1979. In German: Gooß, 1995; Hüsers & König, 1995. For personal and political perspectives: Archivo Lesbico y de Mujeres Diferentes, 1998; Bisexual Anthology Collective, 1995; Hutchins & Kaahumanu, 1991; Off-Pink Collective, 1988; Rose, Stevens & the Off-Pink Collective, 1996; Tucker, 1995; and Weise, 1992.

Bi-Inclusive Books: Under *Psychology, Sociology, and Bisexuality*: Bohan, 1996; D'Augelli & Patterson (1995), Cabaj & Stein (1996), Eliason (1996); Savin-Williams & Cohen, 1996.

Blasingame, Brenda M. (1992). The roots of biphobia: Racism & internalized heterosexism. In **Closer to home** (pp. 47-54).

Eliason, Michele J. (1996). A survey of the campus climate for lesbian, gay, & bisexual university members. **Journal of Psychology & Human Sexuality**, 8, 39-58.

*Eliason, Michele J. (1997). The prevalence & nature of biphobia in heterosexual undergraduate students. **Archives of Sexual Behavior**, 26(3), 317-325.

*Kaplan, Rebecca (1992). Compulsory heterosexuality & the bisexual existence: Toward a bisexual feminist understanding of heterosexism. In **Closer to home** (pp. 269-280).

Mohr, Jonathan J., & Aaron B. Rochlen. (1999). Measuring attitudes regarding bisexuality in lesbian, gay male, and heterosexual populations. **Journal of Counseling Psychology**, 46(3).

*Ochs, Robyn. (1996). Biphobia: It goes more than two ways. In B. A. Firestein (Ed.), **Bisexuality: The psychology & politics of an invisible minority** (pp. 217-239). Thousand Oaks, CA: Sage.

Ochs, Robyn, & Marcia Deihl. (1992). Moving beyond binary thinking. In W. Blumenfeld (Ed.), **Homophobia: How we all pay the price** (pp. 67-75). Boston: Beacon. Reprint appears in M. Adams, W. J. Blumenfeld, R. Castañeda, H. W. Hackman, M. L. Peters, & X. Zúñiga (Eds.). (2000). **Readings for diversity and social justice: An anthology on racism, antisemitism, sexism, heterosexism, ableism, and classism,** (pp. 276-280). New York: Routledge.

Rust, Paula C. (1993). Neutralizing the political threat of the marginal woman: Lesbians' beliefs about bisexual women. **Journal of Sex Research**, 30(3), 214-228. Reprint appears in P. C. R. Rust, **Bisexuality in the United States: A Social Science Reader**, pp. 471-497.

*Spalding, Leah R., & Letitia Anne Peplau. (1997). The unfaithful lover: Heterosexuals' perceptions of bisexuals & their relationships. **Psychology of Women Quarterly, 21**(4), 611-625.

Udis-Kessler, Amanda. (1991). Present tense: Biphobia as a crisis of meaning. In **Bi any other name** (350-358).

Bisexuality and Feminism

For books on bisexuality & feminism, see also the following sections above: *Books Specifically on Bisexuality*: Bisexual Anthology Collective, 1995; George, 1993; Hutchins & Kaahumanu, 1991; Rose, Stevens & the Off-Pink Collective, 1996; Tucker, 1995; and Weise, 1992. In *Spanish*: Archivo Lesbico y de Mujeres Diferentes, 1998.

Bi-Inclusive Books: Under *Identity*: Atkins, 1996; Burch, 1994; Esterberg, 1997. Under *Youth*: Findlen, 1995. Under *Ethnic, Racial, & Cultural Diversity*: Lim-Hing, 1994; Ratti, 1993.

Armstrong, E. (1995). Traitors to the cause? Understanding the lesbian/gay "bisexuality" debates. In **Bisexual politics** (pp. 199-218).

Ault, Amber. (1996). Ambiguous identity in an unambiguous sex/gender structure: The case of bisexual women. **Sociological Quarterly**, 37(3), 449-463.

Ault, Amber. (1996). Hegemonic discourse in an oppositional community: Lesbian feminist stigmatization of bisexual women. In B. Beemyn, & M. Eliason. (Eds.), **Queer studies: A lesbian, gay, bisexual, and transgender anthology** (pp. 204-216). New York: NYU Press.

Baker, Karin. (1992). Bisexual feminist politics: Because bisexuality is not enough. In **Closer to home** (pp. 255-268).

Bisexual Anthology Collective. (1995). Toward a feminist bisexual politic: A discussion. In **Plural desires** (pp. 210-225).

Bloomsbury, Angela. (1998). The politics of erotics: Bisexuality, feminism and S/M. **In the Family: A Magazine for Gays, Lesbians, Bisexuals and Their Relations**, 3(4), 16-19.

Bower, Tamara. (1995). Bisexual women, *feminist* politics. In **Bisexual politics** (pp. 99-108).

Came, Heather. (1996). Towards a free and loose future. In **Bisexual horizons** (pp. 25-29).

Choe, Margaret Mihee. (1992). Our selves, growing whole. In **Closer to home** (pp. 17-26).

Elliott, Beth. (1991). Bisexuality: The best thing that ever happened to lesbian-feminism? In Hutchins & Kaahumanu (Eds.), **Bi any other name** (pp. 324-328).

Eliott, Beth. (1992). Holly near and yet so far. In **Closer to home** (pp. 233-254).

Friedland, Lucy, & Liz A. Highleyman. (1991). The fine art of labeling: The convergence of anarchism, feminism, and bisexuality. In **Bi any other name** (pp. 285-298).

*Golden, Carla. (1994). Our politics and choices: The feminist movement and sexual orientation. In B. Greene G. M. Herek (Eds.), **Lesbian and gay psychology: Theory, research, and clinical applications** (pp. 54-70). Thousand Oaks, CA: Sage.

Gregory, Deborah. (1983). From where I stand: A case for feminist bisexuality. In S. Cartledge, & J. Ryan (Eds.), **Sex and love: New thoughts on old contradictions** (pp. 141-156). London: The Women's Press.

Hemmings, Clare. (1995). Locating bisexual identities: Discourses of bisexuality and contemporary feminist theory. In D. Bell, & G. Valentine (Eds.), **Mapping desire: Geographies of sexualities** (pp. 41-54). London: Routledge.

Higgenbotham, Anastassia. (1995). Chicks goin' at it. In B. Findlen (Ed.), **Listen up: Voices from the next feminist generation** (pp. 3-11). Seattle: Seal Press.

*Kaplan, Rebecca. (1992). Compulsory heterosexuality and the bisexual existence: Toward a bisexual feminist understanding of heterosexism. In **Closer to home** (pp. 269-280).

Matteson, Dave. (1991). Bisexual feminist man. In Hutchins & Kaahumanu (Eds.), **Bi any other name** (pp. 43-50).

Murray, Annie S. (1995). Forsaking all others: A bifeminist discussion of compulsory monogamy. In **Bisexual politics** (pp. 293-304).

Ochs, Robyn. (1992). Bisexuality, feminism, men and me. In **Closer to home** (pp. 127-132). Reprint appears in A. Desselman, L. McNair, & N. Schniedewind (Eds.). (1999). **Women: images and realities: A multicultural anthology** (pp. 155-157). Mountainview, CA: Mayfield Publishing.

Parr, Zaidie. (1996). Feminist bisexuals in the U.K.— Caught between a rock and a hard place? In **Bisexual horizons** (pp. 274-280).

Schneider, Anne. (1991). Guilt politics. In **Bi any other name** (pp. 275-278). Boston: Alyson.

*Sturgis, Susan. M. (1996). Bisexual feminism: Challenging the splits. In **Bisexual horizons** (pp. 41-44).

Terris, Ellen. (1991). My life as a lesbian-identified bisexual fag hag. In **Bi any other name** (pp. 56-59).

*Udis-Kessler, Amanda. (1992). Closer to home: Bisexual feminism and the transformation of hetero/sexism. In **Closer to home** (pp. 205-232).

Uwano, Kei. (1991). Bi-lovable Japanese feminist. In **Bi any other name** (pp. 185-187).

*Weise, Elizabeth R., & Bennett, Kathleen. (1992). Feminist bisexuality: A both/and option for an either/or world. In **Closer to home** (pp. 205-231).

Yoshizaki, Amanda. (1992). Breaking the rules: Constructing a bisexual feminist marriage. In **Closer to home** (pp. 155-162).

*Young, Stacey. (1992). Breaking silence about the "B-word": Bisexual identity and lesbian-feminist discourse. In **Closer to home** (75-87).

Woodard, Victoria. (1991). Insights at 3:30 a.m. In **Bi any other name** (pp. 83-86).

Zabatinsky, Vashti. (1992). Some thoughts on power, gender, body image and sex in the life of one bisexual lesbian feminist. In **Closer to home** (pp. 133-146).

Bisexuality and Spirituality

For books on bisexuality & spirituality, see also the following sections above:
Books Specifically on Bisexuality: Kolodny, 2000.
Bi-Inclusive Books: Under *Identity*: Atkins, 1996; Burch, 1994; Esterberg, 1997. Under *Youth*: Findlen, 1995. Under *Spirituality*: Connor, Sparks & Sparks, 1997; Kimball, 2000; Sweezey, 1997; Tigert, 1996.

Psychological and sociological perspectives

Davidson, Mary Gage. (2000). Religion and spirituality. In R. M. Perez, K. A. DeBord, & K. J. Bieschke (Eds.), **Handbook of counseling and psychotherapy with lesbian, gay, and bisexual clients** (pp. 409-433). Washington, DC: American Psychological Association.

Personal perspectives

Chapman, Guy. (1996). Roots of a male bisexual nature. In **Bisexual horizons** (pp. 62-69).

de Sousa, Elehna. (1995). In the spirit of Aloha: to love is to share the happiness of life here & now. In **Plural desires** (pp. 145-149).

Drake, Kelly. (1996). Bisexuality and spirituality. In **Bisexual horizons** (pp. 111-113).

Farajajé-Jones, Elias. (1994, Spring). Currents of the spirit. **Anything That Moves**, 7, 8-9.

Fehr, Tracy Charette. (1995). Accepting my inherent duality. Bisexual Anthology Collective (Eds.), **Plural desires** (pp. 128-129).

Frazin, Jim. (1994, Spring). An interview with Starhawk. **Anything That Moves**, 7, 24-27.

Hurley, Karen. (1991). Coming out in spirit and in flesh. In **Bi any other name** (pp. 94-102).

Hutchins, Loraine. (1991). Letting go: An interview with John Horne. In **Bi any other name** (pp. 112-116).

Perlstein, Marcia. (1996). Integrating a gay, lesbian, or bisexual person's religious and spiritual needs and choices into psychotherapy. In C. J. Alexander (Ed.), **Gay and lesbian mental health: A sourcebook for practitioners** (pp. 173-188). New York: Harrington Park Press.

Rose, Sharon. (1996). Against marriage. In **Bisexual horizons** (pp. 119-121).

Starhawk. (1995). The sacredness of pleasure. In **Bisexual politics** (pp. 325-329).

Tirado, Leonard. (1991). Reclaiming heart and mind. In **Bi any other name** (pp. 117-123).

Wheaton United Methodist Church Reconciling Congregation Task Force. (1991, Fall). One church's journey toward including bisexuals. **Open Hands: Reconciling Ministries with Lesbians and Gay Men**, 16.

Queer Theory/Cultural Studies/Literary Criticism

For *Books* on queer theory, cultural studies, and literary criticism, see also the following sections above:
Books Specifically on Bisexuality: Bi Academic Intervention, 1997; Bryant, 1997; Garber, 1995; Hall & Pramaggiore, 1996; Storr, 1999. See also the special issue of the *Journal of Gay, Lesbian, and Bisexual Identity* (1997).
Bi-Inclusive Books: Under *Queer theory*: Beemyn & Eliason, 1996.

*Ault, Amber. (1996). Hegemonic discourse in an oppositional community: Lesbian feminist stigmatization of bisexual women. In **Queer studies** (pp. 204-216).

Carroll, Traci. (1996). Invisible sissy: The politics of masculinity in African American bisexual narrative. In **RePresenting bisexualities** (pp. 180-204).

*Connerly, Gregory. (1996). The politics of Black lesbian, gay, and bisexual identity. In **Queer studies** (pp. 133-145).

*du Plessis, Michael. (1996). Blatantly bisexual; or, Unthinking queer theory. In **RePresenting bisexualities** (pp. 19-54).

Eadie, Jo. (1997). Living in the past: *Savage nights*, bisexual times. **Journal of Gay, Lesbian, and Bisexual Identity**, 2(1), 7-26.

Fraser, Miriam (1996). Framing contention: Bisexuality displaced. In **RePresenting bisexualities** (pp. 253-271).

*Hall, Donald E. (1996). Graphic sexuality and the erasure of a polymorphous perversity. In **RePresenting bisexualities** (pp. 99-123).

*Hemmings, Clare. (1993). Resituating the bisexual body: From identity to difference. In J. Bristow, & A. R. Wilson (Eds.), **Activating theory: Lesbian, gay, bisexual politics** (pp. 119-138).

Hemmings, Clare. (1997). Bisexual theoretical perspectives: Emergent and contingent relationships. In Bi Academic Intervention (Ed.), **Bisexual imaginary: Representation, identity and desire** (pp. 14-31). London: Cassell.

Hemmings, Clare. (1998). Waiting for no man: Bisexual femme subjectivity and cultural repudiation. In S. R. Munt (Ed.), **Butch/femme: Inside lesbian gender** (pp. 90-100). London: Cassell.

*James, Christopher. (1996). Denying complexity: The dismissal and appropriation of bisexuality in queer, lesbian, and gay theory. In **Queer studies** (pp. 217-240).

Kaloski, Ann. (1997). Bisexuals making out with cyborgs: Politics, pleasure, con/fusion. **Journal of Gay, Lesbian, and Bisexual Identity**, 2(1), 47-64.

*Loftus, Brian. (1996). Biopia: Bisexuality and the crisis of visibility in a queer symbolic. In **RePresenting bisexualities** (pp. 207-233).

Morris, Sharon, & Merl Storr. (1997). Bisexual theory: A bi academic intervention. **Journal of Gay, Lesbian, & Bisexual Identity**, 2(1), 1-6.

Pramaggiore, Maria. (1996). Straddling the screen: Bisexual spectatorship and contemporary narrative film. In **RePresenting bisexualities** (pp. 272-297).

Shugar, Dana R. (1999). To(o) queer or not? Queer theory, lesbian community, and the functions of sexual identities. In D. Atkins (Ed.), **Lesbian sex scandals: Sexual practices, identities, and politics** (pp. 11-20). New York: Haworth.

Bisexual Community & Bisexual Politics

For *Books* on bisexual community & politics, see also the following sections above:
Books Specifically on Bisexuality: For psychological and sociological perspectives: Rust, 1995. In German: Feldhorst, 1996; Hüsers & König, 1995. For personal and political perspectives: Bisexual Anthology Collective, 1995; Hutchins & Kaahumanu, 1991; Ochs, 2000; Rose, Stevens, & Off Pink Collective, 1996; Tucker, 1995; Weise, 1992. In *Spanish*: Archivo Lesbico y de Mujeres Diferentes, 1998.

Bi-Inclusive Books: Under *Identity*: Esterberg (1997). Under *LGBT Communities*: Harris, 1999; Hertzog, 1996; Shephard, Yeskel & Outcalt, 1996; Swan, 1997; Working Group on Funding Lesbian & Gay Issues, 1999.

Geographic Bisexual Communities

Barr, George. (1985). Chicago Bi-ways: An informal history. **Journal of Homosexuality,** 11(1/2), 231-234.

Berry, Dave. (1996). A history of the Edinburgh Bisexual Group. In **Bisexual horizons** (pp. 281-286).

Dworkin, Andrea Sharon. (2001). Bisexual histories in San Francisco in the 1970s and early 1980s. **Journal of Bisexuality,** 1(1), 87-119.

Euroqueer, A. (1996). Bisexuality in Brussels. In **Bisexual horizons** (pp. 287-288).

Esterberg, Kristin G. (1996). Gay cultures, gay communities: The social organization of lesbians, gay men, & bisexuals. In R. C. Savin-Williams, & K. M. Cohen (Eds.), **The lives of lesbians, gays, & bisexuals: Children to adults** (pp. 337-392). Fort Worth, TX: Harcourt Brace.

Hüsers, Francis. (1996). Bisexual associations in Germany. In **Bisexual horizons** (pp. 293-297).

Kaal, Wouter. (1996). A history of the bi movement in the Netherlands. In **Bisexual horizons** (pp. 289-292).

Roberts, Beth C. (1997). "The many faces of bisexuality": The 4th International Bisexual Symposium. **Journal of Gay, Lesbian, and Bisexual Identity,** 2(1), 65-76.

Roberts, Wayne. (1996). The making of an Australian bisexual activist. In **Bisexual horizons** (pp. 149-153).

Ross, Jeff. (2001). The San Francisco field of dreams: A history of the San Francisco Bi Film Festival 1997-1999. **Journal of Bisexuality,** 1(1), 181-185.

Rubenstein, Maggi, & Cynthia A. Slater. (1985). A profile of the San Francisco Bisexual Center. **Journal of Homosexuality,** 11(1/2), 227-230.

Tucker, Naomi. (1995). Bay Area bisexual history: An interview with David Lourea. In **Bisexual politics** (pp. 47-62).

Weise, Beth R. (1996). The bisexual community: Viable reality or revolutionary pipe dream? In **Bisexual horizons** (pp. 303-313).

The Broader Bisexual Community and Bisexual Politics

Arnesen, Cliff. (1991). Coming out to Congress. In **Bi any other name** (pp. 233-239). Boston: Alyson.

*Donaldson, Stephen. (1995). The bisexual movement's beginnings in the 70s: A personal retrospective. In **Bisexual politics** (pp. 31-46)

Eadie, Jo. (1993). Activating bisexuality: Towards a bi/sexual politics. In J. Bristow, & A. R. Wilson (Eds.), **Activating theory: Lesbian, gay bisexual politics** (pp. 139-170).

Chandler, Paul. (1996). Coming in from the cold: Bisexuality and the politics of diversity. In **Bisexual horizons** (pp. 277-235).

*Farajajé-Jones, Elias. (1995). Fluid desire: Race, HIV/AIDS, and bisexual politics. In **Bisexual politics** (pp. 119-130).

Hemmings, Clare, & Warren J. Blumenfeld. (1996). Reading "monosexual". **Journal of Gay, Lesbian, & Bisexual Identity,** 1(4), 311-321.

Highleyman, Liz A. (1995). Identity and ideas: Strategies for bisexuals. In **Bisexual politics** (pp. 73-92).

*Highleyman, Liz, Robert Bray, David Chapman, Adrienne Davis, Lani Ka'ahumanu, & Elliot Ramos. (1996). Identity and ideas: A roundtable on identity politics. **Journal of Gay, Lesbian, & Bisexual Identity,** 1(3), 235-253.

Hutchins, Loraine. (1995). Our leaders, our selves. In **Bisexual politics** (pp. 131-142).

*Hutchins, Loraine. (1996). Bisexuality: Politics & community. In B. A. Firestein (Ed.), **Bisexuality: The psychology & politics of an invisible minority** (pp. 240-259). Thousand Oaks, CA: Sage.

Ka'ahumanu, Lani. (1995). It ain't over 'til the bisexual speaks. In **Bisexual politics** (pp. 63-68).

Lano, Kevin. (1996). Bisexual history: Fighting invisibility. In **Bisexual horizons** (pp. 219-226).

Ochs, Robyn, & Highleyman, Liz. (1999). Bisexual Movement. In B. Zimmerman (Ed.), **The encyclopedia of lesbianism**. New York: Garland.

Orlando, Lisa. (1991). Loving whom we choose. In **Bi any other name** (pp. 223-232).

Randen, Heidi. (2001). Bi signs and wonders: Robyn Ochs and the Bisexual Resource Guide. **Journal of Bisexuality,** 1(1), 7-26.

Rust, Paula C. Rodríguez. (2000). Popular images and the growth of bisexual community and visibility. In P. C. R. Rust (Ed.), **Bisexuality in the United States: A Social Science Reader** (pp. 537-553). New York: Columbia University Press.

Shuster, Rebecca. (1991). Considering next steps for bisexual liberation. In **Bi any other name** (pp. 266-274). Boston: Alyson.

*Udis-Kessler, Amanda. (1996). Identity/politics: Historical sources of the bisexual movement. In **Queer studies** (pp. 52-63).

Resources from India

Bi Sherry and Deep

BOOKS (NON FICTION)

1. **World of Homosexuals** by Shakuntala Devi, Vikas, 1979. *One of the first books published in India on homosexuals and their relatively anonymous and unknown lives.*
2. **Invisible Minority** by Arvind Kala, Dynamic Books, 1992. *Interviews of homosexual men who frequent cruising areas in Delhi and Bombay.*
3. **Less than Gay: A citizen's report on the status of homosexuality in India,** AIDS Bhedbhav Virodhi Andolan, 1991. *A comprehensive account of the status of homosexuality (and bisexuality) in India. It presents metculous facts, and is through in arguments. Deals with homosexuality in an emapathetic manner.*
4. **Sakhiyani: Lesbian desire in Ancient and Modern India,** Giti Thadani, Cassel, 1996. *The product of intensive field based research which delves into the forgotten traditions of love between women in India and the status of female homosexuality today.*
5. **A Lotus of Another Colour: An Unfolding of the South Asian Gay and Lesbian Experiences,** edited by Rakesh Ratti, Alyson Publication, 1993. An anthology of poems, stories and articles by gays, lesbians and bisexual of South Asian origin in the US.
6. **Panjabi Sufi Saints- AD1460-1900,** by Lajwanti Rama Krihna, Ashajanak Publications, 1973. *A collection of short biographies of Sufi saints of Panjab including those who celebrated homosexual love.*
7. **Ganesa: Lord of Obstacles, Lord of Beginings,** by Paul B Courtright Oxford University Press, 1985. *An examination of Ganesa, a Hindu God, including an analysis of his homosexaual aspects.*
8. **Tamil Temple Myths: Sacrifice and Divine marriage in South Indian Saiva Tradition,** by David Shulman, Priceton University Press, 1980.
9. **The cult of Draupadi Mythologies: From Gingee to Kurukshetra,** by Alf Hieltebietl, Motilal Banarsidass Publishers, 1998. *About a popular Goddes cult, among other things also anlyzes transvestism and gender-reversed homosexuality as reflected in some myths associated with the cult of the Mother Goddess.*
10. **Kali's Child: The mystical and erotic in the life and teachings of Ramakrishna,** by Jeffrey Kripal, University of Chicago Press and Mediamatics, 1997. *A study of the saint and mystic of Bengal, Ramakrishna Paramahamsa which looks at him in a new light. It examines his spiritual practices in the context of his erotic relationshilps to his disciples.*
11. **Shiva and Dionysue: The religion of Nature and Eros,** by Alain Danielou, translated by K F Hurry, Inner Traditions International Ltd, 1984. *A book about the cult of the Hindu god Shiva and its comparison with cult of Dionysus in ancient Greece. It also talks about homosexuality in the context of myths and rituals of the Shaiva Cult.*

PLAYS

1. **Inside Gayland,** by Rajesh Talwar, 1995. *A satirical play on Section 377 of the Indian Penal Code which criminalise sodomy.*
2. **O Come Bulky Stomach,** by Shantanu Nagpal, 1994. *About a married, unhappy HIV+ homosexual man.*

3. **The Alien Flower,** by Sapphiere Creation Dance Workshop, 1997. *The first ballet on homosexuality in India based on poems of Rakesh Retti and Sanjay.*
4. **Coming Out with Music,** by Sarani, 1998. *Bengali songs and dance performance on the pain and pleasure of coming out in the Indian Society.*

BOOKS (FICTION)

1. **Sabdangal (Voices) in Poovan Banana and other stories,** by Vaikom Muhammad Basheer, Disha Books 1994.
2. **Mallika Bahar,** by Kamal Kumar Majumdar, Rachanabali. *A short story about two women in love with each other.*
3. **Randu Penkuttikal,** by V T Nandakumar, 1972 (Malayalam). *A novel describing the story of two teenage girls frrom rural Kerala who fall in love with each other.*
4. **Funny Boys,** Shyam Selvadurai. *A semi-autobiographical novel centered on a homosexual Tamil by growing up in Colombo, Sri Lanka.*
5. **Strange Obsession,** by Shobha De, Penguin India Ltd, 1992. *Novel based on a theme of same sex love between a women who falls for another women who if confused about her sexuality.*
6. **Lihaf (The Quilt)** by Ismat Chughtai. *A short shory of the lesbian relationship between an aristocratic women and her servant which brought the auther to court and exile.*
7. **Dew Drop Inn,** Leslie de Noronha, Writers Workshop, 1997.
8. **One day I locked my flat in Soul City,** by Raja Rao, Rupa 1995.
9. **Santap,** by Manav Chakraborty, Ananda Publishsers, 1993. *A deeply sensitve portrayal of the agony of hijras or eunuchs of India.*

POEMS

1. **Narman,** Ifti Naseem, 1995. An anthology on homosexual love.

FILMS

1. **Umbartha,** directed by Jabbar patel, 1982 (Marathi). *The first Indian film with two lesbian character, Jangam and Sunanda, in the context of women's prison.*
2. **Holi** directed by Ketan Mehta, 1984 (Hindi). *Centered around homosexual blackmail in boarding schools. It depicts the grave consequence of breaking the unspoken pact of secrecy that gays use to survive in closely knit communities.*
3. **Adhura,** directed by Ashish Nagpal, 1995, Hindi. *A tragic story of a rich industrialist falling in love with a male newspaper editor. Yet to be released in India. Under the cloud of censership.*
4. **Fire** directed by Deepa Mehta, 1996. *About a sexually dissatisfied housewife who discovers sensualilty and solace in a relationship with her young sister-in-law. Not yet released in India.*
5. **Daayra,** by Amol Palekar, 1996, Hindi. Award winning film about a man who believes that he is a women trapped in a male body.
6. **Darmiyaan,** by Kalpana Lajmi, 1997, Hindi. *Film about an aging actress and her hermaphrodite son and their efforts to come in terms with the latter's hermaphroditism.*
7. **BOMgAY,** directed by Riyad Wadia, 1996.
8. **Jodie,** directed by Pratibha Parmar.

Reel Bisexuals:
Bisexuality on the Big Screen
compiled bi Wayne Bryant

The following is a list of notable films containing one or more bisexual characters. Most of these films are available on video and described in further detail in the compiler's book, **Bisexual Characters in Film: from Anaïs to Zee.** For each film listed, the format is as follows:

Name of film (alternate name, if any) • *Country* • Director • Year of release

If you have trouble finding bi films at your nearby lackluster video store, nearly all of the movies listed here are available at the Bisexual Videostore on the web. The URL is:

http://www.biresource.org/videostore

Videos purchased through this site help to finance projects of the Bisexual Resource Center, such as this Bisexual Resource Guide.

Comedy

Better Than Chocolate • *Canada* • Anne Wheeler • 1999

An excellent lesbian romantic comedy with a strong bisexual character.

Beyond Therapy • *USA* • Robert Altman • 1986

Offbeat comedy starring Jeff Goldblum as the bisexual and Glenda Jackson as his therapist.

Billy's Hollywood Screen Kiss • *USA* • Tommy O'Haver • 1998

Gay photographer Billy tries to get Gabriel to model for his latest project — remakes of famous Hollywood screen kisses, featuring male couples.

Beyond Therapy

Chasing Amy • *USA* • Kevin Smith • 1997

Ostensibly the story of a straight male cartoonist who falls in love with a lesbian female cartoonist. Beneath the surface it's really about the two guys, their complex relationship, and the difficulty of defining one's sexuality. Highly recommended. [Editor's note: I found the dialogue most obnoxious!)

Dallas Doll • *Australia* • Ann Turner • 1994

Bisexual actress Sandra Bernhard stars as an American golf pro who moves in with an Australian family and ends up sleeping with all the family members who are of legal age.

Entertaining Mr. Sloane • *USA* • Douglas Hickox • 1970

An adaptation of Joe Orton's play about a handsome bisexual killer who is in relationships with a brother and sister.

Even Cowgirls Get the Blues • *USA* • Gus van Sant • 1993

Uma Thurman plays Sissy Hankshaw, a bisexual woman who was born to travel. Based on the Tom Robbins novel. Uneven acting throughout, but excellent music by kd lang.

Even Cowgirls Get the Blues

French Twist (Gazon Maudit) • *France* • Josiane Balasko • 1995

A French farce in which a housewife falls in love with a lesbian whose van broke down at her doorstep. Stars Victoria Abril.   A fun film despite some heavy-handed stereotypes.

Go Fish • *USA* • Rose Troche • 1993

A humorous look at lesbian relationships in the 90s. Lesbian attitudes toward bisexual women examined through a character who also sleeps with men.

Grief • *USA* • Richard Glatzer • 1993

Alexis Arquette plays the bi character in this comedy about the soap opera going on behind the production of a TV soap opera. Paul Bartel, who has directed other films with bisexual characters, plays the judge.

The Hotel New Hampshire • *USA* • Tony Richardson • 1984

Includes a love scene between Jodie Foster and Nastassja Kinski. Also starring Rob Lowe and Wallace Shawn.

The Incredibly True Story of Two Girls in Love • *USA* • Maria Maggenti • 1995

Same-sex love crosses race and class boundaries. Multiple bisexual characters. The director identifies as "omni-sexual."

Late Bloomers • *USA* • Julia Dyer • 1997

Two married women discover the unexpected pleasures of a same-sex relationship.

Love and Human Remains • *Canada* • Denys Arcand • 1993

Combination comedy and thriller. A serial killer is stalking the streets of Toronto. Ruth Marshall plays the main character's bisexual roommate.

My Father is Coming • *Germany/USA* • Monika Treut • 1990

A German woman's father is coming to visit her in New York and doesn't know that she is single and unemployed. Co-stars Annie Sprinkle as herself.

New Year's Day • *USA* • Henry Jaglom • 1990

A Californian (Jaglom) rents an apartment in Manhattan, only to discover that the previous tenants have not yet moved out. "Everybody out there [in Los Angeles] is bisexual."

The Opposite of Sex • *USA* • Don Roos • 1998

Christina Ricci stars as a bad-assed teen who seduces her brother's boyfriend.

Relax, It's Just Sex • *USA* • P.J. Castellaneta • 1998

Sex and relationships in the '90s. Serena Scott Thomas plays the bi character.

A Rose By Any Other Name • *USA* • Kyle Schickner • 1997

A straight man and a "lesbian" fall in love. Their friends don't get it. Written and directed by a bisexual who definitely does.

Scenes from the Class Struggle in Beverly Hills • *USA* • Paul Bartel • 1989

It's the servants vs. the elite in this sex farce starring Jacqueline Bisset, Mary Woronov, Wallace Shawn, and Ed Begley Jr.

Their First Mistake • *USA* • George Marshall • 1932

Laurel and Hardy perform simply the finest gender-bending roles of their era.

Biographical:

Becoming Colette • *Germany/France/USA* • Danny Huston • 1991

The story of a young bisexual woman who became one of France's greatest writers.

Carrington • *UK* • Christopher Hampton • 1995

This historical drama ignores its Bloomsbury Group setting and curiously neglects Carrington's bisexuality, while highlighting her husband's. Starring Emma Thompson.

Chanel Solitaire • *France/UK* • George Kaczender • 1981

The story of a young bisexual woman who became one of France's greatest designers.

Henry and June

Gia • *USA* • Michael Cristofer • 1998

Angelina Jolie plays bisexual supermodel Gia Marie Curangi, the first American female celebrity to die of AIDS.

Henry and June • *USA* • Philip Kaufman • 1990

The story of a young bisexual woman who kept one of France's greatest diaries. Stars Uma Thurman as June.

Total Eclipse • *UK* • Agnieszka Holland • 1995

A film about the stormy relationship between poets Paul Verlaine and Arthur Rimbaud. Not the most positive portrayal of bisexuals.

Wilde • *UK* • Brian Gilbert • 1998

The best of several films about the tribulations and trials of Oscar Wilde.

Musical

The Adventures of Priscilla, Queen of the Desert • *Australia* • 1994

Three drag queens (a gay man, a bisexual, and a transsexual) lip sync their way across the Australian outback. Great music and fabulous costumes, but gratuitous sexism.

Cabaret · *USA* · Bob Fosse · 1972

Based on stories by gay author Christopher Isherwood. Stars Joel Grey, Liza Minelli, and Michael York.

Zachariah • *USA* • George Englund • 1970

Billed as "the first electric western." Stars drummer Elvin Jones. Great music by the New York Rock Ensemble, Country Joe and the Fish, The James Gang, and Doug Kershaw.

Historical

The Bostonians • *UK* • James Ivory • 1984

Written by gay author Henry James, the main character is based on his bisexual sister. Like most Ivory films, it is a period piece with beautiful costumes and scenery.

Queen Christina • *USA* • Rouben Mamoulian • 1933

Greta Garbo stars as the bisexual queen of Sweden. She kisses the countess and dresses in male drag.

Spartacus • *USA* • Stanley Kubrick • 1960 (restored 1991)

The restored version depicts Crassus (Laurence Olivier) as bisexual, attempting to seduce his slave. This scene was cut from the original release. Also stars Peter Ustinov, Laurence Olivier, Tony Curtis, Woody Strode, Charles Laughton and Kirk Douglas.

Drama

2 Seconds (Deux Secondes) • *Canada* • Manon Briand • 1998

A champion bi-cyclist retires from racing and struggles to make a life for herself in the real world. In French with subtitles.

Advise and Consent • *USA* • Otto Preminger • 1962

A political struggle in the U.S. Senate causes the revelation of many secrets. Stars Henry Fonda, John Granger, and Charles Laughton (as the Jesse Helms character).

All Over Me • *USA* • Alex Sichel • 1997

Major teen angst about sexuality, drugs, home life and more.

Bar Girls • *USA* • Marita Giovanni • 1994

A lesbian film with lots of bi women and "sudden conversions." Most of the action takes place in an upscale L.A. lesbian bar. Look for a cameo by Chastity Bono.

Basic Instinct • *USA* • Paul Verhoeven • 1992

Every bisexual or lesbian woman in the film is a killer. Stars Sharon Stone and Michael Douglas.

Bedrooms and Hallways • *USA* • Rose Troche • 1998

Kevin falls in love with another man in his group therapy session, then complicates his life by getting together with his high school sweetheart, Jennifer.

Bound • *USA* • Andy & Larry Wachowski • 1996

A gangster moll conspires with a female ex-convict to steal a fortune from the mob. In the process they fall in hot, passionate lust.

Chantilly Lace • *USA* • Linda Yellen • 1993

Made for TV movie about women and friendship in the 90s. Lots of improvised dialogue. The b-word is actually used.

Claire of the Moon • *USA* • Nicole Conn • 1992 • 102m

An anal-retentive lesbian and a sloppy bisexual woman share a cabin at a writers retreat. They are at each other's throats until they finally fall in lust. The ending, though highly predictable, is worth the wait.

Crash • *Canada/UK/France* • David Cronenberg • 1996

The story of group of people (some of whom are bisexual) with a fetish for bodies which have been deformed by car crashes. Decidedly not for the weak of stomach.

The Crying Game • *UK* • Neil Jordan • 1992

A bisexual British soldier is taken hostage by the Irish Republican Army. His captor's life is changed forever.

Dakan • *Guinea* • Mohamed Camara • 1997

A rare African film with bi male characters. Sori and Manga are schoolmates who are attracted to women, but ultimately come to understand that their first love is each other.

Desert Hearts

Desert Hearts • *USA* • Donna Deitch • 1985

Breakthrough film about a conservative woman going through a divorce who falls in love with a wild, young lesbian (Patricia Charbonneau) in the desert.

El Diputado (The Deputy or Confessions of a Congressman) • *Spain* • Eloy de la Iglesia • 1978

A married Spanish congressman with a particular interest in young men is framed by the fascists.

Dog Day Afternoon • *USA* • Sidney Lumet • 1975

Al Pacino plays a bisexual who robs a bank to get money for his lover's sex-change operation. Based on a true story.

The Doom Generation • *USA* • Gregg Araki • 1995

It isn't easy to shock movie-viewers these days, but Araki gives it his best shot. This road movie features foul-mouthed teens, psycho killers, and sweaty bi sex.

Erotique • *USA/Germany/Hong Kong* • Lizzie Borden, Monika Treut & Clara Law • 1993

Three short films by women directors. Two have bisexual characters. The first of these, "Let's Talk About Sex" was co-written by bisexuals, Lizzie Borden and Susie Bright.

Exotica • *Canada* • Atom Egoyan • 1995

An excellent film about some very disturbed people who work at or frequent a strip club. This movie is a study in eroticism, secrecy, and despair.

Fire • *Canada/India* • Deepa Mehta • 1996

Two Indian women in arranged marriages take comfort and eventually pleasure in each other.

Flirting with Disaster • *USA* • David O. Russell • 1996

The character called Tony actually calls himself bisexual. Not the world's most likable guy, but no worse than the other characters.

The Fourth Man (De Verde Man) • *Netherlands* • Paul Verhoeven • 1983

A man falls in love with another man whom he passes on a train, only to find that they are both in love with the same dangerous woman.

High Art • *USA* • Brandon Williams • 1998

A young and aspiring magazine editor learns that her drugged-out upstairs neighbor was once a well-known photographer. The two women mix work with play.

Higher Learning • *USA* • John Singleton • 1995

A film about racism and the struggle for identity. Loaded with cardboard characters, including a student who is "confused" about her sexuality.

I've Heard the Mermaids Singing • *Canada* • Patricia Rozema • 1982

Polly, an inept temp worker, falls in love with her new boss. She later discovers the woman's darkest secrets.

Law of Desire (La ley del deseo) • *Spain* • Pedro Almodóvar • 1987

Almodóvar's semi-autobiographical film about the loves and losses of a gay film director. A wide range of sexualities are represented.

Mass Appeal • *USA* • Glenn Jordan • 1984

Jack Lemon as a parish priest who hates confrontation, but finds himself defending a bisexual divinity student.

Nea • *France* • Nelly Kaplan • 1976

Comic drama about a teenage girl who writes a best-selling erotic novel. She encourages her mother's love for another woman.

Nowhere • *USA* • Gregg Araki • 1997

The third film in Araki's generation X trilogy. Bisexual characters abound (along with sex, drugs, music, and a space alien). Shortly after the film was released, the director, known as a gay icon, revealed that he has a girlfriend.

Paris France • *Canada* • Gerard Ciccoritti • 1993

Lucy decides that her writer's block can be broken if she can just recreate the wild sexuality of her Paris years. Her husband and lover are both bi.

Peter's Friends • *UK* • Kenneth Branagh • 1992

Peter invites his old school friends for a New Year's reunion and the sharing of revelations. An appalling bit of overacting by the director.

Pigalle • *France/Switzerland* • Karim Dridi • 1994

Fifi, the bisexual hustler, Vera, the private dancer, and Divine, the transvestite hooker are among the denizens of this seedy Paris neighborhood.

The Pillow Book • *France/UK/Netherlands* • Peter Greenaway • 1997

A sumptuous visual treat, this is the story of a Japanese woman obsessed with the human body as calligraphy canvas. Her father and lover are both bisexual.

The Rainbow • *UK* • Ken Russell •1989

Amanda Donohoe and Sammi Davis play teacher and student who fall in love. Glenda Jackson as the mother. Based on the novel by D.H. Lawrence.

Savage Nights (Les Nuits Fauves or Wilde Maechte) • *France* • Cyril Collard • 1993

Writer/director/star Collard's story of a self-absorbed bisexual man who is HIV positive and makes no attempt to protect his lovers. Won four César awards just days after Collard's death.

Steam • *Italy/Turkey/Spain* • Ferzan Ozpetek • 1997

Francesco inherits a Turkish bath from his aunt. He leaves his wife in Rome and heads for Istanbul to dispose of his property. When he sees the bathhouse, he falls in love with it, and the caretaker's son.

Sunday Bloody Sunday • *UK* • John Schlesinger • 1971

The trials of triads. Murray Head appears in the role of a young artist whose older lovers are played by Peter Finch and Glenda Jackson.

The Talented Mr. Ripley • *USA* • Anthony Minghella • 1999

A talented young forger uses his wiles to escape poverty by taking over another man's identity.

Three of Hearts • *USA* • Yurek Bogayevicz • 1993

A lesbian hires a male "escort" to seduce and then dump her bisexual ex-lover in hopes that she can win her back.

Threesome • *USA* • Andrew Fleming • 1994

A woman is mistakenly assigned to the dorm room of two men. Each becomes attracted to the roommate who is not attracted to them. The bisexual character is treated as "confused."

La Truite (The Trout) • *France* • Joseph Losey • 1982

Frederique is so attractive that her gay husband falls in love with her. So do lots of other people, of various sexualities.

Velvet Goldmine • *UK/USA* • Todd Haynes • 1998

Return with us now to the thrilling days of Glamrock with the rise and fall of young bisexual rockstar Brian Slade.

Victim • *UK* • Basil Dearden • 1961

Dirk Bogarde plays a bisexual lawyer whose marriage and career are threatened by a blackmail scheme.

The Watermelon Woman • *USA* • Cheryl Dunye • 1997

A young African-American woman searches for the identity of an actress identified in old film credits only as The Watermelon Woman. In the process she finds a lot more, including (briefly) a bisexual lover.

When Night is Falling • *Canada* • Patricia Rozema • 1995

Love story between a previously-straight woman teaching at a religious school and a lesbian who is a performance artist in a circus. Highly recommended.

Wild Things • *USA* • John McNaughton • 1998

Neve Campbell, Kevin Bacon, and Matt Dillon star in this less-than-thrilling thriller. The bisexuality is treated matter-of-factly, but the sex is mostly gratuitous.

X, Y and Zee

Women in Love • *UK* • Ken Russell • 1970

Based on the D.H. Lawrence novel. Features an extended nude male wrestling scene. Stars Alan Bates and Glenda Jackson.

X, Y & Zee (Zee and Company) • *USA* • Brian Hutton • 1971

Elizabeth Taylor seduces Susannah York in order to get her away from Michael Caine. A decidedly bad and dated film that must be seen.

Your Friends and Neighbors • *USA* • Neil LaBute • 1998

If you have friends and neighbors like this, run far away, change your name, and start a new life. Definitely *not* a date movie. Excellent acting by Amy Brenneman and the ensemble.

Cult

Black Lizard • *Japan* • Kinji Fukasaku • 1968

An actor in drag plays a bisexual female master thief. One of the campiest films of all time. Screenplay by bisexual author, Yukio Mishima, who also appears in the film.

The East Is Red • *Hong Kong* • Ching Siu-Tung & Raymond Lee • 1993

A classic Hong Kong martial arts film in which the hero is a transgendered bisexual. Bloody.

Faster Pussycat! Kill! Kill! (Leather Girls, Mankillers) • *USA* • Russ Meyer • 1965

The classic 60s sexploitation film. Three go-go dancers (one lesbian, one bi, and one straight) drive their sports cars into the desert and terrorize everyone they meet.

Flesh • *USA* • Paul Morrissey • 1968

A young and beautiful Joe Dallesandro plays a bisexual hustler who is trying to raise money for an abortion for his wife's girlfriend. One of the best of the Warhol films.

Liquid Sky • *USA* • Slava Tsukerman • 1983

Alien beings in search of opiates discover that orgasms produce the very best. They lands atop the apartment building of the bisexual Margaret and change her life.

The Rocky Horror Picture Show • *UK* • Jim Sharman • 1976

This science fiction parody is the queen of camp cult films, starring Tim Curry and Meatloaf as two of many bisexual characters. Great music by Richard O'Brien, who plays Riff Raff.

The Sticky Fingers of Time • *USA* • Hilary Brougher • 1997

This low-budget, campy sci-fi flick features several bisexual characters. A writer goes out for a cup of coffee in 1953 and ends up in the East Village in 1997, unaware that a nuclear explosion has mutated her soul.

Mysteries

The Color of Night • *USA* • Richard Rush • 1994

Bruce Willis as a psychologist who takes over his murdered friend's therapy group to discover who killed him. Jane March is excellent as the bisexual character, Rose.

Deathtrap

Deathtrap • *USA* • Sidney Lumet • 1982

Michael Caine is a writer who plans a murder in order to overcome a bad case of writer's block. But who is the intended victim? His wife? His lover? Lots of great plot twists.

The Last Of Sheila • *USA* • Herbert Ross • 1973

James Cockburn sets an elaborate trap to discover the hit-and-run driver who killed his wife. Many more discoveries are made along the way. Star-studded cast.

Horror

Blood and Roses (Et Mourir de Plaisir) • *France/Italy* • Roger Vadim • 1960

Carmilla is obsessed with her vampire ancestor of two hundred years earlier. She is taken over by the vampire's spirit.

Dracula's Daughter • *USA* • Lambert Hillyer • 1936

The first in a long tradition of female bisexual vampires on film. She falls in love with her (male) doctor and seduces a (female) prostitute.

The Hunger • *USA* • Tony Scott • 1983

Beautifully filmed story about a bisexual vampire in search of a new lover. Hot love scene between Catherine Deneuve and Susan Sarandon. Also starring David Bowie.

Interview With the Vampire • *USA* • Neil Jordan Scott • 1994

Starring Tom Cruise, Brad Pitt, and Antonio Banderas. Not as explicitly bisexual as the book, but the erotic tension can be cut with a knife.

Lair of the White Worm • *UK* • Ken Russell • 1988

Amanda Donohoe is a vampirish snake-woman who seduces her prey, both male and female, before feeding them to the snake god.

Lust for a Vampire (To Love a Vampire) • *UK* • Jimmy Sangster • 1970

A student seduces and kills classmates and teachers at a boarding school.

The Vampire Lovers • *UK* • Roy Ward Baker • 1970

A young woman is left at houses of the wealthy by her mother. She seduces their daughters and drains their blood.

Vampyres, Daughters of Dracula • *UK* • Joseph Larraz • 1975

A pair of female vampires live in a castle together in England. They are lovers, but also enjoy the men they seduce before killing them.

WWW.BISEXUAL.ORG

BRINGING
BISEXUALS
TOGETHER

YOUR INTERNET HOME
FOR *EVERYTHING* BISEXUAL

INTERNET RESOURCE LINKS

CITY BI CITY

BI NEWSGROUPS & LISTS

UPCOMING BI CONFERENCES

BI PERSONAL ADS

BI CHAT ROOMS

BI BOOKS

AND MORE!

Getting Bi on the Internet

A group effort by Gilly Rosenthal, Audrey Beth Stein, Laure Vulpierres (aka Voop), Katherine Foote, & John Valentine.

The Internet has become a wonderful and popular place to share ideas, discussion, and resources. But although it is a great place to find bi and bi-related information, it can also be quite overwhelming to the newcomer. Without a good working knowledge of how to use search engines and navigate the Internet, it is very easy to just become lost and not find anything useful at all!

The resources here are listed by type: web pages, e-mail lists, IRC (chat), and newsgroups. Each section has a description of what types of resources are listed and how to use them, with a list of some of the most popular and useful bisexual-related items.

Since there's way too much on the Internet to cover here, and because it is always changing, we've attempted to compile only what we think are some of the most general and helpful resources to someone new to the Internet (or to bisexuality!). By no means is this an attempt to include ALL bisexual or bi-inclusive Internet resources, but rather it is an attempt to provide some good jumping-off points to get you started.

Web

Bi Audrey Beth Stein

URLs for all sites mentioned in boldface are included at the end of this section.

The web has become a great resource for bisexuals in recent years. The Bisexual Resource Center (BRC), which publishes the Bisexual Resource Guide, also publishes a number of pamphlets on the web and in print. Titles include "Bisexuality: Some Questions Answered," "10 Things Your Congregation Can Do To Become More Welcoming," and "How to Start a Bisexual Support Group." The BRC also hosts an online bisexual bookstore in conjunction with Amazon.com as well as the Bisexual Resource List which is part of the Queer Resource Directory.

General

Bisexual Resource Center http://www.biresource.org/

Planet Out http://www.planetout.com/

Bisexual Options http://www.bisexual.org/

News, information

GLAAD http://www.glaad.org

Rainbow Icon Archive http://www.enqueue.com/ria/

Poly-bi http://www.polybi.com

Links

Queer Resources Directory http://www.qrd.org/

Bi.org http://bi.org/

Bisexual Hell http://www.tiac.net/users/danam/bisexual.html

Bi All Means http://www.biallmeans.org/

Delta V http://www.dv-8.com/index1.html

Chats

Queer Resources Directory—list of electronic mailing lists http://www.qrd.org/electronic/mail/

Articles

E-Directory of Lesbigay Scholars http://newark.rutgers.edu/~lcrew/lbg_edir.html

Bisexuality And How To Use It: Toward a Coalitional Identity Politics: http://eserver.org/bs/16/sandell.html

The Fine Art Of Being Come Out To: A Straight Person's Guide To Gay Etiquette: http://www.io.com/~wwwomen/queer/etiquette/intro.html

BiNet USA: http://www.binetusa.org/:

Gay, Lesbian, and Bisexual Politics http://polisci.about.com/science/polisci/cs/gayslesbians/

Youth

ELIGHT http://www.elight.org/

!Outproud! http://www.outproud.org/

International listings

Khushnet - Extensive listings for South Asian GLBs http://www.khushnet.com/

Religious

Links to BGLT religious groups http://www.lavenderlinks.com/topics/religion.html

God loves gays http://www.godlovesgays.com/

Al-Fatiha Links - connected to to Al-Fatiha-News this links page offers a comprehensive list of online communities existing around the globe for LGBTQ Muslims. http://groups.yahoo.com/group/al-fatiha-news/links

Bi Mailing Lists
Bi Gilly Rosenthol

Imagine being able to have a conversation with other people just like you all over the world - observant Jewish bisexuals, bi librarians, bi women with male partners. Or people who just share a similar interest - other people who want to chat about bi theory, activism, or local events. How can you do that without running up a phone bill to challenge the national debt? Join some email lists!

An email list is way of talking via email with not just one person at a time, but a whole group. You can sit back and just read the messages that come by, or be an active participant in the conversation. You send messages to a central address that sends them out to everyone who's subscribed to the list. Some lists are closed - only women, or bisexuals, or bisexual women with purple hair, are allowed to join, and subscriptions requests are filtered through a human being. Others are open, and anyone who's interested can join. Some have an option for digest format--you get one email with a bunch of messages, rather than thirty email messages throughout the day. In addition to the address used to send messages to the list, there is usually a separate address for administrative tasks such as joining and leaving the list. This address usually goes to one of two common programs used to maintain mailing lists, Majordomo and Listserv. If the subscription address is in the form of listserv@anywhere.com, you can send an email with the body "info listname" for more information, or "sub listname your name" to subscribe. It the address is majordomo@anywhere.com, the format for information is the same, and to subscribe simply write "subscribe listname your-email-address" in the body of your message. Try not to include your signature file, if you use one; it will only confuse the computer. Very quickly, you should get back information about where to send messages that you want to go to the list, and how to unsubscribe. Save this message - it makes it much easier once you're getting three hundred messages a day and need to cut down on your mailing lists!

The Mailing List List

Regional mailing lists are included in the Directory section with their respective regions; general and topic-specific mailing lists are listed below.

Biachad Biachad, which means "together" in Hebrew, is an international discussion list for religious Jews who are bisexual or bi-curious. Regular topics of discussion are religion, sexuality, culture, and politics. In the future, we are hoping that the list will also grow to include regional, national, and possibly international gatherings. majordomo@byz.org subscribe biachad your-email-address.

BIACT-L Bisexual Activists Discussion List (listserv@brownvm.brown.edu info biact-l)

BiW-MP This is a list for bi women in relationships with men to discuss any particular issues which relate to these relationships, covering general issues like relationships with the lesbian community, contradictions in being a feminist dyke in love with a man, and handling one's desires for women whilst maintaining a relationship with a male partner. majordomo@bi.org http://bi.org/biw-mp/

BIFEM-L A discussion list for issues of interest to bisexual women. listserv@brownvm.brown.edu info bifem-l

BISEXU-L A general discussion list on issues of interest to bisexuals. listserv@brownvm.brown.edu info bisexu-l http://drycas.club.cc.cmu.edu/~julie/bisexu-l.html

BITHRY-L Bisexual Theory Discussion List listserv@brownvm.brown.edu info bithry-l

disabled-bi The Disabled Bisexual list is open to anyone who defines themselves as disabled. Disabled is defined as anything that impairs your standard of living majordomo@queernet.org subscribe disabled-bipagan-bi

The Pagan Bisexual list is for any Bisexual, male or female, who defines themself as Pagan. Open to any path. majordomo@queernet.org subscribe pagan-bi

bi-pagan For pagan bisexuals. Based in the UK. listserv@ogham.org. subscribe bi-pagan {your name}. http://www.maghmell.demon.co.uk/bi-pagan/

RuBIfruit Moderated mailing list for bi women only. majordomo@queernet.org info rubifruit

WOMBAT "Women of Beauty And Temptation" Wombat is a women-only list for discussion of bisexuality. While only women are allowed, it's not required that you be bisexual to join. Info: WomBAT-request@listserv.aol.com Subscribe: listserv@listserv.aol.com SUBSCRIBE WomBAT your name http://drycas.club.cc.cmu.edu/~julie/wombat.html

Gay, Lesbian, Bisexual People of Color to Subscribe: majordomo@abacus.oxy.edu with the text "subscribe glbpoc" or for information on the list, with the text "info glbpoc".

APLBN Asian Pacific-Islander Lesbian & Bisexual Women's Network Messages include various discussion topics, announcements of community events, and networking. Requests for subscription or info: APLB-REQUEST@kwaj.engr.sgi.com. APLBN is human run; please send a human-readable message. Web page: expage.com/page/aplbn.

Vidaguei List Spanish-language discussion group.VIADGUEI@listbot.com.

Activistaguie List Spanish-Language e-mail list intended for the sharing of political and act ivist information. ACTIVISTAGUE@listbot.com.

IRC
Bi John Valentine

Interrelay chat, or IRC, is very much in flux. Anyone at anytime can create a channel (chat room)...and the channels are constantly changing. There are some "reliable" bi channels under the names #bi, #bisexual, and #bisexuals_anonymous. To complicate matters, there are hundreds of IRC servers around the world. There seem to be three main networks of IRC servers: DALnet, Undernet, and EFnet. Each of these three networks seem to have the three above mentioned channels on a regular basis as well as dozens of other bisexual related channels that come and go.

The character of the channels varies. Some are for non-sexual discussion only, while others are purely sexual. The channels listed above seem to be the most tame and friendly to people new to IRC.

Web sites where one can learn about IRC, download IRC software, and search for currently available channels include

http://www.liszt.com/chat/

http://www.irchelp.org

http://www.funet.fi/~irc

http://light.lightlink.com/irc/

Newsgroups
Bi Kathryn Foote

Newsgroups, like e-mail lists (listservs), are electronic forums through which people all over the world can connect on the basis of common interests and characteristics. Newsgroups, however, are easier to use than e-mail lists in some ways. As long as a particular newsgroup exists on the server to which your computer is networked (for example, on the aol.com server if your internet access is through America Online) all it takes to get started is to locate it on the list of groups available and then click to subscribe. That group you selected is then instantly accessible for you to participate in at your convenience (although "netiquette" generally dictates that you "lurk"--that is, just read--a given group for a month or so before posting yourself). So, with a newsgroup, there is no waiting for a listowner or listserv program to process your subscription request--and no danger of hundreds of messages suddenly appearing in your personal mailbox, as with a high-volume mailing list.

Despite these advantages, or in some measure because of them, the trend for sexuality-related discussion is currently toward listservs and away from newsgroups. Ease of access makes newsgroups (especially unmoderated ones) obvious targets for "spam" (irrelevent, irritating, and often commercial messsages sent to many newsgroups at once, much like traditional direct mail), "hate-mail" posts by bi/homophobic bigots, and sometimes a combination of the two. Relatedly, e-mail lists afford their subscribers greater privacy than do newsgroups. They also offer a better opportunity to discuss narrowly-focused topics (such as bis/LGBTs in a certain profession or religion) without being interrupted by someone relatively clueless who is "just passing by" in cyberspace.

Nevertheless, there are still several internationally-oriented bisexual and related newsgroups on the internet that are usually filled with more posts than you could read in one sitting. Some regional/national newsgroups (described in the regional sections of this guide) still get a fair number of legitimate posts as well. You will also be able to find out about new/other groups through your newsreader's search program or through search engines like Yahoo! on the worldwide web. The primary bisexually focused newsgroup on the internet is soc.bi. (There is also alt.personals.bi, but even many of the non-spam posts there are of the "bi-curious" and/or "seeking hot bi babe" variety and so may not be of interest to many.) The discussion is wide-ranging (from bi self-definition, to politics, to gossip) and often quite interesting and informative. The group can seem, however, to have wild mood swings--from threads (groups of related posts) composed of little more than allusions to newsgroup in-jokes, to protracted and vicious "flamewars" (exchanges of nasty, often *ad hominem* attacks), sometimes over seemingly minor differences. It is an especially good idea, therefore, to read the FAQ (Frequently Asked Questions) document that is posted periodically to the newsgroup itself and is permanently on the web at http://bi.org/~jon/soc.bi (the soc.bi homepage). Doing so will allow you to familiarize yourself with some of the pet peeves and the folklore that have developed among longtime posters. (Reading a newsgroup's FAQ, when one exists, is always advisable.) There are two other newsgroups that are not just about bisexuality but are explicitly inclusive of bis. These are soc.women.lesbian-and-bi (swlab) and soc.support.youth.gay-lesbian-bi (ssyglb). Unlike soc.bi, these forums are moderated. That is, posts to the group get forwarded to a moderator who filters out the spam, hate mail, and anything else that is deemed inappropriate or irrelevant. Please note, however, that these groups are not exclusive in terms of who can post. Swlab will post messages from men or heterosexual women as long as they are civil and concern the group's topic: the lives of lesbians and bi women. Ssyglb, as the title suggests, focuses on support, discussion, news and networking for LGB youth but does not prohibit appropriate messages from older people (like those who are thirty or even more ancient). The FAQs for swlab and ssyglb are on the web at http://welcome.to/swlab/http://welcome.to/swlab/ and http://www.youth.org/ssyglb/ssyglb-faq.html, respectively. These FAQs are quite comprehensive, chock full of links and other resources, and are great resources in and of themselves. Finally, there are two other well-populated groups that may be of interest to bisexuals and that already have many bi posters: soc.motss and alt.polyamory. The "motss" in soc.motss stands for "members of the same sex," and is an acronym generally understood on the net to pertain at least to lesbians and gay men and often extended (as in the case of this newsgroup) to include bisexual, transgender, and other. Soc.motss is for social discussion among LGBTQ people. Alt.polyamory is a group for discussions of interest to polyamorous people. The FAQ provides the basics on polyamory (and beyond), so that those new to the concept can be prepared to engage in meaningful discussion.

If you do not have newsgroup access or your system does not carry one of the newsgroups described here, you can still read and post through a web site called dejanews (http://www.deja.com/usenet) as long as you can provide them with an e-mail address. If you do not have an e-mail address, or if that server is busy, you can still read some groups through search engines on the web.

However you get there, here's hoping you have a happy experience in bi newsgroup land.

DIRECTORY OF BISEXUAL AND BI-INCLUSIVE ORGANIZATIONS

This directory has been compiled with the help of editors throughout the world. International resources are listed first, followed by listings arranged alphabetically by country, from Argentina to Zimbabwe. It is certainly not comprehensive — most likely it is only the tip of the iceberg. It is intended to give those looking for support some idea of where to begin. It is also interesting to take a look around the world and see what is out there.

Interesting quotes and photographs are interspersed throughout these pages. As you're traveling through the listings, you will find the words of Margaret Mead, Alfred Kinsey, Ani DiFranco, Marjorie Garber, Marge Piercy, Lani Ka'ahumanu, Robyn Ochs, Elias Farajajé-Jones, Deb Kolodny, Hélène Cixous, Bette Midler, Susie Bright, Collette, Carol Queen, Marlon Brando, Elton John, June Jordan, Georgia O'Keefe, Starhawk, Coretta Scott King, and the Scarecrow from the Wizard of Oz, among many others.

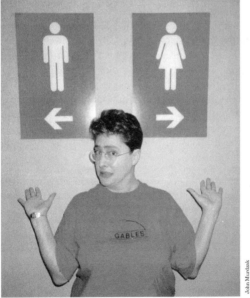

Eve Diana, pondering existential questions backstage at the Donohue Show, 1993

INTERNATIONAL LISTINGS

Bisexual Resource Center PO Box 400639, Cambridge, MA 02140, USA ☎ 617-424-9595 ☒ brc@biresource.org 🖳 www.biresource.org
Educates public & interested organizations about bisexuality. Produces pamphlets, organizes conferences, facilitates Boston area support groups for people who are or think they might be bi, houses the bisexual archives. Website has resources & links to "The Bisexual Bookstore" with 700+ titles. PUB: The Bisexual Resource Guide (300+ pages. US$13.95. 4th edition 2001.)

Bi Without Borders 3010 Hennepin Ave. S., #103, Minneapolis, MN 55408, USA 🖳www.bisexual.org/biwithoutborders
Helps people connect with like-minded individuals, supports local & regional organizations. Projects include: "The Travel Network" of people willing to offer housing & guidance to bis & friends traveling around the US or world; TOO BAD (an action alert network countering prejudice against bis in legislation, media & religious settings); Resource info for those newly out; networking info on issues related to bisexuality; technical assistance to regional & local organizations.

SM/Bi c/o Central Station, 37 Wharfdale Road, London, England N1 9SE, UK ☒ smbi@bi.org 🖳 www.bi.org/~smbi/
Network of bisexuals into BDSM, newsletter, contacts, campaigning. PUB: Ungagged (newsletter), Chainletter (Free w/ SAE: Writers/artists circle, contribution to Chainletter & SAE gets copies of other stories sent.)

International Lesbian & Gay Association rue Marche-au-Charbon 81, Brussels 1000, Belgium ☎/FX:+32-2-5022471 ☒ ilga@ilga.org
Umbrella organization of over 300 glbt groups from 75 countries & over 100 supportive associate & individual members. World/regional conferences, info clearing house, lobbying of international orgs/institutions to fight descrimination based on sexual orientation. Bisexual Information Pool of ILGA c/o ABN, PO Box 490, Lutwyche, Queensland Australia 4030. Email: ausbinet@rainbow.net.au. Permanence every Tu. 8-10pm. PUB: ILGA Bulletin

International Gay & Lesbian Human Rights Commission 1360 Mission St., Suite 200, San Francisco, CA 94103, USA ☎ 415-255-8680; VM:415-553-5558 FX: 415-255-8662 ☒ iglhrc.@iglhrc.org 🖳 www.iglhrc.org/
Mission: to protect & advance the human rights of all people & communities subject to discrimination or abuse on the basis of sexual orientation, gender identity, or HIV status. PUB: Unspoken Rules, Action Alert

Prime Timers Worldwide PO Box 436, Manchaca, TX 78652, USA ☎ 512-282-2861, 8am-10pm Central time ☒ bhwbpt@aol.com.
Social organization for older gay & bi men. Chapters in major cities in Australia, Canada, Sweden & US. Monthly meetings; several other monthly special-interest events.

PFLAG (Parents, Families & Friends of Lesbians & Gays) 1726 M St NW, Suite 400, Washington, DC 20036, USA ☎ 202-638-4200 FX: 202-467-8194 ☒ info@pflag.org 🖳 www.pflag.org
Large annual conference. Local groups in many cities in US & Canada, Australia, UK, France, Argentina, Italy, Israel & South Africa. Referrals to local chapters. Subscribe to mailing list through website. Donations welcome! PUB: PFLAGpole (Quarterly. Various other publications. Catalog available.)

Family Pride Coalition (formerly Gay & Lesbian Parents Coalition International) PO Box 34337, San Diego, CA 92163, USA ☎ 619-296-0199 FX: 619-296-0699 ☒ pride@familypride.org 🖳 www.familypride.org/
Supporting & protecting glbt people & their families. Advocacy & support groups. Pagina en español, informazzione in italiano. Over 85 chapters. International info & referrals on custody, adoption, surrogacy, AI, rights of co-parents.

Straight Spouse Network of Parents & Friends of Lesbians & Gays c/o Amity Pierce Buxton, 8215 Terrace Drive, El Cerrito, CA 94530-3058, USA ☎ 510-525-0200 ☒ info@ssnetwk.org or dir@ssnetwk.org 🖳 www.ssnetwk.org
International organization of heterosexual spouses & partners whose current or former mates are bgl or t. Support groups, state & country contacts & individual spouses provide confidential help & resource info to spouses & partners worldwide. PUB: News & Notes (Published 2x/year)

World Congress of GLB Jewish Organizations PO Box 23379, Washington, DC 20026-3379, USA ☎ 202-452-7424 🖳 www.wcgljo.org/index.html
Aims to end homophobia within the Jewish community & antisemitism in the GLBT community, worldwide. PUB: World Congress Digest Newsletter

Al-Fatiha Foundation 405 Park Av., Suite 1500, NY, NY 10022, USA ☎/FX: 212-752-3188 ☒ gaymuslims@yahoo.com 🖳 www.al-fatiha.org
Int'l org. dedicated to glbtq Muslims & their friends. Holds conferences, works with other interfaith & progressive glbt orgs. Promotes the Islamic ideals of social justice, peace & tolerance through all our work, for a world free from prejudice, homophobia, intolerance & sexism.

"The universe is not only queerer than we supposed, but queerer than we can suppose."

Joseph Haldane

The GaYellow Pages PO Box 533, Village
Station, New York, NY 10014-0533
☎ 212-674-0120 FAX: 212-420-1126
✉ gayellow@banet.net
🖳 www.gayellowpages.com
Free listings for LesBiGay groups & services of all kinds in the USA & Canada.

In addition to these resources, don't forget all of the e-mail lists and web pages listed in "Getting Bi on the Internet."

ARGENTINA

Grupo Bi c/Escrita en el Cuerpo, Perú 1330 4°,
Buenos Aires ☎ (54 11) 4307-6656
✉ escrita@arnet.com.ar
Support group for bisexual & questioning women. Meets 2nd Sat. 5pm at Peru 1330, 4°.

Escrita en el Cuerpo: Archivo y Biblioteca de Lesbianas, Mujeres Bisexuales y Diferentes [Written on the Body: Lesbian, Bisexual & Different Women's Archives & Library] Perú 1330,
4°, Buenos Aires ☎ (54 11) 361 36 43 or 863 91 90
FAX: (54 11) 382 90 95 ✉ escrita@arnet.com.ar
Grupos de apoyo para mujeres bisexuales, producción y distribución de material escrito sobre bisexualidad. [Support groups for bi women, produces & distributes written material on bisexuality.] Coordinates the Working Group on Bisexuality for ILGA Latin America.

Gay, Lesbian, Bisexual, Transvestite & Transsexual Library Parana 157, F (1070), Buenos
Aires ☎ 54 11 4373 89 55 FAX: 54 11 4373 89 55
✉ gaylesdc@arnet.com.ar
Specializes in resources for gay/bi men.

Grupo Nexo Callao 339 4°., Buenos Aires
☎ (54 1) 375 0366 FAX: same ✉ nx@netline.com.ar
Gay & lesbian group, very bi-friendly. Several bi people are working in different cultural activities inside this group. The newly founded Network of GLB Psychologists can be contacted through this group. PUB: NX (The only mainstream GLTB magazine in Argentina. Covers bi issues in a very positive way.)

Lesbian & Bisexual Mothers Support Group Peru
1330, 4°, Buenos Aires ☎ (54 1) 361 36 43
Support group for lesbian, bisexual & questioning mothers meets Sat. 6-8pm in Lesbianas & Escrita en el Cuerpo's premises.

Liga de defensa de las Minorias Sexuales
R. Arabe Siria 3040 1 ° L, Buenos Aires
☎ 054 11 4813-3007 4805-3659

Gays y Lesbianas por los Derechos Civiles
Paraná 157, Buenos Aires 1017
☎/FAX: (054 11)4373 8955 ✉ gaylesdc@arnet.com.ar
Group of attorneys. Legal assistance in the struggle against discrimination.

Amenaza Lésbica Casilla de Correo 12, Sucursal
27 B (1427), Buenos Aires
✉ amenaza@artemis.wamani.apc.org
Grupo de lesbianas que publica una revista abierta a contribuciones por parte de mujeres bisexuales. [Lesbian group that publishes a magazine open to contributions from bi women.]

Asociación Travestis Argentinas c/o Escrita en el
Cuerpo, Peru 1330 4 °, Buenos Aires
☎ (54)1-361-36-49 FAX: (54)1-382-90-95
Grupo de personas transgenero que incluye algunas abiertamente identificadas como bisexuales. [Transgendered group, includes some openly bi-identified people.]

Centro Cristiano de la Comunidad LGTTB
Neuquén 758, Buenos Aires ☎ 41 11 4433-5748
✉ cecristianoglttb@tutopia.com
Religious group, includes bi people in all its activities & literature.

Deportistas Argentinos Gays Defensa 1120,
Buenos Aires ☎ 054 11 4362-9052
✉ info@dag.com.ar 🖳 www.dag.com.ar
Sports group: swimming, soccer, tennis, camps, yoga, theatre, etc. PUB: DAGA

Otras Ovejas Lavalle 376 2°°. E, Buenos Aires
☎/FAX: 54 1 314 59 89 ✉ thanks@wamani.apc.org
🖳 swiftsite.com.otrasovejas
Documentation Centers (40 in L.A.). Study groups on the Bible & other religious texts from a pro-LGB view. PUB: Lesbigay Spirituality & The Bible (Free booklet. Spanish translation from English original.)

Como las Iguanas ▼ Bolivar 553, 4°. B (5000),
Córdoba ☎ (54 51) 56 43 10 ✉ asg@arnet.com.ar
LBTgroup, the 1st of its kind in their city (& in the whole country). Includes bi women & bi FTMs. Offers support groups, street theater & educational activities (lectures at the university).

Colectivo Arco Iris Pasco 994, Rosario, Santa Fe
☎ 54-41-814977 FAX: 54-41-841977
✉ colectivoarcoiris@arnet.com.ar
Focus on sexuality, AIDS, & Human Rights. Provides medical & legal assistance, health education/consulting, psychological help, sex education, hotline, social/support groups (including AA, allies, LBGT groups, HIV, Christian), political action groups. Also runs radio station, publication, & Queer Studies Institute. PUB: INFOCAI (bulletin)

Pardon him Theodotus: he is a barbarian, and thinks that the customs of his tribe and island are the laws of nature.

Julius Caesar in G. B. Shaw's
Caesar and Cleopatra

AUSTRALIA

National

Australian Bisexual Network PO Box 490, Lutwyche, Brisbane, QLD 4030 ☎ +61-7-38572500; tollfree: 1800-653223 (QLD only) ✉ ausbinet@rainbow.net.au 🖳 www.rainbow.net.au/~ausbinet/
National network of bi men, women & transgenders, partners of bis, & regional bi & bi-friendly organisations & services. Based in Brisbane, providing info, web site, some support, sexual health info, policy, advocacy, political action, meetings, social events, Bi Camp, national conferences & outreach to bi & bi-curious people / groups in the Asia-Pacific & Indian Ocean Regions. ICQ: 16442611. PUB: The Australian Bisexual (News, stories, events, information, reviews. ABN Membership/subscription (includes GST): individual/couple: $22/pa; concessional: $17; under 21: $11; groups/services: $28; overseas: $33.)*

Australian Lesbian & Gay Archives PO Box 124, Parkville, VIC 3052 *Preserving the LGB history of Australia.*

Australian Capital Territory

Bi Canberra List Canberra, ACT 🖳 clubs.yahoo.com/clubs/bicanberra *A place for bisexuals in Canberra & local area to chat & meet by e-mail.*

Australian National University: Jellybabies c/o ANU Students' Assn, Canberra, ACT 0200 ☎ (02) 6279 8514 ✉ jellybabiesclub-owner@yahoogroups.com 🖳 student.anu.edu.au/Clubs/Jellybabies. *Campus LGB group.*

New South Wales

NSW Bisexuals List ✉ NSW-Bisexuals-owner@yahoogroups.com 🖳 www.yahoogroups.com/group/NSW-Bisexuals *Adult e-mail list for all NSW Bi Men, Women, Couples, Lovers, & supporters. Must be over 18 & no kiddie porn!*

Bis at Sydney Mardi Gras

Sydney Pride Centre PO Box 7, Darlinghurst, NSW 2007 ☎ (02) 9331 1333 FX: (02) 9331 1199 ✉ mail@pridecentre.com.au 🖳 www.pridecentre.com.au/
Provides venue, support & other services for groups, individuals in Sydney's GLBT community.

Silk Road PO Box 350, Darlinghurst, NSW 2010 ☎ (02) 9206-2080 *Support groups for Asian gay & bi men.*

Cross-Campus Sexuality Network CI- Students' Union, PO Box 10, Kingswood, NSW 2747 *Umbrella group for university / college queer groups in NSW & ACT.*

Macquarie University: Queer Bits Macquarie Univ. Student's Council, PO Box 96, North Ryde, NSW 2113 ☎ Tim Davis: 02-9805-7629

GAMMA NSW 197 Albion St., Surrey Hills, NSW 2010 ☎ toll-free in NSW: 1800-804617 or 02/9207-2800, M-F 6-10pm ✉ gamma@queer.org.au 🖳 gamma.queer.org.au/
Info & support for gay / bi men who are or have been married.

Sydney Bisexual Network PO Box 281, Broadway, NSW 2007 ☎ (02) 9565-4281 ✉ admin@sbn.bi.org 🖳 sbn.bi.org
For bi & bi-friendly people to meet together in welcoming, comfortable, safe, & friendly spaces for serious discussion & fun times.

Gay & Bisexual Peer Support Sydney, NSW ☎ (049) 29 3464

Sydney University: GLOSS/FLOSS Lower Ground Floor, Holme Building, Sydney, NSW 2006 ☎ 02-9660-5222 ✉ gloss@queer.org.au; floss@queer.org.au 🖳 gloss.queer.org.au; floss.queer.org.au/
Social / support groups for non-hetero folks. GLOSS (men) FLOSS (women)

The BiFem Social Group Sydney, NSW ✉ peace@one.net.au 🖳 sydneybifem.freeservers.com/
For bisexual women. Some social event welcome partners & / or their children.

University of Sydney: Queer Collaborations c/o Gay & Lesbian Officers, Sydney Univ.SRC, Lvl 1, Wentworth Bldg., Sydney, NSW 2006 ☎ 02-9660-5222 02-9330-1155 FX: 02-9330-1157 🖳 www.queer.org.au/qc/
Organizes annual national queer student conferences.

University of Technology: Bisexuals/Gays/Lesbians (BIGLUTS) c/o Sexuality Officers, Student Assoc., PO Box 123, Broadway, Sydney, NSW 2007 ☎ 9514-1155; Nicole: 02-9330-1155
Group for lgb & other queer students. Meets Fr. 6pm, Common Area, Level 2, Bon March Bldg.

> **Of course, some people *do* go both ways.**
>
> —The Scarecrow, Wizard of Oz (1939)

Sydney, Australia: winners of 1997
activism awards at national conference

University of Wollongong: Allsorts Collective
c/o SRC Sexuality Officer, Northfields Avenue,
Wollongong, NSW 2522 ☎ (02) 4221-4201
FX: (02) 4221-4233 ✉ sexuality@src.uow.edu.au
🖥 www.uow.edu.au/src
*Parent queer collective at University. Celebrates
sexuality regardless of gender or sexual identity.
Includes Boysorts, Girlsorts & Staffsorts.*

2010 Sydney, NSW ☎ (02) 9552-6130
✉ twenty10@rainbow.net.au
Sydney G/L youth project.

Young Guys Together Sydney, NSW ☎ 02/9515-
3236 ✉ bigayguy@rainbow.net.au
🖥 bigayguy.rainbow.net.au/
Bi/gay/curious males 18-25.

Northern Territory

Northern Territory Bis List ✉ NorthernTerritory-
Bis-owner@yahoogroups.com
🖥 www.yahoogroups.com/group/
NorthernTerritory-Bis
Adult e-mail list for bis in the Northern Territory.

Queensland

Queensland Bisexuals E-mail List QLD
✉ Queensland-Bisexuals-owner@yahoogroups.com
🖥 www.yahoogroups.com/group/Queensland-
Bisexuals
*For bi men,women, couples, or those in search of
these. Also for the bi-curious & bi-closeted to gain
info & support & know they are not alone. Be
tolerant, have fun! 18+ only! No pedophiles,
kiddie porn or doubtful pics to be posted. (Sister
to Yahoo Club -Queensland Bisexuals:
Clubs.yahoo.com/clubs/queenslandbisexuals)*

> ### Bisexuality: The love that dares to speak both names.
>
> *Wayne Bryant*

Bi North Queensland List QLD ✉ Bi-North-
Queensland-owner@yahoogroups.com
🖥 www.yahoogroups.com/group/Bi-North-
Queensland
*For North Queensland Bisexuals to come together
& chat or meet or more! For bis, their partners,
lovers & friends in Rockhampton, Mackay,
Townsville, Mt Isa, Cairns, Atherton, Charters
Towers or anywhere in Queensland North of the
Tropic of Capricorn, including those who plan to
visit the area.*

BifemQld List QLD
✉ BifemQld-owner@yahoogroups.com
🖥 www.yahoogroups.com/group/BifemQld
*List for Women who live in Queensland, who are
bisexual, bi-curious or lesbian. A place to chat &
meet for occasional social gatherings. Not a
personals list, but a friendship based group.*

Bar Bi Brisbane, QLD
*Bar/disco nights for bisexuals & friends
organised by ABN on 2nd & 4th Sat. from 8pm-
2am at Playfords Nightclub, Alliance Hotel,
corner St. Pauls Terrace & Boundary Sreet,
Spring Hill, Brisbane. Check with ABN for latest
details, e-mail to ausbinet@rainbow.net.au or
phone 07-3857-2550.*

Queensland University of Technology: Queer
Students Services Department Brisbane, QLD
☎ (07) 3684 5531 ✉ queer@sq.qut.edu.au
*Support & social services for glbt students &
staff at the University .*

University of Queensland: Queer Sexuality
Collective Student Union, c/o Queer Tribes, Clubs
& Societies, St. Lucia, Brisbane, QLD 4072
☎ +61-7-33652200 (x308) FX: +61-7-33652220
*Social support group for glbt, HIV+ & queer
friendly students at University of Queensland, St
Lucia Campus, Brisbane.*

Metropolitan Community Church Rainbow
Community Center, Brisbane, QLD
✉ mccbris@pronet.net.au
Christian Church with special LGBT outreach.

St. Albans Anglican Church Brisbane, QLD
☎ 07/3870-2566
LGBT welcome.

QldQueer Mailing List , QLD ✉ qldqueer-
owner@listbot.com 🖥 qldqueer.listbot.com
*E-mail list for Queensland LBGT people & friends
for discussion & info.*

South Australia

South-Oz-Bisexuals List SA
✉ South-Oz-Bisexuals-owner@yahoogroups.com
🖥 www.yahoogroups.com/group/South-Oz-Bisexuals
*For bisexuals their lovers, supporters & friends
from South Australia to chat or maybe meet.*

Adelaide Bisexual Support Group Adelaide, SA
☎ Gillian: 08-8395-0318 ✉ Gillian -
gevans@dove.net.au or Jason - merlin@box.net.au
*Social events & meetings for bisexual &
bi-friendly people.*

Gay Adelaide Adelaide, SA
🖳 www.gayadelaide.com
*Excellent website listing glbt resources in
Adelaide.*

Adelaide University Pride Student Union Office,
Univ. of Adelaide, North Terrace, Adelaide, SA
5005 ☎ Ali: (08) 8272 8630
*G/L & non-heterosexual students association of
University. Weekly meetings during teaching
weeks. Organises social events & other functions
for members & the community.*

Flinders University: OUT Adelaide, SA
☎ Contact viaClubs & Societies: (08) 8201 2276
LGB group for students.

Second Story Youth Health Centre 3233 Grenfell
Street, Adelaide, SA 5000 ☎ City: 8232 0233
(9am-5pm)
*LGB Youth Center. Health & esteem education
programs & support groups for people under 26.*

Shangri La c/o Second Story (below), Adelaide, SA
☎ Phillip: 8232 0233 (Tu. only)
*Social support group for young Asian guys up to
30 years old (& partners/friends) who are gay,
bisexual or just attracted to other men. Support,
parties, functions, info on safer sex & on HIV/
AIDS, etc. Confidential, safe & secure.*

Gay & Lesbian Counselling Service of SA
PO Box 2011, Kenttown, SA 5071
☎ (08) 8362-3223, 1800-182-233 FX: (08) 83631046
*A voluntary organisation providing free
confidential counselling & referral services.*

**BAMH (Bi & Married Homosexual Men's Support
Group)** c/o AIDS Council of SA, Kent Town SA
5071, Norwood, SA 5067 ☎ ACSA: (08) 83621611

Tasmania

Tasmanian Bisexual Support Network
✉ teddles@access.net.au
🖳 www.powerup.com.au/~daltoff/bi

Tasmanian-Bisexuals List
✉ Tasmanian-Bisexuals-owner@yahoogroups.com
🖳 www.yahoogroups.com/group/Tasmanian-
Bisexuals
*E-mail list for bisexuals, their lovers, supporters
& friends from beautiful Tasmania!*

Victoria

Victorian Bisexuals E-mail List
✉ Victorian-Bisexuals-owner@yahoogroups.com
🖳 www.yahoogroups.com/group/Victorian-Bisexuals
*Open to ALL Bi Women, Men, their lovers/
supporters, friends, bi-curious people & those that
just Love Bisexuals. Must be 18+.*

Melbourne Bi Married Guys E-Mail List
Melbourne, VIC ✉ melbiguys-
owner@yahoogroups.com
🖳 www.yahoogroups.com/group/melbiguys
*Discussion, support & friendship e-mail list for bi
married men in Melbourne & country Victoria
(Tasmanian men welcome).*

**Australian Bisexual Men's Assoc.- GAMMA
Project** The Franklin Centre, 1B Hamilton Street,
Mont Albert, VIC 3127 ☎ 03-98901068 or 1800-
807-660 (free call w/in rural VIC only)
✉ gpnewst@vicnet.net.au
🖳 www.vicnet.net.au/~abma
*Resource, education & counselling service for
bisexual & married gay men & their partners &
health care professionals working with bi men.
ABMA operates the GAMMA Project & GAMMA-
line info & safe sex counselling line for bi &
married gay men in Victoria.* PUB: Gamma
Project Newsletter (Available online at
www.vicnet.net.au/~abma)

GAMMA-Line Melbourne, VIC ☎ (03) 9899-0509
or 1800-807-660 (free call w/in rural VIC only)
*Confidential counseling & AIDS info service for
married gay & bi men. Operated by the
Australian Bisexual Men's Association Inc.*

Qmelb VIC ✉ qmelb-owner@yahoogroups.com
🖳 www.yahoogroups.com/group/qmelb
*Email list for queer news, created to fill the gaps
that local queer papers BrotherSister &
Melbourne Star Observer don't cover.*

Gay & Lesbian Switchboard Victoria (Inc)
Melbourne, VIC ☎ 03 9510 1846
✉ glswitch@vicnet.net.au 🖳 www.vicnet.net.au/
~glswitch
*Free, anonymous, confidential telephone
counseling, info & referral. Counseling lines 9510
5488 or 1800 631 493 (Free Call Country
Victoria) from 6-10 pm daily & 2-10pm on Wed.*

**Latrobe University: Gay, Lesbian & Bisexual
Society** c/o SRC, Bundoora, VIC 3083
☎ Queer Officers: 03-94792976
✉ woodhouse@LATCS2.LAT.oz.au
*Safe & comfy space to discuss bi & related issues.
All are welcome.*

Hamilton District Alternative Connections
PO Box 366, Hamilton, VIC 3300 ☎ (03) 55712349
Discreet social/ support club for gay & bi men.

**Partners & Families of Gay, Lesbian & Bisexual
People** c/o 831 High St. Road, Glen Waverly or,
PO Box 571 Endeavor Hills, Kew, VIC 3150
☎ Linda: (03) 9700-7190 or A/H - Nan- (03) 9802-
8523, Nancy (03) 9867 7828
Info/support for partners/families of LGB people.

**"I cannot say that I am a lesbian who sleeps with men. For me that's like
saying, 'I'm a vegetarian who eats hamburgers.' Bisexuality says it all,
because it's living with the possibility."**

Lani Ka'ahumanu

Bi Melbourne Mailing list, Melbourne, VIC
✉ bi-melbourne-subscribe@yahoogroups.com
💻 www.yahoogroups.com/group/bi-melbourne
Social/support/discussion group for bis & bi-friendly people in Melbourne & surrounding areas.

JOY-FM PO Box 907, S. Melbourne, VIC 3206
☎ +61 3 969 00 907 FX: +61 3 9699 2646
✉ admin@joy.org.au 💻 joy.org.au
Melbourne G&L/Queer Radio Station. Studio & office location: 268A Coventry St.

Melbourne University: Pride Collective
Melbourne, VIC ☎ Queer Officers: (03)93448159

BrotherSister 87 King William Street, Fitzroy, Melbourne, VIC 3065 ☎ 03-9926 1166
✉ brosisvic_reception@satellitemedia.com.au
💻www.brothersister.com.au/
Free paper informing the glbt community not only about the changing political landscape but also about emerging ideas & ways to express our unique identity. PUB: BrotherSister

Gippsland Gay People's Support Group
PO Box 848, Morwell, VIC 3840
GLB support & social group. 1st Tu.

Swinburne University of Technology: Gay, Lesbian & Bisexual Support Network
c/o Student Union, Swinburne, VIC
☎ Student Union: 03-9214-4440

Warrnambool Gay Group PO Box 1059, Warrnambool, VIC 3280
Social group for LGBs. 3rd Tu at 8pm.

West Australia

West Australian Bisexual Network PO Box 1167, Canning Vale, WA 6155 ☎ Graham or Ian: 08-9354 2737
Counselling & referrals for people coming to terms with their sexuality. Social role passed to Australian Bisexual Network.

WA Bisexuals List WA ✉ WA-Bisexuals-owner@yahoogroups.com
💻 www.yahoogroups.com/group/WA-Bisexuals
Adult e-mail list for all Western Australian Bi Men, Women, Couples, Lovers, & supporters. Must be 18+ & no kiddie porn!!

BiFemWA List WA ✉ bifemwa-owner@yahoogroups.com
💻 www.yahoogroups.com/group/bifemwa
Female only mailing list for bi & bi-curious women (married or single) from W. Australia to give women the opportunity to form a bifem community within Perth city, & hopefully other regions of WA as well, by stimulating chat & discussion amongst WA bifems, offering support, assisting in arranging social events, & assisting bifems to get in touch with others like themselves.

Gay & Lesbian Educator's Network WA
☎ (08) 9486 9855
Support group & network for professionals working in the education field who may identify as glbt.

Curtin University Lesbian, Alternative (Sexuality) & Gay Collective c/o Student Guild, Kent Street, Bentley, WA 6102 ☎ 0419046793
✉ clagcollective@hotmail.com
💻 www.clag-collective.com (password required for some areas or site)

Southwest Friends PO Box 235, Bunbury, WA 6231
☎ Laurie: (08) 9791 1734 after 6pm.
Social/support group for gay/bi/unsure

Gay/Bisexual Fathers' Support Group PO Box 1564, Canning Vale, WA 6155 ☎ (08) 9472 8814
Meets fortnightly Mon at the Carlisle Hotel.

University of Western Australia: Wilde Alliance & Sexuality Information Department
Box 85, Guild of Undergraduates, Stirling Highway, Crawley, WA 6009
☎ termtime: 08-93803902 FX: 08-93801041
✉ sid@gu.uwa.edu.au
Student/staff LGB group. SID: Deals w/all issues of sexuality. Education, referrals, social networking, awareness & visibility campaigns, publications, community events.

Murdoch University Gay & Lesbian Society (MUGLes) Box 406, Student Guild, South Street, Murdoch, WA 6150 ☎ (08) 9360 6759
A safe place on campus that is open to all. Open lunch times M-Th.

West Side Observer PO Box 131, North Perth, WA 6906 ☎ (08) 9228 3277 FX: (08) 9228 1055
✉ editorial@wso.com.au
G/L Community Newspaper for Western Australia. Free at queer venues (try around Northbridge).

Perth Outdoors Group PO Box 47, Northbridge, WA 6865 ☎ (08) 9354 2737
Organising indoor/outdoor activities include car rallies, weekends away, walks, cable skiing, etc.

Bisexual Meeting House Perth, WA ☎ Sundays only, Keith 08/9368-2575
Drop-in centre for bi men providing sexual & social contact, info. & group support.

Australian Bisexual Network abroad at Rome Pride 2000

> **"Sexual identity and sexual desire are not fixed and unchanging. We create boundaries and identities for ourselves to contain what might otherwise threaten to engulf or dissolve into formlessness."**
>
> *Elizabeth Wilson*

Bi Males Perth List Perth, WA ✉ BiMalesPerth-owner@yahoogroups.com
🖳 www.yahoogroups.com/group/BiMalesPerth
E-mail forum for bi males in Perth to share experiences, fantasies, & get togethers.

Enigma Perth, WA ☎ (08) 9446 5092
Support for the spouses of bi people.

Saint Andrew's Anglican Church 259 Barker Road, Subiaco, WA ☎ (08) 9381 1130
A congregation attentive to the needs of glbtq people meets Sun. 6pm.

Freedom Centre PO Box 1510, West Perth, WA 6872 ☎ (08) 9228 0354 ✉ freedom@q-net.net.au
🖳 www.q-net.net.au/~freedom
Confidential, youth-run safe space for young glbtq people to meet, chat, hang out & access info. Drop in centre: 95 Stirling street Northbridge. Open Wed, Fri. 3-9pm & Sat. 12-9pm.

Gay & Lesbian Community Services of Western Australia (inc) Room 2, City West Lotteries House, West Perth, WA 6005 ☎ (08) 9420 7201 (counselling/info); (08) 9486 9855 (admin + fax) ✉ admin@glcs.org.au 🖳 www.glcs.org.au
Offers a range of services, including counseling & an accommodation register. Co-ordinates the Groovy Girls (young women, -27), Breakaway (young men -26); & men 26+ groups.

Western Australian AIDS Council PO Box 1510, West Perth, WA 6872 ☎ (08) 9429 9900 FX: (08) 9429 9901 ✉ waac@waaids.asn.au
🖳 www.waaids.asn.au
Provides a large range of education, support & counseling services for the community.

BAHAMAS

GLBT Hotline & Hope TEA Nassau ☎ 242-328-1816 ✉ hopetea@yahoo.com
Support Group for the glbt community. Profiling laws & providing links to other gay resources in Nassau & the Bahamian Family Islands. Member of ILGA.

Bahamian Gays & Lesbians Against Discrimination ☎ 242-327-1249
✉ bahamianglad@yahoo.com 🖳 www.bglad.org
Support/advocacy group, hotline 9am-midnight daily. PUB: The Outcast Online News Magazine

The Outcast ☎ 242-327-1249
✉ theoutcastnews@yahoo.com
🖳 members.nbci.com/outcastnews/outcastnews/
Online newspaper for Bahama's g/l community.

BELGIUM

HoLeBifoon ☎ +32-(0)9-238 26 26
GLB info line for LesBiGays. Support, listening, & referrals to other resources. Serves the Flemish-speaking part of Belgium.

Télégal ☎ 02/502 79 38 (8pm-midnight)
Info/help line for French speaking lesbigays; does for French speaking part of Belgium what the HoLeBifoon does for the Flemish/Dutch speaking part.

Associaton Culturelle des Gays et Lesbiennes Sourds Francophones de Belgique rue du Marché Charbon 81, Bruxelles 1000
Group for deaf Frenchspeaking lesbigays meet every 2nd Sat. at the Tels Quels Meeting Point (cf. Mailing address) 8pm-12am.

Belgian Gay Motorcycle Club 'De Knalpijp' Vlaanderenstraat 22, Gent 9000 ☎ +32-(0)9-2216056+32-(0)95-185124 FX: +32-(0)9-2226252 ✉ d.factory@innet.be
The name says it all.

Dubbelzinnig Het Roze Huis, Draakplaats 1, Antwerpen, Antwerpen 2018 ☎ + 32 (0) 3 272 44 92 ✉ dubbeldekker@advalvas.be
🖳 surf.to/dubbeldekker
Mixed-group of bisexual people located in Antwerpen; monthly meetings.

Enig Verschil Postbus 144, Antwerpen 1 2000 ☎ (Wed. evening) (03) 213 23 43.
✉ enigverschil@hotmail.com + onthaal@hotmail.com 🖳 bewoner.antwerpen.be/EV
Lesbigay youth group (-26), organises activities +/- once a week, Wed. evening they organise a 'praatcafé' (literally: pub where you can talk). Member of WJNH (umbrella-organisation for lgb youth groups), does onthaal.

Gay Friends Loisirs Boîte Postal 9, Bastogne 6600
French speaking group.

Boomerang p/a Koningin Elisabethlaan 92, Brugge 8000 ✉ postboomerang@hotmail.com
'Young' LBG youth group (-26), weekend activities.

> And why should night and day be so radically divided? / Is there anyone for whom loving and thinking are lived as different beginnings? / Would I have to spend my days with the one and my nights with the other?
>
> *Luce Irigaray*

Tels Quels rue Marché du Charbon 81, second address: BP 888 (do not mention the group name), Bruxelles 1000 ☎ 02/512 45 87
Umbrella organisation for groups such as: International Lesbian & Gay Organisation; Tels Quels Jeunes (youth group); Télégal (telephone helpline - 02/502 79 38 - 8-12pm); Attirent d'Elles (lesbian group); Chorale RoseA Capella (lesbigay chorus group); Parents d'Enfant(s) Homo(s) (parent support group); Parents gays et lesbiens (lesbigay parents). Also offers: a meeting point where activities can be organised (cf. address above + telephone number/secretary open Tu. 7-9 pm); a social service Mon 5-7pm & Wed. 6-8pm); library (Mon.-Fri. 6-8pm & Sat. 5-7pm); monthly magazine; a legal permanence (to give legal advice) Tu. 7.30-9pm & Th. 6.30-8.30pm; a fiscal permanence: Th. 6-8pm; a holiday agency: 04/ 342 05 58 - Tels Quels Meeting Point: bar, social meeting point (daily 5-10pm). See address above.(02/512 32 34) Bar open daily 5pm-2am (open until 4am on Fri., Sat. & evenings prior to holidays) PUB: Tels Quels (monthly)

Alternatives Homosexuelles Brussels
☎ 02/241 64 62 (Philippe Du Bois) or 02/380 49 65 (Philip Turner) ✉ alterhomo@ping.be or pdu@fun.cedeti.be (Philippe Du Bois)
Group for lesbigays & allies. Monthly activity (mostly Sun. afternoon): theatre, cinema, exposition, often followed by an optional dinner.

Parents gays et lesbiens rue Marché au Charbon 81, Bruxelles 1000 ☎ 02/512 45 87 (every 2nd Fri from 8-10pm)
Group for lesbigays parents. 4th Fri. at the Tels Quels (address above) 7-8.30pm

Brussels Gay Sports Brussels ✉ mb10014@tvd.be
"...set up in 1991 to enable homosexual men & women to play sport in an atmosphere free from any ideological, social or sexual discrimination" Sports include: badminton (02/380 49 65. Tu. & Fri.) bodyconditioning (02/537 78 08; Mon.s) swimming (02/648 78 37; On Th. & Sun.) volleyball (02/653 92 07; on Wed.) All the activities are organised not far from Brussels

Fédération Arc-en-Ciel write to: Thierry Glinne , Avenue des saisons 59, Bruxelles 1050
☎ 02/645 25 83
Cultural & sportive association; arc-en-ciel means rainbow.

Cercle homosexuel des étudiants de l'Université Libre de Bruxelles avenue Jeanne 38, Bruxelles 1050 ☎ 02/650 25 40 (answering machine with list of activities) ✉ che@resulb.ulb.ac.be
French speaking; meets Th. 8pm.

Un Sur Dix BP 89, Bruxelles 22 1000 ☎ + 32 (0)2 512 02 02 (Fri 7-9 pm) ✉ unsurdix@infonie.be
French speaking group for lgb -27 organises 'a warm welcome', activities, info sessions...has a magazine (free) permanence: every Fri. 7-9pm at impasse de la Fidélité 11 at 1000 Bruxelles, monthly activity. PUB: Available for free at several lesbigay organisations.

Basta Postbus 1696, Brussels 1 1000
✉ basta@advalvas.be 🖳 surf.to/basta
LGB youth group, organizes activities 2x/month for -27. Activities include going to the cinema, pub, partying, also more educational activities on themes as coming-out, cruising, etc. Member of WJNH, umbrella organisation for lgb youth groups in Flanders. Does onthaal.

Tels Quels Jeunes rue Marché au Charbon 81, Bruxelles 1000 ☎ 02/512 32 34 (Wed. & Sat. 2-5pm)
Meets Wed. & Sat. 2-5 pm.

Liever Spruitjes Postbus 130, Dendermonde 9200 ✉ liever.spruitjes@advalvas.be 🖳 users.pandora.be/liever.spruitjes
LGB youth group member of WJNH BTW, Liever Spruitjes means 'Rather Brussels Sprouts' Subscribe to mailing list for calendar of events. Does 'onthaal.'

Universitaire Campus, Diepenbeek: We Are Gay Gebouw D, Diepenbeek 3590 ☎ +32-(0)11-268109 FX: +32-(0)11-268199 ✉ wag@luc.ac.be
🖳 www.luc.ac.be/~wag/
LGB student organization. Wants to make clear to students that being gay or bisexual is not a problem. Focus on supporting students still fighting with their being gay or bi.

'Holebi Diest' also known as 'Spot' Begijnenstraat 1a, Diest 3290 ☎ +32-(0)13-313505 ✉ holebi.diest@skynet.be 🖳 surf.to/holebi/
GLB workgroup of 'Jeugdhuis Tijl'. For LGB people in the Diest area. PUB: Nieuwsbrief (Free subscription. To subscribe, send e-mail with your mailing address. Electronic subscriptions in plain text or Word-file are available.)

Parents d'Enfant(s) Homosexuel(s) rue Montfort 30, Esneux 4130 ☎ 04/380 34 91
Support group for parents of lesbigays. Meets every 2nd Wed. 6.30-8pm at the Tels Quels (meeting point: rue Marché Charbon 81, 1000 Brussels, Belgium).

HLB - Kring voor homo's, lesbiennes en bi's postbus 32, Etterbeek 3 1040
✉ hethlb@hotmail.com
🖳 igweb.vub.ac.be/kringen/hlb/
Student LBG group, no age limit, part of FWH (Federatie Werkgroepen Homoseksualiteit - see entry) Weekly activities: social (movies, ice-skating, a weekend, a dinner, parties, etc) & educational (coming-out, discrimination, safe sex, debates on different issues).

Federatie Werkgroepen Homoseksualiteit
Kammerstraat 22, Gent 9000 ☎ +32-(0)9-2236929
FX: +32-(0)9-2235821 ⊠ info@fwh.be
🖳 www.fwh.be/
*Umbrella-organization for Flemish GLB societies.
Political & social actions, supports regional
centers & thematical groups with various info
packets, personal info & service through
publication of ZiZo, telephone-service & text-
service on TV, also at www.vrt.be/tt2/
tt.asp?page=527 & http://www.vrt.be/tt2/
tt.asp?page=528.* PUB: ZiZo *(Bimonthly magazine
for LGBs in Flanders. Info about the movement,
politics, culture & society, pink lifestyle,
humour & erotics. Independant editorial team.)*

Verkeerd Geparkeerd Postbus 535, Gent 9000
⊠ VeGe@student.rug.ac.be
🖳 student.rug.ac.be/VeGe/
*Verkeerd Geparkeerd (literal translation: Parked
the wrong way) organizes various activities in
Gent, participates in national meetings &
sometimes has weekend trips. Meetings are
thematic (coming out, safer sex) or social. 2
major lesbigay parties & two smaller parties a
year. Group organises 'onthaal' for new members*
PUB: VG-Verslag *(8 issues/year. Time & location
of actives, deals with lesbigay culture, gay
rights, news, etc.)*

Wel Jong Niet Hetero (bi-werking) Postbus 323,
Gent 1 9000 ⊠ info@weljongniethetero.be
🖳 www.weljongniethetero.be/
*Bi group of Wel Jong, Niet Hetero (WJNH -
"Young, yes, Straight: no way"). Umbrella-
organization for lesbigay youth groups in
Flanders & Brussels. Meeting place for youth -26.
Subcribe to the email list at:
www.weljongniethetero.be/mailinglist/.*

PeperPeper&ZoutZout Postbus 100,
Geraardsbergen 9500 ⊠ pp_zz@hotmail.com
🖳come.to/ppzz
LGB youth group (-26) regular activities.

Dubbeldekker Lombaardstraat 20, 3500 Hasselt
☎ +32-(0)11-212020 FX: +32-(0)11-210054
⊠ lach@tornado.be 🖳 www.tornado.be/~lach/
Mixed bi group, mainly men.

Nota Bene Postbus 137, Hasselt 3500
⊠ nota.bene@freemail.nl
*Meets 8pm 1st & 3rd Fri. at 'Ontmoetingscentrum
Katarina', N. Cleynaertslaan z/n in Hasselt.*

Ja&Dan Postbus 170, Herentals 2200
⊠ jaendan@advalvas.be 🖳 www.go.to/holebi
*Lesbigay youth group organises activities +/- 2x/
month sport, cultural & educational activities.*

Onder Andere(n) Neermarkt 9, Ieper 8900
⊠ onderanderen@hotmail.com
🖳 surf.to/onderanderen
*Lesbigay youth group (-26 years) organizes
activities (educational as well as 'relaxing'):
coming-out, a day at the beach, sports, discussion
on discrimination, relationships, sports, going to
the movies, etc. Member of WJNH (umbrella
organisation for lesbigay youth groups), does
'onthaal'.*

Tandem Boite Postal 70, Jambes 5100
☎ 081/22 19 36 (Mon-Fri 8-10 pm)
*For +18. Active on several levels: - wants to
create a place for 'expression' (where one can
express oneself) - meetings - monthly newsletter -
organises activities: social, cultural, HIV
prevention, etc. permanence: 1st & 3rd Sun 6pm
at the Artisans Brasseurs (cafe in front of the
railway station in Namur).*

GrensGeval Wandelingstraat 31, Kortrijk 8500
⊠ GrensGeval@hotmail.com
*Lesbigay youth group (-26 years). Organizes
activities (educational & 'leisure') during
weekends. Member of WJNH (umbrella
organisation for lesbigay youth groups), does
onthaal.*

De Roze Drempel Postbus 113, Leuven 3 3000
☎ +32-(0)16-200606 ⊠ drempel@ping.be
🖳 www.ping.be/drempel/
*One of the longest existing organizations in the
lesbigay world. Society for students, non-students,
youth, adults from Leuven & sometimes wide
surroundings.* PUB: De Roze Drempel NieuwsBrief
*(Monthly newsletter that keeps you posted
about what the group does, their activities and
gives you insight in things happening in
Flanders & the rest of the world. For BEF 250
or BEF 150 if you're under 26yo, you can
become a member of 'De Roze Drempel' &
receive the newsletter as well as discounts on
activities. To join, deposit the right amount to
bank account 001-1697483-59 and mention
'membership' & 'open' or 'closed,' according to
the kind of envelope they need to send the
newsletter in.)*

**"I have married myself to the conviction that life is only worth living if I
can support my deepest desires to create love. Life is brought to be in
these moments and is sustained by the connections we have with others.
Divinity exists in this promise. Faith rises in my bed when I make love
without reservation. It supports me each time I expose my sexual/
emotional identity."**

Valerie Tobin, in Blessed Bi Spirit

> **"There is no clear dividing line in sexual behavior between gay men or lesbians and bisexuals. People with similar sexual histories identify differently. It is important for us all to recognize this and respect each others choices, not to project our world-view on someone else."**
>
> *Albert Lunde*

&Of Postbus 113, Leuven 3 3000
☎ 016/ 20 06 06 ✉ info@enof.be 🖳 www.enof.be
&of (pronounce: 'enough') Leuven youth gp. run by/for boys & girls under 26, whether scholars or students, employed or unemployed. All activities organised by GLB volunteers -26. Make good friends, discussion in a relaxed & open atmosphere, find a lot of info on topics that are related to homosexuality. Flemish group, but website accessible for French & English speakers. Member of WJNH, umbrella-organisation for lesbigay youth groups. Does 'onthaal.'

Alter Ego rue Roture 52, Liège 4020 ☎ 04/342 24 73 (Mon-Sat 10am-6 pm)
✉ alteregolige@geocities.com
Organizes several activities: permanence every Thurs 8-11pm; dinner 1st Sat of the month; theme parties; evenings with other lesbigay groups, cultural activities, etc.

Parallèle rue Surlet 39, Liège 4020
☎ 04/342 00 56
French speaking group. Meeting centre for lesbigays proposes activities.

Alliage Liège 4000 ✉ alliage@geocities.com
Group (french speaking) that offers services: have a 'library' (mediatheque) on homosexuality.

Cercle Homosexuel Liégeois SIPS, rue des Soeurs de Hasque 9, Liège 4000
☎ 04/223 62 82 ✉ chel@fede.student.ulg.ac.be
Association of lesbigay students in Liège available every Thurs 5pm-7pm (somebody to talk to)

Communauté du Christ Libérateur rue de Fragnée 164, Liège 4000
Group for gay Christians meet every 1st Sun 7pm & every 2nd Tues 8-10pm.

Cercle Homosexuel de Louvain-la-Neuve rue des Wallons 67, Louvain-la-Neuve 1348

Jong Geleerd Postbus 4, Mechelen 2 2800
✉ jonggeleerd@hotmail.com
🖳www.geocities.com/jonggeleerd/
Lesbigay youth group (-26) activities 3x/month. Member of WJNH (umbrella organisation), does onthaal.

KomAf! Postbus 100, Mol 2400
LBG youth group - no age limit. Meets 2nd & 4th Fri. Most activities take place in 'het Wereldhuis'(Corbiestraat 28, 2400 Mol)at 8pm. Organises activities on topics such as safe sex, bisexuality, coming-out (the usual), & also a 'parents' evening'.

Moet Kunnen! Postbus 35, Neerpelt 3910
✉ moet.kunnen@advalvas.be
Lesbigay youth group (-26) only recently founded.

Jo-Jo holebi-jongeren Postbus 659, Oostende 8400 ✉ post_jojo@hotmail.com
New LBG youth group, aspiring to become a part of WJNH (umbrella organisation). Organises activities.

derUIT! Postbus 103, Sint-Niklaas 9100
✉ derUIT@hotmail.com
Lesbigay youth group, organises activities several times a month. Member of Wel Jong Niet Hetero. Does 'onthaal'

Kruispunt Postbus 9, Sint-Truiden 2 3800
Lesbigay youth group (-26) organises activities does not belong to WJNH (umbrella organisation).

BELIZE

Organizations of Friends
c/o PO Box 1294, Belize City

BRAZIL

Bi Brazil List 🖳 clubs.yahoo.com/clubs/bibrasil *A bisexual club onde se fala portugues! [Portuguese-language E-mail list for bisexuals in Brasil.]*

GLB: Grupo de Lesbianas de la Bahia Caixa Postal 6430 - 40.000-000, Rua Frei Vicente 24, Pelourinho, Salvador, Bahia
Work in HIV/AIDS prevention, women's rights, lesbian visibility. Publishes bimonthly newsletter for the Brazilian lesbian community.

Grupo Gay da Bahia Caixa Postal 2552, 40.020, Salvador, Bahia

Quimbanda-DuDu: Grupo Gay Negro da Bahia Rua do Sodré, 45, Salvador, Bahia

Atoba Rua Prof. Carvalho de Melo 471, Magalhaes Bastos, Rio de Janeiro, CEP 21735-11 RJ
Grupo gay/lésbico, abierto a personas bisexuales. [GL group open to bis.]

Associação Diversidade: Rede Paulista de Gays, Lésbicas, Bissexuais e Trangêneros CEAHUSP (Centro Acadêmico de Estudos Homoeróticos da Universidade de São Paolo), Praça da República 426 sobreloja, CEP 01045-000 São Paolo

BULGARIA

Flamingo Agency Tzar Simeon Street 208, Sofia 1680 ☎ +359 48 974647 ✉ post@flamingo.bg.com 🖳 www.flamingo-bg.com/main.htm
Organization for LGBT people. Open 2pm-2am.

CANADA

National

BiNetCanada c/o TBN, 519 Church Street, Toronto, ON M4Y 2C9 ☎ 416-925-9872 ext. 2270 ✉ binet@binetcanada.org 🖳 www.binetcanada.org
National volunteer organization of bisexual Canadians building a national network for sharing information & working together toward greater advocacy & awareness of bisexual issues. Includes bi-positive groups & individuals.

Equality for Gays & Lesbians Everywhere Suite 306, 177 Nepean Street, Ottawa, ON K2P 0B4 ☎ 616-230-1043 FX: 613-230-9395 ✉ egale@istar.ca 🖳 www.egale.ca
Canada's national glbt org. Support & advocacy for the justice, equality & the legal rights of Canadian LGBTs. Info available in English & French. EGALE library, text library, newsletters, related web links & membership info on-line.

Outlooks Magazine Box 439, Suite 100, 1039 17th Avenue SW, Calgary, AB T2T 0B2 ☎ Calgary: 403-228-1157; Vancouver: 604-377-3584; Edmonton: 403-447-3006; 888-228-1157 ✉ outlooks@cadvision.com 🖳 www.outlooks.ab.ca
GLBT monthly news magazine.

March on Washington, 1993

Alberta

BiNet Alberta #6, 23 Sorrel Pl. SW, Calgary, AB T2W 1Z4 ☎ Dan Cohen: 403-259-4098 ✉ dancohen@spots.ab.ca 🖳 www.bisexual.org/g/binetalberta
Internet resource for bisexuals in Alberta & our friends everywhere.

Gay & Lesbian Assoc. of Central Alberta (GALACA) Box 1078, Red Deer, AB T4N 6S5 ☎ 403-340-2198

Calgary Bisexual Network #6, 23 Sorrel Pl. SW, Calgary, AB T2W 1Z4 ☎ Dan Cohen: 403-259-4098 ✉ dancohen@spots.ab.ca
We meet (in person) 1st Th. at the GLCSA offices. Brief agenda, then adjourn to one of Calgary's gay-friendly bars or cafes for the 'real' meeting.

Calgary Bi Women Calgary, AB 🖳 members.tripod.com/~calgarybiw/index.html

The Calgary BiFem Social Group Calgary, AB ☎ 403-620-0361 ✉ CalgaryBiFem@home.com 🖳 members.home.net/calgarybifem/
Open to any woman who is bisexual, lesbian, bi-curious, bi-friendly, bi-single, bi-married, bi-moms, visitors. Coffee Group 2nd Th. 7pm at Rooks, 112 - 16th Avenue NW, Calgary, AB.

Biversity c/o Calgary Birth Control (CBC), Suite 304, 301-14 St NW, Calgary, AB T2N 2A1 ☎ 403-203-5580
Monthly support group, some social activities. Only for city of Calgary. Open to all sexual orientations.

Gay & Lesbian Community Services Association #206 -223 12th Avenue SW, Calgary, AB T2R 0G9 ☎ Gay Lines Calgary (info line): 403-234-8973 FX: 403-261-9776 🖳 www.cglbrd.com/

University of Calgary: Gay & Lesbian Academics, Students & Staff Box 47 MacEwan Student Center, 2500 University Drive, N.W., Calgary, AB T2N 1N4 ☎ 403-220-2872 ✉ glass@ucalgary.ca 🖳 www.ucalgary.ca/~glass/
Open to U of C community. Lesbian, bi, gay, straight, unsure, or 'don't care', all are welcome.

Calgary's Gay, Bisexual & Lesbian Dinner Club! Calgary, AB ✉ andrejhall@hotmail.com 🖳 www.geocities.com/gcdpc

Edmonton Bisexual Support Group c/o Gay & Lesbian Community Centre of Edmonton, Suite 103, 10612 - 124 Street, Edmonton, AB ☎ 403-913-3076 ✉ purplehaze@visto.com 🖳 www.angelfire.com/ab/thepurplehaze
Meetings: info / support for bi men & women. Mtgs. 2nd Tu. 7-9pm at the Gay & Lesbian Community Centre in Edmonton.

Purple Haze Edmonton, AB ✉ purplehaze@visto.com 🖳 www.angelfire.com/ab/thepurplehaze/index.html
Bi social / support group. Monthly meetings.

Gay & Lesbian Community Centre of Edmonton
Suite 103, 10612 - 124 Street, Edmonton, AB
☎ 780-488-3234 ✉ glcce@compusmart.ab.ca
🖳 freenet.edmonton.ab.ca/member/home.shtml or www.edmc.net/glcce
Resources, referrals & support to all members of the general public regarding GLBT issues.

Prime Timers 1093-11444 119th St., Edmonton, AB
T5G 2X6 ☎ Peter: 403-426-7019
✉ mercury@planet.eon.net
Monthly mtgs for G/B men 40+, meets 2nd Sun. 3pm.

Times 10 10121-124 St., Edmonton, AB T5N 1P5
☎ 780-455-5616; Toll Free 1-888-846-3710 FX: 780-455-6540 ✉ times10@telusplanet.net; dcambly@v-wave.com 🖳 www.times10.org
Edmonton's LGB magazine. PUB: Times 10 (10 issues/yr., $35.00 (cdn))

University of Alberta: Outreach Box 75, Students
Union Building, Edmonton, AB T6G 2J7
☎ 877-882-2011 x2029 ✉ outreach@ualberta.ca
🖳 www.ualberta.ca/~outreach/
LBGT discussion/social group. Tu. 5pm in Heritage Room of Athabasca Hall on campus.

Youth Understanding Youth of Edmonton c/o Gay
& Lesbian Community Center of Edmonton, Suite 103, 10612 -124 Street, Edmonton, AB
☎ 1-877-882-2011x2023 ✉ yuyedm@hotmail.com
GLBT social/support group aged 25 & under. Come join in the friendship Sat. 7-9pm at GLCCE.

**Feather of Hope Aboriginal AIDS Prevention
Society** #702, 10242 - 105 Street, Edmonton, AB
T5J 3L5 ☎ 780-488-5773 FX: 780-421-9004
✉ fohaaps@compusmart.ab.ca

Dignity Edmonton Edmonton, AB ☎ 877-882-2011
x2012; Bernard: 780-451-1794; Joseph:
780-481-4218 ✉ trainlvr@compusmart.ab.ca
🖳 www.polarnet.ca/~prince/dignity
For GLB Catholics and friends.

Lambda Christian Community Church Edmonton,
AB ☎ 403-474-0753 ✉ lambdachurch@aol.com
Sun. svcs. A Christian Church with a ministry of healing & social justice in the GLBT community but open to all.

The Unitarian Church of Edmonton 12530 - 110
Avenue, Edmonton, AB ☎ 403-454-8073
✉ uce@compusmart.ab.ca
🖳 www.compusmart.ab.ca/uce
Open, liberal religious community that values diversity & celebrates our GLBT members. Services Sun. 9:30 & 11:15am.

Freedom Fort McMurray, AB ☎ 780-799-4291
Social / support group for members of the GLBT community in Fort McMurray & area.

Northern Rainbow Youth Fort McMurray, AB
☎ 780-790-0775 ✉ nry13_18@hotmail.com
🖳 www.mhenley.com/ashe/nry
Support group for high school students.

**Queer North Gay & Lesbian Community
Association** Box 1492, Grand Prairie, AB T8V 4Z3
☎ 403-539-3325 ✉ spake@telusplanet.net
NW Alberta & NE British Columbia. Open Closet Drop In.

Triangle Alliance Grande Prairie, AB, BC
✉ gprctriangle@hotmail.com
🖳 www.pris.bc.ca/trianglealliance
For GLBT people, their friends & families. Monthly house parties in Grand Prairie, various other events throughout the year in the northern BC & Alberta region.

High Level LGBT Society Bos 3434, High Level,
AB T0H 1Z0 ☎ 926-3989
✉ naltagaygroup@hotmail.com
🖳 www.geocities.com/westhollywood/park/7702/
Social/support group based in High Level w/ counseling services.

Gay & Lesbian Alliance of Lethbridge
Lethbridge, AB ☎ 403-329-4666
Peer support line, M, W 7-10pm. Open meetings every 6 weeks. Coffee nights Th 8-10 at Carole's Bistro.

University of Lethbridge Queers 'n' Allies 4401
University Drive, Lethbridge, AB ☎ 403-329-4666
✉ browra01@uleth.ca
For the students, staff & faculty of the Univ. Primarily social, but also peer support/education, & work with community organizations to meet these ends.

Red Deer College: Pride On Campus PO Box
5005, Red Deer, AB T4N 5H5 ☎ 403-304-6789
Meets Tu, Wed & Th 7pm-11pm. Coordinates a Pride Outreach Program w/a peer helping line (the Pride Outreach Line) providing confidential, non-judgmental assistance with the confusion of sexual identity & stress of sexual realization.

British Columbia

BiNetBC (Bisexual Network of British Columbia)
PO Box 53515, 984 West Broadway, Vancouver,
BC V5Z 1KO ☎ 604-875-6336 ✉ binetbc@bi.org
🖳 www.bi.org/~binetbc
Umbrella organization providing resources & networking for bi & bi-supportive people & groups in BC. Aims to increase visibility, inclusion, & diversity in the glt & straight communities, & to further the development of our own bi community. Hosts annual BC Bisexual Conference. Runs the groups: Biface-support group; Options-social group; Bicycle-activity gp., Biline-phone info line.
PUB: The Fence Post Newsletter (Newsletter is also online at website.)

"I love the person, not the anatomy."

Patrice Donnelly, actress (in Girlfriends, 1995)

Lesbian and Gay Public Employee Association (LGPEA) BC ✉ jim.garbutt@gems9.gov.bc.ca
To achieve a provincial civil service which fully respects & values the contributions of its lgb employees. To be visible as a proud lgb organisation. Open to anyone employed by the BC provincial government, crown corporations, or agencies whose primary funding is from the provincial government.

The Pride Network at the University College of the Fraser Valley C/O C. Magnuson, 33844 King Road, Abbotsford, BC V2T 2C8 ✉ pride_network@ucfv.bc.ca 🖳 www.ucfv.bc.ca/pride

Burnaby College: Take Pride c/o BCIT Student Association, 3700 Willingdon Ave, Burnaby, BC V5G 3H2 ☎ 604-432-6922 x8964

Simon Fraser University: Out On Campus c/o SFSS, Simon Fraser University, Burnaby, BC V5A 1S6 ☎ 604-291-4360 FX: 604-291-5843 ✉ out-on-campus-info@sfu.ca 🖳 www.sfu.ca/out-on-campus
Campus LGBT collective.

Youthquest! Lesbian, Gay, Bisexual & Transgendered Youth Society #200 -2540 Shaugnassy St, Coquitlam, BC V3C 3W4 ☎ 604-944-6293 FX: 604-944-6293 ✉ youthquest@mail.org 🖳 www.geocities.com/WestHollywood/9992
Drop-in programs for youth -22 in Greater Vancouver area: M. 6-10pm at 2732 St Johns St. (Port Moody) Th. 6-9pm at The Lawn Bowling Club (Abbotsford) Sat. 2-6pm at 34 Begbie Street (New Westminster) Sun. 4:30-8pm at 34 Begbie St (Grrrlfriends).

Friends in the Valley Fraser Valley, BC ☎ 604-688-9378x2276
A GLB social club in the Fraser Valley.

Triangle Alliance Grande Prairie, AB & BC ✉ gprctriangle@hotmail.com 🖳 www.pris.bc.ca/trianglealliance
For GLBT people, their friends & families. Monthly house parties in Grand Prairie, various other events throughout the year in the northern BC & Alberta region.

Kamloops Gay, Lesbian & Bisexual Community Box 2071, Stn A, Kamloops, BC V2B 7K6 ☎ 205-376-7311 ✉ galakam@yahoo.com 🖳 www.gaycanada.com/kamloops-gala
Monthly dances, weekly coffee houses, support groups, informational services & outdoor activity group.

Okanogan Rainbow Coalition (ORC) PO Box 711, Station A, Kelowna, BC V1Y 7P4 ✉ okrainbow@hotmail.com
A registered non-profit society dedicated to keeping the glbt community of Kelowna & surrounding areas informed, entertained & represented. PUB: Outwords (outwords@home.com)

Okangan University College: Association for Social Knowledge c/o Student Association, 3333 College Way, Kelowna, BC V1V 1V7 ☎ 250-762-5445 🖳 www.oucsak.bc.ca/askatouc/
Student run collective for glbt people & allies at College. Support, friendship, fun, special events, education & action.

South Okangan Gay & Lesbian Society (SOGALS) Okangan, BC ☎ 250-493-9289
A growing society dedicated to keeping the lgbt community of the South Okanagan entertained & represented.

Rainbow Y North Campus of Okanagan University College, 3333 College Way, Kelowna, BC V1Y 6A6 ☎ 250-470-6067 ✉ rainbowy_ouc@hotmail.com 🖳 www.oucsak.bc.ca/rainbowy/
Safe friendly social support, advocacy, resources for LGBT youth -25.

West Kootenay Gays, Lesbians & Bisexuals Society Box 725, Nelson, BC V1L 5R4 ☎ 250-354-GAYS ✉ wkglbs@kics.bc.ca 🖳 www.kics.bc.ca/~wkglbs/
Non-profit association reporting to the lgb communities of the Kottenay-Boundary area of BC.

Douglas College: Queer Pride Collective c/o Student Society, PO Box 2503, New Westminster, BC V3L 532 ☎ 604-527-5335 x4550; 604-526-5111
Campus group for glbt students & allies.

grrlQuest! 12424 Harris Road, Pitt Meadows, BC V3Y 2J4 ☎ 604/ 460-9115
For lgbq & two-spirited women -22. Regularly scheduled drop-ins.

Rainbow BC c/o 118-8751 General Currie Road, Richmond, BC V6Y 3T7 ☎ 604-244-3765 ✉ cmaynard@home.ca 🖳 www.rainbowbc.com
A loose coalition of individuals & groups who support glbt people in BC.

The Centre 1170 Bute Street, Vancouver, BC V6E 1Z6 ☎ 604-84-5307; toll free 1-800-566-1170 FX: 604/ 684-5309 ✉ thecentre@intergate.bc.ca 🖳 www.intergate.bc.ca\business\thecentre
Community Centre serving & supporting lgtb people & their allies. Lending library, Youth Groups, social, coming out & support groups, community meeting space, free professional counseling, legal clinic, office space rental. Women only & men only groups. Hours: M-F, 10am-10pm.

December 9 Coalition #620 - 1033 Davie, Vancouver, BC V6E 1M7 ☎ 604-687-8752 ✉ dfce@imag.net
Fights for equality for lgbt people under the law & in other areas. Public forums, conferences, public speaks & actions.

Vancouver Bashline Vancouver, BC ☎ 604-899-6203
Short-term counselling, info, referral for LGBT persons regarding instances of anti-queer violence & same-sex relationship violence in Vancouver.

> Even a superficial look at other societies and some groups in our own society should be enough to convince us that a very large number of human beings–probably a majority–are bisexual in their potential capacity for love. Whether they will become exclusively heterosexual or exclusively homosexual for all their lives and in all circumstances or whether they will be able to enter into sexual and love relationships with members of both sexes is, in fact, a consequence of the way they have been brought up, of the particular beliefs and prejudices of the society they live in and, to some extent, of their own life history.
>
> *Margaret Mead (1901-1978) quoted in Redbook, 1975.*

Gay & Lesbian Business Association of Greater Vancouver 20-999 West Broadway, Vancouver, BC V5Z 1K5 ☎ 604-739-GLBA (4522) ✉ glbavancouver@hotmail.com, chaos@axionet.com 🖳 www.glba.org/
Print & online directory of GLBT community & business listings for British Columbia.

Gay, Lesbian & Bisexual Affairs Committee of Capilano College c/o Capilano College Student Union, 2055 Purcell Way, Vancouver, BC V7J 3H5 ☎ 604-984-4969 x2595 FX: 604-984-4995
Raise awareness of sexuality issues & AIDS. Social functions - dances, potlucks, speakers, films, library. Support in the coming out process. M-F 9am-4:30pm.

Gay, Lesbian or Bisexual at Langara College Langara College, 100 W 49th Ave, Vancouver, BC V5V 4L7 ☎ 604-324-3881
Meetings, support, library. Open houses, activities & speakers.

University of British Columbia: Pride UBC 125 N - 6138 SUB Boulevard; Box 9, Vancouver, BC V6T 1Z1 ☎ 604-822-4638 FX: 604-822-9019 ✉ prideubc@pobox.com
Resource group for the campus community . Speakers bureau, queer housing board, library, discussion groups, women's events, beer gardens, dances. other socials.

Gay Youth Services at the Centre c/o the Centre (above) ☎ 604-684-4901
Safe, friendly environment for glbtq youth & their friends -25. Guest speakers, theme nights, events.

Queerlings East Side Youth Group Britannia Community Services Centre Society, 1661 Napier Street, Vancouver, BC V5L 4X4 ☎ 604-718-5828 FX: 718-5858 ✉ jpwatt@unixg.ubc.ca 🖳 www2.vpl.vancouver.bc.ca/DBs/Redbook/orgPgs/3/347620.html
For glbtq & two spirited youth 16-22 who reside in Vancouver's East Side.

Inside Out Vancouver, BC ☎ 604-688-9378
For two-spirited, lgbt youth & their friends, 13-27. Social events, discussions, workshops, guest speakers. Tu 6-8pm.

Two-Spirit Youth Group 1058 Seymour Street, Vancouver, BC V6B 3M6 ☎ 604-254-7746 ✉ kirkd@direct.ca
Support group for queer Native youth. Joint project of Family Services of Greater Vancouver & Urban Native Youth Association. Mts: Th. 7-9pm.

Out On Screen - Queer Film & Video Festival Box 521 - 1027 Davie Street, Vancouver, V6E 4L2, 405 - 207 West Hastings Street, Vancouver, BC V6B 1H7 ☎ 604-844-1615 FX: 604-844-1698 ✉ general@outonscreen.com 🖳 www.outonscreen.com
Non-profit society celebrating the media arts as a powerful tool of communication & cooperation among diverse communities, by promoting the production & exhibition of films & videos of interest to the lgbt communities of BC. Organizes queer film & video festival each August.

Outlook Rogers Television 1865 York Ave, Vancouver, BC V6J 4W3 ☎ 604-734-4611 ✉ outlooktv@outlooktv.org 🖳 www.outlooktv.org
The West Coast's only lgbt magazine show on Rogers Television, Channel 4. Fri. 10pm. 2 new shows monthly.

Fruit Salad Queer Radio - CFRO 102.7FM c/o Vancouver Co-op Radio, 337 Carrall Street, Vancouver, BC V6B 2J4 ☎ 604-684-8494 FX: 604-681-5310 ✉ vcrstaff@vcn.bc.ca 🖳 www.vcn.bc.ca/cfro/
Thursdays 8-9pm, CFRO Radio 102.7FM, Vancouver's only non-profit, volunteer run & funded independent radio.

Queer FM - CITR Radio 101.9 FM University of British Columbia, 233-6138 SUB Blvd., Vancouver, BC V6T 1Z1 ☎ Request line: 604-822-2487 ✉ queerfm@portal.ca 🖳 www.lesbigay.com/queerfm
Variety show for glbt people. Sundays 6-7pm, on CITR Radio 101.9FM.

PFLAG Vancouver 8602 Granville Street, PO Box 30075, Vancouver, BC V6P 5A0 ☎ 604-689-3711 FX: 604-263-0378 ✉ betew@intergate.ca
Support & info for family members of glbt loved ones. Women only & men only groups.

North Okanagan Gay & Lesbian Organization
Box 1419, Vernon, BC V1T 6N7 ☎ 250-558-6198
✉ noglo@yahoo.com 🖳 www3.bc.sympatico.ca/
internetassist/noglo/noglo.htm
*Volunteer group organizing GLBT events in the
North Okanagan.*

Lavender Rhinoceros PO Box 5339, Station B,
Victoria, BC V8R 6S4 ☎ 250-598-6490
✉ lavrhino@home.com 🖳 members.home.net/
lavrhino/
*Facts, focus & forum for lgbt in Victoria &
beyond. Monthly. Subscriptions $30/yr.*

Queerly Canadian - CFUV 101.9 FM PO Box 3035,
Student Union Building, University of Victoria,
Victoria, BC V8W 3P3 ☎ 250-721-8702
FX: 250-727-7111 ✉ cfuv@uvic.ca
🖳 www.cfuv.uvic.ca
*Queer news, music, political discussion, & info
show for the UVIC & Victoria Queer Communi-
ties. CFUV 102FM broadcasts on 101.9FM in
Greater Victoria, & on cable 104.3FM to Greater
Victoria, Vancouver Island, & the Sunshine
Coast. Tu. 8:30pm.* PUB: Offbeat Magazine

University of Victoria: Pride Student Union
Building, PO Box 3035, Victoria, BC V8W 3P3
☎ 250-472-4393 FX: 250-472-4379
✉ pride@uvss.uvic.ca 🖳 www.uvss.uvic.ca/~pride/

Victoria Pride Society Box 8016, Stn Central,
Victoria, BC V8W 3R7 ☎ 250-385-3806
✉ irmaladouche@home.com
*Victoria's political, cultural, & educational
society dedicated to nurturing pride & promoting
visibility.*

Victoria Youth Pride Society c/o Fairfield
Community Place, Victoria, BC V8S 5S1
☎ 250-413-3177 FX: 250-472-4379
✉ vyps@writeme.com 🖳 members.hom.com/vyps
*Safe, comfortable spaces for young people who
are or might be glbt, two-spirited, & their
supporters, to receive support & socialize with
friends. Wed. Discussion Group: 7:30pm,
Fairfield Community Place (1330 Fairfield Road);
Sun. Drop-in: 2-6pm. At Downtown Community
Activity Centre, 755 Pandora Avenue.*

Whistler Gay, Lesbian & Bisexual Friends
Whistler, BC ☎ 604-938-0597
Whistler's first glb group. Meets Monday evenings.

Manitoba

Winnipeg Bi-Pride Group Box 1661, Winnipeg, MB
R3C 2Z6 ☎ (204) 284-5208
*Organization of women & men dedicated to
providing a safe, positive, non-judgmental
environment. Emotional support, to grow & learn
from each other, & to make new friends. While we
support the work of many organizations that
reach out to bisexuals, we believe that it is
important for bisexuals to have our own
community, somewhere we can feel safe, secure,
accepted & loved.*

Rainbow Resource Centre Box 1661, Winnipeg,
MB R3C 2Z6 ☎ 1-888-399-0005 (rural and
northern Manitoba, Northwestern Ontario)
✉ wglrc@escape.ca
🖳 rainbowresourcecentre.homepage.com
*Serving Manitoba's GLBT, & Two-Spirited
Communities.*

Manitoba Queer Winnipeg, MB
✉ teklord@mad.scientist.com
🖳 www.mbqueer.org

Swerve 200-63 Albert Street, Winnipeg, MB R3B
1G4 ☎ 204-942-4599 FX: 204-947-0554
✉ swerve@pangea.ca
Winnipeg's LBG paper. PUB: Swerve (Winnipeg's
Monthly Queer Newsmagazine)

University of Manitoba

GLASS (Gay & Lesbian Associate of Students &
Staff), 312 University Centre, Winnipeg, MB
R3T 2N2, ☎ 204-474-7439 or 204-474-6516
(student center); *The U of M campus connection
to the LGB community of Manitoba. Provides
referral services, social organization, speakers &
films. Involved in community activities, peer
support & small resource library.* **The Rainbow
Pride Mosaic,** Rm 195 Helen Glass Bldg,
Winnipeg, MB, ☎ 204- 474-7439;
✉ uofm_rpm@hotmail.com;
🖳 www.geocities.com/uofm_rpm/

University of Winnipeg

GLBT Resource Center, #I-222 Osborne St.
South, Box 1661, Winnipeg, MB R3L 1Z3,
Email: uwsalgbc@uwinnipeg.ca ,
🖳 www.uwinnipeg.ca/campus/uwsa/
lesgaybi.htm. *Info line, library, legal clinic,
francophone group.* **LGBT Collective,** UWSA
General Office, RM 2624 Lockhart Hall, 513
Portage Ave, Winnipeg, MB R3B 2E9,
☎ 204-786-9025; *Sponsors several visibility
events including: The Homo Hop, Day Without
Hate, & Pink Triangle Week. Info & educational
opportunities about issues relating to homo/
bisexuality & homophobia.*

Winnipeg GLBT Youth Group c/o Winnipeg GLBT
Resource Centre, PO Box 1661, Winnipeg, MB
R3C 2Z6 ☎ 204-244-4526
✉ wlgbyouthgroup@yahoo.com
🖳 www.geocities.com/CapitolHill/4174/
*Safe place for all youth in their teens & 20s who
identify as non-straight or are in the process of
accepting their bi/homosexuality. Topic
discussions & a place to meet others like you.*

Dignity Winnipeg Dignité Box 1912, Winnipeg, MB
R3C 2R2 ☎ Thomas 204-287-8583 or Sandra
204-772-1185 FX: 204-284-0132
✉ dignity-winnipeg@canada.com
🖳 www.polarnet.ca/~prince/dignity/
chapters.html#edmonton

From "BLACK SHEETS"   R Gregory

New Brunswick

Northern Lambda Nord NB
Serving people in n. Maine, USA & n & w New Brunswick. See complete listing under "USA: Maine."

Gai.es Nor Gays Inc. (GNG) PO Box 983, Bathurst, NB E2A 4H8 ☎ 506-783-7440 (F. 8-10pm) ✉ info@gngnb.ca ▨ www.gngnb.ca
Bilingual LGBT group. Dances, suppers & other events in northeast NB. Annual camping/dancing/ fun Labour Day weekend. Runs the only LGBT centre in Atlantic area, at the Complexe Madisco, 702 Main St, office 30, Petit-Rocher. Drop by Fri. 8-10pm. Bilingual. Newsletter.

University of New Brunswick: Spectrum Fredericton, NB ☎ 506-453-4955 FX: 506-453-4958 ▨ www.unb.ca/spectrum
Social/support group for GLBT, two-spirited, queer & questioning students, staff & faculty at the University of New Brunswick & St. Thomas University in Fredericton.

Fruit Cocktail: CHSR 97.9 FM Fredericton, NB ☎ Off air: 506-453-4985; on air 506-453-4979 FX: 506-453-4958 ✉ u5mc@unb.ca ▨ www.unb.ca/web/gala
Mon. 7-8pm radio show syndicated worldwide, lgb news & issues, lesbigay & gay-positive music artists.

Fredericton Lesbians & Gays (FLAG) Station A, Box 1556, Fredericton, NB E3B 5G2 ☎ 506-457-2156 ✉ jwhitche@unb.ca ▨ www.geocities.com/WestHollywood/3074/ contente.htm
Socials/meetings 2nd Wed. 7pm.

New Hope Metropolitan Community Church c/o Unitarian Fellowship Hall, 749 Charlotte Street, Fredericton, NB E3B 1M6
☎ 506-455-4622; 506-457-2156 (FLAG message line)
Services Sun. 7pm. All welcome, regardless of sexual orientation.

PFLAG - Fredericton PO Box 1556, Station A, Fredericton, NB E3B 5G2 ☎ Francis: 506-454-8349 ✉ b84q@jupiter.csd.unb.ca ▨ www.unb.ca/ web/P-FLAG/
Meets 3rd Sun. 2pm in room 19E1 or Alumni Memorial Building on UNB campus. Not related to FLAG or FFLAG.

Safe Spaces 860 Main Street, Suite 303, Moncton, NB E1C 1G2 ☎ 506-869-6224 ✉ safespaces@nb.aibn.com ▨ www.safespaces.org
Services for GLB youth, 14-25.

PFLAG - Moncton (French) 358 rue LaFrance, Dieppe, NB E1A 2B8 ☎ Nicole LeBlanc: 506-382-3269; Pierre Bourgeois: 506-856-7944 ✉ pierre.bourgeois@pwgsc.gc.ca

Mount Allison University: Catalyst c/o Donna Sutton, Counselor, Sackville, NB E0A 3CO ☎ 506-364-2255 FX: 506-364-2263 ✉ ktrotter@mta.ca
Support for lgbt students & info about lgbt issues for members & the university community. Organizes a yearly public forum on lgbt issues & occasional social activities. Meets weekly. Every 2nd meeting open to the public; the remainder are closed support meetings for lgbt students.

Reach Out PO Box 6861, Saint John, NB E2L 4S3 ☎ 506-642-6969; 506-642-1957 ✉ z1fe@unbsj.ca (number 1, not the letter L)
Social group for Saint John area lgb & their families. Video nights, family-oriented activities & other events, some of which are non-smoking or non-alcoholic. Phone line provides info on upcoming AIDS Saint John & LGBT events.

Free To be Me Youth Group Saint John, NB ☎ 506-696-6660 ✉ rainbowpridesj@yahoo.com
For glbq youth 13-19 in Saint John. Confidential group provides education on gay issues, as well as fun social activities.

Saint John Lesbian/Bi Support Network Saint John, NB ✉ sjlesbi@email.com ▨ www.geocities.com/sjlesbi

Newfoundland

Newfoundland Gays & Lesbians for Equality (NGALE) PO Box 6221, St. John's, NF A1C 6J9 ☎ 709-753-4297 (753-GAYS) FX: 709-579-0559 ✉ ngale@geocities.com ▨ www.geocities.com/ WestHollywood/4291
Community-based, non-profit volunteer organization dedicated to providing support, education & advocacy to & for glb & other sexual minorities in NF.

BGLAS: Bisexual, Gay & Lesbian Association for Support Box 20002, Corner Brook, NF A2H 6J5 ☎ 709-634-1066

GLBT Support Corner Brook, NF
✉ glbt_cbs@yahoo.ca 🖳 ngalccb.tripod.com

Gay/Lesbian/Bisexual Support & Infoline St.
John's, NF ☎ 709-753-4297
*24-hour message service. Trained volunteer
available Tu. & Th. 7-10pm & 24 hr. info line.*

**Memorial University: Lesbians, Bisexuals, Gays &
Transgenders at Memorial University** St. John's,
NF ☎ 709-737-7619 ✉ lbgtmun@plato.ucs.mun.ca

PFLAG - St. John's PO Box 6221, St. John's, NF
A1C 6J9 ☎ 709-753-4297

Nova Scotia

**WAYVES: The Atlantic Canadian Lesbian, Gay,
Bisexual, & Transgendered Newspaper** PO Box
34090, Scotia Square, Halifax, NS B3J 3S1
☎ 902-827-1680, advertising; 902-826-7356,
circulation ✉ wayves@fox.nstn.ca
🖳 www.chebucto.ns.ca/CommunitySupport/
Wayves
*Informs Atlantic Canadian LGBT people of
activities in their communities, to promote those
activities & to support their aims & objectives.
An independent publication by a non-profit
collective. PUB: (Published 10 times/year. Free at
various locations throughout Nova Scotia.)*

PFLAG-Amherst 183 East Victoria St., Amherst,
NS B4H 1Y7 ☎ Sydney Russell: 902-667-9091;
Eldon Hay: 506-536-0599
✉ eldonhay@nb.sympatico.ca
*Meets 3rd Th., 12 LaPlance Street, Amherst. Also,
PFLAG-Annapolis Valley (Contact Roger
Bouthillier 902-679-2292, outreach@atcon.com).*

Humans against Homophobia (HAH!) c/o
NSPIRG, 6136 University Ave., Rm. 315, Halifax,
NS B3H 4J2 ☎ 902-494-6662 FX: 902-494-6662
✉ nspirg@is2.dal.ca 🖳 chebucto.ns.ca/
CommunitySupport/NSPIRG
*BLG & straight persons working to dispel sexual
myths & stereotypes in Halifax. Collective with
focus on education & awareness & promoting a
multiplicity of expressions & realities.*

Nova Scotia Rainbow Action Project (NSRAP) c/o
Wayves, RPO Box 34090, Scotia Square, Halifax,
NS B3J 3S1 ☎ 902-832-1900 FX: 902-832-1269
✉ nsrap@ns.sympatico.ca 🖳 nsrap.ns.ca
*Meets quarterly to foster change in our society so
that people of all sexual orientations are valued &
included through community development,
networking, & political activism.*

**JUKA: Nova Scotia Black Gay, Lesbian &
Bisexual Association** c/o AIDS Coalition of Nova
Scotia, #600-5675 Spring Garden Road, Halifax,
NS B3J 1H1 ☎ Les Gray: 902-454-5884
*Monthly social events include pool, coffee & other
events. Also provides peer counseling, community
workshops, open houses, newsletter articles &
support for those infected, affected or concerned
with AIDS. "JUKA" is an African term that
means "Rise up."*

Lesbian Outdoor Club Wayves, Box 34090,
Drawer LOC, Scotia Square, Halifax, NS B3J 1S1
☎ 902-454-0436
Bi-positive organization.

Lesbians & Children Together Halifax, NS
☎ Lena: 902-469-5764
✉ 73654.2033@CompuServe.com
*Social gatherings for lesbians (& supporters) with
children; meets about once a month for parents &
children to meet other lesbian families. Bi-positive
organization.*

**Dalhousie University: Bisexual, Gay & Lesbian
Association of Dalhousie (BGLAD)** Student Union
Building, Rm. 320, 6136 University Av., Halifax,
NS B3H 4J2 ☎ 902-494-1256 ✉ bglad@is2.dal.ca
*Social & support group for LGBTQ university
students. Weekly meetings.*

**Maritime School of Social Work: Lesbian, Gay &
Bisexual Caucus** c/o Rusty Neal, 6414 Coburg
Road, Halifax, NS B3H 2A7 ☎ 902-494-1193
FX: 902-494-6709 ✉ rusty.neal@dal.ca
*Social & support network for social work
students, advocates for curriculum, practice &
policy changes in social work. Some caucus
members available to conduct workshops on
homophobia & heterosexism for groups &
schools. Regular meetings & social events.*

**St. Mary's University: St. Mary's Campus
Outreach Society** Room 516 (5th Floor), Student
Union Bldg., St. Mary's Univ., Halifax, NS B3H
3C3 ☎ 902-496-8717
✉ outreachsociety@hotmail.com
*Safe environment for GLB students to interact &
discuss ideas important to them & show them that
they are not alone.*

**Gay, Lesbian & Bisexual Youth Group at Queen
Elizabeth High School** 1929 Robie Street, Halifax,
NS ☎ 902-421-6797
Contact J. Buffet, guidance counselor.

Lesbian, Gay & Bisexual Youth Project 2281
Brunswick St., Halifax, NS B3K 2Y9 ☎ 902-429-
5429 FX: 902-423-7735 ✉ lgbyp@istar.ca
*Offers social, support & educational groups for
lgb youth -26; conducts educational workshops for
groups & schools; provides support, resources &
advocacy for individuals & youth workers.
Resource library.*

Planned Parenthood Nova Scotia: LGBT Youth Project 6156 Quinpool Road, Suite 100, Halifax, NS B3L 1A3 ☎ 1-800-566-2437; 902-492-0444 (Outline - support line for glbt youth under 26 in NS) ✉ am253@ccn.cs.dal.ca; ppns@istar.ca
Open M-F 9am-4pm. Sexuality info, resource library on sexuality issues, videos, books pamphlets, government reports, LGBT Youth Project resources & workshops on sexuality issues.

Queer News c/o CKDU, 6136 University Av., 4th Fl., Halifax, NS B3H 4J2 ☎ 902-494-6479 FX: 902-494-1110 ✉ ckdufm@is2.dal.ca
Interviews & news from GLBT communities, locally & internationally. Currently airs Wed 12:05-12:30 pm on CKDU FM97.

Men's Sex Project, c/o AIDS Coalition, Nova Scotia Ned MacInnis, 5675 Spring Garden Rd., 6th Fl., Halifax, NS B3J 1H1 ☎ 902-425-4882 FX: 902-422-6200 ✉ acns@kayhay.com
HIV/AIDS prevention, education & support project for gay & bi men in Nova Scotia.

PFLAG Halifax Halifax, NS ☎ Ron: 902-443-3747 ✉ ab274@chebucto.ns.ca
Bi-positive & inclusive.

Red Door Adolescent Health Center 28 Webster Court, Kentville, NS B4N 1H7
☎ Tim: 902-679-1411
Info & resources; support on all aspects of sexuality. Youth group meets Tu. 4pm.

Homosexualist Agenda RR#1, Scotsburn, NS B0K 1R0 ☎ 902-351-2714 ✉ hugmor@north.nsis.com
Promotes freedom & equality for Nova Scotia's LGBT & two-spirited population, confronts homophobia: public education campaign to destroy stereotypes. Future plans: support/outreach for local Pictou County queer community, linking with other groups also fighting for civil rights; participating in the political process for queer liberation.

Cape Breton MsM Group AIDS Coalition of Cape Breton c/o Jean MaQueen, 106 Townsend St., Suite 10, Sydney, NS B1P 6H1
☎ 902-567-1766
Support, educational & social group for gay, bi & non-gay/bi identified men who have sex with men.

Acadia University: Acadia Pride ASU 6836, Wolfville, NS B0P 1Z1 ☎ 902-585-2165 ✉ acadia.pride@acadiau.ca
🖳 dragon.acadiau.ca/apride

> **"You have some queer friends, Dorothy," she said. "The queerness doesn't matter so long as they're friends," was the answer.**
>
> *L Frank Baum, The Road to Oz*

Northwest Territory

Out North Box 2827, Yellowknife, NWT X1A 2R2
☎ 867-669-7279 ✉ Out_north99@hotmail.com
🖳 www.yellowknife.com/ptartan/outnorth.htm

Ontario

Ontario Bisexual Infoline Toronto, ON ☎ 416-925-XTRA x2049 ✉ steve@bi.org
Phone service with info on bisexual groups in southern Ontario & various lgbt organziations in larger cities of northern Ontario.

Lesbian Gay Bi Youth Line of Ontario PO Box 62, Station F, Toronto, ON M4Y 2L4 ☎ 800-268-YOUTH; 416-962-YOUTH FX: 416/962-7967. TDD on all lines ✉ LGBLine@icomm.ca
🖳 www.icomm.ca/lgbline
Peer support/information to LGBT youth in Ontario. Sun-Fri, 4- 9:30pm.

Humber College LGB Club c/o SAC, 205 Humber College Blvd., Etobicoke, ON M9W 5L7
☎ 416-675-6622x5051
✉ lgbclub@hcol.humberc.on.ca
🖳 hcol.humberc.on.ca/html/lgbclub
A positive club for LGB students providing support & education on LGB issues to the college community & organize social events for LGB students.

McMaster University: GLBT Centre c/o Hamilton Hall 406, McMaster University, Hamilton, ON L8S 4K1 ☎ 905-525-9140x27397
✉ glbt@msu.mcmaster.ca 🖳 www-msu.mcmaster.ca/services/glbt/glbt.htm
Social, support groups, including "A Different Voice" radio show. PUB: 10% Plus (newsletter)

RESPECT 276 Hunter Street, West, Hamilton, ON L8P 1S3 ☎ 905-521-1520
Rejuvenate, Excel, Survival, Purpose, Examination, Change, Triumph (RESPECT). Discussion group for GLBT people. Meets 2x/mo. at Melrose United Church, 80 Homewood Ave.

Kingston Lesbian, Gay & Bisexual Association 51 Queen's Crescent, Kingston, ON K7L 3N6
☎ 613-531-8981

Queen's University: Lesbian, Gay & Bisexual Issues Committee c/o Education Commission Office, Kingston, ON K7L 3N6 ☎ 613-545-4816 ✉ lgbic@www.ams.quensu.ca
Responsible for raising awareness & educating on lgb issues on campus (& beyond).

Sisters in Strength 51 Queen's Crescent, Kingston, ON K7L 3N6
A non-judgmental, all womyn's group that tries to provide a safe space for womyn at all stages of discovering their sexuality. Mostly social, but attempts to provide all info needed or requested. Good entry point into the lesbian/bisexual womyn's community. Womyn only, usually youth, but all ages welcome.

Out & About CKWR FM 98.7 Kitchener/Waterloo, ON

LGB entertainment, community info & newsmagazine show.

London Bisexual Network London, ON
☎ 519-433-3762 ✉ LBN_halo@hotmail.com
🖳 www.geocities.com/WestHollywood/Cafe/9790
Support, discussion & networking group, open to all bi / bi-curious men & women. Meets at HALO (649 Colborne St. 2nd floor), 3rd Th. 8-10pm.

Positivity About Youth Sexual Orientation c/o ACOL, 343 Richmond St., London, ON N6A 3C2
☎ David Brownstone: 519-434-1601
Meetings Fri. 8pm, 2nd fl., 343 Richmond St.

University of Western Ontario: Gay, Lesbian & Bisexual Student Affairs UWO, Room 340 UCC, London, ON N6A 3K7 ☎ 519-661-3574 FX: 519-661-3816
Support group for GLB students.

University of Western Ontario: uwOUT! Room 340 UCC, London, ON N6A 3K7 ☎ 519-432-3078

Rainbow Radio Network University of Western Ontario, Rm. 255, UCC, London, ON N6A 3K7
☎ 519-661-3601 business; 661-3600 on-air
CHRW, 94.7 FM, Tu. 10-midnight.

Peel Pride: Gay, Lesbian & Bisexual Youth in Peel c/o Peel Health Dept., 3038 Hurontario St., 3rd floor, Mississauga, ON L5B 3B9
☎ 416-925-9872 x2142
Coalition of Peel youth social agencies & interested individuals who provide support, education & advocacy on behalf of lgb youth. Services includes a drop-in center.

GLIS - Gays, Lesbians in Support Oakville, ON
☎ 905-815-4040x3817
✉ jack.hellewell@sheridanc.on.ca
Social / support groups for glb & friends. Meetings held weekly at the Trafalgar Road Campus of Sheridan College in Oakville.

Gay, Lesbian & Bisexual Youth of Durham Oshawa, ON ☎ 905-665-0051

Al-Anon - Lesbian, Gay & Bisexual Ottawa, ON
☎ Information: 613-237-XTRA 2031
Meets Tu. 8pm at St. Pierre Community Center 172 Gate St. Al-Anon: 12-Step self help group for lgb's affected by someone else's drinking. All welcome. Call main office (above) FMI.

Association of Lesbians, Gays, Transgendered & Bisexuals of Ottawa PO Box 2919 Station D, 318 Lisgar, 2nd Floor, Ottawa, ON KIP 5W9
Home of many lgbt artistic & cultural events.

Carleton College: Gay, Lesbian, Bisexual & Transgendered Centre 427 Unicentre Building, PO Box 401 Unicentre Building, Ottawa, ON K1S 5B6 ☎ 613-520-3723 FX: 613-520-3704
🖳 www.carleton.ca/glbt

Ottawa Bi Women's Discussion Group c/o Pink Triangle Services, 71 Bank Street, 2nd Floor, Ottawa, ON ☎ 613-237-9872 x 2117
✉ bp418@freenet.carleton.ca
Meets 3rd Fri, 7:30pm, at above address.

TORONTO BISEXUAL NETWORK
www.torontobinet.org
416-925-9872 ext.2015

support, discussion, social & pride events, education, political action

BISEXUAL WOMEN OF TORONTO
www.biwot.org
416-925-9872 ext.2198

Ottawa Bi-Poly Group Ottawa, ON
✉ dragon@impertinent.com
🖳 www.polyamory.org/SF/Groups/obpd.html
Meets last Sun. 6pm at Maxwell's, 340 Elgin St.

Pink Triangle Services 71 Bank Street, 2nd Floor, Ottawa, ON ☎ 613-563-4818
Social services agency w / resources including gayline, peer counseling, discussion groups, lending library, speakers bureau. Meeting place for the Ottawa Bi Women's Discussion Group.

Pink Triangle Youth c/o Pink Triangle Services, 71 Bank Street, Ottawa, ON ONT K1P 6H6
☎ 613-563-4818 ✉ pty@doubt.com
🖳 www.gayottawa.net/PTY

Sex Addicts Anonymous (SAA) PO Box 20477, Ottawa, ON K1N 1A3 ☎ 613-786-1060
Sex Addicts 12-Step self help group for lgb's who require support to stop compulsive sex behavior. All welcome.

University of Ottawa: Pride Centre/Centre de la Fierte Box 22, Room 07, 85 University Priv., Ottawa, ON K1N 6N5 ☎ 613-562-5966
FX: 613-562-5969 ✉ pride@aix2.uottawa.ca
Coming out & discussion groups, guest speakers, political action, social events, poster campaign.

Rainbow Service Organization Peterborough, ON
☎ Paul Cummings: 705-876-1845
✉ rmccaugherty@trentu.ca
🖳 www.geocities.com/WestHollywood/3131
Agency catering to needs of lgb's in counties of Peterborough, Northumberland, Victoria & Haliburton. Counseling & social events; monthly dances.

Trent University: Trent Queer Collective
Peterborough, ON ☎ 705-748-1780
✉ queer@trentu.ca 🖳 www.trentu.ca/queer

Community Outreach Project of Algoma (COPA)
Sault Ste. Marie, ON ☎ 705-946-7006
For the lgb community of Sault Ste. Marie. Phone line, social, recreational & gay-positive services.

Gay, Lesbian, Bisexual Youth Group c/o Marco
Theriault, ACCESS Sudbury, 203-111 Elm Street,
Sudbury, ON P3C 1T3 ☎ 705-688-0500
✉ safersex@cyberbeach.net
Meets Mon. September through April. For youth 14- 21. Sponsor: AIDS Committee of Sudbury.

Laurentian University: Pride Association Sudbury,
ON ☎ 705-673-6506 ✉ agll_l@nickel.laurentian.ca
🖳 www.geocities.com/WestHollywood/3859
Meets monthly for students on campus.

Lakehead University: Pride Central Lesbian, Gay & Bisexual Centre c/o LUSU, 955 Oliver Road,
Thunder Bay, ON P7B 5E1 ☎ Jen: 807-343-8813
FX: 807-343-8598 ✉ bgllu@gale.lakeheadu.ca
🖳 www.lakeheadu.ca/~lgbwww
Promotes safety on campus & broadens awareness of lgb issues with the help of a paid Centre coordinator. LGB library.

Toronto Bisexual Network 519 Church Street,
Toronto, ON M4Y 2C9 ☎ 416-925-9872 x2015
✉ tbn@canada.com 🖳 www.torontobinet.org
For bisexuals, their families, friends & lovers. Support, socials, activism & discussion.

BiTO Toronto, ON
Discussion group for the Toronto-area bisexual community. For info on how to join: www.yahoogroups.com / list / bito.

Bisexual Men of Toronto Toronto, ON
☎ 416-536-7373 ✉ borst@chass.utoronto.ca
New group forming in the Toronto area.

Bisexual Women of Toronto 519 Church Street,
Toronto, ON M4Y 2C9 ☎ 416-925-9872 x2198
✉ the_black_orchid@hotmail.com
🖳 www.biwot.org
Support & social network for all bi women or women interested in bisexuality. Discuss various perspectives on current bi issues. Diverse group from the gay & straight communities who try to foster inclusivity by welcoming & encouraging differences. Trans women welcome.

Toronto Poly Discussion Group Toronto, ON
✉ sio@virulent.org 🖳 www.interlog.com/~bcholmes/poly/tpsg.html

Marcia's Bi-Cycle

Healthier Sex Network for Bisexual Men & Women Toronto, ON ☎ 416-925-9872 x 2139
✉ biplayparty@hotmail.com 🖳 www.bi.org/~hsn
Promotes sex-positive, mixed-gender environment for bi people. Occasional parties & social events.

519 Church Street Community Center 519 Church
Street, Toronto, ON M4Y 2C9 ☎ 416-392-6874
City-funded community center.

Coalition for Lesbian & Gay Rights in Ontario Box
822, Station A, Toronto, ON M5W 1G3
☎ 416-533-6824 or 416-925-XTRA x2037
Works toward feminism / LGB liberation. Meets 1st / 3rd Wed, 6-8pm at the 519 Church St. Center.

Lesbian, Gay, Bisexual, Transsexual & Transgender Pride of Toronto 50 Charles Street
East, PO Box 371, Station F, Toronto, ON M4Y
2L8 ☎ 416-92-PRIDE FX: 416-927-7886
✉ parade@pridetoronto.com
🖳 www.pridetoronto.com

Outspoken: Lesbian, Gay & Bi Media Watch Group Toronto, ON ☎ 416-925-XTRA x2212

Gays, Lesbians & Bisexuals International (GLInt)
Toronto, ON ☎ 416-925-XTRA x2187
Support group for interested students & visible minorities whose first language is not English.

Parkdale Gay, Lesbian & Bisexual Group
Toronto, ON ☎ 416-925-XTRA x2012

Portuguese Lesbians, Gays & Bisexuals Toronto,
ON ☎ 416-925-XTRA x2236

University of Toronto at Scarborough: Lesbians, Gays & Bisexuals Toronto, ON ☎ 416-925-XTRA
x2105 ✉ fasc_lgb@fissure.scar.utoronto.ca
🖳 www.scar.utoronto.ca/~fasc_lgb

Coalition of Jewish Gay, Lesbian & Bisexual Students Toronto, ON ☎ 416-925-XTRA x2114

LGB Youth of Toronto 519 Church Street, Toronto,
ON M4Y 2C9 ☎ 416-925-XTRA x2880

Gay, Lesbian, Bi-Youth Support Group York Region Toronto, ON ☎ 416-925-XTRA x2249

Healthier Sex Network for Gay & Bisexual Men
Toronto, ON ☎ 416-925-9872, ext. 2139
✉ dh911@torfree.net 🖳 www.bi.org/~hsn

BGLOW: Bisexual, Gay & Lesbian Organization of Woodstock 377 Buller Street, Woodstock, ON
N4S 4M9 ☎ 519-539-6121; 1-800-755-0394

Prince Edward Island

Abegweit Rainbow Collecive PEI
☎ 894-5776; 1-877-380-5776 (toll free in PEI)
✉ arc@threecats.com
Serving the island's glbt & 2-spirited community.

Island Rainbow Charlottetown, PEI
☎ 902-566-9733

Quebec

Bi-Bec QC ✉ bibec@multimedias.net
📧 wwww.bibec.home.dhs.org/
For bis in Quebec, personal ad, news & very active list (ICQ) Pour les bisexuels du Québec, annonce personelle, forum et une Active List (ICQ) très active !

La cité Bisexuelle ☎418-968-4781
✉ belvox@globetrotter.net 📧 bisexuelle.qc.ca
Resources for francophones. Promotes "Bi pride" & opposes biphobia. Some on-line marketing for bi groups & some Internet expertise. Probably most popular for news of happenings in the bi-French community & help meeting other bisexuals on internet or in real life.

Bi-Montreal Montreal, QC
✉ bimontreal@hotmail.com
📧 welcome.to/bimontreal
Anglophone Group for Montreal bisexuals. Monthly meetings, internet mailing group, online chat & more! Francophones welcome! PUB: Switch Kissers (New independent free local publication for bisexuals. Stories, poems, articles, advice column, classifieds & more! switchkissers@hotmail.com; welcome.to/switchkissers)

Bi Unité Montréal (BUM) C.P. 476 Succursale C, Montréal, QC H2L 4K4 ☎ 514-981-5797
✉ biunitemontreal@hotmail.com
Info & education about bisexuality. Safe place for bisexuals from Montreal. Sports, social, cultural, conference, discussion, community service, education. Vise à informer et éduquer sur la bisexualité et l'identité bisexuelle. Elle vise à doter les bisexuels-les du grand Montréal d'un milieux social et d'outils pour se connaître et se faire comprendre. Elle vise à permettre aux hommes et aux femmes bis d'avoir la possibilité de se former un milieu communautaire et de se doter de ressources appropriées à leur besoins. Nous offrons en plus d'activités sociales, culturelles et sportives, des rencontres-discussions sur des thèmes précis en rapport à la bisexualité, des ateliers / conférences et de la représentation auprès de milieux militants, communautaires GLB et d'éducation .

Montreal bi women (Lana's group) Montreal, QC
✉ lana6855@yahoo.com
Unlisted Yahoo group, a social place where WOMEN from Montreal and surrounding areas can come to meet other bi women. Main language posted is English. Events include pot luck dinners, pajama parties, dance nights, coffee talk, restaurant outings & a regular chat night.

#bisexuelle Undernet Montreal, QC
📧 members.tripod.com/bisex/
Regular social events around Montreal.

McGill University: Lesbians, Bisexual, Gays & Transgendered Students of McGill Shatner Building, Room 416 , 3480 McTavish Street, Montréal, QC H3A 1X9 ☎ 514-398-2106
FX: 514-398-7490 ✉ queer@ssmu.mcgill.ca
📧 ssmu.mcgill.ca/queer/
Small, friendly, social bi discussion group, deals with issues as they specifically relate to bisexual men & women. All bi- & bi-curious people welcome! PUB: Queery (Newsletter 2x/yr.)

Saathi (South Asian Gays, Lesbians & Bisexuals of Montreal/Gais, Lesbiennes et Bisexuels Sud-Asiatiques de Montreal) Montreal, QC
☎ 514-259-2947 ✉ courage@total.net
📧 www.total.net/~courage/saathi.html
Provides a safe space where South Asian Queers may get together socially.

Association des CLSC et des CHSLD du Québec 1801, de Maisonneuve Ouest, Bureau 600, Montreal, QC H3H 1J9 ☎ 514-931-1448
FX: 514-931-9577 ✉ assoc@clsc-chsld.qc.ca
📧 clsc-chsld.qc.ca/
Great resource for teenager & young adults around sexual orientation. Also help for parents with a bisexual teen. They often are the only resource for those who live in area distant.

Platypus: Polyvalence Montreal, QC
✉ mobius67@hotmail.com
📧 www.angelfire.com/pq/polyvalence/
Called Polyvalence because we want people to revel in these multifaceted aspects of sexuality. We try to create a space for everyone, from the brazen to the shy, to feel comfortable, where you can't assume anything about anyone's sexual preference!

> **"You could say love leaps burning / hot in me like the fires / of a star and it needs many / windows, many doors, or it eats / me to ash. Energy forces me / outward expanding like a universe / yet I can stand to leave / nothing, no one I have loved."**
>
> *Marge Piercy*

Saskatchewan

Pridenet - Saskatchewan
💻 www.pridenet.com/sask.html *LGBT website.*

Gay Saskatchewan ✉ bryon@dlcwest.com
💻 gaysask.iwarp.com *LGBT website.*

Pink Triangle Community Services Box 24031
Broad Street PO, 2070 Broad St., Regina, SK
@4P 4J8 ☎ 306-525-6046
✉ ptcsregina@canada.com 💻 members.xoom.com/
ptcs/
*Health education, support, social, counseling,
library, Mon. & Tu. 4-7pm, Wed.-Fri. 7-10pm.*

**Gay, Lesbian & Bisexual Pride Committee of
Regina** Regina, SK
✉ pride-regina@gaycanada.com
💻 www.gaycanada.com/pride-regina/

Men's Monthly Potluck Supper Regina, SK
✉ cschlamp@cableregina.com
💻 www.gaycanada.com/pride-regina/bulletin.htm
Open to all gay/bi men.

The Lavender Social Club Regina, SK
☎ 306-584-7817; 306-775-0169
✉ wanbo@cableregina.com
💻 www.gaycanada.com/pride-regina/bulletin.htm
*Holds women's dances 3rd Sat in the multi-
purpose room at the GLCR 2070 Broad St.*

Prairie Pride Chorus c/o Wesley United Church,
3913 Hillsdale Street, Regina, SK
☎ 306-347-7671; 306-757-0543
💻 www.gaycanada.com/pride-regina/bulletin.htm
*Regina's GLB Chorus. Meets Wed at Wesley
United Church, 3913 Hillsdale St. 7:30-9:30pm,
with coffee afterwards at Magellan's Global Coffee
House, 1800 College.*

Inside Out (Pink Triangle Youth Group) PO Box
24031, 2160 Broad St, Regina, SK S4P 4J8
☎ 306-525-6046
✉ insideout.youthgroup@canada.com
💻 members.xoom.com/ptcs/io.html
*Bi-weekly youth support & social group, 13-24.
Other events.*

**University of Regina: Gays, Bisexuals & Lesbians
at the U of R** c/o University of Regina Students
Union, Regina, SK S4S 0A2 ☎ 306-525-6046
✉ g_blur@hotmail.com
*Biweekly meetings, games/movie nights, special
events, advocacy, hosts pride week every June,
social, support, academic group for students,
faculty & staff at the University.*

Koinonia Wesley United Church, Box 3181, 3913
Hillsdale Ave., Regina, SK S4P 3G7 ☎ 306-525-
8542
Services 2nd & 4th Sat. 7pm.

All Nations Hope Aboriginal AIDS Network Scotia
Bank Building, 1504 Albert Street, Regina, SK
S4P 2S4 ☎ 306-924-8424 or toll free 877-210-7622
FX: 306-525-0904 ✉ makan@sk.sympatico.ca

Perceptions PO Box 8581, 3rd Floor, 241-2 Ave.
S., Saskatoon, SK S7N 4J8 ☎ 306-244-1930
FX: 306-665-9976 ✉ perceptions@the.link.ca
PUB: Perceptions (8x/year. Free distribution.
Subscriptions Can. $22/yr.)

University of Saskatchewan: LGBT PO Box 639,
University of Saskatchewan, Saskatoon, SK S7N
4J8 ☎ 306-652-6080
Support for faculty & staff at the University.

AIDS Programs South Saskatchewan Scotia Bank
Building, 1504B Albert St, Regina, SK S4P 2S4
☎ 306- 924-8420 or toll free: 877-210-7623
FX: 306- 525-0904 ✉ aids.regina@sk.sympatico.ca

CHILE

Centro Lambda Chile Casilla Postal 53575,
Centro Casillas de Santiago, Santiago
✉ redaccom@nova.humanista.cl

**Padres y Familiares de Lesbianas y
Homosexuales (PFLAG)** ✉ chilaids@cchps.mic.cl

CHINA

bi You Yun

Beijing Hotline: 010-64266958. It's
called an "AIDS hotline," but people know
that it's about sexual minorities, too. It's
actually a pager number, not a phone
line. I was told that the volunteers
received thousands of phone calls from all
over China in the months after the
number was publicized in a popular
magazine, so the volunteers had a hard
time finding enough funding to cover
their returning calls. This number was
established in 1997 or 1996, but until the
summer of 1998 was only publicized by
word of mouth within the community.

In Mainland China, although the
visible glbt community has been developing for a few years, there have not been
any formally-named groups until very
recently, because forming non-governmental organizations is a very sensitive
matter there. The first named lesbian
group is Beijing Sister, established in
October 1998, after the first national

lesbian conference in China held on October 2 and 3, 1998. The gay male communities are a lot larger than the lesbian ones in terms of size & number of members, but, to my knowledge, there are also no self-named gay male groups within Mainland China to this day.

Bisexual identity seems to carry somewhat different meanings in China than in the West. To a large extent, the gay or lesbian community does not exclude bisexual people. The absence of the so-called "biphobia" which exists in the West seems obvious, although such an absence is apparently not complete. Indeed, because, in China, the general public still strongly disapproves of same-sex love, some bisexual people see their being able to form heterosexual marriages as real advantage. Although not every bisexual person in China may think that way, it's extremely rare for bis to be accused by gays or lesbians for being "not brave enough to admit." Practically, the prevailing heterosexism puts all people who have same-sex romantic passion in the same boat.

In addition, the Chinese lgbt people (not only in Mainland China, but also in Hong Kong, Taiwan, and some other Asian countries) conceptualize their sexual identity now by a term "Tongzhi" (meaning "comrade." "Tong" meaning "homo," and the Chinese term homosexuality, "tongxinglian," also starts with the same character "tong"), in some sense similar to the English term "queer," but not totally equivalent. In the lgbt context, Tongzhi means people who are not traditionally heterosexual, therefore including gays, lesbians, bisexuals, transgenders and transsexuals, cross-dressers, even S/M, even heterosexual people who are willing to accept sexual minorities. In other words, the Tongzhi community includes bisexual people. Since the late 1980s, gay bars have appeared in almost all major cities in China, while there has not been a single lesbian-exclusive bar. Meanwhile, other alternative community-building means

Robyn Ochs
Meeting at IBC6 on International Bi Organizing

like discussion groups are also developing. For example, in the summer of 1998, a group of glbt people gathered in Lemon Tree Cafe in Beijing for discussion and began a monthly discussion gathering that welcomes anybody to attend. Some activists and scholars have also brought LGBT issues into the discussion in other public settings like the Women's Tea House.

There are regular social gatherings for lgbt people in big cities like Beijing. However, most lgbt people in smaller cities or rural areas still live in tremendous isolation, let alone possible discrimination if one's identity is exposed. So community activists are trying to develop a broader communication network for LGBT people to reduce the isolation most of them have to face in their everyday lives.

As in most other parts of the world, the Internet has also been playing a very important role in connecting LGBT people in China. Here is an incomplete list of the major lgbt websites in China: http://bbs.gzsums.edu.cn/~bbs/. Click "Eden Garden" then click "Homosexuality."

There are quite a few serious gay novels & other good articles. Please note that this website is in mainland China & any erotic materials or radical articles in it may cause its shut-down! I suggest reading the articles while remaining silent, don't cause it to be focused on by security administration. (I quote this entire paragraph from somebody else who is on a Chinese lgbt e-mail list I'm also on.)

http://aizhi.sis.com.cn This site is the on-line version of the AIZHI newsletter, the oldest lgbt advocate newsletter in China started in 1994. This website started in the summer of 1998.

http://www.youmail.com.cn/cafe and http://www.youmail.com.cn/friends (The newsletter "Friends" by dermatologist Dr. Beichuan Zhang, a more academic-oriented newsletter that not only discusses issues related to homosexuality but also intends to bring people in sexual minorities and the so-called "mainstream" together.)

http://www.zg169.net/~les (this is a lesbian and bisexual women—female Tongzhi—website, established in last August 1998. It's pretty active now.)

Besides those in Mainland China, there is a US-based website mainly devoted to the Tongzhi community in Mainland China and the LGBT in the US who are from Mainland China at < http://www.csssm.org >. The organization's name is "the Chinese Society for the Study of Sexual Minorities" (CSSSM), started in September 1997. (I'm one of the founders & current members). The CSSSM publishes a bilingual (Chinese & English), bi-weekly webzine "Tao Hong Men Tian Xia" (direct translation is "pink color all over the world," meaning "we lgbt people are anywhere").

"Lavender Phoenix" is another US-based group, "a network for lesbians & bisexual women in & from Mainland China," started in May 1997 by five lesbians & bisexual women from China in the US (I was one of them). Its web address is members.theglobe.com/tongzhi/ch079802.htmlContact e-mail addresses: < lavender_phoenix@hotmail.com > & < lavphoenix@aol.com >.

COLOMBIA

RIT Apdo Aereo 57724, Santafe de Bogotá ☎ Voicemail: (91) 5007927
Gay/bi group that publishes gay info booklet & coordinates gay conferences, groups, etc.

Equilateros Apartado Aereo 25770, Santafe de Bogotá ☎ (91) 2559814
✉ velandia.sexosida@urc.net.co
Gay-bi group providing support, AIDS education, & activism.

Universidad Anteriormente de U.Andes: GADOS Apdo Aereo 241889, Santafe de Bogotá ☎ Cell: (93)-226-7049; VM: (91) 5051222
📖 www.prof.uniandes.edu.co/~gados/
Weekly social meetings.

Universidad Nacional de Colombia: GAEDS Apdo Aereo 76811, Santafe de Bogotá ☎ (91) 5009100
Lesbigay group.

Proyecto Lambda - Liga Colombiana de Lucha contra el SIDA [Colombian League for the Fight Against AIDS] Avenida 32 # 14-46, Santafe de Bogotá ☎ +57 1 245 4757 FX: +57 1 338 0432
✉ ligasida@latino.net.co 📖 www.aidsnet.ch/i/orgaddress_int_doccentre_col.htm

Comunidad del Discipulo Amado Salon Parroquial Iglesia Santa Teresita, Cra 18 No 43-59, Bogota ☎ (91) 7682100
Gay/bi support group with a religious orientation Meets Sun. 2-4.

ASOCIACION O.G. Apartado aereo 103, Ibague ☎ (982) 620201

COSTA RICA

Costa Rican editor was unable to locate any groups for or inclusive of bisexual people.

CZECH REPUBLIC

Promluv A-club, Milíèova 25, Prague, 100 00 *For lesbians & bisexual women. Focuses on physical & emotional health, contacts & referrals, publication of a magazine (Promluv), & disseminating accurate information about lesbians.* PUB: Promluv
Czech Republic web resources
🖳 www.gay.cz/kontakty_org.htm
Extensive on-line listing of Czech gay groups.

Bi Pride in France

DENMARK

Landsforeningen for bøsser og lesbiske, Forbundet av 1948 Postboks 1023, Teglgårdsstræde 13, Baghuset, Copenhagen, 1007 ✉ lbl@lbl.dk 🖳 www.lbl.dk
☎ +45 33 13 19 48 FX: +45 33 36 00 83
Bisex-Linien Amagertorv 33, Copenhagen
☎ +45 33 33 00 36
Counseling hotline for bi men Mon. & Th. 5-10pm. Support group 1st Wed. for bi men & their partners.

FIJI

Sexual Minorities Project c/o Women's Action for Change, PO Box 12398, Suva ☎011-679-314363 FX: 011-679-305033
Fiji's first gay group!

ECUADOR

Fundación Ecuatoriana de Acción y Prevención para la Promoción de la Salud (FEDAEPS) [Ecuadorian Action & Prevention Foundation for the Promotion of Health] Casilla Postal 165551 Santiago 9, Chile, Baquerizo 166 y Tamayo, Quito ✉ admin@fedaeps.ecuanex.net.ec
☎/FX: 593 2 223 298
Action/prevention health group.

EL SALVADOR

Asociacion Entre Amigos [Among Friends] Avenida y Colonia Santa Victoria, No. 50, Costado Norte Boulevard de los Heroes, San Salvador ☎ 503 225-4213 or 235-1640 ✉ entreamigos@salnet.net
Dutch government-funded 18 page glossy publication, produced by the gay/bisexual program of El Salvador's Foundation for AiDS Prevention, Education & Management (FUNDASIDA). Covers activism, safer sex, community events, & social & legal matters.

ESTONIA

Estonian Association for Lesbians & Bisexual Women (Eesti Lesbiliste ja Binaiste ja Binaiste Ühing (Eesti LesBiÜhing)) Box 3245, 10505, Tallinn ☎ +372 5511132 ✉ eluell@saturn.zzz.ee
Member of ILGA.

FINLAND

Bi Group at SETA Hietalahdenkatu 2 B 16, 00180 Helsinki ☎ +358-9-6123233 (SETA Office) FX: +358-9-6123266 ✉ sossuhki@seta.fi
🖳 www.seta.fi
Meets every 2nd week. Inquire from Seta office on present meeting times.
Women's Bi Group of Helsinki
c/o Naisasialiitto Unioni, Bulevardi 11A, Helsinki ☎ (0)9-643 158 (office hours)
Meets monthly at the above address.
Helsinki University of Technology: Telehpy
Helsinki ✉ telehpy@tky.hut.fi 🖳 www.tky.hut.fi/ ~telehpy/english.html
GLB student group. Meets every other Th. during terms, usually "takkakabinetti" on the ground floor of Jämeräntaival 3A at 7pm. All welcome, regardless of gender or sexual preference.
Homoglobiini PL 288, Fin-20100 Turku ✉ homoglobiini@iname.com
🖳 org.utu.fi/tyyala/homoglobiini/
Turku student glb organisation. Very active & bi-inclusive. Meets during term time (1.9.-31.5.) every 1. & 3. Mon. 7pm Seta office (Rauhankatu 1 c B 22).
Finnish Bi mailing list ✉ bi-lista@netmafia.org
🖳 www.tml.hut.fi/~viu/BI/
The main language of this list is Finnish. Subscribe by sending a message to bi-tilaus@netmafia.org.

FRANCE

Bi-France c/o M. Leo, 1, Montee des Carmelites, Lyon 69001

Au dela du personnel c/o Leo Vidal, 11 rue de l'annonciade, Lyon 69001 ☎ 04 72 008965 FX: 04 72 00 89 65 ✉ lthiers@hol.fr
Libertarian Movement; reflections about feminism, bisexuality, non-monogamy, anarchism. PUB: Au dela du personnel (Book: Editor ACL, 1998 issue)

Groupe Action Gaie (GAG) Initiatives Plurielles, Maison Des Associations, Orleans 45 000 ☎ 02 38 53 2024
Movie club; welcome meetings.
PUB: Le Petit Rose (Black & White; association's news; activities program)

Bi'Cause c/o Centre Gai et Lesbien, 3 Rue Keller, Paris 75 011 ☎ Bi'Cause info line: 01-48-05-13-13; Centre: 01-43-57-21-47
✉ Bi'CauseOnLine@pelnet.com
🖥 www.pelnet.com/bicause
Meets alternate Mon. 8pm at the G/L Centre for discussion/debate; & 2nd Th. in a bar (social). Free monthly writing workshop. Free social support workshop every 2 months, with psychologist. (Bastille/Voltaire or Ledru Rollin metro stop). PUB: Bi'Cause (Black & White: 4-8 pp quarterly; News, association info, outline, books, agenda: available at the CGL)

Let it Bi Paris ✉ letitbe@geocities.com
🖥 www.geocities.com/WestHollywood/Heights/3537
French language news on web. Bibliography, books & bisexuality in the press. List of bi celebrities, bi films, bi organizations & bi web sites.

#bisexuelle (Webnet) Geidex, 13 rue Saint Honoré, Versailles 78180 ✉ admin@bisexuelle.net
🖥 www.bisexuelle.net
Pour les bi et bic-curieux francophones, club privé, dialogue en direct et information. [For French bi & bi-curious, private club, chat & info.]

GERMANY

BiNE - Bisexuelles Netzwerk e. V. Postfach 61 02 14, Berlin 10923 ☎/FX:Bi Helpline 030 -211 74 05 Mon., Wed. 5-6:30pm ✉ zbi@bi.org
🖥 www.bi.org/~bine/ or www.bine.net
National bi group. For info contact Volker at 02761 / 79 01 62 or volker_wielgoss@hotmail.com.

Schwindelfrei Fachschaft Philosophie, Kármánstr. 11, Aachen 52062 ☎ Maria 0241 - 980 10 98 ✉ schwindelfrei@gmx.de
Gesprächskreis, meets every 3rd Sun. at 8pm.

Bi-Frauen Gruppe Berlin Frieda Frauenzentrum e.V., Proskauer Str. 7, 10247 Berlin (Friedrichshain)
Open discussion groups (call for times) & bi women's dances.

Offener Gespräechskreis Bisexualität c/o Sonntags-Club e.V., Greifenhagener Str. 28, Berlin 10437 ☎ 030-4497590 FX: 030-4485457 ✉ info@sonntags-club.de, Subject=Bi-Kreis
🖥 www.sonntags-club.de
Open & theme meetings.

Zentrum für bisexuelle Lebensweisen Nachodstr. 17, Berlin 10779 ☎ Jürgen 030 - 21 47 86 21 ✉ zbi@bi.org

Bisexuellen-Stammtisch Berlin Cri-Cri am Engelbecken, Erkelenzdamm 17, Berlin 10999
Meets 1st Fri. 8pm.

Bisco Berlin (Bi Disco) Ackerkeller, Ackerstr. 12/13 HH, Berlin 10115 ☎ Syivia 030 - 81 49 68 80; Bellus 030 - 681 42 91 ✉ Elfengefluester@aol.com

Lesbenberatung Kulmer Straße 20a, 2.Hinterhof (court), Berlin 10783 ☎ 030-2152000
Anonymous counseling for L & B women over the phone & by appointment. Mon., Tu. & Th. 4-7pm, Fri. 2-5 pm. Library, bi women's dances & other activities, open discussion groups & workshops. Young lesbians day every Wed., 4-5pm on the phone, 5-7pm at above address.

Christopher Street Day, 1998, Cologne, Germany

Referat für Lesben, Schwule, Bi- und Transsexuelle der FU Kiebitzweg 23, Berlin 14195 ☎ 030-83 90 91-18 FX: 030-831 45 36 ✉ schwule@zedat.fu-berlin.de
🖥 userpage.fu-berlin.de/~schwule/referat.html
LGBT Support Group.

Bielefelder Bi-Maennergruppe Bürgerwache, Raum 201, Siegfriedplatz, Bielefeld 33615 ☎ Klaus-Dieter 0521 - 89 18 65 🖥 www.bine.net/german/bigruppen/bielefeld.html

Stammtisch Magnus, August-Bebel-Str. 126, Bielefeld 33602 ☎ Klaus-Dieter 0521 - 89 18 65

Christliche Bi-Gruppe Bonn c/o D. Klein, Postfach 41 02 32, Bonn 53024 ✉ bichthys@gmx.net ▣ members.tripod.de/Bichthys/kontakt.htm

Bi-Gruppe Braunschweig c/o Braunschweiger AIDS-Hilfe, Eulenstrasse 5, Braunschweig 38114 ☎ Irmgard 0531 - 280 79 71 ✉ iroesch@aol.com ▣ www.bine.net/german/bigruppen/ braunschweig.html

Bi-Gruppe-Bremen c/o Rat und Tat Zentrum, Theodor-Körner-Strasse 1, Bremen 28203 ☎ 0421-7000007 FX: 0421-7000009

BiNe Jugendtreffen Addi Keil, Postfach 104 261, Bremen 28042 ☎ Addi 0421 - 794 97 49 ✉ jugend@bine.net

homland Gruppe für Lesben, Schwule + Bisexuelle Postfach 1116, Dessau 06812 ☎ 0340 - 882 69 34 ✉ homlandberatung@gmx.de

Bi-Gruppe Erfurt SwiB-Zentrum, Windhorststrasse 43a, Erfurt 99096 ☎ David 0361 - 373 22 83 ✉ DavidBenAvram@t-online.de

Gesprächskreis MixBis Frankfurt 60. ☎ Thomas & Harald 06192 - 4 28 68 Winnie 069 - 50 93 01 82

Frauengruppe Frankfurt 60. ☎ Winnie 069 - 50 93 01 82

Stammtisch bisexueller Frauen und Maenner Weinstube, Egenolffstr. 17, Frankfurt (Nordend) 60316 ☎ Thomas & Harald: 06192 - 42868;Winnie: 069 - 50 93 01 82 ✉ frankfurt-main@bine.net

Bi-gruppe Gelsenkirchen c/o AIDS-Hilfe Gelsenkirchen, Husemann Str. 39-41, Gelsenkirchen 45879 ☎ Juergen: 0201-8554599 (evening), Petra: 0209-399789 (evening) or Inge and Jutta: 0234-332987 (evening) ✉ xuferlos@aol.com ▣ www.bine.net/german/ bigruppen/gelsenkirchen/rubi.html *Meets monthly.*

Bi-Gruppe Göttingen Gemeindehaus der Reformierten Gemeinde, Untere Karspüle 11, Göttingen 37073 ☎ Johanna: 0551 - 531 19 24 ▣ bine.net/german/bigruppen/goettingen.html

LesBiSchwuler Chor Belle Alliance Magnus Hirschfeld Zentrum, Borgweg 8, Hamburg *LGB Choir, meets Fri. 18:00.*

Schwule und Bisexuelle zwischen 30 und 40 Cafe Magnus, Borgweg 8, Hamburg *Gay & bisexuals 30-40, meet Fri. 20:00.*

B6Y-Treff Heidelberg 69. ☎ 06227 - 542 62; Joachim 06221 - 2 91 89

Frauen-Bi-Treff Heidelberg 69. ☎ Margret 06227 - 542 62

Christopher Street Day, 1998, Cologne: Germany

Hilde Vossen

BI-ings, Bi-Gruppe Hildesheim c/o Hildesheimer AIDS-Hilfe, Zingel 14, 31134 Hildesheim ☎ Birgit Jost: 05121-133127

Stammtisch Kassel 34127 ☎ Sascha 0561 - 890 69 34 ✉ d.rennek@gmx.de

Ansprechperson Koblenz 560. ☎ Andreas 02638 - 66 52

Koelner Bi-Frauengruppe Schulz, Karthaeuserwall 18, Koeln/Cologne (Suedstadt) 50678 ☎ Iris Wallerath 9221-875699 *Open discussion group only for women.*

UFERLOS Kölner Bi-Gruppe e.V. c/o Bürgerzentrum Ehrenfeld, Venloer Str. 429, Köln/ Cologne 50823 ☎ Peter 0214 - 471 40, Armin 0221- 61 37 30 ✉ uferlos-koeln@gmx.de ▣ bine.net/german/bigruppen/koeln/koeln.html *Meetings for open discussion group, special discussion group & organisation team.*

Uferlos Party Köln SchuLZ Koelner Schwulen- und Lesbenzentrum , Karthaeuserwall 18, Köln/ Cologne (Ehrenfeld) 50678 ☎ Peter 0214-47140 ▣ bine.net/german/bigruppen/koeln/koeln.html

LesBiSchwule Jugendgruppe Konstanz Konstanz ☎ Stefan 0173 - 3257939 or Ute 0179 - 5052613 ✉ StefanBaier@gmx.de or sfinxx@gmx.net

Bi-Gruppe Laatzen c/o Kontaktzentrum, Kiefernweg 2, Laatzen 30880 ☎Volker von Thenen 05102 / 3799 *Meets 2nd Wed. every month 7:30pm.*

Bi-O-Logisch Mainz-Wiesbaden c/o Mainzer Aids-Hilfe, Hopfengarten 19, Mainz 55116 ☎ Werner: 0611-598947 Petra 06131-678332 *Bi Stammtisch meets every 2nd Wed. Bi Gruppe meets every 4th Wed.*

Bi-Gruppe München c/o SUB, Müllerstr 43, München 80469 ☎ 089-2603056

Bi Stammtisch - München München 80469

Eltern homo- und bisexueller Jugendlicher und Erwachsener Neumünster 24530 ☎ Ingrid 04321 - 21875 *A group for parents of homo- & bisexual youths & adults.*

> The girl was getting used to queer adventures, which interested her very much.
>
> *L Frank Baum, The Road to Oz*

Bi-Gruppe Nürnberg Morrison Glockenhofstr. 39, 90478 Nürnberg ☎ Christina: 0911-4180091; Edwin: 0911-3609944; Fred: 0911-3939271 ✉ edwin.goebel@t-online.de

Kontaktpersonen Olpe (Südwestfalen) 57462 ☎ Volker, Silke 02761 - 79 01 68 ✉ BiGruSWF@gmx.de

Bi-Gruppe Potsdam Potsdam ☎ 0331-901313

Bi-Gruppe Stuttgart Stuttgart 70199 ☎ Andreas 0711 - 262 13 55 Gyula 07146 - 86 185 ✉ stubigru@hotmail.com

Bi-Gruppe Trier SchmiT-Zentrum, Mustorstr. 4, Trier 54290 ☎ John 0651 – 241 63 or 970 44 11 daytime
Meets 2nd & 4th Th. 8pm.

GUATEMALA

OASIS: (Organizacion de Apoyo a una Sexualidad Integral frente al SIDA) Apto Postal 1289, Guatemala ☎ 502-253 3453; 502-220 1332 FX: 502-232 1021 ✉ oasisgua@terra.com
🖳 www.maxpages.com/oasis
Works with marginalized groups including glbt, sex workers, & ghetto youth. Various educational activities/groups: health/HIV/AIDS/sexuality education, self-esteem, codependency, alcohol/ drug addiction, & human rights work. Also sponsors cultural activities: films, art shows, parties. Members of ARCEGAL (Asociacion Regional Centroamericana de Gays y Lesbianas).

Asociación de Talleres Holísticos (ATH) Apdo. Postal 1289, Ciudad de Guatemala ☎/FX: 502/22-33-35 ✉ pmpasca@guate.net
Primarily gives sessions/lecture & conductions discussions on sexuality, mostly for youth in the capital. Support & services for HIV/AIDS. Contacts: Ruben Mayorga, Fernando Arevalo, Jose Mario Maza.

HONDURAS

Grupo PRISMA Apartado Postal 4590, Tegulcigalpa ☎ 504-232-8342 ✉ prisma@sdnhon.org.hn 🖳 504-232-6058/ 232-8342
Social/educational group working for empowerment of the LBG community in Honduras within the greater context of human rights. Publication has articles & information about local events.

HONG KONG

HK-QUEER ✉ majordomo@sqzm14.ust.hk
For glb people in Hong Kong. To subscribe send message to majordomo@sqzm14.ust.hk. In the body of message write: "subscribe hkqueer"

Zi Mei Tong Zhi - Queer Sisters Hong Kong Central Post Office #9313 ☎ 852-23144348 (answered live Thursdays 7:30-10pm) ✉ qs@qs.org.hk 🖳 www.qs.org.hk
Feminist organization advocating & fighting for women's sexual rights, comprised of women who are tired of "being told to stick to one SEXual ID & one kind of feminist idea" & never can we be named or explained by one (whatever) ism. We are playful & serious, personal & political, involved in a movement fighting for a more inclusive, more open & better world with larger space for women, as sexual beings & as subjects, who have different, various & ever-changing routes in the immense domain of sexuality. We believe in a never ending search for the indeterminacy, heterogeneity, multiplicity, transgressiveness & variance of sexuality & sexual choices. Projects include research, a hotline, a quarterly newsletter, workshops, fundraising parties & having fun.

Hong Kong Ten Percent Club GPO Box 72207, Kowloon
Gay & lesbian group.

Joint College Queer Union
🖳 www.asiaonline.net.hk/~skjliu
For Hong Kong's GLB students.

Hong Kong Blessed Minority Christian Fellowship PO Box 20516, Hennessy Road Post Office ☎ (852) 2834 6601 ✉ minoritychurch@geocities.com
🖳 www.geocities.com/WestHollywood/6262/
GLB Christian Fellowship. 1st Sun. 4-6pm at Li Hall, St. John Cathedral.

HUNGARY

Lambda Budapest - Association of Gay Friends (Lambda Budapest - Meleg Baráti Társaság) PO Box 388, 1461 Budapest ☎ 266-9959 ✉ masok@masok.hu 🖳 www.masok.hu

Gay Switchboad Budapest Postbox 752, H-1437, Budapest ☎ +36-30-323334 FX: +36-1-3512015 ✉ budapest@compuserve.com
🖳 gaytoday.badpuppy.com/garchive/tech/ 030998te.htm
Hotline 4-8pm for questions ranging from social events to HIV/AIDS education to navigating as a tourist in Budapest (including money, travel, weather, etc). Staff fluent in English, German, & Hungarian.

Kesergay PO Box 50, 1554 Budapest
Hungarian Jewish group of lesbians & gays.

ICELAND

Samtokin '78: Icelandic Organisation of Lesbians & Gay Men Postholf 1262, 121 Reykjavik, Reykjavik 121 ☎ 354-5528539 FX: 354-5527525 ✉ gayice@mmedia.is 🖳 www.gayiceland.com/reykjavik/
National organization w/several groups, including a small group for bisexual people. "The organisation of course welcomes bisexual people in all of its activities. We have a gay center at Lindargata 49 with a coffeeshop & a library open M, Th 8-11pm & Sat. 9:30pm-1am." Also in Iceland: "semi-gay" bar at Laugavegur 22, & gay guesthouse "Room With a View" at Laugavegur 18 (ph/fax: +354 522 7262), gay radio 89.3 (24 hours/day)" PUB: Samtakafrettir (Small newsletter which gives details on what's happening each month. In Icelandic.)

INDIA

LGBT India ☎91-80-548120; 91-98440-10022 ✉ owaiskhan@hotmail.com 🖳 www.geocities.com/WestHollywood/Cafe/8033/
Communication collective of Indian glbt organizations & activists. Staged 1st annual "Friendship Walk" 7/2/99 in Calcutta, visiting the offices of various non-governmental & community-based organizations to teach "about the significance of the Stonewall Riots."

BiIndia listserv ✉ biindia@hotmail.com
Email list for bisexuals living in India or of Indian origin.

Khushnet India: Indian South Asian Network Online 🖳 www.khushnet.com/directory/india.htm
Extensive listings for South Asian glb groups in India, including Secunderabid, New Dehli, Bombay, Lucknow, Dehli, Banglore, Calcutta, Cochiri, etc.

SANGAMA 1st Floor, No.7, 8th Main, 3rd Phase, Domlur 2nd Stage, Banglore, Karnataka 560071 ☎ 080-5309591 ✉ admin@sangama.ilban.ernet.in
Resource center on sexuality. Provides info, action & support for sexual minorities, their families & friends & helps enlarge social, cultural & political space for sexual minorities. Sensitization workshops, public lectures & film screenings on issues related to sexual minorities & sexual health. Helps sexual minorities to come to terms with their sexuality & live with self-acceptance, self-respect & dignity.

The only abnormality is the incapacity to love.

—Anaïs Nin, French writer, 1903-1977

Stree Sangam PO Box No 16613, Matunga, Bombay 400 019 ✉ admin@faow.ilbom.ernet.in
A collective of lesbian & bisexual women.

Counsel Club c/o Pawan, Post Bag 10237, Calcutta 700 019
For glb people. Annual membership of Rs 200/ $10 for Naya Pravartak subscription, penpal listing, access to archives, counseling help.

Sappho c/o A.N., PO Box EC-35, Calcutta - 10, Calcutta, West Bengal 700010 ✉ malvi99@hotmail.com

Humsafar Trust (India) Post Box 6913, Santa Cruz West, Mumbai, Maharastra 600 056 ☎ 91-22-972-6913 ✉ humsafar@vsnl.com 🖳 www.humsafar.org/
Drop-in centre for men who have sex with men (MSM). In person & phone counseling, condom distribution, outreach work.

Humrahi Editor-Darpan, PO Box-3910, Andrews Ganj, New Delhi 110 049 ☎ "Humraz" Helpline: 685-9113 Mon & Thu 7-9pm; to volunteer call 685-1970/71. ✉ owais@bigfoot.com 🖳 www.geocities.com/WestHollywood/Heights/7258/
Meets Sat. 7-8:30pm (& 'tries' to move on to a bar) at Naz, C-1/E Green Park Extension, off Aurobindo Marg, New Delhi. PUB: Darpan

AASRA Circle GPO BOX 68, Patna, Bihar 800 001 ☎ 91-0612-271598 ✉ aasra@dte.vsnl.net.in
Health & Human Rights Advocacy & Support group for BGLT people working to place recognition & action for GLBT rights on the wider 'mainstream' community agenda. PUB: Timeshare (Bulletin with community news, views, & global information. Language: English with space for vernacular content (Hindi & Nepali))

INDONESIA

GAYa NUSANTARA (GN) Jln Mulyosari Timur 46, Surabaya, Ja-Tim 60112 ☎ (62-31) 593-4924 FX: 599-3569 ✉ gayanusa@ilga.org
Provides personal contacts, HIV/AIDS counseling, community outreach & gay awareness workshops. Coordinates the Indonesian l/g network, consisting of l/g organizations & individual activists throughout the nation. Many of the organizations in the network comprise transgendered people (waria) & lesbians. Other coordinating bodies are IPOOS/Gaya Betawi for the Jakarta metropolitan area and Sumatra, Gaya Dewata for Bali, Nusa Tenggara & East Timor, and Gaya Celebes for Celebes, the Moluccas & Irian Jaya (West Papua). PUB: GAYa NUSANTARA (Monthly.)

Indonesian BGay Society (IGS) PO Box 36/ YKBS, Yogyakarta 55281 ✉ ambrossi@idola.net.id

---

Buku Seri IPOOS Gaya Betawi Kotak Pos 7631/ JKBTN, JKBT, Jakarta Barat 11470 (62-21)
☎ 566-0589 (9-6, except Tuesdays)
Indonesian periodical put out by Indonesian gay organization.

Zaqzim Gaya Metropolitan Jln Tanah Tinggi IV RT4 RW03 No. 15A, Jakarta Pusat, 10000
☎ 62-21-442-3874 Mitras
Kotak Pos 3308/JKP, Jakarta Pusat 10038
✉ blue_blue@rocketmail.com
Indonesian lesbian group, publish LaMitraS newsletter.

GUCHI - Gabungan Cowok Homo Indonesia Jln Sukolilo 311, Semarang, Ja-Tang 50000
Society of Gay Men in Indonesia.

Kang Bakak 1211 PO Box 183, Serang, West Java 42101

IRELAND

Bi Irish c/o OUThouse, PO Box 4767, Dublin
☎ Darragh, (h) +353 1 670 56 80
✉ bi.irish.@bi.org 🖳 bi.org/~bi.irish/
"For bisexuals & others who feel not quite straight...main focus is on the exploration & validation of bisexual identities..."

Gay Ireland Website 🖳 gayireland.com
Sister to 'Irish Queer' website. Similiar in info, but different in tone. Largely Dublin-based info.

Lesbian & Gay Resource Centre 8 South Main St, Cork ☎ 021-278470 FX: 021-287471
Married Gay Men Group Wed. 7-9pm, Sat. 3-5pm. Contact 021-271087.

The Other Side Bookshop & Cafe 8 South Main St., Cork ☎ (021) 278 470
Open Tu.-Sun. 11am-7:30pm. Holds a range of community center meetings & workshops.

L&G Resource Group The Other Place, 8 South Main Street, Cork City, Cork County
A group connected to Cork's wider gay scene, with access to bookshop, cafe & club.

Queer Na Nog Cork City, Cork County
☎ code - 278 470
Ask for Emmet when phoning. Aimed at -25s.

Lesbian Phone Line, Cork City, Cork County
☎ code - 271 087
Answered live Th. 8-10pm.

Reach: Gay Christian Group, Cork City, Cork County ☎ code - 291 371
Gay Christian group meets Tu. 7.30-9pm.

University College Cork: Orientation & Sexual Identity Society (OASIS) Box 50, Student Accommodation Office ☎ +353 21 902276; +353 21 902353 FX: +353 21 274483 ✉ oasis@www.ucc.ie
🖳 www.ucc.ie/ucc/socs/oasis
For lgb students & their friends.

OUThouse: LGB Community Resource Center 6 South William St., D2, Dublin ☎ (01) 670 6377
Organizes many support / social groups. Coffee shop & drop-in resource center. M-F 10-6. Coffee shop: M-Sat. 12-6, Sun. 3-6.

Dublin City University LGB Society Dublin
☎ code - 711 0760 ✉ lgbsoc@redbrick.dcu.ie
University-based society. Meets Tu. 7.30pm.

Lesbians Organising Together 5-6 Capel Street, Dublin 1 ☎ code - 872 7770
Phone for further info. The number listed can be used Mon-Fri from 10-6. Also 24 hour line on code - 155 012.

AIDS Alliance 53 Parnell Square, Dublin City
☎ code - 873 3799
AIDS information centre.

Les/Gay/Bi Drop-ins c/o Galway Gay Helpline, PO Box 45, Eglington Street, Galway
☎ (091) 564-611, Wed. 8-10pm.
Meets Sun. 4pm for films, workshops, chats & coffee.

National University of Ireland, Galway: Pluto Galway ✉ plutosoc@yahoo.com
🖳 www.geocities.com/WestHollywood/7116/ index.html
LGB society of the university. Meets Tu. 7:30pm during termtime in Rm. 307, Tower 2.

Ensemble Galway City, Galway ☎ code - 566 134
Fortnightly drop-in for gay & bi men. Sat. 3-6.

COTHU Tralee, Kerry ☎ code - 2155 559 (Thursdays)
Support group meets 1st & 3rd Th.

Gay Switchboard PO Box 151, GPO, Limerick
☎ code - 310 101 (Mon./Tu. 7.30-9.30pm)
Phoneline for information in the area.

Assembly L&G Group PO Box 24, GPO, The Quay, Waterford City, Waterford County
☎ code - 799 07 (Wednesdays 7.30-9.30)
Bisexual-inclusive. Social & political group.

German bi activist, Peter Bell

Robyn Ochs

ISRAEL

Association of Gays, Lesbians & Bisexuals in Israel 28 Nachmani St., PO Box 37604, Tel Aviv 61375 ☎ (011) 972-3-620-4327; (011) 972-3-629-3681 FX: (011) 972-3-525-2341 ✉ sppr@netvision.net.il 🖳 www.geocities.com/WestHollywood/Stonewall/2295
Aims to advance legal, social & cultural rights of glbt's in Israel in order to become fully equal citizens. Political action, education programs, & collaboration with social change agents, enhance a sense of solidarity & congregational cohesion within the community, & to assist & support those in need. Support groups, help lines, social events, youth groups & pride celebrations & an international email network. (Formerly the Society for the Protection of Personal Rights)

HaZman HaVarod (The Pink Times) PO Box 14595, Tel Aviv 61144 ☎ 972-3-620-1977 FX: 972-3-525-2341 ✉ to@zmanvarod.co.il 🖳 www.zmanvarod.co.il
Israel's national LGBT monthly newspaper.

Gay Bar: The Israeli Association of LGBT Lawyers ✉ israel_gaybar@hotmail.com

Tehila (PFLAG) ☎ 972-9-958-7779 ✉ tehila@poboxes.com 🖳 www.poboxes.com/tehila
Israel's PFLAG with local groups in Jerusalem, Tel Aviv and Haifa

Zahal Bet ✉ klali@hotmail.com 🖳 members.xoom.com/zahalb/
Israel's national youth organization (for ages 15-22) with local groups meeting in Jerusalem, Tel Aviv & Haifa.

Israel's Foreign Lesbos ✉ i_f_l@netvision.net.il 🖳 homepages.gayweb.com/IFL/index.html
Discussion group for lesbian/bi women who are originally from outside of Israel & now live in Israel, either temporarily or permanently.

KLAF PO Box 26221, Jerusalem 91261 ☎ 972-2-625-1271 ✉ klaf_israel@hotmail.com 🖳 www.aquanet.co.il/vip/klaf
Israel's lesbian, feminist community.

Ben Gurion Univresity: Sagol Be'er Sheva ✉ sagol@bgumail.bgu.ac.il
LGBT student union.

The Jerusalem Open House PO Box 33107, Jerusalem 91037 ☎ (011) 972-2-625-3191 FX: (011) 972-2-625-3192 ✉ gayj@hotmail.com 🖳 www.poboxes.com/gayj
Jerusalem's LGBT umbrella organization & community center. Support groups, social events, political activism, info. lines, speakers bureau, sports clubs, art workshops, religious study, youth groups & pride celebrations.

Hebrew University: HaAsiron HaAcher (The Other 10 Percent) PO Box 6916, Jerusalem 91068 ☎ 972-2-653-5454 ✉ asiron@hotmail.com 🖳 www.poboxes.com/asiron
LGBT student union.

Tel Aviv University: Gay Studies/Queer Theory Reading Group Tel Aviv ✉ qttau@hotmail.com 🖳 www.gay.org.il/qttau/
Reading group which reads & discusses texts. Usually we read texts & discuss them, but occasionally guest speakers or members of the reading group present their own work.

ITALY

Up to the present in Italy bisexuality has never been considered an authentic identity, but rather, an alternative word for understanding homosexuality. The majority of women don't like bisexual men, and ridicule them. This is the truth in the south especially. In the big cities (es. Milano, Torino, Roma) we are beginning to see affirmations of a new culture (similar to the socio-sexual culture of the United States) and people are becoming a bit curious about bisexual men and especially bisexual women. So far, bisexual identity has been considered an option only inside of the gay (and particularly the gay male) movement. In Italy there are no pubs, bars, or discotheques exclusively or mostly bi. Bi people often going to traditional heterosexual or homosexual meeting-places. There are a lot of mix hetero-homo pubs and discotheques, but we can't understand them as bisexual places.
— Kripton

Bisex Italy ✉ bisex@cybercore.com 🖳 www.cybercore.com/bisex
This is the 1st Italian bi group. Members mostly in northwestern Italy, but also in other cities. Social events, IRC, email list.

Ireos (centro servizi autogestito per la comunità queer) Via Ponte all'Asse, 7, attn: Alessandra, Firenze/Florence 50144 ✉ ireos@freemail.it
"A great association" that includes a small bi group that meets in Florence 1-2 times/month, for cultural activities & socializing.

JAMAICA

J-FLAG: Jamaica Forum of Lesbians, All-Sexuals & Gays P O Box 1152, Kingston 8 ☎ 876 978-1954 FX: 876 978-7876 ✉ jflag@hotmail.com
🖳 village.fortunecity.com/garland/704/
Committed to working towards a Jamaican society in which the human rights & equality of lesbians, all-sexuals & gays are guaranteed, engaging in initiatives that will foster the acceptance & enrichment of the lives of same-gender loving persons who have been, & continue to be, an integral part of society. "All-Sexual" is a term used to indicate that it considers all-sexual behaviour to be part of a sexual continuum in which classifications such as "gay", "lesbian" & "bisexual" often cannot be rigidly applied.

JAPAN

HIP's Home Page ✉ hibino@mbox.kyoto-inet.or.jp
🖳 web.kyoto-inet.or.jp/people/hibino/
Maintained by HIBINO, Makoto. Contains 5MB of HIBINO's literature, including essays on sexuality & gender with LesBiGay pride march photos. Most pages are in Japanese, some in English.

Project P c/o PONPOKO-House, 58 Higashikubota-cho, Kita-sirakawa, Sakyo-ku, 606-8285, Kyoto ☎ +81-75-723-4421 ✉ hibino@mbox.kyoto-inet.or.jp 🖳 web.kyoto-inet.or.jp/people/hibino/group/ProjectP/index.html
An all-welcome/active/political/friendly group in Kyoto, Japan. We try to understand, communicate, & enjoy our differences. Issues with sexual orientation, gender roles, gender identity, sex, & sexual violence are our important interests, but not all. Events, workshops, monthly cafes, occasional publications. (Inquiry in English takes long time for answer.)

KAZAKHSTAN

KONTRAST Box 108, AlmatyKazakhstan ☎ 7(3272) 338610 FX: 7(3272) 338610 ✉ casdin@kaznet.kz; kontrast1@members.gayweb.com; kontrast1@nlrk.kz
Human rights protection foundation for g/l people. See www.blakout.net/nuuz/20000428/ homofobia_in_kazakhstan.htm for info on difficult conditions in Kazakhstan. Member of ILGA. Needs donations.

Gay KZ - Kazakhstan Queer Web 🖳 members.nbci.com/gaykz/

Kazakhstanigay 🖳 www.yahoogroups.fr/group/kazakhstanigay
Email list.

KOREA

Ditto (Katten-Maum) Pusan ☎ 051-809-2583
The meaning of ditto (katten-maum) is sameness, homogenity. All of our members are sexual minorities & we chose the name for the purpose of "becoming one". There are few local queer groups in Korea. Most of the groups exist in Seoul & Ditton (katten-maum) is a local queer group in Pusan & Kyungnam. The queer culture of this region differs from Seoul & other regions so our org. is specific to the region. Acitivites include: counseling, AIDS activism, aiding HIV+ people, political activism.

ChinGu-sai PO Box #1246, Kwanghwamun, Seoul 110-612 ☎ (82-2) 464-7916 or 462-8425 (M-F 7-10pm) ✉ ebahn@chollian.net
Gay men's group whose name means "between friends." Activities include: advocating gay pride, political activism, safer sex education, AIDS activism, self-esteem workshops, summer gay rights camp, phone & individual counselling.

Dae Dong In PO Box 97, Kwanghwamun, Seoul ☎ 02-923-0609 FX: 02-923-2175
Composed of members from Seoul, welcomes all concerned about sexual minority rights. Sexual orientation or preference does not matter (transgender, queer, heterosexual...) Advocates gay/lesbian rights & strives to gain visibility. PUB: Dyke (Monthly newsletter describing various activities & news about the organization.)

Kiri Kiri PO Box #1816, Kwanghwamun, Seoul 110-618 ☎ 02/363-7213
The 1st, largest & most political lesbian org. In recognition of the exclusion of lesbian issues & agenda from gay discourse, subculture & feminism in Korea, Kiri Kiri stives for lesbian visibility & to raise lesbian rights as a social issue. Activities include: lesbophobia criticism, political activism, safer sex education, & providing a safe & supportive environment for lesbians (phone & individual counseling too). PUB: Alternative World (1st Lesbian publication: lesbophobia criticism, safer sex education, practical info for lesbians, film/book/event reviews.)

Sappho Seoul ✉ sapphorok@yahoo.com
Lesbian group. Monthly get-togethers. Foreign women welcome.

"In today's society, it is easier for a woman to marry a man. But being bisexual means you can't choose what body the love of your life will come in...and mine came in the body of a woman."

Vivienne Esrig

Queer Film Festival Organization Midong Building #301, Nakwon-Dong 195-1, Chongno-Ku, Seoul
☎ 02/766-5626 FX: 02/766-0598
✉ queer21@interpia.net
This org. planned to hold the 1st queer film festival in Seoul in 1997, but the festival was cancelled several times due to government censorship. They will continue to attempt to hold the festival. Furthmore, they wish to make the existence of queer visible in a heterosexist society such as Korea & promote a positive understanding of queer identities. PUB: Queer Cinenews: Irregular Magazine (Official news & activities related to Queer Film Festival. Reports latest happenings in the queer cinema community.)

Seoul National University: MaUm 003 Seoul
☎ (82-15) 844-7137
LGB student group. Welcomes all sexual minorites. The original name of this group was MaEum 001. Heterosexuals can be seen as having 100% of rights whereas homosexuals are just recently gaining rights & recognition. To symbolize this struggle, the group increases the number each time a positive social change for LGB rights happens.

Yonsei University: Come Together Seoul
☎ 015/357-3769
1st gay group in Korea, contributing greatly to raising gay rights as a social issue in Korea. Strives to provide a space where individuals can share their personal experiences & support each other. Members translate & read various foreign books on gay discourse. Currently trying to network with other university gay/lesbian groups.

LITHUANIA

Lithuanian Gay League P.D.862, 2000 Vilnius 2000 ☎ +370 2333031 FX: +370 2333031
✉ lgl@gay.lt ▣ www.gayline.lt/
National NGO aiming to raise awareness about LGB discrimination in Lithuanian society. Educational programming about AIDS & STDs. Activism for creating anti-discrimination legislation, project for registered partnerships.

Kaunas County Organization of Sexual Equality (KASLO) P.D. 1045, 3042 Kaunas ☎ +370 7705737
✉ robejona@takas.lt

Sapho P.D. 2204, 2049 Vilnius ✉ sphinfo@is.lt
▣ www.is.lt/sappho/

MALAYSIA

Pink Triangle PO Box 11859, 50760, Kuala Lumpur
☎ 444-4611 FX: 444-4622 ✉ isham@pop7.jaring.my
A voluntary, non-profit, NGO involved in community-based work on sexuality & AIDS.

MEXICO

Taller Reflexivo de Mujeres Bisexuales (TREMUB c/o El Closet de Sor Juana, Nevado 112, Depto. 8, Col. Portales, México ☎/FX: 525 549 11 91
✉ tremub@yahoo.com
Cuenta con un espacio permanente sobre el ser bisexual y su inserción en otros movimientos sociales - feminista, lésbico, democrático, derechos humanos. Cuenta con un proyecto de difusión a través de una revista informativa recién iniciada. [Space for discussion about bisexual identity & involvement in other movements: feminist, lesbian, democratic, human rights. Recently produced a publication.]

Acion Humana Por La Comunidad Apartado Postal 27-131, México 06761 ☎ 52-5-772-0778
✉ amac@laneta.apc.org
Activism on HIV-AIDS, gay life, human rights.

Las Amantes de la Luna Apto. 27- 029. Adm Correos 27, México DF CP 06061 ☎ 52 (5) 5738 5153 ✉ amlunas2@laneta.apc.org
Publication for lesbians & bisexual women.

Colectivo Sol Cerrada Cuauhnochtli 11, Pueblo Quieto, Tlalpan, México, D.F. CP 14040
☎ 52 (8) 5606-7216 ✉ colsol@laneta.apc.org
Center for information & documentation about Mexican homosexualities.

Boys & Toys, DesnuDarse Rio Tiber 40-502, México, D.F. CP 06500 ☎ 52 (5) 5525-1825
✉ boystoys@prodigy.net.mx
Publication about sexology for the gay community.

Genesis. Grupo cristiano ecumenico GLBTT Articulo 123 No. 134 (casi esq. Bucareli), México, D.F. ☎ 52 (5) 5608 2196
✉ genesis_mexico@hotmail.com

Shalom Amigos Apartado 67 CAP Polanco, México, D.F. CP 11550 ☎ 52 (5) 5264-6888
✉ shalomamigos@hotmail.com
Jewish Mexican GLBT group.

Iglesia de la Comunidad Metropolitana de Monterrey Diego de Montemayor 219 sur (entre Washington y M. Arreola), Monterrey, NL CP 64000 ☎/FX: 52 (8) 340 3789
✉ icmmty@hotmail.com
Metropolitan Community Church for glbt people. Daily services.

Homo sapiens sapiens AC AP 1-1796, Guadalajara, Jalisco CP 44101 ☎ 52 (3) 181 2609
✉ homosapiens@members.gayweb.com

OASIS - Center for Diversity Hamburgo 2801, J. Altavista, Monterrey, NL CP 64840
☎/FX: 52 (8) 358 2401 ✉ gess@prodigy.net.mx
GLBT community center. Workshops. Conferences.

> **"If God meant people to be bisexual, there would be two sexes."**
>
> *Don Hopkins*

NAMIBIA

Rainbow Project, Sister Namibia Collective PO Box 40092, Windhook FX: 00264 61 230618 ✉ sister@iafrica.com.na
"Namibia's first rights group for glbt people."

NEPAL

Nepal Queer Society G.PO 8975, EPC 5203, Kathmandu 🖳 www.khushnet.com/directory/nepal.htm
For queer people of Nepal. Linked on Khushnet.

NETHERLANDS

Vereniging Landelijk Netwerk Biseksualiteit (Dutch Bi Network) Postbus 75087, Amsterdam 1070 AB ☎ +31-(0)6-22938519 (M, W, Th. F, 20-21h) FX: +31-(0)10-2449059 ✉ lnbi@lnbi.demon.nl 🖳 www.lnbi.demon.nl/
National bi-organization/action-group. PUB: Bi-Nieuws (Quarterly newsletter in Dutch only. 35 Dutch guilders to join society & receive Bi-Nieuws by mail in a discrete envelope. Transfer 7.50 dutch guilders on giro-account 5459383 of LNBi in Amsterdam to receive sample issue. Exchange subscriptions accepted, foreign memberships add 10 guilders.)

Dutch Bisexuals Mailing List
✉ binl-l@lnbi.demon.nl
General mailing list for Dutch speaking bisexuals. To subscribe, send e-mail to majordomo@lnbi.demon.nl without subject & the text 'subscribe binl-l' in the body of the message.

Stichting Werkgroep Biseksualiteit Amsterdam Blauwburgwal 7-9, Amsterdam 1015 AS ☎ +31-(0)72-562.95.45 ✉ t.witkamp@hetnet.nl

Twente Technical University: HoBiHe, Enschede ✉ hobihe@student.utwente.nl 🖳 hobihe.srd.utwente.nl/
Youth group for integration of homo- & bisexuality. To join e-mail list, send e-mail to listserv@student.utwente.nl with 'subscribe hobihe-l First Last' (without quotes) in the body of the message, where you replace 'First' & 'Last' with your first & last name.

Bi-women group Bijou, Gouda ☎ +31-(0)6-23.03.53.91
Women's group that organizes meetings during weekends, varying activities. Exchange of opinion & meeting other bi-women.

Jongerengroep PéPé Taco Mesdagstraat 32-1, Groningen 9718 KM ☎ +31-(0)50-5132620 ✉ gaygron@xs4all.nl
LGB youth group. Social evening for youngsters, theme-evenings.

Gobi Initiatiefgroep Biseksualiteit Nijmegen PO Box 552, Nijmegen 6500 AN ☎ +31-(0)24-3234237
Various social & thematical gatherings. Men's, women's, youth, & mixed groups.

Rotterdam Bi! Speedwellstraat 176, Rotterdam 3029 BL ☎ +31-(0)10-244.90.66 FX: +31-(0)10-244.90.59 ✉ maurice@lnbi.demon.nl
Social meetings, for fun & meeting people.

Apollo PO Box 1490, Rotterdam 3000 BL ☎ +31-(0)10-436.14.44 ✉ apollohj@dds.nl 🖳 huizen.dds.nl/~apollohj/
The lgb youth group of Rotterdam. Maximum age: 26. PUB: 32 (Newsletter for members.)

Discussion group 'De Samenkomst' Tilburg ☎ +31-(0)13-463.00.43 (Ton)
Social & theme evenings alternate. Focuses on the surroundings of Tilburg.

Dark Passions Tilburg ☎ +31-(0)13-534.34.05 (Judith) ✉ dark_passions@hotmail.com
SM group for bi's.

Discussion Groups: De Kringen Kanaalweg 21, Utrecht 3526 KL ☎ +31-(0)30-2888636 (Paul) ✉ info@kringen.nl 🖳 www.kringen.nl/
Monthly meetings at members' homes. Call to inquire if openings are available. New groups formed regularly & can carry on for years. PUB: Keerkring (Information newsletter for members.)

Dutch Society Orpheus PO Box 14121, Utrecht 3508 SE ☎ +31-(0)20-639.07.65 ✉ orpheus@xs4all.nl 🖳 www.xs4all.nl/~orpheus/
Discussion & support group for glbs & partners. Meetings for married couples with one lg or b partner. Various locations around the Netherlands. PUB: Orpheus Nieuwsbrief (Quarterly newsletter for members.)

Dutch Bi Network, "Rose Zaturday," 1997

Dutch Bi Network, "Rose Zaturday," 1997

Foundation Group 7152 PO Box 1402, Utrecht 3500 BK ✉ mcta.rigter@chello.nl 🖳 www.geocities.com/WestHollywood/Stonewall/2951/

National organization for lesbian & bisexual women. All women, young, old, married or single can join, privacy respected.

PUB: *Amarant (6/year & contains info & articles pertaining to women, lesbianism, & bisexuality.)*

Bi-evening at Café Sebas Zoetermeer
☎ +31-(0)6-23.03.53.91 (Hennie)

NETHERLANDS ANTILLES

Orguyo Montaña di Rei 447, Curaçao ☎ 599 9 67 85 43 FX: 599 9 65 05 85 ✉ curamere@ibm.net

NEW ZEALAND

New Zealand Bisexual Network PO Box 5426, 281 Karangahape Road, Auckland ☎ 64 +9-302-0590 FX: 09-302-2042 ✉ grieve@ihug.co.nz; oceannz@hotmail.com 🖳 bisexual.cjb.net
Social group, meets monthly. Welcomes all bisexual & bi-curious. Involved in ongoing political change.

Bi New Zealanders List
🖳 clubs.yahoo.com/clubs/binewzealanders
A place where Bi New Zealanders can chat online.

New Zealand Gays, Bisexuals, Lesbians & Friends Electronic Mail List (NZGBLF) ✉ To subscribe: nzgblf-sub@qrd.org.nz. For inquiries: nzgblf-info@qrd.org.nz
Email list for the queer community in New Zealand / Aotearoa. Overseas visitors welcome.

QRA: Guide to the GLBT communities in New Zealand 🖳 nz.com/NZ/Queer
Website with a comprehensive list of queer groups in New Zealand.

New Zealand Pink Pages 🖳 nz.com/NZ/Queer/PinkPages
Web site lisitng LGBT & Queer resources in New Zealand.

Express: New Zealand's Newspaper of Gay Expression PO Box 47-514, Ponsonby, Auckland ☎ 64-9-361-0190 FX: 64-9-361-0191 ✉ editor@expressnewspaper.co.nz
Excellent newspaper found all over the inner city of Auckland. Has listing for all queer events around New Zealand.

OUT! Magazine Private Bag 92126, Auckland
☎ +64-9-377-9031 FX: +64-9-377-7767
✉ out@nz.com

New Zealand Gay & Lesbian Accommodation Guide No. 2 RD, Palmerston, Otago
☎ 64 + 3 + 465-1742 FX: 64 + 3 + 465-1748
✉ RON.HARRIS@xtra.co.nz
New Zealand Accommodation guide for queer friendly hotels, hostels & bed & breakfasts. (NZ$10 for the latest guide)

Icebreakers Icebreaker Referrals, PO Box 9247, Marion Square, Wellington ☎ Wellington Gay Switchboard: 7:30-10pm: (04) 385-0674 ✉ ice-breakers@geocities.com
🖳 www.geocities.com/WestHollywood/village/2622/
Nationwide network of support & social groups for young gay / bi / questioning men (16-26) to develop healthy self-esteem. Icebreaker groups also in Hamilton, Auckland, Dunedin & Christchurch.

Aukland Pride Centre Box 5426, 281 Karangahape Road, Auckland ☎ +64-9-302-0590 ✉ pride@xtra.co.nz 🖳 www.geocities.com/auckland_pride
For GLBT communities in Tamaki Makaurau / Auckland, People's Centre, 281 Karangahape Road, Newton Auckland. Social events, space for groups & projects, drop-in & phone venue, newsletter, info & referral, political lobbying.
PUB: *Pride Newsletter*

Gayline Auckland Level 2, 39 Anzac Ave, Auckland ☎ (09) 303 3584
Referrals for anyone requiring support, counselling, or info about their sexuality. Telephone counselling Men / Women Mon. - Fri. 10am-10pm. Weekends 5-10pm.

AIDS Hotline ☎0800 - 802 437
AIDS information & counselling. Calls can be forwarded to Gayline Auckland for toll free access to the services of Gayline.

Tamaki Makaurau Lesbian Newsletter PO Box 44-056, Pt Chevalier, Auckland 2
☎ 64 + 9 + 376-2454
Monthly newsletter, 11 issues per year.

Icebreakers for Men Auckland
☎ (09) 376-4155 (Rainbow Youth)
Social / support group for young men, 16 - 26, who think they might be gay or bisexual.

Icebreakers for Women Auckland
☎ (09) 376 4155 (Rainbow Youth)
Social/support group for young women who think they might be lesbian or bisexual.

Dinner Club for Women PO Box 68 922, Newton, Auckland ☎ 64 + 09 + 360-9550
✉ dcw@outnet.co.nz
Social dining group for women.

Auckland University:

Uni-GoBLeT: For staff & students; **Women Loving Women:** BOTH: c/o Auckland Univ. Students Association, Private Bag 92019, Auckland.

Rainbow Youth Auckland Box 5426, Wellesley St., Auckland ☎ +64-9-376-4155; infoline:+64-9-376-4156 ✉ info@rainbowyouth.org.nz
📖 nz.com/nz/queer/rainbowyouth
Social/support/educative group for GLBT youth.
PUB: Rainbow Youth

BLG (Bisexual, Lesbian, & Gay Support Group)
c/o UCSA, Christchurch ☎ Nick or Rebecca: (03) 365 2620 ✉ sbh25@student.canterbury.ac.nz
Social/support group for blgt/unlabelled students.

Icebreakers Christchurch c/o198 Youth Health Centre, 198 Hereford, Christchurch ☎ Gayline 379-4796 or Ettie Rout Centre 379-1953
✉ icebreakers_chch@hotmail.com
📖 nz.com/NZ/Queer/ChchIcebreakers
Support group for gbq young men 16-24. Explores issues related to sexuality & provides a safe, secure & fun environment for youth.

University of Canterbury: UniQ Christchurch
Christchurch ☎ 64 + 3 + 364-2652 extn 3912
✉ uniq canterbury@hotmail.com
Th. 12 -2pm Lower Common Room wing of the University of Canterbury Students association Union Building, 90 Ilam Road, casual drop in style. Also more organised stuff during the year. Group is very inclusive of bisexuals.

Ice breakers PO Box 1382, Dunedin
☎ 64+3+477-2077
Social/Support group for young men, -26 who think they may be bisexual or gay.

Otago University: PUMP c/o Gayline, Dunedin
☎ 64+3+477-2077
LGB group at University.

P Flag South PO Box 5266, Dunedin
✉ gouldint@es.co.nz
Support group for parents of GLB.

Members of the New Zealand Bisexual Network, Auckland, on a day trip

Angus Astutter

Otago Gaily Times c/o The AIDS Project, 57 Hanover St, Dunedin ☎ +64-3-474-0221
Otago queer magazine. PUB: Otago Gaily Times

Gisborne Gay Support 21 Walsh Street, Gisborne
☎ 64 + 6 + 863-0413
Social & support organisation. Bi-monthly social gatherings & parties.

BLG Hamilton (Bi/Lesbian/Gay) Hamilton
☎ 64 +7 + 855-5429
24 hour telephone line, with info on groups around Hamilton, HIV/AIDs, queer friendly bars & publications in the area. This phone line is personed 8-10pm on Wed.

Waikato University: BLG Collective/Queers on Campus Hamilton East ✉ wql@list.waikato.ac.nz
Email list available to all students & staff at the University.

Gaylink Hamilton ☎ 64 + 7 + 855-5429
📖 www.geocities.com/WestHollywood/1102
Wed 8-10pm: Social support group for men. Link House, Hamilton. There are also some separate women's group. Phone line open same hours, these have info on queer friendly bars.

Outpost PO Box 7038, Hamilton
Yearly subscription $10

Club 40 PO Box 8341, Havelock North, Hastings
Bi inclusive club.

Gayline Hokitika Hokitika ☎ +64-3-755-6270
Mon. , Tu., Th 7-10pm. ·

Gayline Invercargill Invercargill
☎ 64+3+477-2077
Support & info phone line, staffed 7:30-10pm Fri.

> **Actually, the main thing now...is to become an individual. The art of mastering life is the prerequisite for all further forms of expression...**
>
> *Paul Klee, 1902*

Spectrum (Nels Inc.) Box 4022, Nelson South
☎ Kevin:+64-3-547-2827 ✉ kevin@ts.co.nz
🖳 www.co.nz/~kevin
Social/support group for gay & bi men. Drop-in centre Thurs 7:30-10:30pm for coffee & conversation at 42 Franklin St. $2.00 entry. They also put Gaytime FM on air every week.

Ascent Nelson ☎ Brian +64-3-548-3304
For gay/bi Catholic men.

Taranaki Pride Alliance PO Box 6074, New Plymouth
PUB: Rainbow Times

Palmerston North Bisexual Group Box 1491, Palmerston North ☎ (06) 358-5378
✉ krysbaker@hotmail.com 🖳 nz.com/NZ/Queer/MALGRA/

Gayline Rotorua Rotorua ☎ 64 + 7 + 348-0193
Phoneline to inform visitors of queer venues and groups in the local area.

Gayline Tauranga ☎ 64 + 7 + 577-0481
24 hour recorded phone line with queer friendly groups & venues listed. Staffed Wed. 6-10pm.

Aoraki Lesbian & Gay Club Timaru
☎ 64 + 3 + 684-7016 ✉ maccat@timaru.com
Local group that is inclusive of all groups. Call for information on local queer venues.

Wellington Bisexual Women's Group PO Box 5145, Wellington ☎ 64 4 499-1401
✉ pamelajmorgan@hotmail.com
1 support & 2 social meetings a month.
PUB: Bi-lines

First Out Wellington ☎ c/o Lesbianline:
(04) 499-5567
A group for young women -27 who think they might be lesbian or bisexual.

Galaxies: Lesbian, Gay & Bisexual Christian Community of Wellington PO Box 5203, Thorndon, Wellington ☎ St. Andrews+64-4-472-9211 or 389-1777 FX:+64-4-472-9211
For GLB Christians & their families. "Non-hierarchical, non-judgmental & open in its theology."

Victoria University of Wellington: UniQ
c/o VUWSA, PO Box 600, Wellington
☎ 64 4 473-8566 🖳 cic-uniq.tripod.com
Group for LGBTQ students. Inclusive, safe, friendly environment for all queer people on campus. Helps people start up more specific groups (eg. bi men's support group, queer chocoholics, etc).

Bloom 56 Victoria Street, Wellington ☎ Serena on 64 + 4 + 389-5380 or Lesbianline 4 + 499-5567
For bisexual & lesbian women -26. Safe confidential venue. Meets every 2nd Fri. 7-9pm at Wellington Womens Centre, 56 Victoria Street.

Overt PO Box 12-270, Thorndon, Wellington
✉ overt@mailcity.com
🖳 www.crosswinds.net/~overt
GLBT group, promotes visibility & offer advocacy to combat homophobia & heterosexism. A pro-queer action group, with affiliate groups in Auckland & Nelson.

"Whether we like it or not, and no matter how much we think that we are assimilated, our very lives are a great threat to the great wall of either-or. Some of us fought damn hard to carve out identities as lesbians or gays. We weren't in a place to question that wall. We made an uncomfortable peace with it. Now here come the bisexuals, the transgender and the intersexed folk challenging that wall. And that's pretty irritating. Why do they want to ruin our movement? And we had accepted the existence of the wall. We had accepted the existence of the fence. Now some of our own are saying that the wall doesn't even exist! This is painful. It's time consuming. You have to keep having all these workshops on inclusion within the queer community. It's brain racking. Somebody's confused. (Not us!) But if we are all to survive with our lives, let the decolonizing begin. Queer-in-intersection identity can then spill out into queer heterosexual identity, for heterosexual identity exists only by virtue of defining itself as the norm against queer deviations. But if there really is no norm, then there really aren't any deviations! We're all then just a big mix of possibilities of desire just waiting to happen. But we have to resist, resist, resist, with our very beings! That is what we need to do if we are to reinvent family and to survive with our lives. We don't have alternative families. We have families that we create and define as we choose. We don't have alternative lifestyles. We have lives.

Elias Farajajé-Jones, in "Loving Queer" from In the Family, Vol. 6, No. 1, Summer 2000.

Lesbian Quarterly PO Box 11-882, Wellington
*Quarterly Wellington magazine & newsletter.
Formerly called the Lesbians Newsletter.*

Wellington City Council's Guide to GBLT PO Box
2199, Wellington ☎ 64 + 4 + 499-4444
*Free guide provided by Wellington City Council
with a directory of all GLBT services & venues.*

NICARAGUA

Centro Nicaragüense de Derechos Humanos
Apartado 4402, Managua
Has LGBT human rights project.

Colectivo de Mujeres Autonomas Apartado
Postal Ciudad Sandino 038, Managua
*Group for autonomous women; includes lesbians
& bisexual women.*

Fundación Xochiquetzal Apartado No. 112,
Managua ☎ 505/2-490585 FX: 505/2-491346
✉ quetzal@tmx.com.ni
*Non-profit NGO based in Managua w/ offices in 5
cities in northern Nicaragua. (Contact in
Matagalpa: Angela Rocha Mairena 505/61-
490585) Provides HIV testing & counselling.
Youth work, hotline, radio programs, documenta-
tion of injustices. Also members of Arcegal, a
Central Amercan LGBT organization, & the
Central American Confederation of NGOs Against
AIDS.* PUB: Fuera del Closet (Out of the Closet)
(Published 3 times/yr: March (dedicated to
women), June (to sexual preferences), Sept (to
youth), Dec (to the International Day in the
Fight Against AIDS).

NORWAY

Bikuben Postboks 296, Skoyen, Oslo

**Landsforeningen for Lesbisk or Homofil figjoring
(LLH - Norway)** St. Olavs plass 2, Pb 6838, Oslo n-
0130 ☎ 47/22-36-19-48 FX: 47/22-11-47-45
✉ llh@c2i.net 📇 www.llh.no
*Nat'l organization for liberation of LGB people.
Establishes social, political, & educational
agendas. Norway's largest & most important
LBG organization. Receives state funding, but
operates independently. Coordinates local adult &
youth groups all over Norway.* PUB: BLIKK

Ungdomsgruppa/LLH-Oslo Postboks 0838, St.
Olavs Plass, Oslo N-0130 ☎ support lines:+47 810-
00-277 ✉ ungdomstelefonen@hotmail.com
*Runs a support hotline for LGB youth. Regular
meetings, social events, nights out. Part of LLH-
Norway.*

Bilaget Landsforeningen for Lesbisk og Homofil
frigjøring i Rogaland, Pb. 1502 Kjelvene,
Stavanger 4093 ☎ +47 51 53 14 46
FX: +47 51 53 65 01 ✉ post@llh-rogaland.com
📇 llh-rogaland.com

It's better to be hated for what one is than to be loved for what one isn't.

—Andre Gide, Frenh Novelist, 1869-1951.

Nettverk for forskning om homoseksualitet Turid
Eikvam, Institutt for kriminologi, Postboks 6706
St. Olavs plass, Oslo 0130 FX: + 47 22 85 02 52
📇 www.uio.no/~turide/
Research network addressing lgbt issues.

Løvetann Postboks 6745, St. Olavs plass, Oslo
0130 ☎ +47 22 36 00 78 FX: +47 22 20 61 75
✉ lovetann@online.no
*Magazine published 6 times a year covering lgb
topics.*

Raadgivingstjenesten for homofile og lesbiske
Senter for Seksuell Helse (SSH-Grensen) ,
Grensen 5-7 0159 Oslo ☎ + 47 22 08 29 50
*Professional counseling for lgb people & their
partners.*

PAKISTAN

Khushnet Pakistan Hum-Khayal Publications,
Attn: Anjum, 2 Jinnah Colony, Faisalabad
📇 www.khushnet.com/
*Publishers of Pakistan's first book of gay poetry,
Narman, by Ifti Nasim.*

PERU

Gayperu ✉ gperu@geocities.com
📇 www.geocities.com/WestHollywood/Stonewall/
6067/
On-line resource. IRC, info, etc.

PHILIPPINES

Bisexual Network of the Philippines. ✉Manila Bi
Group: Danny: sioldan@hotmail.com Cebu Bi
Group: Brian: argao@rocketmail.com. 📇
www.rainbow.net.au/~ausbinet/binetph.htm. *A
new network still in its formative stage but eager to
hear from bisexual & bi-curious men &women from
throughout the Republic of the Philippines. You are
welcome to attend any meetings & social events that
may be organised or go on our private e-mail list
for BiNet Philippines news updates. We are
developing social groups in the Manila Metro area
& in Cebu City. We hope other groups will develop
as more people contact us & get involved.*
Can't Live In the Closet. PO Box 2356, CPO 1163
, Quezon City. FX: (632) 911-6239. ☎ ✉
CLIC@phil.gn.apc.org. Philippino lesbian group.

University of the Philippines: UP Sappho. ✉ up_sappho@hotmail.com. 🖳 members.tripod.com/up_sappho_society/. *Caters mainly to lesbian students from the University. Currently enrolled lesbians from any UP unit are welcome to join the organization. At present, UP Sappho has 25 members.*

ZONE Convergence of Gay Humanists & Friends. 42 - B Lake View Drive, Pasig City. ☎ 63/2-671-73-72 ✉ zone@misa.irf.ph.net. *To end discrimination & inequality, denounce violence in any form be it physical, religious, economic or sexual in origin. To move towards a world of diversity & multiplicity in beliefs & ideas in ethnicity, language, work, lifestyle. Believe in freedom & the meaning of life. Imagine a world that is flexible, changing & responding to the dynamic needs of people. For anyone! Including gay-friendly heteros.*

Pro-Gay (Progressive Organization of Gays in the Philippines). PO Box 1764, Quezon City CPO 1157. ✉progay@yahoo.com. 🖳 members.tripod.com/~progay_philippines/. *Gay rights, support & social group. Led the first Gay March in Asia on June 26, 1994. They define the struggle for gay liberation as a part of the struggle of the Filipino people for national freedom, & at the same time, with a distinct concern for the concrete demands of Filipino gay men.*

POLAND

University of Warsaw: ALG Board 24/26 Krakowskie, Przedmiescie Street, 00-927 Warszawa 64

Lambda Bydgoszcz PO Box 111, 85-956 Bydgoszcz 13

Lambda Krakow PO Box 249, 30-960 Krakow 1

Lambda Poznan PO Box 176, Poznan 2 ☎ 61-537655 (Fridays 5-8pm only)

Lambda Torun PO Box 115, 87-116 Torun 17

Lambda Warsaw 24/26 Krakowskie, Przedmiescie Street, 00-927 Warszawa 64

Lambda Wroclaw PO Box 812, 50-950 Wroclaw 2 *Ruch Lesbijek i Gejow.*

Ruch Lesbijek i Gejow RGL (Lesbians & Gays Movement) PO Box 63, 00-504 Warszawa 15

--It feels so good, Masha. --I'm not Masha, I'm - Misha. --It feels good anyway...

Russian joke from gay.ru

RUSSIA

From the Gay.Ru web page: Only a decade ago Russian gays were reduced to underground, our love did not dare to speak its name. Perestroika has made changes in our country possible. Russian gays threw off the yoke of Soviet-time constraints, the homosexuality has been decriminalized, and general attitudes have become more tolerant. The Internet greatly contributed to the increase of the public awareness and it was Gay.Ru that brought together Russian gays giving them a sense of unity.

Gay Russia: Russian National Gay, Lesbian, Bisexual & Transsexual Website PO Box 1, 109457, Moscow ✉ Russian: ed@gay.ru; English: nikita@gay.ru 🖳 www.gay.ru *Resources, info throughout Russia. Contains its own bi section.*

rus-bi ✉ natasha@amber.he.net 🖳 bi.org/~russia/rus-bi.html *Discussions on lesbianism & bisexuality in Russia & Russian-speaking countries.*

Rainbow Sphere Foundation PO Box 1, 109457 Moscow ✉ sphere@gay.ru 🖳 www.gay.ru/sphere (Russian only) *Info on gay life in Moscow. Assistance to gays & lesbians. Support to g/l professional associations. Publishing projects.*

The League Irkutsk ✉ aegoroff@hotmail.com 🖳 members.nbci.com/daboy2/index.html *Member of ILGA.*

Tsentr Treugolnik (Triangle Center) Moscow 129348 ☎ 7 095 163-8002 ✉ triangle@glas.apc.org *Moscow regional GLB organization.*

Mi y Vi (We & You) bldg. 2, 15 8-ya ulitsa Sokolinoy Gory , (Metro Shosse Yentouziastov), Moscow 129626 ☎ 7-095-916 48 68 FX: 7-095/916-48 68 ✉ weandyou@online.ru; weandyou@mail.ru 🖳 www.glasnet.ru/~weandyou/we_you.htm (in English) *Support for HIV+ GBL, spreading legal & medical info on AIDS & HIV in CIS countries.* PUB: Life Goes On

Moscow Lesbian "Rozovaya Svecha" (Pink Candle) Group 107140, p/o box 129, Moscow

Murmansk Regional Public Organization: "The Circle/Krug" Murmansk ✉ polarstar@ilga.org 🖳 www.rfsl.se/pitea/archangelsk.html *For GLB people in Northern Russia.*

Wings PO Box 108, 191186 St. Petersburg ☎ 312 31 80 ✉ krilija@ilga.org; alex@kukharsky.spb.su 🖳 www.home.axon.ru/~krilija
G/L association, ILGA member. Protection of g/l rights, increase of gay awareness, struggle against homophobia & for legalization of same-sex partnerships. Travel advice for gays & lesbians coming into Russia.

Labrys Women Public Foundation PO Box 45, 191123 St. Petersburg ✉ labrys@mail.admiral.ru
Protection of rights & lawful interest of lesbians, increase of public awareness, support to public & creative lesbian actions. Publishes an info bulletin & maintains a lesbian archive.

St. Petersburg Gay Guide , St. Petersburg ☎ +7-812- 233-88-83 ✉ admin@gay.spb.ru 🖳 www.gay.spb.ru
Info on gay resources in St. Petersburg.

SINGAPORE

People Like Us PO Box 299, Raffeles City Post Office 9117

Singapore: Action for AIDS 62-B Race Course Rd S-218568 🖳 www.khushnet.com/singapore.htm
AIDS action, local group. Listed in Khushnet.

Oriental Sensation 134 Bukit Batok, West Avenue 6 2365

SLOVAKIA

Atribút g/l vydáva HaBiO PO Box 233, Prazská 11, 810 00 Bratislava 1 ☎ +4217/52492013 FX: +4217/52492013
Gay/bi group.

Ganymedes Košice MARS A&E Ganymedes, c/o PO Box B-18, 040 98 Košice ✉ levan@pobox.sk 🖳 www.gay.sk/ganymed/index.html
Gay organization of eastern Slovakia.

SLOVENIA

SiQRD: Slovenian Queer Resources Directory ✉ siqrd@mila.ljudmila.org 🖳 www.kud-fp.si/~siqrd/index.html
Comprehensive on-line listing.

Roza klub Kersnikova 4, SI-1000, Ljubljana ☎ 386/61-130-4740 FX: 386/61-329-185 ✉ siqrd@ljudmila.kud-fp.si 🖳 www.ljudmila.org/siqrd/rk-e.html
Political & social group for women & men. Publishes magazine Revolver, organizes g/l film festival, works on education & social events (clubs Roza disco & Propaganda), cooperates at preparing law on registered partnerships.

Magnus Kersnikova 4, SI-1000, Ljubjana ☎ +386-61-1304740 FX: +386-61-329185 ✉ skuc_magnus@slo.net 🖳 www.ljudmila.org/siqrd/magnus/index.html
Social organization for men only. They own a gay club Tiffany, organize trips, work on safer-sex education & AIDS/HIV prevention.

SKUC LL Metelkova 6, SI-1000, Ljubljana ☎ 386/61-132-7368 FX: +386-61-329185 ✉ siqrd@mila.ljudmila.org 🖳 www.ljudmila.org/siqrd/ll.html
Political & socal organization for women only. They publish magazine Lesbo, work on lesbian visibility, co-operate at preparing law on registered partnerships. They also own lesbian club Monokel (Eyeglass).

Youth Group - Ljubljana skupina Legebitra, p.p.106, 1001 Ljubljana ✉ Minus26@hotmail.com 🖳 www.kud-fp.si/~siqrd/legebitra/index.html
Youth group for lgbt people -26.

SOUTH AFRICA

Bisexual in South Africa List 🖳 clubs.yahoo.com/clubs/bisexualinsouthafrica
Adult e-mail list for bisexuals in South Africa.

Mazibuko Kanyiso Jara: Equal Rights Project National Coalition for Gay & Lesbian Equality PO Box 27811, Yeoville 2143 ☎ +27 (0)11 487 3810/1/2 FX: +27 (0)11 4871670 ✉ admin@ncgle.org.za; mazibuko@ncgle.org.za
Voluntary association of more than 74 LGBT organizations. Lobbied successfully for the retention of sexual orientation as one of the grounds of non-discrimination in the Constitution. Works for legal & social equality. Work includes law reform, lobbying, litigation, advocacy, employment equity, leadership training.
🖳 www.q.co.za/
On line "gayteway to South Africa." News, lots of travel info, community venues & organizations."

Capetown Gay, Lesbian & Bisexual Helpline ☎ 021 422-2500 (Paging)
Also, Triangle Project: Safe sex info, HIV Counselling.

University of Cape Town: Rainbow Organization Private Bag, RONDEBOSCH , Cape Town 7700 ✉ GALA@its.uct.ac.za
🖳 www.uct.ac.za/depts/src/societies/gala/

Gay & Lesbian Collective 11 Battersea Avenue, Reservoir Hills, Durban ☎ Christopher David: (31) 821-309

Gays & Lesbians of Pretoria PO Box 26197, Arcadia 0007 ☎ 012 - 344 6500 ✉ glop@gay.co.za 🖳 www.glop.org.za/
Located at 133 Verdoorn St., Sunnyside, Pretoria. Nonprofit, non- racial, democratic community service organisation for the well-being of lgbt individuals.

University of South Africa: Sexual Orientation Forum c/o Ian Alderton, Dept. of Mathematics, UNISA, PO Box 392, Pretoria 0003 ☎ (012) 429-6752 FX: (012) 429-6064 ✉ alderiw@alpha.unisa.ac.za 💻 www.glop.co.za/unisa.html
Interest group at Unisa speaking & raising concerns on behalf of a (till recently) voiceless & invisible grouping at this University. Deals with issues relating to discrimination on the campus on the grounds of sexual orientation, the extension of employment benefits to same-sex partnerships & highlights issues of equality of treatment as part of the broader transformation process at Unisa.

Gay & Lesbian Organization of Witwatersrand PO Box 23297, Joubert Park, Johannesburg 2044 ☎ + 11 648 5873 FX: + 11 487 1670
Founded in 1988 by a group of South African black gay & lesbian activists. Campaigns for lesbian/gay rights.

SPAIN

Casal Lambda C/Ample, 5, Barcelona 08002 ☎ 34+93-412-72 72 FX: 34+93-412-74-76 ✉ lambda@pangea.org 💻 www.pangea.org/org/lambda
Centro asociativo sin ánimo de lucro que tiene como objetivo la normalización del hecho homosexual. Ofrece a gais y lesbianas un espacio de encuentro y orientación, y un Centro de Información y Documentación. Tarea de proyección social y a partir de sus activities culturales y del trabajo continuado de sensibilización hacia las instituciones públicas, las partidos políticos y el conjunto de la sociedad. [Non-profit organization works to normalize homosexuality & for civil rights. Cultural programming, public & legislative reform. Meeting space, info, resource center.]

Asociación de Lesbianas y Gais de Cantabria - ALEGA Centro Arcoiris, Barrio Camino 10, bajo, Santander, Cantabria 39004 ☎ Int+34+(9)42+291370 ✉ alega@nodo50.org 💻 www.nodo50.org/alega PUB: Gaizeta

ANAT - CP Apdo. 126, 348805, Guardo, Palencia ☎ 0034/902-11-49-49 ✉ anat@dragonet.es
NGO whose ojectives are attention, info for people with drug dependency &/or HIV/AIDS infection. Services & activities include: info/education, rehab, youth group, social activities, self-support, education, cultural groups, sport group.

Arcadia Cadiz C/Cervantes 19, bajos, Cadiz 11003 ☎ 34+(9)56+212200 ✉ arcadia@mixmail.com

Aldarte Barroeta Aldamar 7, Pral. Izqa., Bilbao, Euskadi 48001 ☎/FX: 34+(9)4+4237296 ✉ aldarte@euskalnet.net
Support center for GLBT. Study centre. Psychological & sexual support. Legal info. Safer sex workshops. GLBT support groups. PUB: Aldarte Informa

Ben Amics - Agrupació Gai i Lesbian de les Illes Balears C/ Imprenta 1, 1º, Palma de Mallorca, Illes Balears 07001 ☎/FX: 34+(9)71+723058 ✉ benamics@espanet.com 💻 www.espanet.com/benamics
Ben Amics PUB: Col.lectiu Lambda de Gais i Lesbianes del Pais Valencia
c/ Salvador Giner, 9 b. izq., Valencia, País Valencià 46003 ✉ lambda@arrakis.es 💻 www.arrakis.es/~lambda
Various associated groups: youth, lesbian, AIDS prevention, Christian gays, university groups. Telephone info, library, medical, social, & mental help services, legal assistance.

HERAKLES - SAFO Assemblea per la Llibertat Sexual [Assembly for Sexual Liberty] C/ Los Centelles 29-10, Valéncia, País Valencià 46006 ☎/FX: 34 96 334 03 28 ✉ herasafo@arrakis.esfils@xarxaneta.org (FILS)
Somos abiertos a todos/as los/as que estamos por la libertad sexual. Coordinados con el movimiento alternativo que denuncia le homofobia. Se ha creado el Fórum Internacional para la Libertad Sexual FILS. Nuestro grupo gestiona una base de datos con contenidos de libertad sexual y alternativos. [Open to all those who believe in sexual liberty. Works with the alternative movement that denounces homophobia. Created FILS, the International Forum for Sexual Freedom. Maintains a database of information about sexual freedom & alternatives. Organizes concerts & a film series.]

SRI LANKA

Friendship Sri Lanka c/o Shan Gunawardane, 1049 Pannipitiya Rd, Battaramulla, Colombo
For lesbians & bisexual women.

Companions on a Journey 1003 /5 Park Lane, Welikada, Rajagiriya, Wattale
☎ (941) 072-876754764 ✉ coj@sri.lanka.net; sherman@srilanka.net
💻 www.khushnet.com/directory/sri_lanka.htm
LGBT group. Runs a drop-in center in Colombo. Homosexuality even amongst consenting adults (Male / Female) in private is illegal under the section 365 of the Sri-Lankan Penal code with a maximum penalty of 12 years rigorous imprisonment. Yet despite this the country generally has a relaxed approach towards the issue of homosexuality.

SWEDEN

Swedish Regional Bi Networks *During the B iconference 2000, 3 loosely shaped regional networks were founded: BiSyd (south Sweden), contactperson, Hanna Bertilsdotter, hanna.bertilsdotter@spray.se; BiÖst (the middle-east part of Sweden), contactpersons, Stina Flink , stinaflink@zeta.telenordia.se, or Karin Ekström, nirakekstrom@hotmail.com; BiLandsbygd ("Bicountryside, or everything which is not south or middle east of Sweden) contaktperson, Camilla Jönsson, camilla@bredband.net*

Swedish Bi Email Lists *Bigrupp: mailing list for Swedish biactivists BiPride: national Swedish social mailinglist for bisexuals & others interested in discussing birelated subjects BiA: The national biactivistgroup of RFSL (the Swedish national GLB rights organization) BiBrev: Swedish electronic bi-newsletter. Contact person for all lists: Hanna Bertilsdotter, hanna.bertilsdotter@spray.se*

RFSL The Swedish Federation for Gay & Lesbian Rights website 💻 www.rfsl.se/
Extensive Swedish LGB website, including resources for bisexuals.

Walking back from lunch at IBC4,

Robyn Ochs

Bi i Göteborg (BiG) c/o RFSL Göteborg, Box 4033, 400 40 Göteborg ☎ RFSL: 031-775 40 18
✉ frema@user.bip.net 💻 www.rfsl.se/goteborg
(select bigruppen from menu)
Social & educational group.

Bikupan c/o RFSL, Stockholm, Box 350, S-101 26, Stockholm ☎ Christopher Arnold: (+46) 8 628 89 08 ✉ bikupan@rfsl.se 💻 www.rfsl.se/stockholm/bikupan/
Mts. Tu. 7pm at the RFSL-huset, Sveavägen 57, 1 tr.

Dalarma County contact person ✉ John Thornander: john.thornander@rfsl.se

Helsingborg contact person , Helsingborg
✉ Pelle Strandh: plusmeny@hotmail.com

Linköping contact person ✉ Anna-Karin Skantz: annsk190@student.liu.se

Malmö contact person ✉ Hanna Bertilsdotter: hanna.bertilsdotter@spray.se

Örebro contact person ✉ Camilla Jönsson: camilla@bredband.net

Östersund contact person ✉ Lars Hjalmarsson: LarsE_H@hotmail.com

Uppsala contact person ✉ Erika Reinedahl: syster_sol@hotmail.com

SWITZERLAND

biswiss 💻 biswiss.x2.nu/
News group & email list in three languages for Switzerland.

Rainbowline ☎ 0041-0848 80 50 80
National phone line in three languages French, German, Italian.

Bi-group-Basel c/o Stephan Kalt, Delsbergerallee 55, Basel, Basel-Stadt 4053 ☎ 061 331 66 14
✉ stephan@bidule.com

HABS, Gruppe fuer schwule Vatern, verheiratete Schwulen und bisexuelle Maenner PO Box CH-4001, Basel ☎ 061-692 66 55
✉ steilacotschna@compuserve.com; info@habs.ch
💻 www.habs.ch
For fathers & / or married men.

Bisexuelle Frauen Gruppe Postfach 5505, 3001 Bern ☎ 031-331 01 78 ✉ lesbiruf@swissonline.ch

Les-Bi-Ruf Postfach 7046, 3001 Bern
☎ 0041-31-311 07 73 ✉ lesbiruf@swissonline.ch
Phone line.

Coming Inn & Other side c/o HABS, Mühleplatz 11, 3000 Bern 13 ☎ 0041-31-311 63 53
💻 www.datacomm.ch/cominginn

Freedom Bienne ☎ 0041-79-470 50 92

Association 360° CP 411, 1211 Geneve 4 ☎ 0041-0878 878 360 ✉ espace360@360.ch 💻 www.360.ch
trans inclusive also PUB: 360° (public magazine)

Dialogai, Gays Mariés CP691, 1211 Genève 21, 11,13 Rue de la Navigation, Genève, Genève ☎ 022-906 40 40 or 45 FX: 022-906 40 44 ✉ dialogai@hivnet.ch 🖳 www.dialogai.ch *For married glb people.* PUB: Dialogai Info (Free publication. Articles & information about French-speaking Switzerland.)

Infobi (Antenne Bisexuelle Romande) 13 des Oiseaux, CP 894, 1000 Lausanne 9 ☎ 0041.21.646.25.35 FX: 0041.21646.29.29 ✉ infobi@gmx.ch 🖳 www.vogay.ch

Groupe de Femmes Bi Lausanne ☎ 0041-78-790 49 49 ✉ amies_bi@hotmail.com

VoGay, jeunes gays, bis et lesbiennes (GLB Youth Group) 13, av des Oiseaux 13, CP 894, CH-1000 Lausanne 9 ☎ 41-21/646 25 35 FX: 41-21/646 29 29 ✉ vogay@worldcom.ch 🖳 www.vogay.ch

Lilaphon, Zentrum für Frauen ZEFRA Postfach 2309, 6000 Luzern 2, Vonmattstr. 44, 6003 Luzern, Luzern ☎ 041-360 30 26 ✉ lilaphon@yahoo.de

LesBiSchwul Zug Zeuhausgasse 9, Zug 041-710 48 75 ☎ 041-710 48 75 ✉ lesbischwul@zugernet.ch *Books & video library*

Woman to Woman Frauenzentrum, Mattengasse 27, Zürich 8005 ☎ 01-272 05 04 FX: 01-272 81 61 ✉ frauenzentrum@access.ch 🖳 www.fembit.ch *Discussion forum for lesbian & bisexual women.*

Artemisia Sihlquai 67, Zürich ☎ 0041-01-242 02 70 *Phone line.*

THAILAND

Pink Ink MBE Surawong #227, 173/3 Surawong Road, Bangkok 10500 ☎ (02) 661-3150 ext 1515 ✉ pinkink@khsnet.com 🖳 http://www.khsnet.com/pinkink/ *"Listings of all things queer in Thailand."*

Anjaree PO Box 322, Ratchadamngoen BKK 10200 ☎ 477-1776 ✉ anjaree@hotmail.com *Lesbian organization aimed at Thai speakers, with occasional social, educational, or travel events that welcome visiting woman. They also put out a Thai language newsletter.*

UKRAINE

The Foundation to Defend the Rights of Sexual Minorities a/r 8506, Kharkov 310055 ☎ 011-38-0572-934264 FX: 38-0572-934264 *Seeking contacts & assistance from abroad.*

Nash Mir: Regional Information & Human Rights Defense Center for Gays & Lesbians PO Box 62, 91051 Lugansk-51 ☎ (0642) 479422 ✉ ourworld@cci.lg.ua 🖳 www.gay.org.ua/ PUB: Nash Mir (Monthly magazine)

> **What is new is not bisexuality but rather the widening of our awareness and acceptance of human capacities for sexual love.**
>
> *Margaret Mead (1901-1978), quoted 1975 in Redbook*

Kiev Regional Intellect Club for Gays & Bisexuals PO Box 99, 254080 Kiev ✉ nick@nym.alias.net *Revival of the spirituality among GLB, leisure activities, & info on GLB in Ukraine. Contact person: Nickolay Yanko.*

My S Vami (We Are With You) Anti-AIDS Center Room 201, 9 Gueorguievsky pereulok, 252034 Kiev ☎ 044 228 73 85

UNITED KINGDOM

National

National Bisexual Helpline ☎ 020 8569 75000 *Tu. 7:30-9:30pm Wed. 7:30-9:30pm. Sat. 10:30am-12:30 pm.*

Bi Community News BM RiBBit, London, England WC1N 3XX ✉ bcn@bi.org 🖳 www.bi.org/~bcn/ *Back issues available on the webpage. National newsletter for UK bisexuals; upcoming events, bi-related publications & films, interviews & articles, cartoons, letters. UK's only regular listing of bi news, groups & events nationwide.* PUB: Bi Community News (12 issues UK £8 (Unwaged) UK £10 (Standard) £15 (Supporter and EU) £25 (Super supporter & those outside EU))

British Bisexual Federation c/o LBG, PO Box 3325, London, England N19EQ ✉ bbf@bi.org 🖳 bi.org/~bbf *Nationwide Umbrella Organization for groups & individuals.*

Soc.Bi 🖳 bi.org/~jon/soc.bi *Long running usenet friendly group for all bi's.*

Both Sides Now ✉ bothsidesnow-subscribe@yahoogroups.com 🖳 members.xoom.com/bothsidesnow/bothsidesnow *Email discussion group for Bi's into Indie, punk music, lively & friendly chatter.*

UK-BI 🖳 www.maghmell.demon.co.uk/uk-bi/ *Mailing list for bisexuals in the UK. To subscribe, send a message to listserver@ogham.org with no subject, reading subscribe uk-bi {yourname}.*

UK-SMBI 🖳 bi.org/uk-smbi/ *Email list to discuss issues related to BDSM & Bisexuality in the UK*

Bi-Academic Intervention University of York , Women's Studies Centre, 5 Main St., York, England YO1 5DD ✉ eakn1@york.ac.uk
Resource for students & researchers interested in work related to Bisexuality & Queer theory.

Bisexual Therapists Forum England ☎ Contact through Bisexual Phoneline (London): 020 8569 7500
For those involved in counseling work.

Bi-Q 7 Hill Cottages, Rosedale East, Pickering, North York, England YO18 8RG
🖳 www.neilhudson.freeserve.co.uk/contents.htm
16 page 'zine, "The antidote to bisexual seriousness."

Off Pink Publishing Collective 24 Shandon Rd., Clapham Park, London, England SW4 9HR
✉ OffPink@bi.org
Publishers of Bisexual Lives & Bisexual Horizons.

Burning Issues Group A Behr, 50 Moundfield Road, London, England N16 6TB
✉ bissues@yahoo.com 🖳 croydon/gov.uk/bissues
Librarian group working to improve library provisions for LGBT.

Bi Parents' Network BPN, c/o BM Ribbit, London, England WC1N 3XX ☎ 020 8692 8417 before 10.30pm
When writing for info, include SAE.

Pink Parents Box 55 Green Leaf Bookshop, 82 Colston St, Bristol BS1 5BB ☎ 011 7377 5794
For parents of glbt people. Helpline Th. 7-10pm.

Happy Families PO Box 1060, Doncaster, England DN6 9QE ☎ 01302 702601
Support groups for lgb parents.

Outrage P O Box 17816, London SW14 8WT
☎ 0208 240 0222 🖳 outrage.cygnet.co.uk
LGBT Direct Action Campaign Group.

...It's just that things don't always happen as you predict, or even because you strive for them to be so. Rather, change comes from the accumulated dreams and yearnings of the many who break out of the mold—not because they think they should, but because they can't help it. We become visible because our parade is just too damn obvious to avoid, because fear is simply in the way, and we're too big to go around it any more. We become desirable as soon as we put away the ugly stick—and then we find real beauty, waiting for us, without complaint.

Susie Bright

Sexual Freedom Coalition P O Box 4ZB, London, England W1A 4ZB ☎ 0207 460 1979
Pansexual Campaign Group.

University GLBT Organisations in the UK
🖳 www.umu.man.ac.uk/lgbsoc/services/links/unilgbtsocieties.htm
Website listing dozens of GLBT university-based organisations in the UK.

Vigour ✉ vigouruk@hotmail.com
Support group for visually impaired LGBT.

At Ease 28 Commercial St., London, England E1 6LS
Armed forces support.

Youth

Youthline ☎0800 169 7384 OR 0161 273 7190
Phone line run for young glb people, aged 14-25. Run by Peer Supporters (other young LGBs) who offer support, info & advice. Operates on Tues 6:30pm-9pm, & Sat 1-3pm.

Lesbian, Gay & Bisexual Youth Line ☎ 01908 587 677 (Milton Keynes, Wed. 7:30-9:30 pm.)

HIV

National AIDSLINE ☎0800 567123
Information on referral & support services.

Religious

Quest LinkLine LGB Catholics London & Scotland
☎ London 020 7792 0234; Scotland 0141 948 0397
London Fri. 7-10, Scotland Sun. 7-10.

Christian Science LGB Group ☎ 020 7515 6427

Jewish LGB Group ☎ 020 8922 5214

L & G Christian Helpline ☎ 020 7739 8134

Action for Gay & Lesbian Ordination
PO Box 5716, London, England W10 6WN
☎ 0207-813 5247

Al Fatiha Muslim Group 424 37 Store Street, London, England WC1 ✉ alfatiha-London@hotmail.com

Called to be One PO Box 24632, London, England E9 6XF
Support for Catholic parents of LGBS.

GAON London, England ☎ 07957 485365
Orthodox or formally Orthodox Jews.

Quest L & G Catholics BM Box 2585, London, England WC1N 3XX

London

London Bisexual Group 86 Caledonia Road, London, England N1 9DN ☎ 020 8569 7500
✉ LondonBi@bi.org 🖳 www.bi.org/~LondonBi
Meets Fri 8pm, at London Friend, 86 Caledonian Road N1 (Kings Cross- St. Pancras tube). Mixed social group & personal support group.

> **I tried to persuade myself that I was three-quarters normal and that only a quarter of me was queer —whereas really it was the other way around.**
>
> *—Somerset Maugham, English novelist/ playwright, 1874-1965*

SM/Bi c/o Central Station, 37 Wharfdale Road, London, England N1 9SE ✉ smbi@bi.org
🖳 www.bi.org/~smbi/
Network of bisexuals into BDSM, newsletter, contacts, campaigning. Meet 2nd Sun. 7.30pm. at above address. PUB: Ungagged, Chainletter (Ungagged (Newsletter) Free with SAE Chainletter : Writers/artists circle, contribution to Chainletter & SAE gets copies of other stories sent.)

East Bi South East London, England
✉ michale19@hotmail.com
Informal gatherings of bis based in East London.

Gemma BM Box 5700, London, England WC1N 3XX
Friendship network of lesbian & bi women with/ without disabilities.

Lesbian & Bi Women Artists London ☎ Tracey: 020 8925 4315

GLAD c/o Central Station, 37 Wharfdale, London, England N1 9SE ☎ 020 7837 5212
Legal advice.

Post Adoption LGB Group 5 Torriano Mews, Post Adoption Centre, London, England NW5 2RZ
☎ 020 7284 0555

Gay & Lesbian Policing Initiative 2G Leroy House, 436 Essex Road, London, England N1 3QP
☎ Ofc: 020 7704 6767
Assistance for dealing with homophobic violence & abuse. Works with the Police service to educate about the LGBT community. Helpline 020 7704 2040 (Mon. 5-8pm, Tu. 1-3pm, Wed. 3-6pm, Fri. 12-2pm).

Lesbian & Gay Anti-Racist Alliance PO Box 150, London, England WC1X 9AT ☎ 0207 278 6869

Rank Outsiders BCM Box 8431, London, England WC1N 3XX ☎ 0207 652 6464
Support for currently serving & retired LGB armed forces.

School's Out Institute of Education, 20 Bedford Way, London, England WC1
☎ Geoff: 020 7582 2325
London LGB's working in education.

Lesbian, Gay & Bisexual Alcohol Project London, England ☎ 020 7737 3579

Narcotics Anonymous LGB London W11
☎ Helpline daily 10am-10pm: 020 7351 6794
Meets Tu., 7:30pm, Church Hall, Portobello Rd., London.

PROJECT LSD 32a Wardour St., London, England W1 ☎ 0207-439-0717 (Wed. 6-9)
Drug info & advice for LGBs.

REGARD BM Regard, London, England WC1N 3XX
☎ 020 7738 6191
Help line Tu. 7-9pm organization for Disabled LGB.

Out Take London, England
☎ Derek: 0207-613-5326; Lynne: 0207-613-3616
Support for LGBs with mental health problems.

Brother & Sisters Club 109 Kessock Close, Ferry Lane Estate, London, England N17
Support for LGB people with hearing difficulties.

Brothers & Sisters Club 25 Cruickshank St., London, England WC1X 9HF ☎ 0207 837 5561
For calf LGBs.

Gay Spiritual Group BCM Zeal, London, England WC1N 3XX ☎ 020 8846 8593 FX: 020 8563 1082

Metropolitan Community Churches BM/MCC, London, England WC1N 3XX ☎ 020 7485 6756

NAZ Project 241 King Street, London, England W6 ☎ 020 8741 01879
Support for South Asian, Middle Eastern, North African, Horn of Africa & Latin American communities.

Orientations London, England ☎ 0956 535 871 ✉ jsun@ic.ac.uk
South East & East Asian LGBs.

Beit Klal Yisrael PO Box 1828, London, England W10 5RT ☎ 020 8960 5750
Alternative Jewish community.

Black Gay & Bisexual Group London, England ☎ 020 8675 6001, 020 8674 1511
Support & social group for black brothers.

Black Lesbian & Gay Centre Room 113, 5/5a Westminster Bridge Road, Room 113, London, England SE1 ☎ 020 7620 3885
Helpline Tu./Th. 11:30am-5:30pm.

Big Up Unit 41,Eurolink Centre, 49 Effra Road, England SW2 ☎ 020 7501 9264
For black men who have sex with men. Helpline 0207 501 3915.

Blackliners ☎ 020 7738 5274
Help line for Blacks & Asians M-F, 9:30am-6pm.

Rainbow Moffies London, England
☎ Gregory: 07957 322115
Support & social group for South & Southern Africans.

Amach Linn c/o Hammersmith Irish Centre, Blacks Road, Hammersmith, London W6
☎ 020 8450 4022
Support for Irish LGB in London. Helpline Thurs.

Japanese Rainbow Group London, England
☎ 0795 747 9981 ✉ pe_uk@yahoo.co.jo

Jewish Lesbian & Gay Group BM/JGLG, London, England WC1N 3XX ☎ 020 8922 5214
Helpline 020 7706 3123 Mon. & Th. 7-10pm.

KISS London, England ☎ 020 8741 1879 (Parminder)
South Asian, Middle Eastern lesbian/bi women support group.

Cypriot Lesbian & Gay Group Central Station, 37 Wharfdale Road, Kings Cross, London, England N!

DOST London, England ☎ 020 8741 1879
South Asian, Turkish, Arab & Irani gay men. Meets Wed. 7-9 pm.

Diaspora London, England ☎ 020 8533 2174
-25 LGB of colour meet Thurs.

Latin American Gay Support Group London, England ☎ 020 8741 1879

Metroline LGB London, England ☎ 020 8865 3355
Helpline Mon.-Th. 7-10pm.

Metronet L&B Women's Drop In Greenwich, South East London, England ☎ 020 8265 3311/ 8265 3355 Natalie
Tu. 1-3:30pm.

Metronet LGB Mental Health Drop In- Greenwich, South East London, England ☎ 020 8265 3311/ 8265 3355
Clive or Natalie available for advice & support Th. 1-4pm.

GB Harlow Harlow, (Essex) London England ☎ Alex: 0973-541974 (24 hrs./day)
Meet Harlow Tu. 7-9:30pm.

Youth

Albert Kennedy Trust Unit 305a 16/16a Baldwin Gardens, London, England EC1N 7RJ ☎ 020 7831 6562 ✉ info@akt.org.uk 🖳 www.akt.org.uk/
Support for homeless LGB Youth.

Camden Young Lesbian & Bi Women's Group Camden, London ☎ 0207-267 2898 (Mon. 6-9pm)
Lesbian & bi women -25.

Croydon LBG Group London ☎ 07071-225 577 *-25.*

Divas London, England ☎ 020 8533 2174
For lesbian & bi women under 21. Meets Fri. 6-8 in Hackney.

Diverse Divas Camden, London, England ☎ 020 7267 8595
Women -25.

First Move London, England ☎ 020 8205 0006 (Mon. 4-6) ✉ firstmove@baeu.demon.co.uk
Collindale-based YGB -25.

First Step PO Box 1992, London, England WC1N 3XX ☎ 020 8461 4112
-21s meets Mon. 7:30-10.

Forbidden Fruit London, England ☎ 020 8533 2174
-25; Hackney; Graham/Gareth.

Freedom London, England ☎ 020 8533 2324 (Tu. 2-4)
LGB youth.

Greenwich Freedom Youth London, England ☎ 020 8316 4397 (Loraine or James)
LGB -26.

> ## I don't care what people do, as long as they dont do it in the street and frighten the horses!
>
> *—Mrs. Patrick Campbell, English actress, 1865-1940.*

HARROW LGB Youth Support Service London, England ☎ Lorraine: 020 8863 6684 (M-Th. 14-10pm)

Hounslow Young Lesbian & Bisexual Group Hounslow, London, England ☎ 0956-459 223
Women -26; meet Sun. 6-8:30pm.

Identity Chiswick, London, England ☎ 0208-742 2381
Meet Sun. 6:30-8:30, Chiswick; gay & bi men -26.

LGB Teenage 6-9 Manor Gardens, London, England N7 6LA ☎ 020 7263 5932 (Sun. 4-7, Wed. 7-10)

MALE OUT London, England ☎ 020 7267 8595
Camden male youth; meet Wed. 6:30pm.

MYNORS (Merton Youth Not of Rigid Sexuality London, England ☎ 020 8646 3033
Wed. 6:30-9:30pm.

Masala London, England ☎ 020 8741 1879
LGB Youth of South Asian origin.

Metro Tribe London, England ☎ 020 8865 3355
-26 support group Sat. 2-5.

NRG Youth Project London, England ☎ 0207 620 1819
LGB -25 Th. 6-10 pm & weekends. Near Waterloo.

North London Line Youth Project London, England ☎ 0207 607 8346
Mon.: Mixed 6-9pm Tu.: L & B women 6-9pm Wed.: Mixed 2-5pm.

North Seven Social Old Fire Station, 84 Mayton St., London N7 ☎ 0207-700 4658
Gay & bi men 16-25; meet Tu. 7-10.

Open Door London, England ☎ Louise/Rachel: 0208-698 9453/6675
Lesbian & bi women -26; meet Wed. 7-10pm.

Out on Thursday London ☎ 0207-386 9131
Hammersmith gay & bi men -25; meet Th. 6-10pm.

Outlinks: LGB Youth Project London, England ☎ (0207) 378- 8732
1 on 1 meeting with youth worker. Mixed social group Tu. 7-9pm.

Outzone London ☎ 0207-348 8008 Pete
Support & social for gay & bi men -25 in London.

Phase Tower Hamlets Youth Project London, England ☎ 0207 515 4617
LGB group. Mixed Drop in Wed. 3-5 pm, L&B women 6-9pm Th., G&B men 6-9pm Sat. & Sun.

Lisa and Fritz at IBC5, Boston

QT Youth Group London, England
☎ 020 8427 5505 (VM)
LGB group (16-25) 020 8427 1799, Fri. 6-10pm.

SHOUT London, England ☎0208 675 0306
SW London LGB Youth Group Fri. 7-10pm

Staying Out London, England ☎ 0208-533-2174
*For LGB people -25. Meets Tu. 7-10pm in
Hackney for -25. -17, 1st Sat. 2-5pm.*

Strength Progression Diversity London, England
☎ 0589-422854
Lesbian & bi women -26.

The Mix London, England ☎ 0207 867 8595
*LGBT -25 in Kentish Town Tuesday 6:30-9:30pm.
Minicom 0207 387 2404.*

Waltham Forest Lesbian/Bi Women London,
England ☎ Al/Vicky: 0589-422854
Lesbian & bi women -26.

Youth Out Pastures Youth Centre, Davies Lane,
London, England E11 ☎ 020 8532 8008
Gay and bi men - 26; meet Mon. 7-10pm.

Hillingdon LGB Youth Group Hillingdon, London,
England ☎ Paul/Sam: 01895-235777
🖳 www.geocities.com/WestHollywood/Heights/2314
LGB -21.

ACAPS 34 Electric Lane, Brixton, London,
England ☎ 0207 737 3579
*Counseling for LGB's & their partners with
drinking problems.*

BOY BLUE The Old Fire Station, 84 Mayton St.,
London, England N7 ☎ 020 7609 4059 (Wed. 5-8 pm)
*Sexual health drop-in for gay & bi men -25,
Wed. 5-8pm.*

South East England

Allsorts Brighton, England
☎ Jessica: 07932 852533

Pink Parenting Group Morley Street Family
Centre, Morley Street, Brighton, England

University of Brighton: LGBT Society Students
Union, Falmer House 232, Brighton, Sussex,
England BN1 9PH ✉ lgbtsoc-ubu@bris.ac.uk
🖳 www.bris.ac.uk/Depts/Union/LGBTsoc/

The Outhouse LGB Centre 19 East Hill,
Colchester, Essex, England

Colchester Bi Group c/o The Outhouse
☎ 01206 869 191
Meets 1st Th. 7 pm at the Outhouse.

L & Bi Women Essex Essex, England
☎ Julia: 01702 618886

Southend Women's Coming Out Group
Southend, Essex, England ☎ 01072 344355

Hampshire LGB Youth Group Hampshire, England
☎ 023 9247 2813

Freedom Youth Basingstoke, Hampshire, England
☎ 01256-376486
LGB youth group.

University of Portsmouth LGB Portsmouth,
Hampshire, England ☎ (01705) 81914101705 755
866 (nightline, 8pm-8am) ✉ lgb@port.ac.uk
🖳 www.port.ac.uk/sunion/clubs/lgb/

Southern Bisexual Network 82a Northam Road,
Unit 4, Southampton, England SO14 0SN
☎ Chris: 07901 570646
*Social network of bi's around Portsmouth,
Southampton & Solent area.*

Herts LGB Helpline Hertfordshire ☎ 01727 858567

WOW Health and Social Group The Priory
Centre, 11 Priory Road, High Wycombe, Bucks
HP13 6SL

Women of Wycombe PO Box 781, High
Wycombe, Bucks HP12 3GJ

Bexley LGB Group 8 Brampton Road, Kent,
England DA7 4 EY ☎ 020 8316 5954 M-Th 5-8pm

Bexley Area Youth Bexley, Kent, England
☎ 020-8265 3311
Meets Fridays, -26.

Outside In PO Box 119, Orpington, Kent, England
BR6 9ZZ
Volunteer support for LGB's in Prison.

Bisexual Groups in formation, Oxford c/o Richard
01865 727023

Oxford LGB Centre St. Michaels St, Off
Cornmarket, Oxford, England

**Oxford University: Lesbian, Gay & Bisexual
Society** Student Union, 28 Little Clarendon
Street, Oxford, England ✉ lgbsoc@sable.ox.ac.uk
🖳 users.ox.ac.uk/~lgbsoc/

Wayout Oxford, England ☎ 01865 243389
Youth group.

Space LGB Youth Oxted, Surrey, England
☎ 01372-731011

DLAGGS 7 Victoria Ave., South Croydon, Surrey,
England CR2 ☎ 0208 660 2208
Deaf Group.

Out Crowd Woking, Surrey, England
☎ 01483-727667

Brunel University: LGB Society c/o Union of Brunel
University, Uxbridge, Middx, England UB8 3PH
☎ 01895 462200 FX: 01895 462200
✉ sugsoc@brunel.ac.uk 🖳 www.brunel.ac.uk/
~xxsugsoc/

East Anglia

Cambridge University LBG Society CUSU, 11/12 Trumpington Street, Cambridge, England CB2 1QA ☎ Termtime: 01223-333313 Tuesdays 8-11pm. **FX:** 01223-7-40777
✉ lesbigay@cusu.cam.ac.uk
🖳 www-lbg.cusu.cam.ac.uk/

Kite Club c/o Box Kite Club, Arjuna 12 Mill Road, Cambridge, England CB1 2AD
✉ kiteclub@hotmail.com
  -19.

Sister Act Social PO Box 294, Cambridge, England CB4 2XR

Freedom Club Huntington, Cambridgeshire, England ☎ 01480 398036
✉ lgbfreedom@hotmail.com
  LGB 16-23.

Standout c/o Matthew Project, Pottergate, Norwich, Norfolk, England

Women on Women Drop In c/o 7a St. Benedicts St., Norwich, Norfolk, England

Oasis LGB Youth Group Suffolk, England
☎ Julie: 01473 212 165

South West England

Bath University: LGB Society - Square Pegs Bath, Somerset, England ☎ Tuesdays 6-7pm on Bath (01225) 465793 ✉ lgb@bath.ac.uk.
🖳 www.bath.ac.uk/~su4lgbs/
  Regular informal meetings in 4E 3.22on Tu. 6-7pm.

Freedom Youth Bristol, Somerset, England
☎ 0117 955 3355

Sh-Out c/o 12 Litchdon Street, Barnstable, Devon, England EX32 8ND
  LGB Social Group.

Exeter University LGB Friend Group LGB Officers, Guild of Students, Top Corridor, Devonshire House, Stocker Road, Devon, Devonshire, England ☎ 01392 263541 ✉ lgb@exeter.ac.uk
🖳 gosh.ex.ac.uk/societies/lgb/
  Open to all university students & local people.

LGB Switchboard Dorset ☎ 01202 318822

Quaker Lesbian & Gay Fellowship 3 Hallsfield, Ruth, Cricklade, Swindon, England SN6 6LR
  Bi-positive Quaker group.

Wiltshire & Swindon L & Bi Women's Link Wiltshire, England ☎ 07713 225854
  Counseling service.

Young & Gay Awareness Project Swindon, Wiltshire ☎ 01793 694700 (M. 6-8)

Midlands England

Birmingham University Lesbian, Gay, Bisexual Society Birmingham, West Midlands, England ✉ LGB@bham.ac.uk 🖳 www.guild.bham.ac.uk/lgb/
  Separate lesbian & bi women's group as well.

Friend West Midlands P O Box 2405, Birmingham B5 6SF

Cotswold LGBT Social Group Cotswolds, Gloucestershire, England ☎ 01386 701363

Coventry Friend P O Box 8, Coventry, Warwickshire, CV1 3ZT

L & Bi Women's Group c/o Terrance Higgins Trust, 10 Manor Road, Coventry, Warwickshire,England

DeMontfort & Leicester University LGB Group Leicester, Leicestershire, England ☎ DeMontfort contact: Ray, LGB Officer: 0116-2555576. Leicester contact: Jazz: 0116-2556282x143 or ansaphone 0116 2555394. ✉ lgb@leister.ac.uk

Northampton Lesbian, Gay & Bisexual Alliance 1st Floor, Charles House, 61-69 Derngate, Northampton, England NN1 1UE

Nottingham Women's Bi Group Nottingham Women's Centre, 30 Chaucer St., Nottingham, England NG1 5LP
  Women only social group, meets 8pm 3rd Tu. at above address. Press buzzer marked "library."

Black Lesbian & Bisexual Support Group Nottingham, England. ☎ Krys 0115 953 9828

If bisexuality is in fact, as I suspect it to be, not just another sexual orientation but rather a sexuality that undoes sexual orientation as a category, ... then the search for the meaning of the word "bisexual" offers a different kind of lesson. Rather than naming an invisible, undernoticed minority now finding its place in the sun, "bisexual" turns out to be, like bisexuals themselves, everywhere and nowhere. There is, in short, no "really" about it. The question of whether someone was "really" straight or "really" gay misrecognizes the nature of sexuality, which is fluid, not fixed, a narrative that changes over time rather than a fixed identity, however complex. The erotic discovery of bisexuality is the fact that it reveals sexuality to be a process of growth, transformation, and surprise, not a stable and knowable state of being.

—Marjorie Garber, in Vice Versa: Bisexuality and the Eroticism of Everyday Life *(NY: Simon & Schuster*

> **There's no limit on how complicated things can get, on account of one thing always leading to another.**
>
> E.B. White

Nottingham Trent University: Lesbian, Gay & Bisexual Society Nottingham, England
✉ lgb@su.ntc.ac.uk 🖳 www.geocities.com/nottinghamtrentlgb/
Non-students welcome.

Telford Bisexual & Lesbian Drop In Centre Telford, Shropshire, England. ☎ 01952 223222

Keele University LGB Society c/o Students' Union, Staffordshire, England ST5 5BJ
✉ ksc07@cc.keele.ac.uk 🖳 www.keele.ac.uk/socs/ks07/

North Staffs LGB Association 57-59 Piccadily, Hanley, Stoke on Trent, Staffs ST1 1HR

North East England

Darlington Women on Women & Drop In Darlington, England. ☎ 01325 462418

Rainbow Centre LGB Support Line Hartlepool, England. ☎ 01429 285000 (Mon 7-9pm)

GALYIC Halifax, West Yorkshire, England. ☎ 01422 320099 (Wed. 7-9)

Leeds Bisexual Group c/o Leeds LBG Sitchboard, PO Box HH29, Leeds, West Yorkshire, England LS8 2UA ✉ Leeds@Bi.org
Meets 2nd Tu. Metz cafe bar.

Libby & Out Leeds, West Yorkshire, England. ☎ 0113-245 3588
Lesbian & bi women 15-25.

Bi Womens Group PO Box 1 JR, Newcastle Upn Tyne, NE99 1JR

ComBiNe (Community of Bisexuals in the North East) PO Box 1JR, Newcastle-Upon-Tyne, England NE99
Monthly social / support group for bisexual women, men, partners of bis & allies. Meets 7.30pm 1st Sat of the month, at MESMEC NE Floor 3 11 Nelson Street Newcastle on Tyne.

Gay Girls Group Sheffield PO Box 487, Sheffield, South Yorkshire, England S1 2JL
Lesbian & Bi women 14-25.

Lesbian & Gay Foster & Adoptive Parents Network Northern Support Network, PO Box 2078, Sheffield, South Yorkshire, England S2 4YQ

Next Generation LGB Sheffield, South Yorkshire, England ☎ 0114 2700298
Youth info & support Centre.

Sheffield University Bisexual Group FAO Natalie Dell, Sheffield Uni LGB, Students Union Building, Western Bank, Sheffield, England S10 2TN
☎ 0114 222 8673 Luchtime during term
✉ lgb@shef.ac.uk 🖳 usit.shef.ac.uk/~lgb
Meets 1st & 3rd Mon. during termtime. Open to students & nonstudents.

North West England

LGB Outreach Cumbria ☎ 01228 603075

Icebreakers LGB c/o Quaker Meeting House, Chean Walk, Frodsham Street, Chester, Cheshire ☎ Peter 012 44 342066

Utopia c/o Calypso Youth Information Shop, The Groves, Chester, England CH1 1SD
GLB youth group.

GLYAM 33 Great Kings Street, Macclesfield, Cheshire, England ☎ 01625 501 203
Ages 14-25. Meets Wed.

GLYSS Runcorn, Cheshire, England
☎ Kerry: 01928 580270

Gay Healthy Alliance PO Box 9, Widness, Cheshire, WA8 0GP

Dorothy's Drop In c/o Friends Meeting House, Sliverwell Street, Bolton, Lancashire

Lancaster University UniQ Lancaster, Lancashire, England 🖳 www.lancs.ac.uk/socs/lgb/

South Ribble One in Ten South Ribble, Central Lancashire, England. ☎ 01772 621 165
Youth group.

West Lancs One in Ten Lancashire, England ☎ 0498 924 164

Chorley L & Bi Women's Link Chorley, Lancashire ☎ 01257 234738

Friend Helpline Liverpool, England ☎ 0151 708 0234 (Thurs. 7-10pm)

Liverpool University: Lesbian, Gay, Bisexual & Transgender Society Guild of Students, PO Box 187, Liverpool, England L69 3BX
☎ 0151 794-4165 ✉ livlgb@hotmail.com
🖳 members.netscapeonline.co.uk/liverpoollgbt/

Biphoria LGF, 15 Pritchard Lane,Manchester, England M1 7DA ☎ (0161) 235-8000
✉ manchester@bi.org 🖳 bi.org/~manchester/
Meets 1st Thurs 8pm at the L&G Centre on Sydney St. Mixed social / discussion group.

Albert Kennedy Trust - Manchester 23 New Mount Street, Manchester, England M4 4DE
☎ 0161 953 4059
LGB homeless teenagers.

Befriending Project Peer Support Project, PO Box 153, Manchester, England M60 1LP ☎ 0161 274 4664 ✉ office@peer-support.org.uk 🖳 www.peer-support.org.uk/support/befriending.htm
New project created for young lgb people, 14-25. Meet & chat with other young lgb people on a friendly one to one basis. We don't judge you & it is a confidential service.

Families & Friends of Lesbians and Gays
PO Box 153, Manchester, England M60 1LP
☎ 01392 279 546

Lesbian & Gay Youth Manchester Peer Support
Project, PO BOX 153, Manchester, England M60
1LP ☎ 0161 274 4664 ✉ lgym@peer-
support.org.uk 🖳 www.peer-support.org.uk/lgym
Meets 2x/week 7pm Tu. & 3pm Sat. For lgb -26.

**Manchester University: Lesbian Gay & Bisexual
Society** Manchester Univ. Students Union,
Manchester, England M13 9PR
✉ lgbsoc@umu.man.ac.uk 🖳 www.umu.man.ac.uk/
lgbsoc/
Also Lesbian & Bi Women's Group, email list.

Peer Support by Post Peer Support Project,
PO Box 153, Manchester, England M60 1LP
✉ penpals@peer-support.org.uk 🖳 www.peer-
support.org.uk/support/penpals.htm
*Written support service where young lesbian, gay
& bisexual people can write to a Peer Supporter
for support, info & advice. Not a dating service.*

Peer Support project Peer Support Project, PO
Box 153, Manchester, England M60 1LP
☎ 0161 274 4664 ✉ office@peer-support.org.uk
🖳 www.peer-support.org.uk
*Offers info & support to lgb -26. This is in the
form of Youthline, Peer by Post, Befriending
Scheme & many PSP run groups.*
PUB: Peer Pleasure (A magazine of articles
submitted by young people who use the Peer
Support Project. Call the office to receive a
copy.)

Positive Parenting Campaign Dep 7, 255
Wilmslow Road, Manchester, England M14 5LW

Queer Youth Manchester Manchester, England
☎ 07092 031 086 ✉ david@queeryouth.org.uk
🖳 www.queeryouth.org.uk
*Social support group for lgbt young people in the
Greater Manchester Area. Based in the Heart of
Manchester's Gay Village we believe we provide a
safe meeting place for gay young people to come
& relax. Main group runs Th. 6-10pm.*

Triangle Group - Deaf LGB's Manchester
*Group for Deaf LGB's & their friends. Sign
Language used at these meetings. Meets 1st Sun.
at 2pm outside the Rembrant on Canal St.*

Young Lesbian/Bisexual Women c/o Alison,
PO Box 93, Stockport, Greater Manchester,
England SK1 3FJ

Stockport Lesbian, Gay & Bisexual Group PO
Box 93, Stockport, Greater Manchester, England
SK1 3FJ ☎ 0161 477-4096
🖳 www.thebase.free-online.co.uk
*Men: mtgs Wed. & Fri. evenings. Women:
Th. evenings discussion for -26.*

Wales

DASH LGB Drug Alcohol Resource 74 Nolton St.,
Bridgend, Wales

Cardiff University: LGB Students University Union
Cathays Park, Park Place, Cardiff, Wales/Cymru
CF1 3QN ☎ (01222) 398903 FX: (01222) 396608

WOW Bute Terrace, Cardiff, Wales

Lampeter University LG&B Group LGB Officer c/o
Student Union, Lampeter, Wales/Cymru SA48
7ED ✉ lampeterlgb@angelfire.com
🖳 www.angelfire.com/ga/lampeterLGB/

LGB Switchboard Swansea, Wales
☎ 01792 480044
Th. 7-9:30pm.

UCMC/NUS Wales LGB Campaign c/o 107 Walter
Road/ Heol Walter, Swansea, Wales/Cymru SA1
5QQ ☎ (01792) 643-323 FX: (01792) 648-554
✉ nus.wales@enablis.co.uk 🖳 www.enablis.co.uk/
nus.wales/fwhoarew.html#english

**University of Wales Swansea: Lesbian, Bisexual,
Gay Society** Societies Centre, Union Building,
3rd Floor, L Pigeonhole, Swansea, Wales/Cymru
SA2 8PP ☎ 07968 252455 (the LGB mobile phone)
✉ swansealgb@bigfoot.com
🖳 swansealgb.members.beeb.net/
*Drop-in sessions on Tu. 6-7pm in the Advice &
Support Centre. LGB meetings Tu. 7:30-8pm.*

Big & Tall Association P O Box 1, Prestatyn,
North Wales LL19 8ZL

Scotland

Lesbian & Bi Women in Central Scotland
Scotland ☎ 01786 471285 (Mon 7:30-9:30)

Lesbian & Bi Group Aberdeen c/o Women's
Centre, Shoe Lane off Queens St., Aberdeen,
Scotland

**DiversiTay Lesbian Gay Bisexual Transgender
Group** PO Box 53, Dundee, Scotland DD1 3YG
☎ (01382) 202620 ✉ diversitay@hotmail.com
🖳 www.dundeelgb.freeserve.co.uk/
*Helpline for counseling & info: M. 7-10pm. This
Way Out support group confidentially serves
LGBT people aged -25; meets Sun. PUB:
ELIGIBILITY (Regional newsletter available
from organization or at other local sources.)*

Dundee University: LGBT Society Airlie Place,
Dundee, Students' Association, Dundee, Scotland
✉ lgbt-society@dundee.ac.uk
🖳 www.dusa.dundee.ac.uk/lgb/

Bi Archive 58a Broughton Street, Edinburgh EH1
3SA
Archive of Bi leaflets, magazines etc.

Edinburgh University: Blogs, Bisexual, Lesbian, Gay or Transgender Society c/o BLOGS, 60 The Pleasance, Edinburgh, Scotland EH8 9TJ
☎ 0131 557 3620 Th. 7:30-9:30pm
✉ blogs@ed.ac.uk 🖳 www.ed.ac.uk/~blogs/

LGB Centre - Edinburgh 58a-60 Broughton Street, Edinburgh, Scotland

Stonewall Girlz PO Box 4040, Edinburgh, Scotland EH3 3UU
Young women's group.

Stonewall Youth Project PO Box 4040, Edinburgh, Scotland EH3 3UU

Moray LGB PO Box 5763, Elgin, Scotland IV30 4ZE

University of St. Andrews Lesbian, Gay, Bisexual & Transgendered Society Students' Union, Fife, Scotland KY16 9AJ ✉ LGBTsoc@st-andrews.ac.uk
🖳 www.st-and.ac.uk/~lgbtsoc/
Weekly meetings Mon. 8pm in the Chaplaincy Centre (Opposite the Union), followed by social in Westport Pub at 10pm.

LGB Centre - Glasgow 11 Dixon , Glasgow, Scotland

Forth Friend PO Box 28, Stirling, Scotland FK9 5YW

Glasgow Bisexual Group c/o HumanSpace, 17 Queens Crescent, Glasgow, Scotland G4 9BL
☎ Neil: 0141 945 2672; Sarah 07980 855801
✉ glasgow@bi.org 🖳 www.quine.org.uk/support/gbwg/
Meets 1st Mon.

Edinburgh Bisexual Group in San Francisco, 1990

UNITED STATES

National Organizations

BiNet USA 4201 Wilson Blvd. #110-311, Arlington, VA 22203 ☎ 202-986-7186 ✉ binetusa@aol.com 🖳 www.binetusa.org
National bisexual network. Collects & distributes info. on bisexuality; facilitates the development of bisexual community & visibility; works for the equal rights & liberation of bisexuals & all oppressed peoples; multicultural & political agenda, does media & educational work, coalition building with g/l communities. Open to all. National coordinators: BiNet News Editor - Gerard Palmieri (biNet phone); Media Spokesperson - Michael Szymanski (mikeszy@aol.com); Treasurer - Deborah Kolodny; Secretary - Kris Roehling. Also has regional delegates who serve as liaisons to their local regions. For contact info. on your Regional Delegate, call BiNet's main phone number. See display ad. PUB: BiNet News (Quarterly newsletter with regular columns: tips for organizers, news & events of national & regional interest, resources, activism.)

Bisexual Foundation 6700 SW 52nd St., Miami, FL 33155 ☎ 305-661-2310 FX: 305-669-3155 ✉ gawen@igc.org
"National not-for-profit organization dedicated to building bisexual community & providing a physical gathering space for the bisexual community."

Gay & Lesbian Alliance Against Defamation (GLAAD) Bi Visibility Project Team (BVPT) 150 W. 26th St. Suite 503, New York, NY 10001 ☎ Wombo Woo: 212-807-1700x24 ✉ bi-vis@glaad.org 🖳 www.glaad.org/glaad/bi_visibility/
Helping expand GLAAD media monitoring to be sensitive to bi issues. Call for meeting dates.

GLAAD 1360 Mission St., Ste. 200, San Francisco, CA 94103 ☎ 800-GAY-MEDIA, 415-861-2244 FX: 415-861-4893 ✉ glaad@glaad.org 🖳 www.glaad.org
Works for fair & diverse coverage of les/gay/bis, & fights stereotypical portrayals in the print & electronic media. To report a defamation, call hotline at above telephone number. PUB: GLAADNote, Media Alert

National Gay & Lesbian Task Force Policy Institute 121 West 27th Street, Suite 501, New York, NY 10001 ☎ 212-604-9830 FX: 212-604-9831 ✉ ngltf@ngltf.org 🖳 www.ngltf.org
Lobbies, organizes, educates, & demonstrates for full GLBT civil rights & equality. Holds annual Creating Change Conference, a skills-building event for activists.

Lambda Legal Defense & Educational Fund 120 Wall Street, Suite 1500, New York, NY 10005-3904 ☎ 212-809-8585 FX: 212-809-0055 ✉ vbaeta@lambdalegal.org 🖳 www.lambdalegal.org
National organization committed to achieving full recognition of the civil rights of l/g & people with HIV/AIDS through impact litigation, education, & public policy work. Test cases selected for the likelihood of their success in establishing positive legal precedents. Offices in NY, LA, Chicago, & Atlanta & nat'l network of volunteer Cooperating Attorneys.

GLSEN National: Gay, Lesbian & Straight Teachers Network 121 West 27th St., New York, NY 10001 ☎ 212-727-0135 ✉ glsen@glsen.org 🖳 www.glsen.org
National organization fighting to end anti-gay bias in K-12 schools. 80 or so chapters.

Human Rights Campaign 919 18th Street, NW, Suite 800, Washington, DC 20006 ☎ 202-628-4160 FX: 202-347-5323 ✉ hrc@org 🖳 www.hrc.org
National organization lobbies Congress, participates in elections, mobilizes grassroots political support for equal rights for lgb Americans. [Editor's note: They do important lobbying work but sometimes have a very hard time with the "b" & "t" in GLBT. They could be said to represent the gay & lesbian "mainstream."]

National Organizers Alliance, Les/Bi/Gay/Trans Caucus 715 G St. SE, Washington, DC 20003-2853 ☎ 202-543-6603 FX: 202-543-2462 ✉ noa@igc.org
For professional, community, labor, progressive social change organizers. Annual gathering, newsletter, pension plan, resource center, job bank. PUB: The Ark (quarterly) (Subscriptions to newsletter & job bank $50/year.)

The Allies Project 1322 Rhode Island Avenue, NW, #5, Washington, DC 20005 ✉ info@alliesproject.org 🖳 www.alliesproject.org
Envisions a world free from discrimination on the basis of gender identity & sexual orientation & seeks to create a society where the struggle for justice & equality is not seen as the sole responsibility of those who are already oppressed. We will challenge straight America, through the media, the Internet, & grassroots organizing, to actively engage in the struggle for BGLT equality.

National Black Lesbian & Gay Leadership Forum. 14366 U St., NW #200, Washington, DC 20009 ☎ 202-483-6786 FX: 202-483-4790

> **We in the movement must learn to honor, embrace and defend our diverse selves. If we do this, we can win.**
>
> Dee Moschbacker at Creating Change Conference, Los Angeles, CA, 11/14/92.

This is what (some) bis look like. group photo, 1st National Bi Conference, San Francisco 1990

National LLEGO: The National Latina/o Lesbian, Gay, Bisexual & Transgender Organization 1612 K Street NW, Suite 500, Washington, DC 20006 ☎ 202-466-8240 FX: 202-466-8530 ✉ aquiLGBT@llego.org 🖳 www.llego.org *Assistance & organizational support for the Latina/o LBGT community in the US & Puerto Rico. Associations with 100+ organizations: HIV/ AIDS service, social/cultural, spiritual, university, educational, & youth groups.*

American Psychological Association Division 44: Committee on Bisexual Issues in Psychology c/o Ron Fox, PhD, Co-Chair, PO Box 210491, San Francisco, CA 94121-0491 ☎ 415-751-6714 ✉ rcf@wenet.net; m742ehp@aol.com 🖳 www.apa.org/divisions/div44/ about_us.html#Committee on Bisexual Issues in Psychology; additional contact: Emily Page, Psy.D., Co-Chair, 350 Massachusetts Ave., #183, Arlington, MA 02474, 781-641-3980

American Psychological Association Division 44: Society for the Psychological Study of Lesbian, Gay, & Bisexual ISsues (SPSLGBI) 750 First Street, NE, Washington, DC 20002-4242 ☎ 202-336-5500 🖳 www.apa.org/divisions/div44/ *Part of American Psychological Association. For social scientists & students, regardless of orientation or gender, interested in applying psychological knowledge to the study of glb issues.*

American Psychological Association: Committee on Lesbian, Gay, & Bisexual Concerns (CLGBC) 750 First Street, NE, Washington, DC 20002-4242 ☎ 202-336-5500 🖳 www.apa.org/pi/lgbc/ *Michael Stephens, Chair (1999)*

> **This is the new bisexual movement in a nutshell: hard fought, hard thought, and distinctly individual.**
>
> *John Leland, Newsweek, 17 July 1995*

American Political Science Association: Gay, Lesbian & Bisexual Caucus c/o Shane Phelan, Univ. of New Mexico/Dept. Political Science, Albuquerque, NM 87131 ☎ 505-277-5104; APSA main #: 202-483-2512 ✉ sphelan@unm.edu *Holds annual meeting.*

American College Personnel Association Standing Committee for Lesbian, Gay, Bisexual & Transgender Awareness One Dupont Circle, NW, Suite 300, Washington, DC 20036-1110 ☎ 202-835-ACPA FX: 202-296-3286 ✉ info@acpa.nche.edu 🖳 www.acpa.nche.edu/ comms/scomma/sclgbta.htm *List-serve is open to members of the association at listproc@ucdavis.edu, with message "subscribe ACPA-SCLGBA". PUB: Out on Campus: Beyond Tolerance: Lesbians, Gays, & Bisexuals on Campus (Newsletter w/ACPA membership; available from University Press of America, 800-462-6420 - US$29.)*

National Association of Student Personnel Administrators GLBT Issues Network Bill Geller, VP for Student & Community Services, University of Maine at Farmington, Farmington, ME 04938 ✉ geller@maine.edu 🖳 ecuvax.cis.ecu.edu/~rllucier/naspaglb.html *Mission: to increase the acceptance & understanding of glbt faculty, staff, & students & their allies within the student affairs profession. Quarterly newsletter. Annual conference.*

American Library Association: Gay, Lesbian, Bisexual & Transgendered Round Table c/o Faye Chadwell, Collections Department, 1299 University of Oregon, Eugene, OR 97403-1299 ☎541-346-1819 ✉ chadwelf@oregon.uoregon.edu 🖳 isd.usc.edu/~trimmer/ala_hp.html *Nation's first GLBT professional organization. Awards the annual GLBT Book Award (bisexual added to name in 1994). Maintains clearinghouse of GLB related bibliographies, directories, reading lists.*

The Bisexual Resource Guide 4th edition

Gill Foundation 2215 Market St., Denver, CO 80205
☎ 303-292-4455
Fabulous GLBT grant making organization. Also administers Colorado's Gay & Lesbian Victory Fund (supports non-glbt progressive organizations).

GLB Veterans of America PO Box 29317, Chicago, IL 60629 ☎ James Darby, Nat'l Contact: 773-752-0058
✉ glbva@glbva.org
🖥 www.glbva.org
National veterans' organization with local chapters in cities including: Chicago, Denver, Palm Springs, San Antonio, San Diego, St. Louis, Albuquerque, Orange County, Tucson, & the New England region. Call for local contact information. PUB: The Forward Observer

Digital Queers 560 Castro St., Suite 150, San Francisco, CA 94114 ☎ 800-GAY-MEDIA
✉ digiqueers@aol.com or info@dq.org
🖥 www.dq.org
National nonprofit group of computer professionals & technology aficionados supporting nonprofit organizations through consultation, training, & hardware/software upgrades related to technology. Also a forum for social & professional networking. PUB: Newsletter in both print & email format.

Lavender Caucus: The LGB Caucus of the SEIU (Service Employess Int'l Union) Western Conference 560 20th Street, PO Box 10593, Oakland, CA 94160 ☎ 415-821-1142
Social, on-the-job support, employment, & political issues. Distributes newsletter. All union members welcome at meetings. Biennial conference seeks to educate LGBTs about labor issues, & vice versa. Other contacts: Northwest: Marcy Johnsen 206-706-1588 (tel), 206-783-7245 (fax), MARCYJ1199@aol.com Southern CA: Bill Strachan nursebear@loop.com 818/985-9115 (fax).

Pride At Work, AFL-CIO 815 16th Street, NW, Room 4020, Washington, DC 20036
☎ 202-637-5085 FX: 202-508-6923
✉ paw@aflcio.org 🖥 www.prideatwork.org
Int'l coalition of lgbt workers & their supporters. Mobilizes mutual support between organized labor movement & LGBT communities around organizing for social & economic justice. We seek full equality for LGBT workers in their workplaces & unions, & educate the LGBT community about benefits of union membership. Biennial convention. PUB: Pride At Work Newsletter (Newsletter comes with membership ($25 per year). Additional donations appreciated! No one denied membership for lack of funds.)

Bisexual Resource Center receives award from the National Gay & Lesbian Task Force, 1996

AT&T LGB United Employees (League) 11900 Pecos St., Denver, CO 80234-2703 ☎ 703-713-7820; TDD: 1-800-855-2880
✉ ATTLEAGUE@aol.com
🖥 www.league-att.org/index.html
Addresses workplaces issues affecting LGBT employees or employees with LGBT family members.

CompaqPlus c/o Director of Diversity Programs, 20555 SH 249, Houston, TX 77070 ✉ CompaqPlus.INFO@compaq.com
🖥 www.ziplink.net/~glen/compaqplus/
Compaq People Like Us: for LBGT employees (present & past) of Compaq Computer Corporation. Formerly DECPLUS (Digital Equipment Company People Like Us).

Federal GLOBE PO Box 45237, Washington, DC 20026-5237 ✉ webmaster@fedglobe.org
🖥 www.fedglobe.org
GLBT Employees of the Federal Government. Aims to eliminate prejudice & discrimination based on sexual orientation in the federal government through education on GLBT issues. Particular attention to inclusion of bisexuals. PUB: newsletter (bimonthly): globalview (UP to GS6-$12; GS7 to GS11-$24; GS12 and above-$36)

Deptartment of Labor GLOBE Washington, DC
✉ diane@fedglobe.org 🖥 www.fedglobe.org
GLBT employees of the US Dep't of Labor. See Federal Globe for desc.

Commerce GLOBE Washington, DC ☎ 202-482-8120 ✉ docglobe1@aol.com 🖥 www.fedglobe.org
Provides info & networking. See Federal GLOBE.

Celta Lambda Phi Washington, DC
🖥 www.dlp.org
National social fraternity for g/bi & progressive men. "When it comes to diversity, what others hide in shame, we boldly embrace in pride."

DOT GLOBE PO Box 23239, Washington, DC 20029 ☎ 202-366-2548 ✉ ericwdc@aol.com
🖥 www.fedglobe.com
GLBT employees at US Dept. of Transportation. See Federal Globe for description.

IRS GLOBE PO Box 7644, Washington, DC 20044
🖥 www.fedglobe.org
GLBT employees at the IRS. See Federal GLOBE for description.

Lavender Families Resource Network PO Box 21567, Seattle, WA 98111 ☎ 206-325-2643 (V/TTY)
Info, referrals, emotional support for lgb parents in custody & visitation, parenting, donor insemination & adoption. PUB: Mom's Apple Pie (Newsletter $15/yr.)

Momazons PO Box 82069, Columbus, OH 43202 ☎ 614-267-0193 ✉ momazons@momazons.org 🖳 www.momazons.org
For lesbian mothers & lesbians who want children in their lives. One of the organizers says that Momazons is inclusive of bi women, regardless of the gender of any current relationship.

Family Diversity Projects, Inc. PO Box 1209, Amherst, MA 01004-1209 ☎ 413-256-0502 FX: 413-253-3977 ✉ info@lovemakesafamily.org 🖳 www.familydiv.org
Non-profit organization to educate students, parents, teachers, politicians, religious leaders & the general public about family diversity to help eliminate prejudice, stereotyping, name-calling, & harassment on the basis of race, gender, sexual orientation, or mental & physical ability. PUB: Love Makes A Family (Photo/text exhibit & book.)

COLAGE - Children of Lesbians & Gays Everywhere 3543 18th St. #1, San Francisco, CA 94110 ☎ 415-861-KIDS FX: 415-255-8345 ✉ colage@colage.org 🖳 www.colage.org
National support group run by & for the children of glbt parents. Newsletter, confererences, email lists, & support groups for children & for adult children of all ages. See also Family Pride Coalition. PUB: Just For Us ($25 for membership & quarterly newsletter.)

National Youth Advocacy Coalition (NYAC) 1638 R Street, NW, Suite 300, Washington, DC 20009 ☎ 202-319-7596 FX: 202-319-7365 ✉ nyac@nyacyouth.org 🖳 www.nyacyouth.org
Advocacy, education, & information on GLBT youth issues; resources, technical assistance, & national referrals. Sponsors Bridges Project, a national clearinghouse on glbt youth. Sponsors a annual national summit & regional conferences. PUB: Crossroads (2x/year. No charge, but contributions welcome.)

Advocates for Youth Washington, DC ☎ 202-347-5700 🖳 www.youthresource.com
They have a publication called "I think I'm Bi ... Now what do I do?" available on the web & as hard copies. (www.youthresource.com/library/bisexual.htm) & other great bi links.

National Queer Student Coalition, USSA 1413 K St., NW, 9th fl., Washington, DC 20005 ☎ 202-347-USSA or 347-8772 FX: 202-393-5886 ✉ comm@usstudents.org 🖳 www.usstudents.org
National grassroots student lobbying organization.

National Union of Jewish LGBT Students Bernard Cherkasov, Ex. Dir., 1500 Mass. Ave., NW, Washington, DC 20005 ✉ nujls98@hotmail.com 🖳 www.wcglo.org/index.html
Educational & supportive resource group for Jewish lgbt students, with affiliate groups on most major campus & students from all over the US & Canada.

Lambda 10 Project Office of Student Ethics/Anti-Harassment Programs, 705 E. 7th St., Indiana University, Bloomington, Bloomington, IN 47405 ☎812-855-4463 FX: 812-855-4465 ✉ lambda10@indiana.edu 🖳 www.indiana.edu/~lambda10
National organization providing educational resources & info. pertaining to GLB fraternity/sorority members.

Pride Institute 14400 Martin Drive, Eden Prairie, MN 55344 ☎ 1-800-54-PRIDE FX: 612-934-8764 ✉ info@pride-institute.com 🖳 www.pride-institute.com
Inpatient alcohol & drug treatment, intensive day treatment programs, & halfway houses specifically for GLBTs. Facilities in Minneapolis, Chicago, NYC, NJ, Fort Lauderdale, FL, & Dallas, TX. Other sites include non-chemical dependency mental health services.

Unitarian Universalist Association Office of Bisexual, Gay, Lesbian & Transgender Concerns 25 Beacon Street, Boston, MA 02108-2800 ☎ 617-948-6475 ✉ obgltc@uua.org 🖳 www.uua.org/obgltc
Provides resources for UU congregations working toward being more affirming & welcoming to BLGT folks, including info, resolutions & pamphlets encouraging support for BLGTs; a list of welcoming congregations; free organizational start-up kits, bibliographic materials, sample same-sex union services, pink triangle stickers, & info on public speaking.

Interweave 167 Milk St, #406, Boston, MA 02109-4339 🖳 qrd.tcp.com/qrd/www/orgs/uua/uu-interweave.html
Membership organization affiliated with the UUA (above), dedicated to the spiritual, political, & social well-being of UU's confronting oppression as lgbt persons, & their heterosexual allies. Celebrates the culture & the lives of its members. PUB: Interweave World

---

When the wall of homophobia is just too damn high and the mountain of intolerance too wide, it's easier to just drop some of the weight, which usually means elderly gays, queer youth, drag queens, leather folks, sexual outlaws, bisexuals. I've always believed, to be honest with you, that there is no dress codes for civil rights in this country.

—Robert Bray, Field Organizer for the National Gay & Lesbian Task Force.

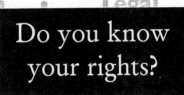

Adoption • Legal Planning
Employm **Do you know** entiality
Lawyer R **your rights?** ge / Civil
Unions • Custody
• Harassment • Discrimination •
HIV-related issues • Student rights

We Do.

Gay & Lesbian Advocates & Defenders (GLAD) has worked for over 21 years on behalf of gay men, lesbians, bisexuals, transgendered individuals and people with HIV in the six states of New England. Whether the issue is employment discrimination, denial of health care, the right of glbt students to get an education in safety, fair treatment for glbt parents, the recognition of families of same-sex couples or housing discrimination, GLAD is your resource.

Call the Legal Information Hotline

▼ For Information About Your Rights
▼ For Help Finding an Attorney
▼ To Find Ways to Get Involved

TTY (617) 426-6156
1:30-4:30
Monday - Friday
English and Spanish
www.glad.org
(800) 455-GLAD

GLAD

equal justice under law

Dignity USA 1500 Massachusetts Avenue NW #11, Washington, DC 20005 ☎ 202-861-0017 FX: 202-429-9808 ✉ dignity@aol.com 📖 www.dignityusa.org
For glbt Catholics & their family & friends.
PUB: Dignity Journal (quarterly)

Brethren/Mennonite Council for Lesbian & Gay Concerns PO Box 6300, Minneapolis, MN 55406-0300 ☎ Amy Short: 612-722-6906 FX: 612-343-2061 ✉ bmcouncil@aol.com 📖 www.webcom.com/bmc/
Support for Brethren & Mennonite GLBTs & their parents, spouses, relatives & friends. Fosters dialogue between gay/non-gay people in the churches; provides accurate info about human sexuality from the social sciences, biblical studies & theology. The Supportive Congregations Network, a program of BMC, encourages congregations to publicly declare their welcome to LGBTs. Also a College Network which offers support & networking opportunities for LGBT youth, college students, & adults. PUB: Dialogue/ BMC Newsletter (Dialogue is a newspaper for all churches published 3x/yr. addressing theology, biblical studies, church life, and publicizing upcoming events. The BMC Newsletter is specifically for GLBT persons & includes announcements, idea exchange, & reports on LGBT-related events. It is also published 3x/yr.)

National Publications

Anything That Moves 2261 Market Street #496, San Francisco, CA 94114-1600 ☎ 415-626-5069 ✉ info@AnythingThatMoves.com 📖 www.AnythingThatMoves.com
Non-profit organization publishing a 64-page magazine for bisexuals. Also a community resource & activist organization.

In The Family: The Magazine for Queer People & their Loved Ones PO Box 5387, Takoma Park, MD 20913 ☎ 301-270-4771 ✉ Lmarkowitz@aol.com 📖 www.inthefamily.com
Quarterly magazine addressing glb families. Sponsors annual family therapy conference. (Editors note: a really bi-positive magazine to which I happily subscribe!)

BLK PO Box 83912, Los Angeles, CA 90083-0912 📖 www.blk.com/
National LGB newsmagazines for people of color in the life: BLK, Blackfire, Black Lace, Kuumba & Black Dates.

XY Magazine 4104 24 St. #900, (see below for subscription address), San Francisco, CA 94114 ☎ 1-877-996-0930 domestic (toll free) or 415-552-6668 (int'l # is out of order) FX: 415-552-6664 ✉ Subscriptions: XY@PUB-SERV.COM; info: WAZUP@xy.com 📖 www.xy.com
Bi-monthly breakthrough periodical for young queers. Includes a wide range of features & news bites covering music, politics, activism, fashion, technology & more.

Sometimes Robyn woked the Guide's staff too hard. Pixel is exhausted from proofreading.

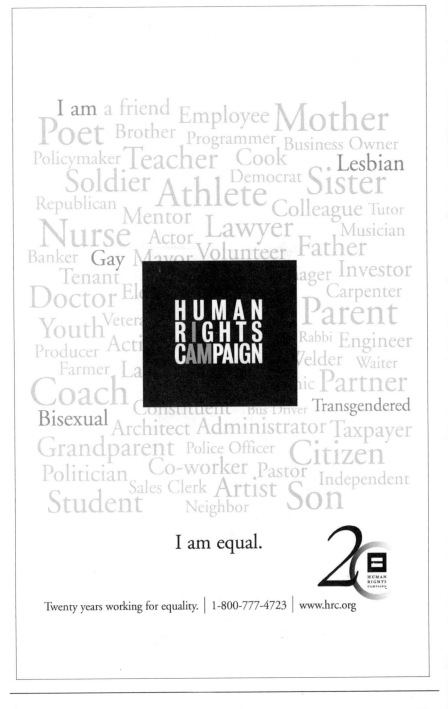

Black Books Box 31155, San Francisco, CA 94131
☎ 415-431-0171 FX: 415-431-0172
✉ info@blackbooks.com 🖳 www.blackbooks.com
*Catalog of products, which give information
"from the erotic world" & which promote bisexual
visibility. Catalog costs $1. Statement of age
required.* PUB: Black Sheet Magazine/Black Book
(Black Sheets is a humorous magazine on
alternative sexuality & popular culture. Bi-
annual directory to alternative sexuality
resources in North America.)

Journal of Gay, Lesbian & Bisexual Identity
Warren J. Blumenfeld, Editor, PO Box 929,
Northampton, MA 01061 ☎ 413-585-9121
FX: 413-584-1332 ✉ blumenfeld@educ.umass.edu
*Interdisciplinary journal. Peer-reviewed original
articles, personal essays, clinical studies, research
papers, etc. For submission guidelines write to
editor, above. For subscription information:
Human Sciences Press, Inc., Attn. Dept. HGL94,
233 Spring St., New York, NY, 10013-1578.*

Girlfriends c/o HAF Enterprises, 3415 Cesar
Chavez, Ste. 101, San Francisco CA 94110
☎ 415-648-9464; subscriptions: 800-GRL-FRND
✉ staff@girlfriendsmag.com
🖳 www.girlfriendsmag.com
*Bi-positive monthly magazine for women
addressing "lesbian culture, politics &
entertainment." I subscribe!*

Curve 1 Haight St., Suite B, San Francisco CA
94102 ☎ 800-705-0070EMAIL
🖳 www.curvemag.com
*"The best-selling lesbian magazine" in the US.
Also bi-friendly. I subscribe!*

Alabama

PFLAG Anniston PO Box 1213, Anniston, AL
36202-1213

Auburn University Gay & Lesbian Association
Auburn University, AL ✉ au-agla@gay.com
🖳 www.auburn.edu/~aglassn/
*Provides support for GLBT people, their friends
& supporters. Educates the campus & community
about glbt issues To join their email list: send a
blank email to agla- subscribe@yahoogroups.com*

Covenant Metropolitan Community Church 5117
First Avenue North, Birmingham, AL 52210
☎ 205-599-3363 ✉ CovenantMCC@aol.com
🖳 www.geocities.com/WestHollywood/7903/
*Welcoming congregation for ALL. Services, choir
pratice, bible study, special events.*

**Gay & Lesbian Information Line: Lambda
Resource Center** Suite 201, 205 32nd St. South,
Birmingham, AL 35233-3007 ☎ 205-326-8600
Info. phone/TDD line, Mon.-Sat. 7-10pm.

Metropolitan Community Church Huntsville 3015
Sparkman Dr., Huntsville, AL
*"With the gay brochures & pride flags flying in
the main entrance, you KNOW all kinds of
families are welcome here."*

Rocket City Rainbow Squares 416 Homewood Dr.
SW , Huntsville, AL 35801 ☎ Clara: 205-881-
6531: Mark: 256-882-9053 ✉ Clara:
cwelch@hiwaay.net or Mark: mrfhrt@hiwaay.net
🖳 fly.hiwaay.net/%7Ecwelch/rainbow/
*Western Square Dancing with or without a
partner regardless of race, religion, sex, national
origin, or sexual orientation.*

Unitarian Universalist Church, Huntsville 2222
Governors Dr., Huntsville, AL
Gay friendly church.

PFLAG Mobile 957 Church Street, Mobile, AL
36604 ☎ 334-438-9381

**University of South Alabama: Alliance for Sexual
Diversity** Student Center, Mobile, AL 36688
✉ usaasd@hotmail.com
🖳 www.southalabama.edu/asd/
Student-run confidential safe & social space.

Tuscaloosa Gay, Lesbian, Bisexual Alliane
Tuscaloosa, AL ☎ 205-348-7210

**University of Alabama: Gay, Lesbian, Bisexual &
Transgender Alliance** Ferguson Student Center,
1st Flr, Tuscaloosa, AL 35486
✉ glbta_pathfinders@hotmail.com
🖳 bama.ua.edu/~glbta/index.html
*Supportive environment for GLBT students.
Promotes understanding & education within the
university & surrounding community about
GLBT individuals & the discrimination that exists
against them. Hosts the Pathfinders support group
& the Educational Panel.*

Alaska

Anchorage Gay/Lesbian Helpline Anchorage, AK
☎ 907-258-4777

Anchorage IMRU2 Anchorage, AK
☎ 907-566-4678
Youth group.

University of Alaska, Anchorage: The Family c/o
Campus Center, Anchorage, AK 99508-8000
✉ uaa_the_family@yahoo.com
🖳 cwolf.alaska.edu/~abfam/

Anchorage PFLAG PO Box 203231, Anchorage,
AK 99520-3231 ☎566-1813
*3rd Tu. at Anchorage Unitarian Universal
Fellowship, 3201 Turnigan Blvd. (at 32nd St.).*

Fairbanks Lesbian/Gay Info Hotline Fairbanks,
AK ☎ 907-458-8288
*Community information, club event & meeting
schedules, referrals, personals, or just to chat.*

> On the open range, fences exist because
> there are no natural boundaries.
> - *Marge Garber*

P-FLAG Fairbanks PO Box 84680, Fairbanks, AK 99708 ☎ 907-457-3524 ✉ pflag@mosquitonet.com 🖳 www.mosquitonet.com/~pflag/
2nd Th. 6:30pm at the Midnight Sun House, 581 University Av.

South East Alaska Gay & Lesbian Alliance (SEAGLA) PO Box 21542, Juneau, AK 99802 ☎ Helpline: 907-586-4297 ✉ seagla@ptialaska.net 🖳 www.ptialaska.net/~seagla/
Support network for glbt people in SE Alaska.

PFLAG Juneau PO Box 32245, Juneau, AK 99803 ☎ 907-463-4203
1st Sat. 10:30am-12:30pm in the Mendenhall Mall Library .

Arizona

BiNet Arizona 24 W. Camelback Road, #B-105, Phoenix, AZ 85013 ☎ 602-280-9074 FX: 602-675-8551 ✉ binetaz@binetaz.org 🖳 binetaz.org
Provides support groups for women, men, co-gender, trans, youth & spouses of bis.
PUB: BiNet AZ newsletter (Monthly.)

Northern Arizona Bi Email Discussion Group AZ 🖳 globelists.theglobe.com/people_lifestyle/ gay_lesbian_bisexual/bisexual/biflag-L/list.taf

Northern Arizona Bisexual Resources Flagstaff, AZ 🖳 members.xoom.com/_XMCM/biflag/ index.htm

The Closet Times Newsletter & Verde Valley Alternative Lifestyles Directory AZ ☎ 520-634-4842 ✉ mertimac@sedona.net

Northern Arizona Rainbow Community Center 1300 South Milton Road, Suite 221, Flagstaff, AZ 56001 ☎ 520-774-6416 ✉ robert.mclean@nau.edu

The Mountain Rainbow Reporter Flagstaff, AZ ☎ 520-522-7894 ✉ llubet@co.coconino.az.us
PUB: The Mountain Rainbow Reporter

Northern Arizona University: Lesbian, Bisexual, Gay Alliance PO Box 6036, Flagstaff, AZ 86011 ☎ 520-523-7110 ✉ lbga-p@dana.ucc.nau.edu; rkf4@dana.ucc.nau.edu 🖳 members.xoom.com/ _XMCM/biflag/gaychat.htm

PFLAG Flagstaff PO Box 29527, Flagstaff, AZ 86002 ☎ 520-773-7811 ✉ dh70481@goodnet.com

PFLAG Lake Havasu City 2494 Rainbow Ave. North, Lake Havasu City, AZ 86403-3840 ☎ 520-505-4730 ✉ Havasu@aol.com

Mesa Community College: Gay, Lesbian, & Bisexual Education League 1833 W. Southern Ave, Student Activities & Services, Mesa, AZ 85202 ☎ 480-461-7277 (Student Activities & Services)

The Community Center 24 W. Camelback Road #C-100, Phoenix, AZ 85013 ☎ 602-265-7283 FX: 602-234-0873 ✉ vsglcc@swlink.net 🖳 www.phxcenter.org
Board voted in May 1998 to drop "Gay & Lesbian" in order to be more inclusive & changed their bylaws. Voted for 1st ever out bi as co-chair of Board of Directors. Includes "Young & Bi" youth group.

Valley of the Sun Gay & Lesbian Community Center PO Box 33367, Phoenix, AZ 85067-3367 ☎ 602-265-7283 FX: 602-234-0873 ✉ vsglcc@swlink.net 🖳 www.swlink.net/~vsglcc/ index_refresh.html

PFLAG Phoenix & the Valley of the Sun PO Box 7265, Phoenix, AZ 85011-7265 ☎ 602-843-1404 ✉ info@pflag-phoenix.org 🖳 www.pflag-phoenix.org

Dignity/Integrity Phoenix PO Box 60953, Phoenix, AZ 85082-0953 ☎602 222-8664 ✉ DigInPHX@Netzone.com
Queer-friendly Catholic church.

Gentle Shepherd Metropolitan Community Church PO Box 33758, Phoenix, AZ 85067-3758 ☎ 602-864-6404 FX: 602-864-6405 ✉ gsmcc@gsmcc.org
Truly unique Church for many reasons, including outreach to the Lesbian, Gay, Bi-sexual, Transgendered & Straight Allied community.

Emergence International (Gay Christian Scientists) PO Box 26237, Phoenix, AZ 85068 ☎ 800-280-6653 ✉ Emerge800@aol.com 🖳 www.cslesbigay.org/emergence
Annual conferences PUB: Emerge! (bimonthly); In Between Times (monthly)

> **"So. When you have sex with men, you are straight, and when you have sex with women you are a lesbian. As a bisexual woman, this is what I hear; again and again, this is what I hear. Your sexuality comes in compartments, like your heart has two chambers and you cannot feel with both; your soul is like Berlin before the wall came down. And the truth of my experience is this: my sexuality is whole. I am not straight with men and lesbian with women; I am bisexual with both."**
>
> *Greta Christina in Bisexual Politics*

> Theories of lesbian and gay development have typically regarded establishing a lesbian or gay identity as the end point of the coming out process. Bisexuality was thought to be a transitional experience and identification, whereas, in reality, it can be an endpoint, phase, or place of recurrent visitation.
>
> Dr. Ron C. Fox, *(in BiNet USA presspacket)*

Arizona State University

Lambda League, Student Organizations, Tempe, AZ 85287; ☎ 480-965-8690;) lambdaleague@asu.edu; 📖 www.asu.edu/studentprgms/orgs/lambda_league/; Umbrella org. for glbt groups on campus, including: **Bi Necessity,** a bi group, contact: John Bashford (jon.bashford@asu.edu). **Gay & Bisexual Men's Group,** contact Jose Madera (asu_mens_group@hotmail.com). **Lesbian & Bisexual Women's Group,** contact Connie Engel (connie.engel@asu.edu). **Act Out,** a glbt political activist group; 📖 www.asu.edu/studentprgms/orgs/act_out/, ✉ Brandon Moore (beatnikasu@aol.com). **Progression,** for graduate students, contact Marcia Darcy (maria.darcy@asu.edu). **Coming Out Discussion Group,** contact Melissa Soto (traylors@hotmail.com). **Our Space,** for GLBT social work students, contact Donna Henault (dhenault35@yahoo.com). **Gay & Lesbian Legal Alliance (GALLA),** for glbtq students at the College of Law, 📖 www.asu.edu/studentprgms/orgs/GALLA.

Crossroads Proto Nest of the Church of All Worlds Box 857, Tempe, AZ 85280-0857 ☎ 480-894-5121 ✉ ryuujin@digitalf.com 📖 www.caw.org
Pagan religion based loosely on the ideals described in the book Stranger in a Strange land by Robert Heinlein. Accepting of all sexual orientations & relationship styles, & is particularly supportive of polyamory. Crossroads is the local grouping of a worldwide organization. PUB: Tri-Via

Wingspan 300 E. 6th St., Tucson, AZ 85705 ☎ 520-624-1779 (Info line; live 11-7 Mon.-Sat.) FX: 520-624-0364 ✉ Wingspan@wingspanaz.org 📖 www.wingspanaz.org/
Southern Arizona's GLBT community resource center. PUB: Center Newsletter

GLB Support Group St. Francis in the Foothills Methodist, 4625 E River, Rm 43, Tucson, AZ 85718 ☎ Dave (facilitator) 520-745-9059 FX: 520-299-9099
Open to everyone, not just for religious folks. Meets Th. 7:30.

Married Gay & Bi Men's Support Group c/o Daniel Overbeck, Ph.D., 5650 E. 22nd St., Tucson, AZ 85711 ☎ 520-745-6977 FX: 520-748-2609
Free, weekly support group facilitated by professional psychologist.

University of Arizona

Pride Alliance: Building 19 Room 215, Tucson, AZ 85721; ☎ 520-621-7585; ✉ Pride@ps.asua.arizona.edu; 📖 ps.asua.arizona.edu/~pride; **BGALA:** ☎ 520-626-4692; ✉ dorschel@u.arizona.edu. **LGBT Graduate Students:** ✉ gbtgrad@clubs.arizona.edu. **Committee on Lesbian, Gay & Bisexual Studies,** PO Box 210431, Tucson, AZ 85721-0431; ☎ 520-626-7580; ✉ lgbs@u.arizona.edu. **Faculty & Staff for Gay, Lesbian, & Bisexual Equity:** ✉ matkin@ccit.arizona.edu. **Safe Zone:** 📖 www.arizona.edu/~out/safe.html; Program aimed at creating a more appreciative & accepting campus climate. Workshops offered throughout the year. **U of AZ Library Allies of Lesbian, Gay, & Bisexual Staff:** ✉ idols@bird.library.arizona.edu.

Metropolitan Community Church of Tucson 3269 N. Mountain Avenue, Tucson, AZ ☎ 520-791-7676

Rainbow Interfaith Community of Tucson Tucson, AZ 📖 www.dakotacom.net/~rholmes/ric
Group of interdenominational churches open & welcoming to GLBT people.

PFLAG Tucson PO Box 36264, Tucson, AZ 85740-6264 ☎ 520-575-8660 ✉ PFLAGTucson@aol.com 📖 members.aol.com/pflagtucson/

Arkansas

Bisexual, Gay, Lesbian Action Delegation of Northwest Arkansas PO Box 2897, Fayetteville, AR 72702 ☎ 501-582-INFO
Social, safety, education, fundraising, awareness.

The Flamingo Moon 4627 N. Oakland, Fayetteville, AR 72703 ☎ 501-443-5452
Film society, hosts monthly viewings of glbt films. All are welcome.

University of Arkansas: Gay Student Alliance ARKU 504, Fayetteville, AR 72701 ☎ 501-575-4633 ✉ glbsa@comp.uark.edu 📖 www.uark.edu/~glbsa/
Wed. 7pm, ARKU Rm 311-South.

PFLAG of Fayetteville/NW Arkansas PO Box 2897, Fayetteville, AR 72702 ☎ 501-443-4159
Local chapter of national support/advocacy organization. Meetings, 2nd Sun. 3-5pm at the Unitarian Universalist Fellowship, 901 Cleveland.

Regional AIDS Interfaith Network (RAIN)
Fayetteville, AR ☎ 501-444-9206 (Caile Spear, Fayetteville); 1-800-851-6301
Faith-based program of services for people affected by HIV disease & its related issues. Care Teams, Compassionate HIV/AIDS education programs, support groups, networking. Also offers HIV/AIDS education programs statewide.

AIDS Resource Center of Northwest Arkansas
Fayetteville, AR ☎ Leslie: 501-443-2437
Help and assistance programs, including an emergency hot-line, information phone line, lending library, panel of speakers, testing referral, & food or financial assistance to those with HIV. Also hosts a monthly game night & other activities.

Arkansas State University: Students of Alternative Lifestyles Chickasaw Student Services Center, Room 202, Jonesboro, AR
✉ ASU_SAL@hotmail.com 🖳 www.geocities.com/asusal/
Support & social organization for LBGTQ invididuals/friends in the Jonesboro/Northeast Arkansas area. Meets monthly.

BiGALA of Arkansas Tech University PO Box 7182, Russellville, AR 72801
✉ techbigala@yahoo.com 🖳 stuserv.atu.edu/clubs/bigala/
Support/advocacy organization. Meets Th. 9pm.

> **"We already know that a bisexual identity is not sufficient to ensure agreement or conformity—we are too diverse in every way. Let us make that a strength, not a failing, of our movement. If we begin to reify "bisexual" (as if in saying the word we agree to the specifics of its meaning— already a mistake, in my opinion, and not yet possible at this stage of our community development) we may be tempted to leave out the wonderful, difficult complexity of acknowledging the diverse spectrum our community holds. I would prefer us to mindfully write it in— we may not fuck anything that moves, but, in our rainbow of difference, we are all practically everything that moves, and if we welcome each other in these differences as well as in our similarities we will weave community of a strong cloth indeed."**
>
> *Carol Queen in Bisexual Politics*

San Francisco Freedom Day Parade

Robyn Ochs

California

So many California listings! They are arranged (more or less) by region. Los Angeles, San Diego, Long Beach the San Francisco Bay Area and San José are listed first under their own heading, followed by California groups, arranged by zip code, south to north.

Los Angeles

BiNet Los Angeles PO Box 94161, Pasadena, CA 91109-4161 ☎ 323-882-4402 ✉ info@BiNetLA.org 🖳 www.BiNetLA.org
Social get-togethers 3rd Sat. for bis & friends. $5 donation requested. Also organizes conferences.

Los Angeles: Gay & Lesbian Community Services Center, Bisexual Support Groups The Village at Ed Gould Plaza, 1125 N. McCadden Place, Los Angeles, CA 90038 ☎ 213-860-7302
✉ conversation@laglc.org 🖳 www.laglc.org/village/village_index.html
Bi Men's Discussion Group 1st & 3rd Mon. 8-10pm; Bi Women's Discussion Group 1st Mon. 8-10pm. $2 suggested donation.

Chingusa - Los Angeles PO Box 741666, Los Angeles, CA 90004-1666 ☎ 213-553-1873
✉ chingusai@writeme.com 🖳 home.LACN.org/LACN/chingusai/default2.htm
Korean-American glbt co-gender, multi-generational & bilingual coalition of 3 sub-groups: 1st & 2nd generation women, 1st generation Korean-speaking men; & one-point-five/second generation English-speaking men. Twice a year, Chingusai meets as a coalition.

Different Spokes of Southern California
PO Box 291875, Los Angeles, CA 90029-1875
☎ 213-896-8235 ✉ dccs@differentspokes.com
💻 www.differentspokes.com
LGB bicycling club. Beginning riders to advanced. Weekly organized rides & social events. Membership $20 yr. single or $40 yr. couple.
PUB: Different Spokes Southern Calif. Newsletter (visit website for comp. copy)

Occidental College: Gay/Straight Alliance 1600 Campus Road, Box 707, Los Angeles, CA 90041
☎ 323-259-2500 ext. 4298 ✉ neel@oxy.edu
💻 www.oxy.edu/departments/stulife/clubs/

University of California Lesbian Gay Bisexual Transgendered Campus Resource Center Dr. Ronni L. Sanlo, Director, 220 Kinsey Hall, Box 51579, Los Angeles, CA 90095-1579
☎ 310-206-3628 FX: 310-206-8191
✉ lgbt@ucla.edu 💻 www.saonet.ucla.edu/lgbt/
Organizes many support groups including one which is specifically bi. PUB: OUTlist (Published in the UCLA Daily Bruin during National Coming Out Week in October. Gaybruins tradition that names out & proud LGBT individuals & allies in the UCLA community.)

University of Southern California: Gay, Lesbian, Bi, Trans Assembly USC Student Union, Rm. 415 , Univ. Park Campus, 830 Childs Way, Los Angeles, CA 90089-0898 ☎ 213-740-7619 ✉ glbausc@usc.edu
💻 www.usc.edu/student-affairs/glba/

Affirmation: Gay & Lesbian Mormons - Los Angeles Chapter PO Box 46022, Los Angeles, CA 90046 ☎ 323-255-7251
✉ LASaints2@earthlink.net
💻 www.home.earthlink.net/~lasaints2/
Sun. evening meetings, monthly social event.
PUB: Reflections (Monthly news magazine.)

Affirmations/Los Angeles: United Methodists for Gay, Lesbian, Bisexual & Transgendered Concerns PO Box 691283, West Hollywood, CA 90069-9283 ☎ 323-969-4664 ✉ affirmLA@aol.com (local) or umaffirmation@yahoo.com (national)
💻 www.umaffirm.org (national)
Meets 2nd Sun. 7pm at Holman United Methodist Church, 3320 W. Adams Blvd., Los Angeles.

Long Beach

Bis at the Center/ BiNet Long Beach-Orange County Gay & Lesbian Community Center of Greater Long Beach, 2017 E. 4th St., Long Beach, CA 90814-1001 ☎ 562-434-4455; 562-437-0511 (same as 800-JULY-DOT) FX: 562-495-7502
✉ bisexuals@aol.com 💻 www.centerlb.org/ or www.biconsult.com
Meetings held at The Center Fri .8:00pm, & hosts parties & conferences.

Bi Consultation Service PO Box 20917, Long Beach, CA 90801 ☎ Gary North: 562-437-0511, or1-800-585-9368 (1-800-JULY-DOT)
✉ bisexuals@aol.com 💻 members.aol.com/bisexuals
One to one counsultation & small support groups for people just starting out. Also information about bi-supportive therapists. BiMarried men's group. Other specialty groups created as needed.

California State Univ., Long Beach: Lesbian/Gay/Bisexual/Transgender Resource Center FO4 Room 165, CSULB, 1250 Bellflower Blvd., Long Beach, CA 90840 ☎ 562-985-4585: main line; 562-985-4588: event line ✉ lgbtrc@hotmail.com
💻 www.csulb.edu/web/centers/lgbtrc
Office hours: Mon.-Thurs. 10a-7p; Fri. 10a-2p. Groups include: Women's Rap; Men's Rap; Speaker's Bureau; Book & Video Library; Gay Lesbian Bisexual Transgender Students United; Delta Lambda Phi (men's fraternity); & Eastern Ethnicity & Pacific Islander Discussion Group.

San Diego

Bisexual Forum 4545 Park Blvd, Suite 260 (but group doesn't meet there), San Diego, CA 92116 ☎ 619-692-2077 (San Diego glbt center) or 619-542-0088 (Fritz Klein) ✉ fritzsd@aol.com
Meets 2nd Tu., 7:30pm at the Community Church, Thorn & First Street.

BiPol San Diego c/o LGMCS, PO Box 3357, San Diego, CA 92163 ☎ 619-542-0088 Fritz (#10)
✉ kbaker@rohan.sdsu.edu
Promotes visibility, educates, and fights homophobia & biphobia.

Bill at San Francisco Pride, 1990

Woman 2 Woman Lesbian & Gay Men's Community Center, 3909 Centre St., San Diego, CA 92103 ☎ 619-692-2077
Support/discussion group for bi women. Meets 4th Th. 8pm at above address.

University of California, San Diego

Chancellor's Advisory Committee on LGBT Issues & GLBT Resource Office, 9500 Gilman Drive, La Jolla, CA 92093; ☎ 858-822-3493; FX: 858-822-3494; ✉ caclgbti@ucsd.edu (for the task force) or rainbow@ucsd.edu (for the resource office); 🖳 orpheus.ucsd.edu/caclgbi/home.html; *Administrative body comprised of UCSD students, staff, & faculty to identify & analyze the needs & concerns of LGBT faculty, staff, students, alumnae/alumni, & affiliates at UCSD, to inform & educate the entire UCSD community about the issues affecting LGBTs at UCSD. Resource Center offers support & outreach.* **Lesbian, Gay, Bisexual, Transgendered Association**, c/o GLBT Resource Office; ☎ 858-534-4297 (534-GAYS); ✉ ucsdlgba@sdcc.13.ucsd.edu or rainbow@ucsd.edu; 🖳 sdcc.13.ucsd.edu/~ucsdlgba/home.html; *Meets Mon.s at 7pm. Bisexual Forum meets Mon., 3:30pm at the LGBT Resources Office.* **Women's Support Group & Gay Men's Support Group**, c/o Psycological & Counseling Services, Galbraith Hall #190, La Jolla, CA 92093; ☎ 858-534-3755, ✉ Dlgba@sdcc.13.ucsd.edu; 🖳 sdcc13.ucsd.edu/~ucsdlgba/support/support.htm/; *UCSD's Psychological & Counseling Services. Groups available for registered students.*

San Diego State University: Lesbian, Gay, Bisexual & Transgender Student Union 500 Campaile Dr., San Diego, CA 92182 ☎ 619-594-2737 ✉ lgbtsu@rohan.sdsu.edu 🖳 www.sdsu.edu/studentlife/ (no direct website yet)

"There is no need for bisexual people to reach consensus on the best way to organize and build community. To achieve both useful short-term reforms and far-reaching long-term social change, we can benefit from all of the various strategies: alliance with the gay and lesbian movement, an independent bi-focused movement, a broad sexual and gender liberation movement, and a push to de-emphasize identity politics and re-define binary conceptions of sexuality and gender."

Liz A. Highleyman, in Bisexual Politics

San Francisco Bay Area

BIPOL c/o Ka'ahumanu , 20 Cumberland St., San Francisco, CA 94110 ☎ 415-821-3534

Bi Men of Color San Francisco, CA ☎ Bill: 510-540-0869

Jewish Bisexual Caucus c/o James A. Frazin, PO Box 78261, San Francisco, CA 94107 ☎ Jim: 415-337-4566 ✉ jf@shibboleth.com
Support & advocacy group welcoming all Jewish bisexuals at monthly gatherings. Mixed-heritage people or those unsure or exploring bisexual & Jewish identity are welcome.

Bay Area Bi Women's Group PO Box 190493, San Francisco, CA 94119 ✉ babw-owner@yahoogroups.com; also: asgaya@earthlink.net (calendar info); sdell99@aol.com (meetings & event planning) 🖳 home.earthlink.net/~asgaya/babw.html
Activities calendar, resource listings.

Bi-Friendly Network San Francisco/East Bay c/o E. Clary, PO Box 1088, Alameda, CA 94501 ☎ 415-289-2222 ✉ bifriendly@frap.org 🖳 www.frap.org/bifriendly
Unstructured social gatherings that focus on fun, folks, conversation, food and drink, & general silliness. SF group- 2nd Mon. 7:30pm at Muddy Waters Coffee House, 262 Church Street at Market. East Bay- 3rd Tu. 7:30pm at Au Coquelet, 2000 University at Milvia, in Berkeley.

Bisexual Men's Support/Personal Growth Group Ron Fox, Ph.D., MFCC, PO Box 210491, San Francisco, CA 94121-0491 ☎ 415-751-6714 ✉ rcf@wenet.net
Men's therapy group, with focus on communication & relationship issues. Fee.

San Francisco Bay Times 3410 19th St., San Francisco, CA 94110 ☎ 415-626-0260 FX: 415-626-0987 ✉ sfbaytimes@aol.com
GLBT bi-weekly newspaper for the Bay Area. This paper has the best (only) regularly published list of bi (& many other) . resources in the Bay Area. PUB: San Francisco Bay Times (Bi-weekly)

Harvey Milk Institute 584 Castro St., PMB 451, San Francisco, CA 94114 ☎ 415-552-7200 FX: 415-552-0179 ✉ harvmilk@aol.com 🖳 www.harveymilk,.org
Mission is to foster the development and examination of lesbian, gay, bisexual, transgender & queer culture & community in the Bay Area & beyond. Has included some of the first courses in bisexuality. PUB: Class catalogs (Printed and online class schedules.)

Pacific Center 2712 Telegraph Avenue, Berkeley, CA 94705 ☎ 510-548-8283 ✉ info@pacificcenter.org 🖳 www.pacificcenter.org/
Sponsors various bi support groups. Call about current groups. Quarterly newsletter includes free announcement section for other BGLTQ groups.

Rainbow Community Center of Contra Costa County 2118 Willow Pass Rd., Concord, CA 94520 ☎ 925-692-0090 FX: 925-692-0091 ✉ mwalker@rainbowcc.org 🖳 www.rainbowcc.org *Peer group support, referral services, social opportunities, & educational programs.* PUB: Prism (Free monthly newsletter with calendar, articles, ads, center schedule.)

Gay Lesbian Straight Education Network San Francisco-East Bay 436 14th Street, Suite 209, Oakland, CA 94612-2708 ☎510-338-0880 (newsletter: 510-234-3429) ✉ respect@glsensfeb.org (newsletter: boblatham@aol.com) 🖳 (for GLSEN) www.glsen.org *Advocates equality in education & change in education environments to make them safe & supportive for LGBTQ youth. Part of national org. Other chapters throughout the state & in Norther Calif.* PUB: GLSEN/SF-EB Newsletter (Monthly. Lists meetings & school workshops. Articles about GLBT education news. Samples mailed on request. Also available on website.)

Lyric (Lavender Youth Recreation & Information Center) 127 Collingwood St., San Francisco, CA 94114 ☎ ofc: 415-703-6150; youth talkline: 800-246-PRID(E); TDD: 415-341-8812 FX: 415-703-6153 ✉ office: lyric@lyric.org youth talkline: lyricinfo@tlg.net 🖳 www.lyric.org *Many groups for young people's programs for lgbtq. Programs include academic tutoring, after school support, job training, leadership training, youth talkline/infoline, arts & media, health education, young, loud & proud conference, & wellness programs.*

BA-CYBERDYKES San Francisco, CA ✉ ba-cyberdykes-owner@queernet.org *BA-CYBERDYKES is a San Francisco Bay Area lesbian/bi discussion list for self-identified dykes. For more information, send an e- mail message to majordomo@queernet.org with only "info ba-cyberdykes" in the body of the message.*

Gay Asian/Pacific Alliance PO Box 421884, San Francisco, CA 94142-1884 ☎ Info/events tape 415-282-4272 ✉ info@gapa.org 🖳 www.gapa.org *Dedicated to furthering the interest of gay & bi Asian & Pacific Islander men through awareness, positive identity development, & establishing a supportive community. Social, cultural (chorus, theater, dance), political awareness, HIV/AIDS advocacy, 35+ group, publications, scholarship.* PUB: Lavender Godzilla Newsletter

San Francisco State University: Queer Alliance (formerly Les/Gay/Bi Alliance [LGBA]) Student Union Building M-100A, 1650 Holloway, San Francisco, CA 94132 ☎ 415-338-1952 ✉ queer@sfsu.edu 🖳 www.sfsu.edu/~queer *Support, newsletter, events.*

Stanford University

Lesbian, Gay & Bisexual Community Center PO Box 18265, Stanford, CA 94309, ☎ 650-725-4222, ✉ lgbcc-staff@lists.stanford.edu 🖳 www.stanford.edu/group/QR/ (case-sensitive). *Info/referral resource, meeting center, "safe space" for members of Stanford's LGBQT community. Groups include (with links from main website):* **BLG Alliance at Stanford:** ☎650-725-4222; **OUTLAW - BGL Law Students Association:** ☎650-723-0362; **SUSEQ: LGB Students, Faculty, & Staff at the School of Education:** ☎650-723-2109; **GSB Out4Biz** *(for LGB members of the Graduate School of Business).*

LYRIC, a San Francisco youth Group

Mills College: Queer Alliance c/o Associated Students at Mills College, 5000 MacArthur Blvd., Oakland, CA 94613 ℅ 510-430-2255 (main) or 510-430-2130 (student life office) FX: 510-430-3314 (main office) V www.mills.edu/LIFE/ASMC/asmc.homepage.html or www.mills.edu/PUBS/STUDHBK_UG_CURR/sh-ug_studorgs.html *Committees include: Lesbian Avengers (direct action to fight queerphobia & promote glbt women's issues & visibility on campus & in the larger Oakland community) & BLAST (Bisexuals, Lesbians, & Straights Talking (organization educating the straight community about what it means to be gay through movie nights, discussions, lectures).*

> I am black and I am female and I am a mother and I am a bisexual and I am a nationalist and I am an anti-nationalist. And I mean to be fully and freely all that I am! ... I believe I have worked as hard as I could, and then harder than that, on behalf of equality and justice — for African-Americans, for the Palestinian people, and for people of color everywhere. And no, I do not believe it is blasphemous to compare oppressions of sexuality to oppressions of race and ethnicity: Freedom is indivisible or it is nothing at all.
>
> June Jordan

Lyon-Martin Women's Health Center 1748 Market Street, Suite #201, San Francisco, CA 94102 ☎ 415-565-7667
Primary care services for women, special sensitivity to lesbian, bis & trans women, including routine physical examinations, internal medicine, gynecology, family planning, & prevention & screening. HIV services include counseling, testing, prevention education, support groups, case management, & comprehensive medical care.

New Leaf Services for Our Community 1853 Market St., San Francisco, CA 94103 ☎ 415-626-7000 ext.205 FX: 415-626-5916 ✉ (none yet) 🖳 www.newleaf.org
New Leaf provides psychotherapy for HIV-positive men & women in the LGBT community. Both long & short-term therapy offered. Bisexual therapists available on request.

Proyecto Contrasida Por Vida 2940 16th St. #308, San Francisco, CA 94103 ☎ 415-864-7278 FX: 415-575-1645
Latino/a LGBTQ HIV service agency; includes youth drop-in group MWTh, call for times.

Asian Pacific Islander Wellness Center (includes Vietnamese Lesbians Gays & Bisexuals) 730 Polk Street, 4th Floor, San Francisco, CA 94109-7813 ☎ 415-292-3420 FX: 415-292-3404; tty 415-292-3410 ✉ info@apiwellness.org 🖳 www.apiwellness.org/
Education, support, empowerment, advocacy for Asian & Pacific Islander communities - particularly those living with or at-risk for HIV/AIDS. Staff speak 16 languages. Free confidential HIV treatment case management, mental health & substance abuse counseling, medical & psychiatric care.

San Francisco Network for Battered Lesbians & Bisexual Women 3543 18th Street, Box 28, San Francisco, CA 94110 ☎ voice mail: 415-281-0276; hotline 415-864-4722 or 415-333-HELP
Brief phone counseling & referrals for women emotionally, phsyically, or sexually battered by women lovers. Community education & training re: woman to woman battering.

Q Action 2128 15th St., San Francisco, CA 94114-1213 ☎ 415-575-1050 FX: 415-575-0116 ✉ qaction@stopaids.org 🖳 www.stopaids.org
Peer-based group of young gay & bi men (25 & under) committed to stopping the spread of HIV in our community. Part of the Stop AIDS project.

Many human beings enjoy sexual relations with their own sex, many don't; many respond to both. The plurality is the fact of our nature and not worth fretting about.

—Gore Vidal 1991 (from "The Birds and The Bees" in The Nation 10/28/91.)

Gaylesta: Gay, Lesbian, Bisexual & Transgender Psychotherapist's Association of the Bay Area 5337 College Avenue, Suite #713, Oakland, CA 94618 ☎ 888-869-4993 (referral service; toll-free); 510-433-9939 (membership & info)
Professional networking, community education, social events & psychotherapist referral service.
PUB: Gaylesta News (A newsletter to inform members of events, ads, classifieds & organization news.)

University of California, Berkeley

Queer Resource Center, 305 Eshleman Hall, Berkeley, CA 94720, ☎ 510-642-8429; ✉ events@queer.berkeley.edu; 🖳 queer.berkeley.edu. *Umbrella groups for campus groups.* **Fluid**, c/o QRC; ✉ fluid@queer.berkeley.edu; 🖳 queer.berkeley.edu/fluid/; *Discussion & social group for bis, those questioning, & anyone going without a label.* **Cal Q&A**, c/o QRC; ✉ calqa@queer.berkeley.edu; 🖳 queer.berkeley.edu/calqa/; *For queer-identified Asians/Pacific Islanders.* **GLOBE (Gays, Lesbians, Or Bisexuals Everywhere)**, c/o QRC; ✉ globe@queer.berkeley.edu; 🖳 queer.berkeley.edu/globe/; *Support & social group for queer & questioning students in the Residence Halls.* **Queer Council**. c/o QRC, ✉ council @queer.berkeley.edu; 🖳 queer.berkeley.edu/council/; *Consists of leaders of the queer groups at Cal as well as other leaders on campus. Other campus groups include:* **Women's Rap Group** (✉lgbt@uclink.berkeley.edu; 🖳 http://queer.berkeley.edu/rap/); **Y QUE** (🖳 http://queer.berkeley.edu/yque/; jaimeg00@hotmail.com; ☎ 510-832-2588); **Queer Latina/o. Gay, Lesbian, Bisexual Catholics Support Group** Newman Hall-Holy Spirit Parish, 2700 Dwight Way, Berkeley, CA 94704 ☎ 510-848-7812 or 510-848-7813 FX: 510-848-0179 🖳 www.support.net/HolySpirit. *There is a student group & an adult/non-student group.*

San José

Bi-Friendly South Bay c/o Billy DeFrank Lesbian & Gay Community Center , 938 The Alameda , San Jose, CA 95126 ☎ 408-793-5131 (voicemail/info line) ✉ poetgrrl@myfamily.com; bifriendly@frap.org 🖳 www.southbaybi.org/ (info)
Bisexual peer support group Tues from 7:30-9pm at the Center. Coffee social after the support group, at 9pm at Cafe de Matisse, 371 South First St., downtown San Jose. Host is Joe (joe@bi.org). Look for the Bi Pride flag or a large, friendly group of people. Project of the South Bay Bisexual Organizers & Activists (SoBOA), & affiliated with the Billy DeFrank Lesbian & Gay Community Center of San Jose. PUB: Bi the Way (Bi Monthly newsletter available on the web, at the Center, or by subsription.)

Billy DeFrank Lesbian & Gay Community Center
938 The Alameda, San Jose, CA 95126
☎ 408-293-4525 or 2429 FX: 408-298-8986
✉ dfcreception@defrank.org 🖳 www.defrank.org
A community center with many programs & courses including a bi group.

South Bay Bisexual Organizers & Activists (SoBOA) c/o Billy DeFrank Lesbian and Gay Community Center , 938 The Alameda , San Jose, CA 95126 ☎ 408-793-5131 ✉ info@southbaybi.org
🖳 www.southbaybi.org
Monthly potluck brunches from 2nd Sun. 11am-1pm to plan Bi-Friendly South Bay socials, bi education & outreach programs, publicity, & fundraising events. Non-profit affiliate of the Billy DeFrank Lesbian & Gay Community Center of San Jose. PUB: Bi the Way (online)

South Bay Queer & Asian c/o Billy DeFrank Center, 938 The Alameda, San Jose, CA 95126
☎ 408-293-4525 or 2429 FX: 408-298-8986
✉ dfcreception@defrank.org 🖳 www.defrank.org
SBQ&A is a support & social group which provides South Bay Gay Asian & Pacific Islanders a safe place to come out & be comfortable with their sexual identity & race. Meets every other Tu. 7-9 p.m. in Room C. PUB: DeFrank News (free, monthly)

South Bay/Santa Clara Mixed Bi Support Group
c/o Billy DeFrank Lesbian & Gay Community Ctr., 938 The Alameda, San Jose, CA 95126
☎ Community Center: 408-293-2429 or 4525
FX/tdd: 408-298-8986 ✉ dfcreception@defrank.org
🖳 www.southbaybi.org or www.defrank.org
Guided rap & discussion group Tu. 7:30-9pm.

Trikone PO Box 21354, San Jose, CA 95151
☎ 408-270-8776 (magazine) or 415-789-7322 (group) FX: 408-274-2733 ✉ trikone@rahul.net or info@trikone.org 🖳 www.trikone.org
A socio-political organization for glb South Asians. Organizes & participates in several Bay Area events & publishes national newsmagazine. Send E-mail for events mailing list. PUB: Trikone magazine (published quarterly.)

San Jose State University: Gay, Lesbian , Bisexual, Transgender Alliance Box 55 SAS, San Jose, CA 95192-0038 ☎ 408-924-7238
✉ glbta@email.sjsu.edu 🖳 www.sjsu.edu/orgs/glbta/
Social & educational.

More California (in zip code order)

Pasadena Bi Group & Married Bisexual Men's Group PO Box 90814, Pasadena, CA 91109 ☎ 626-568-7991 FX: 562-495-7502
General bi group by appointment; also: married bisexual men's group for men who are or have been in long-term relationships; 8-10-week closed group where bi married men can share their frustrations & strengths with each other. Professional counselor facilitates both groups.

> **Asked of Bette Midler: "Are you bilingual?" Her response: "Once, in college."**
> ☙

California Institute of Technology (CalTech)

Lesbigay Union, Mail Stop 104-58, Pasadena, CA 91125; ☎ 626-395-8331; ✉ CLU@its.caltech.edu or CLU-request@cco.caltech.edu; 🖳 www.cco.caltech.edu/~clu; *Open to Caltech students, faculty, & staff.*
Pride Association, ✉ cspa@pride.caltech.edu;
🖳 www.ugcs.caltech.edu/~cspa/; *Gay-straight alliance & social group for glbt undergraduates.*

Jet Propulsion Laboratory: Lambda JPL Mail Stop 264-860, Pasadena, CA 91125
☎ 818-354-3680 or 818-393-0664 ✉ lambda-request@godzilla.jpl.nasa.gov (to subscribe); lambda@godzilla.jpl.nasa.gov (for discussions & announcements) and lambda-announce@jpl.nasa.gov (announcements only)
🖳 www.cco.caltech.edu/~clu/lambda/lambda.html
Official glb group at JPL.

California State University, Northridge: Lesbian , Gay Bisexual Transgender Community Resource Center & LGBT Alliance LGBT CRC, 18111 Nordhoff St., Northridge, CA 91330-8261
☎ 818-677-1200 (main campus #), -2390 (student development) ✉ lgbtcrc@csun.edu
🖳 www.csun.edu/lgbtcrc
Galen Hammond, administrative director.

Bi-Line (previously Pansocial Center) 7136 Matilija Av., Van Nuys, CA 91405 ☎ 818-989-3700 ✉ larisem@pacbell.net
Hotline, free counseling & referrals.

Claremont Colleges: Queer Resource Center 700 N. College Way, Pomona College, Claremont, CA 91711 ☎ 909-607-1817 🖳 www.pomona.edu/Parents/ParentsGuide/Support.html#qrc
Meets in Walker Hall. Office open Sun.-Th. 1-5pm & 7-11pm, Fri.-Sat. 1-5pm.

San Francisco Freedom Day Parade, 1990

Robyn Ochs

Cal Poly Pomona: Lesbian, Gay, Bisexual &Transgender Student Resource Center/Pride Center 3801 W. Temple Ave., Building #1, Room 206, Pomona, CA 91768 ☎ 909-869-3064 FX: 909-869-5259 ✉ jjowens@csupomona.edu ▣ www.csupomona.edu/~pride_center/

Mira Costa College: Lesbian Gay Bisexual Transgendered Student Association 1 Barnard Drive, Oceanside, CA 92056-3899 ☎ 760-757-2121 x8918 of 1-888-201-8480 ✉ lgba@kes.miracosta.cc.ca.us ▣ www.miracosta.cc.ca.us/clubs/lesbigay/lgbtsapage2.htm
Monthly drop-in support group co-facilitated by peer counselors & students; O.U.T.E.D. The Organization of Unification Through Education of Diversity; What's the Buzz monthly Coffee Talk & new Hollywood films; Membership meetings for "out" members; members who are not comfortable gather at a undisclosed location — members are notified by email about these meetings.

University of Redlands: Gay, Lesbian, Bisexual Straight Union c/o Student Leadership & Involvement Center, PO Box 3080, Redlands, CA 92373-0999 ☎ 909-793-2121— Advisor: Daniel Kiefer, x5103; Joyce Larson, x7241 ▣ www.redlands.edu/student_life/Clubs_Orgs.htm

University of California, Riverside: Lesbian, Gay, Bisexual & Transgender Resource Center 250 Costo Hall, Riverside, CA 92521 ☎ 909-787-2267 ✉ lgbtrc@ucr.edu ▣ lgbtrc.ucr.edu/
Queer Alliance & various discussion groups.

Seventh Day Adventist Kinship PO Box 7320, Laguna Niguel, CA 92607 ☎ 949-248-1299 ✉ sdakinship@aol.com ▣ www.sdakinship.org/
Ministers to the well being of individuals with diverse sexual orientations who have ties with the Seventh-day Adventist denomination along with their families & friends

The use of the phrase "sexual orientation" to describe only a person's having sex with members of their own gender or the other sex obscures the fact that many of us have other strong and consistent sexual orientations--toward certain hair colors, body shapes, racial types. It would be as logical to look for genes associated with these orientations as for "homosexual genes."

Ruth Hubbard, "False Genetic Markers, in *The New York Times*, 8/2/93.)

Orange Coast College: Pride 2701 Fairview Road, Costa Mesa, CA 92626 ☎ 714-432-5738 (student svcs.); 714-432-5613 (advisor) or 714-342-0202 ▣ www.occ.cccd.edu/
Weekly meetings during term time Th 5-6pm.

University of California, Irvine: Lesbian Gay Bisexual Transgender Resource Center 106 Gateway Commons, University of California, Irvine, CA 92697-5125 ☎ 949-824-3277 (LGBTRC) or 949-824-3169 (Pat Walsh, Director) FX: 949-824-3412 ✉ lgbtrc@uci.edu or plwalsh@uci.edu ▣ www.lgbtrc.uci.edu/
Peer counseling, speakers bureau, meeting space, coming out program. GLBSU meets Wed., 6-8pm at the LGB Resource Center. Rainbow Coalition meets 1st & 3rd Mon.; Irvine Queers (IQ) meets Tu. 7-9 p.m.

California State University, Fullerton: Lesbian/Gay/Bisexual Association University Center 256, Box 67, Fullerton, CA 92831 ☎ 714-524-7093 or 7734 ✉ kto19637@student.fullerton.edu ▣ www.fullerton.edu/deanofstudents/clubs_and_orgs/club_directory.htm
Mts. Wed 6 pm.

The Center Orange County 12832 Garden Grove Blvd., Suite A, Garden Grove, CA 92843 ☎ 714-534-0862 FX: 714-534-5491 ✉ administration@centeroc.org ▣ www.centeroc.org

BiNet Santa Barbara - Bi Now Santa Barbara, CA ☎ 805-687-2535 ✉ BiNetSBBiNow@aol.com
Mostly a social group w/open discussions.

Pacific Pride Foundation 126 E. Hailey St. #A-11, Santa Barbara, CA 93101 ☎ 805-963-3636 FX: 805-963-9086 ✉ yessprogram@hotmail.com (youth program) ▣ www.silcom.com/~pride/
Bi youth encouraged to attend the youth groups that meet Mon. 3:30-5pm at the Santa Barbara office (above), & Mon 5-6:30pm at the Santa Maria office, 819 West Church Street, 805-349-9947 PUB: The Bulletin

University of California, Santa Barbara

Queer Student Union, CAC Box 78, Santa Barbara, CA 93106; ☎ 805-893-3778 (advisor); ✉ acker-d@sa.ucsb.edu or queersu@geocities.com ; ▣ www.geocities.com/WestHollywood/Stonewall/9379/; *Meets Tu. 7:15pm in the Multicultural Center on campus.* **Multicultural Queer Grad Network**, PO Box 162 UCSB, Santa Barbara, CA 93106; ☎ Queer Resource Coordinator: 805-893-5846; ✉ bazarsky-d@sa.ucsb.edu ; ▣ orgs.sa.ucsb.edu/mcq/.

California Polytechnic State University San Luis Obispo: Gays, Lesbians, Bisexuals United Box 234, UU Room 218, San Luis Obispo, CA 93410 ☎ 805-761-1281 (Associated Students Inc.) ✉ gays-lesbians-bisexuals@calpoly.edu ▣ www.calpoly.edu/~glbclub/

SLO Bi Women's Group 4650 San Anselmo, Atascadero, CA 93422 ☎ 805-461-1178

California State University, Fresno: Lesbian, Gay, Bisexual & Sraight Alliance 5280 N. Jackson, Box SU36, Fresno, CA 93740 ☎ (559) 278 5721 [Dr Linda Garber] ✉ JJ1GK@aol.com

Bi-Life Marin c/o Marin AIDS Project, 1660 Second Street, San Rafael, CA 94901 ☎ 415-457-2487 x420 FX: 415-457-5687 ✉ BiLifeNBay@aol.com *An outreach of the Marin AIDS Project. Provides social events to strengthen the bi community, & provides an environment for bisexual & bi-curous men & women to meet like-minded individuals. Also presents educational forums where people meet to discuss important issues of self-discovery.*

Sacred Space Institute PO Box 4322, San Rafael, CA 94913-4322 ☎ 415-507-1739 ✉ info@lovewithoutlimits.com 🖳 www.lovewithoutlimits.com *Supports loving, committed, ethical, multi-partner relationships. Workshops, ongoing groups, speakers bureau, quarterly newsletter. All sexual preferences welcome. Includes online bookstore that also links to Loving More Magazine (previous magazine was Polyamory).*

Sonoma State University: Bisexual Gay & Lesbian Alliance of Sonoma State 1801 East Cotati Ave. (SSU main address), Rohnert Park, CA 94928 ☎ Jed Burchett, 707-586-3431 & Elizabeth Rey, 707-824-2854 (Advisor: 707-664-3127) ✉ Owlstorm7@aol.com 🖳 www.sonoma.edu/ CampusLife/clubs/clublist.html *For students exploring their sexual identity. Informational networking, social activities. Weekly meetings Tu. @ 12, Club Room, Student Union.*

Spectrum

1000 Sir Francis Drake Blvd. #10, San Anselmo, CA 94960-1743 ☎415-457-1115 X 203; FX: 415-457-2838; ✉ spectrumVL@aol.com; *Community center with programs for youth, adults, seniors, men, women, mixed gender groups. Volunteer opportunities. Book discussions. Most programs open to bisexuals.* **Bisexual Support & Discussion Group**; ☎ Joelle x203; (Sponsors occasional community forums & holds support/discussion group meetings); **New Horizons** (Group for TBLG & questioning people 20-29 years old); Rainbow's End (For lgbtq youth, 14-25, Th. 7-9pm)

Cabrillo College: Queer Club Student Center, 6500 Soquel Drive, Aptos, CA 95003 ☎ 831-479-6231 FX: 831-479-5743 🖳 www.cabrillo.cc.ca.us/ (for campus only)

De Anza College: Bisexual, Lesbian, Transgendered, & Gay Association 21250 Stevens Creek Boulevard, Cupertino, CA 95014 ☎ Advisor: Jean Miller: 408-864-8488 ✉ ol_myth@yahoo.com 🖳 clubs.yahoo.com/clubs/ deanzalgbaclub

Intel Gay, Lesbian, Bisexual, or Transgendered Employees, 2200 Mission College Blvd., Santa Clara, CA 95052 ☎ 408-765-4199 (Liz Parrish) 🖳 www.glyphic.com/iglobe *An Intel-sanctioned employee diversity group for networking of Intel employees.* PUB: The Rainbow Connection (A benefit for members published monthly, lists activities at Intel sites worldwide.)

Bi-Friendly Santa Cruz PO Box 7095, Santa Cruz, CA 95063-7095 ☎ 831 427 4556 ✉ scruz-bi@yahoogroups.com 🖳 www.yahoogroups.com/ group/scruz-bi *Monthly meetings. All welcome.*

Women's Bisexual Network of Santa Cruz & the Greater Monterey Bay Area PO Box 3536, Santa Cruz, CA 95063-3536 ☎ 831-427-4556 *Meets 4th Wed.*

University of California, Santa Cruz: Gay, Lesbian, Bisexual & Transgender Resource Center 1156 High Street, UC Santa Cruz, Santa Cruz, CA 95064, ☎ 831-459-2468; FX: 831-459-4387; ✉ glbtcenter@cats.ucsc.edu; 🖳 www2.ucsc.edu/ glbtcenter/; *Central organization for campus & allied groups.* **The Gay, Lesbian, Bisexual, Transgender, Allied, & Questioning Network** *(umbrella organization for many of the queer groups on campus. Allies & friends welcome to attend meetings).* **Bi-the-Way** *(social/support/ discussion group for students who identify as bisexual, queer, or non-labeling)* **Sappho** *(Group for women who are les, bi or questioning). All groups c/o GLBTRC.*

Camp Lavender Hill PO Box 11275, Santa Rosa, CA 95406 ☎ 707-544-8150 *Summer camp in Nevada City, CA, for children (7-17) of GLB families. Counselors are ages 18-23 & have either grown up in GLB families or are themselves GL or B. Non-profit staffed entirely by volunteers. Annual golf tournament fundraiser held on women's weekend in Guerneville.*

> In another life, dear sister, I too would bear six fat children. In another life, dear sister, I too would love another woman and raise one child together as if that it pushed from both our wombs. In another life, sister, I too would dwell solitary and splendid as a lighthouse on the rocks or be born to mate for life like the faithful goose. Praise all our choices. Praise any woman who chooses, and make safe her choice.
>
> Marge Piercy

University of California at Davis: Lesbian Gay Bisexual Transgender Resource Center
University House Annex, 1 Shields Avenue, Davis, CA 95616 ☎ 530-752-2GLB
✉ lgbtcenter@ucdavis.edu
🖳 lgbcenter.ucdavis.edu/
Provides education, info & advocacy services. Works to create & maintain an open, safe, inclusive environment for lgbt students, staff, faculty, their family & friends, & the entire campus.

Sacramento Area Bisexual Network Sacramento, CA 95814 ✉ desireedd@excite.com
🖳 www.bisexual.org/g/sabn/
Meets 2nd & 4th Tues, 7:30-9:00pm at The Open Book bookstore, 910 21st St, Midtown Sacramento.

California State University at Chico: Pride Bell Memorial Union, Chico, CA 95929 ☎ 530-898 6345 [ask for Lana Burris] ✉ lburris@csuchico.edu
🖳 www.ecst.csuchico.edu/~pride
Also open to non-Chico State students in the area. Student group. providing education, support & social activities for GLBT students & allies.

Colorado

BiNet Colorado PO Box 886, Denver, CO 80306 ☎ 303-499-5777
Monthly activities.

Rainbow Planet Rainbow Planet, LLC, PO Drawer 2270, Boulder CO 80306-2270 ☎ 303-443-7768
✉ planet@RainbowPgs.com
🖳 www.rainbowpgs.com/loc/bldrc.htm
Excellent print & online directory of glbt organizations & businesses in Colorado (& neighboring states)

Equality Colorado PO Box 300476, Denver, CO 80203 ☎ 303-839-5540; 303-852-5094; crisis line 888-557-4441 toll free in CO only FX: 303-839-1361
✉ equality@equalitycolorado.org
🖳 www.equalitycolorado.org
Educational & outreach statewide to increase awareness of GLB experience, civil rights & the effect of Amendment 2. Political advocacy, legislative work & PAC. Anti-violence project & training programs. 24 hr crisis line.

GLSEN/Colorado PO Box 280346, Lakewood, CO 80228-0346 ☎ 303-936-6562 FX: Same # (call first)
✉ glsenco@glsenco.org 🖳 www.glsenco.org
A nonprofit group that strives to assure that each member of every school community is valued & respected, regardless of sexual orientation.
PUB: GLSEN/Colorado Newsletter (brief quarterly update on activities & news)

Bisexual Women's Voice Boulder PO Box 886, Boulder, CO 80306 ☎ 303-499-5777

Boulder Pride PO Box 1018, Boulder, CO 80306
🖳 www.boulderpride.org

Proud Lockheed employee

OASOS Program: Coming Out Boulder/Longmont Boulder, CO ☎ 303-678-6139
🖳 www.oasos.com
Support groups meet weekly in Boulder & Longmont.

University of Colorado, Boulder: Gay, Lesbian, Bisexual, Transgender Resource Center 103 UCD, Boulder, CO 80309-0103 ☎ 303-492-1377
✉ glbtrc@colorado.edu 🖳 www.colorado.edu/glbtrc

University of Colorado Boulder LGB Alumni Association Boulder, CO ☎ 800-492-7743
✉ killinger_m@cusund.colorado.edu

Pikes Peak Gay & Lesbian Community Center: Pride Center PO Box 607, Colorado Springs, CO 80901 ☎ 719-471-4429 ✉ mail@ppglcc.org
🖳 www.ppglcc.org

ALSO (All Lifestyles & Outlooks) 730 N. Tejon St, Colorado Springs, CO 80903 ☎ 719-685-4773
✉ asuc@asuc.net
Potluck 3rd Sat. 5:30pm church annex, call to confirm. Support group at All Souls Unitarian Church.

Women's Social Group Colorado Springs, CO ☎ 719-471-4429

Colorado College EQUAL: Gay, Lesbian, Bisexual Alliance 902 N. Cascade WB2166, Colorado Springs, CO 80946 ☎ 719-389-7817
✉ l-skolnik@ColoradoCollege.edu
🖳 www.cc.colorado.edu/students/BGALA/

University of Colorado, Colorado Springs: BGALA Colorado Springs, CO ☎ 719-570-6069
✉ bgala@mail.uccs.edu 🖳 www.uccs.edu/~bgala/

Community Council for Adolescent Development
Pride Center, 125 N Parkside, Colorado Springs,
CO 80909 ☎ 719-328-1056
*Runs: Inside/Out (a youth support group). Meets
5:30 Wed, for -23.*

Pikes Peak Metropolitan Community Church 1102
S. 21st St., Colorado Springs, CO 80904
☎ 719-634-3771 FX: 719-634-3015
✉ admin@pikespeakmcc.org
🖳 www.pikespeakmcc.org
Worship service Sun 10:30am.

Denver Grrrls email list Denver, CO
*Email list for bisexual women in the Denver
Colorado area. To subscribe email denvergrrrls-
subscribe@yahoogroups.com*

Crossroads c/o John Barry, 3955 E Exposition
Ste 408, Denver, CO 80209 ☎ 303-698-2385
*Support group for married bisexual men.
Referrals for bi women & spouses.*

**Gay, Lesbian & Bisexual Community Services
Center of Colorado, Inc.** 234 Broadway, Denver,
CO 80203 ☎ 303-733-7743
✉ center_info@coloradoglbt.org
*Support groups, counseling, library, speakers
bureau, youth groups (18-25), helpline, referrals.*

**Denver University: Lesbian, Gay & Bisexual
Alliance** Denver, CO ☎ 303-871-2321

Dignity - Denver PO Box 3072, 1100 Fillmore,
Denver, CO 80201 ☎ 303-322-8485
Organization for lgbt Catholics. Liturgies Sun. 5pm.

**Metropolitan State College of Denver: Gay
Lesbian Bisexual Transgender Student Services**
CB 74, PO Box 173362, Denver, CO 80217-3362
☎ 303-556-6333 FX: 303-556-3896
✉ BensenK@mscd.edu 🖳 clem.mscd.edu/~glbtss
*Karen Bensen, LCSW, Coordinator. Resource
center, provides info related to glbt issues to
students, staff, & faculty.* PUB: Out Around
Campus (Published twice a semester)

Rainbow Alley Youth Drop-In Center
PO Box 9798, 919 E. 14th St., Denver, CO 80209
☎ 303-831-0442
Drop in center for GLBT youth -26.

P-FLAG Denver, CO ☎ 303-333-0286 help line,
303-573-5861 administrative office
*Meetings include a rap group for bisexuals &
their families. Meets 1st Th.*

Pagan Rainbow Network Herbs & Arts Bookstore,
2015 E. Colfax Ave., Denver, CO 80218
☎ 303-388-2544
Spirituality circle for LGBT community.

Metropolitan Community Church of the Rockies
980 Clarkson, Denver, CO 80218 ☎ 303-860-1819
🖳 www.mccrockies.com
*LGBT religious organization offers foodbank &
pastoral counseling. Sun & Wed services.*

Gay/Lesbian Association of Durango (GLAD)
Box 1656, Durango, CO 81302 ☎ 970-247-7778
✉ gladurango@juno.com

**Fort Lewis College: Gay, Lesbian & Bisexual
Alliance** 1000 Rim Drive, Durango, CO 81301
☎ Prevention Office: 970-247-7097
✉ focglbta@hotmail.com
🖳 student.fortlewis.edu/~glba/
Support network for GLBT & allies.

Lambda Community Center of Fort Collins 149 W.
Oak St #8, Ft. Collins, CO 80524 ☎ 970-221-3247
✉ lambda@lambdacenter.org
🖳 www.lambdacenter.org/
*For GLBs in northern Colorado & southern
Wyoming. Group for gay/bi men; Rocky
Mountain Youth Group for GLB & questioning
youth; Also mixed gender Bisexual Support
Group.* PUB: Lambda Line (Bi-monthly.)

Weird Sisters PO Box F, Ft. Collins, CO
☎ 970-482-4393 ✉ weirdsisters@worldnet.att.net
*Newspaper for lesbian, bisexual, & alternative
women*

Colorado State University

GLBT Student Services Office, 18 Lory
Student Center, Ft. Collins, CO 80523;
☎ 970-491-4342; *Resources, referrals, support,
education & outreach.* **Student Organization
for Gays, Lesbians & Bisexuals, Gathering
of Womyn & Straight But Not Narrow,** all at:
CSU, Box 206, Activities Center, Ft. Collins, CO
80523; ☎ 970-491-7232.

Rocky Mountain Youth Group 149 W Oak #8, Ft.
Collins, CO ☎ 970-221-3247
✉ lambda@lambdacenter.org
🖳 www.lambdacenter.org

Western Equality Grand Junction, CO
☎ 970-242-8949
Associated with Equality Colorado in Denver.

Mesa State Gay, Lesbian & Bisexual Alliance PO
Box 2647, Grand Junction, CO 81502
☎ 970-248-1664
✉ jzeigel@mesa5.mesa.colorado.edu; or
philhellas@aol.com

P-FLAG Grand Junction PO Box 4904, Grand
Junction, CO 81502 ☎ 970-242-8965

University of Northern Colorado

Greeley Queer Alliance ☎ 970-351-1484
DESC: Support & social group for UNC
& Greeley residents. **GLBT Resource Center:**
☎ 970-351-2906; DESC: provides education &
information for the UNC & Greeley
communities. Referrals to local social groups,
counseling & medical services, & supportive
religious/spiritual organizations.

As far as I'm concerned, being any gender is a drag.

Patti Smith

Pueblo After 2 PO Box 1602, Pueblo, CO 81002
☎ 719-564-4004 ✉ puebloafter2@juno.com
Pueblo's main glbt social/political organization.

PFLAG Pueblo PO Box 4484, Pueblo, CO 81003
☎ 719-542-6359

Pueblo Metropolitan Community Church 1003
Liberty Lane (corner Bonforte), PO Box 1918,
Pueblo, CO 81002-1918 ☎ 719-543-6460
✉ revcwolf@aol.com
5pm Sun. services.

University of Southern Colorado: One in Ten
c/o Associated Student Government, 2200
Bonforte Boulevard, Pueblo, CO 81005

Connecticut

Conn-Bi-Nation c/o Project 100 Community
Center, 1841 Broad St., Hartford, CT 06114
☎ 860-224-4015; 203-634-6511
*Statewide educational, political and social
organization for bisexuals & allies. Meets 2nd &
4th Sun. at 7pm.*

Bisexual Ladies of Connecticut (BLOC) CT
✉ karina@ctbifemales.com
🖥 www.ctbifemales.com
*Not-for-profit group. Provides bi women in
Connecticut with a discreet, safe, comfortable
environment to meet other bi women for support,
friendship, fun, & more. Meant for mature women
of all ages, races, religion & statures. Regular
outings at area nightclubs & gathering spots, &
other "get-togethers". Single men NOT welcome.*

Metroline 495 Farmington Ave., Hartford, CT
06105 ☎ 860-570-0823, 860-233-9241
✉ mol@hartnet.org
*Bi-weekly GLBT news magazine for CT & New
England.*

**Connecticut Coalition for Lesbian, Gay, Bisexual
& Transgender Civil Rights** CT ☎ 860-521-4710
✉ cgfeminist@aol.com
*State-wide organization promotes & develops
political awareness in the LGBT community.
Organizes LGBT people & allies for LGBT civil
rights, politically empowers LGBT people through
ongoing involvement in the legislative process &
creates related educational programs.*

**True Colors, Inc.: Sexual Minority Youth & Family
Services (Children from the Shadows
Conference)** PO Box 1855, Manchester, CT 06045
☎ 860-649-7386, 888-565-5551
✉ CFshadows@juno.com
*Non-profit to improve & enrich the lives of sexual
minority youth & families. Hosts excellent annual
conference addressing LGBT youth issues for
youth & service providers, semi-annual youth
leadership training including conflict resolution &
leadership skills. Great source of referrals to
youth groups.*

Connecticut Pride Committee c/o GLB
Community Center, 1841 Broad Street, Hartford,
CT 06114 ☎ 860-524-8114
🖥 www.connecticutpride.com
*Meets @ Community Center in Hartford. Holds
annual festival in West Hartford.*

Stonewall Speakers Association CT
☎ 860-633-5111; 203-453-1395
*Speakers bureau addressing sexual orientation.
SSA puts on programs at over 60 High Schools
& Colleges each year.*

**Straight Spouse Network - Western
Massachusetts & Connecticut** see Western Mass
listing for contact info. ☎ 413-625-6033
✉ aharris@valinet.com
*Provides free non-phobic info, a lending library
& monthly area support groups in West Hartford,
CT & Northampton, MA.*

**Connecticut Private High Schools: Gay/Straight
Alliances** CT ☎ 860-649-7378 or 888-565-5551
(True Colors, Inc.) ✉ gsa-info@ourtruecolors.org
🖥 www.ourtruecolors.org
*There are groups at many private schools,
including: Loomis Chaffee, Windsor; Watkinson
School, Hartford; Choate Rosemary Hall,
Wallingford; Hamden Hall Day School, Hamden.
See the True Colors' web page for a complete list.
Call True Colors at the above numbers for contact
info. for each school.*

Connecticut Public High Schools: Gay/Straight Alliances CT ☎ 860-649-7378 or 888-565-5551 (True Colors, Inc.) ✉ gsa-info@ourtruecolors.org 💻 www.ourtruecolors.org

There are groups at many public high schools, including Amity HS; Branford HS; Brookfield HS; Bunnell HS, Stratford; Cheshire HS; Conard HS, W. Hartford; Coventry HS; Danbury HS; Daniel Hand HS, Madison; EO Smith HS, Storrs; Guilford HS; Greenwich HS; Hall HS, W. Hartford; Ledgeyard HS; Lymon Hall, Wallingford; New London HS; Newtown HS; Ridgefield HS; Sheehan HS, Wallingford; Southington HS; S. Windsor HS; Staples HS. Check True Colors' web site for a complete list. Call True Colors at the numbers listed above for contact info. for each school.

Queer & Active CT ☎ 860-568-9376 ✉ queerandactive@yahoo.com

Young people, 2-25. Builds bridges among youth in the community, high schools, colleges & universities.

RAYS (Rainbow Accepting Youth), Northeastern CT CT ☎ Bob Brex: 860-564-6100

Meets Sun. 3:30-5:30pm at United Services.

Lifestyles United Bridgeport, CT ☎ Ryan: 203-576-7679

Support group for LGBTQ youth in the greater Bridgeport area. The group writes & performs various works about their experiences.

Bi Rap Group Triangle Community Center, PO Box 4062, E. Norwalk, CT 06855 ☎ 203-853-0600

Meets 2nd & 4th Wed. 7:30pm.

Triangle Community Center PO Box 4062, East Norwalk, CT 06855 ☎ 203-853-0600 FX: 203-964-1133 ✉ TCCenter@aol.com

GLB center serves the GLB communities from New Haven county to Westchester county in N.Y. & all of Fairfield county; located at 15 River Street in Norwalk. Meetings, activities, cultural & educational programs, area's largest lgb resource room. PUB: New & Views (Monthly.)

Outspoken - Norwalk Youth Group PO Box 4062, East Norwalk, CT 06855 ☎ 203-227-1755 FX: 203-227-3035 ✉ dwoog@optonline.net 💻 www.ctgay.com

Fairfield County's support group for LGBTQ youth, 16-22. Mixed gender, h.s. & college-aged young people. Support, info, speakers, opportunity to get involved in the political arena.

Bisexual Rap Group c/o GLB Community Center, 1841 Broad St., Hartford, CT 06114 ☎ 860-724-5542

Monthly topic meetings.

March on Washington, 1993

Robyn Ochs

Project 100, Gay, Lesbian & Bisexual Community Center 1841 Broad St., Hartford, CT 06114-1780 ☎ 860-724-5542 FX: 203-724-3443 ✉ project100htfd@aol.com 💻 www.project100htfd.com

Non-profit community center. Provides safe & supportive meeting space w/ game room, full kitchen & private offices for area groups. Dances, entertainment. Wheelchair accessible. PUB: Update (Monthly newsletter.)

Hartford Commission on Gay, Lesbian & Bisexual Issues c/o City Hall, 550 Main Street, Hartford, CT 06106 ☎ Hartford Town Clerk: 860-543-8581

Meets 2nd Tu. 7pm, Rm. 401 City Hall. Advisory committee, recommends legislation to City Council.

Married Men's Support Group Hartford, CT ☎ Norman: 203-264-5605

Gay & bi men. Therapist facilitated. 1st & 3rd Mon.

Orgullo Latino: A Gay/Bi Men's Health Project Hispanic Health Council, 175 Main Street, Hartford, CT 06106 ☎ 860-527-0856

Culturally sensitive AIDS risk reduction programs, outreach, & a support group for Latino men who have sex with men.

Trinity College: EROS (Encouraging Respect of Sexualities) Student Activities, 300 Summit Street, Hartford, CT 06106 ☎ Fatou-Maty Diouf, 860-297-3355 ✉ FatouMaty.Diouf@trincoll.edu 💻 www.trincoll.edu/orgs/eros

Support group for GLBT students, as well as educational outreach to the Trinity community.

University of Connecticut: Lambda Law Student Association School of Law 55 Elizabeth Street, Hartford, CT 06105 ☎ Sandy Goldberg: 860-570-5131

GLBT law students, alumni & allies.

Your Turf Youth Group, Hartford c/o LGB Community Center, 1841 Broad St., Hartford, CT 06114 ☎ Rich: 860-278-4163

Facilitated support & social group for lgbt youth.

"You could move."

Abigail Van Buren, responding in her Dear Abby column to a reader who wrote about a gay couple moving in across the street and asked, How can we improve the quality of the ...neighborhood? (from *The Equal Times*, Denver Colorado)

Wesleyan University

Queer Alliance: *Umbrella organization including:* **LBQ** *(women's social group),* **GBQ** *(men's social group),* **Step One** *(confidential support group for people questioning their sexuality). Brings speakers to campus.* **BGLT Awareness (BiLeGaTA).** **GBLOCQ (Gays, Bisexuals, Lesbians of Color and Questioning):** *Desc: Social group for lgbt people of color at Wesleyan.* All groups c/o Queer Resource Center, c/o WSA, 190 High Street, Middletown, CT 06457; ☎ 860-685-2425; ✉queer@wesleyan.edu

New Haven Gay & Lesbian Community Center PO Box 8914, New Haven, CT ☎/FX: 203-387-2252. ✉ NHGLCCinfo@aol.com 📖 www.i-out.com/nhglcc *Serves the GLBT community; located at 50 Fitch Street in New Haven. Safe place where GLBT people can meet for professional, social services & peer support.* PUB: NHGLCC news

Southern Connecticut State University: LGB Prism Student Center 501 Crescent St., New Haven, CT 06515

Yale University

Lesbian, Gay, Bisexual & Transgendered Cooperative, PO Box 202031, New Haven, CT 06520-2031; ☎ 203-432-1585; ✉ lgbt@yale.edu; 📖 www.yale.edu/lgbt; *Umbrella organization. Sponsors confidential discussion groups & social & educational events. Monitors Yale policies.* **BiWays,** c/o LGBT Cooperative, *Confidential discussion group open to LGBT, straight, curious & questioning men and women. Tu. 9pm in the Wimmin's Center.* **GAYalies,** c/o LGBT Cooperative; *Social/support/discussion group for men to discuss gay/bi issues Sun. 10pm at the Wimmin's Center.* **YaLesbians,** c/o LGBT Cooperative; *Confidential discussion group for all women. Wed. 8pm in the Wimmin's Center.* **PRISM: Queers of Color,** c/o Women's Center Yale Station, Box 2031, New Haven, CT 06520; ☎ 203-432-0388; ✉ erw23@pantheon.yale.edu; *Discussion (& more!) group for queer & questioning people of color. Works to create inter-campus networks with other groups at other colleges & universities.* **Outlaws: LGBT Students' Association at Yale Law School;** , Box 208215, New Haven, CT 06520-8215; ☎ Associate Dean's Office 203-432-7646; ✉ lgblsa@yale.edu; 📖 www.yale.edu/outlaws/; *Holds meetings, sponsors speakers, & travels to conferences & events at the intersection of sexuality & the law.* **Yale Divinity School Gay Lesbian Straight Bisexual Coalition,** 409 Prospect Street, New Haven, CT 06511; ☎ 203-865-8556; ✉ michael.s.thomas@yale.edu. **Pathways Peer Counseling,** c/o LGBT Cooperative. *Counseling hotline for LGBT people. Line open Sun. & Tu. 9pm-midnight during academic year; students may also leave a message at any time.*

BGLAD4YOUTH c/o AIDS Project New Haven, 850 Grand Ave., New Haven, CT 06511 ☎ John Ginnetti: 203-624-0947x232 *Safe space for LGBTQ youth in greater New Haven area to discuss issues of orientation & identity.*

New Haven Youth New Haven, CT ☎ 203-387-2252 *School/community based LGBT youth support group sponsored by the New Haven Gay & Lesbian Community Center. Meets Mon. 4:30-6:30 at the Community Center, 50 Fitch Street.*

Ever notice how so many bisexuals refuse to call themselves bisexual? Many people who lead bisexual lives would rather call themselves nothing at all before calling themselves bi. Now some people are simply anti-label. You ask them why they don't call themselves bisexual, and they tell you that labels are too limiting. That they don't want to exclude themselves from any groups of people. Other people aren't anti-label *per se*, they just don't like the "b" word. They say they can't relate to it, that they don't even know what it means. You even come across certain "extreme" types, who definitely aren't squeamish about labels given that they adopt other stigmatized labels like sado-masochist, anarchist, pagan, or punk, but even THEY wouldn't call themselves bisexual. ... The BLAS, the Bisexual Label Avoidance Syndrome, seems to affect a large segment of the bi population. Now I believe that everyone has the right to label or not to label themselves. We don't need a bunch of people becoming the Label Police. But the consequences of the BLAS-- invisibility, discrimination, biphobia --are truly damaging. Until more of us start taking on the bisexual label, the growth of the bi community and the bi political movement will be stymied.

Lucy Friedland in Bi Women (V7,), Oct-Nov, 1989.

Connecticut College: SOUL (Sexual Orientations United for Liberation) Box 1295, New London, CT 06320 ☎ 860-447-1911 x2896
▣ camel2.conncoll.edu/ccinfo/soul/soul.html

One-in-Ten Youth, New London New London , CT ☎ 860-439-2363
Provides peer and social support to LGBTQ youth in the Greater New London area. Meets twice a month on Sun 4:30-6:00pm in New London.

Connecticut Bisexual Women's Network 77 Myrtle St., Shelton, CT 06484 ☎ 203-922-1058 ✉ msfontaine@juno.com
Support group, social gatherings, bi-monthly publication. Many members married or have male partners. PUB: BiWays (c/o GFontaine msfontaine@juno.com)

University of Connecticut

Rainbow Center, Martha Nelson, Director, U-96, 1315 Storrs Road, Storrs, CT 06269 ☎ 860-486-5821; FX: 860-486-6674; ✉ rnbwdir@uconnvm.uconn.edu; ▣ www.rainbowcenter.uconn.edu. *Provides info, SafeSpace program, educational guest speakers, resource referral, listserv.* **AQUA (Allies & Queers Undergraduate Alliance)**, Box U-8G, 2110 Hillside Rd., Storrs, CT 06268-3008AA, ☎ 860-486-3679; *Student-run group for college community. Focus on educating; social & political components.* **School of Social Work: Lesbian/ Gay/Bisexual Alliance**, 1800 Asylum Av., W. Hartford, CT 06117; ☎ 860-570-9152; FX: 860-241-9786; *Academic & social support group for LGB social work students.*

Biosphere PO Box 270171, West Hartford, CT 06127 ☎ 860-424-4555
✉ biosphere1999@yahoo.com
Day trips, camping, retreats, hiking, film festivals, fun runs, Prides & annual Biosphere weekend adventure for (primarily) Connecticut bisexuals.

Out for Life The Bridge Family Center, 1022 Farmington Ave, West Hartford, CT 06107 ☎ 860-231-8459; 860-521-8035
Biweekly LGBT/Q youth group facilitated by Elliot Strick, MA, LMFT, family therapist. Coming out to family & at school, what it's like being gay/bi, dating, making new friends. Supportive, confidential, no fee.

University of Hartford: Spectrum c/o SGA 200 Bloomfield Ave., West Hartford, CT 06117 ☎ 860-768-5108 ✉ bigalaf@uhavax.hartford.edu
For GLBT students & allies. Weekly meetings, peer counseling, support group, social events, political actions.

Eastern Connecticut State University: ABiGayLe & Friends (the Association of Bisexuals, Gays, Lesbian & Friends) c/o Unity Center,182 High St., Willimantic, CT 06226 ☎ 860-465-4459
Library, peer counseling, dances, National Coming Out Day, homophobia seminars in freshman residence halls.

ATT employee group at the March on Washington, 1993

Robyn Ochs

Delaware

University of Delaware: Lesbian, Gay & Bisexual Student Union Room 304, Perkins Student Center, Academy Street, Newark, DE 19716 ☎ 302-831-8066 ✉ lgbsu-ud@udel.edu
▣ copland.udel.edu/stu-org/lgbsu/
Student organization for lgb people in the local community, with a mailing list for general members. To subscribe, send an e-mail to: majordomo@udel.edu with the words: subscribe lgbsu-list in the message body.

BGLAD: Bisexuals, Gays, Lesbians and Allies at DuPont PO Box 2192, Wilmington, DE 19899-2192 ☎ 302-571-9112
✉ BGLAD.BGLAD@usa.DuPont.com
▣ www.dupontbglad.com
For LGB & ally DuPont employees.

Gay Lesbian & Bisexual Youth Social Group Wilmington, DE ☎ 302-652-6776 or 1-800-810-6776
Meets Sat. 1-4pm.

Cautious, careful people, always casting about to preserve their reputation and social standing, can never bring about a reform. Those who are really in earnest must be willing to be anything or nothing in the world's estimation, and publicly and privately, in season and out, avow their sympathies with despised and persecuted ideas and their advocates, and bear the consequences.

Susan B. Anthony

PFLAG of Northern Delaware PO Box 26049, Wilmington, DE 19899 ☎ 302-654-2995 ✉ travelcompany@worldnet.att.net 🖳 www.pflag.org
Local chapter of national organization which promotes the health & well-being of GLBT People & their friends & families.

District of Columbia

BiNetwork DC [DC Metropolitan Area] PO Box 7657, Langley Park, MD 20787-7657 ☎ Activities recording: 202-828-3080 ✉ bndc@obscure.org 🖳 www.bndc.org
Social & support group for bisexuals & our friends in the Washington DC Metropolitan area, including MD & Northern VA. We sponsor parties, potlucks, & various subgroups, including a women's group & BiPOC, Bisexual People Of Color. PUB: Side Bi Side, *our quarterly newsletter*

BiNetwork DC - e-mail list Washington, DC ✉ greg@ogburn.net 🖳 www.bndc.org
Listserv providing online social space for members of the BiNetwork DC & our friends. Also sponsors a weekly chat room. Please visit our website for more info .

Bisexual Insurgence PO Box 33662, Washington, DC 20033-3662 ☎ 202-518-1158; 301-891-7428 ✉ bi_insurgence@yahoo.com 🖳 www.bisexualinsurgence.org
Local activist group w/mission to increase bisexual visibility within the gay & straight communities through demonstrations, media campaigns, educational outreach, lobbying, & direct action.

Bi Women's Cultural Alliance PO Box 2254, Washington, DC 20013-2254 ☎ 202-828-3065 🖳 members.tripod.com/~BiWCA
"Monogamous, duogomous, traditional, feminist. Not for s/m, polyamorous." Groups include: Jewish Women's Spirituality Group; Bi Women's Dinner.

At the March on Washington, 1993

The Washington Blade 1408 U St. NW, 2nd floor, Washington, DC 20009-3916 ☎ 202-797-7000 🖳 www.washblade.com
GLBT weekly newspaper. Covers local, national, & int'l news.

Lambda Sci-Fi: DC Area Gaylaxians PO Box 656, Washington, DC 20044 ☎ 202-232-3141 🖳 www.lambdasf.org
For fans of science fiction & horror. Live long & prosper!

Pride At Work, AFL-CIO, Baltimore-Washington Chapter c/o 501 Third Street, NW, Suite 200, Washington, DC 20001-2797 ☎ 202-637-5085 ✉ prideatwork@yahoo.com 🖳 www.prideatwork.org
Works within the the LGBT community for a better understanding of the trade union movement; to work within the labor movement to foster better understanding of the needs of LGBT union members; and to work to organize the vast majority of unorganized LGBT workers into the trade union movement. PUB: Pride At Work *Newsletter (Newsletter w/membership ($25 per year). Donations welcome! No one denied membership for lack of funds.)*

Asian/Pacific Islander Queer Sisters (APIQS) Washington, DC ☎ 202-483-0236 ✉ patayaann@hotmail.com
Social/support group, creates a space for Asian & Pacific Islander Queer women through potlucks, discussion, poetry slams, rap sessions.

Black & White Men Together PO Box 73111, Washington, DC 20056 ☎ 202-452-9173 ✉ bwmtdc@hotmail.com 🖳 www.bwmtdc.org
Black & white gay men work together to understand racial & cultural differences & celebrate diversity.

Black Lesbian Support Group c/o Whitman-Walker Clinic, 1407 S St. NW, Washington, DC 20009 ☎ 202-797-3593 ✉ blsg@blsg.org 🖳 www.blsg.org
Social/cultural discussion & support group for black lesbian/bi women. Meets 2nd & 4th Sat. 3-5pm. Over 35 group meets 1st Sat. at above.

Khush - DC PO Box 53149, Temple Heights Station, Washington, DC 20009 ☎ 202-728-3870 ✉ khushdc@geocities.com 🖳 www.geocities.com/WestHollywood/4786/
For South Asian LGB people in the DC Metro area. Monthly meetings 1st Sat.

American University: Gay, Lesbian, Bi, Transgender & Ally Resource Center 226 Mary Graydon Center, 4400 Massachusetts Ave, NW, Washington, DC 20016-8164 ☎ 202-885-3347 FX: 202-885-3354 ✉ glbta@american.edu 🖳 www.american.glbta
Undergraduate group. Open 9-6 for students to relax, study, & socialize. Lending library with current subscriptions. Join their listserve by calling 202-885-3346 & leaving a message.

George Washington University: Lesbian, Gay, Bisexual Alliance c/o Student Activities, 800 21st. St. NW, Box 16, Washington, DC 20057 ✉ gwpride@gwu.edu
Open to the public, support, social, awareness.

Georgetown University Pride Washington, DC ☎ 202-687-5558
Fosters greater awareness of glb legal issues.

Sexual Minority Youth Assistance League (SMYAL) 410 7th St. SE, Washington, DC 20003 ☎ 202-546-5940 (ofc); 202-546-5911 (talk line) FX: 202-544-1306 ✉ smyal@aol.com 🖳 www.smyal.org
Youth 13-21; Free. Open for drop-ins M-F 3-8pm & Sat. 1-4. Computer & resource center, support groups including youth of color group. Anonymous HIV testing available.

Interweave: All Souls for LGB Concerns (Unitarian-Universalist) c/o All Souls Unitarian Church, 16th & Harvard Street, NW, Washington, DC 20009 ☎ 202-332-5266 🖳 www.all-souls.org

Whitman-Walker Clinic 1407 S St., NW, Washingon, DC 20009 ☎ 202-797-3500; TTY: 939-1528 ✉ wwcinfo@wwc.org 🖳 www.wwc.org
Non-profit volunteer GL community health organization serving the DC metro area. Open to anyone in need of HIV-related services. Includes Lesbian Services Program, offering supportive, culturally-sensitive & caring services addressing the mental & physical health needs of lesbians, bi women, all women who partner with women, & transgender individuals (lsp90@aol.com).

US Helping US, People Into Living, Inc. 811 L St., SE, Washington, DC 20003 ☎ 202-546-8200 FX: 202-546-4511 ✉ uhpil@erols.com 🖳 www.ushelpingus.org
HIV/AIDS prevention, outreach & support services for African-American gay & bi men. Website, Support groups, group & individual psychotherapy, holistic health workshops, & community theatre & forums.

Florida

Florida Atlantic University: Lambda United 777 Glades Road -UC, Boca Raton, FL 33431 ☎ 561-394-2712 FX: 561-394-0488 ✉ info@lambdaunited.com 🖳 www.lambdaunited.com/
Active student organization.

University of Miami at Coral Gables: Gay, Lesbian & Bisexual Community Smith-Tucker Involvement Center, University Center, Room 209, Coral Gables, FL 33124 ☎ 305-284-4505 FX: 305-284-5987 ✉ umglbc@umiami.ir.miami.edu

BiNet Fort Lauderdale Fort Lauderdale, FL ☎ GLCC: 954-563-9500 🖳 www.bicafe.com/Info/I199905038.asp
Bi Support Group meets 1st & 3rd Wed at the new GLCC Community Center at 1717 N. Andrews Ave.

"Your Fence is Sitting on Me" at March on Washington,

Bisexual Community Building Group c/o GLCC, 1717 N. Andrews Av., Fort Lauderdale, FL 33311 ☎ Michael Page 954-581-5001; GLCC: 954-463-9005; FX: 954-764-6522 🖳 www.glccftl.org
1st & 3rd Wed. 7:30 at Center. Also thru the Center: Lesbian & Bi Spirituality & Support Gp.; GLBT youth groups; Girth & Mirth; Front Runner; coming out groups,

Gainesville Bisexual Alliance PO Box 14151, Gainesville, FL 32604-2151 ☎ 904-335-6359 🖳 www.afn.org/~bialli/

University of Florida at Gainesville: Lesbian, Gay, Bisexual Student Union 300-48 J. Wayne , Reitz Union, Gainesville, FL 32611-8505 ☎ 352-392-1665 x.326 ✉ pride@sg.ufl.edu 🖳 sg.ufl.edu/pride
Weekly bisexual discussion groups; library; roommate referral; speakers' bureau; lectures; film festivals; speak outs.

University of North Florida: Gay, Lesbian Bisexual Association Student Services, Bldg. 14, 18000 UNF Drive, Jacksonville, FL 32224 ✉ glba@unf.edu 🖳 www.unf.edu/groups/glba/

GLBT Youth of Miami PO Box 014340, Miami, FL 33101 ☎ 305-571-9601 FX: 305-571-9602 🖳 www.pridelines.org/
Weekly support groups for youth 13-26, annual prom for glbt youth. One of the groups sponsoring the Sun Conference (annual youth conference for all of Florida) & dances, movie nights. Adult volunteers facilitate support groups & assist at events. Mtg. spaces in downtown Miami & Kendall.

I am bisexual. I am not confused. I am confusing. I am sorry if you are confused by that.

Michael Langlois

BiWays, Orlando c/o GLBCC (below), Orlando, FL ✉ krisr@biways.org 🖳 www.biways.org
Meets Mon. 7pm at the GLBCC.

Gay Lesbian Bisexual Community Center 946 N. Mills Ave., PO Box 533446, Orlando, FL
☎ 407-228-8272 FX: 407-228-8230 🖳 glbcc.org/
M-Th 11-9; F 11-6; Sat 12-7; Sun 12-5. Sponsors several groups, including BiWays & Rainbow Connection.

Rainbow Connection Orlando, FL ☎ G/L Community Center: 403-843-4297
Social/discussion group for glb people 18-25.

Gay/Bi Married Men's Group Orlando, FL
☎ 407-777-9833

University of Central Florida: Gay, Lesbian, Bisexual Student Union c/o Student Activities, PO BOX 163245, Orlando, FL 32816-3245
✉ ucfglbsu@ucf.edu 🖳 pegasus.cc.ucf.edu/~ucfglbsu/

Delta Youth Alliance c/o Gay & Lesbian Community Services of Central Florida, Inc., 714 East Colonial Drive, Orlando, FL 32803
☎ 407-843-4297 ; GLCS: 407-425-4527
Explicitly includes bisexual people. Rap group Mon. at 6. Ages 13-19.

University of West Florida: Queer Student Union 11000 University Parkway, Pensacola, FL 32514
☎ Adviser: 850-474-2923 ✉ Global@uwf.edu
🖳 www.uwf.edu/global/?ti2Xdw=www.uwf.edu/~global/
Student group. Weekly meetings during termtime.

Florida State University: Lesbian, Gay, Bisexual Transgender Student Union FSU Student Gov't Assoc. , A205 Oglesby Student Union, Tallahassee, FL 32306-4027 ☎ 850-644-8804
✉ lgbtsu@admin.fsu.edu 🖳 www.fsu.edu/~activity/sga/lgbtsu/
Discussion groups, library, educational services, roommate referral service, open to everyone.

The Family Tree: A Lesbian, Gay, Bisexual, Transgender Community Center 1406 Hays Street, #4 (32301), PO Box 38477, Tallahassee, FL 32315 ☎ 850-222-8555 FX: 850-222-4211
✉ staff@familytreecenter.org
🖳 www.familytreecenter.org
Peer & phone counseling, support groups, youth program, social events, community education, resource library, diversity activism, monthly newsletter, website, community outreach. PUB: Branching Out

Compass: The Gay & Lesbian Community Services Center of Palm Beach County 1700 North Dixie Hwy, West Palm Beach, FL 33407
☎ Main/TDD: 561-833-3638; Teen Line: 561-833-8388 FX: 561-833-4941 ✉ CompassWPB@aol.com
🖳 www.gopbi.com/community/groups/compassWPB/
Support, educational, social & referral services to the lgb community of W. Palm Beach. Programs include: HOPE (youth group); SAGE (Senior Group); PFLAG, 12-step groups, HIV services; lesbian & gender social/support groups.

Georgia

West Georgia Gay & Lesbian Resource Center GA ✉ atheist@bravenet.net
🖳 www.truthtree.com/westga
Non-profit, 100% volunteer social & political organization in west Georgia. Our services include personal ads, chat rooms, message boards, & local community information.

University of Georgia: Lambda Alliance 325 Tate Student Center, Athens, GA 30602 ☎ 770-549-9368 ✉ lambda@uga.edu 🖳 www.uga.edu/lambda/
Social, educational, speakers bureau. Open to the public. Other campus group: GLOBES *(GLB Employees & Supporters): organization for LGB faculty & staff as well as students (PO Box 7864, Athens, Ga. 30604 or call 546-4611).*

Classic City Youth Athens, GA ☎ 404-546-4611
✉ support@athenseen.org
🖳 www.athenseen.org/
Athens' lgb youth group. Support network for teens dealing with sexuality issues. Meets Sat. 2 pm at the Presbyterian Student Center (1250 South Lumpkin St.). Social & recreational programs.

BiNet Atlanta PO Box 5240, Atlanta, GA 31107
☎ 404-256-8992 ✉ binet@mindspring.com
🖳 www.mindspring.com/~binet/
Social events & discussion group.

Some folks say that bisexuals are not oppressed because at least we are accepted by mainstream society when we are involved with members of the opposite sex. Agreed, society may like us when we show that piece of who we are. But conditional acceptance is not really acceptance at all. When we show our other side, our gay side, we suffer the same discrimination as other gay men and lesbians. We don't lose only half our children in custody battles. When homophobia hits, we don't get just half fired from our jobs (put on half time, perhaps?). We don't get just half gaybashed when we are out with our same-sex lovers (oh please, only hit me on my left side. You see, I'm not gay, I'm bisexual!). We, too, get discriminated against because we are gay.

Robyn Ochs

Color Bi Numbers Atlanta, GA ☎ 404-881-1985 ⊠ colorbinumbers@geocities.com 🖳 www.geocities.com/WestHollywood/Park/6927/
Social network of bi men, women & couples of all races coming together to celebrate diversity while networking & socializing. We are African American, Asian, Latin & bi-racial people who welcome all people of color & those who enjoy relating to people of color. Meets 1st Fri. 7:30 at Lambda Center, 828 West Peachtree St.

Emory University: Office of Lesbian/Gay/Bisexual Life Dobbs Univ. Center 246E, Atlanta, GA 30322 ☎ 404-727-0272 ⊠ schesnu@emory.edu 🖳 www.emory.edu/LGBOFFICE/
Programs & services to improve the campus climate & create an open & welcoming environment for lgbt students & employees. Two listservs, LGBannounce & EmoryGLB, provide access to info and information-plus-discussion, respectively, about current lgb events/issues. To subscribe, send subscription request to listserv@listserv.emory.edu.

Georgia State University: Alliance of GLBT Students Box 1831, Atlanta, GA 30303 ☎ 404-651-4741

Georgia Tech: Gay & Lesbian Alliance 350291 Georgia Tech Station , Atlanta, GA 30322-1550 ☎ 404-894-5849 ⊠ gala@gatech.edu 🖳 cyberbuzz.gatech.edu/gala/
Support, acceptance & friendship among peers. Also on campus: OUTTECH, a forum for discussing issues of concern to glbt employees of Georgia Tech & for developing strategies to improve the campus climate.

State University of West Georgia: Gay, Bisexual & Straight Alliance Carrollton, GA 30118 ☎ Mark Faucette, advisor: 770-836-4344 ⊠ galawgc@westga.edu 🖳 www.westga.edu/~galawgc/
Campus group. Weekly meetings. Open to others in the Carrollton area.

The Zacchaeus Society PO Box 447, Covington, GA 30015 ☎ 404-522-1444
Confidential outreach to the straight & glbt citizens of Rockdale & Newton counties. Services: referrals, visiting the sick, counseling, education of the straight & gay community, emotional & spiritual support (including family support) A non-profit, volunteer program. Monthly meetings.

Agnes Scott College: Lesbians, Bisexuals & Allies 141 East College Avenue, Box 501, Decatur, GA 30030 ☎ 404-638-6614
Creates comfortable & safe space for l/b members of the Agnes Scott Community & strives to educate the campus about lbg issues & to raise consciousness & promote acceptance.

Youth Pride 302 E. Howard Ave., Decatur, GA 30030 ☎ 404-378-6175 ⊠ info@youthpride.org 🖳 www.youthpride.org/

> **"There's a lot of pressure on me to toe the line. Dykes say I waffle, but I can only be myself.... I don't care so much about labels. To me, there's not a big line down the middle of the human race. I mean, how much more out can I be?"**
>
> —Ani DiFranco, interview in Deneuve Jan/Feb 1995.

Armstrong Atlantic State University: Unity & Diversity League 11935 Abercorn Ext., Savannah, GA 31419 🖳 www.armstrong.edu/Activities/Clubs/UDL/udl.html

Georgia Southern University: Triangle PO Box 12491, Statesboro, GA 30460 ☎ 871-1723

Valdosta State College: Gay & Lesbian Association c/Doug Carver, VSC Box 7097, Valdosta, GA 31698 ☎ 912-247-0181 ⊠ dcarver@grits.valdosta.peachnet.edu
Inclusive of bi folks.

Hawaii

Bisexual Network PO Box 2022, Kaua'i, HI 96746 ☎ 808-821-1690 ⊠ evolved@aloha.net

Lambda Aloha PO Box 921, Kapa'a/Kaua'i, HI 96746 ☎ 808-822-7171 ⊠ lambda@aloha.net; evolved@aloha.net 🖳 www.aloha.net/~lambda
Excellent on line listing of Hawaii's resources at: Gay Kuai'i Online: http://www.aloha.net/~lambda/not4prof.htm.

Civil Unions - Civil Rights Movement, Honolulu, HI 96828 ☎ 808-951-7000; 808-944-4598 ⊠ info@civilunions-civilrights.org 🖳 www.civilunions-civilrights.org
Statewide coalition of glbt & allies, organizations/institutions to achieve equality & justice for glbt citizens in Hawaii. A project of Marriage Project - Hawaii.

Gay & Lesbian Community Center 2424 Beretania St., PO Box 22719, Honolulu, HI 96823-2718 ☎ 808 951 7000 FX: 808-951-7240 ⊠ GLCC-News@juno.com
Library, support groups, speakers bureau, Marriage Project Hawaii.

Na Mamo O Hawai'i (Hawai'ian Lesbian &Gay Activists) Honolulu, HI ☎ 808-595-0402 ⊠ lgomes@hawaii.edu
Group dedicated to fighting racism in the Gay Community AND homophobia in the Hawai'ian Community.

University of Hawaii, Honolulu: Gay/Lesbian/Bisexual 'Ohana Honolulu, HI ☎ 808-955-6152

Gay-Lesbian 'Ohana Maui PO Box 5042, Kahului / Maui, HI 96733 ☎ 808-244-4566 🖳 maui-tech.com/glom/
Education, outreach, political action, health & social agenda.

Both Sides Now, Inc. PO Box 5042, Maui, HI 96733 ☎ 808 244 4566
Dances, picnics, women's gatherings & other social events.

Bridges: LesBiGayTrans Questioning Youth Group Maui Lesbian/Gay Youth Project, Suite 171, Box 356, Paia, HI 96779 ☎ 575-2681 or 573-1093
Weekly support group in Wailuku. Education & outreach to adults working with LGBT youth, classroom presentations, & a speakers bureau. Information, referrals, & confidential phone contact for youth exploring their sexual identity.

Idaho

Diversity Online: Idaho's Gay, Lesbian, Bi & Trans News PO Box 323, Boise, ID 83701 ☎ 208-323-0805 FX: 208-323-0805 ✉ editor@tcc-diversity.com 🖳 www.tcc-diversity.com/diversityhome.htm
Also available in print.

Online Listing of GLBT Resources in Idaho ID 🖳 www.geocities.com/WestHollywood/2025/org.htm

Boise Bisexual Network PO Box 15471, Boise, ID 83715 ☎ 208-331-1101
Random meetings & social events.

The Community Center 919-A N. 27th, Boise, ID 83702 ☎ 208-336-3870
Meeting center & referrals. Game night 2nd & 4th Mon. 7pm. Movie Night Tu. 7:15pm.

Your Family Friends & Neighbors PO Box 768, Boise, ID 83701 ☎ 208-344-4295 ✉ yffn@yffn.org 🖳 www.yffn.org
A nonprofit 501 (c)(3) grass-roots organizing corporation promoting respect, understanding, & tolerance for lgb people.

Mark Silver (then editor of *Anything that Moves*) & Robyn Ochs at Creating Change Conference, 1997

Ada County Human Rights Task Force Boise, ID 83701 ☎ 208-388-8213

Idaho Log Cabin Republicans 1117 Kimberly Lane, Boise, ID 83712 ☎ 208-331-7873

Treasure Valley Pride Association Boise, ID ☎ Rob Wetzel: 208-853-2551 🖳 www.pridedepot.com
Pride Festival planning organization.

Triangle Connection: Bi, Gay & Lesbian Social Group PO Box 503, Boise, ID 83701 ☎ 208-939-1627

Victims of Hate Crimes Support Committee Boise, ID ☎ Leslie Drake: 208-375-8712

Women's Night PO Box 768, Boise, ID 83701 ☎ 208-344-4295 box3 ✉ womensnight@yahoo.com 🖳 www.idahowomen.org
Music, art, theatre & outdoor activities for women.

Boise Gay Couples Supper Club Boise, ID ☎ 208-853-1110 🖳 www.idahodesigns.com/bgcg
Social group for glbt couples in Boise & surrounding areas. Last Sat. at a member's house.

Spontaneous Productions Boise, ID ☎ 208-368-0405 🖳 www.idahodesigns.com/sponprod
LGBT theater company.

Boise State University: Bisexual, Gay & Lesbian Allies for Diversity (B-GLAD) Boise, ID 83725 ☎ Mike Esposito: 208-426-1590 FX: 208-426-1391 ✉ mesposit@boisestate.edu
Meets weekly during termtime on campus. Open to the public.

PFLAG Boise/Treasure Valley 3773 Cayuga Place, Boise, ID 83709 ☎ 208-362-5316; Helpline: 208-362-5397 ✉ rhgarrison@aol.com

Treasure Valley PFLAG 3773 Cayuga Place, Boise, ID 83709 ✉ Rbarr83703@earthlink.net
Meetings at the Southminister Presbyterian Church 6500 Overland Rd. in Boise 2nd Fri. 7:30-9pm. Dues $30.00 a year or $35.00/couple.

Treasure Valley Metropolitan Community Church at Boise 408 N. Garden Street, Boise, ID 83702 ☎ 208-342-6764 🖳 www.aol.com/tvmcc
Inclusive church services Sun. 5:45pm.

Youth Alliance for Diversity Boise, ID ✉ yad@yffn.org
Support & social group for youths & their allies.

PFLAG Caldwell 1415 Filmore, Caldwell, ID 83605 ☎ 208-459-9535

PFLAG Coeur d'Alene PO Box 1444, Hayden Lake, ID 83835 ☎ 208-765-8209 ✉ pflagcda@geocities.com 🖳 www.icehouse.net/sysrq/pflag/indexjq.html

Inland Northwest Gay People's Alliance PO Box 8135, Moscow, ID 83843 ☎ 208-882-8034
Meetings 2x/month. Newsletter.

PFLAG Mountain Home Route 2 Box 488, Mountain Home, ID 83647 ☎ 208-587-5497

PFLAG New Meadow/McCall 3196 Branstetter Lane, New Meadows, ID 83654 ☎ 208-347-2681 ✉ gkimball@ctcweb.net

Idaho State University Bisexuals Gays Lesbians & Allies for Diversity Pocatello, ID ☎ 208-238-7402 🖳 www.isu.edu/departments/isubglad *University Club.*

PFLAG Sandpoint/Bonner County 214 Churchill Road, Sagle, ID 83860 ☎ 208-255-1506 ✉ redog@televar.com

PFLAG Twin Falls/Magic Valley c/o Alex Herzinger, 143 Pierce St, Twin Falls ID 83301 ☎ Connie: 208-733-9172 ✉ pflag@magiclink.com 🖳 www.magiclink.com/web/axellh

Illinois

Chicago

Chicagoland Bisexual Network PO Box 14385, Chicago, IL 60614-0385 ☎ 312-458-0983 🖳 www.bisexual.org/chicagoland/ *Includes: Bi Womyn's Discussion Group; Bi Men's Discussion Group; Bi PAAC; Bi Socials (1st Saturdays).* PUB: *Bi...the Way (bi monthly newsletter includes local calendar & local & national news. Submissions welcome.)*

Bi PAAC Chicago, IL ☎ 312-458-0983 *Bisexual Political Action/Awareness Coalition.*

BAM - Bisexual AOL Members Chicago, IL ☎ 773-908-9054 *Bi social group. Meets monthly.*

Windy City Times 1115 W. Belmont, Chicago, IL 60657 🖳 www.outlineschicago.com *Weekly free LGBT newspaper. Includes other publications from same publisher: Blacklines (monthly), En La Vida (monthly), Nightlines (weekly events listing).*

Alternative Phone Book 619 W. Stratford Pl. #406, Chicago, IL 60657-2643 ☎ 773-472-6319 ✉ yellow@xsite.net 🖳 www.prairienet.org/apb *LGB community listings, updated twice a year. Distributed free of charge throughout Chicago. Also available on the Web.*

OutChicago: GLBT Electronic Resources Consortium Chicago, IL ✉ webmaster@outchicago.org 🖳 www.outchicago.org/index.html

Lesbigay Radio/WDNZ AM750 Chicago, IL ☎ 1-888-WE-ARE-GAY 🖳 www.lesbigayradio.com/ *5-7pm CST. Can be listened to on the radio or online.*

CrossRoads Chicago, IL ☎ 773-866-8824 *Support group for married bi men.*

Going On Chicago, IL ☎ 708-524-1323 *Support group for wives of gay & bi men.*

Spouse's Group Chicago, IL ☎ 847-299-1658 *Support group for straight spouses of gay/bi people. Suburban Chicago area.*

Affinity 5650 S. Woodlawn Ave, Lower Level, Chicago, IL 60637 ☎ 773-324-0377 ✉ affinity95@aol.com 🖳 www.affinity95.org *Serving black lesbian & bi women, many ongoing events & presentations, Social & support & informational. Drop-in center with library.*

AXIOS! c/o 5601 N. Sheridan, #5-B, Chicago, IL 60660 ☎ 773-271-1027 *LGB's of Greek or Eastern Orthodox heritage.*

Amigas Latinas lesbianas/bisexuales Chicago, IL ☎ 312-409-5697 *For Latina lesbians/bisexuals.*

Harambe Jahard Chicago, IL ☎ 773-492-2055 *suburban African-American bi & gay men's support group.*

Imani/Umoja Chicago, IL ☎ 773-907-8993 *Gay & bi African-American men's support group.*

SANGAT Chicago PO Box 268463, Chicago, IL 60626 ☎ 773-506-8810 FX: 773-271-4024 ✉ youngal@aol.com; sangat@juno.com 🖳 hometown.aol.com/youngal/sangat.html *LGBT organization & support group for people from India, Pakistan, Bangladesh, Sri Lanka, Nepal, Afghanistan, Iran, Burma & other South Asian countries. Non-profit organization for international brotherhood/sisterhood for peace & harmony, regardless of sexual orientation, religious or boundaries of the country. Monthly dinner- call for info.*

All of us--bisexuals, lesbians, gay men, and heterosexuals--have the right to exist and to choose whom we will love. In answer to the question, "Are you gay or straight?" bisexual activists have begun to challenge this artificial polarization and create a lifetime identity that need not change with the gender of our lovers. Honesty demands flexibility, and by dissolving the barriers created by old static categories, all of us can focus less on our own differences and more on our common goals of political empowerment. Bisexuals are not fence sitters. There *is* no fence. Instead of a fence, we see a field, with mostly lesbian and gay people on one side and mostly heterosexual people on the other. ... Sometimes we travel toward one end or the other--in a day, in a year, or in a lifetime.

Robyn Ochs and Marcia Deihl, "Moving Beyond Binary Thinking" in Homophobia: How We All Pay the Price.

> **"Our national debates over issues of equality and tolerance must not be restricted to 'gay and straight' issues, but broadened to include bisexual people in our human community. When our leaders include bisexual people's needs in public policy and public comment, when our communities and families welcome a complex understanding of sexuality, when members of the gay, lesbian, and transgender community appreciate and understand the experiences of their bisexual neighbors - when our society acts with intelligence and compassion, we are all made greater."**
>
> NGLTF Executive Director Elizabeth Toledo, September 2000.

DePaul University: Pride DePaul Programs & Organizations Office, , 2nd Fl. Stuart Ctr., 2311 N. Clifton Av., Chicago, IL 60614-3212 ☎ 773-687-2000x4041 ✉ pride@condor.depaul.edu 🖳 www.depaul.edu/~pride/
For glbtq & ally students.

Illinois Institute of Technology: Gay, Lesbian, Bisexual Student Alliance 3241 S. Federal Street, Chicago, IL 60616 ☎ 312-808-6400 ✉ glbsa@charlie.cns.iit.edu 🖳 www.iit.edu/~glbsa/
Student group.

Loyola University: Gay, Lesbian & Bisexual Alliance Centenial Forum-Student Union, 6525 N. Sheridan Road, Box #25, Chicago, IL 60626 ☎ 773-973-6910312-915-6502 ✉ glaba@luc.edu 🖳 www.luc.edu/orgs/glaba/
Offers support & a safe place of LGB & friends to gather together.

Northeastern Illinois University: GLBA 5500 N. St. Louis Ave, Chicago, IL 60625

University of Chicago: Queers & Associates 5706 S University Ave Rm 004 , Chicago, IL 60637 ☎ 773-702-9734 FX: 773-702-7718 ✉ qa@listhost.uchicago.edu 🖳 gay-lesbian.uchicago.edu/
For queers & allies on campus. "queer by nature, nerds by choice" "not just for College students — we're open to students in the Divisions & Professional Schools & to faculty & staff."

University of Illinois, Chicago

Office of Gay, Lesbian, Bisexual & Transgender Concerns, 1007 W Harrison St 1180 BSB, Chicago, IL 60607-7140, ☎ 312-413-8619, FX: 312-996-4688; ✉ oglbc@uic.edu; 🖳 www.uic.edu/depts/quic/oglbc, *Open M-F 8:30-4:45.* **Pride,** 750 S. Halsted, M/C 118, Chicago, IL 60608, ☎ 312-996-4424, ✉ pride@uic.edu, 🖳 www2.uic.edu/stud_orgs/pride/. *LGB student organization providing social, educational & supportive services as well as events for the UIC community.*

Horizons Community Services 961 W. Montana Avenue, Chicago, IL 60614 ☎ 773-472-6469 FX: 773-472-6643 ✉ horizons@horizonsonline.org 🖳 www.horizonsonline.org
Youth services, counseling, support groups, anti-violence project, legal services, speakers service.

Other Illinois

Prairie Flame PO Box 2483, Springfield, IL 62705 ✉ pflame@eosinc.com
Monthly LGBT newspaper covering Central Illinois.

Aurora University: GLOBAl (Gay, Lesbian, Bisexual, Transgender & our Allies League) 347 South Gladstone, Aurora, IL 60506 ☎ 630/844-5789
Student support/social group; meets twice a month (one closed meeting & one open meeting)

Advocacy Council for Human Rights PO Box 5048, Bloomington, IL 61702-5048 ☎ 309-830-2521 FX: 309-827-0456 ✉ achr@mailcity.com 🖳 www.angelfire.com/il2/achr/
The Rainbow Connection (Monthly newsletter mailed to 300+ individuals & businesses.)

Woman at March on Washington, 1993

Southern Illinois University: Saluki Rainbow Network c/o Office of Student Development, Mailcode 4425, Carbondale, IL 62901-4425 ☎ 618-453-5151 M-F 5-9pm 🖳 www.siu.edu/~glbf/
For people on campus & in the larger community.

Community Members Against Discrimination PO Box 852, DeKalb, IL 60115 ☎ 815-748-6415
CMAD advocates on public policy issues concerning LGBT people in DeKalb & beyond.

Northern Illinois University

Lesbian Gay Bisexual Transgender Programs, c/o Programming & Activities, Northern Illinois University, DeKalb, IL 60115, ☎ 815-753-2235, FX: 815-753-2905; ✉ mcook@niu.edu, 🖳 www.niu.edu/lgbt/,
Provides educational materials on LGBT life & culture & offers info, support, & referral to LGBT individuals, support & advocacy for LGBT students, educational programs, speakers bureau, & consultation with organizations for enhancing LGBT services. **Prism: Lesbian, Gay, Bisexual, Transgender & Allies Coalition**, Campus Life Building, 190M, DeKalb, IL 60115, ☎ 815-753-0584, ✉ PrismNIU@gay.com, 🖳 www.geocities.com/WestHollywood/2222/,
Provides a support network & positive social outlets for the LGBT & ally communities of Northern Illinois University & the surrounding area. Info, social activities & referrals for educational, legal, civic & counseling concerns for the LGBTA community, & educational activities & services about LGBT topics to all interested persons within & outside the university community. **Northern Pride**, c/o LGBT Programs. *Social support network for LGBT faculty & staff.* **Fruit Cocktail**, c/o LGBT Programs. *Informal social network for LGBT graduate, law, & non-traditional students.* **Presidential Committee on Sexual Orientation**, Office of General Counsel, Northern Illinois University, DeKalb, IL 60115, ☎ 815-753-8365, ✉ norden@niu.edu, 🖳 www.niu.edu/pcso. *Monitors campus climate issues for LGBT students, faculty, & staff, & makes recommendations to the University President regarding needed changes in policies, programs, & services.* **Safe Zone Program**, c/o LGBT Programs. *Creates a visible network of allies to provide support, info, & referral to LGBT people, & to contribute to a positive campus climate.*

Project Alliance PO Box 852, DeKalb, IL 60115 ☎ 815-748-6415
Community outreach organization, providing opportunities for community service & social interaction for LGBT people & their allies.

Gay & Lesbian Association of Decatur PO Box 3783, Decatur, IL 62524 ☎ 217/422-3277 FX: 217-422-3277 ✉ GLAD@GLADdecatur.org
Gay/Lesbian social group. PUB: GLAD Newsletter (Eight-page newsletter for Gay community)

Millikin University: Gay, Lesbian, & Allies' Association of Millikin Office of Student Programs, RTUC, 1184 W. Main St., Decatur, IL 62522 ☎ 217-424-3541 FX: 217-424-3544 ✉ glaam@mail.millikin.edu 🖳 www.millikin.edu/campuslife.orgs/glaam/
Committed to dismantling oppression in all forms, provides safe space, support, & council for glbt & questioning students & allies. Facilitates discussion for the student body, faculty, staff & administration on issues pertinent to the Community. Numerous activities.

DuPage Questioning Youth Center 900 Ogden Avenue, Suite 326, Downers Grove, IL 60515 ☎ 630-415-2053 ✉ QYCExec2@aol.com 🖳 www.dupageqyc.com
Weekly drop-in centers in Hinsdale, Naperville, Aurora & Woodstock.

PFLAG Hinsdale PO Box 103, Downers Grove, IL 60516 ☎ 630-968-9060; 630-415-0622 🖳 www.dpliv.com/pflag

Northwestern University Gay & Lesbian University Union (GLUU) c/o Campus Activities Office, Norris Univ. Center, 1999 South Campus Drive, Evanston, IL 60208-2500 ✉ gluu@nwu.edu 🖳 www.nwu.edu/gluu/index.html
Providing education on BLG issues, social opportunities, coming out support & activism for GLB grad students, faculty & staff.

Northwestern University

Northwestern BGALA, 1999 South Campus Drive, Northwestern University, Evanston, IL 60208, ☎ 847-491-2375, ✉ bgala@northwestern.edu, 🖳 www.studorg.northwestern.edu/bgala, DESC: *Multifaceted university umbrella organization providing social opportunities, coming out support, education & activism for the campus LGBTQSA community. Also sponsors a bisexual discussion group called* **BIONIC**. **QWYR (Queer Women You Rock)**, c/o M. Phillips, 614 Clark Street Apt 3e, Evanston, IL 60201, ☎ 847-869-8465 ✉ chelle@nwu.edu, *Social group for queer women - in the closet or out of it. Providing social opportunities, coming out support & activism for GLB female grad students, faculty & staff.*

> **Freedom and justice cannot be parceled out in pieces to suit political convenience. Like martin, I don't believe you can stand for freedom for one group and deny it to others.**
>
> Coretta Scott King

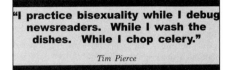

> **"I practice bisexuality while I debug newsreaders. While I wash the dishes. While I chop celery."**
>
> *Tim Pierce*

Affirmation: United Methodists for Lesbian/Gay/ Bisexual Concerns PO Box 1021, Evanston, IL 60204 ☎ 847-733-9590 ✉ umaffirmation@yahoo.com 🖳 www.umaffirm.org/
Independent, not-for-profit organization with no official ties to The United Methodist Church. Affirmation is 100% supported by contributions from interested individuals. PUB: Affirmation Newsletter (All contributors of $25 or more considered members & will receive the quarterly newsletter.)

Knox College: Gay, Lesbian & Bisexual Community Alliance Mailbox K-1648, Galesburg, IL 61401 ✉ mbonilla@knox.knox.edu 🖳 knox.knox.edu:5718/~glbcawww/
Student organization offering support & raising awareness.

PFLAG Glenview 332 Wright Court, Libertyville, IL 60048 ☎ 773-472-3079 (helpline number) ✉ pflagw@aol.com 🖳 www.PFLAG.org (has link to chapter info)
Meets monthly for support, education & advocacy.

Western Illinois University: Bisexuals, Lesbians, Gays, & Friends SOC Union, 1 University Circle, Macomb, IL 61455 ☎ 309-298-1674 ✉ mibglf@wiu.edu 🖳 www.wiu.edu/users/mibglf
Support, unity, & strength, & works toward educational, social, & political goals for lgb people & their allies.

The Stonewall Group PO Box 4554, Naperville, IL 60567 ☎ 630-585-3827 ✉ stonewallassoc@aol.com 🖳 www.stonewallassociation.com
Support group meets Tu.. 6:30-8pm at DuPage Unitarian Church, 4S.535 Old Naperville Rd. Monthly discussion group plus social activities. For those 18+ & out of high school.

Illinois State University: PRIDE—GLBTQA Student Organization c/o Student Services, Normal, IL 61790-2200 ☎ 309-438-2429 ✉ isu.pride@hotmail.com 🖳 www.ilstu.edu/depts/studentlife/RSO/gen/PRIDE

Prism Youth Network Box 784, Oak Park, IL 60303 ☎ 708-386-3463 🖳 www.opalga.org
For LGBT youth 14-18. Weekly drop-in meetings. Near west suburbs of Chicago.

Spectrum Oak Park, IL ☎ 708-848-0273
LGBT young adult 18-25, Oak Park area (near west suburban Chicago).

William Rainey Harper Community College: Gay, Lesbian & Bisexual Students of Harper c/o Student Development, 347 Building A, Harper College, Palatine, IL 60607 ☎ 847-935-6346 FX: 847-925-6033

Quad Citians Affirming Diversity Plaza Office Building, 1705 Second Avenue, Rock Island, IL 61201 ☎ 309-786-2580 FX: 309-788-1681 ✉ qcad@revealed.net 🖳 www.qcad.net
Brings GLBT people together to learn from each other & create an affirming environment; youth drop-in center 2x weekly. PUB: QCAD News (Monthly newsletter about upcoming programs; essays by members & kids.)

Diversity of Rockford 117A South Third Street, Rockford, IL 61104 ☎ 815-964-2639 ✉ robyntrans@aol.com
A non-profit organization that serves the BGLT community in the Rockford area.

University of Illinois, Urbana-Champaign

Office for Lesbian, Gay & Bisexual & Transgender Concerns, 322a, Illini Union, 1401 West Green Street, Urbana, IL 61801, ☎ 217-244-8863 or 217-244-3277, 🖳 www.odos.uiuc.edu/gblt/, *Safe, affirming, inclusive place for all students, faculty, & staff, particularly LGBT.* **Queer Action Forum**, URU 292 Allen, MC-050 Campus, Urbana IL 61801, ☎ 217-332-3336, ✉ klambert@uiuc.edu. **Sexual Orientation Diversity Allies (SODA) Committee**, 1610 John Street, Champaign, IL 61820, ☎ 217-333-3704. *Queer-friendly & queer faculty & staff at the U of I. Look for the pink triangle labeled "Ally" displayed in their offices.* **Queers on Campus**, c/o Office for LGBT Concerns, ✉ qoc@uiuc.edu. *Social organization for UIUC graduate & professional students, faculty, & staff, who are lgbt. Meetings are very casual—they are opportunities for LGBT people from around campus to get together & chat. Friends & partners welcome to all of our activities.* **Safe Zone**, 280 Illini Union, Cubicle #44, 1401 W. Green Street, Urbana, IL 61801, ☎ 217-333-1187, 🖳 www.uiuc.edu/ro/SafeZone, *Group formed to educate the campus community about issues of concern to LGBT people.*

Review: Bi/Gay Married Men's Support & Conversation Groups Box 7406, Villa Park, IL 60181 ☎ 630-627-1990 ✉ Reviewgrp@aol.com 🖳 members.aol.com/reviewgp/advice/index.htm
Informal meetings, about 20 people per meeting. $5/meeting. Meets in Oak Park.

> **There are not two discrete populations, heterosexual and homosexual... Only the human mind invents categories and tries to force fact into separated pigeon holes. The sooner we learn this... the sooner we shall reach a sound understanding of the realities of sex.**
>
> Alfred Kinsey

Indiana

Gay, Lesbian & Bisexual Coalition PO Box 5731, Bloomington, IN 47407 ☎ 812-855-5688 ✉ the_glbt_coalition@yahoo.com 🖳 www.bloomington.in.us/socserv/iris/Bloomington_Gay.html
Community based organization dedicated to enhancing the climate for glb people through active political, educational & social means.

Indiana University

Office of Gay, Lesbian, Bisexual, Transgender Student Support Services, 705 E.Seventh St., Bloomington, IN 47408-3809, ☎ 812-855-4252, FX: 812-855-4465, ✉ glbtserv@indiana.edu, 🖳 www.indiana.edu/~glbtserv/. **OUT (GLBT Student Union),** Indiana Memorial Union, Suite 473-474, IU, Bloomington, IN 47405, ☎ 812-855-5OUT, ✉ out@Indiana.edu, 🖳 www.indiana.edu/~out, *Umbrella organization working closely with various support groups.*

Bi-Versity of Indianapolis & Central Indiana , Indianapolis, IN ☎ Jenny: 765-287-0395 ✉ Brad: PNDZ90A@Prodigy.com 🖳 www.bisexual.org/indianapolis

Indiana Youth Group Box 20716, Indianapolis, IN 46220-0716 ☎ 317-541-8726 FX: 317-545-8594 🖳 www.indianayouthgroup.org
Drop-in center offering medical & mental health care & life skills. Trains youth for community outreach. Nat'l pen-pal program for GLB youth.

LGBT Fairness Indianapolis, IN ☎ Marla Stevens: 317-582-2910 ✉ lgbtfair@aol.com

Ball State University: Spectrum Student Center Box 16, Muncie, IN 47306 ✉ spectrum@bsu.edu 🖳 www.bsu.edu/students/pride/spectrum/

Earlham College: Rainbow Tribe Richmond, IN 47374 ☎ 765-983-1436 ✉ owner-rtribe-l@earlham.edu 🖳 www.earlham.edu/~rtribe/

Indiana State University: Alliance of Bisexual, Lesbian & Gay Students & Allies Box 18, ISU, Hulman Memorial Student Union, Terre Haute, IN 47809 ☎ 812-237-6916x1 ✉ ablgsa@mama.indstate.edu 🖳 mama.indstate.edu/ablgsa/

Purdue University: LesBiGay Network 1001 Stewart Center, Box 642, West Lafayette, IN 47906 ✉ triangle@expert.cc.purdue.edu 🖳 expert.cc.purdue.edu/~triangle

---

Erotic energy holds the universe together. What is gravity but the desire of one body for another?

—Starhawk, Washington DC 4/24/93.

Iowa

Central Iowa Bisexual Social Group PO Box 2425, Ames, IA 50010 ☎ 515-233-3189 ✉ vraymond@iastate.edu 🖳 www.public.iastate.edu/~vraymond/BiSocial.html
Meets monthly: bi theme matinees & evening cafe socials. informal, no agenda. Sponsors [IowaBiSocial] mailing list: see website. Some members do bi oriented community service projects.

Borderbandits IA 🖳 www.yahoogroups.com/group/borderbandits-IA
Iowa e-mail list, ongoing discusssion of the fluidity of gender & desire & defying either / or dicotomies, i.e., bis, trans, etc.

ACCESS line: A Resource for Midwestern Gays, Lesbians, Bisexuals & Friends PO Box 1682, Waterloo, IA 50704 ☎ 319-232-6805 ✉ access@forbin.com
Monthly newspaper for, by, about LGB people in Iowa & vicinity.

QUAD Citians Affirming Diversity IA
See full QCAD listed under Illinois, USA.
PUB: QCAD News

GLB Ames PO Box 1761, Ames, IA 50010-1761 ☎ 515-232-0000 ✉ glbames@aol.com 🖳 members.aol.com/GLBAmes/
GLBT community organization. Monthly meetings; various topics & speakers.

Iowa State University

Lesbian, Gay, Bisexual & Transgendered Student Services, 1010H Student Services Bldg., Ames, IA 50011; ☎ 515-294-1020; ✉ lgbtss@iastate.edu; 🖳 www.public.iastate.edu/~lgbtss. **Lesbian/Gay/Bisexual/Transgendered/Allies Alliance,** EG-46 Memorial Union, 2229 Lincoln Way, Ames, IA 50014-7163; ☎ 515-294-2104; ✉ alliance@iastate.edu; 🖳 www.alliance.stuorg.iastate.edu/. *Weekly meetings, social & educational events.*

University of Northern Iowa: UNIGLO 244A Bartlett Hall, Cedar Falls, IA 50613 ☎ 319-222-0003 ✉ uniglo@uni.edu

Gay & Lesbian Resource Center 305 2nd St SE Suite 324, Cedar Rapids, IA 52406 ☎ 319-366-2055 ✉ crglrc@crglrc.org 🖳 www.crglrc.org/

Luther College: AWARE FPO 45, Decorah, IA 52101 ☎ 319-387-1277

Drake University: Bisexuals Gays and Lesbians At Drake (B-GLAD) Student Life Center, Drake University, Des Moines, IA 50311 ☎ 515-271-3711 ✉ bglad@acad.drake.edu

Fairfield Bisexual Network Fairfield, IA ✉ exam_us@yahoo.com
Completely confidential! Support for bis, partners, allies & persons questioning. Individual & small group counseling. Good for making bi friends.

...all too many of us are content to be just like everyone else. Here's the reality. Not all of us want to be like everyone else. We make a serious mistake when we create a dress code for civil rights. As a young woman, I was taught that bisexuals were fence sitters, unwilling or unable to choose a sexual orientation, unwilling to face the stigma of being gay or lesbian, seeking comfort in heterosexual privilege. What harm was done to me and others with these very notions cannot be calculated, but the harm to our movement has been enormous. I believe that our process as a community must reflect the world that we want to build. If we want to be like everyone else, we will act like everyone else. We will be greedy, we will value style over substance, and we will cast out those that challenge us and our comfortable assumptions. If we want to build a movement that is transformational, we will model honesty, we will model openness and we will take the risks that challenge conventional thinking. We will act with integrity in our personal relationships and in our relationships with our colleagues. We will seek out and lift up every voice, challenged by what we hear but not afraid. We will listen to every voice. The true test of democracy is how it embraces those who look, act, and think differently, not just those who are the same. This is the world we dream of--a more compassionate society. One that values the worth and dignity of all people. We can't subscribe to the 'I'll get mine now and we'll add you later' modeof politics. As a woman, as a lesbian, as a Jew, I can't be a woman on Thursday, a lesbian on Friday, and a Jew on Saturday. And I challenge any organization that requires that I make that choice. Perhaps it is an old fashioned notion, but I believe that to move forward, each of us must move forward together.

Kerry Lobel, excerpted from a keynote address given by Kerry Lobel at the fifth International Bisexual Conference, Cambridge, MA April 5, 1998

Grinnell College: Stonewall Resource Center Younker Memorial Resource Center, 1211 8th Ave, Grinnell, IA 50112 ☎ 515-269-3327 FX: 515-269-3710 ✉ srcenter@ac.grin.edu 💻 www.grinnell.edu/www/tour/stonewall.html *Open community space, library, meeting rooms for Grinnell lbgt.*

Simpson College: Lesbian/Gay/Bisexual/ Transgender Alliance 508 N C ST, Indianola, IA 50125 ☎ 515-961-1520 ✉ Mike Wright, advisor: wright@storm.simpson.edu

The Iowa City Bisexual Discussion Group University of Iowa, WRAC: Bi-Group moderator., Iowa City, IA 52242 ☎ 319-335-1486 ✉ icbi@gay.com 💻 www.bisexual.org/g/icbi *In person & online discussion of bi issues. To attend: ph. interview with moderator, be bi-friendly & respect confidentiality. No pressure to decide sexual orientation, come out or participate in specific activities, which have included: publishing locally, public speaking, help researchers, help other LGBT groups. Frequent socials & mass e-mail one another.*

University of Iowa

Gay, Lesbian, Bisexual, & Transgender Union & Iowa's Pride; 203 Iowa House, Iowa Memorial Union, Iowa City, IA 52242-1317; ☎ 319-335-3251; FX: 319-335-3407; ✉ glbtu@uiowa.edu; 💻 www.uiowa.edu/~glbtu/. **Lesbian, Gay & Bisexual Staff & Faculty Association**, 130 North Madison Street, Iowa City, IA 52242; ☎ 319-335-1125; ✉ Michael Blake: michael-blake@uiowa.edu; 💻 www.uiowa.edu/~lgbsfa. Open to university employees. Monthly meetings *& ongoing work in AIDS/HIV+ policy, curricula development, domestic partnership, & advocacy/referral.*

Morningside College: Gay Lesbian Bisexual Student Group Timothy Orwig, 1501 Morningside Ave, Sioux City, IA 51106 ☎ 712-274-5333 FX: 712-274-5101 ✉ tto001@alpha.morningside.edu

Wartburg College: Gay Bisexual Lesbian Educational Support (GABLES) c/o Social Work Department, Waverly, IA 50677 ☎ 319-352-8250 ✉ Susan Vallem: vallem@wartburg.edu

Kansas

The Liberty Press PO Box 16315, Wichita, KS 67216-0315 ☎ 316-652-7737 FX: 316-685-1999 ✉ editor@libertypress.net 🖳 www.libertypress.net
Statewide news magazine w/current info about Kansas groups & events.

Emporia State University: PRIDE 1200 Commercial, Campus Box 65, Emporia, KS 66801 ✉ ESU_PRIDE@yahoo.com
Pride = People Respecting Individuality & Diversity in Education.

Freedom Coalition PO Box 1991, Lawrence, KS 66044 ☎ Tim Brownlee 785-843-1889 ✉ brownlee@ukans.edu 🖳 www.freedomcoalition.org
Grassroots, community organization supporting civil rights for all regardless of sexual orientation. Best known for helping pass Lawrence's gay civil rights law, the only one of its kind in the state of Kansas. Monthly meetings. Organizes events, works with schools & community to end homophobia; legislative lobbying.

First Fridays Lawrence, KS ☎ 785-841-2345
A potluck for women who love women.

Lawrence Men's Group Lawrence, KS
Open support group for all men. Meets Wed., 7-9:15pm at Ecumenical Christian Ministries. Gay & straight mixed, one of its goals is to end homophobia in all men.

Kansas Cookboys P O Box 1692, Lawrence, KS 66044 ✉ liquidstiv@aol.com or olin@sunflower.com
A monthly culinary-themed potluck & social event.

Women's Activities Group Lawrence, KS ✉ emily4601@yahoo.com
Monthly lunch meeting at restaurants around Lawrence.

KU Libraries Queer Resources Lawrence, KS ☎ Contact: Rob Melton 🖳 www.ukans.edu/~rmelton/gayles/index.html

University of Kansas, Lawrence: Queers & Allies 423 Kansas Union, Box 13, Lawrence, KS 66045 ☎ Contact: Matthew Skinta 785-864-3091 ✉ QandA@raven.cc.ukans.edu 🖳 www.raven.cc.ukans.edu/~quanda/
Meetings are the 1st, 3rd, 5th Th. at 7pm in Parlor ABC of the Kansas Union

A Different Light: GLBT AA 714 Vermont, Lawrence, KS ☎ Jan: 785-865-2774
LGBT Alcoholics Anonymous meetings Sun. 11am at 714 Vermont & Tu. 7pm at Ecumenical Christian Ministries.

Flint Hills Alliance PO Box 2018, Manhattan, KS 66505-2018 ☎ 913-776-6743 ✉ fha.kansas@usa.net 🖳 www.debtaylor.com/fha
GLBT community organization.

University of Kansas: Oread Rainbow Alliance Oread, KS ☎ Maggie Childs: 785-864-3378 ✉ mhchilds@ukans.edu
A group for GLBT faculty & staff advocates.

Kansas State University: Queer Straight Alliance Office of Student Activities and Services, Ground Floor - K State Student Union, Topeka, KS 66506 ✉ qsa@ksu.edu 🖳 www.ksu.edu/qsa
Open to students, faculty & area residents.

Support to Express Yourself 708 SW 6th Ave., Topeka, KS 66603 ☎ 785-232-3100 ✉ moonbeamrainbow@aol.com
For teens. Mtgs. Tu. 7pm.

PFLAG - Topeka PO Box 8162, Topeka, KS 66608-0162 ☎ Lawrence: 785-841-2345; Topeka: 785-246-0730 ✉ pflagks@freewwweb.com
Confidential meetings 1st Sun. 2:30pm.

The Gay Information Line & Land of Awes Information Services P O Box 16782, Wichita, KS 67216-0782 ☎ 316-269-0913 FX: 316-269-4208 ✉ awes@fn.net 🖳 www.awes.com
Automated, voice-mail system. Operator usually available weeknights 6-10pm.

Wichita Prime Timers 6505 E. Central #109, Wichita, KS 67206 ☎ 316-691-0917
Affiliate of Prime Timers Worldwide. For mature gay men.

Wichita Bears P O Box 16751, Wichita, KS 67216-0751 ✉ isotopehbr@aol.com 🖳 www.bear.net/clubs/witchita.bears/
Monthly Potlucks held at Mother's Lounge, 3102 E. 31st South.

Project Acceptance PO Box 686, Wichita, KS 67201-0686 ☎ 316-68P-FLAG ✉ pflag@southwind.net
Support group sponsored by Wichita PFLAG for ages 14-18. Safe, affirming place for glb youth & friends w/adult facilitators. Info about sexuality, prevention of suicide, violence & school, family & work concerns & many life-affirming issues. Mtgs. Tues. 7pm. "We want you to know that you are not alone."

Transitions P O Box 686, Witchita, KS 67201-0686 ☎ 316-68P-FLAG ✉ pflag@southwind.net
Support group sponsored by Wichita PFLAG for young adults 18-24. Safe, affirming place of acceptance for glb youth & friends w/adult facilitators. Info about sexuality, suicide prevention, violence & school, family & work concerns. "We want you to know that you are not alone."

College Hill United Methodist Church 2930 E. 1st Street, Wichita, KS 67214 ☎ 316-683-4643
A welcoming group open to all people regardless of sexual orientation, 9:40 am, Sundays. Open Door Fellowship - a monthly gathering of gay men & lesbians, 3rd Th.

First Metropolitan Community Church of Kansas 156 S. Kansas Avenue, Wichita, KS 67211 ☎ 316-267-1852 FX: 316-267-1859 ✉ mccwitchita@aol.com
Sunday Services: 10:30am, ASL signing at every service.

First Unitarian Universalist Church of Witchita 1501 N. Fairmount, Wichita, KS 67208 ☎ 316-684-3481
GLBT welcoming congregation.
PFLAG - Wichita P O Box 686, Wichita, KS 67201-0686 ☎ 316-68P-FLAG ✉ pflag@southwind.net
📧 www.pflag.org
Monthly programs, parents support group.

God Loves All The Beautiful Rainbow of Sexual Orientation Do Not Exclude Lesbians, Gays And Bisexuals

March on Washington, 1993.

Kentucky

Western Kentucky University: Lesbian/ Bisexual/ Straight/ Gay Alliance c/o Dr. Karen Schneider, Cherry Hall Room 20B, 1 Big Red Way, Bowling Green, KY 42101 ☎ 502-745-0111
College queer club dedicated to social support & political activism.

Centre College: BGLAD Box 1212, Randy Hayes, Advisor, Danville, KY 40422 ☎ 606-238-5471
✉ hays@centre.edu 📧 web.centre.edu/~bglad/
B-Glad was conceived to provide social support network for persons dealing with issues concerning their or other individual's homosexuality or bisexuality; non-profit organization

Northern Kentucky University: Common Ground
c/o Student Life, University Center Suite 10, Highland Heights, KY 41099 ☎ Student Life: 606-572-6514 ✉ outfront@nku.edu
📧 www.nku.edu/~commonground/
Meets Tu. 3-5pm University Center 303.

University of Kentucky: LAMBDA Patterson Office Tower, Lexington, KY 40506 ☎ 606-257-3151
📧 www.geocities.com/WestHollywood/Chelsea/ 1195/
Meets Th. 7:30 pm in Student Center room 231.

Transylvania University: TUnity 300 North Broadway, Lexington, KY 40508 ☎ 606-233-6490 ✉ tunity@mail.transy.edu 📧 http:// www.transy.edu/homepages/tunity/
Student-run group for glbt issues at TU.

University of Louisville: Common Ground SAC W301, Louisville, KY 40292 ☎ 502-635-1905
✉ commong@ulkyvm.louisville.edu
📧 www.louisville.edu/rso/commonground
College social support, political group with meetings & on- line discussions.

Louisville Youth Group PO Box 4664, Louisville, KY 40204 ☎ (502) 589-3316
Meets bimonthly as a peer support group for self-identified GLB youth 14-21. Invites speakers to present at the group & holds proms.

Louisiana

LAMBDA Group, Inc. PO Box 1911, Baton Rouge, LA 70821 ☎ 225-383-0777 ✉ info@lambdabr.org
📧 www.lambdabr.org
Non-profit group covering Baton Rouge & area. Provides programs on LGBT issues. Fights discrimination in the gay & heterosexual community, & runs Baton Rouge Community Center at 1733 Florida Blvd. (225-346-0670) PUB: The Lambda Letter (Bi Monthly newsletter.)

Louisiana State University: Gays, Bisexuals, Lesbians & Supporters United Baton Rouge, LA ✉ GBLSU235@aol.com 📧 hometown.aol.com/ gblsu235/myhomepage/business.html
Purpose: to have fun & coordinate events to create a family atmosphere within the group. Provides speaker to other groups & classes.

Lesbian & Gay Community Center 2114 Decatur, New Orleans, LA 70116 ☎ 504-945-1103 FX: 504-945-1102 ✉ lgccno@aol.com; 📧 lgccno.homepage.com
Bi-inclusive community center that has hosted a bi support group. PUB: The Center Line

Hate Crimes Hotline c/o Lesbian & Gay Community Center, 2114 Decatur, New Orleans, LA 70116 ☎ 504-944-HEAL (4325)
Hotline for victims of hate crimes based on sexual preference, gender, race, religion, age, physical or mental disability. Referrals to appropriate assistance & documentation of hate crimes in the state.

> **My definition of a free society is a society where it is safe to be unpopular.**
>
> Adlai Stevenson

Loyola University: GOAL: Gay/Lesbian Outreach @ Loyola 6363 St. Charles Ave. Box 1, New Orleans, LA 70118 ☎ 504-861-5881 ✉ goal@loyno.edu 🖳 www.loyno.edu/~goal *Education, awareness, support, service to members of the Loyola community interested in GLBT issues. Panel discussions & community service outside of the university.*

Tulane University's Bisexual, Gay, & Lesbian Alliance 6823 St. Charles Avenue, New Orleans, LA 70118 ✉ bigala@mailhost.tcs.tulane.edu 🖳 www.tulane.edu/~bigala

Nicholls State University: Gay, Lesbian, Bisexual, Friends Alliance c/o University Counseling Center, 227 Elkins Hall, Thibadoux, LA 70310 ☎ 504-448-4080 ✉ org-glbfa@nich-academic.nich.edu 🖳 www.nicholls.edu/GLBFA/index.html *Safe & friendly atmosphere for all people to discuss issues relevant to the gay community. Educate people in the community to help create an environment conducive to a healthy lifestyle for all.*

Maine

Maine Bisexual People's Network PO Box 10818, Portland, ME 04104-6818 *Resources, referrals, support. Currently no regular meetings.*

BINNE (Bi in Northern New England) PO Box 10818, Portland, ME 04104-6818 ✉ owner-binne@rulesthe.net 🖳 binne.rulesthe.net/ *Email list for Bi people in Northern New England (USA). Although originally intended for Maine, it's open to anyone bi or bi friendly.*

Maine GayNet ME ✉ me-gaynet@queernet.org 🖳 www.qrd.com/maine *Excellent resource for links & info.*

Maine Rural Network 51 Shore Road, Standish, ME 04084 ☎ 207-642-2015 ✉ nomad@watchic.net *Rural organizing project for Maine, formed in 1998 when the civil rights law in Maine was repealed. We believe in connecting communities (LGBT & Progressive) as a way to create safe, open, inclusive places to live. We encourage anyone rural or urban to join us and help bring about social change in rural Maine. Network News (Quarterly newsletter about our activities, community events, & what it is like to live in rural Maine as a member of the LGBT/Progressive commiunity. Sample newsletter by request.)*

Maine Lesbian & Gay Political Alliance PO Box 232, Hallowell, ME 04347-0232 ☎ 800-556-5472; 207-761-3732 ✉ mlgpa@javanet.com *Statewide political association/advocacy for the bglta communities. Very Bi/Trans/Diversity friendly. Networking/organizing, strategizing, educating, & campaigns. Advocacy/legislative work for safer schools. Monthly meetings & newsletter.*

Am Chofski, Maine's GLB Chavurah

Maine Speak Out Project for Equal Rights PO Box 15303, 7 Dana St., Portland, ME 04112 ☎ 207-879-0480; toll free 1-866-879-6767 FX: 207-775-4903 ✉ msoproject@gwi.net 🖳 www.mainespeakout.org *Trains & deploys volunteers statewide to speak with citizen groups in their towns & regions about their lives & the lives of others who experience discrimination in Maine.*

Northern Lambda Nord PO Box 990, Caribou, ME 04736-0990 ☎ 207-498-2088; 1-800-468-2088 (in Maine). (M, W, F, 7-9), voice/tty. 🖳 www.ctel.net/~lambda *Serving n. Maine & n. & w. New Brunswick in Canada. Social activities, discussion group, speaker's bureau, lending library, phoneline. Meetings 2nd Th.s at 6:30pm (ME), 7:30pm (NB) G/L Community Services Ctr, 568 Main St., Caribou. Religious/spiritual gathering Sun. at the Community Center.* PUB: *Communiqué (6x/year by subscription. Monthly calendar of activities.)*

Gay, Lesbian & Straight Education Network (GLSEN) Downeast Maine PO Box 373, Ellsworth, ME ✉ rees@midmaine.com *Working to make schools safer for & more respecting of GLBT youth & staff. Teacher training, advocacy, youth support, workshops. A chapter of national GLSEN.*

Dyke Dates ME ✉ alyse@psouth.net 🖳 www.psouth.net/~alyse/dd.html *Online resource & activities for Southern Maine lesbian & bi women. Listing of area resources, & night clubs.*

National Association of Social Workers, Maine Chapter. Sexual Minorites Issues Committee PO Box 5065, Augusta, ME 04332-5056 ☎ 207-622-7592 FX: 207-623-4860 ✉ nasw99me@aol.com; Email for Sexual Minorites Issues Committee: fbrooks@maine.edu *Assists social workers & other allies advocating for GLBT people in Maine. Political activism, lobbying, & education & social service resources to sexual minority groups & individuals. Safe & supportive environment for Maine social workers to discuss sexual minority issues.*

Robyn Ochs

PFLAG/Brunswick, ME ME ☎ 207-725-6390;
207-729-9895 ✉ marg@ime.net
*Meets 4th Wed. in Pilgrim House of 1st Parish
Church, 9 Cleaveland St., Brunswick, 7-9pm.
Support, education & advocacy for GLBT
persons, their parents, families & friends.*

Bisexual Men's Discussion Group Dayspring,
One Weston Court, Augusta, ME 04330
☎ 207-621-6201 ✉ daysprg@mint.net
*Meets 2nd & 4th Wed. 7pm at Dayspring Office.
Not exclusively for married bis but inclusive of
married bis.*

Central Maine Gay Men's Support Group c/o
Brian Kaufman, 52 Green Street, Augusta, ME
04330 ☎ 207-778-7379 ✉ bjkpma@maine.edu
*Meets Tu. 7pm at the Winthrop St. Unitarian
Church. Gay, bi, married men, & youth welcome
to attend for discussion, info, social support
(often followed by a group outing for coffee).*

Man 2 Man PO Box 2038, Bangor, ME 04402
☎ 207-990-2095 FX: 207-990-2286
✉ AIDSNtwk@aol.com
🖳 WWW.maineaidsnetwork.com
*HIV prevention program for men who have sex
with men. Education, testing, support groups,
HIV/AIDS hotline, workshops.*

Outright Bangor Bangor, ME 04401
☎ Shawn Box: 207-990-2095; 800-429-1481
*Supportive, informative & social mtgs for GLBQ
youth -23. Safe space for questions, growth, & fun.*

**University of Southern Maine: Alliance for Sexual
Diversity** Campus Center, University of Southern
Maine, Bedford, ME 04103 ☎ 207-780-4996
FX: 207-780-4463 🖳 usmcug.usm.maine.edu/~asd/

Coastal Outright Coastal AIDS Network,
PO Box 956, Belfast, ME 04915 ☎ Emily Graves:
207-338-6330 or 800-207-4064 FX: 207-338-4540
✉ coastaloutright@yahoo.com 🖳 www.acadia.net/
wkacAIDS/
*Meets 2nd/4th Fri. in Rockland for GLBTQ youth
-23. Through collaboration of youth & adults, we
provide support, education, advocacy & social
activities.*

**Bowdoin College: Bisexual, Gay & Lesbian
Alliance for Diversity (BGLAD)** Moulton Union
Info. Desk, Brunswick, ME 04011 ☎ 207-725-3000
(ask for BGLAD)

Midcoast Outright, Brunswick PO Box 581,
Brunswick, ME 04011 ☎ 207-729-8747
🖳 www.qrd.org/maine/outright.midcoast.html
Supportive & affirming spaces for glbtq -22.

> Its a crime, it's an evil, dangerous
> thing / To stifle the gift of love and
> the joy it surely brings / Well, I'll
> love who I please, I'm gonna give
> the best of me / Walking tall, and
> blessed with the right to be.
>
> Mary Watkins

University of Maine, Farmington

Gay-OK!, c/o Brian J. Kaufman, Ph.D., 111
South St., Farmington, ME 04938, ☎ 207-778-
7379, FX: 207-778-7378, ✉ BJKPMA@maine.edu,
*Meets weekly during termtime for discussion &
social support. LGBTQ, Intersex & Ally
individuals welcome to join our safe space for a
variety of activities including LGBTIQA videos,
games (Jenga, "Truth or Dare", The Rainbow
Gayme), or "tea & sympathy" to discuss civil
rights setbacks in the state. Serving Franklin
County & Northern Kennebec County to the
Canadian border, & open to university faculty,
staff, students, community members, alumni, etc.*
**Rainbow Educational Alliance for Diverse
Individuals (READI)**, c/o Mary Schwanke,
Ph.D., 111 South St., Farmington, ME 04938,
☎ 207-778-8151, ✉ BJKPMA@aol.com, DESC:
*Student group programs, LGBT events, meetings
& activities.*

Women Singing OUT PO Box 693, Kennebunkport,
ME 04046 ☎ 207-892-6286
✉ womensingingout@aol.com
🖳 www.rainbowbeacon.com/womensingingout
*A tri-state (NH/ME/MA) lesbian-based chorus.
Welcomes all women of diverse sexual orientations who are dedicated to musical excellence and
& change. "Even though we are a lesbian based
group, we are an inclusive organization to which
all women are welcome."*

**Bates College: Gay/Lesbian/Bisexual/Straight
Alliance** Box 77, Lewiston, ME 04240

Lewiston/Auburn Outright c/o AIDS Coalition of
Lewiston-Auburn, PO Box 7977, Lewiston/Auburn,
ME 04243 ☎ 207-786-2717 ✉ Nancy Bullett:
acla@gwi.net 🖳 www.qrd.org/maine/outright.l-
a.html
For youth. Fri. 6-8:30pm in Lewiston.

**University of Maine, Orono: Wilde-Stein Alliance
for Sexual Diversity** C. Max Hilton Room,
Memorial Union, Orono, ME 04469-0000
☎ 207-581-1596 ✉ wilde.stein@umit.maine.edu
🖳 www.ume.maine.edu/~wstein

Gay/Lesbian/Bisexual Parents Group PO Box
10818, Portland, ME 04104

PFLAG/Portland PO BOX 8742, Portland ME
04104 ☎ 207-774-3441
✉ PFLAGportlandme@aol.com
*Promotes the health & well-being of glbt people,
their families, & friends through support to create
a society healthy and respectful of diversity.*

Outright Portland PO Box 5077, Portland, ME
04101 ☎ 207-828-6560; 888-567-7600 FX: 207-828-
4606 🖳 www.outright.org
*For LGBTQ young people. Support group Fri.
7:30-9:30pm, Sunday **QTurn** hangout for 20-26
yr. olds.6-8pm, Monday Night Q&A - support
group for 12-16 yr. olds & parents, 6-8pm,
Informal Drop-In Tu. 6-9pm, **Whatabout** Wed.
6-8pm at 3 Ellsworth St. Other activities
throughout the week.*

Maryland

Bi Group Gay & Lesbian Community Center, 241 W. Chase St., Baltimore, MD 21201 ☎ 410-837-5445 FX: 410-837-8512
Community center sponsors many groups, including bi group.

Johns Hopkins University: Diverse Sexuality & Gender Alliance Second Floor, 3505 N. Charles Street, Baltimore, MD 21218 ☎ 410-516-4088 FX: 410-516-4986 ✉ dsaga@jhu.edu
💻 www.jhu.edu/~dsaga
Events & entertainment, political & social activities, discussions. General meetings Mon. 8:30pm in Gilman 12. PUB: Closet Space

Maryland Institute College of Art: ANGLE c/o Student Activities, 1300 Mt Royal Avenue, Baltimore, MD 21217 ☎ Student Activities: 410-225-2284
"Awareness Now for Gays, Lesbians & Everyone."

Inner Light Unity Fellowship 400 I St SW, Bethesda, MD ☎ 202-544-6588
African-American house of worship for GLBT people. PUB: Coming Out Pagan (Quarterly Journal with international readership celebrating glb spirituality/nature religions.)

> There are few people in this country who are as out as I am. I have a husband, and I have a woman companion. There is an obsession with trying to define women by their sexuality. People don't know how to deal with you if they can't define your sexuality. I'm just perverse enough to like that.
>
> —Patricia Ireland, President of NOW, 1993

Dignity/Maine PO Box 8113, Portland, ME 04104 ☎ Rosemary or Janet: 207-646-2820
Supportive Masses for LGBT Catholics, their friends & families Sun.s 6pm in St. Luke's Cathedral, 143 State St., Portland.

University of Southern Maine GLBTQA Resources Program 135G Woodbury Campus Center, PO Box 9300, Portland, ME 04104-9300 ☎ 207-228-8235 FX: 207-780-4463 ✉ sholmes@usm.maine.edu
💻 www.usm.maine.edu/glbtqa
Seeks to ensure a University environment that is positive, safe & supportive for members of GLBTQ & Allied community through a series of educational opportunities, support services & advocacy work.

University of Maine at Presque Isle: Rainbow Alliance Presque Isle, ME ✉ Advisor: Dr. David Rolloff: rolloffd@polaris.umpi.maine.edu
💻 www.qrd.org/maine/umpi.html
For glbtq people on the campus, & from the community.

Rainbow Business & Professional Association PO Box 6627, Scarborough, ME 04070-6627 ☎ 207-775-0077 💻 www.rbpa.org
Statewide, non-profit org. established to create a GLBT "chamber of commerce" for Maine. Meetings/dinners held in Portland area, 2nd Mon.

Out on Mount Desert Island PO Box 367, Southwest Harbor, ME 04679 ☎ 207-664-0328 ✉ oomdi@geocities.com 💻 www.geocities.com/WestHollywood/Heights/5011/
Supporting the LGBT & allied community of downeast Maine. Very active social/support group. Meets Tu. 7pm. Newcomers always welcome.

Colby College: The Bridge - Colby's GLBTA Community 5920 Mayflower Hill Dr., Waterville, ME 04901 ☎ 207-872-3635 ✉ bridge@colby.edu
💻 www.colby.edu/bridge/

> "I'm a Kinsey pi... (irrational, transcendental, and memorable to sixteen decimal places)."
>
> *Kay Dekker*

Boston Pride, 2000

> The Bible contains 6 admonishments to homosexuals and 362 admonishments to heterosexuals. That doesn't mean that God doesn't love heterosexuals. It's just that they need more supervision.
>
> Lynn Lavner

University of Maryland, College Park: Pride Alliance Stamp Student Union, Room 3104, College Park, MD 20742 ☎ 301-314-8347 🖳 www.inform.umd.edu/StudentOrg/lgba/
Mon. 6pm for SafeSpace, our weekly peer support group in Student Union Room 1137; Pride Forum every other Wed. 5 pm in Jimenez Hall Room 1117—varied events, where we disucuss community issues, upcoming social events, learn about the LGBT movement.

Hood College: Tolerance, Education & Acceptance Box 1200, Hood College, Frederick, MD 21701 🖳 www.hood.edu/student/tea
Student group, including people of all sexual/affectionate orientations and open to all students, faculty & staff who advocate the rights of sexual minorities.

Towson State University

Diverse Sexual Orientation Collective, c/o Student Government Association, TU Box 1983, Towson, MD 21204-7097; ☎ 410-830-2340; DESC: Office in University Union, Room 324.
Gay, Lesbian & Bisexual Issues Committee, c/o David Bergman Chair, English Dpt, Towson, MD 21204-7097; ✉ Bergman@midget.towson.edu; 🖳 www.towson.edu/~tinkler/lgb/ · homepage.html. *Addresses issues related to sexual orientation for students, faculty & staff. Open to all members of the TSU community.*

Massachusetts

Statewide

New England Queer College Organization 001 Leverett Mail center, Cambridge, MA 02138 ✉ neqco@neqco.org 🖳 www.neqco.org
NEQCO is a student-run organization that acts as a network between all of the BGLT campus groups in New England. We host leaders meetings, and our website lists all of the BGLT activites in each school's campuses, so that members of other schools can attend.

Pridenet MA ✉ pride@pridenet.com 🖳 www.pridenet.com/mass.html
Statewide GLBT Information.

KARAMA: The New England Lavender Arabic Society MA ☎ Bassam Kassab: 650-579-1876
Social group for Arab, Armenian & Persian LGBT & supporters.

Massachusetts Department of Education: Safe Schools Program 350 Main Street, Malden, MA 02148-5023 ☎ 781-338-6322; 338-6313 ✉ Kim Westheimer: kwestheimer@doe.mass.edu, Abigail Kinnebrew, akinnebrew@doe.mass.edu 🖳 www.doe.mass.edu/lss/program/ssch.html
Massachusetts DOE project working in conjunction with the Governor's Commission on Gay & Lesbian Youth to make schools safe for "gay & lesbian" youth. PUB: Gay/Straight Alliances: A Student Guide (27 minute video - "Safe Schools Program for Gay & Lesbian Students" - free for in-state residents. Others send blank 30min videotape.)

MassQ-Net MA 🖳 www1.wsc.ma.edu/massqnet/
Web page sponsored by the Massachusetts Governor's Commission on Gay & Lesbian Youth of GLB contacts at Massachusetts State & Community Colleges to serve glb members of our campus communities in a more comprehensive way.

Lesbian & Bisexual Rights Task Force of the National Organization for Women 214 Harvard Ave, Allston, MA 02134 ☎ 232-1017 FX: 617-232-4162 ✉ massnow@gis.net 🖳 www.NOW.org
Helping to fight racism & homophobia in our communities, while working to expand the diversity of chapter issues, outreach & membership.

National Association of Social Workers, Mass Chapter, Committee on Gay/Lesbian/Bisexual Issues 14 Beacon St., Suite 409, Boston, MA 02114 ☎ 617-227-9635
Includes a MA GLB Training Committee, which does training on working with GLB clients.

New England Gay, Lesbian & Bisexual Veterans, Inc. JFK Station, PO Box 6599, Boston, MA 02114 ☎ Rick Buchanan: 978-249-5921 ✉ cliff4vets@aol.com 🖳 www.glbva.org
Resource referral, advocacy & networking for GLBT military veterans.

Cliff Arneson & NE GLB Veterans, Boston 1994

Rebecca E. Rosenblum, Psy.D.

Licensed Psychologist
Bilingual English/Portuguese

**857 Mass Ave (nr Central Sq)
Cambridge, MA 02139
617-661-1422**

Specializing in individual, couples, and group psychotherapy for adults. Addressing issues related to bisexuality, relationship issues, immigration, behavioral medicine, depression, and trauma.

La violencia doméstica afecta a las lesbianas, mujeres bisexuales, y gente transgénero, vengan de doude vengan
Domestic Violence happens to lesbians, bisexual women, and transgender folks from all walks of life

Llámenos para refugio, para advocacía, o simplemente para hablar.
Call for shelter, for advocacy, or just to talk

617- 423 - SAFE

Hotline/Linea de Crisis v/tty

www.nblbw.org

The Network

La Red

Robyn Ochs

March on Washington, 1993

The New England Leather Alliance

(a.k.a. NLA: New England)

For the past decade, NELA has worked to support the growth of all segments of the leather community in New England, through inclusive events, publications, programming, and charitable giving. Our Activist Roundtables have brought together groups from all six New England states to solve common problems and our Safe SM campaign has distributed over 8000 Safe Sex/Safe SM booklets throughout the region.

- **Fetish Fair Fleamarket**
  Our semi-annual vendor fair draws 4000+ attendees and attracts top vendors from the US, Canada, & Europe. Gay, straight, bi, married, single, polyamorous, young, old, all segments of the BDSM population come together at the FFF.

- **Events**
  We meet monthly at varying locations, depending on the topic. We hold activist roundtables, invite speakers to teach classes, and go on social outings which have included a BDSM camping trip, classes by Fetish Diva Midori and Carol Queen, a seminar on leather history, safety, and much more!

- **The Scarlet Leather**
  Our newsletter has always been a resource for the community at large. Free copies are distributed though local fetish shops, and we mail to hundreds of individuals. **The Scarlet Leather** provides a local calendar, reports on the activities of local organizations, and publishes valuable information about safety, activism, legislation, and more.

NELA: New England Leather Alliance
P.O. Box 35728
Brighton, MA 02135-0013
(617) 864-0655 Voice Mail/Events Line
http://www.nla-newengland.org

Gay, Lesbian, Bisexual, Transgender Youth Initiative The Medical Foundation, Prevention Support Services, 95 Berkeley St., Boston, MA 02116 ☎ Fraelean Curtis: 617-451-0049x268 ✉ fcurtis@tmfnet.org
📖 www.ultranet.com/~pss/projects.html#gay
Resources & technical assistance to groups around Massachusetts that work with GLBT youth or want to address homophobia.

The Pink Pistols of New England MA
✉ boston@pinkpistols.org, admin@pinkpistol.org
📖 www.pinkpistols.com/local/boston/index.html
GLBT gun afficionados.

in newsweekly: New England's Gay, Lesbian & Bisexual Newspaper 544 Tremont St, Boston, MA 02116 ☎ 617-426-8246 FX: 617-426-8264
✉ info@innewsweekly.com
Serving New England. Covers news & nightlife. PUB: in newsweekly (Weekly. Subscription rate: $140/yr. 1st class. Also free at certain community locations.)

Amherst

Amherst College

Lesbian, Gay & Bisexual Alliance, Heath Center, 204, Box 1817, Amherst, MA 01002-5000
☎ 413-542-8106 ✉ lgbta@unix.amherst.edu
📖 www.amherst.edu/~lbga/. *Political, social, support, weekly meetings.* **Queer/Straight Alliance,** Amherst, MA 01002 ☎ 413-582-5714
✉ qsa@unix.amherst.edu 📖 www.amherst.edu/~qsa/. *Political organization dedicated to LGBT awareness & fighting homophobia. Meets Tu. 8:30pm during termtime in Campus Center 207. All students invited.*

Amherst/Pelham Regional High School: Making Schools Safe for Gay, Lesbian, & Bisexual Students Committee/GSA 21 Mattoon St., Amherst, MA 01002 ☎ Michael Bardsley: 413-549-3710

Family Diversity Projects, Inc. PO Box 1209, Amherst, MA 01004-1209 ☎ 413-256-0502 FX: 413-253-3977 ✉ info@lovemakesafamily.org
📖 www.familydiv.org
Non-profit organization to educate students, parents, teachers, politicians, religious leaders & the general public about family diversity to help eliminate prejudice, stereotyping, name-calling, & harassment on the basis of race, gender, sexual orientation, or mental & physical ability. PUB: Love Makes A Family (Photo/text exhibit & book.)

Gay, Lesbian & Bisexual Group of the Jewish Community of Amherst 742 Main Street, Amherst, MA 01002 ☎ 413-256-0160 (Ask for GLB group)
For GLB Jews & their families. Sabbath & holiday services as well as social, educational & community action programs.

Hampshire College: Queer Campus Alliance Amherst, MA 01002 ☎ 413-582-5714

University of Massachusetts, Amherst

Stonewall Center: A Gay, Lesbian, Bisexual & Transgender Education Resource Center, Crampton House/ SW, Amherst, MA 01003
☎ 413-545-4824 FX: 413-545-6667
✉ stonewall@stuaf.umass.edu 📖 www.umass.edu/stonewall/. *Info / referral, education & cultural programming, speakers bureau for 5-college community. Free library (including videos). Crisis & discrimination response, training & consulting. Activities for graduate & older undergraduate students. Also, QueerE, an e-mail network of GLBT events in the Pioneer Valley.* PUB: The Blatent (Monthly newsletter of area GLBT events.)
Pride Alliance RSO Box 66, Amherst, MA 01003 ☎ 413-545-0154 ✉ lgba@stuaf.umass.edu.
Sponsors info-socials Tu. 7-9pm in the Campus Center to provide glbt students with a safe space to socialize & discuss relevant issues. Open to all. Great place to meet people & find community resources if you are just coming out. Also sponsors bisexual (mixed gender) discussion group.
Bisexual Focus Group c/o Stonewall Center
✉ levchuck@student.umass.edu. *Affilliated with the Pride alliance. Meets Sun. 7:30, Campus center or student union.* **Gay, Lesbian, Bisexual Speakers Bureau** 406G Student Union, Box 41, Amherst, MA 01003 ☎ 413-545-4824. *We talk about our lives as lgbt people & heterosexual allies. We are committed to change through communication.*

Graduate Student Gay, Lesbian & Bisexual Group c/o Stonewall Center. *GLBT graduate students across the campus interested in gathering to socialize & create connection across departments.*

Lesbian, Bisexual & Gay Political Caucus c/o Pride Alliance. **Lesbian, Bisexual, Gay Counseling Collective** 406G Student Union, Box 41, Amherst, MA 01003 ☎ 413-545-2645. *"Free, confidential peer counseling for local community, supervised by mental health professsionals. Weekly rap group, drop in or phone counseling."* **Alumni Pride Alliance at Amherst** c/o Stonewall Center
📖 www.umass.edu/stonewall/alumni.html. *Allows alumni to stay in contact, network, & keep in touch with the GLB campus community.*

Boston Pride, 1994

Boston, Cambridge, & environs

Bisexual Resource Center PO Box 1026, Boston, MA 02117-1026 ☎ 617-424-9595
✉ brc@biresource.org 🖳 www.biresource.org
Located at the Boston Living Center, 29 Stanhope Street, Boston, MA. See listing under "International."

Biversity - Boston 29 Stanhope St., Boston, MA 02116 ☎ 617-424-9595 ✉ biversity@blank.org
🖳 www.biresource.org/biversity
Mixed gender network in Boston for bis & allies. 2 brunches / month, discussion groups, movie outings, games nights, bicycling, etc. To subscribe to b-monthly postal mail events calendar: write or call w / your name / address; to email events list only: email biversity-request@blank.org; to discussion list: biversity-chat-request@blank.org or biversity-chat-digest-request@blank.org (for a day's worth of posts in one email). For any subscription write only 'subscribe' (no quotes) in message body.

Boston Bisexual Women's Network PO Box 400639, Cambridge, MA 02140 ☎ 617-424-9595
Publishes newsletter. Monthly potluck brunches & other social events. Periodic bi women's coming out groups. PUB: Bi Women (Sliding scale $20-30 +/-. Bi-monthly, 12-16 pages. Submissions from women welcome.)

Bisexual Women's Rap c/o The Women's Center, 46 Pleasant Street, Cambridge, MA 02139
☎ Women's Center: 617-354-8807
Free, open discussion on previously chosen topics.

Bi People of Color Gatherings c/o Bisexual Resource Center ☎ 617-424-9595 (leave message)
✉ Maria Christina Blanco: brctina@shore.net
Potluck & Discussion group. "A chance to connect & celebrate who we are." 4th Mon. 7-9pm at the Boston Living Center (above). All genders, diverse ethnicities welcome.

Bisexual & Bi-Curious Men's Group c/o FCHC, 7 Haviland St., Boston, MA 02115 ☎ 617-927-6032
✉ Marshall Miller: mmiller@fenwayhealth.org
Drop in support group, meets 2nd Tu. Free.

March on Washington, 1993

Coming Out as Bisexual c/o Bisexual Resource Center ☎ BRC Office: 617-424-9595
✉ info@biresource.org 🖳 www.biresource.org
Sponsored by the BRC. Informal support group for people who think they may be bisexual & / or who are attracted to more than one gender. 1st Wed. & 3rd Tu. 7-9pm.

Married Bisexual Women's Support Group
Women's Center, 46 Pleasant Street, Cambridge, MA 02139 ☎ 617-354-8807
New support group for married women who are bisexual or questioning their sexuality.

Gay & Bisexual Married Men's Support Group
c/o Bisexual Resource Center ☎ 781-316-1985; 781-545-2516 ✉ boston_bmmg@hotmail.com
🖳 world.std.com/~ewk/
Meets 1st & 3rd Mon., 7:30-10 at the Living Center.

Gay & Lesbian Advocates & Defenders (GLAD)
294 Washington Street, Suite 740, Boston, MA 02108 ☎ 617-426-1350 FX: 617-426-3594
✉ gladlaw@glad.org 🖳 www.glad.org
New England-wide legal rights & education organization for LGBT people & people living with HIV.

SpeakOut: GLBT Speakers Bureau PO Box 1358, Boston, MA 02117 ☎ 617-450-9776
✉ info@SpeakOutBoston.org
🖳 www.speakoutboston.org
Offers presentations on speakers' personal LGBT experiences. Gives special workshops targeting individual audiences: managers, human resource professionals, teachers, dorm counselors, police officers, or other groups. Provides speaker training. PUB: The Speaker (Board-produced newsletter that appears bi-monthly.)

Lesbian, Gay & Bisexual Freedom Trail Band of Boston PO Box 600486, Newton, MA 02460
☎ Jon 617-267-6311; toll free 877-FRDMTRL
✉ FrdmTrlBnd@aol.com
🖳 www.rdrop.com/~lgba/boston/
Provides entertainment & background music for special Lesbian & Gay community events. All year, all over New England. Need twirlers, banner carriers, band-aides & instruments. No auditions required.

LiLac: Lesbian, Gay & Bisexual Employees of Lotus 55 Cambridge Parkway, Cambridge, MA 02142 ☎ Kay Wilkins: 617-693-1230
✉ kay_wilkins@lotus.com
Provides a way for lgbt & other Loti & friends / supporters throughout the company to meet, network & get support.

The Gaylactic Network PO Box 127, Brookline, MA 02146 ✉ network@lambdasf.org
🖳 www.lambdasf.org/gaylacticnetwork/network.html
Club for GLBT (& friends) science fiction & fantasy fans. Meets locally in several areas, including Boston & DC. PUB: GNAPA (Yahoogroups list - www.yahoogroups.com/community/GNAPA or GNAPA-subscribe@yahoogroups.com)

Boston Pride 1994

Robyn Ochs

Cambridge Lavender Alliance PO Box 380884, Cambridge, MA 02238 ☎ 617-492-6393 Sue Hyde ✉ shyde@hgltf.org
Social & political activist organization for improving the quality of life for LGBT people in Cambridge.

Massachusetts Area South Asian Lambda Association (MASALA) PO Box 1182, Cambridge, MA 02142 ☎ 617-499-9669 ✉ bostonmasala-owner@yahoogroups.com
Discussion/support/social group for South Asian LGBT folks. PUB: MASALA monthly newsletter (Free trial subscription)

Girlfriends c/o Cambridge Family & Children's Service, 929 Mass. Ave, Cambridge, MA 02136 ☎ 617-876-4210
Free, weekly peer support group for lesbians & bi women of color. Currently meets on Saturdays.

Queer Asian Pacific Alliance PO Box 543, Prudential Station, Boston, MA 02119 ☎ 617-499-9531 ✉ qapa@geocities.comqapa@ccae.org, qapa_2000@yahoo.com 🖳 www.geocities.com/WestHollywood/heights/5010
For lgbtq women & men of both Asian & Pacific Islander heritages. Social gatherings 1st Sun. To subscribe to the QAPA email list, send to majordomo@ccae.org: subscribe qapa-news subscribe qapa.

Boston Prime Timers, Inc. 29 Stanhope Street, Boston, MA 02116-5111 ☎ 617-338-5305 ✉ BosPT@aol.com 🖳 home.earthlink.net/~chuck200/bostonpt.html
For mature gay & bi men & their admirers. Monthly events calendar.

Boston University Lesbian, Gay Bisexual People in Medicine Boston University School of Medicine, 715 Albany Street, Boston, MA 02118 ✉ Jason Smith (smithj@bu.edu); Adam Lebowitz (alebowit@bu.edu) 🖳 homepages.go.com/~adleb/lgbpm.html
Combined group for students, faculty, & staff at BU Medical Center including Medicine, Public Health, Dentistry, Graduate Medical Sciences, & other health-related sciences. Social group for lgbt & friends. Notification about all activities is by e-mail. Mailing list confidential. To SUBSCRIBE to the e-mail listserve, send message to majordomo@bu.edu, with : "subscribe lgbpm-list" in the body of the message.

Boston University: Spectrum Office #6, Stud.Cntr, George Sherman Union, 775 Commonwealth Avenue, Boston, MA 02215 ☎ 617-353-9808 ✉ spectrum@bu.edu 🖳 people.bu.edu/spectrum/
Weekly mtgs., with films, guest speakers, etc. during termtime.

Harvard Medical School: Kinsey 2-to-6ers 25 Shattuck Street, Boston, MA 02115
LGB Harvard Medical School affiliates. Produces events & annual resource brochure: "abOUT HMS."

New England Conservatory of Music Lesbian, Gay, Bisexuals 33 Gainsborough St., c/o Cordelia Chenault or David Devoe, Boston, MA 02115 ☎ 617-585-1295 - Student Life office ✉ jazzdiesel@aol.com
Social & political group.

Northeastern University: Bisexual, Lesbian & Gay Association (NUBiLAGA) 360 Huntington Av., Room 240, Curry Student Center, Boston, MA 02115 ☎ 617-373-2738 ✉ nubigala@yahoo.com

Northeastern University School of Law: Lesbian, Gay & Bisexual Association 59 Cargill Hall, 360 Huntington Ave., Boston, MA 02115 ☎ 617-373-2738 (NuBiLAGA) ✉ jscarborough@nunet.neu.edu (Faculty Advisor) 🖳 www.queercaucus.homestead.com

Simmons College: Lesbian, Bisexual & Allies Association 300 The Fenway, Boston, MA 02115 ☎ 617-521-2446 ✉ LBA2@artemis.simmons.edu

The Art Institute of Boston: The Alliance 700 Beacon St., Boston, MA 02215 ☎ 617-262-1223; 617-349-8509 ✉ sturner@mail.lesley.edu 🖳 www.lesley.edu/diversity.html
LGB group for students, faculty & staff.

University of Massachusetts - Boston: Queer Student Union Boston, MA ☎ 617-287-7983 ✉ lgbc@umb.edu

> **"When one understands bisexuality as the sum total of all of the implications of loving others at the level of the SOUL, and not merely at the level of the physical BODY, one understands that this capacity is indeed our most fortunate destiny, and a state of exquisite grace."**
>
> *Deb Kolodny, in Blessed Bi Spirit*

Northeastern University GLB group, Boston Pride

Harvard University

BGLTSA PO BOX 380232, Cambridge, MA 02138 ☎ 617-493-1193) ✉queer@hcs.harvard.edu, 🖳 www.digitas.harvard.edu/~queer/ *Campus undergraduate group.* **Association of Lesbian, Bisexual & Gay Graduate Students (LBGGS)** Dudley House, Harvard Yard, Cambridge, MA 02138) lbggs@hcs.harvard.edu. *Social Mixers 8-10pm 1st Th. in Grad. Student Lounge, Dudley House, open to all. Email list: to subscribe send message with name & e-mail address to lbg-request@katla.harvard.edu.* **BOND** ✉ bond@hcs.harvard.edu. *BGLT group with a social, non-political focus.* **Girlspot** 3 Sacramento St., Cambridge, MA) ✉ girlspot@hcs.harvard.edu 🖳 www.hcs.harvard.edu/~girlspot/. *Harvard's group for queer women & allies.* **Bagels** ✉bagels@hcs.harvard.edu. *Harvard BGLT group for Jewish students & supporters.* **Cornerstone** Harvard/Radcliffe Catholic Student Center, 20 Arrow Street, Cambridge, MA 02138 ✉ jlandry@pobox.harvard.edu. *Bi-monthly gathering to discuss sexual identity & spirituality in a comfortable, non-judgmental atmosphere for glb Catholics. Harvard / Radcliffe students only.*

Lesley College: Association of Gays, Lesbians & Bisexuals
29 Everett St., Cambridge, MA 02138-2790 ☎ 617-349-8540 (Student Affairs) *For undergraduates.*

MIT: Gays, Lesbians, Bisexuals, Transgendered, & Friends at MIT (GAMIT)
142 Memorial Drive, Room 50-306, Cambridge, MA 02139 ☎ 617-253-5440 ✉ gamit-admin@mit.edu 🖳 www.mit.edu/activities/gamit/ *Primarily serving the MIT community, but open to everyone. Coming out group, organization meetings, social events.*

Boston College: Lesbian, Gay & Bisexual Community
Box L-112, Chestnut Hill, MA 02467 ☎ 617-552-2979 FX: 617-555-0050 ✉ murayda@bc.edu

University of Massachusetts, Boston: Queer Student Union
c/o Student Life, Harbor Campus, 100 Morrissey Blvd., Dorchester, MA 02128-3393 ☎ 617-287-7983

> Never doubt that a small group of thoughtful, committed citizens can change the world; indeed, it's the only thing that ever does.
>
> Margaret Mead

Boston College Law School: LAMBDA Law Students Association
885 Centre Street , Newton Centre, MA 02459 ☎ 617-552-0955 ✉ suffredk@bc.edu 🖳 www.bc.edu/lambda/ *Coalition of LGBT students, staff, faculty & supporters who: foster a supportive social network, educate the community about lgbt identities, sponsor panels on legal issues affecting lgbt individuals, promote diversity in law. school & the legal profession, & strive toward equality before the law.*

Tufts University

Lesbian, Gay, Bisexual & Transgender Resource Center 226 College Avenue, Medford, MA 02155 ☎ 781-627-3770; Director: 617-627-5770 FX: 617-627-3574) Director's email: ✉ jbrown@emerald.tufts.edu. *Programming & resources for LGBT & straight communities on campus.* **Tufts Transgendered, Lesbian, Gay & Bisexual Collective** c/o Student Activities, Campus Center, Medford, MA 02155 ☎ 781-627-3770. *Student group, meets weekly.*

Project 10 East, Inc. PO Box 382401, Cambridge, MA 02238 ☎ 617-864-GLBT, Cambridge Rindge & Latin High School group 617-349-6486 ✉ info@project10east.org 🖳 www.project10east.org/ *Builds bridges between communities & glbt & straight youth alliances, creating its model from the successes of existing school- & community-based programs. Drop-in center weekday afternoons during the school year at Old Cambridge Baptist Church, 1145 Mass Ave., & runs GSA groups in several local high schools, including Cambridge Rindge & Latin HS.*

Boston Pride, 1990s

> **"After reading the fine anthology of African American women writers entitled "This Bridge Called My Back", I am sometimes tempted to write something called "This Fence Called My Butt."** It seems that wherever I sit down, that is where the fence is. No matter how hard I try to belong to a group, sooner or later someone draws a line and it inevitably ends up going right through my body, my desire, my soul, my gods...I refuse to choose one or the other, no matter where they'd like to split me. I choose both, again and again, every time, because I truly believe that this is the only real choice, the one that my God/dess would make if S/he were Me."
>
> *Raven Kaldera, in Blessed Bi Spirit*

BAGLY: Boston Alliance of Gay, Lesbian, Bisexual, Transgendered, & Questioning Youth
PO Box 814, Boston, MA 02103 ☎ 617-227-4313, (TTY) 617-983-9845 FX: 227-3266
✉ bagly@bagly.org 🖳 www.bagly.org
Youth led, adult supported social support organization for glbtq youth & straight allies, - 23. Also offers peer-counseling program, speaker's bureau, referrals, sponsors events & activities for youth. BAGLY is also the primary contact for the GLBT Youth Group Network of Mass.

Boston GLASS- Gay & Lesbian Social Services
93 Massachusetts Ave, 3rd fl, Boston, MA 02115
☎ 617-266-3349 ✉ GLASS@jri.org
Community Center for LGBT youth, 13-25. Formalized programs, discussions, support & social groups. Safe place to meet, talk & hang out. No hassles, no pressures, just a great group of people who understand.

At Boston pride

Robyn Ocha

Latino Health Institute Project Luna 95 Berkeley Street, Boston, MA 02116 ☎ 617-350-6900 x184 ✉ luna@lhi.org 🖳 www.lhi.org
For Latino GLBT youth.

Fenway Community Health Center 7 Haviland St., Boston MA 02115:

Color Me Healthy ☎ 617-927-6244 ✉ Orlando Colon: ocolon@fenwayhealth.org
Social/support group for gay/bi men of color. Free. **Delta Project** ☎ David Young: 617-927-6300 ✉ dyoung@fchc.org
🖳 www.fenwayhealth.org/services/wellness/delta.htm. *Monthly topic discussions for gay/bi men on cultural, social, economic, political & health issues. 3rd Tu..6:30-8:30pm at Fenway.*
Coming Out Group ☎ Ann: 617-927-6202; main # 888.242-0900 (in MA) 🖳 www.fchc.org/calendar.htm. *A co-ed, short term group for men & women in the process of coming out as gay or bisexual. Call for meeting times & to arrange an initial evaluation. Fee-based on sliding scale.*
Essence of a Woman ☎ 617-927-6134 ✉ Dede Thomas: dthomas@fenwayhealth.org. *Monthly sex rap series for women who have sex with women.* **HIV- Negative Gay/Bi Men's Support Group** ☎ 617-927-6300; Vin Longo 617-927-6231 ✉ vlongo@fenwayhealth.org. ✉*3-session series each month. Teaches risk assessment & risk reduction strategies. Free.*
Queer Women's Polyamory Discussion & Support Group ☎ 617-927-6058
✉ starfurry@worldnet.att.net. *Discussion/support group for lesbians & bi women interested in polyamory & alternatives to monogamy. All women are welcome. Meets 2nd Tu. at Fenway.*
SASSIE (Sisters Acquiring Safer Sex Information & Education) ☎ 617-927-6134 ✉ Dede Thomas: dthomas@fenwayhealth.org
SASSIE stands for "Sisters Acquiring Safer Sex Information & Education." 8 week group: self esteem, relationships, sexuality. **Victim Recovery Program - VRP** ☎ 617-927-6300 or 800-834-3242 ✉ Dave Shannon: dshannon@fenwayhealth.org
Services for glbt victims of domestic violence, hate crimes, sexual assault, & police misconduct. Support groups available. All services available in Spanish.

The Network/La Red: Ending Abuse in Lesbian, Bisexual Women, & Transgender Communities
PO Box 6011, Boston, MA 02114 ☎ 617-695-0877 Hotline:423-SAFE FX: 617-423-5651
✉ nblbw@erols.com 🖳 www.nblbw.org
Bilingual TTY accessible hotline, free wheelchair accessible support group, legal & other referrals, newsletter, community education. Added Bisexual to their name in 1996.

AIDS Action Committee 131 Clarendon St, Boston, MA 02116 ☎ 617-450-1286

Am Tikva PO Box 1268, Brookline, MA 02446 ☎ 617-883-0893 ✉ Info@amtikva.org 🖳 www.amtikva.org
Boston LGBT Jews, offering Sabbath & holiday services, educational / discussion groups & social events.

Dignity/Boston PO Box 408, Boston, MA 02117-0408 ☎ 617-421-1915 ✉ dignityinfo@dignityboston.org 🖳 www.dignityboston.org
LGBT Catholic group. Weekly mass.

Interweave 167 Milk St, #406, Boston, MA 02109-4339 🖳 qrd.tcp.com/qrd/www/orgs/uua/uu-interweave.html
Membership organization affiliated with the UUA, dedicated to the spiritual, political, & social well-being of UU's who are confronting oppression as lgbt persons, & their heterosexual allies. Celebrates the culture & the lives of its members. PUB: Interweave World

Keshet: Jewish Gay, Lesbian, Bisexual, & Transgender Advocacy & Education Group of Boston c/o Jewish Family & Children's Service, 1340 Centre Street, Newton, MA 02459 ☎ 617-558-1278 x212 FX: 617-558-5250 ✉ ALederbe@JFCSBoston.org 🖳 www.boston-keshet.org/
Advocates mequality & integration of GLBT folks in the Jewish community to strengthen the Jewish identities of GLBT Jews. PUB: Kol Keshet (newsletter)

Unitarian Universalist Association Office of Bisexual, Gay, Lesbian & Transgender Concerns 25 Beacon Street, Boston, MA 02108-2800 ☎ 617-948-6475 ✉ obgltc@uua.org 🖳 www.uua.org/obgltc
Provides resources for UU congregations working toward being more affirming & welcoming to BLGT folks, including info, resolutions & pamphlets encouraging support for BLGTs; a list of welcoming congregations; free organizational start-up kits, bibliographic materials, sample same-sex union services, pink triangle stickers, & info on public speaking.

Metro Southeast Youth Alliance 792 North Main St., Brockton, MA 02401 ✉ jltk80a@prodigy.com
GLBTQ & supportive youth -22 welcome. Meets Th. 7-9pm at 792 North Main St.

Concord-Carlisle High School: Spectrum 500 Walden Steet, Concord, MA 01742 🖳 www.colonial.net/cchsweb/clubs.html
LBG & straight alliance.

Triangle Divers 26 Saxton Street, Dorchester, MA 02125 ☎ 617-422-1775 ✉ Info@Triangledivers.org,jmcbride@tiac.net 🖳 www.triangledivers.org/
New Englands only g/l SCUBA club & the first gay SCUBA web site! Monthly meetings 3rd Wed. 7:30pm at Club Cafe, 209 Columbus Ave. in Boston's South End.

Stonehill College: PRIDE Easton, MA ✉ jdemarco@stonehill.edu, garp97@hotmail.com

Valuable Families PO Box 60634, Florence, MA 01062 ☎ 413-585-1257 ✉ valfams@mailcity.com 🖳 www.valuablefamilies.org
Non-profit organization of glbt parents, their children, & allies.

Venture Out PO Box 60271, Florence, MA 01062 ☎ 413-584-8764 ✉ ventureout@geocities.com 🖳 www.geocities.com/WestHollywood/2956
Activities group based in Western MA.

Metro West Bis 14 Main St. #2, Framingham, MA 01712 ☎ 508-872-3720 ✉ ultrarifka@ncounty.net 🖳 www.yahoogroups.com/group/metrowestbis
Newly forming social / peer support group for those living in the suburbs west of Boston.

Mount Wachusett Community College, Lesbian, Gay, Bisexual, & Straight Alliance 444 Green Street, Gardner, MA 01440-1000

CAMEN - Cape Ann Gay & Bi Men's Discussion Group Gloucester, MA ☎ David Goudreau 978-281-0311

Lexington High School: Gay/Straight Alliance Science Building, 251 Waltham Street, Lexington, MA 02173 ☎ Michael Lerner: 781-861-2362 ✉ mlerner@sch.ci.lexington.ma.us
Support & social action group for students.

Other Massachusetts

Cape Lesbian, Gay, Bisexual Coalition PO Box 148, Brewster, MA 02631 ☎ 508-430-9939
Phone evenings or leave message. PUB: Directory of gay & gay-friendly businesses & services on Cape Cod (call for free copy).

Bridgewater State College: Bisexual, Lesbian & Gay Alliance BSC Campus Center, 131 Summer St., Bridgewater, MA 02325 ☎ 508-697-1200 x2032

Brockton High School Gay/Straight Alliance Forest Ave., Brockton, MA 02401 ☎ 508-580-7624

Massasoit Community College Gay/Straight Alliance One Massasoit Blvd, Brockton, MA 02402 ☎ 800-227-3377x1679 FX: 508-427-1250

At Boston Pride

Northampton GLB Pride March, 1991

A. Dubois

Cape Islands Gay & Straight Youth Alliance (CIGYA) PO Box 805Y, Monument Beach, MA 02553-0805 ☎ 508-778-7744x12; 877-429-7743 ✉ cigyahouse@aol.com 🖳 www.capecod.net/gayyouth/
Facilitated discussion group Th. 7-8:30pm at 56 Barnstable Rd, Hyannis. Also workshops, social activities & trips. Youth -23.

Merrimack College - Gay-Straight Alliance N. Andover, MA ✉ merrimackgsa@aol.com

University of Massachusetts, Dartmouth: Bisexual, Gay & Lesbian Alliance PO Box 144, Campus Center, Old Westport Road, N. Dartmouth, MA 02747 ☎ 508-999-8163
Support for students on campus.

Brockton Area Alliance of Gay & Lesbian Youth PO Box 119, N. Easton, MA 02356 ☎ 877-4-BRAGLY ✉ bragly@hotmail.com 🖳 www.brdk.org/bragly/
Part of the Metro Southeast Youth Alliance. Safe place for GLBTQ & supportive-straight youth. MSPCC BUILDING, 3rd Floor, Main St. Brockton. Mon. 8-10pm. Founded & supported by Healthcare of SE Massachusetts, South Shore AIDS Project, Massachusetts Dept. of Public Health in cooperation with Governors Commission on Gay & Lesbian Youth, GLBT Youth Group Network of Massachusetts.

Southcoast Diversity Alliance c/o Child & Family Services, 1061 Pleasant St., New Bedford, MA 02740 ☎ 508-996-8572 FX: 508-991-8618
Social support group providing a safe & nurturing environment for LGBTQ youth -21.

Unity Church of North Easton 13 Main Street, North Easton, MA 02356 ☎ 508-238-6373 ✉ office@unity-church.com 🖳 www.brdk.org/uc/index.htm
Organized religious society & a member of the Unitarian Universalist Association. GLBT friendly. PUB: The Unity News (508-238-6373 c/o Unity Church 9 Main St., North Easton, MA 02356. Editors: Cathy Adler & Sue Meunier Email: news@unity-church.com.)

Lesbian, Gay & Bisexual, Transgender Political Alliance of Western Massachusetts PO Box 1244, Northampton, MA 01061 ☎ 413-586-8876 🖳 www.wmassalliance.org/ 🖳 info@wmassalliance.org
Works in local communities around Western Massachusetts to ensure that LGBT interests are being served by our local politicians & to support initiatives that benefit our community.

Men With Men Room 311, 16 Center Street, Northampton, MA 01060 ☎ 413-585-1012
Social/discussion group for gay & bi men. Meets 1st & 3rd Fri.s 7:30-9pm.

Northampton Area Lesbian & Gay Business Guild PO Box 593, Northampton, MA 01061-0593 ☎ 413-585-8839 ✉ NALGBGinfo@aol.com 🖳 www.westmass.com/nalgbg/
A LGB & Allied business association.

Out Now!: Lesbian, Gay & Bisexual Youth Group of Greater Springfield PO Box 833, Northampton, MA 01061 ☎ 1-888-429-9990 ✉ hmrichar@javanet.com
Free, voluntary support group for -22. Meets weekly at Trinity Church in Springfield. Wheelchair accessible. When leaving message, leave any special instructions regarding calls back. 413-586-2627 M-F 10am-1pm gets live person. Lifecourse also offers counseling for bi folks (fee for service).

Smith College

The Lesbian Bisexual Transgender Alliance Student Government Office, Clark Hall, Northampton, MA 01063 ☎ 413-585-4907 ✉ lba@sophia.smith.edu 🖳 www.smith.edu/lba
Political & social organization serving the Smith LBT & allied community. **Prism** Clark Hall SGA Office, Northhampton, MA 01063, ✉ tstcloud@mail.smith.edu, 🖳 www.smith.edu/lba/prism. *Provides resources to the LBT/Ally/Questioning women of color community through social events, films, discussions, & speakers. Meets weekly.* **School of Social Work: Lesbian, Gay, Bisexual Transgendered Alliance** Lilly Hall, Northampton, MA 01063

Homo-Bi-Hetero Society Northfield Mt. Herman School, Northfield, MA 01360-1089 ☎ Vicky Greenbaum: 413-498-4440

Wheaton College

Lesbian Gay Bisexual Alliance Norton, MA 02766 🖳 marylyon.wheatoncollege.edu/Club/lgbta/.

Lesbian, Gay, Bisexual, & Transgender Alumnae/i (LGBTA) c/o Sharon Howard, Wheaton College Alumnae/i Relations, Norton, MA 02766 ☎ 508-285-8207 ✉ maguilar@bcpl.net 🖳 marylyon.wheatoncollege.edu/Club/lgbta/home.html *LGBT Alumnae/i Group for Wheaton College Web site lists events of LGBT interest sponsored by Wheaton College, the LGBTA Steering Committee, & the LGBT Alliance.*

> **i speak without reservation from what i know and who i am. i do so with the understanding that all people should have the right to offer their voice to the chorus whether the result is harmony or dissonance. the worldsong is a colorless dirge without the differences that distinguish us, and it is that difference which should be celebrated not condemned. should any part of my music offend you, please do not close your ears to it. just take what you can use and go on.**
>
> Ani DiFranco

Salem State College: Gay, Lesbian & Bisexual Peer Action Group of the Salem Community Salem, MA 01970 ☎ 508-741-6436

Straight Spouse Network - Western Massachusetts & Connecticut 53 Elm St., Shelburne Falls, MA 01370 ☎ JaneHarris: 413-625-6933 ✉ aharris@valinet.com
Support for spouses whose partners are GL or B in a non-homophobic, confidential environment.

GLBT Organization of Somerville Somerville, MA ☎ 617-623-8692 ✉ Emailsomerville_glbt@hotmail.com
Goal: to build and organize a stronger, politically present GLBT community in Somerville.

Mount Holyoke College Lesbian Bisexual Alliance Box 105, Mary Wooley, So., South Hadley, MA 01075 ☎ 413-538-3822

Mount Holyoke College SYSTA Box 1943, South Hadley, MA 01075
LBQ Women of Color.

Southern Worcester County Bisexual Alliance (SWCBA) PO Box 145, Southbridge, MA 01550
"Open to bis & bi-friendly people of either gender. In the process of forming a bi support group, a group for married bisexuals, and a bi/gay/les walking group. We could use the help of anyone in the area."

Gay/Lesbian Info Service Springfield, MA ☎ 413-731-5403

Springfield Technical Community College: Gay, Lesbian, Bisexual Alliance c/o Student Activities, 1 Amory Square, Springfield, MA 01105 ☎ 413-748-3750
Meets Tu. 12:30-1:30 during termtime. Open to all college-aged people in the greater Springfield area.

Cape Cod Community College: LGB Alliance at 4 C's #2240 Lyanough Rd., W. Barnstable, MA 02668 ☎ John French: 508-362-2131 x4320
Meetings on Tu. at 1 pm.

Brandeis University: Triskelion c/o Student Center, PO Box 9110, Waltham, MA 02254-9110 ☎ 781-736-3749 ✉ trisk@brandeis.edu 🖳 www.undergrad.brandeis.edu/~trisk
BGLT group for students at Brandeis. Brandeis also has a bi group: BiSpace.

Wellsley College Lesbians, Bisexuals, Transgendered & Friends Schneider Center, 106 Central St., Wellesley, MA 02181 ☎ 781-283-3417 ✉ wbltf@wellesley.edu

Westfield State College: Gay/Straight Alliance 577 Western Avenue, Westfield, MA 01086-1630 ☎ Advisors: Brian Cahillane 413- 572-5401, Kath Bradford 413-572-5404 🖳 rlserver.wsc.mass.edu/qnet/westfield.htm

Williams College: Queer/Straight Alliance Student Union, Williamstown, MA 01267 🖳 wso.williams.edu/orgs/qsa
Meets Mon. 10pm during termtime.

Assumption College: Gay & Lesbian Discussion Group 500 Salisbury St, PO Box 15005, Worcester, MA 01615-0005

Clark University: Lesbian, Bisexual & Questioning c/o Women's Center Collective, Box B-5, Worcester, MA 01610-1477 ☎ 508-793-7287

Holy Cross College: Allies 1 College St., Worcester, MA 01610 ☎ 508-793-3487 (student activities)
Mixed group (LGBT & straight). Educates the Holy Cross community on gay issues by holding weekly meetings in the Hogan Center & organizing events throughout the year.

MSM Services Program AOW, Inc., 85 Green St., Worcester, MA 01604-4134 ☎ 508-770-1308 x32 or 508-775-3773 x32
Specialized assistance & support to G & B men & other men who have sex with men. Professional clinicians provide counseling, groups, educational programs, & social activities. Free & confidential. Funded by the Mass DPH.

Worcester Polytechnic Institute: BiLAGA c/o Student Activities Office, 100 Institute Rd., Worcester, MA 01609 ✉ bilaga@wpi.edu

Worcester State College: Delta c/o Student Center, 486 Chandler Street, Worcester, MA 01602 ☎ Student Center: 508-929-8073

Morning Star Community Church PO Box 687, Worcester, MA, MA 01602 ☎ 508-892-4320; 508-949-7939 🖳 www.mccweb.org
A Metropolitan Community Church, Provides support, love, & guidance in a caring, nonjudgmental, Christian environment. All welcome. Services in Auburn.

Michigan

Between the Lines 20793 Farmington Rd., Suit 25, Farmington, MI 48336 ☎ 888-615-7003 FX: 248-615-7018 ✉ pridepblis@aol.com 🖥 www.betweenthelinesnews.com
Statewide newspaper for LGBT & Friends.

Triangle Foundation 19641 West Seven Mile Road, Detroit, MI 48219 ☎ 313-537-3323 FX: 313-537-3379 ✉ trijeffm@aol.com 🖥 www.tri.org
Statewide civil rights, advocacy & anti-violence organization for lgbt people. Projects: Anti-Violence Project; Human Rights Project; Legislative Education; People of Faith Network; Media Watchdog; Legal Advocacy Fund; Community Response/Speaker's Bureau

Albion College: Break the Silence c/o CPO, Albion, MI 49307 ☎ 517-629-1469

Grand Valley State University: Out n' About 1 Campus Drive, Allendale, MI 49401 ☎ 616-895-2345 ✉ out_n_about48@hotmail.com

Alma College: Pride LGB Students Gayle Passaretti, Faculty Advisor, 614 W. Superior, Alma, MI 48801 ☎ 517-466-7225

VisiBIlity c/o Holly Ferrise, 1955 McKinley, Ypsilanti, MI 48197 ☎ 734-484-4614 ✉ nanette@umich.edu
Ann Arbor based, multi-gender group for bisexual, pansexual, omnisexual, multisexual, bi-affectional folks & their partners, friends, & allies. Support group meets 2nd Sun. 4-6. Discussion group 4th Fri. 7-9. Both at WRAP Office, Braun Ct., Ann Arbor. Both followed by socials.

Poly Positive Ann Arbor, MI ☎ Stephanie: 734-913-8895 ✉ Doug: bolero156@netscape.net; bolero@ibm.net 🖥 www.blackrose.org/~bolero/pp_faq.html
Social/support group for polyamorous people of all orientations.

Unscouts: Bisexual Women's Support & Social Group Ann Arbor, MI ☎ Stephanie: 734-913-8895. ✉ Tammy: tammy@intranet.org 🖥 home.intranet.org/~hope/unscouts.html
Informal support/social group for bisexual & bi-friendly women 21+. New members welcome.

Bi folk showing off bi t-shirts, March on Washington, 1993

University of Michigan

Lesbian Gay Bisexual & Transgender Affairs, 3200 Michigan Union, Ann Arbor, MI 48109-1349, ☎ 313-763-4186; FX: 734-647-4133 (attn: to LGBTA), ✉ lgbta@umich.edu, 🖥 www.umich.edu/~inqueery. **Lavender Information & Library Association**, School of Information, 304 West Hall, 550 East University, Ann Arbor, MI 48109, ✉ LILA@board.umich.edu, 🖥 www.si.umich.edu/LILA/, *Active, professional organization for School of Information students, University libraries & archives staff, & related professionals. LILA promotes awareness of glbt issues through educational, networking, social & political activities.* **Delta Lambda Phi, Alpha Mu Chapter** PO Box 980280, Ypsilanti, MI 48198 ☎ 734-651-2431 ✉ LambdaMen@hotmail.com 🖥 dlp.org/ or www.emunix.emich.edu/~centaur
For the University of Michigan, Eastern Michigan University, & Washtenaw Community College. National social fraternity for gay/bi & progressive men. "When it comes to diversity, what others hide in shame, we boldly embrace in pride."

Ozone House: Support/Social Group for Lesbian, Gay, Bisexual, Transgender, & Questioning Youth 1705 Washtenaw, Ann Arbor, MI 48104 ☎ Rob: 662-2265 ext. 18 ✉ ozonehouse@aol.com
Support/Social Group for LGBTQ youth 13-18. Free, totally confidential. Discuss, watch videos & participate in recreational & educational activities within a supportive environment.

Ford Gay, Lesbian or Bisexual Employees 23814 Michigan Avenue #187, Dearborn, MI 48124 ☎ 313-438-1970 ✉ info@fordGLOBE.org 🖥 FordGLOBE.org
Formal organization for employees & active agency contractors at Ford Motor Company who are glb or who support glb concerns to foster an inclusive & supportive atmosphere. Monthly membership meetings, lunch meetings, coffee socials & other social events.

Wayne State University: Lesbian, Gay, Bisexual, Transgender Services 5221 Gullen Mall, 573 SCB, Detroit, MI 48202 ☎ 313-577-3398 FX: 313-577-3257 ✉ s.schoeberlein@wayne.edu 🖥 www.studentcouncil.wayne.edu/GLBU/main.html
Office in Student Center Bldg. 756.2. Counseling programs, support groups, educational presentations, info & referrals.

Michigan State University: Alliance of Lesbian, Bi Gay & Transgendered Students 441 MSU Union, East Lansing, MI 48824-1020 ☎ 517-353-9795 FX: 517-353-4717 ✉ alliance@pilot.msu.edu 🖥 www.msu.edu/user/alliance
Open to community members & MSU students, faculty & staff.

> **Like many men, I too have had homosexual experiences and I am not ashamed.**
>
> *Marlon Brando, 1980s.*

Bi-Married Men's Group Ferndale, MI
☎ 248-680-0133
Support/Social group for bi/gay men who are or have been married. Safe place to get support, gain info, & make friends. Monthly meetings, 4th Tu. 7pm at Affirmations (195 West 9 Mile, Ferndale).

Affirmations L&G Community Center Ferndale, MI ☎ 800-398-GAYS
✉ affirmationsglbt@juno.com
Has "bi & bi-friendly group" that meets 2nd Wed. 7-8:30pm.

University of Michigan at Flint: Lesbian, Gay, Bisexual & Transgender Center 365 UCEN, Flint, MI 48502-2186 ☎ 810-766-6606
✉ lgbt@list.flint.umich.edu
🖳 www.flint.umich.edu/departments/lgbt_center

Michigan Tech: Keweenaw Pride PO Box 501, Houghton, MI 49224 ✉ pride@mtu.edu
🖳 www.sos.mtu.edu/ccglba
Student group for glbt people & friends. Provide support, educate ourselves & others, & promote a "queer positive" atmosphere on campus. Active in the campus community, participating in events such as Winter Carnival & Spring Fling.

Western Michigan University: LBG Student Services A327 Ellsworth Hall, Kalamazoo, MI 49008 ☎ 616-387-2123 FX: 616-387-3348
✉ salp_lbg@wmich.edu 🖳 www.salp.wmich.edu/lbg/glb

Northern Michigan University: Outlook Box 4, University Center, Marquette, MI 49855
☎ 906-227-1557 ✉ outlook@nmu.edu

Central Michigan University

Office of Gay & Lesbian Programs, 130 Sloan Hall, Mt. Pleasant, MI 48859 ☎ 517-774-3637 FX: 517-772-2022. **Prism**, 129 Sloan Hall, Mt. Pleasant, MI 48859 ☎ 517-774-7470
✉ prism@cmich.edu *Social & support organization for GLBs & friends.*

Palland University: Pride Forum 49 Oakland Center, Rochester, MI 48309 ☎ 248-370-4122 FX: 248-370-4293 🖳 www.oakland.edu/prideforum

> **I got a girl in every port and a couple of guys in every port, too.**
>
> *Sal Mineo, American actor, 1939-1976*

Dignity Detroit PO Box 558, Royal Oak, MI 48068 ☎ 313-278-4786
"An affirming, loving community of glbt individuals, their friends & families who gather to worship in the Catholic tradition." Mass Sun at 6pm in the Sacred Heart Chapel located at Marygrove College in Detroit on the corner of Wyoming & McNichols. Dignity announces the formation of a spiritual, social support group for women. Meets 3rd Sat 10am-12noon at Marygrove College.

Eastern Michigan University

Lesbian, Gay, Bisexual & Transgender Support Services Office, c/o Campus Life, 201-C Goodison, Ypsilanti, MI 48197 ☎ 734-487-4149 ✉ LGBTRC@emich.edu, 🖳 www.emich.edu/public/vso/lgbt.html. **Lesbian & Gay, Faculty & Staff at EMU**, c/o Prof. Michael McGuire, PO Box 80438, Ypsilanti, MI 48198-0438 ☎ 734-487-0292 ✉michael.mcguire@emich.edu.

Minnesota

BECAUSE Conference (Bisexual Empowerment Conference A Uniting Supportive Experience) Planning Committee c/o OutFront Mininesota, 310 E. 38th St. East, Minneapolis, MN 55409 ☎ 612-822-0127 x503
✉ because2001@hotmail.com
🖳 www.bisexual.org/g/because2001/
Annual Midwest bisexual 3-day empowerment conference held in midwest in the spring.

OutFront Minnesota 310 38th Street East, #204, Minneapolis, MN 55409 ☎ 612-822-0127; 800-800-0350 FX: 612-822-8786 ✉ outfront@outfront.org
🖳 www.outfront.org
Provides assistance in legal matters, domestic violence, & acts as a political spokesgroup for g/l concerns in Minnesota. Some services are bi-inclusive.

Northland Gay Men's Center 8 North Second Avenue E. Suites #308-309, Duluth, MN 55802 ☎ 218-722-8585
Non-profit organization providing services to gay/bi men of the upper Midwest.

OutWest Teens Alone, 915 Main St., Hopkins, MN 55343 ☎ 952-988-TEEN (8336)
FX: 952-988-5358 🖳 www.teensalone.com
Support & discussion group for youth 10-17 who are questioning their sexual identity.

Mankato State University: Lesbian, Gay, Bisexual Center Centennial Student Union 242, Mankato, MN 56002 ☎ 507-389-5131
🖳 www.csu.mankato.msus.edu/lgbc/

The Bisexual Connection Minneapolis, MN
☎ Gary Lingen: (651) 645-2851
✉ lingenmagick@compuserve.com
Support & resources for bi, bi-supportive & bi-curious people.

> **Okay, okay.** If you're asking am I one, I'll go that route—good public relations. If it's good enough for Gore Vidal and Elton John, it's good enough for me. I am bisexual, happy and proud. A woman in every bed... and a man, too. Satisfied?
>
> *Rock Hudson, American actor 1925-1985*

Twin Cities' Bisexual Organizing Project
Minneapolis, MN ✉ demodave@usinternet.com
💻 www.tcbop.org
Regional organizing group for the Twin Cities (Minneapolis & St. Paul) area. Currently working on establishing a Bisexual Resource Center in Minneapolis & expanding local social & support activities for bisexuals.

Bi Women's Social Group Minneapolis, MN
✉ tina_haines@hotmail.com
💻 beta.communities.msn.com/ BisexualWomensSocialGroup/homepage
Currently meets 2nd Fri. at Vera's Cafe in Minneapolis.

Bisexual Women's Support c/o Chrysalis (below)
Support group for bi women to discuss self worth, uncoupling, isolation & relationship issues. Meets weekly for 8 weeks. $9 donation per meeting requested, but not required.

Chrysalis: A Center for Women 4432 Chicago Ave.
S., Minneapolis, MN 55407 ☎ 612-871-0118,
TTY 612-871-3652 FX: 612-870-2403
✉ info@chrysaliswomen.org
💻 www.chrysaliswomen.org
Women's resource center. Individual & group therapy; legal & mental health resources; support groups for women & their families, incl. a coming out support group for lesbian & bi women; ongoing bisexual support group; ongoing lesbian support group; chemical dependency counseling; parenting education; & resource counseling & referral.

District 202: A Center for Gay/Lesbian/Bisexual/ Transgender Youth 1601 Nicollet Avenue,
Minneapolis, MN 55403 ☎ 612-871-5559
FX: 612-871-1445 💻 www.dist202.org
Community organization & hang-out space for glbtq-identified youth or youth who have questions about sexual orientation issues. Dances, meetings, weekly movie nights, drag king shows, etc. Call for open hours or just drop by.

Keshet G'vah Minneapolis, MN ☎ 612-824-4226;
612-374-8638 ✉ keshetgaavah@mac.com
Social & religious organization for Jewish LGBT people.

Augsburg College: Bisexual, Gay & Lesbian Services (BAGLS) 2211 Riverside Avenue,
Minneapolis, MN 55454 ☎ Doug Green, Faculty
Adviser: 612-330-1187 ✉ green@augsburg.edu
💻 www.augsburg.edu/bagls
Student group making this a safe place for GLBT students. Also has a women's group called AWARE.

University of Minnesota

Queer Student Cultural Center, 720 Washington
Ave. SE, Lower Level, Room 4, Minneapolis, MN
55455 ☎ 612-626-2344 ✉ qscc@tc.umn.edu
💻 www.tc.umn.edu/~qscc/,
Houses a number of GLBT groups such as: the University Gay Community; University Bisexual & Transgender Community; Queer Graduate & Professional Association; Straight Friends & Allies of QSCC; Queer Women; the fraternity Delta Lambda Phi; ALPHA: Allied Lavender Public Health Association.

Steven J. Schochet Center for Gay, Lesbian, Bisexual & Transgender Studies
320-16th Ave. SE, Suite 132 (Klaeber Court),
Minneapolis, MN 55455 FX: 612-625-3499
FX: 612-624-9028 💻 www.glbtstudies.umn.edu/
Newly founded center for scholarship in glbt studies. Houses archives on GLBT history & scholarship, coordinates GLBT degree programs, & supports academics and research in areas related to GLBT people & communities.

Project Offstreets 41 N. 12th Street,
Minneapolis, MN 55403 ☎ 612-252-1200
FX: 612-252-1201
Safe space for street youth. Come in the back door off of the parking lot. Drop-in center open most evenings & also offering day programs. Offers shelter referrals, hang-out space, help with getting medical care & support for youth who have been kicked out of their homes or just need someone to talk to. The center is for all youth but has a strong GLBT youth population & group.

> **Ever since I had that interview in which I said I was bisexual it seems twice as many people wave at me in the streets.**
>
> *Elton John, 1980s.*

The Bridge for Runaway Youth 2200 Emerson Avenue S., Minneapolis, MN 55405 ☎ 612-377-8800 FX: 612-377-6426 🖳 www.bridgeforyouth.org
Resource center for runaway youth, including GLBT youth & parents. Support groups, family counseling, social groups, & training programs. Open 24 hours a day.

H.I.M. Program/Red Door Clinic 525 Portland Avenue, Lower Level, Minneapolis, MN 55415 ☎ 612-348-6641 FX: 612-348-2904 ✉ charles.tamble@co.hennepin.mn.us
Safer sex program for men who have sex with men. HIV testing. Sponsors Married Men's Lunch for men aged 18+. E-mail to receive updates on scheduled events.

Pride Institute Outpatient Center Minneapolis, MN ☎ 1-800-54-PRIDE ✉ info@pride-institute.com 🖳 www.pride-institute.com
Evening outpatient alcohol & drug treatment program for GLBT people. Call for location & current activities.

Twin Cities Men's Center 3249 Hennepin Avenue South, Suite 55, Minneapolis, MN 55408 ☎ 612-822-5892 ✉ tcmc@freenet.msp.mn.us 🖳 www.tcmc.org
Nonprofit organization primarily for men but also offering mixed gender groups including partners' groups, a 20-something group, support & educational programs for gay, bi & heterosexual men.

Moorhead State University: Tri-College Ten Percent Society PO Box 266, Moorhead, MN 56563 ☎ Larry Peterson: 701-231-8824, Christine Smith: casmith@mnstate.edu ✉ ndsu-ten-percent@plains.nodak.edu OR tenpercentsociety@yahoo.com 🖳 www.acm.ndsu.nodak.edu/Ten_Percent/
Moorhead State University, Concordia College & North Dakota State University.

University of Minnesota, Morris: E-Quality Group 600 E. 4th St., PO 45SC, Morris, MN 56267 ☎ 320-589-6091 ✉ equality@cda.mrs.umn.edu 🖳 www.mrs.umn.edu/~pehng/Equality/

Carleton College: Lesbian, Gay, Bisexual & Transgender Community One N. College Street, Northfield, MN 55057 ☎ Kaaren Williamson, Staff LGBT Advisor 507-646-5222 ✉ kwilliam@acs.carleton.edu
Weekly meetings. Occasional social events & dances.

St. Olaf College: GLOW! (Gay, Lesbian or Whatever) 1500 St. Olaf Avenue, Northfield, MN 55057-1001 ☎ 507-646-3923 🖳 www.stolaf.edu/orgs/glow
Also alumni group: "AfterGLOW."

St. Cloud State University: GLBT Services Atwood Memorial Center, Suite 216, St. Cloud, MN 56301 ☎ 320-654-5166 FX: 320-654-5190 ✉ glbt@stcloudstate.edu 🖳 www.stcloudstate.edu/~glbt/

Hamline University: Spectrum, GLBT and Allies 1536 E. Hewitt Ave., St. Paul, MN 55104-1284 ☎ 651-523-2395 ✉ spectrum@gw.hamline.edu 🖳 www.hamline.edu/~gaylesb/index.html
Everyone welcome, regardless of orientation.

Macalester College: Queer Union 1600 Grand Avenue, St. Paul, MN 55105 ☎ 612-696-7613 ✉ qu@macalester.edu 🖳 www.macalester.edu/~qunion/
Student-run glbt/Two-Spirited/Intersexed advocacy group. For Macalester students.

Quatrefoil Library 1619 Dayton Street, St. Paul, MN 55104 ☎ 651-641-0969
LGBT-themed library with both lending & archival collections. Books, videos, tapes, games, periodicals & historical material.

St. Paul Schools Out For Equity Program 1930 Como Avenue, St. Paul, MN 55108 ☎ 612-603-4942; 651-603-4946 (Alan Horowitz) ✉ mtinucci@mail.stpaul.k12.mn.us
Creating supportive public school environments for GLBT students, staff & families.

Wingspan Ministry St. Paul-Reformation Lutheran Church, 100 N. Oxford Street, St. Paul, MN 55104 ☎ 651-224-3371 FX: 651-224-6228 ✉ wngspan@aol.com NOTE: No "i" 🖳 www.stpaulref.org
LGBT ministry. Worship: Sun. 10:30am. Adult education: Sun., 9am. Also provides info & resources for congregations around the country working with the GLBT community.
PUB: Soaring With Wingspan (Quarterly newsletter)

> **"Jesus the holy leper speaks to my bisexuality by offering me a model for life outside the boundaries of destructive hierarchical dualisms. Jesus does not appear to have spent much energy worrying about the impossibility of his status, since there was too much kingdom work to do and since his experience was that nothing was impossible with God. If I am to follow Jesus in this way, I can and must relinquish my concerns and anger about people who deny the existence of bisexuality. Let them believe what they believe. In the meantime, I'd rather work on bringing the kingdom a little closer than wrangle over the 'truth' of my sexual identity."**
>
> *Amanda Udis-Kessler, in Blessed Bi Spirit*

Mississippi

Mississippi Gay Lobby MS
✉ MsGayLobby@msgaylobby.org
🖳 www.msgaylobby.org
MGL exists to educate glb Mississippians about their community, its history, & relevant issues, & advance the cause of full equality & civil rights for all of the glb community. Bi-inclusive, & actively seeking bi & lesbian board members.

University of Southern Mississippi: Family for Diversity, Box 5549, Hattiesburg, MS 39406-5549
✉ planforchange@hotmail.com
Promotes gay visibility on campus & in community to educate & end prejudice, discrimination, & homophobia.

Mississippi State University: GLBF, Gays, Lesbians, Bisexuals & Friends of MSU Mississippi State, MS
✉ glbf@ra.msstate.edu 🖳 www.msstate.edu/org/glbf
Confidential organization of members from the University & surrounding community. Friendly, open forum to discuss and find peer support on issues related to sexual diversity. Anonymous legal, counseling, & medical referrals for serious issues (including harassment, abuse, "outing," issues with family/friends, self-acceptance, suicide prevention, sexual health, etc.).

Camp Sister Spirit 444 Eastside Drive, Ovette, MS 39464 ☎/FX: 601-344-1411
✉ sisterspir@aol.com
🖳 www.rainbowpriderv.net/css
Holds some women-only festivals throughout the year. Facilities include: RV hookups, women-only bunkhouse, camp site, private cabins that can include mixed gender, fully equipped shower-house & kitchen, donated library of over 1,500 titles. Group rentals available. Alcohol-free (entire camp is a free and sober space). Violence-free (no violence in word or deed).

University of Mississippi: GLBA, Gay Lesbian & Bisexual Association PO Box 3541, University, MS 38677 ✉ glba@olemiss.edu 🖳 www.olemiss.edu/orgs/glba/
To provide support for glb's, their friends, & supporters. To educate the campus & community about glb issues. To provide a social setting conducive to positive interaction for the aforementioned individuals.

Missouri

Pridenet Missouri 🖳 www.pridenet.com/mo.html
GLBT Resources for the State of Missouri.

University of Missouri: Triangle Coalition A022 Brody Commons, Columbia, MO 65211
☎ 573-882-4427
✉ triangle@showme.missouri.edu.
🖳 web.missouri.edu/~triangle/home.html

Passages Gay & Lesbian Youth Group PO Box 45377, Kansas City, MO 64111 ☎ 816-691-8740
✉ passages@passageskc.org
🖳 www.passageskc.org/
Social & educational opportunities in a safe environment for youth exploring their sexual orientation. Youth Discussion Groups Sun. 7-8:30pm at Metropolitan Community Church-Gentle Souls (3801 Wyandotte, Kansas City, MO).

Bisexual Alliance of Saint Louis (BASL) St. Louis, MO ☎ 314-995-4629 🖳 www.bisexual.org/basl
Bimonthly social & support group. Wheelchair accessible. Free, all welcome. 4th Mon. 7-9pm, Trinity Episcopal Church, 600 N. Euclid (cor. Washington). Also two e-mail lists: BiStLouis, a discussion list, and basl-info, an information list. To subscribe, send a message to - subscribe@yahoogroups.com.

Privacy Rights Education Project PO Box 24106, St. Louis, MO 63130 ☎ 314-862-4900 FX: 314-862-8155 ✉ prepstl@prepstl.org 🖳 www.prepstl.org

Pride St. Louis: Annual Celebration of LGBT Pride PO Box 2826, St. Louis, MO 63111
☎ 314-772-8888 ✉ pride@pridesaintlouis.com
🖳 www.pridesaintlouis.com/

St. Louis Gay & Lesbian Chavurah Central Reform Congreagation, 77 Maryland Plaza, St. Louis, MO 63108 ☎ 314-361-3919

Metropolitan Community Church of Greater St. Louis 5000 Washington Place, St. Louis, MO 63108 ☎ 314-361-3221 FX: 314-361-3221
✉ mccstlouis@worldinter.net
🖳 www.geocities.com/~mcc_st_louis/

My people are Iqvrim, Hebrews. Some say that the word comes from a root which means boundary crossers, transgressors. Some say that it was a word of contempt, given by masters who saw us as out of control. As a bisexual feminist I will not, I cannot, live in the boxes created for me by others. I cross the invisible line and say, 'I love whomever I love. Regardless of the package they come in, I love all of who they are...the softness and the hard, the courage and the fear, the broken and the healed. I love them and that love is good, and that love is honored by God.' Every day I hold the whole.

Deb Kolodny, in Blessed Bi Spirit

Homosexualies Latinos Saint Louis, MO
☎ 314-567-8701 ✉ holastl@hotmail.com
🖳 hola.stlouis.homepage.com/
*Meetings first Th., 7pm. Trinity Episcopal
Church, 600 N. Euclid.*

Southwest Missouri State University

Bisexual, Gay & Lesbian Alliance, 901 S.
National Avenue, Springfield, MO 68504;
✉ bigala@hotmail.com;
🖳 studentorganizations.smsu.edu/BIGALA/;
Meets Wed. 7pm in Student Union room
308-B. Lambda Peter Groenendyk, Chair:
✉ pcg295t@mail.smsu.edu
🖳 studentorganizations.smsu.edu/bigala/
lambda.htm; *LGBT Faculty & Staff group.*

Drury University: Allies 900 N. Benton, Springfield,
MO 65802 ☎ (417) 873-7226, Dr. Ruth
Bamberger, sponsor ✉ allies@drury.edu
🖳 www2.drury.edu/allies/
*Open organization on campus dedicated to
promoting diversity in & understanding about
sexual identity within the student body.*

Montana

Pridenet 🖳 www.pridenet.com/mt.html *Mailing
list; listings for Montana's bars, restaurants,
bookstores, accomodations, local groups, resources.*

Montana State University: QMSU SUB 51, Strand
Union Building, Mail Code 4051, Bozeman, MT
59717 ☎ 406-994-4551 ✉ q-msu@montana.edu
🖳 www.montana.edu/wwwstuac/osa%20spec.htm
*Meets Tu. 7pm, RM145 Strand Union Bldg.
Occasional films, speakers.*

Outspoken PO Box 7105, Missoula, MT 59807-
7105 ☎ 406-543-2224 ✉ OutSpknMT@aol.com
🖳 missoula.bigsky.net/outspokn
*Monthly print & online newspaper which "gives a
voice to the gay community of Missoula &
surrounding communities."*

University of Montana: Lambda Alliance

University Center 209, Missoula, MT
☎ 406-243-5922 ✉ lambda@selway.umt.edu

KISMIF Missoula, MT
*GLB AA meeting, Mon. 7pm at Lifeboat, 532
University Ave.*

There is no **"female sexual
experience,"** no **"male sexual
experience,"** no unique
heterosexual, lesbian or gay
experience. There are instead the
different experiences of different
people, which we lump according
to socially significant categories.

*Ruth Hubbard (in "There is No Natural Human
Sexuality," Sojourner, April 1985)*

Nebraska

University of Nebraska, Lincoln

GayLesBiTrans Resource Center, Rm. 234
Nebraska Union 14th & R Streets, Lincoln, NE
68588-0455 ☎ 402-472-5144. **Allies Against
Heterosexism & Homophobia**, c/o GLBT
Resource Center ☎ 402-472-5644
🖳 www.unl.edu/allies/; *GLBT support /
advocacy; works in straight community to combat
attitudes & actions of heterosexism &
homophobia.*

Bi Choice NE 9505 R Plaza, #106, Omaha, NE
68127 ☎ 402-592-4250 ✉ quest15@juno.com
*Brunch 2nd & 4th Sun., 1pm, McFoster's 38 &
Farnam, Omaha. Other monthly events.*

Rainbow Outreach Center 1719 Leavenworth St.,
Omaha, NE 68102 ☎ 402-341-0330
✉ rainbow@rocc.org 🖳 www.rocc.org
Omaha area GLBT community center PUB: The
Gayzette (Contact Bruce Bufkin 402-932-3273,
lastdwarf@aol.com for submissions & calendar
events.)

PFLAG Omaha PO Box 390064, Omaha, NE
68139-0064 ☎ 402-291-6781 ✉ info@pflag-
omaha.org 🖳 www.pflag-omaha.org
Support, education, advocacy. PUB: PFLAG
Omaha - Newsletter (Penny Mahnel 5303 S 172
St Omaha, NE 68135)

MPower - Nebraska AIDS Project 139 S 40th ST,
Omaha, NE 68131 ☎ 402-552-9260 ext 120
✉ briand@nap.org 🖳 www.nap/mpower.org
*Tools & support to keep gay, bisexual, & trans
men HIV negative.*

Nevada

Bi-sexuality Support Group 1006 E. Sahara, Las
Vegas, NV 89104 ☎ 702-593-4345

**The Center: Serving the GLBT Community of
Southern Nevada** 912 E. Sahara, Las Vegas,
NV 89104 ☎ 702-733-9800
🖳 www.lasvegasglbtcenter.org/

**University of Las Vegas: Gay Straight Freedom
Alliance** Las Vegas, NV
Wed. 7pm in the Moyer Student Union.

**University of Nevada, Reno: Queer Student
Union** Mail Stop/056, Reno, NV 89557
☎ 702-327-5342 ext. 502 (voice mail)
✉ qsu@asun.unr.edu 🖳 www.asun.unr.edu/clubs/
qsu
*Promotes the understanding of LGBT people,
issues & culture through social interaction,
outreach, education, community service.
Membership open to anyone including, but not
limited to, University of Nevada, Reno students,
alumni, & members of the community of any age.*

New Hampshire

New Hampshire Bisexuals c/o Mr. Bruce Gillis, PO Box 711, Dover, NH 03821 ☎ 603-749-4156 ✉ nh_bi@yahoo.com 📖 www.geocities.com/nh_bi
NH's only bisexual on-line resource. Info, resources, monthly newsletter. Discussion listserv at www.yahoogroups/group/nh-bisexuals.

Gay Info Line of New Hampshire (NH) 26 South Main St, Box 181, Concord, NH 03301 ☎ 603-224-1686 📖 www.rainbowresources-nh.org/gil.htm
NH's only informational GLBTQA organization. Info on all GLBTQA resources in NH.
PUB: *Lifeline Directory*

Rainbow Resources of NH Gay Info Line of NH, 26 South Main St, Box 181, Concord, NH 03301 ☎ 603-224-1686
✉ webmistress@rainbowresources-nh.org
📖 www.rainbowresources-nh.org
Electronic arm of the the Gay Info Line of NH. Provides access to resource information for NH's sexual minority community. PUB: GILNH *Lifelines GLBT Resources Directory (Resource guide directory of NH glbt/straight resources in NH. Print copies of the directory can be purchased from GILNH.)*

PFLAG NH Concord Chapter 158 Liberty Hill Road, Bedford, NH 03110-5627 ☎ 603-472-4944 ✉ FJGreaney@aol.com
Meets 3rd Sun. at the First Congregational Church in Concord.

The Lakes Mountains Connection Women PO Box 164, Campton, NH 03223 ☎ 603-744-2489 📖 www.barney.org/acalendar/calendar.html
Socials for women, outdoor activities. Monthly meetings, newsletter.

Mountain Valley Men PO Box 36, Center Conway, NH 03814 ☎ Dave or Paul: 207-925-1034
[Primarily gay] men's group for N. New Hampshire & W. Maine. Meets monthly.

Capital Gay Men PO Box 985, Concord, NH 03302-0985 ☎ 603-224-6884 ✉ jer2@mediaone.net 📖 people.ne.mediaone.net/jer2/cgm.html

Minotaurs BC Men PO Box 2141, Concord, NH 03302-2141 ✉ MinotaurBC@aol.com 📖 members.aol.com/MinotaurBC/NH.html

Gay, Lesbian, Bisexual, Transgender Helpline c/o Rick & Jasper Salach-Tate, Apt. 2, 93A Washington St., Dover, NH 03820 ☎ 603-743-GAY2 ✉ mail@dovernhsupport.org 📖 www.geocities.com/WestHollywood/Village/1425/HELP.html
GLBT info, referral, support. Leave a message & we'll call you back.

Dover Gay/Lesbian/Bi/Transgender & Questioning Support Group c/o Rick & Jasper Salach-Tate, 93A Washington St., Apt. 2, Dover, NH 03820 ☎ Jasper: 603-742-4470; Helpline: 603-743-GAY2 ✉ aboundwsounds@webtv.net 📖 www.geocities.com/WestHollywood/Village/1425
GLBT & Questioning support group.

University of New Hampshire: Campus Gay/Lesbian/Bisexual/Transgender/Allied Alliance Room 7, Memorial Union Building, Durham, NH 03824 ☎ 603-862-4522 ✉ unhalliance@yahoo.com 📖 www.unh.edu/omsa/alliance/alliance1.html

Dartmouth College

Gay, Lesbian & Bisexual Programming, Hinman Box 6181, 220 Collis Center, Hanover, 03755 ☎ 603-646-3635
✉ Pamela.S.Misener@Dartmouth.edu
📖 www.dartmouth.edu/~glbprog. *Located in the Office of Student Life, the LGBT Coordinator provides advising to individual students & to DRA, organizes gay-related educational & social events, provides staff trainings and workshops, & represents the needs & concerns of GLBT students to other areas of the College administration.* **Coalition for Lesbian, Gay & Bisexual & Transgender Concerns**, c/o GLB Programming, ☎ 603-646-3636, cglbtc@dartmouth.edu 📖 www.dartmouth.edu/~dra/resources.html. *Staff & faculty group at Dartmouth working on issues of interest to the glbt community.* **Dartmouth Rainbow Alliance**, c/o LGB Concerns 📖 www.dartmouth.edu/~dra ✉ Dartmouth.Rainbow.Alliance@Dartmouth.edu. *Mixed gender GLBTQ student alliance. Weekly meetings during termtime.* **Bisexual, Gay & Lesbian Alumni**, c/o GLB Concerns, ✉ Dartgala@aol.com 📖 www.dartmouth.edu/~dra/resources.html. *Organization for all glbt alumni & alumnae of Dartmouth College.*

Women Meeting Women PO Box 621, Hollis, NH 03049 ☎ 603-883-9969 ✉ wmw@altavista.net 📖 www.geocities.com/WestHollywood/Stonewall/3842/index.html
Monthly meetings 2nd Sat. 2:30pm, wide range of activities. "Social support & networking" group serving the lesbian community in southern NH & northern MA. Great links for NH women's groups & events.

UNH group at Millenium March on Washington

PFLAG NH North Country Chapter PO Box 3, Jefferson, NH 03583 ☎ 603-586-4346 ✉ dypy@webtv.net 🖳 www.pflag.org/chapters/chapter.html
Meets 3rd Mon.

Out in the Valley Keene, NH 03431 ☎ 802-295-0095 ✉ webmaster@outinthevalley.org 🖳 www.outinthevalley.org
Mixed gender GLBT Resource for the Upper Valley comprised of western NH & eastern Vermont. Monthly social events.

Active Lesbians of the Monadnock Region Area PO Box 1845, Keene, NH 03431 ✉ ALMAKEENE@yahoo.com 🖳 www.barney.org/acalendar/calendar.html
A social lesbian group for women in Southwestern NH & SE VT. Mostly our gatherings are opportunities to meet women in the area, do things together, feel part of a community of acceptance. Events include hikes, bikes, theater, concerts, movies, canoe, kayaking, picnics, potlucks. Also the contact for Brattleboro Area VT Dykes, & AKA VT BAD GRRLS.

Monadnock Gay Men PO Box 1124, Keene, NH 03431 ☎ 603-357-5544 ✉ MonadGay@aol.com 🖳 www.monadnockgaymen.org
Monthly social events for gay men of the Monadnock region of NH.

Switch Hitter

Keene State College: Keene State Pride L.P. Young Student Center, Keene, NH 03431 ☎ 603-358-2639 ✉ kscpride@hotmail.com 🖳 www.angelfire.com/nh/PrideKSC/index.html

Monadnock Outright PO Box 572, Keene, NH 03431 ☎ 877-517-7822, x576 ✉ outright@hotmail.com 🖳 members.aol.com/chapelcoll/outright.html
Safe, confidential place for GLBTQ & ally youth 14 - 22 to meet, talk, & support each other. Two adult facilitators are always present. Free.

PFLAG NH Keene Chapter St. James Episcopal Church, 44 West Street, Keene, NH 03431-3371 ☎ 603-355-1040 ✉ jbleyle1@earthlink.net 🖳 www.pflag.org/chapters/chapter.html
Meets 1st Tues. at St. James Episcopal Church in Keene.

PFLAG NH Lakes Region Chapter 172 Pleasant Street, Laconia, NH 03246-3030 ☎ 603-528-1714 ✉ dandpspink@landmarknet.net 🖳 www.pflag.org/chapters/chapter.html
Meets 2nd Sun. in Laconia NH.

Amelia's Women PO Box 746, Lebanon, NH 03766 ✉ bev@barney.org 🖳 www.rainbowresources-nh.org/amelias_home.htm
Lesbian social group sponsors occasional potlucks, & other events. Sends out email of interest to the local women's community & quarterly electronic newsletter. Welcomes bi women.

PFLAG NH Upper Valley Chapter Headrest Organization, Church street, Lebanon, NH 03766 ✉ deb@headrest.org 🖳 www.pflag.org/chapters/chapter.html. Listserver: mail.digitaldawn.net/mailman/listinfo/pflag.

Manchester Outright 816 Elm St., PO Box 344, Manchester, NH 03101 ☎ 603-645-5274 ✉ manchesteroutright@yahoo.com
Confidential social / support group for glbtq -22. Weekly support group meetings for youth & Community Education speakers upon request. No newsletter, but frequent e-mail updates to members.

Nashua Outright 443 Amherst Street, Suite 220, Nashua, NH 03063 ☎ 603-889-8210 ✉ nashuaoutright@hotmail.com 🖳 nashuaoutright.simplenet.com
Social support group for glbtq & ally youth -22.

Gay Men's Reading Group of Nashua NH c/o Southern NH AIDS Task Force, Nashua, NH 03064 ☎ 603-595-8464 ✉ gerryred@yahoo.com
Monthly book group for men sponsored by Southern NH AIDS Task Force of Nashua NH.

Gay & Proud Men's Group Piermont, NH ☎ BJ: 603-272-5815
Social men's Group for GBT men in western NH. Meets monthly. Alcohol & Drug free meetings.

Portsmouth NH Bi Women's Resource & Support Group c/o Women's Health Consortium, 29 Vaughan Mall, Portsmouth, NH 03801 ☎ 630-431-1669 ✉ Sue Corcoran: schmoo@nh.ultranet.com
Confidential, bi-monthly, drop in, discussion group to share information about area resources, issues & topics of interest of the group members. Bi friendly & questioning women welcome. Registration NOT necessary.

Out And About Women PO Box 5691, Portsmouth, NH 03802-5691 ☎ 603-740-1429 or 1-877-422-0702 ✉ out_and_about98@yahoo.com 📇 outandabout.cjb.net
Open to all women & lesbians. Social group with meetings, potlucks, dances, movie nights, occasional speakers and / or topical discussions. Monthly meetings sometimes include potlucks.

Seacoast Gay Men PO Box 1394, Portsmouth, NH 03802 ☎ 603-430-4052 ✉ board@seacoastgaymen.org 📇 www.seacoastgaymen.org
Meets Mon. Celebrating their 20th anniversary, provides a safe & open environment for men in all stages of coming out. An association of gay men of all ages & of many diverse backgrounds who get together socially to share similar interests & to celebrate our common bond.

Seacoast Outright PO Box 842, Portsmouth, NH 03802-0842 ☎ 603-431-1013; 800-639-6095 teen crisis line ✉ seacoastoutright@hotmail.com 📇 www.lgbt.net/seacoastoutright
GLBTQ youth -22 in Southern ME & NH.

AIDS Response Seacoast 1 Junkins Avenue, Portsmouth, NH 03801 ☎ 603-433-5377 or 800-375-1144 ✉ ARSadmin@aol.com 📇 members.aol.com/ARSadmin/public/ars_home.htm
Non-profit, community-based HIV/AIDS service organization. Education, direct assistance & advocacy to persons & communities affected by HIV infection who live in NH counties of Rockingham & Strafford, southern York, Maine counties & educational programs throughout NE.

Gay Men Fight AIDS Inc. PO Box 4342, Portsmouth, NH 03802-4342 ☎ 603-436-5445; 207-641-8702 ✉ gmfaids@aol.com 📇 www.dartmouth.edu/~hivnet/nh.orgs.html
HIV prevention for men who have sex with men. Including GBQ MSM. Safer sex & HIV prevention workshops at a private home with peer facilitators who are also gay & bi men.

The Lifeguards PO Box 4342, Portsmouth, NH 03802-4342 ✉ gmfaids@aol.com or Mac9531@aol.com 📇 www.dartmouth.edu/~hivnet/nh.orgs.html
Health sexuality groups for gay / bi men. A multi-week get together for men to explore coming out, sexuality, dating, HIV/STD risk, & building community. Joint project of AIDS Response Seacoast, Gay Men Fight AIDS, & So. NH HIV Task Force.

> **We bisexuals are not confused. We're not fence-sitters, because maybe there really is no fence. But we do refuse to accept the paradigm of mono-sexuality that says that you're either gay or straight. I am a recovering bi-phobe, so I know what it's like to struggle with what doesn't fit into the either-or categories. Bisexuals challenge with our bodies and our lives that way of thinking, and define ourselves as we choose while still acknowledging our place in queer community, which we will not abandon in times of oppression.**
>
> *Elias Farajajé-Jones, in "Loving Queer" from In the Family, Vol. 6, No. 1, Summer 2000.*

Ladybugs North 114 Chester Road, Raymond, NH 03077 ☎ 603-463-9061 ✉ ladybugs_north@yahoo.com 📇 www.geocities.com/ladybugs_north
Social events for women. Meetings & bimonthly newsletter.

PFLAG NH Plymouth Chapter PO Box 20, Rumney, NH 03266 ☎ 603-786-9812 ✉ rjlarson@coopresources.net 📇 www.pflag.org/chapters/chapter.html
Meets 1st Sun. in Plymouth.

PFLAG NH Seacoast Chapter PO Box 138, Stratham, NH 03885 ☎ 603-772-5196 ✉ sgwool@aol.com 📇 www.pflag.org/chapters/chapter.html
Meets 1st Tu.. 7-9 at Stratham Community Church.

New Jersey

BiZone (formerly Bisexual Network of New Jersey) The Pride Center of NJ, 211 Livingston Ave, New Brunswick, NJ 08903 ☎ 732-246-3769 ✉ info@bizone.org 📇 www.Bizone.org
Support / social group. for bisexual, bi-curious, bi-friendly people, their partners, & allies.

NJ BiWomen c/o The Pride Center, 211 Livingston Avenue, New Brunswick, NJ 08901 ☎ 732-846-2232 ✉ info@biwomen.org 📇 www.biwomen.org.
A social / discussion group for bisexual, bi-curious, & bi-friendly women living in the NJ area. Meets 1st Tuesdays 7:30-9pm at the Pride Center. Transgendered people welcome.

> **For now I look you in the eye and say / I will not be the skeleton in our family closet / I will not be your homo or heterosexual assumption / I will not be your scapegoat / I will not be controlled / I will not be contained / I will not betray my truth**
>
> *Lani Ka'ahumqanu, from That Naked Place*

Pride Center of New Jersey PO Box 11335, New Brunswick, NJ 08906-1335 ☎ 732-846-2232 ✉ info@pridecenter.org 🖳 www.pridecenter.org
LGBT community center, 211 Livingston Ave. Discussion / support mtgs for youth, older men, bisexuals, co-dependents, lesbian mothers, gay men & women in straight marriages, Republicans, educators, families of glb people, & other groups.

New Jersey Lesbian & Gay Coalition PO Box 11335, New Brunswick, NJ 08906-1335 ☎ 732-828-6772 ✉ mail@njlgc.org 🖳 www.njlgc.org
NJ's political coalition of LGBT, AIDS & supportive straight organizations.

Jersey Pride, Inc. PO Box 10976, New Brunswick, NJ 08906 ☎ 732-21-GAY-NJ; 732-214-2965 ✉ info@jerseypride.org 🖳 www.jerseypride.org
Organizes NJ's LGBT Pride Parade in Ashbury Park. Hosts Nat'l Coming Out Day Cultural Heritage Festival. PUB: Jersey Gaze (Quarterly Magazine)

NJ Education Association - Lesbian, Gay, Bisexual Caucus PO Box 314, Roosevelt, NJ 08555 ☎ 609-448-5215 FX: 609-448-9550 ✉ carolwchlr@aol.com
Support & info on lgb issues in education; protect rights & interests of glb members & their supporters.

Burlington County Gay & Lesbian Alliance NJ ☎ 856-866-5527
Burlington County LGBT social group.

Rutgers University, Camden: Lambda Alliance CMS #68, Rutgers, 328 Penn Street, Camden, NJ 08102 ✉ ims2kc@crab.rutgers.edu
Support group for glb students at Rutgers.

Gays, Bisexuals & Lesbians (GABLES) of Cape May County PO Box 641, Cape May Court House, Cape May, NJ 08210-0641 ☎ 609-861-1848 ✉ gables99@email.com PUB: Cape May County Gay/Gay-Friendly Business Directory

GALY-NJ (Gay and Lesbian Youth-NJ) PO Box 137, Convent Station, NJ 07961-0137 ☎ 973-285-1595 (helpline); 973-285-5590 (business); 973-285-0889 (TDD) FX: 973-539-8882 ✉ galynj@galynj.org 🖳 www.galynj.org
Youth group. Meets in South Orange & other locations.

Gay Activist Alliance in Morris County PO Box 137, Convent Station, NJ 07961-0137 ☎ 973-285-1595 (helpline); 973-285-5590 (business line); 973-285-0889 (TDD) FX: 201-539-8882 ✉ gaamc@gay.com 🖳 www.gaamc.org
Mon 7pm: support groups, speakers, dances, socials at Morristown Unitarian Fellowship, 21 Normandy Heights Road, Morristown. State's largest G&L organization. "Acceptance of bis is improving. Worth the trip." PUB: Challenge (Newsletter includes news, views, poems, editorials, contact info & local events info.)

Jersey City State College: Gay, Lesbian, Bisexual & Friends Association Student Union Bldg., 2039 Kennedy Blvd., Jersey City, NJ 07305

Drew University: Gay, Lesbian, Bisexual & Straight Person's Alliance c/o Student Center, Madison, NJ 07940

Rumapo College: Gay, Lesbian, Bisexual Coalition c/o Student Activities505 Rampo Valley Road, Mahwah, NJ 07430 ☎ 201-825-2800 x547 ✉ Advisor: mgolsch@ramapo.edu
Supports GLB people. Open to off-campus community.

Cumberland County Gay, Lesbian, & Bisexual Alliance PO Box 541, Millville, NJ 08332-0541 ☎ 609-563-1872
Positive, safe social & supportive environment for everyone.

Rutgers University

BiGLARU: Bi/Gay/Lesbian Alliance of Rutgers University; Rutgers Student Center, SAC Box 91, New Brunswick, NJ 08903, ☎ 732-932-1306 ✉ biglaru@mariner.rutgers.edu 🖳 mariner.rutgers.edu/biglaru. *Open to all.* **Bisexual, Gay & Lesbian Outreach Hotline**, SAC Box 146, 613 George Street, New Brunswick, NJ 08903 ☎ 732-932.7886. **Lesbians & Bisexual Womyn in Action**, ✉ _labia_@yahoo.com 🖳 www.geocities.com/CollegePark/Library/1174/main.htm; **Rutgers Union for Gay & Bisexual Men**, 🖳 www.eden.rutgers.edu/~rugbi. **Latina/o & People of Color Lesbian-Gay-Bisexual-Transgender Union**, ✉ bjork@eden.rutgers.edu. **Gay, Lesbian & Bisexual Alumni/ae**, Office of Diverse Community Affairs & Lesbian/Gay Concerns, Bishop House- Rutgers University, New Brunswick, NJ 08903; ☎ 732-932-1711 🖳 www.rci.rutgers.edu/~divcoaff/

> **Whence come I and on what wings that it should take me so long, humiliated and exiled, to accept that I am myself?**
>
> *Collette*, The Vagabond

Princeton University

Lesbian, Gay & Bisexual Alliance, 306 Aaron Burr Hall, Princeton, NJ 08544 ☎ 609-258-4522 ✉ lgba@princeton.edu 💻 www.princeton.edu/~lgba/. Includes: **Lesbian/Bisexual Task Force**, weekly meetings of **Gay/Bi Men** & **Gay/Bi Women**, & **BIG (the Bisexual Interest Group)**. **Lesbian Gay Bisexual Coordinator**, 313 West College, Princeton University, Princeton, NJ 08544 ☎ 609-258-1353 FX: 609-258-3831 ✉ mseldin@princeton.edu.

Raritan Valley Community College: Lesbian, Gay, Bi Student Group (GET OUT!) c/o RVCC Student Activities, PO Box 3300, Somerville, NJ 08876 ☎ 908-526-1200

Rainbow Place of South Jersey PO Box 2132, Voorhees, NJ 08043-2132 ☎ 856-866-5527 ✉ R-P-S-J@webtv.net 💻 www.homestead.com/RPSJ
Info services, support network, youth group, social events. PUB: South Jersey's Rainbow Pride *(Newsletter includes articles & event listings of interest to South Jersey LGBT community. New South Jersey BiZone section.)*

Generation Q c/o Rainbow Place of South Jersey (above)
LGBT youth group.

New Mexico

OUT! magazine PO Box 27237, Albuquerque, NM 87125 ☎ 505-243-2540 FX: 505-842-5114 ✉ mail@outmagazine.com 💻 www.outmagazine.com
Monthly GLB news magazine. Both the magazine & web site list GLB resources for New Mexico. PUB: OUT! magazine

Bis R Us 10623 Castillo St., SW, Albuquerque, NM 87121 ☎ Rachel 505-836-5239
Meets 2nd Sun. for fun & fellowship.

University of New Mexico: Del Otro Lado Student Activities Center, Box 100, Albuquerque, NM 87106 ☎ 505-277-6739 ✉ smiths@unm.edu 💻 www.unm.edu/~dol/
Includes Men's Rap Group, Women's Rap Group, & Bisexual Rap Group. General discussion groups & social/political activities.

MPower 120 Morningside, NE, Albuquerque, NM 87108 ☎ 505-232-2990 ✉ MPowerABQ@aol.com 💻 www.MPowerOnline.org/
Community Center & community building program for gay & bi men, 18-29.

Gay, Lesbian, & Straight Education Network of Albuquerque, NM PO Bos 7875, Albuquerque, NM 87194 ☎ 505-268-1771 or 505-286-3235 ✉ doyle@apsicc.aps.edu
Educational org. for all members of the community, including LBGTs & others.

Mike Syzmanski & his proud mom at the March on Washington, 1993
Robyn Ochs

Common Bond, Inc. POB 26836, Albuquerque, NM 87125 ☎ 505-891-3647 FX: 505-891-3647 ✉ commonbond@aol.com 💻 members.aol.com/commonbond/index.html
LesBiGay Info for Albuquerque & the NM area. Also LesBiGay support group for -21.

Emmanuel Metropolitan Community Church PO Box 80192, Albuquerque, NM 87198 ☎ 505-268-0599 ✉ EMCCAbq@aol.com 💻 www.nmia.com/~sundance
Special outreach to the LBGT community. Social justice group. "Come as you are; believing as you do." Meets at 341 Dallas NE, Albuquerque. PUB: The Advent (Quarterly)

New Mexico AIDS Services 4200 Silver Ave., SE, #D, Albuquerque, NM 87108 ☎ 505-266-0911 💻 http://www.nmas.net/
Referrals to nearest HIV+/AIDS support -service group. People can be referred to groups that include & welcome them.

Lesbians, Bisexuals, Gays & Friends of New Mexico State University PO Box 30001, Dept. 3WSP, NMSU, Las Cruces, NM 88003 ☎ 505-646-4312 FX: 505-646-3725 ✉ lbg@nmsu.edu 💻 www.nmsu.edu/~lgbf
Meets weekly during termtime. Mostly students, but people of all ages from the university & community are welcome. Th. at 7:30 in Emerson Building Rm. 229.

Lesbian, Gay, & Bisexual Diversity Working Group MS M704 Los Alamos National Laboratory, Los Alamos, NM 87544 ☎ 505-667-8390 (chair) FX: 505-665-3891 ✉ rfuchs@lanl.gov 💻 www.lanl.gov/people/franks/lgblanl.htm
Working group under the Diversity Office at Los Alamos National Laboratory. Membership limited to LANL employees & subcontractors.

Southwest Gay Men's Association PO Box 168, Mesilla, NM 88046 ☎ 505-522-1390 ✉ shelmrei@crl.nmsu.edu
Although the group has kept its original name, it includes glb members.

Santa Fe Lesbian, Gay & Bi Pride Committee 369 Montezuma #399, Santa Fe, NM 87501 ☎ 505-989-6672
Community resource & networking group. Events include Santa Fe LGB Pride, Santa Fe Gay Film Festival, & National Coming Out Day.

Human Rights Alliance 1121 Calle Largo, Santa Fe, NM 87501 ☎ 505-982-7017 505-982-3301 hotline
Hotline provides names & telephone numbers for GLB groups in the Santa Fe area.

New Mexico Institute of Mining & Technology: Gays & Friends P.O, Box 3681 C18, Socorro, NM 87801-3681 ☎505-835-6297 ✉ gaf@nmt.edu 🖳 www.nmt.edu/~gaf
Easy-going, non-political, social club for GLB students & friends at New Mexico Institute of Mining & Technology. Open to anyone else in Socorro area. Semi-regular monthly meetings.

New York

New York City (in the following order: bi groups, glbt community groups, professional groups, university groups, youth groups, health groups, other)

New York Area Bisexual Network PO Box 497 Times Square Station, New York, NY 10108 ☎ 212-459-4784 or 212-714-7714 (Bi Request Info Line)
Communications network for bi groups. Helps new groups form; publishes events calendar; hosts various groups & meetings.

BiRequest PO Box 396, Ansonia Station, New York, NY 10023-0396 ☎ 212-714-7714 (recorded info.) ✉ birequest@yahoo.com 🖳 www.birequest.org/
Discussion group for bisexual & bi-friendly people. Th. 6-8pm at NY Spaces, 131 West 72nd Street in Studio 1. Wheelchair accessible. Followed by socializing at local restaurant. Group outings, dances, special events, e-mail list.

Bisexual Public Action Committee (NYABN) c/o NYABN, PO Box 497, Times Square Station, New York, NY 10108 ☎ 212-459-4784 (NYABN)
Educational/activist group fighting for LGB rights.

Bisexual S/M Discussion Group c/o NYABN, PO Box 497, Times Square Station, New York, NY 10108 ☎ NYABN: 212-459-4784
Monthly discussion of S/M interests & experiences. Affiliated with NYABN.

New York Pride

Bisexual Women's Support Group c/o The Center (below), New York, NY ☎ The Center: 212-620-7310
Weekly discussion & consciousness-raising group.

Bisexuals in Long-Term Relationships c/o The Center (below), New York, NY ☎ Judy: 718-788-7512 ✉ marks6@soho.ios.com
Monthly discussion/support group to deal with issues & feelings involved with being in a committed relationship while still actively bisexual. Spouses & partners welcome.

Bisexual 12 Step Meetings New York, NY ☎ NYABN: 212-459-4784
Open meetings Sat. 8pm at the Center (below). Anyone in any kind of recovery is welcome.

A Different Drummer Guide New York, NY ✉ drum@bway.net 🖳 www.bway.net/~drum/
On-line listing of bi groups & events in New York City & region.

Gay/Lesbian Identified Bisexuals c/o NYABN, PO Box 497, Times Square Station, New York, NY 10108 ☎ Bryan: 718-338-1866 ✉ bryan@glib.com 🖳 www.glib.com/glib.html
Monthy meeting followed by socializing at a nearby restaurant. Safe space for people exploring their sexuality. Transgendered & bi people welcome.

House of Anjea New York, NY ☎ 212-479-7886
Exclusively for bisexual women of color.

Bisexual Information & Counseling Services, Inc. 599 West End Av., Suite 1A, New York, NY 10024 ☎ 212-595-8002 ✉ wwedin@rr.com
Educational programs/materials, individual/group/couples therapy. Technical assistance on bi issues to other non-profits & agencies. Outreach programs to communities of color, incarcerated & formerly incarcerated, students, health professionals. Se habla espanol. Non-profit, tax exempt.

New York Gay & Lesbian Community Center One Little West 12th St., New York NY 10014 ☎ 212.620.7310 ✉ webmaster@gaycenter.org 🖳 www.gaycenter.org
Enormous glbt community center. Home to many NYC bi groups, as well as dozens of other groups.

Uptown Manhattan Pride Columbia University Station, PO Box 250085, New York, NY 10025 ⌨ www.uptownmanhattanpride.org
Social & cultural org. for glbt people living in uptown Manhattan.

Pride House Queens: LGBT Community Center 120-55 Queens Blvd., New York City, NY 11315 ☎ 718-261-7068 ✉ mudang@ix.netcom.com

Lavender Heights New York, NY ☎ 212-465-3100
Washington Heights group welcomes bisexuals.

Shades of Lavender c/o Bklyn AIDS Task Force, 502 Bergen St., Brooklyn, NY 11217 ☎ 718-622-2910
Multicultural center in Park Slope, Brooklyn, for lesbians & bi women. Self-help, discussion, workshops, retreats, etc. Writers Collective, Bi/ Lesbian Youth -21 group, Women 20s/30s group, Narcotics Anonymous Group, movie nights, 1 on 1. PUB: Shades (Monthly. Events listings.)

Gay & Bi Fathers' Forum c/o The Center (above), New York, NY ☎ 212-721-4216 or 718-768-1358
Support & social group for gay & bisexual fathers & others in child-nurturing situations. 1st Fri. 8-10:30.

Men of All Colors Together/New York PO Box 237107, Ansonia Station, New York, NY 10023 ☎ 212-330-7678 ⌨ www.mactny.org/
Men of all colors create a multicultural community. Bi-friendly. General meeting: 1st/ 3rd/4th Fri. 8-11pm, LG Community Center. Board mtg: 2nd Fri. PUB: MACT Information Bulletin (Monthly newsletter.)

Orthodykes, c/o The Center (above), New York, NY ☎ 212-539-8804 ✉ orthodykes@hotmail.com ⌨ www.orthodykesny.org/
Discussion, socializing & support for lbt women who identify with Orthodox Judaism.

Sistahs in Search of Truth, Alliance & Harmony (SiSTAH) c/o The Center (above), New York, NY ☎ 212-479-7886
Deals with spiritual & emotional growth, as well as acceptance for all womyn of color.

Irish Lesbian & Gay Organization c/o The Center (above) ☎ 212-967-7711x3078 ⌨ www.geocities.com/Broadway/5421/ilgo.html
Social, Cultural & Political group for Irish & Irish American l/g.

People of Color Queers of Multi-Racial & Ethnic Descent Box 7045, New York NY 10116-7045 ☎ 212-969-8724, 718-857-4723 ✉ alpinfo@alp.org
Open to anyone who defines themself as a multi-racial or ethnic Person of Color & queer.

Relaxed Agnostic Bisexual -- I don't know, I don't care, and maybe I'll sleep with it.

Kateri

Gay Asian & Pacific Islander Men of NY PO Box 1608 Old Chelsea Station, New York, NY 10113-1608 ☎ 212-802-RICE (7423) ✉ gapimny@gapimny.org ⌨ www.gapimny.org/
Safe & supportive social, political, & educational forum for GBTQ Asian & Pacific Islander men in the NYC area. General mtgs (open to all men): 3rd Fri. 8pm at the Center. Business meetings (open only to Asian & Pacific Islander men): 1st Fri. at 8pm. PUB: PersuAsian (www.gapimny.org/ newsletter/newsletter.html)

Kilawin Kolektibo A. Ubaldo 43-07 39th Place #5A, Sunnyside, New York, NY 11104 ☎ 718-706-7220 ✉ kilawin@aol.com
Pinay lesbian & bisexual identified gathering of sisters.

Assal New York, NY ☎ 718-596-0342x35 ✉ labwas@yahoo.com
For Arab & Iranian LBT women based in New York City, with members throughout the east coast. Support network, organizes cultural events & social activities, & political activism.

Gay Officers Action League c/o The Center (above), New York, NY ☎ 212-NY1-GOAL (691-4625) ✉ ny1goal@aol.com ⌨ www.goalny.org
Professionals currently or formerly employed in law enforcement & criminal justice. Other supporters members of Friends of GOAL (FOG). Supports, advocates for membership, empowerment of blg community, social justice. 2nd Tu. 7pm at the Center.

Columbia University

Queer Alliance, 106 Earl Hall, Mail Code 2000, New York, NY 10027 ☎ 212-854-1488, ✉ lbgc@columbia.edu ⌨ www.columbia.edu/cu/ lbgc/. *The primary social, political, & educational organization for the undergraduate queer community at Columbia, although membership & events are open to all. Other groups at Columbia include* **Queer Coop,** **Bionic** *(bi discussion gp.),* **LABIA** *(Lesbians & Bi Women in Action, c/o QA),* **Queers of Color** *(c/o QA),* **Campus Queers for Christ** *(c/o QA),* **Queergrads** *(c/o QA),* **Queer Studies Group** *(c/o QA),* **GABLES-CU** *(employee group,* ⌨ www.columbia.edu/cu/gables/), **Gayava** *(Jewish group),* **ClusterQ** (Columbia Business School, ⌨ www.gsb.columbia.edu/students/ organizations/clusterq/ *(fosters a positive environment & builds a professional network for our members, by visibility, education, & preventing discrimination. Networking between existing students & alumni, w/students at other business schools, & w/professionals in the lbgt community at large.)*

Columbia University Teachers College: Lesbian, Bisexual, Gay & Transgender Community Office of Student Activities, Box 42, 525 W. 120th St., New York, NY 10027

Bi buttons for sale, New York Pride, 1998

Brooklyn College Lesbian, Gay Bisexual & Transgendered Alliance (LGBTA) 2900 Bedford Avenue, Brooklyn, NY 11210-2889 ☎ 718-951-4234 ✉ bclgbta@yahoo.com 🖳 lgbta.tripod.com/welcome.html

Kingsborough Community College: Gay, Lesbian & Bisexual Alliance 2001 Oriental Blvd., Brooklyn, NY 11235
Student / academic group focused on GLB issues. Annual Gay Awareness Day, weekly rap sessions, end-of-term social events.

Pratt Institute: Gays, Lesbians & Bisexuals at Pratt Office of Student Activities, Chapel Hall, 200 Willoughby Ave., Brooklyn, NY 11205 ☎ Student Activities: 718-636-3422

John Jay College: Lambda Association Ofc. of Student Activities, 445 West 59th St., New York, NY 10019 ☎ Student Activities Ofc: 212-237-8738/2
LBGT student union group. Educates student community on LBGT issues.

New York University

Office of Lesbian, Gay, Bisexual & Transgender Student Services, 244 Greene St., Room 305, New York, NY 10003 ☎ 212-998-4424 ✉ lgbt.office@nyu.edu 🖳 www.nyu.edu/lgbt/.
Queer Union at NYU, 21 Washington Place, Box 200, New York, NY 10003, ☎ 212-998-4938, ✉ queer.union.club@nyu.edu 🖳 pages.nyu.edu/clubs/queerunion/, *Social, support, & political organization for undergraduate glbt students.*
LGBTIPS: Lesbians, Gay, Bisexuals, Transgenders in Public Service, Wagner Graduate School of Public Services ✉ lgbtips.club@nyu.edu 🖳 pages.nyu.edu/clubs/lgbtips *(Resources & listings of NYU-wide LGBT events)*. **Bisexual, Gay & Lesbian Law Students**, 240 Mercer St., New York, NY 10012 ☎ 212-996-6574.

Green Chimney Children's Services New York, NY 10010 ☎ 212-491-5911 ✉ info@greenchimneys.com
🖳 www.pcnet.com/~gchimney/programs/nyc/nyc.htm
Operates a wide range of residential, social service & educational programs that specifically focus on the needs of glbtq youth & their families. Supervised living, group homes, Audre Lorde School (NYC Board of Ed GED Preparation program for GLBTQ youth 16-21).

Bi, Gay, Lesbian, & Transgender Youth of NY (BIGLYNTY) c/o The Center (above), New York, NY ☎ 212-620-7310 🖳 www.gaycenter.ordf/bigltyny.html
Youth-run group for LBGTQ youth -22.

Center Youth Enrichment Services (YES) c/o The Center (above), New York, NY ☎ 212-620-7310 🖳 www.gaycenter.org/programs/mhss/yes.html
Activities-based empowerment / prevention program for lgbt youth, 13-22. Theater, art, writing, TV, journalism, leadership training, job-seeking, advocacy, referrals. PUB: OutYouth

Hetrick-Martin Institute 2 Astor Place, New York, NY 10003 ☎ 212-674-2400; TTY 212-674-8695 FX: 212-674-8650 ✉ info@HMI.ORG
🖳 www.hmi.org/
The world's first & largest not-for-profit, multi-service, education, & advocacy organization dedicated to providing services to LGBTQ youth, & all youth coming to terms with sexuality issues.

Like homosexuality, bisexuality can be poison to the heterosexist power structure. Bisexuality, in its own way, makes everyone more difficult to control, to coerce. Bisexuality confounds the paradigm that pits straights against gays, and the so-called "normal" people against the "deviants."

-Lucy Friedland, in "Bi Pride & Gay Sensibility" in *Bi Women* (V6, No3, June/July 1988)

The Door 555 Broome St., New York, NY 10013
☎ 212-941-9090 FX: 212-941-0714
*For youth 12-20: crisis intervention, long-term
counseling, drop-in center, medical care,
alternative high school, housing referral services,
legal, education/vocational programs. Support
group for glb youth.*

Identity House PO Box 572, Old Chelsea Station,
New York, NY 10011 ☎ 212-243-8181
✉ identityhouse@erols.com 🖳 www.erols.com/
identityhouse
*At 39 W. 14th St. Walk-in peer counseling &
therapy referral center for the LGBT community.
Short-term groups, workshops & special events.
Therapist referrals. Drop-in coming out groups
for men & women over 40. Small donations for
meetings & counseling.*

More New York

Capital District Bisexual Network c/o ABN342
Madison Ave. #B, Albany, NY 12210
☎ 518-462-6138, Box 48
Bi brunch — call for details.

Lesbian/Gay/Bisexual Youth Group Albany
Community Center, Albany, NY ☎ 518-462-6138
*Albany Community Center also has meetings for
GLB adults. Th., Fri. 7-8:30.*

SUNY Albany: PRIDE Alliance Campus Center 116
1400 Washington Avenue, Albany, NY 12222
☎ 518-442-5672 ✉ pride@csc.albany.edu
🖳 www.albany.edu/~pride
*Goal: to provide safe space, & through solidarity
& visibility on our campus, community &
throughout our lives to ensure LGBT equal rights.*

Alfred University: Spectrum c/o Student
Activities, Alfred, NY 14802-1232
✉ spectrum@alfred.edu

Bard College: BiGayLA PO Box 5000, Annandale-
on-Hudson, NY 12504-5000

**Wells College: Lesbian, Bisexual, Questioning,
Transgendered & Allies** Aurora, NY

Pride for Youth 2050 Bellmore Avenue, Bellmore,
NY 11710 ☎ 516-679-9000
*24 hr crisis hot line, support groups, counseling,
peer education, community education & a weekly
coffeehouse for glbt youth -25.*

Binghamton University: Rainbow Pride Union
Student Union, Binghamton, NY 13902-6000
☎ 607-777-2202 ✉ rpu@sa.binghamton.edu
🖳 www.sa.binghamton.edu/~rpu/
Social & political group for students.

**SUNY Brockport: Sexual Orientations United for
Liberation (SOUL)** c/o Brockport Student
Government, 350 New Campus Drive, Brockport,
NY 14420 ☎ 716-395-5269
✉ soul_of_brockport@yahoo.com
🖳 www.acs.brockport.edu/'glbsfa/
*Open to anyone, student or non-student, nothing
assumed.*

Bronx Lavender Community Center Poe Building,
2432 Grand Concourse, Suite 504, Bronx, NY
10458 ☎ 718-601-9404 ✉ agoldcrow@aol.com
*Educational, cultural, social, political, spiritual,
human service, & health providers, service
organizations, agencies & peer groups. Safe space
for LGBT & two-spirited people to meet old &
new friends. Monthly calendar of events available.
Wheelchair accessible.*

Entre Hombres - The Bronx 886 Westchester Ave.,
Bronx, NY 10459 ☎ 718-328-4188 FX: 718-328-2888
*Outreach & counseling services & community
building events that specifically address the
complex cultural & psychosocial issues presented
by Latino men who have sex with men. Regular
weekly meetings for Latin gay, bisexual or MSM.*

Pride in da Bronx 2488 Grand Concourse Suite
#326, Bronx, NY 10458 ☎ 718-364-9529 FX: 718-
364-0667
*Drop-in center GLBTQ youth in the Bronx.
Includes bi support group.*

**Sarah Lawrence College: QVC (Queer Variety
Coalition)** Student Activities, Student Affairs
Office, 1 Mead Way, Bronxville, NY 10708

Buffalo State College LGBA 209 Cassety Hall,
1300 Elmwood Ave, Buffalo, NY 14222

SUNY Buffalo: Lesbian, Gay, Bisexual Alliance
362 Student Union, Buffalo, NY 14260-2000
☎ 716-645-3063 ✉ bruschi@acsu.buffalo.edu
🖳 www.buffalo.edu/sa/lgba
*Support, social, educational, & lesbigay events
for grad & undergrad students. Annual film
festival.*

**GLYS: Gay & Lesbian Youth Services of Western
NY** 190 Franklin St, Buffalo, NY 14202 ☎ 716-855-
0221 ✉ glys@glyswny.com 🖳 www.glyswny.com/

Hamilton College: Rainbow Alliance 198 College
Road, Clinton, NY 13323 ☎ 315-859-4830

Chautaqua County Gay & Lesbian Info Line
PO Box 254, Fredonia, NY 14063 ☎ 716-679-3560

**SUNY Fredonia: Gay, Lesbian, Bisexual Student
Union** Campus Center, Fredonia, NY 14063
☎ Center for Multicultural Affairs: 716-673-3149
✉ glbsu@hotmail.com 🖳 www.fredonia.edu/
department/maffairs/glbu/welcome.html
*Phone for student union; leave message with
secretary. Relaxed, safe & supportive atmosphere
for LGB & their friends. Educating the campus &
community.*

NYC Pride

SUNY Geneseo: Gays, Lesbians, Bisexuals, Friends CU Box 128, Geneseo, NY 14454 ☎ 716-245-5889 ✉ glbf@geneseo.edu 💻 www.geneseo.edu/~glbf/

Hobart & William Smith College Pride Alliance Geneva, NY 14456 ☎ 315-781-GLBF 💻 www.hws.edu/act/sll/pride/
GLBTQ & friends. Activist, social, support. Seeks equality for people of all sexual orientations on campus & in the world. Provides info, resources & a listening ear.

Hofstra University: PRISM 220 Student Center, Hempstead, NY 11550 ☎ 516-463-6301 💻 www.gayhofstra.com
For people of diverse sexual orientations to meet & learn from one another. Campus-focused, members of the community welcome.

Ithaca Lesbian, Gay & Bisexual Task Force PO Box 283, Ithaca, NY 14851 ☎ Bill Abeles: 272-0851 ✉ wabeles1@twcny.rr.com 💻 www.ilgbttf.org/
Coffeehouse, quarterly newsletter, monthly calendar & activities. PUB: Outlines (Outlines: outlines@ilgbttf.org, www.ilgbttf.org/ outlines.shtml)

Cornell University: Lesbian, Gay, Bisexual, Transgender Resource Center G-16 Anabel Taylor Hall, Ithaca, NY 14853-1601 ☎ 607-254-4987 ✉ lgbtrc@cornell.edu 💻 lgbtrc.cornell.edu
Groups include: **BiOm** *(a social support group for bisexuals);* **Direct Action to Stop Homophobia***;* **Ga'avah***;* **Greeks United***;* **Lambda Law***;* **Lesbian, Bisexual, Questioning Women***;* **Men Supporting Men***;* **MOSAIC***;* **Out in the World***;* **QuASAR***;* **Safe Space***;* **Vets for Diversity***. Hours: M-F, 10am-4pm.*

Ithaca College: BiGAYLA c/o Student Center, Ithaca, NY 14850 ✉ bigayla@ic3.ithaca.edu, rprosse1@ic3.ithaca.edu 💻 www.ithaca.edu/ bigayla
Meets Mon.8pm in Friends 210.

New York City Pride March

> There is always a moment in any kind of struggle when one feels in full bloom. VIVID. ALIVE. To be such a person or to witness anyone at this moment of transcendent presence is to know that what is human is linked, by a daring compassion, to what is divine. During my years of being close to people engaged in changing the world I have seen fear turn into courage. Sorrow into joy. Funerals into celebrations. Because whatever the consequences, people, standing side by side, have expressed WHO THEY REALLY ARE, and that ultimately they believe in the love of the world and each other enough TO BE THAT."
>
> *Alice Walker, in Anything We Love Can Be Saved: A Writer's Activism*

Sojourner's Wimmin's Gathering Space PO Box 398, New Paltz, NY 12561

SUNY New Paltz: BiGAYLA Student Union Building, 338, New Paltz, NY 12561 ☎ 845-257-3097

Hartwick College: Bi-Gala+ Oneonta, NY 13820 ✉ bigala@hartwick.edu 💻 users.hartwick.edu/ ~bigala/
Campus student organization.

SUNY Plattsburgh: Lesbian, Gay, Bisexual Alliance Angell College Center, Plattsburgh, NY 12901

Vassar College: Queer Coalition 124 Raymond Av., Box 3038, Poughkeepsie, NY 12601 ✉ queer@vassar.edu 💻 vsa.vassar.edu/~qcvc
Social awareness & political umbrella organization for those whose sexual preference is not exclusively hetero or whose gender designation is not limited to their sex: **Gay/Straight Alliance**, *"***HIM***" (He's Into Men),* **QULOR** *(queer people of color issues),* **Womyn's Group**, **First Step** *(coming out), &* **ACT 29** *(for those whose religion does not approve of their sexuality).*

SUNY Purchase: G/L/B/T Union CCS 3004, Purchase College, 735 Anderson Hill Rd., Purchase, NY 10577 ☎ 914-251-6976 💻 www.purchase.edu/stulife/clubs/glbtu/
Support group, social outlet, political voice & education resource for the entire Purchase community. Invite speakers, sponsors movies, gives support, plans Gay Pride Month on campus & throw annual, world famous cross dressing Fall Ball.

Bi Support Group: Northern Dutchess County, NY
PO Box 531, Rhinebeck, NY 12572-0531
*Monthly or bi-weekly. Respectful & safe
environment for bi's to share concerns about our
lives, loves, friends, communities, & bisexuality.
Definitely not for cruising.*

Gay Alliance Genesee Valley 179 Atlantic Ave,
Rochester, NY 14609 ☎ 716-244-8640 (voice/tty)
✉ info@gayalliance.org 🖳 www.gayalliance.org/
*5 week support group "Coming to Terms With
Bisexuality". Membership in GAGV includes
publication.* PUB: Empty Closet (Oldest LGB
paper in Upstate NY. Published Monthly.
716-244-9030.)

Rochester Gay Married Men's Support Group c/o
Don Hall, PO Box 10514, Rochester, NY 14610-
0514 ☎ 716-461-3799
*Helps men balance marriage & erotic attractions
to men.*

COAP: Come Out & Play c/o Gay Alliance of the
Genesee Valley, 179 Atlantic Avenue, Rochester,
NY 14609 ☎ 716-244-8640 ✉ coap@webcom.com
🖳 www.geocities.com/WestHollywood/2995
*Large social group for people in 20s & 30s. No
membership dues. Plans parties, weekend trips, &
day activities. Meets monthly.*

Lilac Rainbow Alliance for the Deaf c/o GAGV,
179 Atlantic Av., Rochester, NY 14607-1255
✉ lrad@deafqueer.net
🖳 www.deafqueer.net/lrad/
2nd Sat. 7pm at Gay Alliance.

Nayim Box 18053, Rochester, NY 14618
☎ 716-546-8853
Lesbigay Jewish group. Youth + adult.

Nazareth College: Lambda Association
c/o Student Organizations, 4245 East Avenue,
Rochester, NY 14618

Rochester Institue of Technology Gay Alliance
c/o Student Government, RIT Gay Alliance,
1 Lomb Memorial Drive, Rochester, NY 14623
✉ ritga@rit.edu 🖳 www.rit.edu/~ritga/
*Student run organization provides support &
advocacy for all lgb, & allies within RIT & the
Rochester area. Increase positive awareness of the
glb community by hosting speakers, fundraisers,
& participating in coming out week, drag show,
etc. Education to curtail homophobia.*

University of Rochester: GLBFA Wilson Commons
#101J, Rochester, NY 14627 ☎ 716-275-9379
✉ glbfa@mail.rochester.edu
🖳 www.cif.rochester.edu/sa-org/glbfa/
*Serves all members of the University community.
Highlights include pride week & Lambda Alumni
Association.*

**SUNY Stony Brook: Lesbian Gay Bisexual &
Transgendered Alliance** Student Union 045A ,
Stony Brook, NY 11790 ☎ 516-632-6469
✉ pride@ic.sunysb.edu 🖳 www.sinc.sunysb.edu/
Clubs/pride/
*Educational, political & social organization.
General mtgs: Th. Support gp: Wed. All welcome.*

New York City Pride

Pride Community Center PO Box 6608, Syracuse,
NY 13217 ☎ 315-446-4436
✉ syracusepride@yahoo.com
🖳 syracusepride.tripod.com/contact.htm

Syracuse University: Pride Union 750 Ostron
Avenue, Syracuse, NY 13210 ☎ 315-443-3599
✉ prideunion@hotmail.com
🖳 www.angelfire.com/ny/prideunion/
*Undergraduate student group. Library, social
activities, disussion groups, referrals, etc.*

**Rensselaer Polytechnic Institute: Gay, Lesbian &
Bisexual Alliance** Box 146, Troy, NY 12181-0146
☎ 518-276-2655 (events line) FX: 518-276-6920
Mark Fax to GLBA ✉ glba@rpi.edu
🖳 www.rpi.edu/dept/union/glba/public_html/
index.html

Center Lane Westchester Jewish Community
Services, 845 N. Broadway, Suite 2, White Plains,
NY 10603 ☎ 914-948-1042
*Workshops, theatre, coffeehouses, trips, & more
for g/l/b youth 15-21.*

The Loft & Helpline Services 180 East Post Rd.,
White Plains, NY 10601 ☎ 914-948-2932
✉ loftcenter@aol.com 🖳 www.loftgaycenter.org/
*Lesbian & Gay Community Center, 180 E. Post
Rd., White Plains. 20 groups for people in the
Greater Westchester Area.*

....**It's just that things don't always
happen as you predict, or even
because you strive for them to be
so. Rather, change comes from the
accumulated dreams and yearnings
of the many who break out of the
mold—not because they think they
should, but because they can't help
it. We become visible because our
parade is just too damn obvious to
avoid, because fear is simply in the
way, and we're too big to go around
it any more. We become desirable
as soon as we put away the ugly
stick—and then we find real beauty,
waiting for us, without complaint."**

Susie Bright

BiNet, USA Southeast Regional Conference

North Carolina

Triangle Bisexual Network - Raleigh Chapter
4205 Pleasant Valley Road, Suite 232, Raleigh,
NC 27612-2632 ☎ 919-406-7555, 919-856-8370
✉ rtbn232bi@aol.com
*Serves Wake, Franklin & Johnston counties.
Resources & social events. Support & social
group for bisexuals, their partners, & bi-friendly
people. Also a Non-Bi Partners of Bisexuals group.*

**North Carolina Lesbian, Gay, Bisexual &
Transgender Pride, Inc.** PO Box 3284, Durham,
NC 27715-3284 ☎ 919-990-1005
✉ NCPrideInc@aol.com
*Moves around the state, in a different city each
year.*

Equality North Carolina PAC PO Box 28768,
Raleigh, NC 27611-8768 ☎ 919-829-0343
FX: 919-828-3265 ✉ equalityncpac@aol.com
🖳 equalitync.org
LGB political action committee. PUB: Equality
North Carolina PAC Newsletter

The Front Page PO Box 27928, Raleigh, NC 27611
☎ 919-829-0181 FX: 919-829-0830
✉ frntpage@aol.com 🖳 www.frontpagenews.com
*Statewide newspaper which prints statewide
directory. Web site serving the Carolinas gl
communities.*

Men of All Colors Together, Greensboro Triad
NC ☎ 336-274-9259 ✉ mactnews@technotriad.com
🖳 www.technotriad.com/mact/aboutus.html

Community Connections PO Box 18088,
Asheville, NC 28814 ☎ 828-251-2449
✉ lmorphew@earthlink.net

Community Connections Publications PO Box
18088, Asheville, NC 28814 ☎ 828-285-8861
FX: 828-285-9390
Publication for the GLBT community.
PUB: Community Connections (See above.)

CLOSER PO Box 2911, Asheville, NC 28802
☎ 828-277-7815
*Community Liaison Organization for Support,
Education & Reform. Contact Dan or Joan
Marshall*

Gay & Bi Fathers Asheville, NC ☎ 828-252-6951
Support group for fathers.

University of North Carolina at Asheville Out
One University Heights, Asheville, NC 28801
✉ uncaout@bulldog.unca.edu 🖳 www.unca.edu/
uncaout

OutFit PO Box 5978, Asheville, NC 28813-5978
☎ 828-277-7815
*Youth service providing council for those
questioning their sexual identity or confronting
gender issues.*

PFLAG Asheville West North Carolina All Souls
Parish, PO Box 5978, Asheville, NC 28813-5978
☎ 828-277-7815

Metropolitan Community Church Asheville
PO Box 2359, Asheville, NC 28802 ☎ 828-232-0062

Unitarian Universalist Church Asheville 1 Edwin
Place, Asheville, NC 28801 ☎ 828-254-6001

Camp Pleiades 114 Abby Road, Bakersville, NC
28705 ☎ 888-324-3110 🖳 www.starcamp.com/
*A 'summer camp' for women. Season runs May-
October.*

Appalachian State University BGLAD
ASU Box 8979, Boone, NC 28608 ☎ 828-272-2714
✉ B_GLAD@appstate.edu
🖳 www.acs.appstate.edu/dept/bglad/index.html
Students of all sexual orientations invited.

PFLAG Boone 146 Mallard Lane, Boone, NC
28607 ☎ 828-264-4109

Triangle Bisexual Network of Orange County PO
Box 4702, Chapel Hill, NC 27514 ☎ 919-406-7555

Triangle Area Bisexual Women's Support Group
106 Laurel Hill Road, Chapel Hill, NC 27514
☎ 919-688-0223 ✉ brownm.ils@mhs.unc.edu
Support & social activities.

Community Church of Chapel Hill 106 Purefoy Rd,
Chapel Hill, NC 27514 ☎ 919-942-2050
✉ c3huua@mindspring.com
🖳 www.mindspring.com/~c3huua/

Orange Lesbian/Gay Alliance Chapel Hill, NC
☎ 919-929-4053
Local political action group.

**University of North Carolina, Chapel Hill, Queer
Network for Change,** Box 39, CB# 5210, Carolina
Union, Chapel Hill, NC 27514 ☎ 919-962-4401
✉ bglad@email.unc.edu 🖳 www.unc.edu/~bglad;
*Officially recognized student organization, open to
all. Supports glbtq individuals. Educating ourselves
& the greater community on glbt issues & topics.
Activities include: "Coming Out Stories" on
National Coming Out Day.*

Amity Allies Charlotte, NC ☎ 704-362-2635

Charlotte Bisexual Support Group Charlotte, NC
☎ Elizabeth: 704-532-9197 (evenings)
Monthly meeting for confidential support & discussion about issues important to bisexuals held in the Charlotte area. Open to Bisexuals & Bi-friendly folk.

Gay & Lesbian Switchboard PO Box 11144, Charlotte, NC 28220 ☎ 704-535-6277
✉ switchboard@gaycharlotte.com
Provides affirmation, info, support, & referrals to lgbt community & allies.

Mecklenburg GLPAC Charlotte, NC
☎ 704-553-7906
Promoting GLBT equality in Mecklenburg County.

Out Charlotte PO Box 32062, Charlotte, NC 28232-2062 ☎ 704-563-2699 FX: 704-569-8190
✉ OutChar@aol.com 💻 www.outcharlotte.org
Annual cultural festival celebrating the LGBT community as well as film series & cultural events.

Prime Timers of Charlotte PO Box 11202, Charlotte, NC 28220 ☎ 704-561-2257
💻 www.primetimers.org/charlotte
Social organization for mature (30+) gay/bi males to help meet social, cultural, emotional, recreational, health, security, relationship needs.

Q Notes PO Box 221841, Charlotte, NC 28222
☎ 828-531-9988 FX: 828-531-1361 ✉ publisher@q-notes.com, editor@q-notes.com 💻 www.q-notes.com/
Bi-weekly publication covering local & national issues of concern to GLBT community.

University of North Carolina Charlotte PRIDE SGA Office/Cone University Center, UNC-C, 9201 University City Blvd, Charlotte, NC 28223-0001
☎ 704-906-0043 ✉ UNCCPRIDE@aol.com

Time Out Youth 1900 The Plaza, Charlotte, NC 28205 ☎ 704-344-8335 FX: 704-344-8186
✉ toylgbt@aol.com 💻 www.timeoutyouth.com
Support & advocacy for LGBTQ youth, 13-23.

PFLAG Charlotte PO Box 35351, Charlotte, NC 28235-5351 ☎ 704-542-6525; Helpline: 704-364-1474

Western Carolina University BGLAD Cullowhee, NC 28723 ✉ BGLAD@wcu.edu
💻 wcuvax1.wcu.edu/~BGLAD/

B-ME/Black Gay, Lesbian, Bisexual Positive Image Exchange PO Box 48065, Cumberland, NC 28331-8065 ☎ 910-868-6883; 1-888-886-7423
Organization designed to promote healthy, positive self-image for members of the Black lgbt communities. Especially sensitive to bi/trans issues.

Davidson College Friends of Lesbians & Gays (FLAG) PO Box 1325, Davidson, NC 28036 ☎ 704-892-2145 💻 www.davidson.edu/student/organizations/FLAG/flag.html

Robyn Ochs

AC/DC/NC: Member of Triangle Bisexual

Kerr/Lee Community Center/ Information Line PO Box 61032, Durham, NC 27715 ☎ 919-286-1157 ✉ ron@kerr-lee.org, christine@kerr-lee.org
💻 www.kerr-lee.org/
For the lgbt/allies community. Provides space for glbt organizations to hold meetings, etc. & has an info line.

Gay & Lesbian Attorneys of North Carolina (GALA) PO Box 747, Durham, NC 27707 ☎ 919-956-5600 FX: 919-286-2541
✉ cathysurles@mindspring.com

All About Eve 711 Rigsbee Ave., Durham, NC 27701-2138 ☎ 919-688-3002
Women's private club.

GLSEN Triangle PO Box 988, Durham, NC 27702
☎ 919-834-7907 ✉ GLSENTriangle@aol.com

Efrain J. Gonzalez

Loraine Hutchins speaking at BiNet USA, Southeast Regional Conference

Duke University

Center for Lesbian, Gay, Bisexual & Transgendered Life, 202 Flowers Building, Box 90958, Durham, NC 27708; ☎ 919-684-6607 FX: 919-681-8463 ✉ lgbcenter@acpub.duke.edu 🖳 lgbt.stuaff.duke.edu. *Besides friendly talk & a safe space, the Center has info, magazines, AIDS info, safer sex guides, books, & resource guides. Bag lunch series. Karen Krahulik, Director; PUB: Newsletter for the Center for LGBT Life.* **BiGALA Duke**, c/o Center for LGBT Life 🖳 lgbt.stuaff.duke.edu/alumni.html. *Duke's lgb alumni group. Sponsors events at Homecoming & has a periodic newsletter. Write or e-mail for a registration form. Contact: Lee Golusinski.* **Queer Grads**, c/o Center for LGBT Life; ✉ queergrads@duke.edu; lgbt.stuaff.duke.edu/studentgroups.html#queergrads. *Active social & political campus group, open to students (esp. grad & professional students), staff & all others in the Duke LGBT community.* **CHUTZPAH: Queer Jews & Friends**, c/o Center for LGBT Life (above); ✉ chutzpah@duke.edu. *Social group for queer Jews & friends at Duke.* **Gay, Lesbian, & Bisexual Association: Gothic Queers**, Bryan Center 101-3, Durham, NC 27710, ☎✉, c/o Center for LGBT Life (above) *Undergraduate group.* **Task Force on Lesbian, Gay & Bisexual Matters**, c/o Center for LGBT Life ✉ llewis@neuro.duke.edu. *Investigates & promotes better conditions for LGBT students on campus.* **Duke LGB Discussion Group** (E-mail list): dukelgb@acpub.duke.edu. *For those interested in LGB issues at Duke. Provides*

students, faculty & employees at Duke, friends & supporters, with info about events & courses on campus, & about happenings & events of interest in the world outside. Independent & University sanctioned. To subscribe send email to majordomo@acpub.duke.edu with text "subscribe duke lgb".

Gay, Lesbian & Bisexual Society of Durham Technical Community College, Durham, NC 27703 ☎ 919-686-3444

North Carolina Lambda Youth Network 115 Market Street, Durham, NC 27701 ☎ 919-683-3037 FX: 919-683-3194 ✉ nclambda@aol.com 🖳 www.angelfire.com/nc/nclambda/ *Youth-led leadership development network for lgbt & allies ages 13-24.*

Durham Friends Meeting 404 Alexander Ave., Durham, NC 27705-4706 ☎ 919-286-4958 *Quakers*

Eno River Unitarian Universalist Fellowship 4907 Garrett Road, Durham, NC 27707-3443 ☎ 919-489-2575 FX: 919-489-9149 ✉ office@eruuf.org 🖳 www.eruuf.org *Welcoming, friendly UU congregation with active LGBT community. LGBT social group, Pink Triangles, programming for LGBT people, & all our groups welcome participation from all. Many LGBT community groups use our facilities, & our Sun. worship is non-creedal, non-judgmental, & welcoming to all. PUB: Currents (a newsletter)*

All Souls Church, Unitarian Universalist 809 Wilkerson Ave, Durham, NC 27701 ☎ 919-956-8494 FX: 919-667-0258 ✉ allsouls@mindspring.com 🖳 www.rtpnet.org/~ascuu/

Elon College Spectrum 3085 Campus Box, Elon College, NC 27244 ✉ spb137c@prodigy.com

PFLAG Elon College Elon College, NC 27244 ☎ 336-584-7225

Fayetteville Area Bisexual Network (FAB-Net) Fayetteville, NC ☎ 910-483-9792

Fayetteville Area Gay Pride Fayetteville, NC ☎ 910-822-4802; 910-424-7454

Lambda Association of Fayetteville PO Box 53281, Fayetteville, NC 28305 ☎910-822-4802 ✉ LambdaAssocFayetteville@juno.com *Social group for lgbt folks.*

Emmaus Metropolitan Community Church PO Box 346, Fayetteville, NC 28302-0346 ☎ 910-678-8813 ✉ emmausmcc@aol.com 🖳 members.aol.com/mccfaync/index.html *New MCC Church serving the glbt community in Fayetteville & surrounding areas.*

St. Paul's In-The-Pines Episcopal Church 1705 St. Augustine Avenue, Fayetteville, NC 28304-5236 ☎910-485-7098 *Female pastor VERY LGBT-friendly.*

PFLAG Flat Rock Hendersonville 206 Lois Lane, Flat Rock, NC 28731-9709 ☎ 828-696-7250 ✉ allenderry@juno.com

1995

> **...either "bisexuality" is a very common condition, or another artificial category concealing the overlaps. What heterosexuals really fear, is not that "they" — an alien subgroup with perverse tastes in bedfellows — are getting an undue share of power and attention, but that "they" might well be us.**
>
> Barbara Ehrenreich, *1989*

PFLAG Gastonia Western Piedmont PO Box 101, Gastonia, NC 28052-0101 ☎ 704-629-4881

Alternative Resources of the Triad PO Box 4442, Greensboro, NC 27404 ☎ 336-748-0031; 336-855-8558
Winston-Salem group. Hotline 7-10pm nightly, referral center, sponsors support groups.

Guilford College: Gays, Lesbians, Bisexuals & Allies PO Box 17725, Greensboro, NC 27410 ☎ 336-316-2374 ✉ glba@rascal.guilford.edu 🖳 www.guilford.edu/studorg/glbta

University of North Carolina Greensboro Gay, Lesbian, Bisexual & Transgender Association Box 27 Eliot University Center, Greensboro, NC 27412 ☎ 336-334-4282 ✉ pride@uncg.edu 🖳 www.uncg.edu/students.groups/pride/

Gay & Lesbian Adolescent Support System (GLASS) Greensboro, NC ☎ 336-272-6053 ✉ glassemail@yahoo.com 🖳 www.people-places.com/glass
Youth support group for glbtq youth ages 15-21.

Gay, Lesbian & Straight Education Network PO Box 41199, Greensboro, NC 27404-1199 ☎ 336-288-6836 ✉ contact@GLSENGreensboro.org 🖳 glsengreensboro.org
Advocates for LGBT staff & students in school communities.

PFLAG Greensboro PO Box 41534, Greensboro, NC 27404 ☎ 336-852-8489
Meets monthly. Helpline: 336-855-8558

Friendship Friends Meeting 1103 New Garden Rd, Greensboro, NC 27410 ☎ 336-854-5155

St. Mary's Metropolitan Community Church 504 Edwardia Drive, Greensboro, NC 27409 ☎ 336-297-4054

Triad Health Project Greensboro 415 North Edgeworth St, PO Box 5716, Greensboro, NC 27435 ☎ 336-275-1654 FX: 336-275-2209 ✉ thpinfo@aol.com 🖳 www.triadhealthproject.com
Free & confidential HIV/AIDS services & support. Prevention education.

Down East Gay, Lesbian, Bisexual & Transgendered Information Line PO Box 1691, Greenville, NC 27835-1691 ☎ 252-551-0316 ✉ downeastpride@bigfoot.com 🖳 www.ecu.edu/org/bglad/dep/ or dep.members.gayweb.com
Also put on the Down East Pride Festival.

East Carolina University: Bisexuals, Gays, Lesbians, & Allies for Diversity (B-GLAD) c/o Office of Student Leadership Development, 109 Mendenhall Student Center, ECU, Greenville, NC 27858 ☎ 252-551-0316#3 ✉ bglad@mail.ecu.edu 🖳 www.ecu.edu/org/bglad/
For glb & ally students. Website with very large Index of GLBT student groups in NC.

Unitarian Universalist Congregation of Greenville 131 Oakmont Drive, Greenville, NC 27858 ☎ 252-355-6658

Unitarian Universalist Fellowship Hendersonville PO Box 2359, Hendersonville, NC 28793 ☎ 828-693-3157

Unitarian Universalist Church of Hillsborough 1710 Old NC 10 (@ corner of Lawrence Rd), PO Box 275, Hillsborough, NC 27278 ☎ 919-644-0567 ✉ uuch@rtpnet.org 🖳 www.rtpnet.org/~uuch

BGLAD at Coastal Carolina Community College Jacksonville, NC ✉ cbglad@hotmail.com 🖳 clik.to/coastalBGLAD

Guilford Technical Community College Gay, Lesbian & Bisexual Student Alliance 601 High Point Rd, Jamestown, NC 27282 ☎ 336-334-2797

Unitarian Universalist Fellowship Jamestown 5603 Hilltop Rd, Jamestown, NC 27282 ☎ 336-275-3922

PFLAG Kannapolis 7862 Longbriar Drive, Kannapolis, NC 28081 ☎ 704-932-0949 ✉ needham@vnet.net

All Souls Welcoming Congregation (Unitarian) 200 Century Blvd, Kernersville, NC 27284 ☎ 336-722-0421

Unitarian Universalist Church of the Outer Banks PO Box 1006, Kitty Hawk, NC 27949 ☎ 252-261-2801 ✉ duncarq@interpath.com 🖳 members.tripod.com/~UUCOB/

Outer Banks Gay & Lesbian Club PO Box 1444, Manteo, NC 27954-1444 ✉ outerbanks_glc@geocities.com
Primarily social glbt organization. Recently more inclusive of bi/trans folks.

Unitarian Universalist Coastal Fellowship 1300 Evans Street, Morhead City, NC 28557 ☎ 252-240-2283

PFLAG Mount Airy 1451 Cadle Ford Road, Mount Airy, NC 27030 ☎ 336-320-2431 ✉ snichols@surry.net

Triangle Bisexual Network of Wake County 4205 Pleasant Valley Rd Ste 232, Raleigh, NC 27612 ☎ 919-856-8370 ✉ rtbn232bi@aol.com

---

> **I am sexual**
> **without gendered reference points**
> **riding the chemistry**
> **as it unfolds**
> **I am a free range chicken**
> **Don't fence me in**
> **I can cockadoodle doo your do**
> **and lay with the best of your hens**
>
> *Lani Ka'ahumanu, from That Naked Place*

Triangle Community Works PO Box 5961, Raleigh, NC 27650-5961 ☎ 919-781-7574
🖳 www.tcworks.org
Coaliton w/ member groups dedicated to LGB issues in Raleigh & the triangle area. GL help line weekday nights 7-10pm 919-821-0055.

Raleigh Hopeline Raleigh, NC ☎ 919-231-4525
Support & crisis hotline.

Cape Myrtle Festival PO Box 10043, Raleigh, NC 27605 ☎ 919-851-3512; 919-755-3339
✉ van.early@mindspring.com
🖳 www.crapemyrtlefest.org
A non-profit fundraiser for the community.

Triangle Sports (LGB Athletics) PO Box 6564, Raleigh, NC 27628

ASPYN - A Safer Place Youth Network PO Box 5961, Raleigh, NC 27650 ☎ 919-839-2912
Non-threatening, social outlet for GLBQ youth in Raleigh & surrounding areas. Meetings facilitated by adults, but run by the youth.

North Carolina State University Bisexuals, Gays, Lesbians & Allies PO Box 7314, Raleigh, NC 27695 ☎ 919-512-8629 ✉ bgla@ncsu.edu
🖳 www2.ncsu.edu/ncsu/stud_orgs/lgsu/

P-FLAG Raleigh-Durham/Triangle Chapter PO Box 10844, Raleigh, NC 27605-0844 ☎ 919-380-9325
✉ rhallen@intrex.net 🖳 www.pflag.org/chapters
Parents & friends of lesbians & gays.

Unitarian Universalist Fellowship of Raleigh 3313 Wade Avenue, Raleigh, NC 27607 ☎ 919-781-7635
✉ UUFRaleigh@aol.com 🖳 www.uufr.org

Winthrop University: Gay, Lesbian, Bisexual & Ally League (GLOBAL) c/o Student Activities Office, Rock Hill, NC 29733 ☎ 803-323-2248 (ask for GLOBAL)

PFLAG Rocky Mount 712 York Street, Rocky Mount, NC 27803 ☎ 252-442-7423
✉ Lchesson@aol.com

Warren Wilson College Gay, Lesbian, Bisexual, Transgender & Straight Alliance PO Box 9000, Swannanoa, NC 28815-9000 ☎ 828-298-3325
✉ alliance@warren-wilson.edu 🖳 www.warren-wilson.edu/~alliance

GROW Resource Line 341-11 S. College Rd. Suite 182, Wilmington, NC 28403 ☎ 910-762-0301
✉ GROWNews@aol.com
GLB resource line & community service organization.

University of North Carolina Wilmington: PRIDE Wilmington, NC ☎ 910-675-9222 x452
✉ PRIDE@uncwil.edu
🖳 vxd.ocis.uncwil.edu:8000/~pride/

St. Jude's Metropolitan Community Church 4326 Market St. Suite 170, Wilmington, NC 28403
☎ 910-762-5833 ✉ stjudes@bellsouth.net
🖳 www.stjudesmcc.org

Wake Forest Gay Straight Student Alliance PO Box 7203, Winston Salem, NC 27109
🖳 www.wfu.edu/Student-organizations/GALBA/gssa.htm

Youth Flag Winston Salem, NC ☎ 336-765-6694
Support group for youth organized by PFLAG Winston Salem.

PFLAG Winston-Salem PO Box 15477, Winston-Salem, NC 27113 ☎ 336-760-8865
✉ jose.isasi@internetmci.com
Meets monthly.

GLSEN Winston Salem PO Box 173, 1959 N Peacehaven Rd, Winston Salem, NC 27106
✉ plumedejj@aol.com

Interweave Winston Salem 4055 Robinhood Rd, Winston Salem, NC 27106

Metropolitan Community Church of Winston Salem 2315 Huff St, Winston Salem, NC 27107
☎ 336-784-8009

Unitarian Universalist of Winston Salem 4055 Robinhood Rd, Winston Salem, NC 27106
☎ 336-659-0331

Unity Church of Winston Salem Stratford Rd & Hews Rd, Winston Salem, NC 27101
☎ 336-760-8300

Winston Salem Friends Meeting 3151 Reynolds Rd, Winston Salem, NC 27106 ☎ 336-726-8801

North Dakota

PFLAG Bismarck Central Dakota PO Box 2491, Bismarck, ND 58502-2491 ☎ 701-223-7773
🖳 redrival.com/pflagcd

North Dakota State University: Ten Percent Society see listing under Minnesota (Moorhead State University: Tri-College Ten Percent Society), NDSU Dept History, Minard Hall 412J, PO Box 5075, Fargo, ND 58105-5075 ☎Larry Peterson: 701-231-8824 🖳 www.ten-percent.org ✉ tenpercentpsociety@yahoo.com

PFLAG Fargo Moorhead PO Box 10625, Fargo, ND 58106 ☎ 701-232-8361 ✉ fmpflag@fmpflag.org
🖳 www.fmpflag.org/

University of North Dakota 10% Society Box 8385 Memorial Union, Grand Forks, ND 58202 ☎ 701-777-3269 (vm) ✉ tenps@sage.und.nodak.edu
🖳 www.und.edu/org/tenps/index.html

PFLAG Grand Forks 3210 Cherry Street Apt 24, Grand Forks, ND 58201 ☎ 701-775-4447 🖳 www.geocities.com/WestHollywood/Chelsea/ 6537/ ✉ pmoore@medicine.nodak.edu

PFLAG Minot Uni Med South, 600 17th Avenue SE, Minot, ND 58701 ☎ 701-857-2402 🖳 www.geocities.com/lmwarner73/

Ohio

Statewide

Ohio WOMBAT (Women of Beauty & Temptation) OH ✉ Kimbirly25@aol.com 🖳 www.egroups.com/ group/OhioWombats
Email list for bi women in Southern Ohio. Social events scheduled through the list.

Gay People's Chronicle PO Box 5426, Cleveland, OH 44101-0426 ☎216-631-1052 ✉ calendars@chronohio.com 🖳 www.gaypeopleschronicle.com/home.htm
Free Ohio GLBT newspaper. A list of distribution points available on their website.

Outlook Free Newspaper 700 Ackerman Road, Suite 600, Columbus, OH 43202 ☎ 614-268-8525 ✉ editor@outlooknews.com 🖳 www.outlooknews.com
Free Ohio GLBT newspaper. List of distribution points is on the website.

Rainbow Pride Hotline PO Box 8104, Columbus, OH 43201 ☎ 1-800-291-9190 ✉ support@kaleidoscope.org 🖳 www.kaleidoscope.org
24 hour toll free support & info. line for GLBT youth in Ohio.

Local

Ohio Northern University: Open Doors Prof. Compton, Psychology Dept, Ada, OH 45810 ☎ 419-772-2139 ✉ p-compton@onu.edu
Faculty advisor: Prof. Phil Compton.

Akron Pride Center

PO Box 22254, Akron, OH 44302 ☎ 330-253-2220 ✉ pride@rainbow-akron.com 🖳 rainbow-akron.com/stonewall/index.htm *Community center at 71 N. Adams St. serving the Akron area. Open Wed. 11am-4pm, Th. 6-9pm, closed weekends.* Groups include: **Bi Pride** *(Potluck & discussion of bisexual issues, 1st Fri., 7pm);* **Women's Pride** *(Open discussion, 2nd & 4th Mon., 7pm);* **Men's Pride** (Open discussion group, meets 2nd & 4th Wed., 7pm); **Teen Pride** *(Support & discussion for GLBT youth 13-18. 1st & 3rd Tues. 7pm);* **AA Pride** *(Support for alcoholic & drug dependent GLBT people. Meets Th. 7pm.);* Akron **Area Pride Collective** (☎ 330-657-2977; ✉ aapc@rainbow-akron.com. *Meets 2nd/4th Tu. 7pm. Produces Akron's Annual GLB Pride Weekend).*

Stonewall Akron Box 3216, Akron, OH 44309 ☎ 330-849-1520; 330-453-2609 ✉ stoneakron@aol.com 🖳 www.rainbow-akron.com/stonewall/index.htm
Aims to achieve social & political equality through the elimination of discrimination against the glb community.

University of Akron: Lesbian, Gay, Bisexual, Transgender Union Gardner Center #14, Akron, OH 44325-4601 ✉ lgbu@uakron.edu or lgbtu@hotmail.com 🖳 www.uakron.edu/lgbu/
Open to students & non-students. Informal, supportive, educational resource lgbt & allies. Weekly topic meetings cover a wide range of topics. Guest speakers, videos, field trips. Meets Mon. 8pm in the Elm Room of Gardner Student Center during termtime.

PRYSM (Akron) East Akron YMCA, 100 Goodyear Blvd., Akron, OH 44305-4034 ☎ VM: 330-258-3652 or 216-375-2437 (NE Task Force on AIDS)
Discussion/social/support for GLBT teens & adults to age 22. Meets Sats 11:30-1:30 at above address. May currently be on hiatus, call to verify meeting times.

PFLAG Alliance 2541 Pleasant Place, Alliance, OH 44601 ☎ 440-821-0177, helpline: 800-956-6630

PFLAG Elyria/Lorain County 730 Park Ave., Amherst, OH 44001 ☎ 440-988-8215
Meets 3rd Mondays, 8pm. First Congregational Church, 4th & Washington, Lorain.

Kent State University (Ashtabula Campus) LGBU 3325 W. 13th St., Ashtabula, OH 44004 ☎ 440-964-4289 🖳 www.ashtabula.kent.edu/ campuslife/studentmain.htm
Student organization, run by students, that advocates the rights of all glbt & heterosexuals. Supports, educates, informs the general public.

PFLAG Ashtabula 1710 Walnut Blvd., Ashtabula, OH 44004 ☎ 440-964-3350
Meets last Fri. 7pm, Donohoe Center conference room, U.S. 20 East, Ashtabula.

Bi activists piled up at the International Bi Conference, NYC 1994

Ohio University

Open Doors: GLBT Student Union, 18 N. College St., Athens, OH 45701 ☎ 740-594-2385 ✉ open_door_glbt@hotmail.com 🖳 welcome.to/opendoors. *Serves all, including straights. Social, support & (some) political activism group. Weekly discussions Wed. 8pm in the living room of United Campus Ministry, 18 North College Street during termtime.* **GLOBE Gay, Lesbian, or Bisexual Employees**, Athens, OH 45701 ☎ 740-593-1935 ✉ cinoman@ohio.edu or globe@www.ohiou.edu 🖳 www.ohiou.edu/globe/index.html. *GLBT Faculty/Staff advocacy group. Membership $10/yr.* **Delta Lambda Phi** Box 5604, Athens, OH 45701 ✉ centaur@oak.cats.ohiou.edu 🖳 oak.cats.ohiou.edu/~centaur/contact.html. *Local branch of national social fraternity for gay, bi & progressive men.*

Baldwin Wallace College

Lambda ✉ lambda@bw.edu 🖳 www.bw.edu/~lambda/. *Confidential group meets weekly on campus. "Safe space" for discussion & support to all those dealing with sexual orientation issues.* **Allies** ✉ allies@bw.edu 🖳 www.bw.edu/~allies/. *Educate ourselves & others about glbt issues; support for people of all sexual identities. Mts Thurs, 6-7pm in the Grindstone Room of the Student Union. Address/☎ for both groups: 275 Eastland, Berea, OH 44017; 440-826-2356.*

GLSEN/Cleveland PO Box 433, Berea, OH 44017 ☎ 216-738-7525 ✉ GLSENcleve@aol.com 🖳 www.geocities.com/glsencleve/index.htm *National organization fighting to end anti-gay bias in K-12 schools.*

Bowling Green Gay-Lesbian Info Line Bowling Green, OH ☎ 419-352-5242 *Info Line: Mon/Wed/Fri 7-10pm.*

Stonewall 25 March, NYC, 1994

Bowling Green State University

Vision University Hall Box 22, Bowling Green, OH 43403 ☎ 419-372-0555 ✉ vision@members.gayweb.com, 🖳 www.bgsu.edu/studentlife/organizations/vision, *Weekly meetings. Also a support group,* **VisionLite. Women's Action Coalition**, 463 Saddlemire Student Services, Bowling Green University, Bowling Green, OH 43403 ☎ 419-372-2343 ✉ acbgsu@hotmail.com 🖳 www.bgsu.edu/studentlife/organizations/womens-action/main.html. *Mtgs: Th 6:30pm in Suite 450 Saddlemire, then out to Java Supreme (on Court Street) for coffee & conversations.*

Awakenings 8211 Brecksville Rd, Bldg #4, suite 104, Brecksville, OH 44141 ☎ 440-526-0468; 1-800-486-0904 *Free professionally facilitated support group for GLBT folk.*

Side by Side PO Box 9096, Canton, OH 44711 ✉ funbunz@aol.com *Social organization for gay & bi men & women. Monthly social events.*

Cincinnati Gay & Lesbian Center PO Box 141061, Cincinnati, OH 45250-1061 ☎ 513-591-0200 ✉ mail@glbtcentercincinnati.com 🖳 www.glbtcentercincinnati.com/ *Community Service Center, serving the Cincinnati area. Located at 4119 Hamilton Ave. Open: 6-9pm M-Th, 6-11pm Friday, 12-4pm Saturday.*

GLBT Coalition c/o Cincinnati G&L Center (above) *Delegates from local GBLT organizations. Meet monthly to exchange info about community activities & initiatives, & increase awareness, communication, cooperation, & unity among GBLT organizations. Meets 3rd Sun. 10am. at St. John's Unitarian Church (320 Resor Av. in Clifton).*

Cincinnati GLBT Hotline (24-hr) Cincinnati, OH 45250 ☎ 513-591-0222 *24 hr. Cincinnati GLBT Hotline, run by the Cincinnati GLBT Center.*

Brother II Brother, Cincinnati, Inc. 5531 Hamilton Ave, PO Box 6001, Cincinnati, OH 45224 ☎ 513-542-5186 Terry Payne; 513-684-1348 Voice Mail *Meets monthly. Family of diverse African American communities dedicated to empowerment, education & improvement of the quality of life. Seek to create nurturing environment by organizing & providing social, spiritual, civic & health care networks. Embraces & affirms all GLB of African descent.* PUB: Brother II Brother newsletter

Cincinnati Youth Group c/o Cincinnati G&L Center (above) ☎ Missy Sachs: 513-684-8405; 513-591-0200 ✉ bearluvr@one.net or mail@glbtcentercincinnati.com 🖳 www.geocities.com/WestHollywood/Stonewall/1166/ *Support & discussion group for GLBT youth 13-21, trained adult facilitators. Meets Sun. 6pm at the Cincinnati GLBT Center, 4119 Hamilton Ave. Also, youth drop-in nights, Th., 6-9pm.*

Crazy Ladies Center 4039 Hamilton Ave., Cincinnati, OH 45223 ☎ 513-541-4198 ✉ info@crazyladies.org 🖳 www.crazyladies.org
A center for the lesbian community & all feminists. Safe space where diverse groups of women come together for discussion, work & education. Groups include: **Women's Coming Out Group** *- (Tu. 7:30-9pm. Contact: Kathy P., 451-5552. Open meeting for lesbians or women exploring their sexual identity or who are in any part of the "coming out" process) &* **One Step Beyond (Coming Out)** *(Open meeting for women who have explored the coming out process & are looking for expansion in their lives. Contact: Jan E. 683-2024).*

Pink Paradigm 3511 Wabash Ave., Cincinnati, OH 45207 ☎ 513-396-6738
A queer social network for cultural change.

Rainbow Cincinnati Cincinnati, OH ✉ info@gaycincinnati.com 🖳 www.gaycincinnati.com
Electronic community for glbt people in Cincinnati.

Stonewall Cincinnati PO Box 954, Cincinnati, OH 45201 ☎513-651-2500 ✉ dtcswc@aol.com 🖳 www.stonewallcincinnati.org
Works on behalf of all glbt people to end discrimination & violence, & to promote cultural inclusion through education, advocacy & outreach.

GLSEN/Cincinnati PO Box 19856, Cincinnati, OH 45219 ☎ 513-624-6963, 513-923-2137
FX: 513-345-5543 ✉ GLSENcincy@aol.com
Making schools safe for all students. $35 membership fee (includes both local & national membership). Meets at the G/L Community Center, last Tu. 7pm.

Gay & Bisexual Married Men Group 2183 Central Pkwy, Cincinnati, OH 45214 ☎ 513-481-8185

Men of Color Outreach Project 3458 Reading Road, Cincinnati, OH 45229 ☎ 513-487-6520
FX: 513-281-0455 ✉ tpayne@gcul.org 🖳 www.gcul.org
Meetings 2nd, 4th Th. 6:30-8pm. SIMBA (Safe in My Brother's Arms): meeting/training for men interested in being buddies or peer-to-peer trainers meets 1st, last Fri. 6-8pm. Literary Club 1st Mon. PUB: Parity 2000 newsletter, Brother II Brother newsletter

People of All Colors Together (PACT)
PO Box 2526, Cincinnati, OH 45201-2526 ☎ 513-395-PACT ✉ PACTCINOH@aol.com 🖳 members.nbci.com/rebinoh/PACT.html
Co-chairs- Roger Burgess 591-2833, Jim Wagner 961-4475. Cultural, educational, political & social activities as a means of dealing with homophobia, racism, sexism & other inequities in our lives & communities. All welcome. Monthly business & social meetings. Rap groups, potlucks, outings.

The Imperial Sovereign Queen City Court of the Buckeye Empire of All Ohio, Inc. PO Box 3414, Cincinnati, OH 45201 ☎ 513-481-5368 ✉ emp6besse@aol.com 🖳 www.geocities.com/WestHollywood/Heights/4001/
With almost 70 courts currently in existence, the Court system is one of North America's largest grassroots lgbt organizations. Although open to everyone, the Court is akin to a "gay Shriners" via its charitable works, & priding itself on the diversity of its membership regarding race, gender, class, & sexual orientation among other characteristics.

Tri State Prime Timers PO Box 34, Cincinnati, OH 45201-0034 ☎ 513-956-1939, 513-956-4398 ✉ primetimoh@aol.com 🖳 www.primetimers.org/tristate
Mature gay/bi men & younger men who admire mature men. Meets monthly.

PFLAG Cincinnati PO Box 19634, Cincinnati, OH 45219-0634 ☎ 513-721-7900, 513-755-6150 ✉ pflagcinci@yahoo.com 🖳 www.geocities.com/pflagcinci/
Meets 2nd Tu. 7:30-10pm at Mt. Auburn Presbyterian Church, 103 William Howard Taft Rd.

University of Cincinnati: Gay, Lesbian, Bisexual & Transgender Alliance PO Box 0136, Cincinnati, OH 45221-0136 ☎ 513-556-1449 ✉ ucalliance@yahoo.com 🖳 www.soa.uc.edu/org/algbp/
Meets Tu. 4:30pm in 429 Tangeman University Center. Office in 209 TUC, open Mon-Fri, 11-3.

What currents, tensions, compromises, and hopes brought us to this point [1987, the beginning of a national US bisexual movement]? Take the dance of solidarity and perceived betrayal within feminism; add in the divisions between the values of culture and community, liberation and freedom; mix liberally with debates over allegiance versus membership, lesbian-feminism versus queerdom; situate the entire concoction within the context of increasingly fragmentary identity politics; and we begin to understand the stories, the stakes, and the priorities of bisexual activists--and of the feminist, lesbian and gay communities with whom we are engaged in our uneasy tango.

Amanda Udis-Kessler, in Bisexual Politics

BiNet USA Meeting, Boston 1998

Robyn Ochs

Cleveland Lesbian/Gay Community Service Center

PO Box 6177, Cleveland, OH 44101 ☎ 216-651-5428 (Hotline 12-10pm M-F, 6-9pm Sat.), 1-888-429-8761 FX: 216-651-6439) info@lgcsc.org V www.lgcsc.org. *Community Center serving GLBT community in Cleveland through a variety of programming, including a GLBT hotline. Located at 6600 Detroit Ave. Office hours 12-7pm M-F, 6-9pm Sun. Computerized Information Line: 216-651-6452. The following groups can be contacted through the Center:* **2B Determined** ⊠ sarah_whitman_young@hotmail.com. *Social, support, educational group for bis, partners, friends, & others. Meets at The Center, 6600 Detroit Ave, 1st & 3rd Fri., 8pm.)* **Bridges** (Formerly Prysm Parents) (🖳 www.lgcsc.org/prysm.htm#parents, **Forum for Parents of LGBT youth.** *1st Mon. 6:30-8:30pm.)* **Brother's Keepers** (Center Men's Group) (*Discussion & support group open to all gay & bi men. Th., 8pm.)* **Men's Coming Out Group** (*Closed (requires Pre-registration) support group in cycles of 6-7 weeks. Call for times/registration info.)* **ACT UP** (☎ 216-861-4946, 888-334-4849. *Branch of national GLBT AIDS activist organization.)* **10% Books** (*Book Club for the GLBT Community. 2nd Mon., 8pm).* **Nubian Women's Forum** (*Discussion & support group for lgbq women of color.)* **Brother's Circle** (*Support, social, prevention, & community networking opportunities to African American men who have sex with men.)* **Prime Timers Cleveland Committee** (*Local chapter of national social group for older gay & bi men, 1st Tu., 8pm)* **Queer Movie Night** (⊠sarah_whitman_young@hotmail.com (*Informal screenings of GLBT films. BYOM (bring your own munchies). At The Center, 4th Fri.).* **Twenty Something** (*Social & entertainment opportunities to people 20-29. 1st & 3rd Tu., 8pm.)* **PRYSM** (Presence & Respect For Youth in a Sexual Minority) 🖳 www.lgcsc.org/prysm.htm. *(Support group for lgbtq youth -21 Sats. 12-3 pm & youth drop in night Wed. 6:30-9pm.)* **Pride Sunday AA** (*GLBT AA Sundays, 7pm).* **Women's Coming Out Group** (*Closed (requires pre-registration) support*

meeting, runs in 6-7 week cycles. Meets at the Center.) **Women's Words** (*Discussion/Support group open to all lesbian & bi women. 2nd & 4th Th., discussion group, 8pm, 1st & 3rd Th., social drop-in, 8pm).*

Cleveland LGBT Pride Committee
PO Box 91031, Cleveland, OH 44101
☎ 216-371-0214 ⊠ prez@clevelandpride.org
🖳 www.clevelandpride.org
Organizing committee for the Annual Cleveland Pride Festival.

Northern Ohio Gender & Sexuality Coalition
10507 Lake Ave, Apt 301, Cleveland, OH 44102
⊠ OhioGSFC-subscribe@yahoogroups.com,
OhioGSFC-owner@yahoogroups.com 🖳
www.yahoogroups.com/group/OhioGSFC
Activism networking & communication & understanding between different "identity" groups, & peer support. Persons of all genders & orientations welcome. Respectful treatment of other list members essential. Queer/Trans/Poly/Kink friendly - open to all, including allies - Cleveland based.

ACLU of Ohio Gay Rights Project
1266 West 6th Street, Suite 200, Cleveland, OH 44101
☎ 216-781-6276 🖳 www.acluohio.org

African-American GLBT Pride
Cleveland, OH 44102 ☎ 216-485-5177
1st & 3rd Sat., 6:30pm, Arabica Coffee House, 11300 Juniper, University Circle.

Asians & Friends, Cleveland
PO Box 29031, Cleveland, OH 44129 ☎ 216-226-6080 x3
⊠ clevndaf@aol.com 🖳 www.geocities.com/WestHollywood/Castro/6101/
Open to Asian & non-Asian GLBT folk. Student's Rate $12/year, Single Rate $20/year, Couples Rate $30. PUB: Asians & Friends (Published spring, summer, fall, winter.)

Cleveland Irish LesBiGay Organization
Cleveland, OH ☎ Diane, 216-281-8384, 440-255-2615

Lambda Amateur Radio Club
PO Box 91757, Cleveland, OH 44101 ☎ 216-381-4774
⊠ DougBraun@aol.com
LGBT ham radio operators. Affiliate of amateur relay league.

Sign of the Rainbow
PO Box 6253, Cleveland, OH 44101
GLBT Deaf & hearing impaired organization.

Straight Spouse Network
Cleveland, OH ☎ 440-354-6683
Meets 4th Tu., 7pm, Euclid Ave Congregational Church, 9606 Euclid Ave.

Western Reserve Historical Society: Gay & Lesbian Archives
www.lgcsc.org/archives.htm, Cleveland, OH 44106 ☎ 216-721-5722
⊠ info@lgcsc.org 🖳 www.lgcsc.org/archives.htm
Document GLB history in NE Ohio.

Gray Pride 2373 Euclid Heights Blvd., Cleveland Heights, OH 44106 ☎ 216-621-7201x213, 216-381-4774 (after 7:30pm), 216-791-8039x328 FX: 216-791-8030 ✉ DougBraun@aol.com or graypride@juno.com
Meets 2nd Tu., locations TBA. 60+year-olds. Interpreting for the deaf provided upon request.

Case Western Reserve University: Gay, Lesbian, Bisexual Alliance c/o Thwing Student Office, 10900 Euclid Av., Cleveland, OH 44106 ☎ 216-754-2215; 216-791-3103; 216-622-2988 (Paul Ellwood) ✉ pxe@po.cwru.edu
Group open to non-students also, educational/social focus. Weekly meetings during termtime.

Cleveland State University: Gay Lesbian & Straight Alliance (GLASA) CSU GLASA, 2121 Euclid Ave, Box 77, Cleveland, OH 44115 ☎ John Calvitta: 440-946-9456 ✉ johnpaul68@hotmail.com 🖥 www.csuohio.edu/gala/index2.html
Bi & Trans friendly. Staff advisor is Bruce Menapace (216) 687- 2277.

Stonewall Union Center 1160 N. High Street, PO Box 10814, Columbus, OH 43201-7814 ☎ GLBT Hotline 614-299-7764 FX: 614-299-4408 ✉ kim@stonewall-columbus.org (Education/Volunteer Coordinator) 🖥 www.stonewall-columbus.org/
GLBT community center. Hotline staffed M-Th 10-7; F 10-5. PUB: *Stonewall Journal (monthly free publications) & Lavender Listings (yearly free business & resource guide for Columbus area)*

Sexual Health Information Line Columbus, OH 43201 ☎ 614-262-3556
Sexual Health Information for all genders & orientations: Tu.- Th., 6-10pm.

Stonewall Anti-Violence Project 1160 N. High St., Columbus, OH 43201 ☎ 614-299-7764 🖥 www.stonewall-columbus.org
Compiles hate-crime statistics for the GLB community, aids victims of hate-crimes, & offers self-defense training.

Men's Coming Out Group c/o The Stonewall Union, 1160 N. High St, P. O. Box 10814, Columbus, OH 43201 ☎ 614-299-7764 FX: 614-299-4408 🖥 www.stonewall-columbus.org
Discussion & support for gay & bi men. Meets 2nd & 4th Mondays, 7pm, at the Stonewall Center, 1160 N. High St.

Diversity of Ohio 263 Crestview Road, Columbus, OH 43202 ☎ 614-486-5664
Contact: Sharifa Williams. Statewide coalition of LGBT people of color.

Authors read from *Bi Any Other Name*, Cambridge MA.

Insight PO Box 360821, Columbus, OH 43236 ☎ 614-470-3111
Newly forming organization of professionals in the glb community. Looking for individuals willing to help lead group.

Ohio Human Rights Bar Association PO Box 10655, 1487 W. 5th Ave #247, Columbus, OH 43212 ☎ 614-265-7530
GLBT lawyers.

GLSEN/Central Ohio PO Box 360952, Columbus, OH 43236-0952 ✉ GLSENCentralOH@aol.com
Local chapter of national organization fighting to end anti-gay bias in K-12 schools.

Prime Timers Columbus PO Box 072167, Columbus, OH 43207 ☎ 614-444-9473
Columbus chapter of Prime Timers, social group for older gay and bi men.

Buckeye Region Anti-Violence Organization (BRAVO) Columbus, OH ☎ 614-268-9622 ✉ bravoavp@earthlink.net 🖥 home.earthlink.net/~bravoavp/
Compiles hate-crime statistics, aids victims of violence, & battles violence against GLBT people.

Asians & Friends, Columbus PO Box 16381, Columbus, OH 43216-0381 ☎ Dexter Ortaliz: 614-793-0422 ✉ afcmh@yahoo.com 🖥 www.afcmh.org
Provides outreach for glbt Asians & non-Asians that is confidential, enjoyable & sociable.

Women's Coming Out Group c/o The Stonewall Union, 1160 N. High St, PO Box 10814, Columbus, OH 43201 ☎ 614-299-7764 FX: 614-299-4408 🖥 www.stonewall-columbus.org
Discussion group for bi & lesbian women. Meets 1st & 3rd Mon., 7pm, at the Stonewall Center.

The Ohio State University

Gay, Lesbian & Bisexual, Transgendered Student Services, 1739 North High Street , #340, Columbus, OH 43210 ☎ 614-292-6200 FX: 614-292-4462 ✉ glbss@osu.edu, 🖥 www.osu.edu/units/Ofglbs/. *University office with paid staff & programming budget. Umbrella for several campus GLBTIA groups.* **Fusion**, c/o GLBTSS, ✉ fusionosu@yahoo.com 🖥 www.ohio-state.edu/students/fusion/indexnf.html. *Student Group, meets Wed. 8pm in the Ohio Union Gray Suite "G".*

Columbus State Community College: GABLE Cougars Nester 116, 550 E. Spring, Columbus, OH 44202 ☎ 614-287-2555; 287-8261 ✉ asignet@cscc.edu 🖥 cscc.edu/docs/stuact/GABLE/index.html
GLBT organization.

Kaleidoscope Youth Coalition 203 King Ave, PO Box 8104, Columbus, OH 43201 ☎ 614-294-7886 ✉ kyc@kaleidoscope.org 🖳 www.kaleidoscope.org/
Phoenix Pride Support Group: Sat., 11am-1pm, 203 King Ave. Drop-in hours: Fri., 7-10pm, Sat, 4-8pm, same location. PUB: GLBT Youth Resource Guide (Resources for youth, educators, counselors, child service agencies.)

Dignity/Greater Columbus 444 E Broad Street, PO Box 82001, Columbus, OH 43202 ☎ 614-451-6528 ✉ dignitygc@aol.com
GLBT Catholics in the Greater Columbus Area.

PFLAG Columbus PO Box 340101, Columbus, OH 43234 ☎ 614-227-9355 🖳 www.geocities.com/WestHollywood/8840
Publishes Resource Guide for GLBT youth, parents, & schools in Columbus & Franklin County area. Info on social svcs., religious orgs., health, legal, support resources, books, articles, videos. 4th Sun. 2pm, Unitarian Universalist Church, 93 West Weisheimer.

PFLAG Columbus African-American Support Group PO Box 340101, Columbus, OH 43234 ☎ Pat Moss: 614-463-1183 🖳 www.geocities.com/WestHollywood/8840/meet.html
Division of PFLAG Columbus, Meets 3rd Sun. 3pm, First English Lutheran Church 1015 E. Main Columbus.

Dayton Lesbian & Gay Center PO Box 1203, Dayton, OH 45401 ☎ 937-274-1776 (Hotline) ✉ dlgc@gaydayton.org 🖳 www.gaydayton.org/dlgc
GLBT Community Center for the Dayton area. Currently operating out of the Faith UCC, 200 Delaware Rd. Hours of operation only during scheduled meetings.

Community Night c/o Dayton Lesbian & Gay Center
Dinner or picnic. A Festive event for all, featuring special guests. 4th Wednesdays, Sept.-June.

Men's Forum c/o Dayton Lesbian & Gay Center
Discussion group for men, meets Wednesday 6:30pm, at Faith UCC, 200 Delaware Rd.

Women's Forum c/o Dayton Lesbian & Gay Center
Weekly discussion & activities, meets at Faith UCC, 200 Delaware Rd, Mondays at 5:30pm.

PACT (People of All Colors Together) Dayton PO Box 3713, Dayton, OH 45401 ☎ 937-275-7629 ✉ pactdayton@aol.com
Meets 4th Sat., 1pm, Eternal Joy MCC, 1630 E. Fifth St.

Team Dayton Dayton, OH ☎ Tom Kohn: 937-277-5125
Sports & cultural opportunities for lgb persons.

Dignity/Dayton PO Box 55, Dayton, OH 45401 ☎ 937-277-7706; 937-640-2468
A supportive community of GLBT & allies within the Catholic community.

GLSEN/Dayton 572 Towncrest Drive, Dayton, OH 45434 ☎ 937-427-1578 ✉ glsenday@aol.com
National organization fighting to end anti-gay bias in K-12 schools.

PFLAG Dayton PO Box 3721, Dayton, OH 45401 ☎ 937-640-3333 ✉ daytonpflag@yahoo.com 🖳 www.pflagdayton.org/
Meets 2nd Tu. 7:30pm, St. John's UCC, 515 E. 3rd St., Dayton, (274-1776).

Safer Sex Support Group Dayton, OH ☎ Brett Rhinehart: 937-461-2437

Sinclair Community College GALA 444 West Third Street, Dayton, OH 45402-1460 ☎937-512-3000 (main college line) ✉ gala_sinclair@hotmail.com 🖳 www.sinclair.edu/studentlife/gala/

University of Dayton, BGLAD c/o Campus Ministries, 300 College Park, Dayton OH 45469-1679 ☎ 937-229-3141 ✉ rossman@trinity.udayton.edu 🖳 www.udayton.edu/~campmin/bglad_group.htm
Identity issues support group for lgb people at Dayton. Weekly meetings. Group advisor: Kathleen Rossman, OSF.

Wright State University: Lambda Union W047 Student Union, 3640 Colonel Glenn Hwy., Dayton, OH 45435-0001 ☎ 937-775-5565; hotline: 937-297-4777 ✉ lambdaunion@yahoo.com 🖳 www.wright.edu/studentorgs/lambda_union/home.htm
Meets Wed. 7pm in W047 Student Union + office hours.

YouthQuest Dayton PO Box 3721, Dayton, OH 45401 ☎ 937-640-3333
✉ youthquestdayton@hotmail.com
🖳 www.youthquestdayton.org
Support system & safe, comfortable environment for sexual minority youth to socialize & meet. Education on risk behavior reduction, including those associated with HIV/AIDS infection & with substance abuse. Meets Wed. 7pm in the Miami Valley Unitarian Fellowship Church at 2001 Far Hills Av.

Ohio Wesleyan University

Gay/Lesbian/Bisexual Resource Center, Hamilton-Williams Campus Center Rm. 225, Delaware, OH 43015, ☎ 740-368-3196 (M-Th 6-8pm). **Pride**, Hamilton Williams Campus Center, Student Activities Office, Delaware, OH 43015, ☎ 740-368-2001, ✉ prideweb@cc.owu.edu, 🖳 pride.owu.edu/index.html, Meets Tu. 10pm at the House of Spirituality, 118 Rowland Avenue.

Bay Area Gays & Lesbians PO Box 13, Fremont, OH 43420
Listed because it's the only known GL group in the area. Acceptance of B/T folk unknown.

Kenyon College: Allied Sexual Orientations (ALSO) Student Affairs Center, Gambier, OH 43022 ☎ 740-427-5661

Denison University OUTLOOK Slater Box 2406, Granville, OH 43023 ☎ 740-587-6696 (Womens Resource Center); 740-587-6366 Leticia Johnson student activities.
GLBT advocacy group.

PFLAG Greenville/Miami Valley NW PO Box 45, Greenville, OH 45331-0045 ☎ 937-548-6730

Hiram College: Lesbian Gay & Bisexual Union c/o Student Activities, Box 8, Hiram, OH 44234 ☎ 330-569-5935 ✉ LGBA@hiram.edu
Meets Mon. 7pm during termtime.

Mother Wit PO Box 265, Kent, OH 44240 ☎ 330-678-4686
Lesbian & bi mothers. This group is for any l/b woman who has ever mothered at any point (could be a niece, nephew, or siblings). Women in opposite-sex relationships are welcome.

Kent State University: Pride Kent Box 17, Office of Campus Life, Kent, OH 44242 ☎ 330-672-2068 ✉ lgbu@kent.edu 🖳 www.kent.edu/stuorg/lgbu
Open to undergrad & grad students, faculty, staff & community members, & allies. Meets Th. 8pm during termtime in Student Center 316.

Bisexual & Married Gay Men PO Box 770932, Lakewood, OH 44107-0041 ☎ Doug: 216-961-7731
Support & social group meets 4th Tu. 7:30pm.

PFLAG Lancaster/Fairfield County 1185 Pleasantville Rd., Lancaster, OH 43130 ☎ 740-645-0565 ✉ graceucc@greenapple.com

Ohio State University: Bi-Global (Lima Campus) 4240 Campus Drive, 66 Galvin, Lima, OH 45804 ☎ 419-221-1641 x415

PFLAG Lima PO Box 5571, Lima, OH 45802 ☎ 419-222-4954 ✉ pflag_lima@yahoo.com 🖳 www.geocities.com/pflag_lima/
Monthly Meetings, Unitarian Universalist, 875 W. Market.

Brothers' Circle 5124 Mayfield Rd, Lyndhurst, OH 44124 ☎ 216-556-0449
African-American gay, bi, TG men.

PFLAG Mansfield/Mid-Ohio 75 Elmridge Rd. , Mansfield, OH 44907-2441 ☎419-756-0460 ✉ bheh@richnet.net

Mentor Center (HUGS East) Rap Group PO Box 253, Mentor, OH 44061-0253 ☎ 440-974-8909 (answered live Wed. 7-9pm) ✉ hugseast@hotmail.com 🖳 www.hugseast.homepage.com
Group of GLB people, singles & couples who share a common desire to create a family" oriented support system to positively affirm, support, & feel more connected with ourselves & each other, &, either individually or as a group move to actively change the way "straight" society relates to us. Meets Th. 7pm at 8521 East Ave, Mentor. Serves Lake, Geauga & Ashtabula counties.

Muskingum College: GLASS (Gay Lesbian & Straight Supporters) 163 Stormont, New Concord, OH 43762 ☎ Advisor: 740-826-8086

PFLAG Norwalk/Firelands 520 Milan Ave., Lot 74, Norwalk, OH 44857 ☎ 419-663-9283 ✉ cliftonspires@hotmail.com

Oberlin College: Lesbian/Gay/Bisexual/ Transgendered Union Wilder Hall, Rm. 202, Box 88, Oberlin, OH 44074-0088 ☎ 440-775-8179 ✉ olgbu@oberlin.edu 🖳 www.oberlin.edu/~lgbu PUB: SNAP: It's a Queer Thing.

Oberlin College: Oberlin Lambda Alumni c/o Oberlin Alumni Assoc., Bosworth Hall, 55 West Lorain Street, Oberlin, OH 44074-1044 ☎ 440-775-8692 FX: 440-775-6748 ✉ ola_oberlin@yahoo.com 🖳 www.oberlin.edu/ ~alumnassc/OLA/
GLBT Alumni group. PUB: OLA News (www.oberlin.edu/~alumassc/OLA/ newsletterOLA.html)

Zeus, to steal boy Ganymede
An eagle's form put on;
And when he wanted the lady Leda
He turned into a swan.
Now some like girls,
and some like boys;
But the moral's plain to see:
If both are good enough for Zeus,
They're good enough for me.

—*Anonymous, Greek poet*

> **[Ceaser is] every man's wife and every woman's husband.**
>
> —*Curio the Elder, Roman writer, 53 B.C.*

Miami University: Gay/Lesbian/Bisexual Alliance
Office of Student Activities, 356 Shriver Center, Oxford, OH 45056 ☎ Roy Boyen Ward: 513-529-4303 ✉ muglbacopres@hotmail.com (Co-Presidents) 🖳 miavx1.acs.muohio.edu/~glbacwis
Collegiate GLBT group - Meets Th. 8pm in 275 Upham, during termtime.

PFLAG Athens 40011 Carpenter Hill Rd., Pomeroy, OH 45769-9645 ☎ 740-698-2120

PFLAG Portsmouth 11 Offnere St, Portsmouth, OH 45662 ☎ helpline: 740-353-1856

PFLAG Akron 723 Tinkers Lane, Sagamore Hills, OH 44067 ☎ 330-342-5825; 330-467-9078
3rd Th., 7:15pm, 671 Canton Rd (Ohio 91), at Albrecht, Akron.

PFLAG Huron, Erie, Ottawa Counties Sandusky, OH ☎ 419-663-9283, 419-627-0380
Meets 3rd Sun., 5pm, Frost Center, Osborn Park, 3910 Perkins Ave, Sandusky.

PFLAG Cleveland 14260 Larchmere Blvd., Shaker Heights, OH 44120 ☎ 216-556-1701 ✉ pflagcleve@pobox.com 🖳 members.aol.com/pflagcleve/
Meets 2nd Tu, 7:30pm, Trinity Cathedral, E. 22 & Euclid, Cleveland, rear.

Wittenberg University

Gay Straight Alliance, PO Box 3926, Springfield, OH 45501, ☎ 937-227-5274, *Student contact for 2000-01: William Cline* c/o above.
Spectrum, PO Box 3848, Springfield, OH 45501, ☎ 937-322-1189, *Contact for 2000-01: student Jackie Motzer at above.*

Gays & Lesbians United PO Box 6552, Toledo, OH 43612-6552 ☎ 419-292-1524; 1-800-362-1524 ✉ glu@toledoglu.org 🖳 www.TOLEDOGLU.org
Political action & educational organization of glbt individuals of Northwest Ohio & Southeast Michigan. Promotes basic civil rights & defend Constitutional guarantees afforded to all citizens of the US. PUB: *World Wide GLBT (Gay) News Digest (Online at Website, updated daily.)*

Lavender Triangle/Womyn's Vineline Box 178079, Toledo, OH 43615 ☎ 419-531-0644 🖳 www.tagala.org/womynsvineline.htm
Social organization for the women of Toledo. Open to all. Please join us. PUB: *Womyn's Vineline*

PRO/Domrose Referral Line John Domrose Foundation for Personal Rights, Inc, PO Box 12607, Toledo, OH 43606 ☎ 419-472-2364
4-11pm. Volunteer GLBT community resource & referral line. Also accepts grant applications for local projects benefiting the GLBT community.

Rainbow Area Youth - Toledo, Inc.
PO Box 12415, Toledo, OH 43606-0015 ☎ 419-327-8686 or 419-255-7510 (ask for Brenda) ✉ toledoray@toledoray.org 🖳 www.toledoray.org
For teenagers 13-19 regardless of race, gender, or sexual orientation. Adult coordinators must be 20 or over. Interested teens should call 255-7510, & ask for Brenda.

University of Toledo: Rocket Rainbow Alliance/ Gay & Lesbian Student Union 1509 Student Union, Toledo, OH 43606 ☎ 419-530-7975 ✉ glsu@pop3.utoledo.edu 🖳 www.utoledo.edu/~rra_glsu/home.htm
Offices 1500 level of the Student Union room 1509. Weekly meetings Th. 8pm during termtime in the Student Union in room SU 3018. Open to both students & non-students regardless of gender or sexual orientation.

PFLAG Toledo PO Box 4619, Toledo, OH 43620 ☎ 419-255-2246 ✉ pflag-toledo@geocities.com 🖳 www.tagala.org/pflag.html
Mtgs: 2nd Tu., 7pm St.Marks Episcopal Church, 2272 Collingwood.

John Carroll Allies 20700 N. Park, Bo 9999, University Heights, OH 44118 ☎ 216-397-2489
GLBT student group.

Otterbein College: Freezone Westerville, OH 43081-2006 ✉ freezone@otterbein.edu
Organization, support, education, movies.

College of Wooster: Gay, Lesbian, Bisexual, Transgendered and Allies Box C-3166, 1189 Beall Ave., Wooster, OH 44691 ✉ COW_GLBTA@hotmail.com
GLBT student organization.

College of Wooster: Student Allies of Sexual Minorities (SASM) SASM, Office of Student Life, Wooster, OH 44691 ✉ buschap@acs.wooster.edu 🖳 www.wooster.edu/sasm/
Campus organization promoting social & political activities relating to the rights of the lgbt community. Provides educational resources for members of the LGBT community, & allies.

PFLAG Wooster 1048 N. Bever St., Wooster, OH 44691 ☎ 330-264-7396 ✉ m2hawk@aol.com

Wayne County Gay, Lesbian, Bisexual Community Wooster, OH ☎ 330-262-4142
Various social events.

The Pride Center of Greater Youngstown 264 Madison Ave, Youngstown, OH 44504 ☎ 330-747-7433 🖳 alt.youngstown.org/pride.htm
Non-profit, all volunteer community center for glbtq persons & allies in the greater Youngstown area.

Out 'n' About 25 Market St, #1401, Youngstown, OH 44503 ☎ 330-746-6816
For lesbian & bi Women.

OutWatch Youngstown, OH ☎ 330-747-8776 🖳 alt.youngstown.org/pride.htm
Political Coalition of LGBT activists in the Mahoning Valley. Meets 2nd Th, 4:15pm, The Beat Coffeehouse, Lincoln Ave, on YSU campus.

PACT (People of All Colors Together) PO Box 1131, Youngstown, OH 44501 ☎ 330-534-5904x3

PFLAG Youngstown 2201 Goleta Avenue, Youngstown, OH 44004 ☎ 330-747-2696, 330-746-4963, 330-427-6238 ✉ smschild@cc.ysu.edu
Meets 3rd Sun, 3pm, Christ Church Presbyterian annex, Hopkins at Canfield (US 62).

Youngstown PFLAG Hotline Youngstown, OH ☎ 330-747-2696
24hr Hotline.

Youngstown State University: LGBT LGBT: Student Activities Office, 1 University Plaza, Youngstown, OH 44555-3571 ☎ Jean Engle: 330-742-3291; Thomas Copeland: 330-742-1640 ✉ jsengle@cc.ysu.edu or tacopela@cc.ysu.edu
To foster a safe & secure community for GLBT persons to express their orientation freely & openly.

Oklahoma

Oklahoma City Gay, Lesbian, Bisexual Community Services Center 2135 NW 39th St., Oklahoma City, OK 73112 ☎ 405-524-6000
Meeting space, info, & referrals. Health education & anonymous HIV testing by appointment. M 7-10pm, Tu-Fr 1-10pm, Sat 7pm-midnight.

University of Oklahoma: Gay, Lesbian Bisexual Transgendered and Friends Ellison Hall 306, Norman, OK 73019 ☎ 405-325-4GLB ✉ albowles@ou.edu 🖥 www.ou.edu/student/glba/
Weekly meetings.

Simply Equal of Oklahoma City PO Box 61305, Oklahoma City, OK 73146 ☎ 405-521-9696
Political group supportive of glbt issues.

Herland Sister Resources, Inc. 2312 N.W. 39th, Oklahoma City, OK 73112 ☎ 405-521-9696
Mostly for lesbians, but bi women welcome. Small pride store & lending library, & social/support organization. Sat/Sun 1-5pm.
PUB: *Herland Voice Newsletter*

Photo courtesy Oklahoma Bisexual Network

Yes, even in Oklahoma!

Central Oklahoma Prime Timers 5030 North May Ave. #134, Oklahoma City, OK 73112 ☎ Art Tassell: 405-840-1910 ✉ atassell@ionet.net 🖥 www.primetimers.org/copt/
Social organization for mature gay & bi men 30+. Younger partners (21-29 yrs. old) may become associate members. Monthly meetings & organized group activities. An affiliate of Prime Timers Worldwide. Monthly newsletter with activity calendar.

Red Rock Behavioral Health Service's Young Gay & Lesbian Alliance 2135 NW 39th St, Oklahoma City, OK 73112 ☎ 405-524-6000, 405-425-0399
Has a bifriendly youth group (for those -25) & offers twice-weekly meetings.

Oklahoma Male Nudists PO Box 12701, Oklahoma City, OK 73157 ☎ 405-498-6224405-947-8827 ✉ okmn1@yahoo.com
Mostly gay; bi's encouraged. Strictly a nude male bonding group, not a sex group. PUB: OkMN Digest (monthly)

Oklahoma State University: Sexual Orientation Diversity Association (SODA) 040 Student Union, Box 601, Stillwater, OK 74078 ☎ 405-744-5252 ✉ nate826@yahoo.com 🖥 www.okstate.edu/osu_orgs/glbca/
"Educational, social & political link for people in Stillwater & surrounding areas. Weekly meetings, events, & educational material on GLB & AIDS/HIV issues."

Tulsa Oklahomans for Human Rights PO Box 2687, Tulsa, OK 74101 ☎ 918-743-4297 (Pride Center)
Runs the Pride Center, 1307 East 38th, Tulsa, OK 74135. Sun-Fri 6-10pm, Sat 12-10pm. 10 different organizations, all bi-friendly. Popular referral center (bars, churches, realtors, doctors, etc.) PUB: Tulsa Oklahomans for Human Rights Newsletter (Local guide to lgbt resources, support/social groups, events.)

Tulsa Area Prime Timers PO Box 52118, Tulsa, OK 74152-0118 ☎ 918-582-6557 ✉ stans@earthlink.net
An affiliate of Prime Timers Worldwide. Social & recreational organization for gay or bi men over 21 in & around Tulsa. Mts. 2nd Sun. at the Pride Center + other activities. PUB: Prime News

HIV Outreach Prevention & Education (HOPE) 3503 East Admiral, Tulsa, OK 74115 ☎ 918-834-TEST
Free, anonymous HIV testing clinic. 6-9pm M-Th by appt. Walk-ins accepted 6-8pm M & Th.

Oregon

BiNet Oregon 23719 Tatum Lane, Monmouth,
OR 97361 ✉ biseverywhere@yahoo.com
*Coalition-building gatherings, including annual
NW Regional Gathering of bi & poly people, with
community-building workshops, hiking, camping
in a beautiful secluded site on Mt. Rainier. 2001
gathering 7/27-8/1, w/overlapping use of site on
8/1-2 with another bi-, straight-, & poly- friendly
group. Binet Oregon strives to build connections
between bisexuals, sponsors community building
gatherings, with others around the state to
enhance bi outreach. Newly forming outdoor/
social group.*

Oregon Bisexual Council PO Box 412, Portland,
OR 97207 ✉ PBA@BiPortland.org,
PortlandBiWomen@aol.com
Quarterly meetings of state bi leaders to strategize.

Coalition to End Bigotry PO Box 13144, Salem,
OR 97309
*Broad-based coalition actively supporting
individuality & securing civil equality & social
justice for GLB people. Sponsors Governor's
statewide LG History Month Proclamation, the
Coalition to End Bigotry & the Mid-Willamette
Lesbian, GLBT Pride Celebration (Salem Gay
Pride), & a quarterly street cleanup.*

Abdill-Ellis Lambda Community Center 281
Fourth Street, Ashland, OR 97520 ☎ 541-488-6990
✉ info@abdellis.org, webmaster@abdellis.org
🖳 www.aelcca.org/
*Oregon's only GLBT community center. Provides
umbrella for wide range of programs including
SOMO-Southern Oregon Men's Outreach, Labrys-
lesbian/bi women's discussion group, & SOYO—
youth outreach. Lending library. Provides only
HIV testing/counseling services in Jackson
County.* PUB: Prizm (Monthly community paper
providing news, info & resources to the
Southern Oregon & Northern California areas.)

**Lesbian Gay Bi & Transgendered Political Caucus
of Southern Oregon** PO Box 1063, Ashland, OR
97520 ☎ 541-482-5829
Southern Oregon political advocacy.

Bisexual Unity Corvallis, OR ☎ Lani: 541-753-7389
✉ lm_ls@hotmail.com
*Monthly potluck 3rd Tu. (Jan.-Oct.) Discussion,
support, other group activities (hikes, movies, etc.)*

**Oregon State University, Corvallis: Rainbow
Continuum** MU East, Snell Hall, Corvallis, OR
97331-4501 ☎ 541-737-6360 🖳 www.orst.edu/
groups/lgba/
Social group for students, faculty & the public.

Womenspace PO Box 50127, Eugene, OR 97405
☎ 541-686-6660; 1-800-281-2800
*Confidential gp for bi/lesbian women who have
been physically, sexually or emotionally battered
in their relationships. Not limited to same-sex
relationships. Drop-in Advocacy Center at 111
East 16th Ave. Peer support, legal svcs. 9-3 M-F,
541-484-6103. Also shelter at a confidential
location, for women & their children.*

**University of Oregon: Lesbian, Gay, Bisexual &
Transgender Alliance** Erb Memorial Union, Ste
34, Eugene, OR 97403 ☎ 541-346-3360
✉ lgba@gladstone.uoregon.edu
🖳 gladstone.uoregon.edu/~lgba

Bisexual Community Forum PO Box 11141,
Portland, OR 97211 ☎ Laury: 503-285-4848
*Casual & wide-ranging discussions, & support.
1st. Mon.: Bi issues; 3rd Mon.: Poly issues.
Possibly the second oldest continuing bi group in
the nation. Open to all, all ages.*

Portland Bisexual Alliance PO Box 412, Portland,
OR 97207-0412 ☎ Bi-Line (announcements/
messages): 503-775-9717 ✉ pba@biportland.org
🖳 www.BiPortland.org
*1st Fri. Workshop, 3rd Fri. Guest Speaker, also
social & political events. Takes "Bi 101"
education & outreach to any interested organizations. Monthly Bi Community Orientation w/one-
on-one support & introduction to bi resources.
Online discussions in Forum. section of web site.
Allied with other local queer, trans, poly, &
BDSM organizations. Annual regional Bi
Conference in spring, Bi Day rally in fall.
Non-profit Motto: "The Freedom to Follow Love"*
PUB: Bisexual Portland (Monthly "Bi Portland"
calendar listing all local bi-related events Also
separate monthly members' newsletter.)

Portland Bisexual Women Portland, OR
☎ 503-768-4293, box #2
✉ PortlandBiWomen@aol.com
*Discussion group for bi & questioning women.
Meets 2x/month for discussion & social events.*
PUB: Bi The Way (Local newsletter, 2x/year.)

**The Bradley-Angle House Bi Women's Caucus
(BAH)** PO Box 14694, Portland, OR 97293
☎ Amy Gitana: 503-282-9940
*Does political & cultural work concerning sexual
violence.*

Brother to Brother PO Box 3182 , Portland, OR
97208 ☎ 503-417-7991
*African American Gay and Bi Men's support
group. Discussions about HIV/AIDS, isolation,
relationships & ways to build community.*

**Desire...is less like a heart, throbbing the same everywhere, and more
like music, and every culture has its own—not only songs, but tonality,
instruments, and occasions.**

Esther Newton (in "Yams, Grinders & Gays," Out/Look, Spring 1988)

Lesbian Community Project PÓ Box 5931, Portland, OR 97228 ☎ 503-233-3913 FX: 503-233-3882 ✉ lcp@webpride.net 🖳 www.europa.com/~lcppdx
Bi-inclusive women centered, women focused group. Referrals, events, forums, discussions, & dances. Although many of these events are open to men & women, LCP remains focused on serving as a resource for lesbians & other women who support the lesbian community.

POLY-PDX Portland, OR 🖳 www.yahoogroups.com/group/POLY-PDX
Public list for the polyamourous community in Portland, Oregon to communicate & create commmunity. Open to poly-friendly & poly-curious folks. Active list with wide-ranging discussions. Many members are bi & all are bi-friendly. Ad hoc real life social events & outings. Necessary to subscribe to group to read postings. Go to URL & follow instructions.

Rose City Discussion Club PO Box 230638, Portland, OR 97281-0638 ☎ 503-972-1869 ✉ rcdc@teleport.com 🖳 www.teleport.com/~rcdc
Monthly open pansexual BDSM, alternative sexuality, & fetish discussion for the Pacific Northwest. Monthly mtgs. in Portland: workshops, speakers, friendly social with 75-100 like-minded friends. Completely bi-friendly & many bi members. Also a clearinghouse for information about all sorts of sexual minorities & resources. Emphasis on safe, sane, consensual.
PUB: RCDC Monthly Newsletter

Rosetown Ramblers PO Box 5352, Portland, OR 97228-5352 ☎ 503-234-9944 🖳 www.rdrop.com/users/ramblers/
Square dance club; also rollerskating, country western dancing. Open to all square dancers, regardless of age, race, gender, religion, ethnic background, or sexual orientation.

Lewis & Clark College: United Sexualities Box 158 , 0615 Palatine Hill Rd., Portland, OR 97219 ✉ us@lclark.edu 🖳 www.lclark.edu/~us/
Student-run, ASLC funded, organization for glbt, queer & questioning youth & allies at Lewis & Clark College. Safe, comfortable arena to express ideas, insights & concerns.

Northwestern School of Law & Lewis & Clark College: Gays, Lesbians or Bisexuals at Law (GLOBAL) 10015 SW Terwilliger Blvd., Portland, OR 97219 ☎ School #: 503-768-6600
Support & advocacy group (allies welcome). Meetings & social events, on & off campus.

Oregon Health Services University: All-Hill Gay, Lesbian, Bisexual Alliance Portland, OR ☎ Scott: 503-494-5227 or 503-632-8569 ✉ ekblads@ohsu.edu
Social gathering monthly. For students, faculty, & staff.

Together Works First Baptist Church125 SE Cowls , McMinnville, OR 97128-6098 ☎ Church 503-472-7941; Don Hutchinson 503-434-6266
Support group for LGBs & friends. Discussion on timely topics; social activities. Neutral, safe environment. Oct-Apr 7pm, May- Sept 7:30pm, 2nd & 4th Mon., First Baptist Church.

Portland State University: Queers & Allies Student Development, Box 751, Portland, OR 97207-0751 ☎ 503-725-5681 FX: 503-725 5680 ✉ queersandallies@mail.pdx.edu 🖳 www.ess.pdx.edu/sfcsg/queersandallies
Student group open to all. Primarily provides a place for queer folks & allies to connect on campus. Meets weekly in Smith Memorial Center. Socio-political events include Queer Prom, Queer Awareness Week, etc.

Reed College: Queer Alliance Signator QA3203 SE Woodstock Blvd., Portland, OR 97202-8199 ☎ Student Activities: 503-771-1112, ask for # of current LGBU signator
Social, educational & support group for interested students, faculty, & staff.

Vanguard Youth Services 424 E. Burnside Ave, Portland, OR 97214 ☎ SMYRC: 503-872-9664 FX: 503-239-8107 🖳 www.smyrc.org
SMYRC is a Queer Youth Recreation Center for glbtq, questioning, allies -24. Open M. 4-8pm, W. 4-9, F./Sat. 4-12. Also a trans youth support group & an art & writing group. Washington County Pride Project offers support & recreational activities in Washington County. Support groups Th. in Beaverton/Tigard & W. in Hillsboro.

Angles - Willamette's Queer-Straight Alliance 900 State Street, c/o Michael Marks, 6932, Politics Department, Salem, OR 97301 ☎ Michael Marks: 503-370-6932; Richard Shintaku: 503-370-6265
GLB support, education, & visibility. Fosters awareness & celebration of diversity. Wed. 7pm, Womyn's Center-3rd Floor, University Center 503-370-6692.

No, she told JJ in her mind,... I can understand you having more than one side in that way. As long as you're on, as you stay on, my side now. .... She had always known from JJ's touch how much he enjoyed her body. She knew it still. Inside her skin. The real question, she felt as she dug deeper, wasn't was JJ "bi" but was he—an old-fashioned term—true?

Elizabeth Searle, A Four-Sided Bed, *p. 199.*

Pennsylvania

Planet Q PO Box 81246, Pittsburgh, PA 15217
☎ 412-784-1500 FX: 412-784-1575
✉ PlanetQ@aol.com 🖳 www.planetqnews.com
*Monthly newspaper serving the tri-state lgbt
community. Local & national news & events.
Submissions are considered, please contact the
Editor.* PUB: PlanetQ News (See above.)

**Muhlenberg University: Gay Straight Alliance
(GSA)** Allentown, PA 18104
✉ bgla@muhlenberg.edu

Gay, Lesbian, Bisexual Helpline of Altoona c/o
Family Services, 2022 Broad Avenue, Altoona, PA
16601 ☎ 814-942-8101
*Provides info, referrals, phone counseling, & one-
on-one-counseling. Open M-F 8:30am-4:30pm.*

Lehigh University: Safe Space c/o Chaplain's
Office, 110 Johnson Hall, 36 University Drive,
Bethlehem, PA 18015-3042 ☎ 610-758-2777
✉ safspace@lehigh.edu 🖳 www.lehigh.edu/
~safspace
*GLBT & ally program. Speakers bureau, speaker
training, peer counseling.*

Bloomsburg University: Free Spirit Adviser: Terry
Riley, Box No. 95, Bloomsburg, PA 17815
✉ lamp@bloomu.edu
*For members of the GLBT community & our
allies - publishes in-house resource guide.*

**University of Pittsburgh - Bradford: Bisexual, Gay
& Lesbian Alliance (BiGALA)** c/o Director of
Student Activities, 300 Campus Drive,
Bradford, PA 16701 ☎ Student Activities Office:
814-362-7654
*A student group that sponsors social activities,
speakers, & other programs on campus.*

Bryn Mawr College: Rainbow Alliance c/o
Student Life Office, Bx C-1725, 101 North Merion
Avenue, Bryn Mawr, PA 19010 ☎ 610-526-7331
*Social, educational, & political group of LB
students of Bryn Mawr College. Also: confidential
Lesbian-Bisexual Support Group (LBSG) for
women, & a speakers' bureau which will send out
speakers upon request.*

**East Stroudsburg University: PRIDE (Gay Lesbian
& Bi-Sexual Student Organization)** Office of
Residence Life, University Center, East
Stroudsburg, PA 18301 ☎ 717-422-3291
✉ jjudicki@po-box.esu.edu
*Campus-wide umbrella organization for faculty,
staff & students. Student organization for GLBT
& allies meets bi-weekly. There is also an ally
organization with faculty, staff & students.*

Edinboro University of Pennsylvania: Identity c/o
Student Government Association, Edinboro, PA
16444 ☎ Dr. Dan Burdick: 814-732-2647
✉ dburdick@edinboro.com
*Support meetings & social get-togethers for lgbq
people & allies.*

At the March on Washington, 1993

Robyn Ochs

**Penn State Behrend: Trigon: Lesbian, Gay &
Bisexual Coalition** Box # 1054, Erie, PA 16563
☎ 814-898-6030 🖳 www.clubs.psu.edu/trigon/
*Serves glb students, staff, & faculty, & allies.
Strives to make homosexuality & bisexuality
more acceptable. Is both a support & social group.*

Gettysburg College: Allies PO Box 2282,
Gettysburg, PA 17325 ✉ allies@gettysburg.edu
🖳 www.gettysburg.edu/project/stuact/allies/
*Student group supportive of lgb concerns on
campus.*

**Gay & Lesbian Switchboard of Harrisburg/ Pride
Festival of Central Pennsylvania** PO Box 872,
Harrisburg, PA 17108-0872 ☎ 717-234-0328
✉ glsh@harrisburgpride.org
🖳 www.harrisburgpride.org
*Information resource center for LGB people.
Organizers of the Harrisburg Pride Festival.
Volunteers available M-F 6-10pm.*

**Haverford College: Bisexual, Gay & Lesbian
Alliance (BGALA)** 370 Lancaster Av., Haverford,
PA 19041 ☎ 610-896-1000 (switchboard)
*Student-run organization. Support group &
hotline for students.*

Indiana University of Pennsyvania: Pride Alliance
c/o Student Activities & Organizations, 319 Pratt
Drive, Indiana, PA 15701 ☎ Student Union:
724-463-8541 ✉ cfdg@grove.iup.edu
*Social & political group designed to foster a safe
& supportive academic & social environment for
the glbt & ally community of IUP.*

**Franklin & Marshall College: Lesbian, Gay,
Bisexual, Transgendered & Allies** PO Box 3220,
Lancaster, PA 17604-3220 ☎ 717-399-6192
✉ Advisor: Anthony Lascoskie:
a_lascoskie@admin.fandm.edu 🖳 www.fandm.edu/
CampusLife/Organizations/LGBTA/Home.html
*Student-run GLB & ally group with weekly
meetings / discussions & LGB related activities.*

Bucknell University: L/G/B/T Concerns Office
100A Roberts Hall, Lewisburg, PA 17837 ☎ 570-577-1609 🖳 www.departments.bucknell.edu/lgb/

Lock Haven University: Lesbian, Gay & Bisexual Student League Office of Human & Cultural Diversity, Box 213, Woolridge Hall, Lock Haven, PA 17745 ☎ 570-893-2154 ✉ ajones@lhup.edu, rsmith6@falcon.lhup.edu

Allegheny College: Committee in Support of Gay, Lesbian & Bisexual People Box 186, Meadville, PA 16335 ☎ 814-332-3338 FX: 814-337-0988
Committee of students, faculty, & administrators working to educate, bring speakers, offer films, & address GLB concerns specific to the Allegheny Community.

BiUnity PO Box 41905, Philadelphia, PA 19101 ✉ biunity@netaxs.com 🖳 www.biunity.org
Philadelphia-area social & support network for bisexuals, their families & friends. Social events, men's & women's discussion & support groups, hosts Death Bi Chocolate (New Year's Day Coffeehouse).

William Way Lesbian, Gay, Bisexual & Transgender Community Center 1315 Spruce St., Philadelphia, PA 19107-5601 ☎ 215-732-2220 FX: 215-732-0770 ✉ wwcenter@yahoo.com 🖳 www.waygay.org
Hosts many political, social & cultural LGBT community organizations and events. PUB: Way Gay News (Monthly newsletter.)

Philadelphia Gay News 505 S. 4th St., Philadelphia, PA 19147 ☎ 215-625-8501 FX: 215-925-6437 ✉ pgn@epgn.com 🖳 www.epgn.com
The larger of the two gay papers in Philadelphia but less bi inclusive.

Phildelphia Family Pride PO Box 4995, Philadelphia, PA 19119 ☎ 215-844-3360
A social, advocacy & support group for LGBT parents & our children.

Philly Pride Presents, Inc. 1315 Spruce St., Suite 227, Philadelphia, PA 19107 ☎ 215-875-9288 or 1-800-937-7968 FX: 215-985-9880 ✉ dopride@aol.com 🖳 www.phillypride.org
Grassroots organizers of the Philadelphia PrideDay in June, OutFest (National Coming Out Day) in October, & WinterPride in January.

At the Millenium March on Washington, 2000

> I was not confused about what I was feeling, which seemed very clear to me, but rather about what to do about what I was feeling. What I wanted to do was lie down with her in a field of daisies and hold her and let her hold me, and then probably kiss. That was as far as my fantasies went. My confusion came mainly from what everybody else would think.
>
> *Joan Baez in* And a Voice to Sing With, *p. 77.*

Gay Married Men's Association (GAMMA)
PO Box 8501, Philadelphia, PA 19101 ☎ 215-477-6003
Peer support group for gay & bisexual men who are or were married or who are in relationships with women. Meets 2nd & 4th Wed. at William Way Community Center.

Men Of all Colors Together / Philadelphia
PO Box 42257, Philadelphia, PA 19101 ☎ 610-277-6595
Gay multiracial, multicultural org. committed to fostering supportive evironents wherein racial, social & cultural barriers can be overcome & the goal of human equality realized. PUB: Newsletter

Men of COLOURS United c/o The COLOURS Organization, Inc., 1201 Chestnut St., 5th Floor, Philadelphia, PA 19107 ☎ 215-496-0330 FX: 215-496-0354 ✉ colours@critpath.org
Meets weekly. Info sharing & mutual support for African-American sexual minority men.

Sisterspace of the Delaware Valley 1315 Spruce St., Philadelphia, PA 19107 ☎ 215-546-4890 TDD: 215-546-4202 ✉ sistrgen@sisterspace.org 🖳 www.sisterspace.org
Sponsors annual women's weekend: music, entertainment, workshops, sports, including Womyn of Color Forum.

The Colours Organization, Inc. 1201 Chestnut St. 5th Floor, Philadelphia, PA 19107-6732 ☎ 215-496-0330 FX: 215-496-0354 ✉ colours@critpath.org
Dedicated to empowering sexual minority people of color. Sponsors several support & discussion groups, including youth, transgender, women, HIV+ & recovery. PUB: Colours Magazine, Pages of Change

South Asian Lesbian & Gay Association-Philadelphia c/o ASIAC, 1201 Chestut, Suite 501, Philadelphia, PA 19107 ☎ 215-563-2424 FX: 215-563-1296 ✉ info@asiac.org 🖳 www.asiac.org
For GLBT South Asians.

Womyn 4 Womyn c/o The Colours Organization, Inc., 1201 Chestnut St, 5th Floor, Philadelphia, PA 19107 ☎ 215-496-0330 FX: 215-496-0354 ✉ colours@critpath.org
Support group by & for sexual minority women of color. Also Sistah 2 Sistah: discussion group for sexual minority women of color 16-24.

University of Pennsylvania

Lesbian Gay Bisexual Transgender Center, 3537 Locust Walk, 3rd Floor, Philadelphia, PA 19104-6225; ☎ 215-898-5044; events line: 215-898-8888; FX: 215-573-5751; ✉ center@dolphin.upenn.edu; 🖳 dolphin.upenn.edu/~center. *University umbrella office for the LGBT community (students, staff, faculty, alumni). Support, advocacy, campus programming, lending library, speakers bureau, mentoring program. Director: Dr. Robert Schoenberg. Publications:* OUTlines: *(Penn community newsletter) &* queer-E *(weekly electronic newsletter).* **Queer Student Alliance**, 104 Williams Hall, 255 South 36th Street, Philadelphia, PA 19104; ☎ 215-898-5270; ✉ qsa@dolphin.upenn.edu; 🖳 dolphin.upenn.edu/~qsa/. *Primary undergraduate queer organization. Weekly meetings, educational & social events.* **Estudiantes Re-estableciendo el Orden Social**, c/o LBGT Center; ✉ espinoza@sas.upenn.edu. *One of the first Latino/Latin American student groups in the US focused on gender & sexual orientation, to: reevaluate Latino/Latin American gender & sex norms & constructions; foster a new masculinity; respect, acknowledge, & grant marginalized men & homosexuals a place in Latino/Latin American patriarchal culture.* **Lesbian Gay Bisexual Social Workers at PENN**, c/o LGBT Center; *For sexual & gender minority students, faculty, & staff of Penn's School of Social Work. Increases visibility for LGBT social workers, educates the School of Social Work about sexual minority issues, provides emotional & social support for members.* Lambda Law, ✉ wproctor@law.upenn.edu; 🖳 www.law.upenn.edu/lgblsa/. *Open to students, faculty & staff at the Law School. Meets regularly. Social events, educational programs, curriculum work.* **LGBT Staff & Faculty Association**, c/o The LGBT Center. *Addresses concerns of PENN's LGBT staff & faculty, sponsors social & informational events, & holds periodic meetings.* **PEARL (Penn's Eagerly Awaited Radical Ladies)**, c/o Penn Women's Center, 3643 Locust Walk, Philadelphia, PA 19104-6230; ☎ 215-898-8611; ✉ hemasara@sas.upenn.edu. *Social organization for lesbian, bi & other aware women. Sponsors dances & potluck dinners. Open to all women at Penn.*

Drexel University: Straight and Gay Alliance Creese Student Center, Rm. 3015 , MacAlister Hall, 32nd & Chestnut Sts., Philadelphia, PA 19104 ☎ 215-895-2063 ✉ saga@drexel.edu 🖳 on.to/saga
Provides a comfortable place for glbtq students. Hosts socials, movie nights, parties, speakers. Meets weekly.

Temple University: Lambda Alliance Student Activities Center, Box 116, 1755 N. 13th St., Philadelphia, PA 19122 ☎ 215-204-5434 ✉ lambda@blue.temple.edu 🖳 www.temple.edu/lambda/
Safe space & community for glbt persons with help from straight allies. Everyone welcome, & privacy & confidentiality respected. Office Location: Student Activities Center Room 205.

Jewish Bisexuals, Gays & Lesbians c/o Hillel of Greater Philadelphia Philadelphia, PA 19104-6227, 202 South 36th St., Philadelphia, PA 19104-6227 ✉ jbagel@dolphin.upenn.edu 🖳 dolphin.upenn.edu/~jbagel/
Students from different colleges in the Philadelphia area who come together to celebrate Jewish culture in a comfortable environment.

Lesbian, Gay & Bisexual People in Medicine Philadelphia Philadelphia, PA ✉ dbilbao@netspace.org, campea@mail.med.upenn.edu 🖳 www.netspace.org/~dbilbao/lgbpm/
Links the efforts of LGBPM chapters in the five Philadelphia-area medical schools. Social gatherings, health info at LGBT celebrations, mentoring program linking LGBT medical students with LGBT physicians. Website lists contacts for each medical school.

The Attic Youth Group 419 South 15th Street, Philadelphia, PA 19146 ☎ 215-545-4331; 24 hr. crisis hotline: 545-2910 ✉ phaedrusoo@aol.com 🖳 hometown.aol.com/phaedrusoo/attic_homepage/index.html
Groups & services for GLBTQ youth 12-21 including HIV related resources, coming out group, drop-in time, counseling, seminars, youth speakers' bureau, library, newsletter, social groups, etc.

40 Acres of Change c/o Colours, 1201 Chestnut St., 5th Floor, Philadelphia, PA 19107 ☎ 215-496-0330 FX: 215-496-0354 ✉ colours@critpath.org
Minority-run support group for sexual minority teens & young adults. Education & mentoring programs. PUB: Pages of Change (Information by & for sexual minority youth of color.)

> ## I don't think there is such a thing as a precise sexual orientation. I think we're all ambiguous sexually.
>
> *Tennessee Williams, American playwright, 1912-1983*

Lutherans Concerned/Delaware Valley 3637
Chestnut St., Philadelphia, PA 19104-2670
☎ 609-582-4692 (Charlie Horn)
✉ LCPhiladelphia@go.com
*Chapter of Lutherans Concerned North America
(LC/NA): Nationwide organization advocating for
glbt inclusion & ordination within the Evangelical
Lutheran Church of America. Attendance &
mailing list info confidential.*

Gay & Lesbian Latino AIDS Education Initiative
1233 Locust St., 3rd Floor, Philadelphia, PA
19107 ☎215-985-3382 FX: 215-985-3388
✉ gloria@critpath.org 🖳 www.critpath.org/
galaei#services
*For GLBT people, focuses on improving the
quality of life for all Latinos/as, LGBT people
&d LGBT Latinos/as, especially in the area of
HIV/AIDS & health related issues.*

Washington West Project 1201 Locust St.,
Philadelphia, PA 19107 ☎ 215-985-9206
FX: 215-985-9214 ✉ washwest@critpath.org
*Health care center serving the lgbt communities.
HIV testing & counseling, support groups,
workshops, clinics, library, counseling.*

Gay & Lesbian Community Center PO Box 5441,
Pittsburgh, PA 15206 ☎ 412-422-0114 (M-F 6:30-
9:30pm; Sat. 3-6pm) FX: 412-422-7913
✉ center@glccpgh.org 🖳 www.glccpgh.org
*At 5808 Forward Avenue, Squirrel Hill. Meeting
spaces, library, youth group (for lgbt, confused
& open-minded youth -22). Web page, Pride
Direct phone book + newsletter. (Pride Direct ¤
listings of GLBT organizations, business &
professional services in the tri-state area. The
Newsletter lists events. Website has events,
resources, links, & support group listings.)*

Gertrude Stein Political Club PO Box 8108,
Pittsburgh, PA 15217 ☎ 412-521-7061
✉ GSPCGP@aol.com 🖳 Coming Soon
*Multipartisan political organization. Screens
candidates with respect to lgbt and women's rights
(especially reproductive rights). Newsletter with
highlights from local, state, national, & school
board candidate visits, published 4x/year.
Meetings occur before each election*

Three Rivers Pride Committee PO Box 5441,
Pittsburgh, PA 15206 ☎ 412-422-0114, x3
✉ trp@trfn.clpgh.org
🖳 www.PittsburghPrideFest.org
*Organizes Pittsburgh's annual LGBT PrideFest (in
June).*

Thursday Night Live PO Box 23700, Pittsburgh, PA
15222-6700 ☎ 412-363-5865 ✉ tnl@trfn.clpgh.org
*Social group for professional glbts. Weekly
meetings & outings.*

After Midnight Pittsburgh, PA ☎ GLCC: 412-422-
0114
*Social club for those in the glbt Black community:
balls, & other social events. Usually meets
monthly.*

Robyn Ochs preparing for San Francisco march,

Asians & Friends International - Pittsburgh
PO Box 99191, Pittsburgh, PA 15233-4191 ☎ 412-
361-1839 FX: 412-521-1368 ✉ afpgh@hotmail.com
🖳 www.qrd.org/qrd/www/orgs/afpgh/index.html
*Annual convention Labor Day weekend, potlucks,
movies, meetings.* PUB: Ring of Fire (Monthly
magazine. See Website.)

Bet Tikvah PO Box 10140, Pittsburgh, PA 15232-
0140 ☎ 412-362-7025 ✉ btikvah@trfn.clpgh.org/
btikvah/news.htm
*Synagogue & community for lgb Jews & their
friends. Monthly newsletter for members.* PUB:
Confidential & restricted to members.

Carnegie Mellon University:
CMU-OUT, CMU Student Activities, Box 99,
5000 Forbes Avenue, Pittsburgh, PA 15238
☎412-268-8794; ✉ OUT+@andrew.cmu.edu;
🖳 www.andrew.cmu.edu:80/user/out. *Student
organization for LGBT people at CMU that holds
weekly meetings. Organizes events & activities.*
Allies, Box 37; ✉ allies@andrew.cmu.edu;
🖳 www.contrib.andrew.cmu.edu/~allies.
*Organization at CMU for people who support glbt
people. Safe space for discussion of sexuality
issues. Includes glbt members.*

Chatham College: Lesbian, Bisexual & Transgendered Alliance Box 345, Woodland Road, Pittsburgh, PA 15232 ☎ 412-365-1261 or 412-365-1527 🖳 www.chatham.edu
Political commitment to promoting visibility of queer/trans women on campus & bringing this into the classroom.

Community College of Allegheny College: Visions AC CCAC Office of Student Life, 808 Ridge Avenue, Pittsburgh, PA 15212 ☎ 412-237-2675
Students committed to building a bridge of understanding about glbt concerns on campus.

PFLAG/Pittsburgh PO Box 81954, Pittsburgh, PA 15217 ☎ 412-421-1250 or 412-363-8839 ✉ pflagpgh@trfn.clpgh.org 🖳 trfn.clpgh.org/pflagpgh/contact.htm
Promotes the health & well-being of glbt people, their families & friends through support, education, & advocacy. Local chapter of national organization.

Persad Center, Inc. 5150 Penn Avenue, Pittsburgh, PA 15224-1627 ☎ 412-441-9786 FX: 412-363-2375
Nonprofit outpatient mental health center for sexual minorities. Clinical counseling & psychotherapy on issues including AIDS, couples issues, gender identity, etc. Consultation, education & speakers available. Sliding scale, Medicaid & ins. accepted.

Pittsburgh Affirmation: United Methodists for Lesbian, Gay, Bisexual & Transgendered Concerns PO Box 10104, Pittsburgh, PA 15232-0104 ☎412-683-5526
Network, advocacy & resourcing group for GLB United Methodists. A chapter of the national organization.

Interweave c/o First Unitarian Church, Ellsworth & Morewood Av., Pittsburgh, PA 15213 ☎ 412-343-2523 FX: 412-243-1781 ✉ kdrust@aol.com 🖳 www.first-unitarian-pgh.org
Religious, activist & social group within the Unitarian Universalist church. Addresses the concerns of glbt communities. PUB: see Unitarian Universalist Gay World (Publication for all UUs; info available group's webpage.)

> **When I finally began coming out to people I had the same feeling one has when, after a long hike, one takes off one's backpack. I felt light and wonderful, and unconstrained -- and surprised, because I had never realized just how much the burden of the closet had weighted me down.**
>
> *Robyn Ochs*

> **The only abnormality is the incapacity to love.**
>
> *Anaïs Nin, French writer, 1903-1977*

University of Pittsburgh: Rainbow Alliance William Pitt Union, Room 500, Pittsburgh, PA 15260 ☎ 412-648-2105 ✉ rainbo+@pitt.edu 🖳 www.pitt.edu/~rainbo
Campus organization offering a social space to meet other lgbt students, raise visibility of glbt issues on campus, & participate in monthly meetings and events, i.e., movies, discussions/lectures, drag shows.

Susquehanna University

Bisexual, Gay, & Lesbian Alliance of Susquehanna Students (BGLASS) c/o Student Life Office, Selinsgrove, PA 17870 ☎ 570-372-4302 ✉ bglass@susqu.edu 🖳 www.susqu.edu/orgs/bglass/. *Confidential support group for lgb students.*
Susquehanna University: Sexual Diversity Awareness Coalition. c/o Scott Manning, Susquehanna University, Selinsgrove, PA 17870 ✉ manning@susqu.edu 🖳 www.susqu.edu/sdac. *Coalition of students, faculty, & staff improving the campus for all sexual minorities.*

Slippery Rock University: Lesbians, Gays, Bi-sexuals & Allies Student Government Assn. Rm. 216, Slippery Rock, PA 16057 ☎ Mr. Vernon Jones/Mr. George Stroud: 724-738-2700

Lesbian, Gay, Bisexual, Transgendered Switchboard of State College PO Box 805, State College, PA 16804 ☎ 814-237-1950 ✉ glbtswitchboard@hotmail.com
Supportive counseling. All-volunteer hotline, referrals 6-9pm nightly.

Penn State College: Coalition of Lesbian, Gay, Bisexual & Transgendered Graduate Students c/o Gay & Lesbian Switchboard , PO Box 805, State College, PA 16804 ☎ 814-237-1950 (6-9pm daily) 🖳 www.lions.psu.edu/lgbt/resources/resources.html
An organization of Penn State grad students. Educational, social & political activities.

Swarthmore College: Swarthmore Queer Union (SQU) 500 College Avenue, Swarthmore, PA 19081-1397 ✉ spain@sccs.swarthmore.edu 🖳 www.sccs.swarthmore.edu/org/glb/
Swarthmore's principle gay group. Sponsors parties, social events, political action, & campus awareness activities. All glbtq students welcome. Meets weekly. Also: **Swarthmore Discussion Group** *(weekly facilitated group - supportive environment for people to discuss & question their sexuality);* **Swarthmore Ourglass** *(discussion group for bisexual women);* **Swarthmore Peer Counseling;** **Swarthmore Sager Committee** *(alumni endowment run by students & faculty to promote awareness of gay issues on campus).*

Pennsylvania State University

Lambda Student Alliance, 310 Hetzel Union Building, University Park, PA 16802; ☎ 814-865-3327; ✉ lambda@psu.edu; 🖥 www.clubs.psu.edu/lambda. *Social, political & educational group. Meets weekly, plus ongoing support groups & social events. Speakers bureau: "Straight Talks." Includes bi support groups.*

Commission on Lesbian, Gay, Bisexual & Transgendered Equity; c/o Susan Shuman, 314 Grange Building, University Park, PA 16802; ☎ 814-863-2294, 814-863-7696; ✉ sbs1@psu.edu; 🖥 www.lions.psu.edu/clgbt/; *University-wide committee addressing a variety of issues of concern to lgbt people on campus.* **Vision,** c/o Rev. Carl Symon, Eisenhower Chapel, University Park, PA 16802; ☎ 814-865-7627; ✉ cas14@psu.edu. *LGBT group for spiritual exploration.*

West Chester University: Lesbian, Gay, Bisexual Alliance Box 233, Sykes Student Union, West Chester, PA 19383 ☎ 610-436-6949

Wilkes University: Ally Intercollegiate Organization c/o Jim Harrington, Wilkes Barre, PA 18766 ☎ Jim Harrington: 1-800-WilkesU, x4428
Open to gay students & allies on college campuses throughout Northeastern PA. Currently 30+ members from 6 local universities. Also interacts with & supports a group for high school-aged gay youth. Many social events, educational programs.

Puerto Rico

Coalición Orgullo Arcoiris [Rainbow Pride Coalition] PO Box 8836, Fernandez Juncos, Santurce, PR 00910-8836 ☎ 787-461-2052
Coalición integrada por organizaciones y personas de la comunidad LGBT. Organiza anualmente la Parada de Orgullo en junio y el Día de Conciaciación en octubre. [Coalition of organizations & individuals from the LGBT community. Organizes annual Pride Parade & Coming Out Day in Oct.]

Coalición Contra el Artículo 103 y Pro Derecho a la Intimidad PO Box 190422, San Juan, PR 00919-0422 ☎ 787-767-3206 ✉ art103@caribe.net
Tiene como uno de sus objetivos la lucha en contra de la ley que criminiliza las relaciones sexuales consentidas entre personas del mismo sexo, por entender que es un delito sin víctimas y no hace otra cosa que crear un ambiente hostil y legitimar la violencia contra la comunidad lgbt. [Has as one of its objectives the struggle against laws criminalizing consensual sexual activity between persons of the samesex, understanding that it is a victimless crime & does nothing more than create a hostile atmosphere & legitimate violence against the lgbt community.]

Fundación Derechos Humanos Av. Ashford 1357, Box 402, San Juan, PR 00907-1432 ☎ 787-722-5027 FX: 787-721-0401
Organización que trabaja en la defensa de los derechos de la comunidad LGBT. [Organization working in defense of the rights of LGBT people.]

Proyecto de Derechos Humanos de LGBT [GLBT Human Rights Project] Box 22029, Estación UPR, San Juan, PR 00931-2029 ☎ 787-0447
Organización que trabaja en la defensa de los derechos de la comunidad LGBT. [Organization working to protect the rights of the LGBT community.]

Universidad de Puerto Rico, Recinto de Rio Piedras CODE UPR Apdo. 21752, San Juan, PR 00931-0752 ☎ 787-764-0000x5683 y 3095
Apoyo a estudiantes lgbt en la Universidad. [Supports LGBT students at the University.]

Madres Lesbianas / Alcoholicos Anonimos Rio Piedras, PR ☎ 787-258-8968; 258-4394; 787-721-6358
Grupo especial para la comunidad glbt. Reuniones jueves 7pm. ICM Cristo Sanador, Calle 44 SE, #1010, Rep Metropolitano Rio Piedras.

COAI, Inc. Proyecot "En Rosa" PO Box 8634, San Juan, PR 00910-0634 ☎ 787-793-7550 FX: 787-793-7530
Prevención VIH/SIDA para homosexuales y bisexuales. Ruiz Soler Calle marginal (al lado de la Sociedad de Epilepsia). [Gay/bi HIV/AiDS prevention.]

Fundación SIDA de Puerto Rico PO Box 364842, San Juan, PR 00936 ☎ 787-782-9600 FX: 787-782-1411

Rhode Island

BiProv PO Box 603094, Providence, RI 02906-0094 ☎ 401-432-2262 (voicemail) ✉ majordomo@aq.org subscribe biprov 🖥 www.aq.org/~js/biprov/
Mixed gender social group for bis & bi-questioning people of all ages & genders. Monthly social event in Providence, Rhode Island (hikes, movies, brunches, etc.) & online discussion/announcement list. Bi support group meets 3rd Wed 6:30-8pm at Rochambeau Library, 708 Hope St—call to verify, or look at schedule on website.

Bayard, Bessie, Baldwin, Bentley Brunch RI ☎ Kathy Townsend-Hurk 401-467-6325
Social group for LGB African-Americans & their significant others of any race. Monthly potlucks.

> **There are 10,000 men AND women on this campus, and I STILL can't find dates on Saturday night!**
>
> *From the mouth of a bi student at the University of Rhode Island*

Boston Pride, 1990s

Gay & Lesbian Victim Assistance 311 Dorie Ave., Cranston, RI 02910-2903 ☎ 401-781-3990 FX: 401-467-9030 ✉ wmhoch@aol.com
Non-profit mental health service.

Adoption Rhode Island 500 Prospect St., Pawtucket, RI 02860-6260 ☎ 401-724-1910 Darlene Allen, Executive Director FX: 401-724-9443 ✉ adoptionri@idf.net
Individual consultation for LGBT issues with respect to adoption. PUB: Tuesday's Child

Brown University

Lesbian, Gay, Bisexual Transgender Resource Center, Box P, Providence, RI 02912, ☎ 401-863-3145; FX: 401-863-1999; ✉ lgbta@brown.edu . **Lesbian, Gay, Bisexual, Transgendered Alliance**, Box 1930, Providence, RI 02912 ☎ 401-863-3062 ✉ lgbta@brown.edu; 🖳 www.brown.edu/students/lgbta/. *Umbrella organization for various LGBT groups at Brown, sponsors social events. Website lists active organizations, calendar of events, links to other resources.* **Lesbian & Bisexual & Questioning**, Box 1930, Providence, RI 02912 ☎ 401-863-2189 ✉ labaq@brown.edu. *Women's discussion group.* **The Next Thing (TNT)**, c/o LGBTA,) kohei@brown.edu; *Lesbigay People of Color Group.* **Quest**, c/o LGBTA, ✉ quest@Brown.EDU *Confidential group for people coming out & / or questioning their sexuality.*

Bryant College: Gay/Lesbian/Bisexual Students 1150 Douglass Pike, Smithfield, RI 02917-1284 ☎ 401-232-6389 ✉ pride@bryant.edu
Weekly meetings, student -led.

Johnson & Wales University: GLBSA 8 Abbott Park Place, Providence, RI 02903 ✉ glbsa@Hotmail.com
GLBSA support group for JWU students.

Rhode Island College: Rainbow Alliance Student Union Room 313, 600 Mt. Pleasant Ave., Providence, RI 02908 ☎ 401-456-8491
Student-led discussion group.

Rhode Island School of Design: Queer Student Union c/o Office of Student Life, 2 College Street, Providence, RI 02903 ☎ 401-454-6602

Dignity/Providence c/o 10 Burleigh Street #5, Providence, RI 02904 ☎ 401-272-2265
Religious & social activities for LGBTs & friends. All welcome.

University of Rhode Island: Gay, Lesbian & Straight Society c/o Student Senate , 346 Memorial Union, Kingston, RI 02881 ☎ 401-874-5480

Youth Pride Inc. 134 George M. Cohen Blvd, Providence, RI 02903-4410 ☎ 401 421-5626 Michelle Duso, Robin Schinnik FX: 401-274-1990
Individual & family counseling; support groups in Providence; peer educators on homphobia, HIV, safer sex; GED help, academic tutoring. Trans discussion group to be announced. Free food pantry & clothing closet.

American Baptists Concerned/RI Chapter RI ☎ Judy 860-446-9933 Diane 401-884-6478 ✉ butter_fly@juno.com
Support, advocacy, networking group of LBG & friends. Meets monthly.

Interweave Westminster Unitarian Church, 119 Kenyon Av., E., East Greenwich, RI 02818 ☎ 401-884-5933; Steve or Dan: 423-0380; or Susan 738-6494
Committee within UU church meets socially for mutual support; does political work on LGBT issues within & outside UU community. LGBT inclusive.

St. James Church St. James Church, 474 Fruit Hill Ave., N. Providence, RI 02911-2636 ☎ Al Barnaby: 401-353-2079
GLBT Episcopalians.

Newport Congregational Church (UCC) Spring & Pelham St., Newport, RI ☎ 401-849-2238 FX: 401-842-0320 ✉ nccflame@aol.com
Self-described as open & affirming of LGB people. Performs commitment services / ceremonies.

Gaymers Providence, RI ☎ Al Esposito: 401-521-0283
Cards & board games for LGBs. Th. 7pm at members' homes.

South Carolina

We Are Family PO Box 30374, Charleston, SC 29417 ☎ 843-937-0000 FX: 843-937-0020
"Gay,lesbian & straight" organization which hosts weekly "Safe Space for Teens" for glq youth 16-23.

Clemson University Gay Straight Alliance Clemson, SC 29634 ✉ cgsa@clemson.edu

University of South Carolina: Bisexual, Gay & Lesbian Association (BGLA) Box 80098, Columbia, SC 29225 ☎ 803-777-3911 ✉ uscbgla@vm.sc.edu 🖳 www.sa.sc.edu/bgla/
Student organization.

Outsmart in the Midlands Columbia, SC ✉ staff@outsmartsc.org 🖳 www.outsmartsc.org/
For high school & college-age sexual minority youth & young adults. Run for & by its members. Weekly mtgs., listserve.

South Dakota

FACES: Free Americans Creating Equal Status of South Dakota 13121 South Creekview Road, Rapid City, SD 57702 ☎/FX: 605-343-5577; 800-354-3417 (toll free in SD) ✉ facessd@aol.com

South Dakota State University: Sons & Daughters c/o Student Activities, PO Box 2815, Brookings, SD 57007 💻 www.sdstate.edu/wsds

Augustana College: Out! c/o Student Activities, Sioux Falls, SD 57197 ✉ out@inst.augie.edu 💻 inst.augie.edu/~out/

University of South Dakota: Gay, Lesbian & Bisexual Alliance USD, Coyote Student Center, 414 E. Clark Street, Vermillion, SD 57069 ☎ Student Activities Ofc: 605-677-5334 ✉ glba@sundance.usd.edu 💻 www.usd.edu/student-life/orgs/glba

Tennessee

Lesbian & Gay Coalition for Justice PO Box 22901, Nashville, TN 37202-2901 ☎ 615-298-5425 ✉ lgcj@lgcj.org 💻 www.lgcj.org/~lgcj/ PUB: Communicator (Provides information about statewide & national action alerts, calendar of events, political campaigns, etc.)

University of Tennessee, Chattanooga: Spectrum Chattanooga, TN ✉ spectrum@cecasun.utc.edu 💻 cecasun.utc.edu/~spectrum/

University of Tennessee, Knoxville: Lambda Student Union 315 University Center, Box 315, 1502 West Cumberland Avenue, Knoxville, TN 37996-4800 ✉ lambda@utk.edu 💻 web.utk.edu/~lambda
Founded to provide a means of communication between glbt, & straight students at UT-Knoxville. Eduational programs, social activities, & political actions.

University of Tennessee, Martin: ALLIES S.T.A.N.D.O.U.T. (Students & Teachers Against Nontraditional Discrimination & Observing Universal Truths) PO Box 119, Martin, TN 38238 ✉ allies@mars.utm.edu,utmallies@yahoo.com 💻 mars.utm.edu/~allies
For people who support glbt persons % glbt rights. Also for people who would like to know more about issues dealing with sexuality. Includes university wide Safe Zone Program.

University of Memphis: BGALA Office of Student Orgs., Box 100, Memphis, TN 38152 ☎ 901-678-5719 ✉ bgala@cc.memphis.edu 💻 www.people.memphis.edu/~bgala

Memphis Area Gay Youth PO Box 241852, Memphis, TN 38124 ☎ 901-335-6249 ✉ magy@gaymemphis.com 💻 www.gaymemphis.com/magy/
Peer discussion group for self-identified glbtq high school youth 13-21 & their friends.

> **"Genetics causes some cats to be black and some cats to be white. But there are also grey cats and all shades and color combinations in between. It follows, therefore, that if sexuality is biologically controlled, then there will be bisexuals."**
>
> *Simon LeVay (neuroanatomist) - "The Pink Paper", May 30, 1997*

Middle Tennessee State University Lambda Association MTSU Box 624, Murfreesboro, TN 37132 ✉ mtlambda@mtsu.edu 💻 www.mtsu.edu/~mtlambda/

Bi The Way - Nashville Nashville, TN ☎ 615-365-0835 ✉ bithewaynashville@yahoo.com 💻 www.nashcenter.org/bitheway.htm
Discussion / support / social group. Meets 2nd Tu., 8-10pm.

The Center for Gay-Lesbian-Bi-Transgendered Life in Nashville 703 Berry Road, Nashville, TN 37204 ☎ 615-297-0008 ✉ nashcenter@yahoo.com 💻 www.nashcenter.org
LGBT community center. Hosts a variety of groups - youth, single gender, transgender, mixed gender, etc. PUB: Center Intrigue (includes calendar of local events. Also available online at www.nashcenter.org/intrig1.htm)

Married & Gay Network (MAGNET) Nashville, TN ☎ 615-297-0008 or 333-8941 💻 www.nashcenter.org/magnet.htm
Support & discussion group for married / divorced gay / bisexual men.

Vanderbilt University

Vanderbilt Lambda Association, PO Box 7076 Station B, Nashville, TN 37235 ☎ 615-322-0236 ✉ lambda@vanderbilt.edu 💻 www.vanderbilt.edu/lambda. *University sponsored organization intended to serve the needs of glbt undergraduates, graduates, faculty, & staff.* **Graduate & Professional Lesbian/Bisexual/Gay Student Association**, Nashville, TN 37240-1111 ✉ vugplbga@yahoo.com. *Umbrella organization for the Vanderbilt Gay / Lesbian Medical Student Association & the Graduate School Lambda.*

Texas

Bisexual Network of Austin PO Box 8439, Austin, TX 78713 ☎ 512-370-9573 ✉ binet_austin@yahoo.com 💻 www.main.org/binetaustin
Weekly socials & special events. Bi women's support group; bi men's group, discussion group. PUB: Bi-News (bi-monthly. $10/yr.)

Trikone-Tejas PO Box 4589, Austin, TX 78765-4589 ☎ Prateek: 512-495-3059
✉ trikonetejas@my-deja.com 🖳 www.main.org/trikonetejas
Pan-Asian alliance of queer & straight students/faculty/staff dedicated to ending sexism, homophobia, biphobia, transphobia & racism. Organizes & participates in several UTAustin events & shares news via website. E-mail for events/mailing list.

Austin Prime Timers PO Box 14892, Austin, TX 78716-4892 ✉ austinprimetimer@aol.com
🖳 http://hometown.aol.com/austinprimetimer/
For older gay & bi men as well as those who prefer their company.

University of Texas: LBJ School Lesbian, Bisexual, Gay & Friends Club c/o Campus Community Involvements, 100-B W. Denton Keeton St. 4-104, Austin, TX 78712 ☎ Faculty adviser: Dagmar Hamilton: 512-471-4962
Political organization to discuss policy issues related to the lgb community, & provide a supportive environment for lbg people at the LBJ School & foster dialogue & understanding for their concerns among the university community. Social activities, policy issues forum, speakers, community service.

University of Texas: Lesbian, Bisexual, Gay Students' Association SOC #275, 100-C West Dean Keeton Street , Austin, TX 78712
✉ lbgsa@www.utexas.edu 🖳 www.lbgsa.org/
Educational & social club. Open to UT students, faculty & staff.

Out Youth: Gay, Lesbian, Bisexual & Transgendered Teens 909 East 49 1/2 Street, Austin, TX 78751 ☎ 512-419-1233 FX: 512-419-1232 ✉ out@outyouth.org 🖳 www.outyouth.org
Drop in center open Tu., W., Th. Sun. 5:30-9:30pm.

Texas A&M University: Gay, Lesbian, Bisexual & Transgendered Aggies Student Activities, 125 John J Koldus Bldg, ATTN: GLBTA, College Station, TX 77843-1236 ☎ 409-847-0321
✉ glbta@gott.tamu.edu 🖳 glbta.tamu.edu
On-campus meetings include speakers, community service, etc. Off-campus meetings are purely social — we go to restaurants, have potlucks, go to movies, etc.

BiNet Dallas PO Box 190869, Dallas, TX 75219 ☎ 214-521-5342 ext 461
✉ BiNet_Dallas@mindspring.com
🖳 www.geocities.com/binetdallas
Egroup address: BiNet_Dallas@yahoogroups.com Bi, Co-sexual, local, support, educational, social, for bis & partners.

Southern Methodist University: Gay, Lesbian & Bisexual Student Organization Dallas, TX 75275
☎ 214-768-4792 ✉ glbso@yahoo.com
🖳 www.smu.edu/~glbso
Campus group.

> **It's preposterous to ask sexual beings to stuff ourselves into the rapidly imploding social categories of straight or gay or bi, as if we could plot our sexual behavior on a contentious, predictable curve.**
>
> Susie Bright (in "Blindsexual," in Sexual Reality: A Virtual Sex World Reader (SF: Cleis, 1992), p. 152)

Out Youth Dallas PO Box 190712, Dallas, TX 75219 ☎ 214-521-5342, ext. 260
✉ bmiskinis@pcico.com 🖳 www.divanet.com/dgla/outyouth
For GLBTQ youth -22. Weekly meetings at the Resource Center of Dallas, 2701 Reagan.

Walt Whitman Community School 4038 Cedar Springs, Box 104, Dallas, TX ☎ 214-855-1535
GLBTQ High School directed by Becky Thompson. The opening of the school received much media coverage.

University of North Texas: UNT Courage PO Box 305069, Denton, TX 76203 ☎ Hot line: 565-6110 Call student center for info. ✉ courage@unt.edu 🖳 orgs.unt.edu/courage/Courageweb.html
Student group. Meetings, social events, ally trainings.

LAMBDA GLBT Community Services PO Box 31321 , 910 N. Mesa, El Paso, TX 79931-0321
☎ 915-562-GAYS ✉ admin@lambda.org
🖳 www.lambda.org/

Texas Christian University: Triangle TCU Box 296933 , Fort Worth, TX 76129
✉ TCUTriangle@hotmail.com
🖳 www.triangle.tcu.edu/

BiNet Houston Houston, TX ☎ 713-467-4380
✉ bihouse@flash.net 🖳 http://home.flash.net/~bihouse/
For men & women exploring their sexuality or already bi- identified.

KPFT AfterHours, Queer Radio With Attitude 90.1 FM 419 Lovett, Houston, TX 77006
☎ 713-526-KPFT 🖳 kpft.splitrock.net
AfterHours, Queer Radio With Attitude, 90.1 FM, airs Sat./Sun. midnight-3am. Monthly bi show 1st Sat. AfterHours is a campy show covering diverse topics. Peridocally we interview national bi activists & writers. Bi segment has been on the air for almost 6 years. Will be setting up a web radio website with all past shows available. Info will be posted on the BiNet USA Webpage when it becomes available. AfterHours available live on web radio at http:kpft.splitrock.net.

University of Houston: Gay, Lesbian Or Bisexual Alliance 4800 Calhoun St. , Campus Activities Box 211, Houston, TX 77004-2610
✉ global@bayou.uh.edu 🖳 www.uh.edu/~global

Hub Triangle Lubbock, TX ✉ dsphd@hotmail.com
🖳 www.geocities.com/duanesimolke/hubtri.html
*Online newsletter for the LGBT community of
Lubbock, Texas.*

**Texas Tech University: Gay/Lesbian/Bisexual
Students** Box 42031-63, Texas Tech, Lubbock, TX
79409 ✉ glbsa@glbsa.com 🖳 www.glbsa.com/
*Mostly students, but members of the community
welcome.*

**Unity Foundation Gay & Lesbian Community
Center** PO Box 15857, San Antonio, TX 78212
☎ 210-822-3533
*Board meetings 7pm 2nd & 4th Th, at the library
- 6017 Soledad Room 613. Open to the public.
Started to provide a home for the social,
emotional, & physical well being of all people,
primarily LGBT persons in San Antonio.*

Utah

**Weber State University's Delta Lambda Sapphos
Union** 2102 University Circle, Ogden, UT 84408-
2102 ☎ 801-626-6782

Utah Valley State College: UV Pride Orem, UT
☎ Lee Mortenson: 801-222-8785; College info #:
801-222-8000 ✉ mortenle@uvsc.edu
🖳 www.uvsc.edu/clubs/special/freedom/
Room 201, Student Center, Tuesday 7-9pm.

Gay & Lesbian Community Center of Utah 361
North 300 West, Salt Lake City, UT 84103
☎ 801-539-8800 🖳 www.glccu.com/
*At 361 N. 300 West. Coffee shop, library,
numerous group mtgs. Call for hours.*

First Thursday Salt Lake City, UT ☎ 801-467-0052
✉ pillarwow@aol.com
Social group for women of all sexual persuasions.

Affirmation: Gay & Lesbian Mormons PO Box
526175, Salt Lake City, UT 84152 ☎ 213-255-
7251 ✉ wasatchweb@aol.com
🖳 members.aol.com/wasatchweb
*Non-profit educational fellowship group serving
glb Mormons & supporters. Meets1st & 3rd Sun
in Salt Lake City, 2nd Sun. is in Ogden & the 4th
is in Utah County. Membership open to all.*

Family Fellowship 1763 N 1500 E, Provo, UT
84604 , Salt Lake City, UT 84109 ☎ 801-374-1447
🖳 http://www.4gayutah.com/groupinfo/
familyfellowship.html
*For Mormon families, to help overcome the pain,
isolation & divisiveness. Quarterly meetings.*

Utah Gay/Straight High School Students' Alliance
8457 S Snowville Dr., Sandy, UT 84093
☎ 801-943-0170
*This is the High School group at the center of a
storm of controversy.*

Vermont's bi group "Both Sides Now"

Vermont

Bisexual Network of Vermont VT ☎ 802-864-3455
*Individuals throughout VT who are Bi, Multi,
2-spirited, or trans identified. Allies welcome.*

Out in the Mountains PO Box 1078, Richmond, VT
05477 ☎ Barbara Dozetos: 802-434-6486 FX: 802-
434-7406 ✉ editor@mountainpridemedia
🖳 www.mountainpridemedia.org
*Free paper. Lists activities & resources in
Vermont, and sometimes NH. Covers GLBTQ
News in the area.*

**Champlain College: Gay/Lesbian/Bisexual/
Friends Alliance** PO Box 670, Burlington, VT
05402 ☎ Ask for GLBFA Contact Person at
802-658-0800 x6425
For students only.

Interweave - Unitarian Universalists Association
First UU Society, 152 Pearl Street, Burlington,
VT 05401-3701 ☎ 802-862-5630
*For glbt people. Meets monthly, When calling,
ask for "The person in charge of Interweave" as
this person rotates.*

R.U.1.2.? PO Box 5883, Burlington, VT 05402-
5883 ☎ 802-860-1044 ✉ thecenter@ru12.org
*Provides venues for the social, cultural, artistic
& educational endeavors of our GLBT & allied
communities. Helps foster other social centers
throughout Vermont* PUB: R.U.1.2.? *(Frequent
newsletter mailed to those on mailing list
(Donations appreciated).)*

University of Vermont: Free to Be: GLBTA B-163
Billings Student Center, Burlington, VT 05405
☎ 802-656-0699 ✉ free2b@zoo.uvm.edu
🖳 www.geocities.com/westhollywood/heights/
3550/glbta.html

Outright Vermont PO Box 5235, Burlington, VT 05402-5235 ☎ 802-865-9677, or in state tollfree: 800-GLB-CHAT (452-2428)
🖳 www.members.aol.com/outrightvt/index.htm
For GLBTQ youth & allies up to age 22. Call for location & hours of drop-in center. PUB: Outright VT (Newsletter sent to dues-paying members)

Castleton State College, One in Ten: Gay, Lesbian, Bisexual Alliance Castleton, VT 05735

Johnson State College: Gay/Straight Alliance 337 College Hill, Johnson, VT 05656
☎ 802-635-2356 x2322 (student association office)
Holds regular meetings & annual events including annual ally party.

Lyndon State College: The Beacon c/o Director of Student Life, Frank Daldo, Lyndonville, VT 05851 ☎ Mary Sue Kelly: 802-626-9371 x6344

Marlboro College: Gay/Lesbian/Bisexual Group c/o The health Center: Linda Rice, Marlboro, VT 05344-0300 ☎ Linda Rice: 802-257-4333
Social group for Marlboro College students, staff, & faculty.

Middlebury College: Middlebury Open Queer Alliance (MOQA) Drawer 9, Middlebury, VT 05753-6033 ☎ 802-443-5000 x3103 (Student Activities) ✉ MOQA@panther.middlebury.edu
🖳 www.middlebury.edu/~MOQA
For students, faculty & staff to communicate on LGBT & Queer lives & living. Weekly meetings. Straight allies & questioning members welcome. Confidential.

Goddard College: Gay, Lesbian, Bisexual Alliance Plainfield, VT 05667 ☎ Ask for the contact for the GLB A 802-454-8311x580
Weekly films, conferences, dances.

Binet USA's New England Regional meeting, April 1994

Landmark College: Gays, Lesbians, Bisexual & Friends Alliance River Road, Putney, VT 05346
☎ Abigail Littlefield: 802-387-1629
✉ alittlefield@landmarkcollege.org

Both Sides Now PO Box 55, Williston, VT 05495
☎ 802-879-1147 ✉ obladida@adelphia.net
🖳 www.angelfire.com/vt/bothsidesnow/
Currently supports a monthly gathering to discuss issues & ideas. Connected with a group in Montreal - hopes to promote sharing of info & activities across the border. PUB: e-zine sent monthly.

Virginia

Virginians for Justice 6 North 6th St.-Suite LL3, PO Box 342, Richmond, VA 23218-0342
☎ 804-643-4816 FX: 804-643-2050
✉ Va4Justice@aol.com 🖳 www.visi.net/vj
Working toward repeal of Crimes Against Nature (CAN)& Sodomy laws. Has lobbyist working with Virginia Government & Legislature. Runs 24 hour Hate Crime Hotline: 1-800-2-JUSTICE.
PUB: ACTION ALERT (Published Bi-Monthly & sent to members. Available in BGLT bookstores.)

Virginia Tech: Lesbian, Gay, Bisexual, Transgender Alliance P. O. Box 686, Blacksburg, VA 24060 ☎ 540-231-7975 ✉ lgba@vt.edu
🖳 www.vt.edu:10021/org/LGBTA/
Mts Th. 8pm during termtime. For LGBT & straight members of the Virgina Tech & surrounding communities.

University of Virginia: Bisexual, Gay, & Lesbian Law Students Association UVA Law School, 580 Massie Road, Charlottesville, VA 22903
✉ kaos@virginia.edu 🖳 scs.student.virginia.edu/~bgallsa/

University of Virginia

Lesbian, Gay & Bisexual Union, PO Box 525, Newcomb Hall Station, Charlottesville, VA 22904 ✉ lgbtu@virginia.edu; 🖳 scs.student.virginia.edu/~lambda1/. **Lesbian, Bisexual & Questioning Women**, c/o LGBU ☎ 804-971-4942; *Meets 7pm at Unitarian House, 808 Rugby Rd. Open to all women.*

George Mason University: Gay, Lesbian, Bisexual Transgender Services Box 190, 4400 University Drive, Fairfax, VA 22030 ☎ 703-993-2895
FX: 703-993-4022 ✉ pride@gmu.edu
🖳 www.gmu.edu/org/pride

Longwood College: UNITY Fayetteville, VA 23909 ✉ unityall@longwood.lwc.edu
🖳 www.lwc.edu/student/UA/
LGB campus group.

Mary Washington College: Gay/Lesbian/Bi Student Association Box 638, Fredericksburg, VA 22401
Campus group. Open to the public.

Central Virginia Affirmation PO Box 501, Hanover, VA 23069-0501 ☎ 804-746-7279
GLBT-affirming Methodist group.

James Madison University: Harmony PO Box 8119, Harrisonburg, VA 22807 ☎ 540-434-8789
Organization for LBG concerns.

Gay, Lesbian & Straight Education Network PO Box 5180, Midlothian, VA 23112
☎ 804-327-8458 ✉ glsenrichmond@yahoo.com
🖳 www.geocities.com/glsenrichmond
Richmond area branch of national group GLSEN.

Bi-Nature Norfolk, VA ☎ 757-490-1719
Tidewater bi group meets Th. 7:30pm at the Unitarian Church of Norfolk, 739 Yarmouth St.

Bisexual, Gay & Lesbian People in Medicine c/o American Medical Students Association, 1902 Association Dr., Reston, VA 20191
☎ 703-620-6600 or 800-767-2266 FX: 703-620-5873
✉ amsa@www.amsa.org and amsa@amsa.org
🖳 www.amsa.org

Richmond Bisexual Network (ROBIN) c/o Phoenix Rising , 19 N. Belmont Ave., Richmond, VA 23221
☎ 804-257-9159 ✉ robinsnet@yahoo.com
🖳 www.geocities.com/robinenet
Social & support organization for bi people in Central Virginia.

Alliance of Black Men Richmond, VA
☎ 804-342-2957 or 228-1867

Gay Fathers Coalition Richmond, VA
☎ 804-330-4090 ✉ GFCRichmond@aol.com
Meets 1st Th. at Fan Free Clinic (downstairs) at 1010 North Thompson Street. Affiliated with Gay & Lesbian Parents Coalition International.

University of Richmond: c/o Student Activities, Richmond, VA 23173-0011 ☎ Adviser, Lee Hawthorne: 804-289-8837 🖳 www.richmond.edu/~safezone/index.html
Safe Zone (allies); New Directions (educational & activist student group for students interested in working on sexual diversity as a social justice issue. URFamily (confidential group for GLBTQ students. Meets weekly for mutual support & social activities together.

Virginia Commonwealth University: Sexual Minority Student Alliance Box 75 , 907 Floyd Av., Richmond, VA 28284
Open to the public. Meets Wed. during termtime in University Student Commons.

Any woman who feels actual horror or revulsion at the thought of kissing or embracing or having physical relations with another woman should reexamine her feelings and attitudes not only about other women, but also about herself.

—Shere Hite, American sexologist, 1976.

Ultimately, the questions of whether someone is 'really' straight or 'really' gay or even 'really' bisexual "misrecognizes the nature of sexuality, which is fluid not fixed, a narrative that changes over time rather than a fixed identity, however complex."

Marge Garber

Richmond Organization for Sexual Minority Youth PO Box 5542, Richmond, VA 23220
☎ 804-353-1699 (office) ✉ The Rosmy@aol.com
🖳 www.rosmy.org
Supports GLBQ Youth 14-21. Offers training for Adults working with GLBT youth & promotes education about GLBT youth. Has a "Youth Support Line": 804-353-2077.

Affirmation: Gay & Lesbian Mormons Richmond, VA ☎ 804-358-3492 ✉ VAGayLDS@aol.com

Interweave c/o Unitarian Universalist Community Church, 8545 Patterson Avenue, Suite 101, Richmond, VA 23229 ☎ 804-741-9253
✉ uuccglenallen@erols.com
🖳 www.stormloader.com.uucc
For all GLBT people, friends & members of UUCC. PUB: UUCC Beginnings (monthly)

P-FLAG Richmond PO Box 36392, Richmond, VA 23235 ☎ 804-744-9016
Meets 2nd Tu. at the Church of the Holy Comforter (Episcopal) at Staples Mill Road & Monument Av.

Washington

The Gay, Lesbian, Bisexual, Transgender & Questioning Youth Info Line ☎206-547-7900
24-hour info on support groups & community activities.

People of Color Against AIDS Network 607 19th Av. E., Seattle, WA 98112 ☎ 206-322-7061
FX: 206-322-7204 ✉ web@pocaan.org
🖳 www.pocaan.org/
Multi-racial AIDS prevention organization. community organizing, community based education/outreach, peer education, community based service liaison. Programs, info, testing, groups. Offices in Seattle, Tacoma & Yakima.

B-GLAD: the Bisexual, Gay, Lesbian Trans & Questioning Adolescent Drop-in Group Youth Eastside Services 16150 NE 8th, Bellevue, WA 98008 ☎ 425-747-4YES (4937)
Free confidential drop-in group for LGBTQ youth 12-19. Th. 6:30-8pm.

Western Washington University: Lesbian, Gay & Bi-sexual Alliance Viking Union 233, Box 1-1, Bellingham, WA 98225-9106 ☎ 360-650-6120 FX: 360-650-6507 ✉ lgba@cc.wwu.edu 🖳 www.as.wwu.edu/lgbta/
Student organization. Supports & affirms the lives of GLBT people & allies. Weekly mtgs., social events, resource library, referrals, speakers bureau.

Evergreen State College: Evergreen Queer Alliance EQA CAB 314, Olympia, WA 98505 ☎ 360-867-6544 FX: 360-866-6685 ✉ evergreen_queer_alliance@hotmail.com 🖳 evergreenqueers.tripod.com/organization/
For all Queers at the College & the surrounding communities.

Washington State University: Gay, Lesbian, Bisexual & Allies Program B-19A Compton Union Building, Box 647204, WSU, Pullman, WA 99164-7204 ☎ 509-335-6388 FX: 509-335-4168 ✉ glbap@mail.wsu.ed 🖳 cub.wsu.edu/glbap
For GLB students, faculty, staff, & allies. Speakers' bureau, newsletter. Center open M-F 8-5. Student group meets weekly, open to all.
PUB: Outspoken: The GLBAP Newsletter

BiNet Seattle Seattle, WA ☎ 206-728-4533 🖳 www.bi.org/~binet-seattle/
Non-profit, mixed gender, social & support organization for bi & bi-friendly people & their partners in the Puget Sound area.

Seattle Bisexual Women's Network PO Box 30645 Greenwood Station, Seattle, WA 98103-0645 ☎ 206-517-7767 ✉ sbwn@hotmail.com 🖳 www.geocities.com/sbwn/
Bimonthly newsletter. Support & discussion groups, newcomer's meetings, social events.
PUB: North Bi Northwest

Seattle Bisexual Men's Union Seattle, WA ☎ 206-728-4533 ✉ alexei_guren@msn.com 🖳 www.bi.org/~binet-seattle/
Men's anti-sexist support & social group. Monthly discussion meetings & social events.

Bi Out Seattle, WA 🖳 www.bi.org/~binet-seattle/
The Bisexual Speakers' Bureau of Seattle. Affliated with BiNet Seattle.

> And the truth of my experience is this: my sexuality is whole. I am not straight with men and lesbian with women; I am bisexual with both. Enjoying sex with both women and men is no more an inherently schizophrenic form of sexuality than enjoying both intercourse and oral sex.
>
> *Greta Christina in* Bisexual Politics.

> It was a while before we came to realize that our place was the very house of difference rather than the security of any one particular difference.
>
> *Audre Lorde, in* Zami *(Persephone Press, Watertown MA, 1982, p. 226)*

Asian Lesbian & Bisexual Alliance PO Box 14232, Seattle, WA 98114 ☎ 206-689-6155 🖳 www.alba.org/alba.asp
Online Resource for Asian Lesbians & Bisexuals, with events listings, an online newsletter, chat room, etc. PUB: Little Sushi (www.alba.org/xsushi/LS01.htm)

Mature Friends PO Box 30575, Seattle, WA 98103-0575 ☎ 206-781-7724 🖳 www.gayscape.com/maturefriends/
Supportive social environment for GLBs 40+. Monthly potlucks, weekly bridge, travel opportunities, garden & theater groups.

Queer & Asian - Seattle PO Box 14153, Seattle, WA 98114 ☎ 206-264-5518 ✉ qasian@drizzle.com 🖳 www.drizzle.com/~qasian/
Network for gay & bi Asian men. Fosters leadership & peer support.
PUB: Mochi Balls (Quarterly newsletter.)

SEAMEC: Seattle Municipal Election Committee for Gays, Lesbians, Bisexuals & Transgenders 1122 E. Pike St. #901, Seattle, WA 98122 ☎ 206-748-1727 🖳 www.seamec.org
Independent non-partisan political action committee. Interviews, evaluates & rates all candidates running for office in Seattle, King County & WA.

Seattle University: Triangle Club Seattle, WA ✉ triangle@seattleu.edu 🖳 www.seattleu.edu/student/clubs/triangle/

University of Washington

Gay, Bisexual, Lesbian & Transgendered Commission Box 352238 / SAO 09, Seattle, WA 98195-2238 ☎ 206-685-4252 ✉ asuwgblc@u.washington.edu 🖳 depts.washington.edu/asuwgblc/index.html.
Office, weekly meetings, special events. Other campus groups include: **QSPH** *(for GLBT students, staff, & faculty in the University of Washington School of Public Health);* **Sexual Orientation Research Group** *(informal association of faculty, professional staff & doctoral students interested in promoting research on lgb issues);* **Social Work GBLT; Queer Curriculum Committee; Out for Business** *(business school group);* **Pride Dawgs** *(political & visibility organization).*

At Millenium March on Washington, 2000

Ellyn Ruthstrom

American Friend's Service Committee's Gay, Lesbian, Bisexual, Transgender & Questioning Youth Program 814 NE 40th St., Seattle, WA 98105 ☎ 206-632-0500 ✉ jfreeman@afsc.org 💻 www.afsc.org
Diverse group of young adults of all sexual orientations. Educating our communities on subjects affecting GLBTQ youth & allies. 24 hr. recorded GLBTQ Youth Info Line at 1-800-425-0192.

Lambert House PO Box 23111, Seattle, WA 98102 ☎ House: 206-322-2515 ✉ webmaster@lamberthouse.org 💻 www.lamberthouse.org/
At 1818 15th Av. (at Denny). Activities & resource center for GLBT youth 14-22.

Seattle Counseling Service for Sexual Minorities 1820 E. Pine St., Seattle, WA 98122 ☎ 206-323-0220 ✉ staffofscs@juno.com 💻 www.gay-lesbian-counseling.org/
Community mental health service for LGBTs & youth & children from sexual minority families. Crisis intervention & counseling service.

Gay City Health Project Seattle, WA ☎ 206-860-6969 FX: 206-860-0195 ✉ info@gaycity.org 💻 www.gaycity.org
Public forums, support groups, many other programs that build community & prevent HIV infection in gay & bi men.

Gonzaga University: HERO. Helping Education Regarding Orientation GU MSC#2436, Spokane, WA 99258-0001 ✉ hero@gonzaga.edu 💻 barney.gonzaga.edu/~hero/main.htm

Pacific Lutheran University: Harmony c/o Student Organizations, Tacoma, WA 98447 ✉ harmony@plu.edu 💻 www.plu.edu/~harmony/
GLTB& Ally group. Weekly meeting during termtime.

Oasis Youth Center Tacoma, WA ☎ 253-534-3204 ✉ oasisyouth@xoommail.com 💻 members.nbci.com/OasisYouth/
For GLBQ youth 14-24. Youth driven program, w/dances & activities.

West Virginia

West Virginia Lesbian & Gay Coalition PO Box 11033, Charleston, WV 25339 ☎ 304-343-7305 ✉ wvlgc@aol.com 💻 members.aol.com/wvlgc
Works toward equality for glbt people, through legislative action, education, & the dissemination of information.

Glenville State College: Colors of Pride 200 High Street, Glenville, WV 26351 ✉ gayatgsc@hotmail.com 💻 www.geocities.com/WestHollywood/Heights/8399/
LGB student organization.

Marshall University

Lesbian, Bisexual & Gay Outreach Office, 137 Pritchard Hall, Huntington, WV 25755, ☎ 304-696-6623, ✉ LGBO@marshall.edu, 💻 www.marshall.edu/LGBO/. *Help students locate gay-friendly housing. Professional counselor on staff. Coming out resources & lending library. Various programs & activities in conjunction with Lambda society.* **Marshall Lambda Society**, Memorial Student Center, c/o Office of Student Activities , Huntington, WV 25755, ☎ 304-696-6623,) muls@marshall.edu, V www.marshall.edu/muls/ *Support/education/activism arou nd LGBT issues. Operate speakers bureau in conjunction with LGB Outreach Office, Safe Space Project, & Allies List. Identify supportive faculty & staff, maintain listserv.*

West Virginia University: Bisexual, Gay & Lesbian Mountaineers PO Box 6444, Morgantown, WV 26505 ☎ 304-293-8200 ✉ biglm@wvusa.u92.wvu.edu 💻 www.wvu.edu/~biglm/
Dedicated to serving the needs of LGB students, faculty & staff, as well as members of the greater Morgantown community.

Allies of Shepherd College c/o Student Affairs, PO Box 3210, Shepherdstown, WV 25443-3210 ☎ Student Affairs: 304-876-5124 ✉ alliesweb@shepherd.edu 💻 www.shepherd.wvnet.edu/alliesweb/
Student group supporting GLBT rights. Meets Wed. 3:30-4:30pm.

> **I've been absolutely terrified every moment of my life and I've never let it keep me from doing a single thing I wanted to do.**
>
> *Georgia O'Keefe*

Wisconsin

Bi? Shy? Why? c/o OutReach, PO Box 168, Madison, WI 53701 ☎ Colin 920-623-4265 ✉ madbee@powerweb.net
Monthly drop-in meetings, participates in gay/lesbian/bi events including pride marches, the MAGIC picnic, political activities, & workshops.

Wisconsin IN Step: Wisconsin's Only LGBT Newspaper 1661 N. Water St. #411, Milwaukee, WI 54202 ☎ 414 278 7840 ✉ editor@instepnews.com 🖳 www.instepnews.com
Contains section called "The Guide" with listings statewide. Good source for current info.

Lawrence University: Pride c/o Information Desk, Box 599, Appleton, WI 54912 ☎ 920-832-7051 (Resource Room) ✉ sarah.e.kesler@lawrence.edu 🖳 www.lawrence.edu/sorg/pride/
Weekly meetings during termtime. Allies welcome.

Frontiers Social Organization for Gay & Bisexual Men 600 Williamson St Suite P1, PO Box 168, Madison, WI 53703 ☎ David: 608-274-5959
Social, discussion & outdoor activity club for gay & bi men. Various programs, seasonal activities and special interest groups. Annual membership dues $20. PUB: The New Frontiersman *(Newsletter mailed monthly to members. Provides info. on upcoming club activities.)*

OutReach, Inc. 600 Williamson Street, Madison, WI 53703 ☎ 608-255-8582 general; 608-255-4297-outline FX: 608-255-0018 🖳 www.ourtreachinc.com* *LGBT center. Referrals, counseling, & general LGBT info. Maintains the Madison G/.L Resource Center Library, the Speakers' Bureau & men's & women's coming out support groups. Good first contact for non-students. (Students see the LGB Campus Center). Open Mon.-Fri., 9am-9pm.*

New York Pride

Morgan co-editor for Oregon, modeling bi fashion

University of Wisconsin, Madison

The Lesbian, Gay, Bisexual & Transgendered Campus Center, 2nd Floor Memorial Union, 800 Langdon, Madison, WI 53706, ☎ 608-265-3344, ✉ staff@lgbtcc.studentorg.wisc.edu, 🖳 www.lgbcc.studentorg.wisc.edu. *Good first contact for students. Open 12-5 M-F during termtime; summer hours vary. Speakers bureau, library, lbt resource info & many social groups & programs. Volunteers welcomed.* **Ten Percent Society**, PO Box 260394, 710 University Avenue Room 201, Madison, WI 53726-0394, ☎ 608-262-7365, FX: 608-265-4495, ✉ tps@tps.studentorg.wisc.edu, 🖳 tps.studentorg.wisc.edu/TPS/default.html, *LGBT & straight-friendly. Mts. weekly, dances.* **LGBT Alumni Council**, WAA, 650 N. Lake St., Madison, WI 53706, ☎ Russell Betts: 608-262-5895, ✉ RussellBetts@badger.alumni.wisc.edu, 🖳 www.uwalumni.com/glbtac/index.html. *Social 3rd Th. Scholarships awarded annually.* PUB: Badger Pride *(Newletter published three times a year).*

Bi Definition c/o Milwaukee LGBT Community Center, 170 S. 2nd St., Milwaukee, WI 53203 ☎ 414-774-5055 ✉ bidef@netwurx.net 🖳 www.netwurx.net/~bidef *Monthly meetings & other events.* PUB: Bi All Means (Quarterly, $15/yr, 12 pp.)

Milwaukee LGBT Community Center 170 S. 2nd St., Milwaukee, WI 53203 ☎ Neil Albrecht: 414-271-2656

Support Group Programs Counseling Center of Milwaukee, 2038 N. Bartlett, Milwaukee, WI 53202 ☎ 414-271-2565
$10 fee/group session unless otherwise noted. **Free Space***: (women only) exploration of sexual/affectional orientation.* **More space***: Support women who are lesbian-identified.* **Breaking Up is Hard to Do***: support group for lesbians.* **Silver Space***: Support group for older lesbians. $3 donation.* **Male Partnered Women** - *dealing with questions of sexual & affectional orientation.* **Gay Men's General Issues***: support group on identity/orientation, intimacy, HIV, relationships, self-esteem.*

University of Wisconsin, Whitewater: IMPACT: Gay, Lesbian, Bi Student Union & Supporters 309 McCutchan Hall, Whitewater, WI 53190 ☎ 414-472-5738 ✉ Impact@mail.uww.edu 🖳 students.uww.edu/stdorgs/impact/
Campus organization open to individuals of all sexual orientations; focuses on campus education, social activities, & providing support & resources to glbt students & allies.

Wyoming

Different & Equal Youth Alliance WY ☎ 1-800-GAYTEEN
LGBTQ youth. Call for info & referrals in Wyoming.

Fund for Social Change PO Box 6837, Cheyenne, WY 82003 ☎ Lynn Griebel: 307-637-6940 ✉ lyn5289@hotmail.com
UGLW political arm. Looking for volunteers to work in coalition building, public education & networking within the LGBT community.

HART Center—HIV/AIDS Resource & Training 1611 Morrie Av., Cheyenne, WY 82001 ☎ Cheyenne: 307-635-5262; Nationwide: 800-364-3104 FX: 307-638-4924 ✉ hartcntr@cheyenneweb.com
HIV/AIDS & LGBT resource center providing LGBT youth group for junior/senior high school students, a GLBT group for high school graduates & adults in their 20s, an adult LGBT Coffee House, a 12-step GLBT program called Rainbo Recovery, & other resources including a transgender program. PUB: HART Beat (Newsletter, 6 issues a year, includes all programs including GLBT support programs.)

United Gays & Lesbians of Wyoming PO Box 6837, Cheyenne, WY 82003-6837 ☎ 307-778-7645 ✉ info@uglw.org 🖳 www.uglw.org/index.html
Seeks to enhance the lives of glbt people in Wyoming through: 1) Education of the general public & ourselves on glbt issues. 2) Advocating the protection & promotion of the civil rights for glbt people. 3) Establishment of a statewide network for dissemination of info regarding glbt issues & events. Annual membership open to all supporters. PUB: United Voice (Monthly newsletter.)

PFLAG Cheyenne Cheyenne, WY 82001 ☎ 307-635-5314 ✉ jalanne@earthlink.net

Metropolitan Community Church (MCC) Light of the Plains PO Box 6853, Cheyenne, WY 82003 ☎ 307-632-4336 ✉ MCCLOTP@aol.com

Project TALK (Together, Aware, Love, Kindness) Laramie, WY ☎ Larry: 307-745-8915
Support group for gay & bi men to connect & talk about their lives.

University of Wyoming: Lesbian, Gay, Bisexual & Transgendered Association PO Box 3625, University Station, Laramie, WY 82071 ☎ 307-766-6340 FX: 307-766-3762 ✉ LGBTA@uwyo.edu 🖳 www.uwyo.edu/lgbta
Social organization to further education about LGBT issues.

Wyoming Youth Pride Project PO Box 1676, Laramie, WY 82073
Creating safe spaces for the youth of Wyoming.

Central Wyoming College: Coalition on Sexual Orientation Riverton, WY ☎ Jewell Dirks: 307-855-2227

SafePlace - Sheridan Sheridan, WY ☎ Kris: 307-672-0310 ✉ krismonson@hotmail.com 🖳 www.geocities.com/spwy99
A youth alliance & support group for glbtq youth & their allies.

Lambda Community Center of Fort Collins 149 West Oak, Suite #8, Ft. Collins, WY 80524 ☎ 970-221-3247 ✉ lambda@lambdacenter.org 🖳 www.lambdacenter.org/

See Colorado listings. For GLBs in northern Colorado & southern Wyoming.

URUGUAY

Grupo Diversidad LGTTB - Comunidad Lésbica, Gay Travesti, Transexual, Intersexual, Bisexual Uruguaya Casilla de Correo 7415, Correo Central, Montevideo ☎ 598 2/915-3021
✉ diversid@montevideo.com.uy
🖳 village.fortunecity.com/etheridge/491/urugay.htm, *LBGTI political activist group; space for support / self-help.*

Gay Uruguay Web Site
🖳 village.fortunecity.com/etheridge/491/urugay.htm. *Listing of GLBT resources in Uruguay.*

VENEZUELA

Movimiento Ambiente de Venezuela
Solis a Munoz, Edificio Augusta,, Piso 1, Apto 1-D, El Silencio, Caracas 1010. ☎ 582 482 4114
✉ accsi@internet.ve

Gay Venezuela
🖳 www.gayvenezuela.com/
Website w/news, chatrooms, etc.

ZAMBIA

LEGATRA: Lesbians, Gays, Bi-Sexuals & Transgender Persona Association
c/Zambia Independent Monitoring Team, 2nd Fl, Muyini House, PO Box 30211, Bombay Rd., Kumwala, Lusaka
☎ 260-1-236856/7; FX: 260-1-236857
✉ zimt@zamnet.zm

ZIMBABWE

Gays & Lesbians of Zimbabwe
35 Colenbrander Road, Milton Park, Harare,
☎(263-4) 74-17-36, FX: (263-4) 77-81-65,
✉ galz@samara.co.zw
Numerous projects & sub-committees devoted to specific campaigns & support work. Frequent well-attended social events. Under direct attack by Zimbabwe government.

Ngongi Chaidzo, c/o GALZ, Bag A6131, Avondale, Harare. *Ngongi Chaido means Great Blessing. Contact c/o GALZ (above). Recently reformed with focus on black lesbians. Social events, as well as safer sex workshops & human rights training.*

GayZim ✉gayzim@hotmail.com
🖳 www.geocities.com/WestHollywood/Stonewall/4946/gayzim.html. *Web magazine for gay & gay-friendly men & women in Zimbabwe.*

BUGLES PO Box 6052, Morningside, Bulawayo *Bulawayo based social / support group for lesbians & gay men in Matabeleland.*

Poet Sheila Mabry at the International Bi Conference, Boston 1998

It's a crime, it's an evil, dangerous thing To stifle the gift of love and the joy it surely brings   Well, I'll love who I please, I'm gonna give the best of me Walking tall, and blessed with the right to be.

Mary Watkins

ANNOUNCEMENTS:
upcoming conferences and events

compiled bi Robyn Ochs

Apparently, bisexuals like to have conferences! There is a real power in getting together with dozens or sometimes hundreds of other people who also identify as bisexual. You remember that you are most certainly not the only one. You get to share stories, make friends, dance, play, and have a good time.

Las Vegas, Nevada, USA, March 16-18, 2001: **2nd M.A.I. Bi Conference for Bisexual and Bi-Curious Men**. Sponsored by Men's Awareness Institute (A subsidiary of American Institute of Bisexuality.). Info available on the web: www.bisexual.org/pages/newconf/lvlasvegas/ or by contacting AIB.

Milwaukee, Wisconsin, USA, May 4-6: **BECAUSE 2001**. At the University of Wisconsin, Madison. For more info: because2001@hotmail.com, Phone: (414) 299-9612; web: http://www.netwurx.net/~because2k1/ or to write to: BECAUSE 2001, PO Box 070845, Milwaukee, WI 53207. Editor's note: I've keynoted this conference — it's EXCELLENT!

The South Central U.S. BiCamp (The South Central Regional Bisexual Retreat) will be held in Texas at the Rainbow Ranch Campground on May 17 - 20, 2001. Co-sponsored by BiNet USA and BiNet Houston. Workshops, campsite, drum circle, more. For info: http://home.flash.net/~bihouse/BiCamp/Main.html or contact BiNet Houston (see listings).

First European Bisexual Conference will be held in Rotterdam, Netherlands on June 22 - 24, 2001. 3 days of workshops and events. All are welcome to attend. For info: http://www.intbiconf.org/ or EBC1 Organizing, PO Box 28210, 3003KE Rotterdam, Netherlands, ebc1-info@intbiconf.org, PH: 31-06-28438124. Registration on sliding scale.

The **First North American Conference on Bisexuality, Gender, & Sexual Diversity** will be held at the University of British Columbia Conference Centre in Vancouver, Canada on August 9-12, 2001. Contact BiNet BC (see listings) for more information, or check out the conference website: http://bi.org/~binetbc/2001/.

Christopher Street Day, 1998,

The annual **Northeast U.S. BiCamp** will be held in West-Central Massachusetts on August 16 - 20, 2001. Informal camping with lots of other bisexuals in a beautiful location. For more info, write: Biversity Boston, 29 Stanhope St., Boston, MA 02116. Info: http://www.biresource.org/biversity/bicamp.html.

The **19th annual UK BiCon** will be held at Coventry University on August 25 - 27, 2001. For info BiCon, London, WC1N 3XX UK or check out their website: http://2001.bicon.org.uk/. **The BiCon UK 2002** organisers are at bicon2002@bi.org. (no other details at present).

International Celebrate Bisexuality Day will be held on September 23. This day is a call for bisexuals, their families, friends and allies to recognize and celebrate bisexuality, bisexual history, culture and community, and the bisexual people in their lives. There will be local events in various cities. For info: http://www.geocities.com/bihouseusa/index.html.

The **Seventh International Bisexual Conference** will be held in Sydney, Australia in October, 2002, in conjunction with the Gay Games! For info contact the Australian Bisexual Network (see listings).

You can access current information about all of these events on the Bisexual Resource Center's website: http://www.biresource.org/conferences.html.

GET INVOLVED IN YOUR LOCAL COMMUNITY. JOIN GROUPS, VOLUNTEER. IT IS AN EXCELLENT WAY TO MEET LIKE-MINDED PEOPLE.

ENORMOUS CHANGES AT THE LAST MINUTE

Trying to get a fixed and definitive picture of an ever-changing grassroots movement is somewhat like trying to get a large group of young children to sit still for a photo. It just can't be done. The bi and glbt movements are in a constant state of transformation, new information comes in on a daily basis. Since I "finished" laying out the listings, here is what has come in:

GROUPS

Botswana

Lesbian, Gay, Bisexual Organisation of Botswana (LEGABIBO)
PO Box 2600, Gaborone
Botswana

Kenya
Kenya Aids Society
 PO Box 76618, Nairobi 2542;
HIV/Aids organisation.

Positive Women's Group
PO Box 30218, Nairobi;
Gay-friendly group.

Mozambique
Jamba House:
Avenida do Trbalho-Mercado, Maputo
Some gays hang out at this hotel. (There are no formally organized lgbt groups in Mozambique)

Namibia
United Gay Organization of Namibia (UGON)
PO Box 21429, Windhoek.

Uganda
Right Companion
c/o: NCGLE, PO Box 27811 Yeoville, 2143, South Africa

United States

New Northeast US E-mail Lists

You are invited to participate in the new NorthBiNortheast e-mail lists.
The three brand new e-mail lists that we (myself and several Tri-State
Conference participants) have
implemented are:

v NorthBiNortheast-announce@yahoogroups.com for announcements related
   to events either concerning bisexuality, of interest to bisexuals, or put on by
   bisexuals in the Northeast (a closed, moderated list). To join, send a blank
   e-mail to NorthBiNortheast-announce-subscribe@yahoogroups.com.

v NorthBiNortheast-discuss@yahoogroups.com for discussion amongst
   bisexuals in the Northeast on any issues concerning them (a closed, lightly
   moderated list) To join, send a blank e-mail to NorthBiNortheast-discuss-
   subscribe@egroups.com.

v NorthBiNortheast-personals@egroups.com a group for posting personals for
   or from
   bisexuals in the Northeast (an open list) To join, send a blank e-mail to
   NorthBiNortheast-personals-subscribe@yahoogroups.com.

The purpose of these lists is to help unite the bisexual community in the
Northeast by increasing communication between local bi communities and
individuals.

BOOKS

Just out from Haworth Press are two anthologies on bisexual
men. *Bisexuality in the Lives of Men: Facts and Fictions*
consists of empirical and theoretical essays; *Bisexual Men in
Culture and Society* contains works on literature, film, and
the media. Both books are edited by Brett Beemyn and Eric
Steinman and are being published simultaneously as special
issues of the *Journal of Bisexuality*.

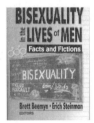

Since laying out the fiction section of the Guide, I have finished two novels that
should be added to the pile:

Palomino, by Australian writer Elizabeth Jolley (NY: Persea Books, 1980) is a
sensuous psychological novel set in the Australian countryside. An older woman,
a disbarred physician, falls in love with a younger woman who has had a long-
lasting incestuous relationship with her brother. It's a captivating read.

The second, ***Three Women*** (NY: Harper Torch, 1999), is yet another by American
Marge Piercy. It's the story of three generations of women in a family and their
struggles to communicate and be close. In her angry and miserable adolescence,
the youngest of the three women is in an intense sexual and emotional triangular
relationship with her two best friends, both male.

HOW TO ORDER MORE COPIES OF THE BISEXUAL RESOURCE GUIDE

Want another (or your own) copy of this book?

1- Go to our web page: http://www.biresource.org/ biproducts/guide.html, pay by credit card, and we'll mail you one.

2 - Send a check or money order for $13.95 to BRC, PO Box 1026, Boston MA 02117-1026 USA and we'll mail you one.

(Note: if you are ordering from outside of the United States, please use an international postal money order or order on the web--our bank will not accept checks from non-US banks for less than US$25.)

3 - Buy online at Amazon.com or from another bookseller.

4 - Go to a bookstore. If they don't have the Guide in stock ask them why not, and ask that they order a copy for you. If you live in an area that has a glbt or feminist bookstore, please consider shopping there.

DID YOU KNOW: All proceeds from the sale of this book go directly to the Bisexual Resource Center, a non-profit organization. Please support us by purchasing this book.

---

http://www.biresource.org/ biproducts/guide.html

Dykes To Watch Out For by Alison Bechdel

WE WANT TO HEAR FROM YOU!

You can update, delete or add listings.

You can let us know about books or films that should be listed.

You can volunteer to be a regional editor for the next edition.

You can send us fabulous quotes!

You can ask us to list your conferences or calls for papers.

You can give us feedback.

Contact us the old-fashioned way or go to our web site:

www.biresource.org/bidir-online

ABOUT ROBYN OCHS

ROBYN OCHS grew up wanting very much to be an activist and to make a BIG difference in the world. But there were already so many really amazing and competent people taking leadership on so many issues that she cared about: women's rights, recycling, saving the whales and the baby seals, and the cats and the dogs, stopping the US from invading the rest of the world (either overtly or covertly), promoting the use of solar power and other renewable energy sources, working against racism and anti-Semitism — the list goes on and on. She graduated high school. She came out (to herself only) as bisexual. She graduated from University. She had her first relationship with a woman. She moved to Boston, and came out to others as bisexual. She and a group of amazing women formed a bi women's support group. She found herself caught up in a vibrant new movement. And at that time there were very few people taking leadership in this movement. Finally, she had found her niche! Here was a place where she felt she could actually make a difference. And that is how Robyn Ochs and the bi movement found each other.

Robyn teaches part-time at Tufts University. Her topics include bisexual identity, and post-War glbt identities and cultures in the United States and Canada. Her most recent course is entitled "Crossing the Lines: Gender and Sexual Orientation" which focuses on those who transgress the cultural binaries of gay/straight and/or male/female: butch women, drag queens, intersexed people, bisexuals and of course the gender rainbow.

She also travels around the US (and sometimes beyond) doing workshops and talks at conferences and on college campuses. If you are interested in bringing her to your school, let her know! She has a lot of experience, and can cover a number of topics from bisexuality 101 to inter-group dialogues, to unlearning homophobia workshops.

You can find out more about Robyn Ochs on the web at: *www.bi.org/~ochs.*